Lecture Notes in Computer Science   11002

Commenced Publication in 1973
Founding and Former Series Editors:
Gerhard Goos, Juris Hartmanis, and Jan van Leeuwen

Advanced Research in Computing and Software Science
Subline of Lecture Notes in Computer Science

More information about this series at http://www.springer.com/series/7408

Andreas Podelski (Ed.)

Static Analysis

25th International Symposium, SAS 2018
Freiburg, Germany, August 29–31, 2018
Proceedings

 Springer

Editor
Andreas Podelski
Universität Freiburg
Freiburg
Germany

ISSN 0302-9743   ISSN 1611-3349 (electronic)
Lecture Notes in Computer Science
ISBN 978-3-319-99724-7   ISBN 978-3-319-99725-4 (eBook)
https://doi.org/10.1007/978-3-319-99725-4

Library of Congress Control Number: 2018952240

LNCS Sublibrary: SL2 – Programming and Software Engineering

This Springer imprint is published by the registered company Springer Nature Switzerland AG
The registered company address is: Gewerbestrasse 11, 6330 Cham, Switzerland

Preface

Static analysis is recognized as a fundamental tool for program verification, bug detection, compiler optimization, program understanding, and software maintenance. The series of Static Analysis Symposia has served as the primary venue for the presentation of theoretical, practical, and applicational advances in the area. Previous symposia were held in Edinburgh, Saint-Malo, Munich, Seattle, Deauville, Venice, Perpignan, Los Angeles, Valencia, Kongens Lyngby, Seoul, London, Verona, San Diego, Madrid, Paris, Santa Barbara, Pisa, Aachen, Glasgow, Namur, and New York. This volume contains the papers presented at SAS 2018, the 25th International Static Analysis Symposium. The conference was held during August 29–31, 2018, at Freiburg, Germany.

SAS 2018 featured two associated workshops: the 9th Workshop on Static Analysis and Systems Biology (SASB 2018), and the 9th Workshop on Tools for Automatic Program Analysis (TAPAS 2017), which were held on August 27, 2018, the day before the conference.

The conference received 37 submissions. Each submission was reviewed by at least three Program Committee members. The Program Committee decided to accept 18 papers, which appear in this volume.

In addition to the regular paper review, we organized a separate evaluation for artifacts submitted by authors, together with their papers. Previous editions of SAS also allowed authors to submit artifacts, but this was the first edition where artifacts were evaluated on their own, by a specific committee. Out of the 16 submissions that came with an artifact, nine were accepted. Only the artifacts of the accepted papers were considered for the evaluation. Each of the nine artifacts was evaluated by two or three members of the artifact evaluation committee. The evaluation aimed at making sure that each artifact allows one to reproduce most or all of the results of the paper. Finally, seven artifacts were found of sufficient quality to pass the evaluation. Authors of accepted artifacts were allowed to add to their paper an artifact-approved badge. We hope that this experience will encourage effort for greater reproducibility of results in static analysis.

The program includes invited talks by Aws Albarghouthi (University of Wisconsin–Madison, USA), Zachary Kincaid (Princeton University, USA), Ruzica Piskac (Yale University, USA), Sharon Shoham (Tel Aviv University, Israel), and invited tutorials by Roberto Bagnara (University of Parma/BUGSENG, Italy), Ken McMillan (Microsoft Research, USA), Oded Padon (Tel Aviv University, Israel), and Peter O'Hearn (University College London/Facebook, UK). We warmly thank these speakers for accepting the invitations.

Many people and institutions contributed to the success of SAS 2018. We would like to thank the members of the Program Committee, who worked hard at carefully reviewing papers, holding insightful discussions during the online Program Committee meeting, and making final selections of accepted papers. We would also like to thank the additional referees enlisted by Program Committee members. The work of the Program Committee and the editorial process was greatly facilitated by the EasyChair conference management system. We are grateful to Springer for publishing these proceedings. Finally, we would like to thank our sponsors: Hahn-Schickard, Facebook, Axivion, ENS Paris, University of Padova, and Springer.

July 2018   Andreas Podelski
                                              (Program Committee Chair)
                                                              Xavier Rival
                                              (Artifact Evaluation Chair)

Organization

Program Committee

Domagoj Babic	Google
Sam Blackshear	Facebook
Marc Brockschmidt	Microsoft
Bor-Yuh Evan Chang	University of Colorado Boulder, USA
Swarat Chaudhuri	Rice University, USA
Jerome Feret	Inria, France
Ashutosh Gupta	TIFR
Nicolas Halbwachs	CNRS/Verimag, France
Lukas Holik	Brno University of Technology, Czech Republic
Barbara König	Universität Duisburg-Essen, Germany
Boris Köpf	IMDEA Software Institute, Spain
Shuvendu Lahiri	Microsoft
Hakjoo Oh	Korea University, South Korea
Andreas Podelski	University of Freiburg, Germany
Sylvie Putot	LIX, Ecole Polytechnique, France
Francesco Ranzato	University of Padova, Italy
Jakob Rehof	TU Dortmund University, Germany
Xavier Rival	Inria/CNRS/ENS Paris/PSL University, France
Sriram Sankaranarayanan	University of Colorado Boulder, USA
Harald Sondergaard	The University of Melbourne, Australia
Alexander J. Summers	ETH Zurich, Switzerland
Ashish Tiwari	SRI International, USA
Caterina Urban	ETH Zurich, Switzerland
Lenore Zuck	University of Illinois at Chicago, USA
Damien Zufferey	MPI-SWS, Germany
Florian Zuleger	Vienna University of Technology, Austria

Additional Reviewers

Allamanis, Miltos	Choi, Wontae	Gange, Graeme
Andrlon, Mak	Chu, Duc Hiep	Ghorbal, Khalil
Balakrishnan, Gogul	Cox, Arlen	Giacobazzi, Roberto
Chakarov, Aleksandar	D'Osualdo, Emanuele	Goubault, Eric
Chen, Yu-Fang	Dubreil, Jeremy	Hollingum, Nicholas
Cho, Sungkeun	Fuhs, Carsten	Journault, Matthieu

Katelaan, Jens
Lengal, Ondrej
Lopes, Nuno P.
Ouadjaout, Abdelraouf
Roux, Pierre

Simon, Axel
Srinivasan, Venkatesh
Stefanescu, Andrei
Stuckey, Peter J.
Sung, Chungha

Ulbrich, Mattias
Unadkat, Divyesh
Wang, Yuepeng
Zanella, Marco

Contents

Fairness: A Formal-Methods Perspective

Aws Albarghouthi[✉]

University of Wisconsin–Madison, Madison, WI, USA
aws@cs.wisc.edu

Abstract. Sensitive decisions of large-scale societal impact are increasingly being delegated to opaque software—a trend that is unlikely to slow down in the near future. The issue of fairness and bias of decision-making algorithms has thus become a multifaceted, interdisciplinary concern, attracting the attention of computer scientists, law scholars, policy makers, journalists, and many others. In this expository paper, I will outline some of the research questions we have been studying about fairness through the lens of formal methods.

1 Introduction

Whether it is at the industrial or governmental level, we are witnessing widespread automation of processes that have the potential to adversely impact individuals or groups. Consider, for instance, automatically assigned credit scores, automated filtering of applicant resumes, predictive policing, or algorithmic pricing. All of these automated processes have the potential to adversely affect the individuals or groups—typically minorities—who are the subjects of the algorithmic decisions. These are not mere academic concerns. Indeed, accounts of automated discrimination are being constantly reported in a range of areas.

Prompted by the importance of addressing bias in automated decision-making, researchers across many disciplines have started studying this problem. Notably, in computer science, multiple formal definitions of fairness have been proposed, and studying their merits, shortcomings, and contradictions is an active area of study (see, e.g., [4,6,7,9]). Relatedly, numerous techniques—mostly in statistical machine learning—have been proposed to enforce some of those fairness definitions (see, e.g., [6,7,12,13]).

In this paper, I will view the fairness problem through the lens of formal methods, and outline a number of research questions we are currently studying. A central technical theme that I wish to highlight is the reduction of probabilistic reasoning to logical reasoning, an approach that allows us to harness the power of established logical techniques—e.g., SMT solvers—for probabilistic reasoning.

© Springer Nature Switzerland AG 2018
A. Podelski (Ed.): SAS 2018, LNCS 11002, pp. 1–4, 2018.
https://doi.org/10.1007/978-3-319-99725-4_1

2   Fairness Through the Lens of Formal Methods

Fairness as a Program Property. Suppose we have a program P that, given an input x representing some individual's information, decides whether to invite them for a job interview. Our view of the problem is broad: P could be a machine-learned classifier, it could be an SQL query filtering out applicants from a database, a Python script, etc.

How do we ensure that P is *fair*? One class of definitions, called *individual fairness*, specifies that P should return a *similar* decision for similar individuals—for some definition of similarity. This is a notion of program *robustness*, ensuring that P is unaffected by input perturbations. Another class of definitions, called *group fairness*, specify that the selection rate for applicants from a minority group is comparable to the selection rate of the rest of the applicants—the majority.

In our work on FairSquare [1], we showed that we can characterize a range of such fairness definitions as formal specifications of programs, and proposed automated verification algorithms to check whether a program satisfies the specification, under a given population. Specifically, we characterize the population as a probability distribution D. Then, P can be viewed as a distribution transformer, and we can ask questions like, what is the probability that P hires an applicant conditioned on them being a minority? By answering such questions, we can check a property like group fairness, e.g., following Feldman et al. [6],

$$\frac{\Pr[P(x) = \textit{true} \mid x \text{ is a minority}]}{\Pr[P(x) = \textit{true} \mid x \text{ is a majority}]} \geqslant 1 - \varepsilon$$

which prescribes that the selection rate from the minority group is at least $1 - \varepsilon$ that of the majority group, for some small ε.

At the algorithmic level, we reduce the problem of computing those probabilities to *weighted volume computation*, where our goal is to compute the volume of the region defined by an SMT formula in linear arithmetic. We demonstrated that we can solve this quantitative problem via iterative calls to an SMT solver, resulting in a sound and complete approach [1,11].

Fairifying Unfair Programs. What should we do when we detect an unfair program? We extended FairSquare with what we like to call a *fairification* algorithm [2], which takes an unfair program P and transforms it into a fair program P', for a provided fairness definition.

Specifically, we cast the problem as follows: Find a fair program P' such that

$$\Pr[P(x) \neq P'(x)] \text{ is minimized}$$

The idea is that P is not trying to be egregiously unfair. What we therefore want to do is nudge it a little bit to make sure that we cover its blind spots that are causing its bias.

At the algorithmic level, we demonstrate how to solve fairification via iteratively solving constraint-based synthesis problems, whose solutions are candidate programs P'. Our approach is inspired by classic results in *probably approximately correct* (PAC) learning, adapted to an SMT-based program synthesis setting.

Fairness and Privacy. Finally, I would like to point out the connection between fairness—particularly, individual fairness—and notions of statistical privacy. *Differential privacy* [5] prescribes that minor modifications to a single record in a database do not yield large changes in the output of a query; this ensures the privacy of the individual to whom the record pertains. Differential privacy is established by randomizing the query evaluation algorithm, instilling noise in its results. The standard definition is that given query q, for all similar databases, d and d', and every possible output o, we have

$$\Pr[q(d) = o] \leqslant e^{\varepsilon} \cdot \Pr[q(d') = o]$$

where $\varepsilon > 0$ is a parameter. As ε approaches 0, the outputs of the query q on d and d' approach each other, increasing privacy.

Perhaps predictably, algorithms for enforcing differential privacy have been ported for ensuring fairness [4,8]. For instance, Kearns et al. [8] employ differential-privacy mechanisms to ensure individually fair selection of individuals from a database—e.g., choosing top football players to send to the world cup.[1] Intuitively, the randomization enforced by differential privacy ensures that minor differences between players do not translate into large changes in the chosen team.

Given the difficulty of designing randomized algorithms for differential privacy (mistakes have been found in published proofs [10]), we have developed automated techniques for proving differential privacy [3]. We demonstrated that we can solve this problem via a careful reduction to solving a system of recursive constraints, defined via *constrained Horn clauses*. Specifically, we showed that a rich space of proofs, called *coupling proofs*, can be logically characterized, allowing us to eliminate probabilistic reasoning.

3 Conclusion

I discussed some of our progress in applying automated verification and synthesis to addressing problems in fairness of decision-making programs. I believe that the formal methods community, broadly defined, has plenty to contribute to the discourse on fairness and bias—for instance, by developing formally verified implementations of fair algorithms, runtime verification techniques for detecting unfairness, programming languages where fairness is a first-class construct, debugging techniques for detecting potential bias, and others.

Acknowledgements. The work described in this talk is in collaboration with a fantastic group of students and researchers: Samuel Drews, Aditya Nori, Loris D'Antoni,

---

[1] World events at the time of writing strongly influenced my choice of example.

Justin Hsu, Calvin Smith, and David Merrell. The work described is generously supported by the National Science Foundation (NSF) grant #1704117.

References

1. Albarghouthi, A., D'Antoni, L., Drews, S., Nori, A.V.: Fairsquare: probabilistic verification of program fairness. In: Proceedings of the ACM on Programming Languages (OOPSLA), vol. 1, pp. 80:1–80:30, October 2017. http://doi.acm.org/10.1145/3133904
2. Albarghouthi, A., D'Antoni, L., Drews, S.: Repairing decision-making programs under uncertainty. In: Majumdar, R., Kunčak, V. (eds.) CAV 2017. LNCS, vol. 10426, pp. 181–200. Springer, Cham (2017). https://doi.org/10.1007/978-3-319-63387-9_9
3. Albarghouthi, A., Hsu, J.: Synthesizing coupling proofs of differential privacy. In: Proceedings of the ACM on Programming Languages (POPL), vol. 2, pp. 58:1–58:30 (2018). http://doi.acm.org/10.1145/3158146
4. Dwork, C., Hardt, M., Pitassi, T., Reingold, O., Zemel, R.S.: Fairness through awareness. In: Innovations in Theoretical Computer Science 2012, Cambridge, MA, USA, 8–10 January 2012, pp. 214–226 (2012)
5. Dwork, C., Roth, A.: The Algorithmic Foundations of Differential Privacy, vol. 9. Now Publishers, Inc., Hanover (2014)
6. Feldman, M., Friedler, S.A., Moeller, J., Scheidegger, C., Venkatasubramanian, S.: Certifying and removing disparate impact. In: Proceedings of the 21st ACM SIGKDD International Conference on Knowledge Discovery and Data Mining, Sydney, NSW, Australia, 10–13 August 2015, pp. 259–268 (2015). http://doi.acm.org/10.1145/2783258.2783311
7. Hardt, M., Price, E., Srebro, N.: Equality of opportunity in supervised learning. CoRR abs/1610.02413 (2016). http://arxiv.org/abs/1610.02413
8. Kearns, M., Roth, A., Wu, Z.S.: Meritocratic fairness for cross-population selection. In: International Conference on Machine Learning, pp. 1828–1836 (2017)
9. Kleinberg, J., Mullainathan, S., Raghavan, M.: Inherent trade-offs in the fair determination of risk scores. In: ITCS (2017)
10. Lyu, M., Su, D., Li, N.: Understanding the Sparse Vector Technique for differential privacy. In: Appeared at the International Conference on Very Large Data Bases (VLDB), Munich, Germany, vol. 10, pp. 637–648 (2017). http://arxiv.org/abs/1603.01699
11. Merrell, D., Albarghouthi, A., DAntoni, L.: Weighted model integration with orthogonal transformations. In: Proceedings of the 26th International Joint Conference on Artificial Intelligence, pp. 4610–4616. AAAI Press (2017)
12. Pedreshi, D., Ruggieri, S., Turini, F.: Discrimination-aware data mining. In: Proceedings of the 14th ACM SIGKDD International Conference on Knowledge Discovery and Data Mining, pp. 560–568. ACM (2008)
13. Zemel, R.S., Wu, Y., Swersky, K., Pitassi, T., Dwork, C.: Learning fair representations. In: Proceedings of the 30th International Conference on Machine Learning, ICML 2013, Atlanta, GA, USA, 16–21 June 2013, pp. 325–333 (2013). http://jmlr.org/proceedings/papers/v28/zemel13.html

The MISRA C Coding Standard and its Role in the Development and Analysis of Safety- and Security-Critical Embedded Software

Roberto Bagnara[1,2]($\boxtimes$), Abramo Bagnara[1], and Patricia M. Hill[1]

[1] BUGSENG srl, Parma, Italy
{roberto.bagnara,abramo.bagnara,patricia.hill}@bugseng.com
[2] Department of Mathematical, Physical and Computer Sciences,
University of Parma, Parma, Italy
bagnara@cs.unipr.it
http://bugseng.com

Abstract. The MISRA project started in 1990 with the mission of providing world-leading best practice guidelines for the safe and secure application of both embedded control systems and standalone software. MISRA C is a coding standard defining a subset of the C language, initially targeted at the automotive sector, but now adopted across all industry sectors that develop C software in safety- and/or security-critical contexts. In this paper, we introduce MISRA C, its role in the development of critical software, especially in embedded systems, its relevance to industry safety standards, as well as the challenges of working with a general-purpose programming language standard that is written in natural language with a slow evolution over the last 40+ years. We also outline the role of static analysis in the automatic checking of compliance with respect to MISRA C, and the role of the MISRA C language subset in enabling a wider application of formal methods to industrial software written in C.

1 Introduction

In September 1994, the "First International Static Analysis Symposium" took place in Namur, Belgium [25]. The *Call for Papers* contained the following:

Static Analysis is increasingly recognized as a fundamental tool for high performance implementations and verification systems of high-level programming languages. The last two decades have witnessed substantial developments in this area, ranging from the theoretical frameworks to the

While Roberto Bagnara is a member of the *MISRA C Working Group* and of ISO/IEC JTC1/SC22/WG14, a.k.a. the *C Standardization Working Group*, the views expressed in this paper are his and his coauthors' and should not be taken to represent the views of either working group.

© Springer Nature Switzerland AG 2018
A. Podelski (Ed.): SAS 2018, LNCS 11002, pp. 5–23, 2018.
https://doi.org/10.1007/978-3-319-99725-4_2

design and implementation of analysers and their applications in optimizing compilers.

In November 1994, MISRA[1] published its "Development Guidelines For Vehicle Based Software" [3]. These listed static analysis as the first automatic methodology to verify software and contained the following paragraphs:

3.5.1.5 Consideration should be given to using a restricted subset of a programming language to aid clarity, assist verification and facilitate static analysis where appropriate.

3.5.2.6 Static analysis is effective in demonstrating that a program is well structured with respect to its control, data and information flow. It can also assist in assessing its functional consistency with its specification.

Paragraph 3.5.1.5 led to the definition of the subset of the C programming language that will later be called *MISRA C*.

While the quoted texts show the passage of time (today we would express things differently), they witness the fact that static analysis was recognized as an established research field at about the same time that it gathered enough industrial recognition to be explicitly recommended by an influential set of guidelines for the automotive industry, one of the most important economic sectors by revenue. The connection between static analysis research and the industrial world —which now encompasses all industry sectors— that recognizes MISRA C as the basis for the development of safe and secure applications in C has been basically unidirectional and mediated by the tool providers. These tool providers are interested in all advances in static analysis research in order to improve the applicability and usefulness of their tools and hence simplify the task of verifying compliance with respect to the MISRA C guidelines. It must be admitted that the static analysis research community has seen the (very pragmatic) industry movement behind MISRA C with a somewhat snobbish and often not well informed attitude.[2] For instance, [10, Sect. 3] suggests that MISRA C concerns coding style and that semantic-based static analysis is not needed to check its guidelines. In reality, while MISRA C encourages the adoption of a consistent programming style, it has always left this matter to individual organizations: "In addition to adopting the subset, an organisation should also have an in-house style guide. [...] However the enforcement of the style guide is outside the scope of this document" [27, Sect. 4.2.2] (see also [28, Sect. 5.2.2]). Moreover, as we will see, semantic-based static analysis is required to check many MISRA C guidelines without constraining too much the way the code is written.

In this paper we try to clear up such misconceptions and to properly introduce MISRA C to the static analysis community. Our ultimate aim is to foster collaboration between the communities, one which we believe could be very fruitful: the wide adoption of MISRA C in industry constitutes an avenue for a wider

---

[1] Originally, an acronym for *Motor Industry Software Reliability Association*.

[2] The authors of this paper are *not* an exception to this statement, at least not until 2010.

introduction of formal methods and a good opportunity to channel some applied static analysis research to the most important subset of the C programming language.

The plan of the paper is the following: Sect. 2 introduces the C language explaining why it is so widely adopted, why it is (not completely) defined as it is, why it is not going to change substantially any time soon, and why subsetting it is required; Sect. 3 introduces the MISRA project and MISRA C focusing on its last edition, MISRA C:2012, with its amendments and addenda; Sect. 4 highlights the links between MISRA C and static analysis; Sect. 5 discusses some trends and opportunities; Sect. 6 concludes.

2 The C Language

The development of the C programming language started in 1969 at Bell Labs, almost 50 years ago, and the language was used for the development of the Unix operating system [40]. Despite frequent criticism, C is still one of the most used programming languages overall[3] and the most used one for the development of embedded systems [7,44]. There are several reasons why C has been and is so successful:

- C compilers exist for almost any processor, from tiny DSPs used in hearing aids to supercomputers.
- C compiled code can be very efficient and without hidden costs, i.e., programmers can roughly predict running times even before testing and before using tools for worst-case execution time approximation.[4]
- C allows writing compact code: it is characterized by the availability of many built-in operators, limited verbosity, . . .
- C is defined by international standards: it was first standardized in 1989 by the American National Standards Institute (this version of the language is known as ANSI C) and then by the International Organization for Standardization (ISO) [17–21].
- C, possibly with extensions, allows easy access to the hardware and this is a must for the development of embedded software.
- C has a long history of usage in all kinds of systems including safety-, security-, mission- and business-critical systems.
- C is widely supported by all sorts of tools.

Claims that C would eventually be superseded by C++ do not seem very plausible, at least as far as the embedded software industry is concerned. In addition to the already-stated motives, there is language size and stability: C++ has become a huge, very complex language; moreover it is evolving at a pace that is in sharp

---

[3] Source: TIOBE Index for June 2018, see https://www.tiobe.com/tiobe-index/.

[4] This is still true for implementations running on simple processors, with a limited degree of caching and internal parallelism. Prediction of maximum running time without tools becomes outright impossible for current multi-core designs such as Kalray MPPA, Freescale P4080, or ARM Cortex-A57 equivalents (see, e.g., [35–37]).

contrast with industrial best practices. The trend whereby C++ rapid evolution clashes with the industry requirements for stability and backward compatibility has been put black-on-white at a recent WG21 meeting,[5] where the following statement was agreed upon [46]: "The Committee should be willing to consider the design/quality of proposals even if they may cause a change in behavior or failure to compile for existing code."

A good portion of the criticism of C comes from the notion of *behavior*, defined as *external appearance or action* [20, Par. 3.4] and the so-called *as-if rule*, whereby the compiler is allowed to do any transformation that ensures that the "observable behavior" of the program is the one described by the standard [20, Par 5.1.2.3#5].[6] While all compiled languages have a sort of *as-if rule* that allows optimized compilation, one peculiarity of C is that it is not fully defined. There are four classes of not fully defined behaviors (in the sequel, collectively referred to as "non-definite behaviors"):

implementation-defined behavior: *unspecified behavior where each implementation documents how the choice is made* [20, Par. 3.4.1]; e.g., the sizes and precise representations of the standard integer types;
locale-specific behavior: *behavior that depends on local conventions of nationality, culture, and language that each implementation documents* [20, Par. 3.4.2]; e.g., character sets and how characters are displayed;
undefined behavior: *behavior, upon use of a non-portable or erroneous program construct or of erroneous data, for which this International Standard imposes no requirements* [20, Par. 3.4.3]; e.g., attempting to write a string literal constant or shifting an expression by a negative number or by an amount greater than or equal to the width of the promoted expression;
unspecified behavior: *use of an unspecified value, or other behavior where this International Standard provides two or more possibilities and imposes no further requirements on which is chosen in any instance* [20, Par. 3.4.4]; e.g., the order in which sub-expressions are evaluated.

Setting aside locale-specific behavior, whose aim is to avoid some nontechnical obstacles to adoption, it is important to understand the connection between non-definite behavior and the relative ease with which optimizing compilers can be written. In particular, C data types and operations can be directly mapped to data types and operations of the target machine. This is the reason why the sizes and precise representations of the standard integer types are implementation-defined: the implementation will define them in the most efficient way depending on properties of the target CPU registers, ALUs and memory hierarchy. Attempting to write on string literal constants is undefined behavior because they may

---

[5] WG21 is a common shorthand for ISO/IEC JTC1/SC22/WG21, a.k.a. the C++ *Standardization Working Group*. The cited meeting tool place in Jacksonville, FL, USA, March 12–17, 2018.
[6] In this paper, we refer to the C99 language standard [19] because this is the most recent version of the language that is targeted by the current version of MISRA C [28]. All what is said about the C language itself applies equally, with only minor variations, to all the published versions of the C standard.

reside in read-only memory and/or may be merged and shared: for example, a program containing ''String'' and ''OtherString'' may only store the latter and use a suffix of that representation to represent the former. The reason why shifting an expression by a negative number or by an amount greater than or equal to the width of the promoted expression is undefined behavior is less obvious. What sensible semantics can be assigned to shifting by a negative number of bit positions? Shifting in the opposite direction is a possible answer, but this is usually not supported in hardware, so it would require a test, a jump and a negation. It is a bit more subtle to understand why the following is undefined behavior:

```
uint32_t i = 1;
i = i << 32;   /* Undefined behavior. */
```

One would think that pushing 32 or more zeroes to the right of i would give zero. However, this does not correspond to how some architectures implement shift instructions. IA-32, for instance [15, section on "IA-32 Architecture Compatibility"]:

> The 8086 does not mask the shift count. However, all other IA-32 processors (starting with the Intel 286 processor) do mask the shift count to 5 bits, resulting in a maximum count of 31. This masking is done in all operating modes (including the virtual-8086 mode) to reduce the maximum execution time of the instructions.

This means that, on all IA-32 processors starting with the Intel 286, a direct mapping of C's right shift to the corresponding machine instruction will give:

```
i = i << 32;              /* This is equivalent to... */
i = i << (32 & 0x1F);     /* ... this, i.e., ...      */
i = i << 0;               /* this, which is a no-op.  */
```

So also for this case, for speed and ease of implementation, C leaves the behavior undefined.

The recurring request to WG14[7] to "fix the language" is off the mark. In fact, weakness of the C language comes from its strength:

- Non-definite behavior is the consequence of two factors:
    1. the ease of writing efficient compilers for almost any architecture;
    2. the existence of many compilers by different vendors and the fact that the language is standardized.

---

[7] Short for ISO/IEC JTC1/SC22/WG14, a.k.a. the *C Standardization Working Group*.

Concerning the second point, it should be considered that, in general, ISO standardizes existing practice taking into account the opinions of the vendors that participate in the standardization process, and with great attention to backward compatibility: so, when diverging implementations exist, non-definite behavior might be the only way forward.

- The objective of easily obtaining efficient code with no hidden costs is the reason why, in C, there is no run-time error checking.
- Easy access to the hardware entails the facility with which the program state can be corrupted.
- Code compactness is one of the reasons why the language can easily be misunderstood and misused.

Summarizing, the C language can be expected to remain faithful to its original spirit and to be around for the foreseeable future, at least for the development of embedded systems. However, it is true that several features of C do conflict with both safety and security requirements. For this reason, *language subsetting* is crucial for critical applications. This was recognized early in [14] and is now mandated or recommended by all safety- and security-related industrial standards, such as IEC 61508 (industrial), ISO 26262 (automotive), CENELEC EN 50128 (railways), RTCA DO-178B/C (aerospace) and FDA's *General Principles of Software Validation* [43]. Today, the most authoritative language subset for the C programming language is *MISRA C*, which is the subject of the next section.

3   MISRA C

The MISRA project started in 1990 with the mission of providing world-leading best practice guidelines for the safe and secure application of both embedded control systems and standalone software. The original project was part of the UK Governments "SafeIT" programme but it later became self-supporting, with MIRA Ltd, now HORIBA MIRA Ltd, providing the project management support. Among the activities of MISRA is the development of guidance in specific technical areas, such as the C and C++ programming languages, model-based development and automatic code generation, software readiness for production, safety analysis, safety cases and so on. In November 1994, MISRA published its "Development guidelines for vehicle based software", a.k.a. "The MISRA Guidelines" [3]: this is the *first* automotive publication concerning functional safety, more than 10 years before work started on ISO 26262 [16].

The MISRA guidelines [3] prescribed the use of "a restricted subset of a standardized structured language." In response to that, the MISRA consortium began work on the MISRA C guidelines: at that time Ford and Land Rover were independently developing in-house rules for vehicle-based C software and it was recognized that a common activity would be more beneficial to industry. The first version of the MISRA C guidelines was published in 1998 [26] and received significant industrial attention.

In 2004, following the many comments received from its users —many of which, beyond expectation, were in non-automotive industries— MISRA published an improved version of the C guidelines [27]. In MISRA C:2004 the intended audience explicitly became constituted by *all* industries that develop C software for use in high-integrity/critical systems. Due to the success of MISRA C and the fact that C++ is also used in critical contexts, in 2008 MISRA published a similar set of *MISRA C++* guidelines [34].

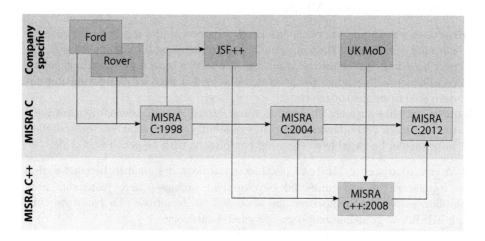

Fig. 1. Origin and history of MISRA C

Both MISRA C:1998 and MISRA C:2004 target the 1990 version of the C Standard [17]. In 2013, the revised set of guidelines known as MISRA C:2012 was published [28]. In this version there is support both for C99 [19] as well as C90 (in its amended and corrected form sometimes referred to as C95 [18]). With respect to previous versions, MISRA C:2012 covers more language issues and provides a more precise specification of the guidelines with improved rationales and examples. Figure 1 shows part of the relationship and influence between the MISRA C/C++ guidelines and other sets of guidelines. It can be seen that MISRA C:1998 influenced Lockheed's "JSF Air Vehicle C++ Coding Standards for the System Development and Demonstration Program" [1], which influenced MISRA C++:2008, which, in turn, influenced MISRA C:2012. The activity that led to MISRA C++:2008 was also encouraged by the UK Ministry of Defence which, as part of its *Scientific Research Program*, funded a work package that resulted in the development of a "vulnerabilities document" (the equivalent of Annex J listing the various behaviors in ISO C, which is missing in ISO C++, making it hard work to identify them and to ensure they are covered by the guidelines). Moreover, MISRA C deeply influenced NASA's "JPL Institutional Coding Standard for the C Programming Language" [2] and several other coding standards (see, e.g., [6,9,42]).

The MISRA C guidelines are concerned with aspects of C that impact on the safety and security of the systems, whether embedded or standalone: they define "a subset of the C language in which the opportunity to make mistakes is either removed or reduced" [28]. The guidelines ban critical non-definite behavior and constrain the use of implementation-defined behavior and compiler extensions. They also limit the use of language features that can easily be misused or misunderstood. Overall, the guidelines are designed to improve reliability, readability, portability and maintainability.

There are two kinds of MISRA C guidelines.

Directive: a guideline where the information concerning compliance is generally not fully contained in the source code: requirements, specifications, design, . . . may have to be taken into account. Static analysis tools may assist in checking compliance with respect to directives if provided with extra information not derivable from the source code.

Rule: a guideline such that information concerning compliance is fully contained in the source code. Discounting undecidability, static analysis tools should, in principle, be capable of checking compliance with respect to the rule.

A crucial aspect of MISRA C is that it has been designed to be used within the framework of a documented development process where justifiable non-compliances will be authorized and recorded as *deviations*. To facilitate this, each MISRA C guideline has been assigned a category.

Mandatory: C code that complies to MISRA C must comply with every mandatory guideline; deviation is not permitted.

Required: C code that complies to MISRA C shall comply with every required guideline; a formal deviation is required where this is not the case.

Advisory: these are recommendations that should be followed as far as is reasonably practical; formal deviation is not required, but non-compliances should be documented.

Every organization or project may choose to treat any required guideline as if it were mandatory and any advisory guideline as if it were required or mandatory. The adoption of MISRA Compliance:2016 [30] allows advisory guidelines to be downgraded to "Disapplied" when a check for compliance is considered to have no value, e.g., in the case of *adopted code*[8] that has not been developed so as to comply with the MISRA C guidelines. Of course, the decision to disapply a guideline should not be taken lightly: [30] prescribes the compilation of a *guideline recategorization plan* that must contain, among other things, the rationale for any decision to disapply a guideline.

Each MISRA C rule is marked as *decidable* or *undecidable* according to whether answering the question "Does this code comply?" can be done algorithmically. Hence rules are marked 'undecidable' whenever violations depend

---

[8] Such as the standard library, device drivers supplied by the compiler vendor or the hardware manufacturer, middleware components, third party libraries, automatically generated code, legacy code, ...

on run-time (dynamic) properties such as the value contained in a modifiable object or whether control reaches a particular point. Conversely, rules are marked 'decidable' whenever violations depend only on compile-time (static) properties, such as the types of the objects or the names and the scopes of identifiers. Clearly, for rules marked 'decidable', it is theoretically possible (i.e., given adequate computational resources) for a tool to emit a message if and only if the rule is violated. However, for rules marked 'undecidable', any tool will have to deal with the *don't know* answer in addition to *yes* and *no* at each distinct, relevant program point. In either case, if it is not practical (or even possible) for the tool to decide if the code is compliant with respect to a guideline at a particular program point, it can:

– suppress the *don't know* answer (i.e., possibly false negatives, no false positives);
– emit the *don't know* answer as a *yes* message (i.e., no false negatives, possibly false positives);
– a combination of the above (i.e., both possibly false negatives and possibly false positives);
– emit the *don't know* answer as a *caution* message (i.e., no false negatives, confined, possibly false positives).

MISRA C rules are also classified according to the amount of code that needs to be analyzed in order to detect all violations of the rule.

Single Translation Unit: all violations within a project can be detected by checking each translation unit independently.

System: identifying violations of a rule within a translation unit requires checking more than the translation unit in question, if not all the source code that constitutes the system.

MISRA C:2012 Amendment 1 [29], published in 2016, enhances MISRA C:2012 so as to extend its applicability to industries and applications where data-security is an issue. It includes 14 new guidelines (1 directive and 13 rules) to complete the coverage of ISO/IEC TS 17961:2013 [22], a.k.a. *C Secure Coding Rules*, a set of rules for secure coding in C.[9] Details of such complete coverage are provided in [32]. A similar document [33] shows that, with Amendment 1, coverage of *CERT C Coding Standard* is almost complete and that, consequently, MISRA C is today the language subset of choice for all industries developing embedded systems in C that are safety- and/or security-critical [4].

For the rest of this paper, all references to *MISRA C* will be for the latest published version MISRA C:2012 [28] including its Technical Corrigendum 1 [31] and Amendment 1 [29]: these will be consolidated into the forthcoming first revision of MISRA C:2012 [5]. It should be noted that both the MISRA C and MISRA C++ projects are active and constantly improving the guidelines and developing new works: for instance, the MISRA C Working Group is currently working at adding support for C11 [21] and, in response to community feedback, at further enhancing the guidance on undefined/unspecified behaviors [5].

---

[9] This technical specification has been slightly amended in 2016 [23].

4   Static Analysis and MISRA C

The majority of the MISRA C guidelines are decidable, and thus compliance can be checked by algorithms that:

- do not need nontrivial approximations of the value of program objects;
- do not need nontrivial control-flow information.

Of course, these algorithms can still be very complex. For instance, the nature of the translation process of the C language, which includes a preprocessing phase, is a source of complications: the preprocessing phase must be tracked precisely, and compliance may depend on the source code before preprocessing, on the source code after preprocessing, or on the relationship between the source code before and after preprocessing.

The rest of this section focuses on those guidelines whose check for compliance requires or significantly benefits from semantic-based analysis. Obviously every undecidable rule has decidable approximations, but these are necessarily characterized by a significant number of false positives unless rigid programming schemes are adopted. For example, Rule 17.2, which disallows recursion, admits a decidable approximation that requires finding cycles in the call graph and flagging, as potentially non-compliant, all function calls via pointers. If function calls via pointers are not used (i.e., the program is written in a smaller subset of C than that strictly mandated by the rule) then there will be no false positives.

The guidelines are listed in Table 1. Note that the text provided for each guideline is just, as indicated, a rough, very rough one-line summary, whereas the proper description can span multiple pages. The reader is referred to [28, 29, 31] for the full details. Note that the list of guidelines in Table 1 begins with four directives: even though checking compliance with respect to them requires information that may not be present in the code, they involve undecidable program properties.

Table 2 classifies the guidelines of Table 1 according to attributes of an approximate representation of the program semantics; an approximation built by a static analysis algorithm to check compliance for the given guideline with adequate precision, that is, no false negatives and relatively few false positives. The attributes are the following:

control-flow: detecting all potential violations with a low rate of false positives requires computing an approximation that allows observing control-flow within the program with relatively high precision;
data-flow: detecting all potential violations with a low rate of false positives requires computing an approximation that allows observing the possible values of objects with relatively high precision; this is further refined with two sub-attributes:
>**points-to:** observing the values of pointer objects is important;
>**arithmetic:** observing the values of other (i.e., non-pointer) objects (including pointer offsets) is important.

Table 1. MISRA C guidelines whose checking requires/benefits from semantic analysis

Guideline	Rough one-line summary
D4.1	Avoid run-time failures
D4.11	Check the validity of values passed to library functions
D4.13	Resource-handling functions should be called in an appropriate sequence
D4.14	Do not trust values received from external sources
R1.3	No undefined or critical unspecified behavior
R2.1	No unreachable code
R2.2	No dead code
R8.13	Point to `const`-qualified type if possible
R9.1	Do not read uninitialized automatic storage
R12.2	Right-hand operand of a shift operator must be in range
R13.1	No side effects in initializers
R13.2	Do not depend on unspecified evaluation order of expressions
R13.5	No side effects in right-hand operand of `&&` or `||`
R14.1	No floating-point loop counters
R14.2	Restricted form of `for` loops
R14.3	No invariant controlling expressions
R17.2	No direct or indirect recursion
R17.5	Actual parameters for arrays must have an appropriate size
R17.8	Do not modify function parameters
R18.1	Pointer arithmetic must not exceed array limits
R18.2	Do not subtract pointers not pointing to the same array
R18.3	Do not compare pointers not pointing to the same object
R18.6	Pointer object must not live longer than corresponding pointees
R19.1	Objects must not be assigned or copied to overlapping objects
R21.13	Functions in `<ctype.h>` must not be passed out-of-spec values
R21.14	Do not use `memcmp` to compare null-terminated strings
R21.17	Use of functions from `<string.h>` must not result in buffer overflow
R21.18	`size_t` argument of functions from `<string.h>` must be in range
R21.19	Do not modify objects through pointers returned by `localeconv`, ...
R21.20	Pointers returned by `asctime`, `ctime`, ... must not be reused
R22.1	All dynamically-obtained resources must be explicitly released
R22.2	Do not free memory that was not dynamically allocated
R22.3	Do not open files for read and write at the same time on different streams
R22.4	Do not attempt to write to a read-only stream
R22.5	Do not directly access the content of a `FILE` object
R22.6	Do not use the value of pointer to a `FILE` after the stream is closed
R22.7	Macro `EOF` must only be compared to values returned by some functions
R22.8	Reset `errno` before calling an *errno-setting-function*
R22.9	Test `errno` after calling an *errno-setting-function*
R22.10	Test `errno` only after calling an *errno-setting-function*

Table 2. MISRA C guidelines and main static analysis properties

Guideline	control-flow	data-flow	
		points-to	arithmetic
D4.1		✓	✓
D4.11		✓	✓
D4.13	✓	✓	
D4.14			✓
R1.3	✓	✓	✓
R2.1	✓		
R2.2	✓		✓
R8.13			✓
R9.1	✓[1]	✓[1]	
R12.2			✓
R13.1		✓	
R13.2	✓		
R13.5		✓	
R14.1	✓	✓	✓
R14.2		✓	✓
R14.3		✓	✓
R17.2	✓	✓	
R17.5		✓	✓
R17.8		✓	
R18.1		✓	✓
R18.2		✓	
R18.3		✓	
R18.6	✓	✓	
R19.1		✓	✓
R21.13			✓
R21.14		✓	
R21.17		✓	✓
R21.18		✓	✓
R21.19		✓	
R21.20	✓	✓	
R22.1	✓	✓	
R22.2	✓	✓	
R22.3	✓	✓	
R22.4	✓	✓	
R22.5		✓	
R22.6	✓	✓	
R22.7	✓	✓	
R22.8	✓		
R22.9	✓		
R22.10	✓		

[1] See Sect. 5.2 for an alternative view on how to check compliance with respect to this rule.

Of course, it is well known that control-flow information depends on data-flow information and the other way around, exactly as points-to information depends on arithmetic values and the other way around: here we only characterize the approximation that is available *at the end* of the static analysis, without reference to how it has been obtained.

Table 2 shows that semantic-based static analysis potentially plays an important role in the checking of compliance with respect to MISRA C. The actual situation, however, is not as clear cut: this brings us to the next section.

5   Discussion

We have seen that 40 MISRA C guidelines out of 173 depend on semantic properties of the program. This implies that research in semantic static analysis is very relevant to the MISRA C ecosystem, provided that a few important points are taken into due consideration. These are discussed in Sects. 5.1, 5.2, and 5.3. A further opportunity for cooperation is outlined in Sect. 5.4.

5.1   MISRA C: Error Prevention, Not Bug Finding

As said earlier, MISRA C cannot be separated from the process of documented software development it is part of. In particular, the use of MISRA C in its proper context is part of an *error prevention* strategy which has little in common with *bug finding*, i.e., the application of automatic techniques for the detection of instances of some software errors. This point is so rarely understood that it deserves proper explanation.

To start with, the violation of a guideline is not necessarily a software error. For instance, let us consider Rule 11.4, which advises against converting integers to object pointers and vice-versa. There is nothing intrinsically wrong about converting an integer constant to a pointer when it is necessary to address memory mapped registers or other hardware features. However, such conversions are implementation-defined and have undefined behaviors (due to possible truncation and the formation of invalid and/or misaligned pointers), so that they are best avoided everywhere apart from the very specific instances where they are both required and safe. This is why the deviation process is an essential part of MISRA C: the point of a guideline is not "You should not do that" but "This is dangerous: you may only do that if (1) it is needed, (2) it is safe, and (3) a peer can easily and quickly be convinced of both (1) and (2)." One useful way to think about MISRA C and the processes around it is to consider them as an effective way of conducting a *guided peer review* to rule out most C language traps and pitfalls.[10]

The attitude with respect to incompleteness is entirely different between the typical audience of bug finders and the typical audience of MISRA C. Bug finders are usually tolerant about false negatives and intolerant about false positives:

---

[10] We are indebted to Clayton Weimer for this observation.

for instance, by following the development of *Clang Static Analyzer*[11] it can be seen that all is done to avoid false positives with little or no regard to false negatives. This is not the right mindset for checking compliance with respect to MISRA C: false positives are a nuisance and should be reduced and/or confined as much a possible, but using algorithms with false negatives implies that those in charge of ensuring compliance will have to use other methods. So, compliance to MISRA C is not bug finding and, of course, finding some, many or even all causes of run-time errors does not imply compliance to MISRA C.

5.2   MISRA C: Readability, Explainability, Code Reviews

Another aspect that places MISRA C in a different camp from bug finding has to do with the importance MISRA C assigns to reviews: code reviews, reviews of the code against design documents, reviews of the latter against requirements. Concerning design documents and requirements this is captured by Directive 3.1. More generally, the need for code readability and explainability is clearly expressed in the rationale of many MISRA C guidelines.

This fact has some counterintuitive consequences on the use of static analysis, which is of course crucial both for bug finding and for the (partial) automation of MISRA C compliance checking. Consider Rule 9.1, whereby the value of an automatic object must not be read before it has been set, since otherwise we have undefined behavior. For bug finding, the smarter the static analysis algorithm the better. Use of the same smart algorithm for ensuring compliance with respect to Rule 9.1 risks obeying the letter of MISRA C but not its spirit.[12] Suppose on the specific program our smart algorithm ensures Rule 9.1 is never violated: we have thus ruled out one source of undefined behavior, which is good. However, the programmer, other programmers, code reviewers, quality assurance people, one month from now or six months from now may have to:

1. ensure that the automatic objects that are the subject of the rule are indeed initialized with the correct value;
2. confirm that the outcome of the tool is indeed correct.

If this takes more than 30 s or a minute per object, this is not good: the smart static analysis algorithm can track initializations and uses even when they are scattered across, say, switch cases nested into complex loops; a human cannot. So, ensuring compliance with respect to Rule 9.1 with deep semantic analysis is counterproductive to the final goal of the process of which MISRA C is part. For that purpose it is much better to use a decidable approximation of Rule 9.1 such as a suitable generalization of the *Definite Assignment* algorithm employed by Java compilers [13, Chap. 16].

---

[11] https://clang-analyzer.llvm.org/, last accessed on July 5th, 2018.

[12] There are many ways to do that.

5.3   Analysis of Code Meant To Comply with MISRA C

As was already recognized in [10], despite the mentioned misunderstanding about the nature of MISRA C, the restriction to a language subset where non-definite behavior and many problematic features are banned or severely regulated "can considerably help the efficiency and precision of the static analysis." This can simplify and guide the design of static analyzers: for example, features of C that are deprecated by MISRA C need not be handled precisely and efficiently when the intended application domain follows MISRA C. It is not a coincidence that such features (e.g., unions, unrestricted pointer casts, backward gotos) pose significant problems to the designers of static analyses tools.

5.4   Annotations

Another area where there is significant potential for collaboration between the static analysis community and the MISRA C ecosystem concerns program annotations. During the last 20 years there have been a number of proposals for annotation languages allowing programmers to provide partial specifications of program components. These languages are usually tied to one specific tool, e.g.: the annotation language of the *Frege Program Prover* [45]; the annotation language of *eCv* (Escher C Verifier) [11], the annotation language of *Frama-C*, *ACSL* (ANSI/ISO C Specification Language) [8], and its executable variant *E-ACSL* [41]; the annotation language of *VCC* [12]; the annotation language of *Veri-Fast* [24,38]. A comparison of these tools, with particular regard to annotation languages and the potential for application in industry, is available in [39].

The MISRA C Working Group is working, among other things, on a tool-agnostic annotation language for C. The main objectives of this endeavor are:

1. to improve the quality (precision) of static analysis by allowing the provision of information regarding the developer's intent, the required state in function preconditions and so on;
2. to make it easier to work with adopted code (legacy code, library code) that has not been written to comply with MISRA C [30];
3. to do this in a way that will be accessible to the majority of C/C++ programmers in a form that is easy to read and understand.

6   Conclusion

In this paper, having explained some of the advantages and disadvantages of using the C language for embedded systems and how the uncontrolled use of C conflicts with both safety and security requirements, we described the background, motivation and history of the MISRA project. We have explained how the MISRA C guidelines define a standardized structured subset of the C language; making it easier, for code that follows these guidelines (possibly with well-documented deviations), to verify that important and necessary safety and security properties hold.

We have looked at the different kinds of the MISRA C guidelines, distinguishing between those that can be automatically verified from the code syntax, those that need information beyond that contained in the source code, and those for which the question as to whether the code is compliant is algorithmically undecidable. We have noted also that, for all guidelines, due to the size and complexity of modern software, automatic tools perform an essential function in the checking or partial checking of compliance. We have highlighted the fundamental differences between so-called bug finding and the application of MISRA C in the context of the error prevention strategy it is part of.

In this paper we have outlined both the role of static analysis in the automatic checking of compliance with respect to MISRA C, and the role of the MISRA C language subset in enabling a wider application of formal methods to industrial software. It is hoped that this will contribute to improved collaboration between the two communities, so that static analysis will be able to play a fuller part in the software development of critical systems leading to improved safety and security.

Acknowledgments. For the notes on the history of MISRA and MISRA C we are indebted to Andrew Banks (LDRA, current Chairman of the MISRA C Working Group) and David Ward (HORIBA MIRA, current Chairman of the MISRA Project). For the information on the ongoing work on annotations, we thank Chris Tapp (LDRA, Keylevel Consultants, MISRA C Working Group, current Chairman of the MISRA C++ Working Group). We are grateful to the following people who helped in proofreading the paper and provided useful comments and advice: Fulvio Baccaglini (PRQA — a Perforce Company, MISRA C Working Group), Dave Banham (Rolls-Royce plc, MISRA C Working Group), Daniel Kästner (AbsInt, MISRA C Working Group), Thomas Schunior Plum (Plum Hall, WG14), Chris Tapp (ditto), David Ward (ditto). We are also grateful to the following BUGSENG collaborators: Paolo Bolzoni, for some example ideas; Anna Camerini for the composition of Fig. 1.

References

1. VV., AA.: JSF Air vehicle C++ coding standards for the system development and demonstration program. Document 2RDU00001, Rev C, Lockheed Martin Corporation, December 2005
2. VV., AA.: JPL institutional coding standard for the C programming language. Technical report JPL DOCID D-60411, Jet Propulsion Laboratory, California Institute of Technology, March 2009
3. The Motor Industry Software Reliability Association: Development Guidelines For Vehicle Based Software. The Motor Industry Research Association, Nuneaton, Warwickshire CV10 0TU, UK, November 1994
4. Bagnara, R.: MISRA C, for security's sake! In: Lami, G. (ed.) Informal proceedings of the 14th Workshop on Automotive Software & Systems, Milan, Italy (2016). http://www.automotive-spin.it/. Also published as Report arXiv:1705.03517 [cs.SE], available at http://arxiv.org/

5. Banks, A.: MISRA C – recent developments and a road map to the future. Presentation slides available at http://www.his-2018.co.uk/session/misra-c-updates-2016, presented at the High Integrity Software Conference 2016, Bristol, UK, 1 November 2016 (2016)
6. Barr, M.: Embedded C Coding Standard. Barr Group, Germantown, MD, USA (2013)
7. Barr Group, Germantown, MD, USA: Embedded Systems Safety & Security Survey, February 2018. http://www.barrgroup.com/
8. Baudin, P., Cuoq, P., Filliâtre, J.C., Marché, C., Monate, B., Moy, Y., Prevosto, V.: ACSL: ANSI/ISO C Specification Language, version 1.13 edn. (2018)
9. CERT: SEI CERT C Coding Standard: Rules for Developing Safe, Reliable, and Secure Systems. Software Engineering, Carnegie Mellon University, 2016 edn. (2016)
10. Cousot, P., Cousot, R., Feret, J., Miné, A., Mauborgne, L., Monniaux, D., Rival, X.: Varieties of static analyzers: a comparison with ASTREE. In: First Joint IEEE/IFIP Symposium on Theoretical Aspects of Software Engineering (TASE 2007), pp. 3–20. IEEE Computer Society, Shanghai, June 2007
11. Crocker, D., Carlton, J.: Verification of C programs using automated reasoning. In: Proceedings of the Fifth IEEE International Conference on Software Engineering and Formal Methods (SEFM 2007), pp. 7–14. IEEE Computer Society, London (2007)
12. Dahlweid, M., Moskal, M., Santen, T., Tobies, S., Schulte, W.: VCC: contract-based modular verification of concurrent C. In: 31st International Conference on Software Engineering (ICSE 2009), Companion Volume, pp. 429–430. IEEE Computer Society, Vancouver (2009)
13. Gosling, J., Joy, B., Steele, G.L., Bracha, G., Buckley, A.: The Java Language Specification: Java SE 8 Edition, 5th edn. Java Ser. Addison-Wesley, Upper Saddle River (2014)
14. Hatton, L.: Safer C: Developing Software for High-Integrity and Safety-Critical Systems. McGraw-Hill Inc., New York (1995)
15. Intel Corporation: Intel 64 and IA-32 Architectures Software Developer's Manual – Volume 2 (2A, 2B, 2C & 2D): Instruction Set Reference, A-Z (2018)
16. ISO: ISO 26262:2011: Road Vehicles – Functional Safety. ISO, Geneva, Switzerland, November 2011
17. ISO/IEC: ISO/IEC 9899:1990: Programming Languages – C. ISO/IEC, Geneva, Switzerland (1990)
18. ISO/IEC: ISO/IEC 9899:1990/AMD 1:1995: Programming Languages – C. ISO/IEC, Geneva, Switzerland (1995)
19. ISO/IEC: ISO/IEC 9899:1999: Programming Languages – C. ISO/IEC, Geneva, Switzerland (1999)
20. ISO/IEC: ISO/IEC 9899:1999/Cor 3:2007: Programming Languages – C. ISO/IEC, Geneva, Switzerland, Technical Corrigendum 3 edn. (2007)
21. ISO/IEC: ISO/IEC 9899:2011: Programming Languages – C. ISO/IEC, Geneva, Switzerland (2011)
22. ISO/IEC: ISO/IEC TS 17961:2013, Information technology – Programming languages, their environments & system software interfaces – C Secure Coding Rules. ISO/IEC, Geneva, Switzerland, November 2013
23. ISO/IEC: ISO/IEC TS 17961:2016, Information technology – Programming languages, their environments & system software interfaces – C Secure Coding Rules. ISO/IEC, Geneva, Switzerland, August 2016

24. Jacobs, B., Smans, J., Philippaerts, P., Vogels, F., Penninckx, W., Piessens, F.:
    VeriFast: a powerful, sound, predictable, fast verifier for C and java. In: Bobaru,
    M., Havelund, K., Holzmann, G.J., Joshi, R. (eds.) NFM 2011. LNCS, vol. 6617,
    pp. 41–55. Springer, Heidelberg (2011). https://doi.org/10.1007/978-3-642-20398-
    5_4
25. Le Charlier, B. (ed.): SAS 1994. LNCS, vol. 864. Springer, Heidelberg (1994).
    https://doi.org/10.1007/3-540-58485-4
26. Motor Industry Software Reliability Association: MISRA-C:1998 – Guidelines for
    the use of the C language in vehicle based sofware. MIRA Ltd, Nuneaton, War-
    wickshire CV10 0TU, UK, July 1998
27. Motor Industry Software Reliability Association: MISRA-C:2004 – Guidelines for
    the use of the C language in critical systems. MIRA Ltd, Nuneaton, Warwickshire
    CV10 0TU, UK, October 2004
28. MISRA: MISRA C:2012 – Guidelines for the use of the C language in critical
    systems. MIRA Ltd, Nuneaton, Warwickshire CV10 0TU, UK, March 2013
29. MISRA: MISRA C:2012 Amendment 1 – Additional security guidelines for MISRA
    C:2012. HORIBA MIRA Ltd, Nuneaton, Warwickshire CV10 0TU, UK, April 2016
30. MISRA: MISRA Compliance:2016 – Achieving compliance with MISRA Coding
    Guidelines. HORIBA MIRA Ltd, Nuneaton, Warwickshire CV10 0TU, UK, April
    2016
31. MISRA: MISRA C:2012 Technical Corrigendum 1 – Technical clarification of
    MISRA C:2012. HORIBA MIRA Ltd, Nuneaton, Warwickshire CV10 0TU, UK,
    June 2017
32. MISRA: MISRA C:2012 Addendum 2 – Coverage of MISRA C:2012 (including
    Amendment 1) against ISO/IEC TS 17961:2013 "C Secure". HORIBA MIRA Ltd,
    Nuneaton, Warwickshire CV10 0TU, UK, 2nd edn. January 2018
33. MISRA: MISRA C:2012 Addendum 3 – Coverage of MISRA C:2012 (including
    Amendment 1) against CERT C 2016 Edition. HORIBA MIRA Ltd, Nuneaton,
    Warwickshire CV10 0TU, UK, January 2018
34. Motor Industry Software Reliability Association: MISRA C++:2008 – Guidelines
    for the use of the C++ language in critical systems. MIRA Ltd, Nuneaton, War-
    wickshire CV10 0TU, UK, June 2008
35. Nélis, V., Yomsi, P.M., Pinho, L.M.: The variability of application execution times
    on a multi-core platform. In: Schoeberl, M. (ed.) Proceedings of the 16th Interna-
    tional Workshop on Worst-Case Execution Time Analysis (WCET 2016), OASICS,
    vol. 55, pp. 6:1–6:11. Schloss Dagstuhl – Leibniz-Zentrum für Informatik, Toulouse
    (2016)
36. Nowotsch, J., Paulitsch, M.: Leveraging multi-core computing architectures in
    avionics. In: Constantinescu, C., Correia, M.P. (eds.) Proceedings of the Ninth
    European Dependable Computing Conference (EDCC 2012), pp. 132–143. IEEE
    Computer Society, Sibiu (2012)
37. Nowotsch, J., Paulitsch, M., Buhler, D., Theiling, H., Wegener, S., Schmidt,
    M.: Multi-core interference-sensitive WCET analysis leveraging runtime resource
    capacity enforcement. In: Proceedings of the 26th Euromicro Conference on Real-
    Time Systems (ECRTS 2014), pp. 109–118. IEEE Computer Society, Madrid (2014)
38. Philippaerts, P., Mühlberg, J.T., Penninckx, W., Smans, J., Jacobs, B., Piessens,
    F.: Software verification with VeriFast: industrial case studies. Sci. Comput. Pro-
    gram. **82**, 77–97 (2014)
39. Rainer-Harbach, M.: Methods and Tools for the Formal Verification of Software: An
    Analysis and Comparison. Master's thesis, Fakultät für Informatik der Technischen
    Universität Wien, Wien, Austria, November 2011

40. Ritchie, D.M.: The development of the C language. SIGPLAN Not. **28**(3), 201–208 (1993)
41. Signoles, J.: EACSL: Executable ANSI/ISO C Specification Language, version 1.12 edn. (2018)
42. Software Engineering Center: Embedded System Development Coding Reference: C Language Edition. Information-Technology Promotion Agency, Japan, version 2.0, July 2014
43. U.S. Department Of Health and Human Services; Food and Drug Administration; Center for Devices and Radiological Health; Center for Biologics Evaluation and Research: General Principles of Software Validation; Final Guidance for Industry and FDA Staff, version 2.0 edn. January 2002. http://www.fda.gov/MedicalDevices/DeviceRegulationandGuidance/GuidanceDocuments/ucm085281.htm
44. VDC Research, Natick, MA, USA: 2011 Embedded Engineer Survey, August 2011
45. Winkler, J.F.H.: The Frege Program Prover. In: 42. Internationales Wissenschaftliches Kolloquium, pp. 116–121. Technische Universität Ilmenau (1997)
46. Winters, T.: C++ stability, velocity, and deployment plans [R2]. Doc. no. P0684R2, ISO/IEC JTC1/SC22/WG21, February 2018. http://www.open-std.org/jtc1/sc22/wg21/docs/papers/2018/p0684r2.pdf

Numerical Invariants via Abstract Machines

Zachary Kincaid$^{(\boxtimes)}$

Princeton University, Princeton, USA
`zkincaid@cs.princeton.edu`

Abstract. This paper presents an overview of a line of recent work on generating non-linear numerical invariants for loops and recursive procedures. The method is compositional in the sense that it operates by breaking the program into parts, analyzing each part independently, and then combining the results. The fundamental challenge is to devise an effective method for analyzing the behavior of a loop given the results of analyzing its body. The key idea is to separate the problem into two: first we approximate the loop dynamics by an abstract machine, and then symbolically compute the reachability relation of the abstract machine.

1 Introduction

Compositional recurrence analysis (CRA) is a method for generating numerical invariant for loops [17,25,26]. The goal of CRA is to compute a *transition formula* that over-approximates the behavior of the program. CRA analyzes programs bottom-up, in the style of an *effective* denotational semantics: we syntactically decompose the program into parts, compute a transition formula for each part independently, and then compose the results. The composition operators for transition formulas correspond to the familiar regular expression operations of *sequencing*, *choice*, and *iteration*.

The essence of the analysis is the *iteration* operator. Given a transition formula that over-approximates the body of a loop, the iteration operator computes a transition formula that over-approximates any number of iterations of the loop. CRA accomplishes this by extracting recurrence relations from a transition formula using an SMT solver, and then computing the closed form of those recurrences. Using this strategy, CRA can compute rich numerical invariants, including polynomial and exponential equations and inequations.

This paper gives an alternate account for this strategy, which is based on extracting an abstract machine that simulates the loop body, and then computing a closed form for the reachability relation of that abstract machine (thus we replace "recurrence relations" with the broader notion of "abstract machine"). Seen in this light, CRA is an answer to the question *given some simple model of computation that admits a closed representation of the reachability relation, how can we make use of it in program analysis?*

Secondly, this paper describes how the compositional approach to program analysis can be used to analyze recursive procedures [25]. A key idea is to exploit

© Springer Nature Switzerland AG 2018
A. Podelski (Ed.): SAS 2018, LNCS 11002, pp. 24–42, 2018.
https://doi.org/10.1007/978-3-319-99725-4_3

the two-phase structure of the iteration operator: we can detect and enforce convergence of procedure summaries using widening and equivalence operations on abstract machines.

The remainder of the paper is organized as follows. Section 2 gives a short introduction to compositional program analysis. The technical core of the paper is Sect. 3, which gives a recipe for analyzing loops by computing the reachability relation of an abstract machine that simulates its body. Section 4 illustrates how abstract machines can be used to analyze programs with (recursive) procedures. Section 5 surveys related work, and Sect. 6 concludes.

2   Outline

We begin by defining a simple structured programming language:

$$x \in \mathsf{Var}$$
$$e \in \mathsf{Expr}::\, = \mathtt{x} \mid n \in \mathbb{Z} \mid e_1 + e_2 \mid e_1 e_2$$
$$c \in \mathsf{Cond}::\, = e_1 \leq e_2 \mid e_1 = e_2 \mid c_1 \wedge c_2 \mid c_1 \vee c_2 \mid \neg c$$
$$P \in \mathsf{Program}::\, = \mathtt{x} \,:\!= e \mid P_1 ; P_2 \mid \mathtt{if}\ c\ \mathtt{then}\ P_1\ \mathtt{else}\ P_2 \mid \mathtt{while}\ c\ \mathtt{do}\ P$$

Our goal is to compute, for any given program P, a transition formula $\mathbf{TF}[\![P]\!]$ that over-approximates its behavior. A transition formula is a logical formula over the program variables Var and a set of primed copies Var', representing the values of the program variables before and after executing a program. In the following, we will make use of several different languages for expressing transition formulas. For the sake of concreteness, we give a definition of polynomial arithmetic transition formulas, PolyTF, below:

$$s, t \in \mathsf{PolyTerm}::\, = \mathtt{x} \in \mathsf{Var} \mid \mathtt{x}' \in \mathsf{Var}' \mid y \in \mathsf{BoundVar} \mid \lambda \in \mathbb{Q} \mid s + t \mid st$$
$$F, G \in \mathsf{PolyTF}::\, = s \leq t \mid s = t \mid s < t \mid c_1 \wedge c_2 \mid c_1 \vee c_2 \mid \exists y \in \mathbb{N}.F \mid \exists y \in \mathbb{Z}.F$$

For any given program P, a transition formula $\mathbf{TF}[\![P]\!]$ can be computed by recursion on syntax:

$$\mathbf{TF}[\![\mathtt{x}\,:\!= e]\!] \triangleq \mathtt{x}' = e \wedge \bigwedge_{y \neq \mathtt{x} \in X} y' = y$$

$$\mathbf{TF}[\![\mathtt{if}\ c\ \mathtt{then}\ P_1\ \mathtt{else}\ P_2]\!] \triangleq (c \wedge \mathbf{TF}[\![P_1]\!]) \vee (\neg c \wedge \mathbf{TF}[\![P_2]\!])$$

$$\mathbf{TF}[\![P_1 ; P_2]\!] \triangleq \exists X \in \mathbb{Z}.\mathbf{TF}[\![P_1]\!][\mathsf{Var} \mapsto X] \wedge \mathbf{TF}[\![P_2]\!][\mathsf{Var} \mapsto X]$$

$$\mathbf{TF}[\![\mathtt{while}\ c\ \mathtt{do}\ P]\!] \triangleq (c \wedge \mathbf{TF}[\![P]\!])^{\circledast} \wedge (\neg c[\mathsf{Var} \mapsto \mathsf{Var}'])$$

where $(-)^{\circledast}$ is an iteration operator: a function that computes an approximation of the transitive closure of a transition formula. Thus, the essential problem involved in designing a program analysis in this style is to define the iteration operator.

3   Approximating Loops with Abstract Machines

This section outlines a general strategy for loop summarization which is based on decomposing the problem into two: (1) find an abstract machine that simulates the action of the transition formula, and (2) express the reachability relation of the abstract machine as a transition formula. We then describe compositional recurrence analysis as an instance of this strategy. We begin with an example.

Example 3.1. Consider the program P given below   •

```
while (i < n) do
    i := i + 1
    if (y < z)
        y := y + i - 1}
    else
        z := z + i - 1
```
$Body$

Recall that $\mathbf{TF}[\![P]\!] = (i < n \wedge \mathbf{TF}[\![Body]\!])^\circledast \wedge n \le i$, where $(-)^\circledast$ is an iteration operator (yet to be defined) and

$$\mathbf{TF}[\![Body]\!] \equiv i < n \wedge i' = i + 1 \wedge \left(\begin{array}{l} (y < z \wedge y' = i + 1 \wedge z' = z) \\ \vee (z \le y \wedge y' = y \wedge z' = z + 1) \end{array} \right) .$$

The formula $F \triangleq i < n \wedge \mathbf{TF}[\![Body]\!]$ defines a transition relation $R \subseteq \mathbb{Z}^4 \times \mathbb{Z}^4$ on the state space $\mathbb{Z}^4$, where each vector $\boldsymbol{u} = \begin{bmatrix} i\ y\ z\ n \end{bmatrix}^T$ corresponds to an assignment of values to the program variables i, y, z, and n. The behavior of F is difficult to analyze directly, so instead we will approximate by a simpler system that is more amenable to analysis. We observe that F is simulated by the affine transformation

$$f(\boldsymbol{x}) = \begin{bmatrix} 1\ 0\ 0 \\ 1\ 1\ 0 \\ 0\ 0\ 1 \end{bmatrix} \boldsymbol{x} + \begin{bmatrix} 1 \\ 0 \\ 0 \end{bmatrix}$$

where the correspondence between the state space of F (i.e., $\mathbb{Z}^4$) and the state space of f (i.e., $\mathbb{Q}^3$) is given by the linear transformation

$$S = \begin{bmatrix} 1\ 0\ 0\ 0 \\ 0\ 1\ 1\ 0 \\ 0\ 0\ 0\ 1 \end{bmatrix} \begin{array}{l} \longleftarrow \text{1st dimension corresponds to i} \\ \longleftarrow \text{2nd dimension corresponds to y} + z \\ \longleftarrow \text{3rd dimension corresponds to n} \end{array}$$

That is, we have that for every $\boldsymbol{u}$ and $\boldsymbol{u}'$ in $\mathbb{Z}^4$ such that $\boldsymbol{u}$ may transition to $\boldsymbol{u}'$ via F, we have $S\boldsymbol{u}' = f(S\boldsymbol{u})$. Phrased differently, we have

$$F \models \begin{bmatrix} 1\ 0\ 0\ 0 \\ 0\ 1\ 1\ 0 \\ 0\ 0\ 0\ 1 \end{bmatrix} \begin{bmatrix} i' \\ y' \\ z' \\ n' \end{bmatrix} = \begin{bmatrix} 1\ 0\ 0 \\ 1\ 1\ 0 \\ 0\ 0\ 1 \end{bmatrix} \begin{bmatrix} 1\ 0\ 0\ 0 \\ 0\ 1\ 1\ 0 \\ 0\ 0\ 0\ 1 \end{bmatrix} \begin{bmatrix} i \\ y \\ z \\ n \end{bmatrix} + \begin{bmatrix} 1 \\ 0 \\ 0 \end{bmatrix} \quad \text{or,}$$

$$F \models \mathtt{i}' = \mathtt{i} + 1 \wedge (\mathtt{y}' + \mathtt{z}') = (\mathtt{y}' + \mathtt{z}') + \mathtt{i} \wedge \mathtt{n}' = \mathtt{n} \ . \tag{1}$$

The analysis of affine systems is classical. We can compute the following symbolic representation of the transitive closure of the transition relation defined by f:

$$c\ell(f) = \exists k \in \mathbb{N}. x_1' = x_1 + k x_2 + \frac{k(k+1)}{2} \wedge x_2' = x_2 + k \wedge x_3' = x_3$$

Since f simulates the behavior of F, then $c\ell(f)$ simulates the behavior of any number of iterations of F. Thus, if we define

$$F^{\circledast} = \exists k \in \mathbb{N}. \mathtt{y}' + \mathtt{z}' = \mathtt{y} + \mathtt{z} + k\mathtt{i} + \frac{k(k+1)}{2} \wedge \mathtt{i}' = \mathtt{i} + k \wedge \mathtt{n}' = \mathtt{n} \tag{2}$$

then we may take $\mathbf{TF}[\![P]\!] = F^{\circledast} \wedge \mathtt{i}' \geq \mathtt{n}'$ to be a conservative over-approximation the behavior of P.

3.1 Approximating Formulas by Machines

Definition 1. *An $(m \times n)$-**formula** is a formula whose free variables range over $m + n$ free variables $x_1, ..., x_m$ and $x_1', ..., x_n'$. For any $(m \times n)$-formula F, we use $\mathcal{R}[\![F]\!]$ to denote the relation that F represents:*

$$\mathcal{R}[\![F]\!] \triangleq \{(\boldsymbol{u}, \boldsymbol{v}) \in \mathbb{Q}^m \times \mathbb{Q}^n : \{x_1 \mapsto u_1, ..., x_n \mapsto u_n, x_1' \mapsto v_1, ..., x_n' \mapsto v_n\} \models F\}$$

*We call an $(n \times n)$-formula an n-**transition formula**. We use $\mathbf{TF}$ to denote the set of all transition formulas (for any n).*

If F is an $(m \times n)$-formula and $\boldsymbol{y} = y_1, ..., y_m$ and $\boldsymbol{z} = z_1, ..., z_n$ are vectors of variables of lengths m and n, we use $F(\boldsymbol{y}, \mathbf{z})$ to denote the result of replacing each x_i with y_i and each x_i' with z_i. If F is an $(\ell \times m)$-formula and G is an $(m \times n)$-formula, we use $F \odot G$ to denote the relational composition of F and G:

$$F \odot G \triangleq \exists \boldsymbol{y}. F(\boldsymbol{x}, \boldsymbol{y}) \wedge G(\boldsymbol{y}, \boldsymbol{x}') \ .$$

We use $\check{F}$ to denote the reversal of F, the $(m \times \ell)$-formula defined by

$$\check{F} \triangleq F[x_1 \mapsto x_1', ..., x_m \mapsto x_m', x_1' \mapsto x_1, ..., x_n' \mapsto x_n]$$

Abstract Machines. Fix some class of abstract machines $\mathbf{M}$, which can be understood as some kind of discrete dynamical system with a numerical state space. We suppose that we are given two functions that related abstract machines to transition formulas:

- $\gamma : \mathbf{M} \to \mathbf{TF}$, which maps each machine M to its *concretization* $\gamma(M)$, a transition formula that represents the action of one step of M.
- $c\ell : \mathbf{M} \to \mathbf{TF}$, which maps each machine M it its *closure* $c\ell(M)$, a transition formula that represents the action of any number of steps of M.

We assume that for any machine M in $\mathbf{M}$, we have $\mathcal{R}[\![\gamma(M)]\!]^* = \mathcal{R}[\![c\ell(M)]\!]$.[1]

Example 3.2. Let **1-LT** denote the set of affine transformations of the form $f(\boldsymbol{x}) = A\boldsymbol{x} + \boldsymbol{b}$, where A is a lower triangular matrix with 1's on the diagonal (e.g., the function f in Example 3.1). For any $f(\boldsymbol{x}) = A\boldsymbol{x} + \boldsymbol{b}$ in **1-LT**, define the concretization of f simply as $\gamma(f) \triangleq \boldsymbol{x}' = A\boldsymbol{x} + \boldsymbol{b}$. The readability relation of an affine transformation in **1-LT** can be expressed in polynomial arithmetic (i.e., PolyTF) and computed in polytime. The procedure is a specialization of the classical one for computing the reachability relation of an affine transformation (which in general does not have a closed form in PolyTF)—see [17, §III.B] for details.

Simulation. Simulation relations are a standard approach to relating the behavior of dynamical systems [31]. Below we specialize the theory to our setting.

Definition 2. *Let F be an m-transition formula and let G be an n-transition formula. A **simulation formula** is an $(m \times n)$-formula S such that*

1. *S is total (for all $\boldsymbol{u} \in \mathbb{Q}^m$ there exists some $\boldsymbol{v} \in \mathbb{Q}^n$ such that $(\boldsymbol{u}, \boldsymbol{v}) \in \mathcal{R}[\![S]\!]$)*
2. *For all $(\boldsymbol{u}, \boldsymbol{v}) \in \mathcal{R}[\![S]\!]$, for every $\boldsymbol{u}'$ such that $(\boldsymbol{u}, \boldsymbol{u}') \in \mathcal{R}[\![F]\!]$, there exist some $\boldsymbol{v}'$ such that $(\boldsymbol{v}, \boldsymbol{v}') \in \mathcal{R}[\![G]\!]$ and $(\boldsymbol{u}', \boldsymbol{v}') \in \mathcal{R}[\![S]\!]$. Diagrammatically,*

$$
\begin{array}{ccc}
\forall\,\boldsymbol{u} & \xrightarrow{\;F\;} & \boldsymbol{v} \\
{\scriptstyle S}\Big| & & \Big\vdots{\scriptstyle S} \\
\boldsymbol{u}' & \dashrightarrow{\;G\;} & \boldsymbol{v}' {\scriptstyle \exists}
\end{array}
$$

We use $S : F \Vdash G$ to denote that S is simulation formula from F to G.

Example 3.3. Consider Example 3.1. For ease of reading, we will refer to original variables i, y, z, n of the system rather than their canonical names x_1, x_2, x_3, x_4. The simulation between relation between the transition formula F and the affine map f is

$$
S \triangleq x_1' = y + z \wedge x_2' = i \wedge x_3' = n \;.
$$

This is a special simulation in that it is functional (each state of the program is related to exactly one state of the affine system), but this need not be the case. For example, suppose that we know (perhaps by running a sign analysis on the program P) that i is non-negative. Let $G = F \wedge i \geq 0$. While we cannot understand the effect of the loop on y and z as an affine transformation, we can so understand lower and upper bounds on them: y and z are incremented by at

---

[1] For our purposes, the weaker hypothesis $\mathcal{R}[\![\gamma(M)]\!]^* \subseteq \mathcal{R}[\![c\ell(M)]\!]$ is sufficient. We use equality to emphasize that $\mathbf{M}$ is expected to be a class of machines that is easy to analyze.

least 0 and at most i. This abstraction can be realized by the function $g \in \mathbf{1\text{-}LT}$ and simulation T defined by

$$
g(\boldsymbol{x}) = \begin{bmatrix} 1&0&0&0&0&0&0 \\ 1&1&0&0&0&0&0 \\ 0&0&1&0&0&0&0 \\ 0&1&0&1&0&0&0 \\ 0&1&0&0&1&0&0 \\ 0&0&0&0&0&1&0 \\ 0&0&0&0&0&0&1 \end{bmatrix} \boldsymbol{x} + \begin{bmatrix} 1 \\ 0 \\ 0 \\ 0 \\ 0 \\ 0 \\ 0 \end{bmatrix} \qquad T = \left(\begin{aligned} &x_1 = i \\ &\wedge\ x_2 = y + z \\ &\wedge\ x_3 = n \\ &\wedge\ x_4 \geq y \\ &\wedge\ x_5 \geq z \\ &\wedge\ x_6 \geq -y \\ &\wedge\ x_7 \geq -z \end{aligned} \right)
$$

The last ingredient we need to be able to define (although not yet *compute*) an approximate transitive closure operator is a way of understanding an $(n \times m)$ simulation formula and a m-transition formula as an n-transition formula. This is given by conjugation:

Definition 3. *Let F be an $(m \times m)$-formula and let S be an $(n \times m)$-formula. The **conjugation of F by S**, $S \triangleright F$, is the $(n \times n)$-formula defined by*

$$
S \triangleright F \triangleq S \odot F \odot \check{S}
$$
$$
= \exists \boldsymbol{y}, \boldsymbol{y'}.S(\boldsymbol{x}, \boldsymbol{y}) \wedge F(\boldsymbol{y}, \boldsymbol{y'}) \wedge S(\boldsymbol{x'}, \boldsymbol{y'})
$$

Example 3.4. In Example 3.1, conjugation of f by S yields the formula in Eq (1), and conjugation of $cl(f)$ by S yields the formula in Eq (2).

Observe that $F \triangleright S$ is the *weakest* among all n-transition formulas G such that S is a simulation from G to F. That is, we have

1. $S : (S \triangleright F) \Vdash F$
2. For all n-transition formulas G, we have $S : G \Vdash F$ if and only if $G \models F \triangleright S$.

Moreover, note that $(R \odot S) \triangleright F \equiv R \triangleright (S \triangleright F)$ and $id \triangleright F \equiv F$, where id denotes an identity relation of appropriate dimension.

Finally, we arrive at the central observation underlying our approach:

Observation 1. *Let F be a transition formula, let M be an abstract machine, and let S be a simulation formula such that $S : F \Vdash M$. Let $F^{\circledast} = S \triangleright cl(M)$. Then $\mathcal{R}[\![F]\!]^* \subseteq \mathcal{R}[\![F^{\circledast}]\!]$.*

That is: provided we can compute for any transition formula F an abstract machine M and a simulation S such that $S : F \Vdash M$, we can over-approximate the transitive closure of F with the transition formula $S \triangleright cl(M)$.

3.2 Computing (best) Abstractions

We now turn to the question of what it means for an abstract machine to be a *best* abstraction of a transition formula. Consider again Example 3.1: the function f is *an* affine transformation in $\mathbf{1\text{-}LT}$ that simulates the given loop, but might there be a better one, whose closure yields more precise information about the loop?

To investigate this problem, it is convenient to use the language of category theory. Fix some class of simulation formulas $\mathcal{S}$, which is quotiented by logical equivalence, contains all identity relations, and is closed under composition (e.g., $\mathcal{S}$ might be the class of simulation formulas that correspond to linear transformations as in Example 3.1). We construct a category $\mathbf{TF}_\mathcal{S}$ where the objects are transition formulas (or perhaps transition formulas of a certain kind, e.g., formulas expressed in Presburger arithmetic), and the morphisms $S : F \to G$ are simulations belonging to $\mathcal{S}$ such that $S : F \Vdash G$. Similarly, we may construct a category of abstract machines $\mathbf{M}_\mathcal{S}$ similarly where the objects are machines and the morphisms are $\mathcal{S}$-simulations. The concretization function γ can now be extended to a functor $\gamma : \mathbf{M}_\mathcal{S} \to \mathbf{TF}_\mathcal{S}$, which maps each machine M in $\mathbf{M}$ to its concretization $\gamma(M)$, and maps each simulation $S : M \to M'$ between $\mathbf{M}$-machines to the same simulation $S : \gamma(M) \to \gamma(M')$ between their associated transition formulas. The closure function cl can likewise be extended to a functor. The question of whether the transition formulas in $\mathbf{TF}$ have best abstractions in $\mathbf{M}$ with respect to simulations in $\mathcal{S}$ can now be phrased as: *does the functor γ have a left-adjoint?*

Recall that a functor $\alpha : \mathbf{TF}_\mathcal{S} \to \mathbf{M}_\mathcal{S}$ is left-adjoint to γ if there is a pair of natural transformations

- $\eta : 1_{\mathbf{TF}_\mathcal{S}} \Rightarrow \gamma \circ \alpha$ (the *unit* of the adjunction)
- $\epsilon : \alpha \circ \gamma \Rightarrow 1_{\mathbf{M}_\mathcal{S}}$ (the *counit* of the adjunction)

such that (1) for all transition formulas F, we have $1_{\alpha(F)} = \epsilon_{\alpha(F)} \circ \alpha(\eta_F)$ and (2) for all abstract machines M, we have $1_{\gamma(M)} = \gamma(\epsilon_M) \circ \eta_{\gamma(M)}$. The best abstraction of a transition formula F can be conceived of as the pair $(\alpha(F), \eta_F)$ consisting of an abstract machine $\alpha(F)$ (*which* machine best captures the behavior of F) and a simulation $\eta_F : F \to \gamma(\alpha(F))$ (*how* the machine $\alpha(F)$ captures the behavior of F). The sense in which $(\alpha(F), \eta_F)$ is *best* abstraction is that for any other machine M and simulation S, there is a unique simulation $\overline{S} : \alpha(F) \to M$ such that $S = \gamma(\overline{S}) \circ \eta_F$; that is, the following diagram commutes:

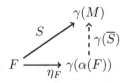

As a consequence, we have that there is no other machine and simulation that yields a better approximation of the transitive closure of a formula F than (α, η_F). This is summarized in the following:

Proposition 1. *Let F be a transition formula, let M be a machine, and let $S : F \to \gamma(M)$ be a simulation. Then $\eta_F \triangleright cl(F) \models S \triangleright cl(M)$.*

Proof. Let $\overline{S}$ be the unique simulation $\overline{S} : \alpha(F) \to M$ such that $S = \gamma(\overline{S}) \circ \eta_F$. Since $c\ell$ is a functor, we have a simulation $c\ell(\overline{S}) : c\ell(\alpha(F)) \to c\ell(M)$. It follows that

$$c\ell(\alpha(F)) \models c\ell(\overline{S}) \triangleright c\ell(M) = \overline{S} \triangleright c\ell(M) \ .$$

Conjugating by η_F yields

$$\eta_F \triangleright c\ell(\alpha(F)) \models \eta_F \triangleright \left(\overline{S} \triangleright c\ell(M)\right)$$
$$= \left(\eta_F \odot \overline{S}\right) \triangleright c\ell(M)$$
$$= S \triangleright c\ell(M) \ .$$

Summing up, we have the following recipe for summarizing loops:

Let $\mathcal{S}$ be a class of simulation relations, $\mathbf{TF}_{\mathcal{S}}$ be a category of transition formulas, $\mathbf{M}_{\mathcal{S}}$ be a category of abstract machines, $\alpha : \mathbf{TF}_{\mathcal{S}} \to \mathbf{M}_{\mathcal{S}}$, $\gamma : \mathbf{M}_{\mathcal{S}} \to \mathbf{TF}_{\mathcal{S}}$, and $c\ell : \mathbf{M}_{\mathcal{S}} \to \mathbf{TF}_{\mathcal{S}}$ be functors, and let $\eta : 1_{\mathbf{TF}_{\mathcal{S}}} \Rightarrow \gamma \circ \alpha$ be a natural transformation such that
1. $\mathcal{R}[\![c\ell(F)]\!] = \mathcal{R}[\![\gamma(F)]\!]^*$
2. α is left adjoint to γ, with unit η.
Then the function $F^{\circledast} \triangleq \eta_F \triangleright c\ell(\alpha(F))$ is an iteration operator.

If we derive an iteration operator $(-)^{\circledast}$ by following this recipe, then it is an easy consequence of Proposition 1 that $(-)^{\circledast}$ is monotone: if $F \models G$, then $F^{\circledast} \models G^{\circledast}$. This property makes it easier to reason about the behavior of program analyses.

3.3 Compositional Recurrence Analysis

We will now present compositional recurrence analysis as a sequence of examples of this recipe.

Example 3.5. The main content of [17, §III, A, B, C] is an algorithm for finding an affine transformation in **1-LT** that simulates a transition formula. We can give a more fine-grained description of the algorithm by describing the sense in which it is best.

The input to the algorithm is a linear arithmetic transition formula F. The algorithm operates in two steps. The first is to compute a best abstraction of F as an affine transformation in **1-LT** with respect to simulations of the form $\boldsymbol{x}' = S\boldsymbol{x}$ where each row of S is a standard basis vector. The fact that the rows of S are required to be standard basis vectors is due to the fact that they correspond to variables that satisfy a recurrence relation. In the light of the perspective of abstract machines, we see an opportunity for improving the analysis by allowing S to be an arbitrary linear transformation—computing best abstractions in this setting is an easy extension of the existing algorithm, and yields a strictly more precise analysis.

Having fixed a **1-LT** affine transformation $f(\boldsymbol{x}) = A\boldsymbol{x} + \boldsymbol{b}$ (of some dimension, say n) and a simulation S with $S : F \Vdash f$, the second step of the algorithm is to compute a best abstraction of F as a **1-LT** affine transformation of the form

$$
g(\boldsymbol{x}) = \begin{bmatrix} A & 0 \\ B & I \end{bmatrix} \boldsymbol{x} + \begin{bmatrix} \boldsymbol{b} \\ \boldsymbol{c} \end{bmatrix}
$$

with respect to linear simulations of the form $\boldsymbol{x}_1' = S\boldsymbol{x} \wedge \boldsymbol{x}_2' \geq S'\boldsymbol{x}$, where $\boldsymbol{x}_1'$ denotes the vector of variables $x_1'...x_n'$ and $\boldsymbol{x}_2'$ denotes the vector of variables $x_{n+1}'...x_m'$. That is, we allow the affine transformation f to be extended with additional dimensions ($n + 1$ through m), which act as upper bounds on linear terms over the variables of F (as illustrated in Example 3.3). This allows CRA to infer invariant polynomial inequations as well as equations. The fact that the lower right corner of the transformation matrix g is restricted to be the identity is a non-trivial restriction: new abstraction techniques are required to lift the assumption while retaining the property of being a best abstraction.   ⌐

Example 3.6. Affine transformations can be used to capture the relationship between the pre-state and post-state of a loop body, but information about the guard of the loop (i.e., relationships between pre-state variables) is lost. This information can be recovered via a *pre-state formula*, which is a transition formula in which only the pre-state variables $x_1, x_2, ...$ appear [17, §III, D]. The concretization of a pre-state formula G is G itself, the closure is defined by

$$
cl(G) = \exists k \in \mathbb{N}.(k = 0 \wedge \bigwedge_{x \in X} x' = x) \vee (k > 0 \wedge G) .
$$

The abstraction function is $\alpha(F) = \exists \boldsymbol{x}'.F$, which is *best* with respect to identity simulations. Post-state formulas can be defined dually.

Given a formula F, we can combine the pre-state, post-state, and affine transformation abstractions of F, by separately computing the closure of each abstraction and then conjoining the results. Better still, we can take a kind of reduced product [14] of the abstractions by synchronizing on the existentially quantified iteration variable k. This combination yields the compositional recurrence analysis described in [17].

Note that although compositional recurrence analysis computes (best) abstractions of *linear* formulas, the closure operator produces *polynomial* formulas. Before applying the abstraction functions, we first linearize the loop body formula [17, §IV]. The abstraction function of CRA is not best for polynomial arithmetic transition formulas (and no non-trivial abstraction function can be, since integer polynomial arithmetic is undecidable), but the fact that the abstraction function is best for linear arithmetic suggests that information is lost *only* because of incomplete reasoning about non-linear arithmetic.

Example 3.7. Affine maps capture non-linear behavior where non-linearity is a function of time, but some systems exhibit non-linear behavior even in a single step. *Solvable polynomial maps* are a class of abstract machines that can capture some such behavior while still being relatively easy to reason about.

Definition 4 ([35]). *A function $f : \mathbb{Q}^n \to \mathbb{Q}^n$ is a **solvable polynomial map** if there exists a partition of $\{1, ..., n\}$, $\boldsymbol{x}_1 \cup \cdots \cup \boldsymbol{x}_m$ with $\boldsymbol{x}_i \cap \boldsymbol{y}_j = \emptyset$ for $i \neq j$ such that for all $1 \leq i \leq m$ we have*

$$f_{\boldsymbol{y}_i}(\boldsymbol{x}) = A_i \boldsymbol{y}_i^t + p_i(\boldsymbol{y}_1, ..., \boldsymbol{y}_{i-1})$$

where $f_{\boldsymbol{x}_i}(\boldsymbol{x})$ denotes $f(\boldsymbol{x})$ projected onto the coordinates, $\boldsymbol{x}_i$, $A_i \in \mathbb{Q}^{|\boldsymbol{x}_i| \times |\boldsymbol{x}_i|}$ and $p_i \in \mathbb{Q}[\boldsymbol{x}_1, ..., \boldsymbol{x}_{i-1}]$.

The concretization of a solvable polynomial is $\gamma(f) \triangleq \boldsymbol{x}' = f(\boldsymbol{x})$. The closure $c\ell(f)$ of f is defined to be the reachability relation of f—[26] gives an algorithm for computing a closed form representation of the reachability relation of a solvable polynomial map in a logic involving polynomials, exponenentials, and also *operators* in the Berg's operational calculus [5], which can be treated as uninterpreted function symbols by an SMT solver.

The abstraction algorithm presented in [26] begins by computing a conjunction of polynomial equations and inequalities that are entailed by the formula. Since the logic is undecidable, we can make no guarantees about the quality of this approximation (however, it is best in the sense that, if the formula is expressed in linear arithmetic, then we compute the convex hull of the formula). A simulating solvable polynomial map is then extracted from this system of equations and inequalities in two steps, just as in [17]. The first step computes the best abstraction of a transition formula as a solvable polynomial map with respect to simulations of the form $\boldsymbol{x}' = S\boldsymbol{x}$. The abstraction is best under the assumption that the input transition formula is of the form $\bigwedge_{i=1}^n p_i(\boldsymbol{x}, \boldsymbol{x}') = 0$, where each p_i is a polynomial and such that

1. For every polynomial $p(\boldsymbol{x}, \boldsymbol{x}')$ such that $F \models p(\boldsymbol{x}, \boldsymbol{x}') = 0$, we have p in the ideal generated by $\{p_1, ..., p_n\}$.
2. F is total—for every $\mathbf{u}$ there exists some $\mathbf{v}$ such that $F(\mathbf{u}, \mathbf{v})$ holds.

Similarly to [17], we then extend this solvable polynomial map with additional dimensions to capture inequalities. However, the algorithm for computing inequalities makes use of polyhedral widening, so it need not be a best abstraction.

4 Control Flow and Recursive Procedures

This section explains how the style of analysis in Sect. 2 can be extended to a more realistic program model that has unstructured control flow and recursive procedures. The foundation is the algebraic view of program analysis pioneered by Tarjan, who developed an efficient algorithm for computing solutions to intraprocedural program analysis problems [39, 40]. The extension to the interprocedural setting is based on [25], which exploits abstract machines to compute approximations of recursive procedures.

We begin by formulating a new program model on top of the simple programming language defined in Sect. 2. Let Proc denote a finite set of procedure names. Define a syntactic category of *instructions*:

$$x \in \mathsf{Var} \qquad e \in \mathsf{Expr} \qquad c \in \mathsf{Cond} \qquad p \in \mathsf{Proc}$$
$$\mathsf{Instr} :: = \; x \; := \; t \mid \mathtt{assume}(c) \mid \mathtt{assert}(c) \mid \mathtt{call} \; p$$

A *control flow graph* $G = (V, \Delta, en, ex)$ consists of a finite set of nodes V, a finite set of instruction-labeled edges $\Delta \subseteq V \times \mathsf{Instr} \times V$, a distinguished entry vertex en, and a distinguished exit vertex ex. A *program* $P = \{G_p\}_{p \in \mathsf{Proc}}$ consists of a collection of control flow graphs indexed by procedure names.

The link from the effective denotational semantics of Sect. 2 to this program model is through the medium of **path expressions**: regular expressions that represent paths through a program. For our purposes, we may define a path expression to be a regular expression over the alphabet of instructions:

$$E \in \mathsf{PathExp} :: = \; instr \in \mathsf{Instr} \mid E_1 + E_2 \mid E_1 E_2 \mid E^* \mid 0 \mid 1$$

Suppose that we fix an iteration operator $(-)^{\circledast} : \mathbf{TF} \to \mathbf{TF}$ that over-approximates the transitive closure of a transition formula. Then given a path expression E and a *summary map* $S : \mathsf{Proc} \to \mathbf{TF}$ that maps each procedure to a transition formula, we can define a transition formula $\mathbf{TF}[\![E]\!](S)$ that over-approximates the paths in the path expression:

$$\mathbf{TF}[\![\mathtt{x} \; := \; \mathtt{e}]\!](S) \triangleq \mathtt{x}' = e \wedge \bigwedge_{\mathtt{y} \neq \mathtt{x} \in \mathsf{Var}} \mathtt{y}' = \mathtt{y}$$

$$\mathbf{TF}[\![\mathtt{assume}(c)]\!](S) \triangleq c \wedge \bigwedge_{\mathtt{x} \in \mathsf{Var}} \mathtt{x}' = \mathtt{x}$$

$$\mathbf{TF}[\![\mathtt{assert}(c)]\!](S) \triangleq \mathbf{TF}[\![\mathtt{assume}(c)]\!](S)$$

$$\mathbf{TF}[\![\mathtt{call} \; p]\!](S) \triangleq S(p)$$

$$\mathbf{TF}[\![E_1 + E_2]\!](S) = \mathbf{TF}[\![E_1]\!](S) \vee \mathbf{TF}[\![E_2]\!](S)$$

$$\mathbf{TF}[\![E_1 E_2]\!](S) = \mathbf{TF}[\![E_1]\!](S) \odot \mathbf{TF}[\![E_2]\!](S)$$

$$\mathbf{TF}[\![E^*]\!](S) = \mathbf{TF}[\![E]\!](S)^{\circledast}$$

$$\mathbf{TF}[\![1]\!](S) = \mathbf{TF}[\![\mathtt{assume}(0 = 0)]\!](S)$$

$$\mathbf{TF}[\![0]\!](S) = false$$

Tarjan gave an efficient algorithm for the *single-source path expression problem*: given a control flow graph $G_p = (V_p, \Delta_p, en_p, ex_p)$, compute for each vertex $v \in V$ a path expression $\mathbf{P}_{G_p}[en_p, v]$ representing the set of all paths from en_p to v in G_p. A summary for the procedure p may be computed by evaluating $\mathbf{TF}[\![\mathbf{P}_{G_p}[en_p, ex_p]]\!](S)$, or we prove that an assertion $(u, \mathtt{assert}(c), v)$ never fails by checking that $\mathbf{TF}[\![\mathbf{P}_{G_p}[en_p, u]]\!](S) \wedge \neg(c[X \mapsto X'])$ is unsatisfiable. The naïve definition of $\mathbf{TF}[\![-]\!]$ given above may use exponentially many transition formula operations due to repeated sub-path expressions. By using memoization or path compression, only linearly many operations are needed [39].

4.1   Interprocedural Analysis

Tarjan's algorithm assumes that we know how to compute a transition formula for each instruction in the programming language. For a language with procedure calls, this means that we require as input a summary map S : Proc $\rightarrow$ **TF**. For programs without recursive procedures, we can use Tarjan's algorithm to compute the summary map: first place the procedures in reverse topological order $p_1, ..., p_n$ (so that if p_i calls p_j then $j < i$), and then compute

$$S_0 = \lambda p.false$$
$$S_i = S_{i-1}\{p_i \mapsto \textbf{TF}[\textbf{P}_{G_{p_i}}[en_{p_i}, ex_{p_i}]](S_{i-1})\}$$

The summary map S_n maps each procedure to a transition formula that over-approximates its behavior.

For programs with *recursive* procedures, however, this process does not work. For recursive procedures we can always fall back on iterative techniques for resolving fixed point equations [13] (as we did in [17]), but this is not a very satisfying solution: we have a methodology for designing powerful invariant generators for loops (Sect. 3), and we would like to be able use this same methodology to analyze recursion.

The first important development in this direction was the work of Reps et al. [34], which showed that Tarjan's algorithm could be used to compute summaries for programs with *linear* recursion (i.e., in each path through each procedure, there is at most call instruction). The intuition behind their approach is illustrated in Fig. 1. Any path that contains a single function call, say $a(\texttt{call bar})b$, can be thought of as a pair consisting of a *prefix* a—a path from entry to the call, and a *continuation* κ—a path from the call to exit. Call the pair consisting of a and b a *tensored path*, and write it as $a \otimes b$. We can construct a *call graph* CG where the vertices are the procedure $\texttt{foo}$ and $\texttt{bar}$ and there is an edge from $\texttt{foo}$ to $\texttt{bar}$ labeled with the tensored path $a \otimes b$ (corresponding to the path in $\texttt{foo}$ that calls $\texttt{bar}$) and similarly an edge from $\texttt{bar}$ to $\texttt{foo}$ labeled $d \otimes e$. We also add a *base* vertex to the graph, and draw an edge from each procedure to *base* representing the path on which there is no recursive call. Tarjan's algorithm can be used to compute for each procedure a regular expression over an alphabet of tensored paths that represents the tensored paths from that procedure to *exit*.

$$\textbf{P}_{CG}[\texttt{foo}, base] = ((a \otimes b)(d \otimes e))^* (c \otimes 1) + ((a \otimes b)(d \otimes e))^* (a \otimes b)(f \otimes 1)$$
$$\textbf{P}_{CG}[\texttt{bar}, base] = ((a \otimes b)(d \otimes e))^* (c \otimes 1) + ((a \otimes b)(d \otimes e))^* (a \otimes b)(f \otimes 1)$$

These regular expressions represent the language of interprocedural paths through their respective procedures, where each tensored path (for instance, the path $(a \otimes b)(d \otimes e)(a \otimes b)(d \otimes e)(c \otimes 1)$ which belongs to $\textbf{P}_{CG}[\texttt{foo}, base]$), can be understood as an interprocedural path by reading the *prefix* of each tensor left-to-right followed by the *continuation* of each tensor right-to-left (that is, the path $adadcebeb$).

We can use transition formulas to represent the behavior of a program along a path; we can also use them to represent the behavior of a program along a

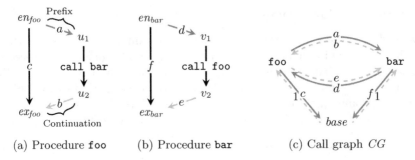

(a) Procedure foo   (b) Procedure bar   (c) Call graph CG

Fig. 1. A schematic recursive program with two procedures foo and bar, along with its call graph labeled with tensored paths. Instructions labeling non-call edges are abstracted away by letters.

tensored path, by using twice as many variables: one set of variables for the prefix, and one set for the continuation. That is:

Definition 5. *Given two n-transition formulas F and G, their **tensor product** $F \otimes G$ is defined to be the (2n)-transition formula*

$$F \otimes G \triangleq F \wedge (G[x_i \mapsto x'_{n+i}, x_i \mapsto x_{n+i}]_{i=1}^n)$$

Observe that we have $(F_1 \otimes G_1) \odot (F_2 \otimes G_2) \equiv (F_1 \odot F_2) \otimes (G_2 \odot G_1)$, so that composition of transition relations respects the left-to-right prefix, right-to-left continuation interpretation of tensored paths.

Summaries for the procedures foo and bar may thus be obtained by recursion on the regular expression of tensored paths, using the tensor product of transition formulas to interpret tensored paths, and finally converting the tensored transition formula back into a transition formula using the following *detensor* operator, which connects the prefix and continuation into a transition formula representing an ordinary path:

$$D(T) \triangleq \left(\exists x'. \left(F \wedge \bigwedge_{i=1}^n x'_i = x'_{i+n} \right) \right) [x_{n+i} \mapsto x'_i]_{i=1}^n .$$

That is, we have

$$S(\texttt{foo}) \triangleq D(\mathbf{TF}[\![\mathbf{P}_{CG}[\texttt{foo}, base]\!]\!])$$

$$S(\texttt{bar}) \triangleq D(\mathbf{TF}[\![\mathbf{P}_{CG}[\texttt{bar}, base]\!]\!])$$

(omitting the S argument to $\mathbf{TF}[\![-]\!]$ since call graph path expressions are free of calls).

Unfortunately, this idea does not extend to non-linear recursive procedures, so in the general case we must fall back on iterative methods for solving semantic equations. Naïve application of the iterative method requires designing an equivalence relation and widening operator for transition formulas. However, this is at odds with our goal of generating invariants in expressive logics, for which such operations are not readily available.

[25] gives an alternate approach, which again exploits abstract machines. The idea is that we can use widening and equivalence operators at the level of *abstract machines* rather than transition formulas. Abstract machines have simpler structure than general transition formulas and are more amenable to this kind of operation.

Example 4.8. In [17], the iteration operator extracts an affine transformation f and a linear simulation S. $S \triangleright \gamma(f)$ is a formula of a particular kind: a convex polyhedron. Widening operators for convex polyhedra are well known [15].   ⌐

Example 4.9. In [26], the iteration operator extracts a solvable polynomial map f and a linear simulation S. The formula $S \triangleright \gamma(f)$ is a conjunction of polynomial equations and inequations. Such formulas can be represented precisely by the *wedge* abstract domain, presented (along with its widening operator) in [26].   ⌐

The idea behind [25] is simple: each time we apply the iteration operator ⊛ to a transition formula F, we will compute an abstract machine that simulates F. Rather than using widening to ensure the convergence of the sequence of procedures summaries for each procedure, we use widening to ensure the convergence of the sequence of abstract machines for each loop. Soundness and termination of this approach relies on the property that every recursive call is contained inside some loop. Obviously, this need not be the case for the original program, but [25] gives an alternative algorithm to Tarjan's path expression algorithm that can be used to obtain *tensored* path expressions for each procedure that do satisfy this property.

5   Related Work

5.1   Abstract Machines with Closure

This section surveys a selection of work that, seen through the lens of Sect. 3, computes closure operators for some class of abstract machines.

Linear machines. (Discrete) linear dynamical systems are a well-studied class of machines, in which the state space is a vector space and the state evolves by applying a linear transformation—i.e., the transition formula of a linear dynamical system is of the form $\mathbf{x}' = A\mathbf{x}$. A formula representing the reachability relation of such a machine can be computed via symbolic matrix exponentiation: $c\ell(A) = \exists k \in \mathbb{N}.\mathbf{x}' = A^k\mathbf{x}$. A symbolic representation A^k can be expressed in terms of exponential-polynomials, where the base of each exponential term is drawn from the eigenvalues of A. However, since the eigenvalues of A may be complex, it is desirable to consider simpler closed forms.

The question of when the reachability relation of an affine dynamical system can be expressed in Presburger arithmetic was answered by Boigelot [8]. Boigelot gave a procedure for computing A^k under the assumption that the multiplicative monoid generated by A, $\{A^i : i \in \mathbb{N}\}$, is finite. Boigelot gives necessary and sufficient conditions for an iterated affine map to be definable in Presburger arithmetic, and also Presburger arithmetic extended with a single function V_r mapping each integer z to the greatest power of r that divides z. Boigelot also considers the case that the linear map is equipped with a polyhedral guard (which can restrict the number of times the linear map is iterated), in which case his conditions are necessary but not sufficient. Finkel and Leroux [18] extends further to guards defined in Presburger arithmetic.

Jeannet et al. developed a technique for *over-approximating* the behavior of linear dynamical systems, which is based on approximating the exponential of the real Jordan form of the transition matrix by an abstract domain of template polyhedron matrices [24].

An *affine program* consists of a finite graph where each edge is labeled by an affine transformation. A special case of interest for our purposes is with only one vertex: such an affine program corresponds to a transition formula of the form

$$\boldsymbol{x}' = A_1 \boldsymbol{x} + \boldsymbol{b}_1 \vee \cdots \vee \boldsymbol{x}' = A_m \boldsymbol{x} + \boldsymbol{b}_m \tag{3}$$

Haase and Halfon gave a polytime procedure for computing a Presburger formula defining the reachability relation of affine programs for which each transition matrix is diagonal and has either 0 or 1 on the diagonal (i.e., an integer vector addition system with states and resets) [20]. Müller-Olm and Seidl give a procedure for computing the smallest affine space that contains the reachability relation of affine programs [32]. Hrushovski et al. [21] gives a procedure to compute the smallest algebraic variety that contains the reachability relation.

Ultimately periodic relations. The transitive closure of difference-bound relations [11,12] and octagon relations [9] has been shown to be definable in Presburger arithmetic, and computable in polytime [27]. The theory of ultimately periodic relations unifies work on linear systems and difference-bound/octagon relations [10].

Polynomial machines. A **solvable polynomial machine** is a dynamical system with a transition formula of the form

$$\boldsymbol{x}' = p_1(\boldsymbol{x}) \vee \cdots \vee \boldsymbol{x}' = p_m(\boldsymbol{x}) \tag{4}$$

where each p_i is a solvable polynomial map. Rodríguez-Carbonell and Kapur [35] showed how to compute an algebraic variety that contains the reachability relation of a solvable polynomial machine with a real spectrum. Kovács improves upon this result, giving an algorithm for computing the smallest algebraic variety that contains the reachability relation of a solvable polynomial machine (without spectral assumptions), and further extends the technique to a broader class of machines with non-polynomial assignments [28]. The class of machines is extended even further in subsequent work by Humenberger et al. [22,23].

5.2 Symbolic Abstraction and Abstract Machines

Approximating programs by finite state machines using predicate abstraction is a classical technique in software model checking [4,19]. Kroening et al. [29] and Biallas et al. [6] present techniques for approximating the transitive closure of loops using predicate abstraction.

Sinn et al. have considered the problem of computing approximations of programs using vector addition systems [37] and difference-bound constraints [38] in the context of resource bound analysis. The technique is based on guessing a set of norms (integer-valued functions of the program state), which amounts to finding a linear simulation.

Recurrence analysis. Recurrence analysis is a family of program analysis techniques initiated by Wegbreit, which approximate the behavior of loops by extracting recurrence relations from the program and computing their closed forms [43]. It is closely related to the approach presented in this paper, with recurrence relations serving an analogous role to abstract machines. Recurrence analysis is a particularly prevalent technique in resource bound analysis, where the ability to compute non-linear expressions representing resource usage (e.g., time complexity) is crucial [1,3,7,16].

Symbolic Abstraction. There has been a body of work on computing best approximations of a logical formulas within abstract domains. For a thorough overview of symbolic abstraction in program analysis, see [33,41]. Here we highlight a few instances in which symbolic abstraction yields a complete instance of the recipe from Sect. 3:

- *Difference bound/octagonal relations*: the best abstraction of a transition formula as a difference bound or octagonal relation with respect to identity simulations can be computed using optimization modulo theories [30,36]. Transitive closure can be computed using the methods of [9,11,12,27].
- *Lossy sums*: the best abstraction of a transition formula in the form $\mathbf{x}' \leq \mathbf{x} + \mathbf{b}$ with respect to linear simulations can be computed using symbolic abstraction in the domain of convex polyhedra [17,42], and the method of Ancourt et al. for finding linear recurrence inequations from polyhedra [2].

6 Conclusion

Abstract machines give a mechanism for developing compositional program analyses that generate precise numerical invariants. There are two categories of work that are directly related to advancing this paradigm:

- Inventing new classes of abstract machines that admit effective closure operators, and which model interesting phenomena in dynamical systems.
- Developing techniques for computing best abstractions of transition formulas by abstract machines. E.g., there are a number of models (some of which referenced in Sect. 5) for which the best abstraction problem has not yet been investigated.

References

1. Albert, E., Arenas, P., Genaim, S., Puebla, G.: Automatic inference of upper bounds for recurrence relations in cost analysis. In: Alpuente, M., Vidal, G. (eds.) SAS 2008. LNCS, vol. 5079, pp. 221–237. Springer, Heidelberg (2008). https://doi.org/10.1007/978-3-540-69166-2_15
2. Ancourt, C., Coelho, F., Irigoin, F.: A modular static analysis approach to affine loop invariants detection. Electron. Notes Theor. Comput. Sci. **267**(1), 3–16 (2010)
3. Bagnara, R., Pescetti, A., Zaccagnini, A., Zaffanella, E.: PURRS: towards computer algebra support for fully automatic worst-case complexity analysis. CoRR abs/cs/0512056 (2005)
4. Ball, T., Majumdar, R., Millstein, T., Rajamani, S.K.: Automatic predicate abstraction of C programs. In: PLDI, pp. 203–213 (2001)
5. Berg, L.: Introduction to the Operational Calculus. North-Holland Publishing Co., Amsterdam (1967)
6. Biallas, S., Brauer, J., King, A., Kowalewski, S.: Loop leaping with closures. In: Miné, A., Schmidt, D. (eds.) SAS 2012. LNCS, vol. 7460, pp. 214–230. Springer, Heidelberg (2012). https://doi.org/10.1007/978-3-642-33125-1_16
7. Blanc, R., Henzinger, T.A., Hottelier, T., Kovács, L.: ABC: algebraic bound computation for loops. In: Clarke, E.M., Voronkov, A. (eds.) LPAR 2010. LNCS (LNAI), vol. 6355, pp. 103–118. Springer, Heidelberg (2010). https://doi.org/10.1007/978-3-642-17511-4_7
8. Boigelot, B.: On iterating linear transformations over recognizable sets of integers. Theor. Comp. Sci. **309**(1), 413–468 (2003)
9. Bozga, M., Gîrlea, C., Iosif, R.: Iterating octagons. In: Kowalewski, S., Philippou, A. (eds.) TACAS 2009. LNCS, vol. 5505, pp. 337–351. Springer, Heidelberg (2009). https://doi.org/10.1007/978-3-642-00768-2_29
10. Bozga, M., Iosif, R., Konečný, F.: Fast acceleration of ultimately periodic relations. In: Touili, T., Cook, B., Jackson, P. (eds.) CAV 2010. LNCS, vol. 6174, pp. 227–242. Springer, Heidelberg (2010). https://doi.org/10.1007/978-3-642-14295-6_23
11. Bozga, M., Iosif, R., Lakhnech, Y.: Flat parametric counter automata. In: Bugliesi, M., Preneel, B., Sassone, V., Wegener, I. (eds.) ICALP 2006. LNCS, vol. 4052, pp. 577–588. Springer, Heidelberg (2006). https://doi.org/10.1007/11787006_49
12. Comon, H., Jurski, Y.: Multiple counters automata, safety analysis and presburger arithmetic. In: Hu, A.J., Vardi, M.Y. (eds.) CAV 1998. LNCS, vol. 1427, pp. 268–279. Springer, Heidelberg (1998). https://doi.org/10.1007/BFb0028751
13. Cousot, P., Cousot, R.: Abstract interpretation: a unified lattice model for static analysis of programs by construction or approximation of fixpoints. In: POPL (1977)
14. Cousot, P., Cousot, R.: Systematic design of program analysis frameworks. In: POPL, pp. 269–282 (1979)
15. Cousot, P., Halbwachs, N.: Automatic discovery of linear constraints among variables of a program. In: POPL (1978)
16. Debray, S.K., Lin, N., Hermenegildo, M.V.: Task granularity analysis in logic programs. In: PLDI, pp. 174–188 (1990)
17. Farzan, A., Kincaid, Z.: Compositional recurrence analysis. In: FMCAD (2015)
18. Finkel, A., Leroux, J.: How to compose presburger-accelerations: applications to broadcast protocols. In: Agrawal, M., Seth, A. (eds.) FSTTCS 2002. LNCS, vol. 2556, pp. 145–156. Springer, Heidelberg (2002). https://doi.org/10.1007/3-540-36206-1_14

19. Graf, S., Saidi, H.: Construction of abstract state graphs with PVS. In: Grumberg, O. (ed.) CAV 1997. LNCS, vol. 1254, pp. 72–83. Springer, Heidelberg (1997). https://doi.org/10.1007/3-540-63166-6_10
20. Haase, C., Halfon, S.: Integer vector addition systems with states. In: Ouaknine, J., Potapov, I., Worrell, J. (eds.) RP 2014. LNCS, vol. 8762, pp. 112–124. Springer, Cham (2014). https://doi.org/10.1007/978-3-319-11439-2_9
21. Hrushovski, E., Ouaknine, J., Pouly, A., Worrell, J.: Polynomial invariants for affine programs. In: Logic in Computer Science, pp. 530–539 (2018)
22. Humenberger, A., Jaroschek, M., Kovács, L.: Automated generation of non-linear loop invariants utilizing hypergeometric sequences. In: ISSAC (2017)
23. Humenberger, A., Jaroschek, M., Kovács, L.: Invariant generation for multi-path loops with polynomial assignments. In: VMCAI, pp. 226–246 (2018)
24. Jeannet, B., Schrammel, P., Sankaranarayanan, S.: Abstract acceleration of general linear loops. In: POPL, pp. 529–540 (2014)
25. Kincaid, Z., Breck, J., Forouhi Boroujeni, A., Reps, T.: Compositional recurrence analysis revisited. In: PLDI (2017)
26. Kincaid, Z., Cyphert, J., Breck, J., Reps, T.: Non-linear reasoning for invariant synthesis. PACMPL **2**(POPL), 54:1–54:33 (2018)
27. Konečný, F.: PTIME computation of transitive closures of octagonal relations. In: Chechik, M., Raskin, J.-F. (eds.) TACAS 2016. LNCS, vol. 9636, pp. 645–661. Springer, Heidelberg (2016). https://doi.org/10.1007/978-3-662-49674-9_42
28. Kovács, L.: Reasoning algebraically about P-solvable loops. In: Ramakrishnan, C.R., Rehof, J. (eds.) TACAS 2008. LNCS, vol. 4963, pp. 249–264. Springer, Heidelberg (2008). https://doi.org/10.1007/978-3-540-78800-3_18
29. Kroening, D., Sharygina, N., Tonetta, S., Tsitovich, A., Wintersteiger, C.M.: Loop summarization using abstract transformers. In: Cha, S.S., Choi, J.-Y., Kim, M., Lee, I., Viswanathan, M. (eds.) ATVA 2008. LNCS, vol. 5311, pp. 111–125. Springer, Heidelberg (2008). https://doi.org/10.1007/978-3-540-88387-6_10
30. Li, Y., Albarghouthi, A., Kincaid, Z., Gurfinkel, A., Chechik, M.: Symbolic optimization with SMT solvers. In: POPL, pp. 607–618 (2014)
31. Milner, R.: Communication and Concurrency. Prentice-Hall Inc., Upper Saddle River (1989)
32. Müller-Olm, M., Seidl, H.: Precise interprocedural analysis through linear algebra. In: POPL (2004)
33. Reps, T., Thakur, A.: Automating abstract interpretation. In: VMCAI (2016)
34. Reps, T., Turetsky, E., Prabhu, P.: Newtonian program analysis via tensor product. In: POPL (2016)
35. Rodríguez-Carbonell, E., Kapur, D.: Automatic generation of polynomial loop invariants: algebraic foundations. In: ISSAC, pp. 266–273 (2004)
36. Sebastiani, R., Tomasi, S.: Optimization in SMT with $\mathcal{LA}(\mathbb{Q})$ cost functions. In: IJCAR, pp. 484–498 (2012)
37. Sinn, M., Zuleger, F., Veith, H.: A simple and scalable static analysis for bound analysis and amortized complexity analysis. In: CAV, pp. 745–761 (2014)
38. Sinn, M., Zuleger, F., Veith, H.: Difference constraints: an adequate abstraction for complexity analysis of imperative programs. In: FMCAD, pp. 144–151 (2015)
39. Tarjan, R.E.: Fast algorithms for solving path problems. J. ACM **28**(3), 594–614 (1981)
40. Tarjan, R.E.: A unified approach to path problems. J. ACM **28**(3), 577–593 (1981)
41. Thakur, A.: Symbolic abstraction: algorithms and applications. Ph.D. thesis, Computer Science Department, University of Wisconsin, Madison, WI, Technical report, 1812, August 2014

42. Thakur, A., Reps, T.: A method for symbolic computation of abstract operations. In: Madhusudan, P., Seshia, S.A. (eds.) CAV 2012. LNCS, vol. 7358, pp. 174–192. Springer, Heidelberg (2012). https://doi.org/10.1007/978-3-642-31424-7_17
43. Wegbreit, B.: Mechanical program analysis. Commun. ACM **18**(9), 528–539 (1975)

Deductive Verification in Decidable Fragments with Ivy

Kenneth L. McMillan[1](✉) and Oded Padon[2]

[1] Microsoft Research, Redmond, USA
kenmcmil@microsoft.com
[2] Tel Aviv University, Tel Aviv, Israel
odedp@mail.tau.ac.il

Abstract. This paper surveys the work to date on Ivy, a language and a tool for the formal specification and verification of distributed systems. Ivy supports deductive verification using automated provers, model checking, automated testing, manual theorem proving and generation of executable code. In order to achieve greater verification productivity, a key design goal for Ivy is to allow the engineer to apply automated provers in the realm in which their performance is relatively predictable, stable and transparent. In particular Ivy focuses on the use of *decidable* fragments of first-order logic. We consider the rationale or Ivy's design, the various capabilities of the tool, as well as case studies and applications.

Keywords: Deductive verification · Distributed systems
Safety verification · Liveness verification · Paxos · Decidable logics
Effectively propositional logic · Cache coherence
Model checking · Specification-based testing

1 Introduction

Ivy is a language and a tool for the formal specification and verification of distributed systems. The rationale underlying Ivy is that, to achieve a high degree of productivity in verification, the system, its representation and its proof must be designed in advance to take maximum advantage of automated provers while avoiding their weaknesses. Ivy is open-source software and is freely available under an MIT license [25].

The use of automated provers in program verification has a long history, going back to the work of Nelson and Oppen [28, 29] and the Boyer-Moore prover [9]. More recent systems include ESC Java [12], Dafny [22] and F* [40]. Program proofs using such tools are typically more succinct than proofs using tactical theorem provers such as Coq [4] and Isabelle/HOL [30] by one or two orders of magnitude (e.g., compare the Ironfleet project [14] using Dafny to the Verdi [42,43] project using Coq). However, it is unclear that this succinctness leads to a proportionate improvement in verification productivity. In practice, users struggle

© Springer Nature Switzerland AG 2018
A. Podelski (Ed.): SAS 2018, LNCS 11002, pp. 43–55, 2018.
https://doi.org/10.1007/978-3-319-99725-4_4

with the unpredictability, instability and lack of transparency of the automated verifiers [11, Sect. 9.1]. Particularly problematic is the heuristic instantiation of quantifiers. This leads to unpredictable failures that are extremely hard to diagnose and may be triggered by small, seemingly irrelevant changes in the prover's input. By lack of transparency, we mean that no clear indication is given of the cause of failures. It is somewhat as if one were trying to develop a software system using a compiler that randomly failed to produce code, without producing any useful error message. In an iterative development process requiring frequent recompilations, this would be untenable.

To try to realize the verification productivity that automated provers promise, the design of Ivy starts with two basic choices: a prover and an application domain in which we wish to produce efficient verified systems. The chosen prover (at least initially) is Microsoft Z3 [27], a high-performance SMT solver [3] that supports satisfiability queries in full first-order logic modulo a variety of theories. The chosen application domain is distributed systems. The primary design goal of Ivy is to allow an engineer to quickly and intuitively reduce the proof of a distributed system to proof goals in a logical fragment for which Z3 is a *decision procedure*. We can think of Ivy as a test of the following three-part hypothesis:

1. Predictability, stability and transparency of proof automation lead to greater verification productivity,
2. Within the decidable fragments used by Ivy, the Z3 prover has these properties, and
3. With appropriate language and tool support, a we can reduce proofs of distributed systems to subgoals in this fragment.

2   Language Design

The use of decidable logics also has a long history in program verification. The choice of a logic generally depends on the application domain. For example, Klarlund proposed the use monadic second-order logic (MSO) for reasoning about manipulations of inductive data structures [15]. For distributed protocols, we posit that decidable fragments of first-order logic are more appropriate, since these protocols usually lack recursive structures, and uninterpreted relations and quantifiers can be used to reason about the multiple nodes or threads, as well as messages, values, and other objects of the system.

The classical example of a decidable fragment of first-order logic is the Bernays-Shönfinkel-Ramsey fragment (also known as EPR, for "effectively propositional"). This consists of formulas without function symbols, whose quantifier structure is $\exists\forall$ in prenex normal form. We can extend this in various ways. For example, in a many-sorted setting, we can allow function symbols that are stratified (*i.e.*, there are no cycles in the graph that the function symbols and the $\forall\exists$ quantifier alternations induce on the sorts). From this we observe that (1) quantifier structure is critical, and (2) function symbols and quantifier alternations should be used cautiously.

2.1 Ivy's Procedural Language

These considerations motivate several important design decisions in Ivy. First, the programming language is imperative rather than functional. Partly this is motivated by decidability. Often, though we are computing a total function, we do not wish to specify it as such, since this could contribute to a function cycle. Instead, we use a procedure and specify only partial correctness. Generally speaking, we avoid any unnecessary assumptions of totality or termination for decidability reasons. Second, the only primitive data type is the Boolean type. This is because primitive data types would introduce both total functions and axioms whose quantifier structure could be problematic. Instead, variables in Ivy hold first-order relations and functions over uninterpreted sorts as their values. This gives the user control of the use of function symbols. By preference, when reasoning about concrete data, we use relational abstractions whose axioms are expressible in the decidable fragment.

Finally, Ivy generates verification conditions (VC's) using the weakest precondition calculus, much like other tools, such as Dafny. The primitive constructs of the language have been chosen so that, not only are the VC's always expressed in first-order logic, but their quantifier structure is apparent from the program source. These considerations are discussed in more detail in [38], which describes the basic procedural language, which has since been extended.

Within these constraints, Ivy's programming language is designed to be as expressive as possible. We can express in Ivy any update to the variables whose transition relation is expressible in first-order logic, using relational and functional updates with free parameters. For example, the following assignment statement removes the pairs (x, Y) from relation r, for all Y:

```
r(x,Y) := false
```

The capitalized symbol Y is treated implicitly as a free parameter. The transition relation of this statement can be expressed as

$$\forall X, Y. \ r'(X, Y) = \text{false if } X = x \text{ else } r(X, Y)$$

We can also create pure first-order function closures. For example, this assignment computes a function f from the current value of the function g and a variable v:

```
f(X) := g(X,v)
```

While the semantics of this is easily expressed in first-order logic, compiling it is a bit more subtle. The compiler creates a closure that captures the values of g and v, allowing function f to be evaluated on demand.

Other first-order expressible updates, such as relational joins, are also possible. With quantifiers and parameterized updates, it is possible to describe procedures that are not actually computable. The compiler handles only a subset of the language in which finite bounds on quantifiers can be statically inferred. Uncomputable updates are still useful, however, in writing specifications.

2.2   Modularity

Another important generalization we can make about decidability is that mixing theories and quantifiers is problematic. For example, quantifier-free integer linear arithmetic with function symbols is decidable, but adding quantifiers makes it undecidable. Moreover, by mixing procedures that use function symbols, we might create a cycle in the function graph and thus also lose decidability.

Ivy's answer to this conundrum is modularity. That is, we hide problematic theories or functions inside modules, to prevent their combinations from taking us outside the decidable fragment. As a very simple example, suppose we require an index type t that forms a discrete total order. We implement this type in a module I which provides an interface with certain operations, such as incrementation (*i.e.,* computing the successor of a value), and guarantees certain properties, such as the axioms of total order. Type t is *interpreted* as the integers, that is, we instantiate the integer arithmetic theory for type t, giving us interpretations for the signature $\{0, 1, +, <, \ldots\}$ over this type. However, only module I sees this interpretation. Since its VC's are quantifier free, Z3 can decide them using its integer arithmetic theory. An application module A using the index type t sees only its abstract specification, and not the integer theory. Thus, it can use quantifiers safely. As we will observe in Sect. 4, this principle can be applied in more complex situations, for example in refining an abstract protocol model to an implementation.

To enforce the separation of theories, modularity in Ivy is quite strict. The specification of a module is never allowed to reference internal state of the module. Rather, the specification of a module provides an abstract notion of state. This consists of a collection of *monitors*: procedures that synchronize with call and return events at the interface, updating the abstract state. The monitors contain assertions that act as either assumptions or guarantees for the modules. Stateful monitors can be used, for example, to specify the interfaces of concrete services, such as networking layers, or abstract models that are used only in the proof.

2.3   The Fragment Checker

The decidable fragment used by Ivy is called the Finite Almost Uninterpreted fragment or FAU [13], which is supported by Z3. FAU generalized the many-sorted extension of EPR, and also allows restricted combination of quantifiers and linear arithmetic. The Ivy verifier generates the verification conditions for a program and checks syntactically that they fall into the FAU fragment. If not, it provides a diagnostic message that explains the failure (for example, it presents an illegal cycle of function symbols). This is important from the point of view of transparency. That is, if a VC cannot be verified, some feedback must be provided to help the user correct the situation and continue developing the proof.

3   Expressiveness of Decidable Fragments of First-Order Logic

Much of the verification using Ivy is done in a many-sorted extension of the EPR fragment of first order logic that allows only allows *stratified* or *acyclic* quantifier alternations and function symbols. Since it is a fragment of first-order logic, it may seem to be too restricted for challenging verification tasks. For example, first-order logic cannot express properties of arithmetic, graph reachability, or inductive data structures. Quite surprisingly, the work on Ivy shows that pure first-order logic, and even a decidable fragment thereof, is powerful enough to capture everything that is needed to verify several complex distributed protocols.

Transitive closure of deterministic paths can be expressed in EPR. This was used in [16–18] for linked data structures, and these ideas can also be used to represent tree topologies, such as forwarding trees of routing algorithms [35]. This also generalizes to other topologies, including rings [38], that can be similarly axiomatized in EPR, and more recently general graphs of out-degree one [32]. The key idea is to take the transitive closure as a primitive relation, and use a formula to represent edges. This allows for a sound axiomatization, which is also complete for finite models. That is, every finite model of the axioms corresponds to a graph of the suitable class. Due to the finite model property of EPR, this completeness ensures that counterexamples obtained in the verification process are never spurious.

Another useful axiomatization is that of *quorums*. Many distributed protocols employ quorums that are defined by thresholds on set cardinalities. For example, a protocol may wait for at least $\frac{N}{2}$ nodes to confirm a proposal before committing a value, where N is the total number of nodes. This is often used to ensure consistency. In Byzantine failure models, a common threshold is $\frac{2N}{3}$, where at most a third of the nodes may be Byzantine. First-order logic cannot completely capture set cardinalities and thresholds. However, we can exploit the fact that protocol correctness relies on rather simple properties that are implied by the cardinality threshold, and that these properties can be encoded in first-order logic.

The idea is to use a variant of the standard encoding of second-order logic in first-order logic. We introduce a sort for quorums, that is sets of nodes with the appropriate cardinality, and use a binary relation *member* to capture set membership. (Alternatively, we can add a sort that represents general sets of nodes, with a unary predicate over it that represents "being a quorum".) Then, properties that are needed for protocol correctness can be axiomatized in first-order logic.

For example, the fact that any two sets of at least $\frac{N}{2}$ nodes intersect is crucial for many consensus protocols. This property can be expressed in first order logic:

$$\forall q_1, q_2 : \text{quorum}_i. \ \exists n : \text{node}. \ member(n, q_1) \wedge member(n, q_2)$$

For Byzantine consensus algorithms that use sets of at least $\frac{2N}{3}$ nodes, they key property is that any two quorums intersect at a non-Byzantine node. This can also be expressed in first-order logic:

$$\forall q_1, q_2 : \text{quorum}_{\text{ii}}. \ \exists n : \text{node}. \ \neg byz(n) \wedge member(n, q_1) \wedge member(n, q_2)$$

These ideas are used in [36,37] to verify multiple consensus protocols from the Paxos [19,20] family, showing that properties that are expressible in first-order logic can be used to prove challenging protocols. For several variants, this provided the first mechanical safety proof.

4 Using Modularity to Verify Implementations

While the techniques outlined in Sect. 3 allow one to verify distributed protocols at the abstract protocol level, they do not suffice to verify an executable implementation. For verified executable implementations, we want to replace the notion of *axioms* with a notion of *interface specification* in a modular, assume/guarantee style. That is, we would like most of the proof to rely on first-order properties such as total order or quorum intersection, but then we would like to produce a concrete implementation, and prove that it satisfies these properties.

Concrete implementations rely on concrete data types such as integers, and data structures such as arrays. Ivy includes a built-in library of several concrete types with their specifications, and allows users to create user defined data types via a module system. Verification of concrete data type implementations is carried out in decidable theories, most commonly the FAU fragment mentioned earlier. This fragment allows restricted combination of quantifiers and arithmetic, and is supported by Z3. In [41], well-known modular verification techniques are applied to separate such theory reasoning, allowing the global protocol verification to be done in pure first-order logic (and EPR), while theories are isolated to particular implementation modules (for example, a module implementing finite sets with a quorum predicate).

An important tactic in that work is to use modularity to break cycles of function symbols or quantifier alternations. For example, if verification requires both a function (or $\forall \exists$ quantifier alternation) from sort A to sort B, and a function from sort B to sort A, then a possible solution is to break the problem into two modules, where each module can be verified with only one of the functions, thus avoiding cycles.

A typical approach is to introduce a "ghost" module that formalizes an abstract model of the protocol. The state of the ghost module is usually encoded using relations, allowing us to verify global properties of the protocol using EPR. The interface of the ghost module is called in the implementation module at the "commit points" of abstract operations. Thus, by assume/guarantee reasoning, we can use the proved properties of the ghost module as lemmas in the proof the implementation module. This allows us to use some quantifier alternations when proving the implementation module, and other quantifier alternations when proving the abstract protocol module, even though combining them would create cycles.

Although the approach uses only modular assume/guarantee reasoning in the proof, this method is still related to approaches based on refinement mappings [2]. In this case, an inductive invariant relating the ghost module's interface state and the implementation state takes the role of the refinement mapping. Although prophecy variables could in principle be used, this was found in [41] to be unnecessary in practice, as we have the flexibility to make the ghost module deterministic.

In [41], these principles are applied to obtain verified implementations of both Multi-Paxos and Raft [31]. The obtained implementations have performance that is on par with other verified and unverified implementations, and the proof burden is much lower compared to other verified implementations such as Verdi [42,43] (using Coq) and IronFleet [14] (using Dafny and Z3). Applying this methodology requires us to carefully consider the functional dependencies in the system while planning the specification and proofs. This effort was more than repaid, however, by the predictability, stability and transparency of Z3 when applied to proof goals in the decidable fragments. Overall, restricting the proof automation to the decidable fragments did not appear to be an insuperable obstacle and in practice resulted in more concise proofs.

5   Liveness and Temporal Verification

Safety properties can be proven using inductive invariants. However, liveness properties of infinite-state systems are usually proven using ranking functions or well-founded relations. Unfortunately, pure first-order logic (without theories) cannot express the required rankings or the notion of a well-founded relation or well-ordered set. Therefore, it may seem that liveness verification cannot be done in pure first-order logic. However, a new technique [33] integrated into Ivy shows that on the contrary, the formalism of first-order logic provides a unique opportunity for proving liveness and temporal properties.

The technique exploits the flexibility of representing states as first-order structures, and uses first-order temporal logic (FO-LTL) (e.g., [1,23]) for temporal specification. This general formalism provides a powerful and natural way to model temporal properties of infinite-state systems. It naturally supports both *unbounded parallelism*, where the system is allowed to dynamically create processes, and *infinite-state per process*. Unbounded-parallelism usually requires infinitely many (or quantified) fairness assumptions (e.g., that every thread is scheduled infinitely often in a program with dynamic thread creation, where an infinite trace can have infinitely many threads). This is fully supported by the formalism and the developed proof technique.

The technique developed in [33] and implemented in Ivy is based on a novel liveness-to-safety reduction, that reduces temporal verification (expressed in FO-LTL) to safety verification of an infinite-state system expressed in first-order logic without temporal operators. This allows us to leverage existing safety verification techniques, and the other techniques implemented in Ivy, to verify liveness and temporal properties. While such a reduction cannot be complete for complexity reasons[1], it is sound, and it was successful in proving liveness of several challenging protocols, including the first mechanized liveness proofs of Stoppable Paxos [21], and the TLB Shootdown algorithm [7].

The liveness-to-safety reduction is based on an abstract notion of acyclicity, using *dynamic abstraction*. For finite-state systems, liveness can be proven through acyclicity (the absence of fair cycles). This is the classical liveness-to-safety reduction of [5]. This also works for parameterized systems, where the state-space is finite (albeit unbounded) for every system instance [39]. For infinite-state systems, the acyclicity condition is unsound (an infinite-state system can be acyclic but non-terminating). The liveness-to-safety reduction with dynamic abstraction defines a finite abstraction that is fine-tuned for each execution trace, while abstracting only the cycle detection aspect (rather than the actual transitions of the system). Such fine-tuned abstraction is made possible by exploiting the symbolic representation of the transition relation in first-order logic, as well as the first-order formulation of the fairness constraints. The full details are explained in [33].

An additional novel mechanism [34] implemented in Ivy that enhances the proof power of the liveness-to-safety reduction is *temporal prophecy* and *temporal witnesses*. Here, the idea is to augment the system with additional temporal formulas that are not part of the specification, and also with additional constant symbols that are essentially Skolem witnesses for temporal formulas. In addition to increasing the proof power, temporal witnesses also facilitate verification of the resulting safety problem using EPR. By introducing a temporal witnesses, one can often eliminate quantifier alternations in the resulting verification conditions. The idea is that a temporal witness is used to name a particular element (e.g., the thread that is eventually starved), and then the inductive invariant can be specified for this particular constant, rather than with a quantifier. In several cases we considered, this allowed to eliminate quantifier alternation cycles. In Ivy, temporal prophecy formulas are derived from an inductive invariant provided by the user (for proving the safety property resulting induced by the liveness-to-safety reduction), which provides a seamless way to prove temporal properties.

6   Additional Topics

6.1   Compositional Simulation

As described in Sect. 2, module specifications in Ivy are stateful monitors. An additional use for these monitors is to generate tests for the module using a compositional testing approach [8]. That is, by symbolically executing the monitor in a given state, we can derive a predicate that represents all of the legal input values for a given procedure in that state. By sampling randomly from the satisfying assignment of this predicate, we can generate sequences of a test inputs.

---

[1] The temporal verification problem in this setting is Π_1^1-complete [1], while safety verification is in the arithmetical hierarchy.

For example, in a client/server protocol, Ivy can take the role of the client in testing the server, or the server in testing the client.

This modular approach to test generation has several advantages. First, compared to traditional unit testing, it has the advantage that it is in a limited sense complete. That is, we have a formal assume/guarantee proof that correctness of the modules implies correctness of the system. This means that if the system does not actually satisfy its specification, there is *some* unit test that exposes this (though this test might be generated with low probability). Compared to integration testing, the advantage is that it is easier to cover the behaviors of a module by stimulating its inputs directly rather than the system-level inputs. This is particularly important in the case of concurrent systems, which suffer from an explosion of interleavings. Because the module has less concurrency than the system, its possible interleavings are more easily explored.

In [26], this method is used to verify the hardware building blocks of a modular cache coherence system for the RISC-V processor architecture, based on a formal specification of the coherent interface. The approach was able to find subtle timing bugs in the RTL-level implementations, and also provides a limited guarantee that, if every block passes all possible tests, then the system as a whole provides the required memory coherence properties.

Specification-based testing also gives a way to check parts of the "trusted base" of Ivy, for example the networking interface, which is based on system services that cannot be formally verified.

6.2   Abstract Model Checking

Propositional LTL is another example of a decidable logic. Satisfiability problems in this logic can be reduced to circuit representations in a standard format [6] that can be checked by highly efficient hardware model checkers such as ABC [10]. Ivy can exploit such model checkers by means of an abstraction. As in an SMT solver, the first-order transition relation is reduced to its "propositional skeleton" by replacing each atomic formula with a free Boolean variable. Though all of the theory information is lost by this transformation, some can be regained by a process of "eager instantiation" of the theory axioms. This process can be controlled by the user by providing a collection of axiom schemata to be instantiated or by applying standard libraries of such schemata. The user can also increase precision by adding history and prophecy variables.

In [24] this approach is tested on a collection of distributed protocols. The ability of the model checker to automatically synthesize part of the system's inductive invariant is seen to substantially reduce the complexity of the invariants that must be provided manually.

6.3   Manual Theorem Proving

It some cases, it may be necessary to fall back on detailed manual proof. For this purpose, Ivy provides a collection of proof tactics that can be used to manually transform proof goals. A standard library provides complete proof rules for first-order logic in the natural deduction style. These can be used where needed for reasoning about specifications that are outside the decidable fragment, for example, to apply induction over the natural numbers using the Peano induction axiom. That is, while Ivy restricts *automated* proof generation to decidable fragments, manual proof is not restricted in this way.

7   Conclusion

A key design goal for Ivy is to allow the engineer to apply automated provers in a realm in which their performance is relatively predictable, stable and transparent. Ivy differs from other program verification tools, such as Dafny and F*, primarily in that its language and features have been designed based on the capabilities of a particular automated prover and the needs of a particular application domain. Ivy's design allows users to structure specifications, implementations and proofs to make maximum use of the capabilities of the prover while avoiding its weaknesses, particularly in the area of heuristic quantifier instantiation.

Case studies have provided preliminary evidence that such a methodology is practical, and that the resulting predictability, stability and transparency of the prover improves overall verification productivity. To some degree, this confirms the three-part hypothesis of the introduction. In particular, it appears that the performance of Z3 is substantially more stable within the decidable fragments, and that, with appropriate language and tool support, the restriction of automation to the decidable fragment is not unduly burdensome. Still, more experience is needed to say with certainty that this trade-off is the right one within the chosen domain and to validate the various design decisions.

Liveness proofs are yet to be integrated with Ivy's modular assume/guarantee reasoning. This is needed to verify liveness of system implementations, rather than abstract protocols. For this, module interfaces may need to be expressed in temporal logic, such that one module's liveness property becomes another module's fairness assumption. Other important issues have yet to be addressed, for example the verification of security or privacy properties. In the long run, the large size of the trusted computing base in Ivy must also be addressed.

Ultimately, the goal of the project is to realize in practice the promise of greater verification productivity inherent in powerful proof tools such as Z3.

Acknowledgements. We thank the many researchers that have contributed to the research agenda reviewed in this article, both as co-authors and via insightful discussions, including: Thomas Ball, Amir Ben-Amram, Nikolaj Bjørner, Tej Chajed, Constantin Enea, Yotam M. Y. Feldman, Jochen Hoenicke, Neil Immerman, Shachar Itzhaky, Ranjit Jhala, K. Rustan M. Leino, Giuliano Losa, Yuri Meshman, Leonardo de Moura, Alexander Nutz, Aurojit Panda, Bryan Parno, Andreas Podelski, Shaz Qadeer, Alexander Rabinovich, Mooly Sagiv, Sharon Shoham, Or Tamir, Zachary Tatlock, Marcelo Taube, James R. Wilcox, Doug Woos, and the anonymous referees and artifact evaluation referees of POPL, PLDI, OOPSLA, CAV, and FMCAD.

Padon was supported by Google under a PhD fellowship and by the European Research Council under the European Union's Seventh Framework Program (FP7/2007–2013)/ERC grant agreement no. [321174-VSSC].

References

1. Abadi, M.: The power of temporal proofs. Theor. Comput. Sci. **65**(1), 35–83 (1989). https://doi.org/10.1016/0304-3975(89)90138-2
2. Abadi, M., Lamport, L.: The existence of refinement mappings. Theor. Comput. Sci. **82**(2), 253–284 (1991). https://doi.org/10.1016/0304-3975(91)90224-P
3. Barrett, C.W., Sebastiani, R., Seshia, S.A., Tinelli, C.: Satisfiability modulo theories. In: Biere, A., Heule, M., van Maaren, H., Walsh, T. (eds.) Handbook of Satisfiability, Frontiers in Artificial Intelligence and Applications, vol. 185, pp. 825–885. IOS Press (2009). https://doi.org/10.3233/978-1-58603-929-5-825
4. Bertot, Y., Castéran, P.: Interactive Theorem Proving and Program Development - Coq'Art: The Calculus of Inductive Constructions. Texts in Theoretical Computer Science. An EATCS Series. Springer, Heidelberg (2004). https://doi.org/10.1007/978-3-662-07964-5
5. Biere, A., Artho, C., Schuppan, V.: Liveness checking as safety checking. Electr. Notes Theor. Comput. Sci. **66**(2), 160–177 (2002)
6. Biere, A., Heljanko, K., Wieringa, S.: AIGER 1.9 and beyond. Technical report 11/2, Institute for Formal Models and Verification, Johannes Kepler University, July 2011
7. Black, D.L., Rashid, R.F., Golub, D.B., Hill, C.R.: Translation lookaside buffer consistency: a software approach. In: Proceedings of the Third International Conference on Architectural Support for Programming Languages and Operating Systems, ASPLOS III, pp. 113–122. ACM, New York (1989). https://doi.org/10.1145/70082.68193
8. Blundell, C., Giannakopoulou, D., Pasareanu, C.S.: Assume-guarantee testing. ACM SIGSOFT Softw. Eng. Notes **31**(2) (2006). https://doi.org/10.1145/1118537.1123060
9. Boyer, R., Moore, J.: A Computational Logic. Academic Press, New York (1979)
10. Brayton, R., Mishchenko, A.: ABC: an academic industrial-strength verification tool. In: Touili, T., Cook, B., Jackson, P. (eds.) CAV 2010. LNCS, vol. 6174, pp. 24–40. Springer, Heidelberg (2010). https://doi.org/10.1007/978-3-642-14295-6_5
11. Ferraiuolo, A., Baumann, A., Hawblitzel, C., Parno, B.: Komodo: using verification to disentangle secure-enclave hardware from software. In: Proceedings of the 26th Symposium on Operating Systems Principles, Shanghai, China, 28–31 October 2017, pp. 287–305 (2017)
12. Flanagan, C., Leino, K.R.M., Lillibridge, M., Nelson, G., Saxe, J.B., Stata, R.: Extended static checking for java. In: Proceedings of the ACM SIGPLAN 2002 Conference on Programming Language Design and Implementation, PLDI 2002, pp. 234–245. ACM (2002). https://doi.org/10.1145/512529.512558
13. Ge, Y., de Moura, L.: Complete instantiation for quantified formulas in satisfiabiliby modulo theories. In: Bouajjani, A., Maler, O. (eds.) CAV 2009. LNCS, vol. 5643, pp. 306–320. Springer, Heidelberg (2009). https://doi.org/10.1007/978-3-642-02658-4_25

14. Hawblitzel, C., Howell, J., Kapritsos, M., Lorch, J.R., Parno, B., Roberts, M.L., Setty, S.T.V., Zill, B.: Ironfleet: proving practical distributed systems correct. In: Proceedings of the 25th Symposium on Operating Systems Principles, SOSP, pp. 1–17 (2015)
15. Henriksen, J.G., Jensen, J., Jørgensen, M., Klarlund, N., Paige, R., Rauhe, T., Sandholm, A.: Mona: monadic second-order logic in practice. In: Brinksma, E., Cleaveland, W.R., Larsen, K.G., Margaria, T., Steffen, B. (eds.) TACAS 1995. LNCS, vol. 1019, pp. 89–110. Springer, Heidelberg (1995). https://doi.org/10.1007/3-540-60630-0_5
16. Itzhaky, S.: Automatic reasoning for pointer programs using decidable logics. Ph.D. thesis, Tel Aviv University (2014)
17. Itzhaky, S., Banerjee, A., Immerman, N., Lahav, O., Nanevski, A., Sagiv, M.: Modular reasoning about heap paths via effectively propositional formulas. In: the 41st Annual ACM SIGPLAN-SIGACT Symposium on Principles of Programming Languages, POPL, pp. 385–396 (2014)
18. Itzhaky, S., Banerjee, A., Immerman, N., Nanevski, A., Sagiv, M.: Effectively-propositional reasoning about reachability in linked data structures. In: Sharygina, N., Veith, H. (eds.) CAV 2013. LNCS, vol. 8044, pp. 756–772. Springer, Heidelberg (2013). https://doi.org/10.1007/978-3-642-39799-8_53
19. Lamport, L.: The part-time parliament. ACM Trans. Comput. Syst. **16**(2), 133–169 (1998). https://doi.org/10.1145/279227.279229
20. Lamport, L.: Paxos made simple. ACM SIGACT News **32**(4), 51–58 (2001). https://www.microsoft.com/en-us/research/publication/paxos-made-simple/
21. Lamport, L., Malkhi, D., Zhou, L.: Stoppable paxos. Technical report, Microsoft Research (2008). https://www.microsoft.com/en-us/research/publication/stoppable-paxos/
22. Leino, K.R.M.: Dafny: an automatic program verifier for functional correctness. In: Clarke, E.M., Voronkov, A. (eds.) LPAR 2010. LNCS (LNAI), vol. 6355, pp. 348–370. Springer, Heidelberg (2010). https://doi.org/10.1007/978-3-642-17511-4_20
23. Manna, Z., Pnueli, A.: Verification of concurrent programs: a temporal proof system. In: de Bakker, J.W., van Leeuwen, J. (eds.) Foundations of Computer Science: Distributed Systems, pp. 163–255. Mathematisch Centrum, Amsterdam (1983)
24. McMillan, K.L.: Eager abstraction for symbolic model checking. In: Conference on Computer-Aided Verification (CAV 2018). Springer (2018, to appear)
25. McMillan, K.L.: Ivy. http://microsoft.github.io/ivy/. Accessed 7 May 2018
26. McMillan, K.L.: Modular specification and verification of a cache-coherent interface. In: Piskac, R., Talupur, M. (eds.) 2016 Formal Methods in Computer-Aided Design, FMCAD 2016, Mountain View, CA, USA, 3–6 October 2016, pp. 109–116. IEEE (2016). https://doi.org/10.1109/FMCAD.2016.7886668
27. de Moura, L., Bjørner, N.: Z3: an efficient SMT solver. In: Ramakrishnan, C.R., Rehof, J. (eds.) TACAS 2008. LNCS, vol. 4963, pp. 337–340. Springer, Heidelberg (2008). https://doi.org/10.1007/978-3-540-78800-3_24
28. Nelson, C.G.: Techniques for program verification. Ph.D. thesis, Stanford, CA, USA (1980). aAI8011683
29. Nelson, G., Oppen, D.C.: Simplification by cooperating decision procedures. ACM Trans. Program. Lang. Syst. **1**(2), 245–257 (1979)
30. Nipkow, T., Wenzel, M., Paulson, L.C.: A Proof Assistant for Higher-Order Logic Isabelle/HOL. LNCS, vol. 2283. Springer, Heidelberg (2002). https://doi.org/10.1007/3-540-45949-9

31. Ongaro, D., Ousterhout, J.K.: In search of an understandable consensus algorithm. In: 2014 USENIX Annual Technical Conference, USENIX ATC 2014, Philadelphia, PA, USA, 19–20 June 2014, pp. 305–319 (2014). https://www.usenix.org/conference/atc14/technical-sessions/presentation/ongaro
32. Padon, O.: Deductive verification of distributed protocols in first-order logic. Ph.D. thesis, Tel Aviv University (2018)
33. Padon, O., Hoenicke, J., Losa, G., Podelski, A., Sagiv, M., Shoham, S.: Reducing liveness to safety in first-order logic. PACMPL **2**(POPL), 26:1–26:33 (2018). https://doi.org/10.1145/3158114
34. Padon, O., Hoenicke, J., McMillan, K.L., Podelski, A., Sagiv, M., Shoham, S.: Temporal prophecy for proving temporal properties of infinite-state systems (in preparation)
35. Padon, O., Immerman, N., Shoham, S., Karbyshev, A., Sagiv, M.: Decidability of inferring inductive invariants. In: Proceedings of the 43rd Annual ACM SIGPLAN-SIGACT Symposium on Principles of Programming Languages, POPL 2016, St. Petersburg, FL, USA, 20–22 January 2016, pp. 217–231 (2016). https://doi.org/10.1145/2837614.2837640
36. Padon, O., Losa, G., Sagiv, M., Shoham, S.: Paxos made epr: Decidable reasoning about distributed protocols. Proc. ACM Program. Lang. **1**(OOPSLA), 108:1–108:31 (2017). https://doi.org/10.1145/3140568
37. Padon, O., Losa, G., Sagiv, M., Shoham, S.: Paxos made EPR: decidable reasoning about distributed protocols. CoRR abs/1710.07191 (2017). http://arxiv.org/abs/1710.07191
38. Padon, O., McMillan, K.L., Panda, A., Sagiv, M., Shoham, S.: Ivy: safety verification by interactive generalization. In: Proceedings of the 37th ACM SIGPLAN Conference on Programming Language Design and Implementation, PLDI 2016, Santa Barbara, CA, USA, 13–17 June 2016, pp. 614–630 (2016)
39. Pnueli, A., Shahar, E.: Liveness and acceleration in parameterized verification. In: Emerson, E.A., Sistla, A.P. (eds.) CAV 2000. LNCS, vol. 1855, pp. 328–343. Springer, Heidelberg (2000). https://doi.org/10.1007/10722167_26
40. Swamy, N., Chen, J., Fournet, C., Strub, P., Bhargavan, K., Yang, J.: Secure distributed programming with value-dependent types. J. Funct. Program. **4**(23), 402–451 (2013)
41. Taube, M., Losa, G., McMillan, K.L., Padon, O., Sagiv, M., Shoham, S., Wilcox, J.R., Woos, D.: Modularity for decidability of deductive verification with applications to distributed systems. In: Foster, J.S., Grossman, D. (eds.) Proceedings of the 39th ACM SIGPLAN Conference on Programming Language Design and Implementation, PLDI 2018, Philadelphia, PA, USA, 18–22 June 2018, pp. 662–677. ACM (2018). https://doi.org/10.1145/3192366.3192414
42. Wilcox, J.R., Woos, D., Panchekha, P., Tatlock, Z., Wang, X., Ernst, M.D., Anderson, T.E.: Verdi: a framework for implementing and formally verifying distributed systems. In: Proceedings of the 36th ACM SIGPLAN Conference on Programming Language Design and Implementation, Portland, OR, USA, 15–17 June 2015, pp. 357–368 (2015)
43. Woos, D., Wilcox, J.R., Anton, S., Tatlock, Z., Ernst, M.D., Anderson, T.E.: Planning for change in a formal verification of the raft consensus protocol. In: Avigad, J., Chlipala, A. (eds.) Proceedings of the 5th ACM SIGPLAN Conference on Certified Programs and Proofs, Saint Petersburg, FL, USA, 20–22 January 2016, pp. 154–165. ACM (2016). https://doi.org/10.1145/2854065.2854081

Experience Developing and Deploying Concurrency Analysis at Facebook

Peter O'Hearn[✉]

Facebook, London, UK

Abstract. This paper tells the story of the development of RacerD, a static program analysis for detecting data races that is in production at Facebook. The technical details of RacerD are described in a separate paper; we concentrate here on how the project unfolded from a human point of view. The paper describes, in this specific case, the benefits of feedback between science and engineering, the tension encountered between principle and compromise, and how being flexible and adaptable in the presence of a changing engineering context can lead to surprising results which far exceed initial expectations. I hope to give the reader an impression of what it is like to develop advanced static analyses in industry, how it is both different from and similar to developing analyses for the purpose of advancing science.

1 Introduction

Static program analysis is a technical subject with well developed principles and theories. We have dataflow analysis and abstract interpretation, inter-procedural and compositional analysis methods, and a great variety of specific abstract domains and logical reasoning techniques. Built upon this foundation we are seeing analysis being applied increasingly to correctness and other problems in the codebases of major companies. It is a very interesting time to work in the area industrially because the applications are so fresh: while there is a wealth of technical information to draw upon, the applications faced are so varied, and the built-up engineering experience so comparatively sparse, that one very quickly encounters challenges at or beyond the edge of both the research and engineering sides of the subject.

In this paper I want to provide an example of what working at the edge of the subject is like in an industrial setting. The presentation is necessarily limited and personal. Nonetheless, I hope that my account might be useful to people who are interested in knowing more about the practice of doing program analysis work from an industrial perspective.

There's no need to build up suspense: The project I describe, RacerD, went much better than I had ever dared hope. It has found over two thousand data race bugs which have been fixed by Facebook programmers before code reaches production, it has been instrumental in the conversion of part of Facebook's Android app from a single-threaded to a multi-threaded architecture, and,

© Springer Nature Switzerland AG 2018
A. Podelski (Ed.): SAS 2018, LNCS 11002, pp. 56–70, 2018.
https://doi.org/10.1007/978-3-319-99725-4_5

unusually for static analysis, it even has received press attention[1]. A research paper presents the technical results of the project, including information on the analysis algorithm, its empirical evaluation, and its impact [1]. I won't repeat this information here.

In most research papers one gets a description of where a project got to, but not how it got there. We get the results of science and/or engineering, but not a picture of how it developed. For the practice of doing science and engineering I've always thought the issue of "how it's done" is an important one, and that examples describing how can have some value. I wouldn't want to force this view on anyone; some might not feel it is worth it to bother with recounting the process in an example, and might therefore prefer to go directly to the research paper and stop reading here. But I personally have derived lots of value from stories I heard from people on how work was done.

In this paper I will tell you about the development of the RacerD project, its twists and its turns, the compromises and design decisions we made to achieve an impactful analysis, and how jumping back and forth between the perspective of an engineer and that of a scientist helped. My aim is to convey what it's like to work on an open research problem in static analysis, while at the same time pursuing the industrial goal of helping people, and how these two activities can even boost one another.

2   A Small Bold Bet

At the start of 2016 I was a manager at Facebook supporting the Infer static analysis team. Infer is an analyzer applied to Java, Objective C and C++ code [5], reporting issues related to memory safety, concurrency, security (information flow), and many more specialized errors suggested by Facebook developers. Infer is run internally on the Android and iOS apps for Facebook, Instagram, Messenger and WhatsApp, as well as on our backend C++ and Java code. It has its roots in academic research [6], which led to a startup company (Monoidics Ltd.) that was acquired by Facebook in 2013. Infer was open sourced in 2015[2], and is used as well at Amazon, Spotify, Mozilla, JD.com and other companies.

I had been in the management role for 2 years, but despite the team doing well (or perhaps, rather, because of it) I was itching to get back to doing technical work myself. I began toying with the idea to go after a problem I had thought about for years, but had never been brave enough to really try to solve to the point of supporting working programmers: concurrency analysis. I had described

---

[1] e.g., thenewstack.io/facebook-engineering-takes-bite-concurrency-racerd/, www.infoworld.com/article/3234328/java/racerd-detects-hard-to-find-race-conditions-in-java-code.html and www.techrepublic.com/article/facebook-open-sources-racerd-a-tool-thats-already-squashed-1000-bugs-in-concurrent-software/.

[2] code.facebook.com/posts/1648953042007882/open-sourcing-facebook-infer-identify-bugs-before-you-ship/.

my aims the year before in an interview with Mike Hicks for his "Programming Languages Ehthusiast" blog:

> I still want to understand concurrency, scalably. I would like to have analyses that I could deploy with high speed and low friction (e.g., not copious annotations or proof hints) and produce high-quality reports useful to programmers writing concurrent programs without disturbing their workflow too much. Then it could scale to many programmers and many programs. Maybe I am asking for too much, but that is what I would like to find.[3]

It was time to see if this was really asking for too much.

It's worth remembering why concurrency analysis is not easy. Say an analyzer wanted to examine each of the different ways to interleave two threads of 40 lines of code. Even if we could process 1 billion interleavings per second, it would take more than 3.4 million years to examine them all! If we extend the number of instructions to just 150 per thread, we get over 10^{88} interleavings, which is greater than the estimated number of atoms in the known universe (10^{80}). The inescapable conclusion is that, even though computers are powerful, we can't explore all the possibilities by brute force.

Yes, there are ways to cut down the number of interleavings, and there have been many interesting research papers on concurrency analysis. But, fundamental problems remained in applying these techniques at scale. Note I am talking here about analyses that do inference about concurrency, not ones that check type hints (e.g., concerning what locks guard what memory) written by programmers. See the companion paper for more discussion of prior work [1].

When I was first thinking of tackling this problem my manager – Bryan O'Sullivan, director of the Developer Efficiency org inside Facebook – was hugely supportive. I remember saying: "you know, Bryan, this is risky, there's a good chance I'll fail completely." To which he replied: "even if you fail, we'll have learnt something and that will be valuable ... I'm completely supportive of you doing this." Bryan and I agreed that it would be good for me to shed a portion of my management responsibilities to free up time for technical work, and Dino Distefano kindly stepped up to take over some of these responsibilities[4].

So with this as backdrop, and surrounded by the upbeat sayings in posters on the Facebook office walls such as

---

[3] http://www.pl-enthusiast.net/2015/09/15/facebooks-peter-ohearn-on-programming-languages/.

[4] I have since shed management responsibilities entirely, moving to a research/engineering role, essentially as a consequence of enjoying doing the technical work on this project.

to offer encouragement, I decided to have a go at making a scalable, low friction, high signal[5] concurrency analysis for the programmers.

3 Understanding the Engineering Problem, Part 1: The Code

At this point I felt had a solid understanding of the scientific side of the problem, and I had a potential way in. I had developed Concurrent Separation Logic (CSL, [9]), and by the work of numerous creative people it had shown how a surprising distance could be gotten in reasoning about concurrent programs without enumerating interleavings (see [4] for a survey). My very general idea was: I will make a CSL analysis that is highly compositional, it will as a result scale to millions of lines of code, and we'll automatically prove some properties of large industrial codebases (see [8] for background and open problems on compositional analysis at scale).

The first property I chose to focus on was absence of data races. This is one of the most basic problems in concurrency. In addition to races putting data structures into inconsistent states, getting rid of them minimizes interference, thus simplifying the task of understanding a program. And, I thought, an effective data race detector could open up other possibilities in concurrency analysis.

The idea "I will make a CSL analysis" is, however, rather abstract from an engineering point of view. I needed to better understand the engineering context where it would be used. My job was to help Facebook's programmers to move fast and produce more reliable code, and I thought I should spend time understanding the concurrent code that they write in order to see if I could serve them. So I spent the next three months scouring Facebook's Android codebases performing mental CSL proofs of race freedom (or, mental bug detection for failed proofs) to understand what I was up against. I made three discoveries.

The first is that Java's explicit thread spawning was seldom seen. This was handled by Android framework code, but also special code in a Facebook UI library called Litho. On the other hand, the programmers were annotating classes with a @ThreadSafe remark, as follows:

```
@ThreadSafe
class C{
    Fields
    T1 m1() { ... }
    ...
    Tn mn() { ... }
}
```

This shortened my path to getting started. I had spent several weeks designing an analysis algorithm for dealing with Java's thread creation, concentrating in particular on carrying around enough information to report errors when a proof failed. Now I would not need that algorithm. Rather, I would choose "the

---

[5] See [7] for further discussion on problems related to friction, signal, etc. in program analysis.

(non-private) methods of a class don't race with one another when run in parallel" as an approximation of the intuitive concept of thread safety: my analyzer could choose specific parallel compositions to shoot for.

The second discovery was that CSL could in principle reason well about all of the code I had seen. I could see how to do manual proofs about the coding idioms I had encountered, the main questions were the level of automation I could achieve and how to give good feedback when proofs failed.

An interesting example I came across was from the file `ComponentTree.java` from Facebook's Litho library, where the following comment indicates a pattern where programmers try to avoid synchronization.

```
// This is written to only by the main thread with the lock held,
// read from the main thread with no lock held,
// or read from any other thread with the lock held.
private LayoutState mMainThreadLayoutState;
```

Litho is open source (https://github.com/facebook/litho) so you can go find the code if you'd like. Boiling down what is happening to an example in "Java with parallel composition", the comment is indicating that

```
 synchronized (lock) { x = 42 } ; y = x;
|| synchronized (lock) { z = x; }
```

is race free. You can read from x outside of synchronization in the first thread because it is not written to in the second. There is a nice proof of this example using CSL with fractional permissions [2,3], which looks like this:

```
Resource Invariant: x:1/2.

[x:1/2] synchronized (lock) { [x:1] x = 42; [x:1] };
        [x:1/2] y = x; [x:1/2]
||
[x:0] sychronized (lock) {[x:1/2] z = x; [x:1/2] } [x:0]
```

With fractional permissions if an lvalue has permission 1 then you can read from or write to it, for fraction >0 but <1 then you can read but not write, and permission 0 means you can neither read nor write. The resource invariant is added when you enter a synch block and subtracted when you leave: we get permission 1 inside the first synch block just because $1/2 + 1/2 = 1$.

I also found examples of ownership transfer, similar to some of the early examples used to illustrate CSL, where the permission to dereference storage transfers from one thread to another. For example, again in `ComponentTree.java`:

```
// The semantics here are tricky. Whenever you transfer
// mBackgroundLayoutState to a local that will be accessed
// outside of the lock, you must set mBackgroundLayoutState
// to null to ensure that the current thread alone has access to
// the LayoutState, which is single-threaded.
private LayoutState mBackgroundLayoutState;
```

Reasoning about the correct usage of `mBackgroundLayoutState` can be done using a disjunctive resource invariant, like

```
mBackgroundLayoutState == null     OR     mBackgroundLayoutState |-> -
```

which we read as saying that either `mBackgroundLayoutState` is `null` or it is a non-null pointer that is owned by a lock. While we could indeed handle such examples with CSL, from looking at the code I hypothesized that the vast majority of it, I guessed 95% to 98%, did not need the kind of disjunctive invariants used to account for ownership transfer, but rather simpler ones like `x:1/2` as above.

The third discovery was that by far the most common synchronization in the codebase was expressed with the `synchronized (this)` construct. There were indeed cases where two locks were used in a single file, there were some instances of read/write locks, and even a counting semaphore. But, the majority of cases involved `synchronized (this)`. Note that these were by no means trivial, because of (for example) idioms like the `ComponentTree.java` example above where programmers would attempt to avoid synchronization. But it suggested: initial impact could be had even without an analysis that attempted to accurately distinguish different locks.

The detective work I did here – reading code and constructing mental proofs and understanding what coding patterns were more and less frequent – while not glamorous was, in retrospect, an incredibly valuable part of the project. The three discoveries above are not novel, but are just part of the kind of normal scoping work one does before embarking on an engineering project. Rather than novelty, the goal is to gather enough relevant information to inform engineering judgement as to the way forward. In this case, the original problem was considerably simplified as a bonus. At this point I had a much better understanding of the engineering context, enough to form a more concrete plan for progress.

4   Pre-α Prototype

By July 2016 I was ready to get started with my tool. It would infer resource invariants for fractional permissions as well as preconditions for threads, and apply these to Facebook's Java codebases. At first the only locking I would treat would be by critical sections `synchronized (this){..}`, and I would aim for simple, un-conditional invariants. Programs using multiple locks within a file or ownership transfer examples, the minority, would be handled either via manually supplied invariants or by an improvement to the algorithm after the simpler majority had been dealt with.

I worked out a pen-and-paper analysis algorithm based on CSL with fractional permissions, and I circulated an internal note to the Infer team. I was very excited at the prospects, as I estimated that we could prove race freedom for hundreds or thousands of classes, and find tens of data race bugs, after the ideas were implemented and deployed. At this point I also sparked up a collaboration with academics, Ilya Sergey from University College London and Nikos Gorogiannis from Middlesex University, to help work on the theoretical foundations of the analyzer. Their input on the theory, and later the practice, would turn out to be important (more on that in the last section of the paper).

The coding was a big task for me, but it was also great fun and very satisfying. I had not programmed for years, and had never in truth written that much code; I was a theorist for most of my career. Sam Blackshear had created a framework I was using, Infer.AI, for writing compositional abstract interpreters, and I convinced him to be my coding mentor (at the same time that I was officially still his manager).

I didn't begin by implementing the algorithm to infer resource invariants and preconditions; that would have been too intricate a starting point. Rather, to learn how to make an inter-procedural analysis which reports inter-procedural errors, I decided that my first prototype would simply search for certain obvious errors: writes outside of any synchronization. Any such write would give rise to a potential self-race, when its enclosing method was run in parallel with itself. Here is an example:

```
SelfRace.java:20: error: THREAD_SAFETY_VIOLATION
   Unprotected write. Non-private method 'SelfRace.foo' writes to field 'this.SelfRace.y'
   outside of synchronization. Reporting because the current class is annotated '@ThreadSafe',
   so we assume that this method can run in parallel with other non-private methods in the
   class (including itself).
   18.    void foo() {
   19.       synchronized(this){ x = 42; };
   20. >     y = 84;
   21.    }
   22.
```

I did not concentrate on these self races because I thought they were so important, but rather to give me something concrete and simple to shoot for in the prototype. I knew that when the real version landed later I would need to provide engineers with effective signal when a potential bug was found, so I optimized my early coding towards that (which I needed to learn about) rather than proof (which I knew better).

By October 2016 I had knocked out a kLOC of code and completed a prototype which I was running on Facebook's Android codebases. The analyzer was not reporting issues to developers but was rather running from time to time silently, in stealth mode. I started planning on converting it over to a CSL prover. I thought I could see how to do this; I could imagine a first prover ready by June 2017 and, after α and β versions shipped to volunteers for feedback, a real launch by the end of 2017.

You might wonder why I thought it would take a whole year. Well, it was only me programming at this stage and, additionally, from the first internal release of Infer in 2014 I remembered how much the tool improved during the $\alpha\beta$ training period. I didn't want to underestimate the importance of the training period. I thought I could calmly and carefully approach a successful launch of a tool for doing concurrency proofs at scale.

So things were going well. I thought I'd have my CSL prover in production in about a year. That would have been scientifically novel I thought, and would likely have produced non-negligible impact and a springboard for doing more. I had no concrete impact thus far after working for 10 months on the project, but my manager Bryan was very happy with this progress and remained supportive. (In fact, he said that he *preferred* that I bet on uncertain long-term work that could fail, rather than more certain short-term work.)

5 Intervention and Pivot

In October 2016 Android engineers inside Facebook caught wind of the project when Sam let the cat out of the bag in a side remark during a status update to an internal Android group.

Sam Blackshear is with Jeremy Dubreil.
October 14, 2016 · Formatted

Infer status update

⋮

There's also a fancier concurrency analysis in the works for checking that `@ThreadSafe` -annotated classes are actually thread safe.

The first question that came in response to Sam's post asked about what in program analysis jargon we would call inter-procedural capabilities.

Will the eventual thread safe annotation be recursive? Will it check that dependencies, at least how they're used, are thread safe?

The story is that a team in NYC was embarking on a new venture, converting part of the News Feed in Facebook's Android app from a sequential to a multi-threaded architecture. This was challenging because hundreds of classes written for a single-threaded architecture had to be used now in a concurrent context: the transformation could introduce concurrency errors. They asked for inter-procedural capabilities because Android UI is arranged in such a way that tree structures like

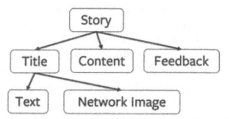

are represented with one class per node. Races could happen via inter-procedural call chains sometimes spanning several classes. Furthermore, the Litho library for UI being developed at Facebook was arranged in such a way that mutations almost never happened at the top level: *intra*-procedural race detection would miss most races.

I was naturally pleased to have engineers express interest in the concurrency project, doubly-pleased in fact because inter-procedural reasoning is one of Infer's strong points. But, I kept my head down working to my planned time-line, which would see release a year later. Then, in November the level of interest ramped up considerably, for example when I received these messages:

11/29/2016 4:21PM

Hey Peter! Jason here from Android Feed Rendering. I usually work in NYC but I'm in LON until Thursday. I hear you wrote @ThreadSafe. I'd love to talk about it and how it could dramatically help us in H1 so your team has some context. Do you have time to chat in person?

⋮

Benjamin

Talking with Jason, one of our managers - we realized that the timeline of background layout in feed might be closely tied to the timeline of static analysis - I'm wondering if you have your roadmap already fleshed out.

At this point I had a decision to make. I could seek to damp down expec-tations and continue with my plan of releasing my prover in a year, or I could pivot to serve the engineers as well as I could, as soon as possible. As a sci-entist I would perhaps have regretted giving up on my "beautiful" prover, but after moving from university to work in an engineering org I found it useful to frequently remind myself of the difference between science and engineering.

"Scientists seek perfection and are **idealists**. ... . An engineer's task is to **not be idealistic**. You need to be realistic as you *have* to compromise between conflicting interests." Sir Tony Hoare[6]

These words of Tony helped me to stay grounded as I contemplated the com-promises that would inevitably be needed were I to choose the second course.

It was in truth an easy decision to make. The job of the Infer team is to help Facebook's programmers: it is only right to respond and help them, and we place this duty above (say) abstract aims concerning the exact shape of an eventual tool. Furthermore, when you try to deploy a static analysis it can sometimes seem like an uphill struggle to convince people that heeding the warnings will be worthwhile. Their time is valuable and one needs to be very careful not to inadvertently waste it. Here, though, we had a team *asking* for static analysis support from a project we were already working on, for an important project they were planning, and where the potential near-term impact of doing so far outstripped anything I had thought about. This seemed like a golden opportunity for someone working in static analysis.

So, I made the decision to pivot to meet the Android engineers' needs as well as we could in a timeframe that would fit their goals. I asked Sam to stop

---

[6] https://reinout.vanrees.org/weblog/2009/07/01/ep-keynote.html.

(only) being my mentor and to join the project immediately as a full contributor himself. He agreed, and this would considerably expand our capabilities.

6   Understanding the Engineering Problem, Part 2: The People

Sam and I met with two Android engineers, Benjamin Jaeger and Jingbo Yang from Facebook's NYC office, and agreed that we should spec out a *minimum viable product* (MVP) for serving them. After discussing what we thought might and might not be possible technically in a three-month timespan, Ben came back to us with a first draft of an MVP, which we iterated on, arriving at something that included the following (in essence).

1. High signal: detect actionable races that developers find useful and respond to. Find many races that would be encountered in practice, but no need to (provably) find them all.
2. Inter-procedural: ability to track data races involving many nested procedure calls.
3. Low friction: no reliance on manual annotations to specify which locks protect what data.
4. Fast: able to report in 15 min on modifications to a millions-of-lines codebase, so as to catch concurrency regressions during code review.
5. Accurate treatment of coarse-grained locking, as used in most of product code, but no need for precise analysis of intricate fine-grained synchronization (the minority, changing rarely, found in infrastructure code).

The requirement for high signal balances false positives and negatives rather than seeking idealistic perfection in either direction. It is common in engineering to accept imperfection but to measure and improve metrics over time. The engineers were comfortable with this requirement; in fact, they suggested it when we said we could not produce a prover with few false positives in three months.

The requirement for low friction was particularly important. Hundreds of classes needed to be placed into a multi-threaded context. If humans were required to write annotations about which locks protected what data, the kind of thing one finds in `@GuardedBy` type systems for Java, then it would take too much time. Inference would help our engineers to move fast.

It is important to note that the specification of the MVP was not arrived at by abstract reasoning alone. It was conceived of by balancing what was technically possible (in our opinion) with the specific needs of people facing a specific problem (convert News Feed), as well as other people in the general engineering population who we needed to help prevent concurrency regressions. By aiming to strike this balance we were able to convert a seemingly intractable problem into a one where an initial success that we could then build on was in sight.

7   Development and Deployment of RacerD

As it happens my pre-α prototype provided a good starting point. It was recording information about accesses and whether any lock was held at a program point. Sam and I set about completing the MVP for RacerD. It was implemented as a special abstract interpreter within the Infer.AI framework. Our design included principles guiding the initial and further developments, specific abstract domains, and a means of determining potential races given what the abstract domains compute. You can see the details in the companion paper [1].

Apart from the specifics, a general design goal of RacerD was simplicity: we were determined not to introduce technical innovations unless they were absolutely necessary. As technical program analysis people it is always tempting to try this or that technique. But we employed occam's razor rigorously, guided by experiment as well as logic, and this was important for how the tool would evolve. If we were to introduce additional complex techniques without extremely good reasons it would have slowed us down, affecting the turnaround time for responding to engineer feedback, and could even have imperiled the project.

After Sam and I completed the MVP, Ben and Jingbo began applying RacerD to classes in our Android codebase. They encountered many false positives, which often had to do with either access to newly allocated entities that had not escaped, and that therefore could not be interfered with. Sam had worked out an ownership analysis for tracking these entities; it was the most challenging part of getting a high-signal analysis, and it was refined over several months. Other problems came up from threading assumptions. Sam and Ben designed an annotation system for expressing assumptions about ownership and threading to help the anlayzer along, and which reflected the way our engineers thought about the code. By this point Sam was doing most of the implementation work responding to false positives and other feedback.

Meanwhile Jingbo was converting vast quantities of Android code to a concurrent context, reporting false alarms to us, and running experiments to keep the conversion moving in the right direction. By October of 2017 it was clear that both projects, RacerD and the conversion of News Feed in Android, were successes. Jingbo announced a performance win for the multi-threaded News Feed, and RacerD had caught thousands of potential data races both in Jingbo's conversions and in automatic comments on code modifications from hundreds of other engineers. I won't belabour the point that the projects went well: you can read more about multi-threading in a blog post[7], and more about RacerD in its own blog[8] and in the companion paper [1]. And there is more to come in the future: already RacerD has enabled further work beyond races, on deadlock detection and starvation, and a modified version of it is in production for C++ as well as for Java. Perhaps the CSL prover will even make an appearance.

---

[7] code.facebook.com/posts/1985913448333055/multithreaded-rendering-on-android-with-litho-and-infer/.

[8] https://code.facebook.com/posts/293371094514305/open-sourcing-racerd-fast-static-race-detection-at-scale/.

Instead of talking more about what was achieved, I want instead to recount some of the further hiccups we had while doing the work, and how we tried to react to them.

8   Hiccups, Theorems, Science and Engineering

We had used reasoning intuition in building an analyzer that quickly searches for likely races, but we did not formalize what we were doing before we did it. However, in parallel, theoretical work was happening, driven mostly by Nikos and Ilya, with Sam and I participating but concentrating more on the in-prod analyzer.

Nikos and Ilya created an idealized analyzer, written in LaTeX, based on CSL with fractional permissions. They then constructed a small prototype, a "baby prover", written in OCaml. There was a gap between the baby prover and the in-prod RacerD. Our original plan was to close the gap, but we found it widening over time because the in-prod analyzer was mutating at a fast rate in response to developer feedback. There was not unanimity of opinion on what to do about this gap.

A non-starter would have been to pause the development of the in-prod analyzer, repeat its work to grow the baby prover, wait until the prover had matured enough to have a low enough false positive rate, and then do the switch-over. The in-prod analyzer was serving our programmers and improving steadily; we did not want to sacrifice this for idealistic purposes.

We wondered if we could instead modify the in-prod analyzer to be sound for bug prevention (over-approximation). I suggested to identify a subset of analyzer runs which corresponded to proofs. We added soundness flags to the analyzer and tried to keep track of sound moves, but this ultimately did not work out. Next, Sam implemented an escape analysis to find race bugs due to locally declared references escaping their defining scope, to reduce the false negatives. The escape analysis led to too many false positives to put into production and we abandoned it. Nikos tried another tack to reduce false negatives: a simple alias analysis, to find races between distinct syntactic expressions that denote the same lvalue. Again the attempt caused too many false positives to put into prod.

The above should not be taken as a commentary on soundness versus unsoundness in general, or as saying unsoundness is necessary or desirable in industrial program analysis. I see no reason why the baby prover could not be grown to the point of being good enough for production. But, having a very effective analyzer in place meant that the priority for doing this became less than if we had no analyzer at all in place.

So we had engineered RacerD to search for probable race bugs rather than to exclude races, we viewed this as a compromise, and we were responding to this compromise by trying to change the analyzer to fit a standard soundness theorem. And we were not succeeding. Then, one day in Sept 2017 I thought to myself: this analysis is actually very effective, the signal is surprisingly good, few false positives are being reported. Those false positives that were turning up often resulted from missing assumptions (e.g., about threading or ownership) rather than problems in the analyzer design. So I thought, rather than try to change the analyzer so it fit a pre-conceived soundness notion, let's try to understand why the already-effective analyzer is effective and formalize a portion of that understanding. I proposed a theorem (or, hypothesis) as follows.

TP (True Positives) Theorem: Under certain assumptions (assumptions reflecting product code), the analyzer reports no false positives.

An initial version of the assumptions was described as follows. Consider an idealized language, IL, in which programs have only non-deterministic choice in conditionals, and where there is no recursion. The absence of booleans in conditionals reflects the idea that in product code very coarse grained locking is typically used. We don't often, for example, select a lock conditionally based on the value of a field, like we do in ownership transfer or fine-grained concurrency examples. The no recursion condition is there because we want to say that the analyzer gets the races right except for when divergence make a piece of code impossible to reach. Now IL does not perfectly represent product code (nothing does as far as we know), but it serves as a useful working hypothesis for theory.

[**Aside.** One can see the TP Theorem as establishing an under-approximation of an over-approximation. Start with a program without recursion. Replace booleans by non-determinism (that's over-approximation). Then no false positives (under-approx). The more usual position in program analysis is to go for the reverse decompostion, an over-approximation of an under-approximation. The "under" comes about from ignored features, and the "over" from a usual sound-for-bug-prevention analysis. In contrast, under-of-over seems like a good way to think about static analysis for bug catching. (And yes, I know the above can even be thought of as under of over of under, where the first "under" ignores recursion.)]

Now, the True Positives Theorem was not actually true of the in-prod analyzer when we formulated it, and it is still not. But we took it as a guiding principle. We would subsequently, when faced with a design choice, take an alternative consistent with the theorem. For example, we implemented a "deep ownership" assumption: If an access path, say x.f, is owned, then so are all extensions, e.g. x.f.g. The analyzer would never report a race for an owned access. The deep ownership assumption goes against soundness for bug prevention (over-approximation), but is compatible with soundness for bug finding (under-approximation). The TP Theorem also provided rationalization for our earlier decisions not to deploy alias or escape analysis.

Since then, Nikos and Ilya have proven a version of the TP Theorem for a version 2 of RacerD, a modified version of the analyzer which is not too far removed from the in-production version. While we had difficulty seeing how to modify RacerD to be sound for bug prevention, we were able to modify it to be consistent with the TP theorem (sound for bug catching, under assumptions). We are in the process of measuring and evaluating the differences between versions 1 and 2. I won't say more on the status of that work as it is in progress, but I would like to talk about science and engineering in program analysis in light of the above.

First, about the role of the TP theorem. We did not think of the theorem before we started, and then go on to implement an analyzer to satisfy the theorem. Rather, the theorem came up later, in response to the surprising behaviour we observed. If you think about the way software is developed in an iterative way then this seems natural: analyzers do not need to be developed according to a (straw man) waterfall model, any more than general software does. And as an aside, if you think about the way research is developed, neither does it usually flow in a neat waterfall fashion.

Second, the role of the theorem is not to provide iron-clad guarantees to rely on. Rather, it has been used to help understand the analyzer and guide the design while it's in flight. This reminds me of something my PhD supervisor Bob Tennent emphasized to me many years ago, which I did not fully appreciate at the time. Bob said that, yes, semantics can be used to show what is true about a programming language after it is set in stone, but it is (arguably) even more valuable in helping inform design when a language is being created [10]. The same is true for program analyzers: RacerD is but one illustration.

Finally, you can see that both science and engineering have played important roles in the development of RacerD. Science gave rise to original ideas on sequential reasoning about concurrent programs, it gave us compositionality, abstraction, and much more. It gave us the basic ideas to get started at all in a way that scales. Then contact with Android engineers led to compromises to get an analyzer that is effective in practice. Trying to understand why the analyzer was effective caused us to go back to science to formulate the TP theorem, and this in turn influenced further development of the analyzer.

This way of having science and engineering playing off one another in a tight feedback loop is possible, even advantageous, when practicing static analysis in industry at present. The subject is not so over developed that exclusively-engineering work is typically the best route to good results, and not so under developed that exclusively-science is the only thing feasible to do. I hasten to stress that exclusively-engineering and exclusively-science remain valuable, things that folks should feel comfortable and well justified in doing. My main point is rather that the current state of the subject, with the possibility of tight science-engineering feedback, makes for a rich variety of ideas and problems to explore.

Acknowledgements. Thanks first of all to Jingbo Yang and Ben Jaeger for being so giving of their time, experience and insight when working with Sam Blackshear and I. And thanks to Sam for taking the engineering of RacerD to another level. I am fortunate to have participated in this collaboration with Ben, Jingbo and Sam. I'm grateful to Nikos Gorogiannis and Ilya Sergey for joining and contributing greatly to the project. Finally, special thanks to Bryan O'Sullivan for consistently and enthusiastically supporting this work, and encouraging me to proceed and be bold.

References

1. Blackshear, S., Gorogiannis, N., Sergey, I., O'Hearn, P.: RacerD: compositional static race detection. In: OOPSLA (2018)
2. Bornat, R., Calcagno, C., O'Hearn, P., Parkinson, M.: Permission accounting in separation logic. In: 32nd POPL, pp. 59–70 (2005)
3. Boyland, J.: Checking interference with fractional permissions. In: Cousot, R. (ed.) SAS 2003. LNCS, vol. 2694, pp. 55–72. Springer, Heidelberg (2003). https://doi.org/10.1007/3-540-44898-5_4
4. Brookes, S., O'Hearn, P.W.: Concurrent separation logic. SIGLOG News 3(3), 47–65 (2016)
5. Calcagno, C., et al.: Moving fast with software verification. In: Havelund, K., Holzmann, G., Joshi, R. (eds.) NFM 2015. LNCS, vol. 9058, pp. 3–11. Springer, Cham (2015). https://doi.org/10.1007/978-3-319-17524-9_1
6. Calcagno, C., Distefano, D., O'Hearn, P.W., Yang, H.: Compositional shape analysis by means of bi-abduction. J. ACM 58(6), 26 (2011)
7. Harman, M., O'Hearn, P.: From start-ups to scale-ups: open problems and challenges in static and dynamic program analysis for testing and verification (keynote paper). In: International Working Conference on Source Code Analysis and Manipulation (2018)
8. O'Hearn, P.: Continuous reasoning: scaling the impact of formal methods. In: 33rd Annual ACM/IEEE Symposium on Logic in Computer Science, Oxford, July 2018
9. O'Hearn, P.W.: Resources, concurrency and local reasoning. Theor. Comput. Sci. 375(1–3), 271–307 (2007)
10. Tennent, R.D.: Language design methods based on semantic principles. Acta Inf. 8, 97–112 (1977)

New Applications of Software Synthesis: Verification of Configuration Files and Firewall Repair

Ruzica Piskac[✉]

Yale University, New Haven, USA
ruzica.piskac@yale.edu

Abstract. The main goal of software synthesis is to automatically derive code from a given specification. The specification can be either explicitly written, or specified through a couple of representative examples illustrating the user's intent. However, sometimes there is no specification and we need to infer the specification from a given environment. This paper present two such efforts.

We first show, using verification for configuration files, how to learn specification when the given examples is actually a set of configuration files. Software failures resulting from configuration errors have become commonplace as modern software systems grow increasingly large and more complex. The lack of language constructs in configuration files, such as types and grammars, has directed the focus of a configuration file verification towards building post-failure error diagnosis tools. We describe a framework which analyzes data sets of correct configuration files and derives rules for building a language model from the given data set. The resulting language model can be used to verify new configuration files and detect errors in them.

We next describe a systematic effort that can automatically repair firewalls, using the programming by example approach. Firewalls are widely employed to manage and control enterprise networks. Because enterprise-scale firewalls contain hundreds or thousands of policies, ensuring the correctness of firewalls – whether the policies in the firewalls meet the specifications of their administrators – is an important but challenging problem. In our approach, after an administrator observes undesired behavior in a firewall, she may provide input/output examples that comply with the intended behavior. Based on the given examples, we automatically synthesize new firewall rules for the existing firewall. This new firewall correctly handles packets specified by the examples, while maintaining the rest of the behavior of the original firewall.

Keywords: Software synthesis · Program repair · Verification
Configuration files · Firewalls

R. Piskac—This research was sponsored by the NSF under grants CCF-1302327, CFF-1553168, and CCF-1715387.

© Springer Nature Switzerland AG 2018
A. Podelski (Ed.): SAS 2018, LNCS 11002, pp. 71–76, 2018.
https://doi.org/10.1007/978-3-319-99725-4_6

1   Introduction

Software synthesis has the potential to transform the software development process, by eliminating software errors before they even occur. The essence of software synthesis is that a programmer must only state *what* should be done, and not *how* it should be done. Instead of writing code manually, a programmer provides a specification and the synthesis tool automatically generates code that satisfies the specification. Consequently, the generated code is correct by construction, thereby avoiding many of the potential errors that could creep into manually written code.

Recent work in this area has focused on manipulating fundamental data types such as strings [5,9,14], lists [4,10] and numbers [15]. The success and impact of this line of work can be estimated from the fact that some of this technology [5] ships as part of the popular Flash Fill feature in Excel 2013 [16].

A common thread to all those tools that they take a given specification and automatically generate code corresponding to that specification. The specification can be explicitly written, in which case we are talking about complete specification, or it can be given in the form of input/output examples. The user provides those examples and they should be chosen so that they illustrate the user's intentions. Nevertheless, this is still an incomplete specification, which means that there might be many programs satisfying the given examples. This type of software synthesis is well known under the name *programming by example* [3,6,8].

In this paper we describe two application domains for software synthesis that have not been not previously studied by the community working in formal methods and verification. One topic is synthesis of a specification for configuration files (Sect. 2, previously published in [12,13]). The second project introduces so-called *repair by example*, which is used for verification and repair of firewall programs (Sect. 3, previously published in [7]).

2   Verification of Configuration Files

Configuration errors (also known as misconfigurations) have become one of the major causes of system failures, resulting in security vulnerabilities, application outages, and incorrect program executions [17,18]. In 2015 Facebook, Tinder, and Instagram all became inaccessible for approximately 52 min. A Facebook spokeswoman reported that this was caused by a change to the site's configuration system [11]. These critical system failures are not rare – a software system failures study [19] reports that about 31% of system failures were caused by configuration errors. This is even higher than the percentage of failures resulting from program bugs (20%).

A recent study [2] showed that in 2016 software errors cost the United States economy approximately \$1.1 trillion. Detecting and preventing software errors plays a major role in a development process, with programmers using techniques like testing, debugging, and verification. However, none of these techniques can be applied to finding errors in configuration files. Effective testing of configuration files is difficult because errors may arise only under certain, hard to simulate conditions, such as heavy traffic loads. Another approach to finding errors in program code is software verification, which has been applied to many complex systems (for example, operating systems, compilers). However, traditional verification techniques cannot be applied to configuration files, because these techniques rely on formal specifications describing the expected behavior of the program. The difficulty with configuration files is that they are mostly simple text files of keywords and values, and there is no traditional sense of a specification. With no formal specification of correctness or semantic program information, verifying configuration files is far outside the scope of existing technologies.

Modern verification technologies inherently depend on the availability of formal specifications, yet they are extremely labor intensive to create and maintain. This is especially the case for configuration files, which rarely have any documentation, even in written English form. We proposed and developed the first tool that can synthesize complex configuration specifications. Our tool combines knowledge discovery techniques with automated reasoning to synthesize constraint models of configuration files.

In the first prototype of our tool, ConfigC [13], we analyzed existing correct configuration files and learned properties that always hold in those configuration files. Some examples of the properties are ordering constraints (e.g., one library should be loaded before another), type constraints (e.g., which keywords act as Boolean flags), and size constraints (e.g., that some memory size always needs to be bounded by some other). Once we have learned such constraints/specifications, ConfigC can verify users configuration files, and report any violations to the user.

We extended this work to a more advanced tool ConfigV [12], which is the first tool that can automatically detect complex errors involving multiple variables, and learn over a training set of partially incorrect configuration files. ConfigV required two core theoretical advances; the first was the introduction of probabilistic types, and the second was an extension to association rule learning [1]. Since configuration files lack helpful semantic information to infer types, we use a probabilistic inference method to learn likely types for keywords based on their values from the training set. We combined this new type information with a generalization of association rule learning that handles not just association rules, but arbitrary, typed predicates.

We evaluated ConfigV by verifying public configuration files on GitHub, and we showed that ConfigV can successfully detect configuration errors in these files.

3 Verification and Repair of Firewalls

Firewalls play an important role in today's individual and enterprise-scale networks. A typical firewall is responsible for managing all incoming and outgoing traffic between an internal network and the rest of the Internet. The firewall accepts, forwards, or drops packets based on a set of rules specified by its administrators. Because of the central role firewalls play in networks, small changes can propagate unintended consequences throughout the network.

We proposed and developed the first framework, called FireMason [7], https://github.com/BillHallahan/FireMason, that not only detects errors in firewall behaviors, but also automatically repairs the firewall. Broadly speaking, a firewall is correct if the rules of that firewall meet the specification of its administrator. While existing tools can identify the cause of an error, administrators still have to manually find an effective repair to the firewall so that it meets the specification. We introduced the concept called *repair by example*. Specifically, a user provides a list of examples of packets and desired routing (e.g., all packets with a certain source IP address should be dropped) to describe the desired behavior of the firewall. The current firewall might or might not route the packets as specified in the examples, but FireMason automatically synthesizes a new firewall that is guaranteed to satisfy the examples. Given the complexity of enterprise-scale networks, finding such a repair requires considerable expertise on the part of the administrator. To the best of our knowledge, there is no other existing effort that automates firewall repairs by examples. The concept of "repair by example" was motivated by the standard practice of how users ask for help with repairing their firewalls. On user forums, users would provide their firewalls and then list a couple of illustrative examples to show how the behavior should change.

The main challenges in firewall repair and verification is that adding a new rule might fix the current problem, but entirely break the behavior on some packages that the user might not have considered. To ensure the correctness of the repair we use techniques from formal methods. We translated a firewall into the formal mathematical language of first-order logic. This allows us to use existing SMT solvers which can automatically reason about these logics. As an illustration, checking if the repair broke some of previously correct behavior reduces to checking a formulas entailment.

By using SMT solvers, FireMason can provide formal guarantees that the repaired firewalls satisfy two important properties:

- Those packets described in the examples will be routed in the repaired firewall, as specified in provided examples.
- All other packets will be routed by the repaired firewall exactly as they were in the original firewall.

Taken together, these two properties allow administrators confidence that the repairs had the intended effect.

By using our formalism we are able to check some important and widely used, but previously out-of-scope, properties, including rate limits. Rate limits, which are frequently used in modern firewalls, put a restriction on the number of packets matched in a given amount of time. Such rules say, for example, that we can only accept 6 packets per minute from a certain IP address. As before, the user provides a list of examples, but with relative times. This requires reasoning about the priorities and permissions of each firewall entry, as well as the temporal patterns of the incoming packets.

In addition to repairing, FireMason is also a stand-alone verification tool. For a given specification, such a checking if a certain packet will be rejected, FireMason can either prove that it holds, or it produce counterexamples.

We evaluated our tool using real-world firewall issues from user forums. We observed that FireMason is able to efficiently generate correct firewalls meeting administrators' examples, without introducing any new problems. In addition, our evaluation shows that FireMason scales well to enterprise-scale networks.

4   Conclusions

More details about the presented projects can be found in [7,12,13].

Two presented projects demonstrated that software synthesis can be successfully applied to problems, such as repair of firewalls and verification of configuration files, which are usually tackled by a system research community. One of the main obstacles was that often the specification does not exist and needs to inferred from the given context or provided examples. In our experience finding a suitable formalism to model the problem and efficiently solve real world instances is crucial. Both presented tools were successfully tested on the real world examples, which motivates us to further pursue addressing non-traditional synthesis problems.

References

1. Agrawal, R., Imieliński, T., Swami, A.: Mining association rules between sets of items in large databases. SIGMOD Rec. **22**(2), 207–216 (1993). https://doi.org/10.1145/170036.170072
2. Cohane, R.: Financial cost of software bugs (2017). https://medium.com/@ryancohane/financial-cost-of-software-bugs-51b4d193f107
3. Cypher, A., Halbert, D.: Watch what I Do: Programming by Demonstration. MIT Press, Cambridge (1993)
4. Feser, J.K., Chaudhuri, S., Dillig, I.: Synthesizing data structure transformations from input-output examples. In: Proceedings of the 36th ACM SIGPLAN Conference on Programming Language Design and Implementation, Portland, OR, USA, 15–17 June 2015, pp. 229–239 (2015)
5. Gulwani, S.: Automating string processing in spreadsheets using input-output examples. In: POPL, pp. 317–330 (2011)
6. Gulwani, S.: Synthesis from examples: interaction models and algorithms. In: 14th International Symposium on Symbolic and Numeric Algorithms for Scientific Computing (2012). Invited talk paper
7. Hallahan, W.T., Zhai, E., Piskac, R.: Automated repair by example for firewalls. In: 2017 Formal Methods in Computer Aided Design, FMCAD 2017, Vienna, Austria, 2–6 October 2017, pp. 220–229 (2017). https://doi.org/10.23919/FMCAD.2017.8102263
8. Lieberman, H.: Your Wish Is My Command: Programming by Example. Morgan Kaufmann, San Francisco (2001)

9. Menon, A.K., Tamuz, O., Gulwani, S., Lampson, B.W., Kalai, A.: A machine learning framework for programming by example. In: ICML (1), pp. 187–195 (2013)
10. Osera, P., Zdancewic, S.: Type-and-example-directed program synthesis. In: Proceedings of the 36th ACM SIGPLAN Conference on Programming Language Design and Implementation, Portland, OR, USA, 15–17 June 2015, pp. 619–630 (2015)
11. Ryall, J.: Facebook, Tinder, Instagram suffer widespread issues (2015). http://mashable.com/2015/01/27/facebook-tinder-instagram-issues/
12. Santolucito, M., Zhai, E., Dhodapkar, R., Shim, A., Piskac, R.: Synthesizing configuration file specifications with association rule learning. PACMPL 1(OOPSLA), 64:1–64:20 (2017). https://doi.org/10.1145/3133888
13. Santolucito, M., Zhai, E., Piskac, R.: Probabilistic automated language learning for configuration files. In: Chaudhuri, S., Farzan, A. (eds.) CAV 2016. LNCS, vol. 9780, pp. 80–87. Springer, Cham (2016). https://doi.org/10.1007/978-3-319-41540-6_5
14. Singh, R., Gulwani, S.: Learning semantic string transformations from examples. PVLDB 5, 740–751 (2012)
15. Singh, R., Gulwani, S.: Synthesizing number transformations from input-output examples. In: CAV, pp. 634–651 (2012)
16. Flash Fill (Microsoft Excel 2013 feature). http://research.microsoft.com/users/sumitg/flashfill.html
17. Xu, T., Jin, L., Fan, X., Zhou, Y., Pasupathy, S., Talwadker, R.: Hey, you have given me too many knobs!: understanding and dealing with over-designed configuration in system software. In: The 10th ESEC/FSEJoint Meeting on Foundations of Software Engineering, August 2015
18. Xu, T., Zhang, J., Huang, P., Zheng, J., Sheng, T., Yuan, D., Zhou, Y., Pasupathy, S.: Do not blame users for misconfigurations. In: The 24th SOSPACM Symposium on Operating Systems Principles, November 2013
19. Yin, Z., Ma, X., Zheng, J., Zhou, Y., Bairavasundaram, L.N., Pasupathy, S.: An empirical study on configuration errors in commercial and open source systems. In: Proceedings of the Twenty-Third ACM Symposium on Operating Systems Principles, pp. 159–172, SOSP 2011. ACM, New York (2011). https://doi.org/10.1145/2043556.2043572

Interactive Verification of Distributed Protocols Using Decidable Logic

Sharon Shoham$^{(\boxtimes)}$

Tel Aviv University, Tel Aviv, Israel
sharon.shoham@gmail.com

1 Extended Abstract

Distributed systems are becoming more and more pervasive in our lives, making their correctness crucial. Unfortunately, distributed systems are notoriously hard to get right and verify. Due to the infinite state space (e.g., unbounded number of nodes and messages) and the complexity of the protocols used, verification of such systems is both undecidable and hard in practice.

Numerous works have considered the problem of *automatically* verifying distributed and parameterized systems, e.g., [1,9,10,17,18,20,23,24,26,38]. Full automation is extremely appealing. Unfortunately, automatic techniques are bound to fail in some cases due to the undecidability of the problem. Some impose restrictions on the verified systems (e.g., [26]), some may diverge (e.g., [24]) and some may report false alarms (e.g., [2]). Moreover, such techniques often suffer from scalability issues and from an unpredictable performance. As a result, most efforts towards verifying real-world systems use relatively little automation [19,25,31].

In contrast, *deductive verification* approaches let a user annotate the verified system with inductive invariants and pre/post specifications, and reduce the verification problem to the problem of proving the validity of the corresponding *verification conditions*. Tools for doing so vary in their expressiveness and level of automation. Some (e.g., [6,12,13,22,33,34]) check the verification conditions by decision procedures, but are limited in their expressivity. Others (e.g., [29]) use undecidable logics and semi-decision procedures, e.g., as provided by satisfiability modulo theories (SMT) solvers (e.g., Z3 [11], CVC4 [4], OpenSMT2 [21], Yices [14]), or by first-order solvers (e.g., Vampire [40], iProver [27]). Tools based on semi-decision procedures might fail to discharge the verification conditions either by non-terminating or by yielding inconclusive answers. Similarly to automatic verification approaches, they also suffer from an unpredictable performance: They might work well on some programs, but diverge when a small change is performed. This is sometimes referred to as a *butterfly effect* [30]. When this happens, it is often extremely difficult to discover, let alone remedy, the root cause of failure in the complex chain of reasoning produced by the algorithm.

Proof assistants such as Coq [5] and Isabelle/HOL [35] offer great expressivity, but require the user to write the proof (possibly exploiting various tactics), while mechanically validating every step in the proof. Verification using

© Springer Nature Switzerland AG 2018
A. Podelski (Ed.): SAS 2018, LNCS 11002, pp. 77–85, 2018.
https://doi.org/10.1007/978-3-319-99725-4_7

proof assistants is extremely labor intensive and requires tremendous efforts even by expert users (e.g., approx. 10 lines of proof were required per line of code in [42,43]). Thus, it is hard to deploy this method to verify complicated systems.

In summary, all of these approaches either (i) handle limited classes of systems, (ii) employ sound but incomplete automatic reasoning which reports too many false alarms, (iii) use semi-algorithms that tend to be fragile, unpredictable and often diverge, or (iv) require too much manual effort, relying on expertise in logic and verification.

Approach. We propose to overcome the shortcomings of existing approaches by using an interactive verification methodology that divides the verification problem into tasks that are well suited for automation and can be solved by decision procedures, and tasks that are best done by a human, and finds a suitable mode of interaction between the human and the machine.

This methodology is based on the conjecture that users usually have high level knowledge of the functionality of the code and interactions between different parts of the program. On the other hand, algorithmic techniques can be effective in reasoning about corner cases missed by the user. The key to success is to exploit these fortes when defining the roles of the user and the automated analysis, and to provide the suitable interface between them.

"One thing all programmers have in common is that they enjoy working with machines; so let's keep them in the loop. Some tasks are best done by machine, while others are best done by human insight; and a properly designed system will find the right balance." — D. Knuth

We argue that letting a user convey her intuition to an automated analysis, and making sure that automation is restricted to decidable problems, will make the verification process more efficient and predictable, and will allow to balance between automation and expressivity.

An attempt at applying this methodology is implemented in Ivy [37]. In this work, we developed an interactive procedure for verifying safety properties of distributed protocols, where the verification conditions are expressed using decidable logic, allowing to check their validity completely automatically with decision procedures, and where the user's creativity guides the construction of the proper annotations. This is achieved by graphically displaying states that violate the verification conditions and letting the user select the relevant parts of the state according to which the annotations (inductive invariants) are updated. We elaborate on this approach in the sequel. We start with some background.

Decidable reasoning in Ivy. Ivy is a verification system based on decidable logic. Decidability greatly improves the predictability of proof automation, resulting in a more practical verification approach. Furthermore, it facilitates an interactive process, where the user may modify the invariants used for verification based on counterexamples.

Ivy supports several decidable fragments of first-order logic, of which [37] uses the **E**ffectively **PR**opositional fragment (EPR). EPR [39] is a fragment of first-order logic where the vocabulary is restricted to constant and relation symbols,[1] and the quantifier prefix is restricted to $\exists^*\forall^*$ in prenex normal form.[2] Satisfiability of EPR formulas is decidable [32] and supported by existing SMT solvers such as Z3 [11] and first-order logic provers such as iProver [27]. Moreover, EPR has the *finite-model property*, which means that every satisfiable formula has a finite model.

EPR is a relatively weak logic, but, perhaps surprisingly, it turns out to be suitable for modeling and verifying interesting systems, including software defined networks [3], heap manipulating programs [16, 22], and, as we do in this work, distributed protocols [36, 37, 41]. We refer the interested reader to the aforementioned works for more details on modeling systems and their properties using EPR.

Safety verification. Safety properties specify bad behaviors that should never be encountered in any run of a system. An example of a bad behavior is the election of more than one leader in a leader election protocol. Safety properties are essential requirements that, when violated, might incur catastrophical outcomes.

One of the most useful techniques for proving safety of infinite-state systems already advocated by Floyd [15] is based on *inductive invariants*. Inductive invariants are an adaptation of the mathematical concept of "induction hypothesis" to the domain of programs. Technically, an inductive invariant I is a property of the system that (i) holds initially (initiation), (ii) implies the safety property (safety), and (iii) is preserved by every step of the system, namely if the system makes a step from any configuration that satisfies I, it reaches a configuration that satisfies I as well (consecution). If an inductive invariant exists, the system is safe. Thus, safety verification reduces to inferring inductive invariants. Similarly to mathematical proofs by induction, the most challenging and creative task in deductive verification of safety properties is coming up with the inductive invariants.

Example 1. As a concrete example, consider a simple distributed protocol for leader election in a ring [8]. The protocol assumes a ring of unbounded size. Every node has a unique ID with a total order on the IDs. Thus, electing a leader can be done by a decentralized extrema-finding protocol. The protocol works by sending messages in the ring in one direction: Each node announces its ID to its immediate neighbor. A node only forwards messages with higher ID than its own ID. When a node receives a message with its own ID, it declares itself as a leader. The safety property of interest here is that no more than one leader is elected. To verify the protocol means to verify that this property holds in every instance of nodes that run the protocol.

---

[1] It is straightforward to extend EPR to allow *stratified* function symbols, i.e., function symbols that do not create cycles among sorts (e.g., if there is a function symbol from sort A to sort B, then no function symbol from sort B to sort A is allowed).

[2] In particular, EPR does not allow the use of arithmetic operations.

In this example, the safety property itself is not inductive. For example, in a configuration where one leader is already elected but there is a pending message to some other node with its own ID, the property will be violated in the next step, hence violating the consecution requirement. Such a configuration is not reachable from the initial configuration of the protocol (where no leader is elected and no message is pending), but the safety property itself is not strong enough to exclude it. In order to exclude the counterexample to induction and make the candidate invariant inductive, it needs to be strengthened by adding (1) a conjecture saying that a message can reach a node with the same ID only if this ID is maximal — this conjecture will exclude the scenario described above, (2) a conjecture saying that the leader has the highest ID, and (3) a conjecture saying that messages cannot bypass nodes with higher IDs.

Verification conditions. We express protocols using a transition relation formula, denoted $Tr(V, V')$, where V is the vocabulary V used to describe the protocol's state, and V' is its copy used to represent the post-state of a transition. Initial state conditions, safety properties and inductive invariants are also specified via formulas, $Init(V)$, $P(V)$ and $Inv(V)$, respectively, over V. Checking whether Inv satisfies initiation, consecution and safety, then corresponds to checking the validity of the following verification conditions:

initiation	$Init(V) \rightarrow Inv(V)$
safety	$Inv(V) \rightarrow P(V)$
consecution	$Inv(V) \wedge Tr(V, V') \rightarrow Inv(V')$

which in turn corresponds to checking the unsatisfiability of the following formulas that encode violations of the requirements:

violation of initiation	$Init(V) \wedge \neg Inv(V)$
violation of safety	$Inv(V) \wedge \neg P(V)$
violation of consecution	$Inv(V) \wedge Tr(V, V') \wedge \neg Inv(V')$

If Tr, $Init$ and $\neg P$ are EPR formulas and Inv is universally quantified, then these formulas fall into the decidable EPR fragment. Indeed, this is the case in the leader election example. If one of the formulas is satisfiable (i.e., the corresponding requirement does not hold), then a *finite* satisfying model exists (due to EPR's finite model property). For example, if consecution is violated, then a finite *counterexample to induction* is found – a state that satisfies Inv but has an outgoing transition to a state that violates it.

Inference of universally quantified inductive invariants via interactive generalization. In [37], we propose an interactive technique for inferring inductive invariants in the form of universally quantified formulas that is able to discover the inductive invariant of Example 1. The approach, implemented in Ivy, is based on iterative strengthening.

Iterative strengthening starts from a candidate inductive invariant, e.g., the safety property, and strengthens it iteratively until it becomes inductive.

Strengthening in Ivy is based on counterexamples to induction: a counterexample to induction s is excluded by conjoining the candidate invariant with a new conjecture that generalizes s into a set of excluded states. Generalization is crucial for the success of the approach. First, the conjecture obtained by generalization must not exclude any reachable state (otherwise, it would not be an invariant). In addition, it needs to be provable by induction with the given language of inductive invariants (otherwise, no further strengthening would turn the invariant into one that is also inductive). Finding a good generalization is extremely difficult to automate, and is a key reason for failure of many automatic techniques.

Therefore, Ivy uses an interactive generalization process, where the user controls the generalization, but is assisted by the tool. Ivy interacts with the user based on a graphical representation of concrete counterexamples to induction, taking advantage of the finite-model property of EPR formulas, as well as of the model-theoretic notion of a *diagram*.

The *diagram* [7] of a finite state (first-order structure) s, denoted $Diag(s)$, is an existentially quantified cube (conjunction of literals) that is satisfied by a state s' if and only if s' contains s as a substructure (where a substructure of s' is a structure obtained by restricting the domain of s' to some subset and projecting all interpretations to the remaining elements in the domain). As such, the negation of the diagram of s is a universally quantified clause that "excludes" s as well as any structure that contains it as a substructure, providing a natural generalization scheme. Additional generalization can be obtained by omitting from $Diag(s)$ some of the literals describing s (equivalently, omitting some "features" from s). These observations were used in [24] as part of an automatic invariant inference algorithm.

Ivy uses the diagram as a means to alternate between counterexamples to induction (which are natural for the user to look at) and universally quantified clauses that exclude them. Namely, when the consecution check fails, the user is presented with a *minimal* finite counterexample to induction, displayed graphically. The user responds by determining whether the counterexample to induction is reachable. If it is, then the inductive invariant is too strong and needs to weakened. If it is not reachable, the invariant can be strengthened to exclude it. In the latter case, the user hides some of the features of the counterexample to induction (e.g., the interpretation of some relation symbol) that she judges to be irrelevant to unreachability (i.e., such that the state remains unreachable with any valuation of these features). In this way, she uses her intuition to focus on the part of the state that really needs to be excluded. The feature selection is performed via a graphical interface. Ivy then computes the diagram of the generalized state, and transforms it into a universally quantified clause (conjecture) that excludes the generalized state and all the states that extend it. It offers the user several additional checks, such as bounded model checking to help verify that the new conjecture does not exclude any reachable state, and additional generalization via interpolation based on the bounded model checking check. All of these checks are implemented using decision procedures (relying on EPR's decidability). In this way, the user controls the generalization process, and is assisted by predictable automation.

Ivy was successfully used to infer invariants for several distributed protocols which are beyond reach of automatic verification algorithms, demonstrating the effectiveness of EPR and the interaction based on counterexamples to induction. Moreover, under the assumption that the user identifies the "correct" features, we are able to bound the complexity of the approach by means of the size of a target invariant.

We note that while the interactive generalization technique is restricted to generating universally quantified inductive invariants, Ivy's graphical interface is useful also in cases where the inductive invariant is more complex. In such cases, Ivy provides counterexamples to induction, and updating the inductive invariant to eliminate them is done entirely by the user. This approach has also proven itself most effective, e.g., in verifying the Paxos consensus protocol [28] and several of its variants [36].

Conclusion. We propose a verification methodology that aims to balance between automation, expressivity and predictability by properly dividing the verification task between the human and the machine. Ivy realizes this methodology by letting the tool check inductiveness of a given candidate inductive invariant using decidable logic, and letting the user update the inductive invariant based on graphically displayed counterexamples to induction. For universally quantified inductive invariants, the latter is also done interactively via a process of interactive generalization. It is left to future work to investigate these ideas with respect to other logics, other inference algorithms (more sophisticated than iterative strengthening), and other interaction modes.

Acknowledgement. This publication is part of a project that has received funding from the European Research Council (ERC) under the European Union's Horizon 2020 research and innovation programme (grant agreement No [759102-SVIS]). The research was partially supported by Len Blavatnik and the Blavatnik Family foundation, the Blavatnik Interdisciplinary Cyber Research Center, Tel Aviv University, and the United States-Israel Binational Science Foundation (BSF) grants No. 2016260 and 2012259.

References

1. Abdulla, P.A., Haziza, F., Holík, L.: Parameterized verification through view abstraction. STTT **18**(5), 495–516 (2016)
2. Alpernas, K., Manevich, R., Panda, A., Sagiv, M., Shenker, S., Shoham, S., Velner, Y.: Abstract interpretation of stateful networks. In: Static Analysis Symposium (SAS) (2018)
3. Ball, T., Bjørner, N., Gember, A., Itzhaky, S., Karbyshev, A., Sagiv, M., Schapira, M., Valadarsky, A.: Vericon: towards verifying controller programs in software-defined networks. In: ACM SIGPLAN Conference on Programming Language Design and Implementation, PLDI 2014, Edinburgh, UK, 9–11 June 2014, pp. 282–293 (2014)

4. Barrett, C., Conway, C.L., Deters, M., Hadarean, L., Jovanović, D., King, T., Reynolds, A., Tinelli, C.: CVC4. In: Gopalakrishnan, G., Qadeer, S. (eds.) CAV 2011. LNCS, vol. 6806, pp. 171–177. Springer, Heidelberg (2011). https://doi.org/10.1007/978-3-642-22110-1_14

5. Bertot, Y., Castéran, P.: Interactive Theorem Proving and Program Development - Coq'Art: The Calculus of Inductive Constructions. Texts in Theoretical Computer Science. An EATCS Series. Springer, Heidelberg (2004)

6. Bouajjani, A., Drăgoi, C., Enea, C., Sighireanu, M.: Accurate invariant checking for programs manipulating lists and arrays with infinite data. In: Chakraborty, S., Mukund, M. (eds.) ATVA 2012. LNCS, pp. 167–182. Springer, Heidelberg (2012). https://doi.org/10.1007/978-3-642-33386-6_14

7. Chang, C., Keisler, H.: Model Theory. Studies in Logic and the Foundations of Mathematics. Elsevier Science, New York (1990)

8. Chang, E., Roberts, R.: An improved algorithm for decentralized extrema-finding in circular configurations of processes. Commun. ACM **22**(5), 281–283 (1979)

9. Conchon, S., Goel, A., Krstić, S., Mebsout, A., Zaïdi, F.: Cubicle: a parallel SMT-based model checker for parameterized systems. In: Madhusudan, P., Seshia, S.A. (eds.) CAV 2012. LNCS, vol. 7358, pp. 718–724. Springer, Heidelberg (2012). https://doi.org/10.1007/978-3-642-31424-7_55

10. Conchon, S., Goel, A., Krstic, S., Mebsout, A., Zaïdi, F.: Invariants for finite instances and beyond. In: Formal Methods in Computer-Aided Design, FMCAD 2013, Portland, OR, USA, 20–23 October 2013, pp. 61–68 (2013)

11. De Moura, L., Bjørner, N.: Z3: An efficient SMT solver. In: TACAS (2008)

12. Drăgoi, C., Henzinger, T.A., Veith, H., Widder, J., Zufferey, D.: A logic-based framework for verifying consensus algorithms. In: McMillan, K.L., Rival, X. (eds.) VMCAI 2014. LNCS, vol. 8318, pp. 161–181. Springer, Heidelberg (2014). https://doi.org/10.1007/978-3-642-54013-4_10

13. Dragoi, C., Henzinger, T.A., Zufferey, D.: Psync: a partially synchronous language for fault-tolerant distributed algorithms. In: Proceedings of the 43rd Annual ACM SIGPLAN-SIGACT Symposium on Principles of Programming Languages, POPL 2016, St. Petersburg, FL, USA, 20–22 January 2016, pp. 400–415 (2016)

14. Dutertre, B.: Yices 2.2. In: Biere, A., Bloem, R. (eds.) Computer-Aided Verification (CAV 2014), vol. 8559. LNCS, pp. 737–744. Springer, Heidelberg (2014). https://doi.org/10.1007/978-3-319-08867-9_49

15. Floyd, R.W.: Assigning meanings to programs. In: Proceedings of Symposium on Applied Mathematics, vol. 32 (1967)

16. Frumkin, A., Feldman, Y.M.Y., Lhoták, O., Padon, O., Sagiv, M., Shoham, S.: Property directed reachability for proving absence of concurrent modification errors. In: Bouajjani, A., Monniaux, D. (eds.) VMCAI 2017. LNCS, vol. 10145, pp. 209–227. Springer, Cham (2017). https://doi.org/10.1007/978-3-319-52234-0_12

17. Ghilardi, S., Ranise, S.: MCMT: a model checker modulo theories. In: Giesl, J., Hähnle, R. (eds.) IJCAR 2010. LNCS (LNAI), vol. 6173, pp. 22–29. Springer, Heidelberg (2010). https://doi.org/10.1007/978-3-642-14203-1_3

18. Gurfinkel, A., Shoham, S., Meshman, Y.: SMT-based verification of parameterized systems. In: ACM SIGSOFT International Symposium on the Foundations of Software Engineering (2016, to appear)

19. Hawblitzel, C., et al.: Ironfleet: proving practical distributed systems correct. In: Proceedings of the 25th Symposium on Operating Systems Principles, SOSP, pp. 1–17 (2015)

20. Hojjat, H., Rümmer, P., Subotic, P., Yi, W.: Horn clauses for communicating timed systems. In: Proceedings First Workshop on Horn Clauses for Verification and Synthesis, HCVS 2014, Vienna, Austria, 17 July 2014, pp. 39–52 (2014)

21. Hyvärinen, A.E.J., Marescotti, M., Alt, L., Sharygina, N.: OpenSMT2: an SMT solver for multi-core and cloud computing. In: Creignou, N., Le Berre, D. (eds.) SAT 2016. LNCS, vol. 9710, pp. 547–553. Springer, Cham (2016). https://doi.org/10.1007/978-3-319-40970-2_35

22. Itzhaky, S., Banerjee, A., Immerman, N., Nanevski, A., Sagiv, M.: Effectively-propositional reasoning about reachability in linked data structures. In: Sharygina, N., Veith, H. (eds.) CAV 2013. LNCS, vol. 8044, pp. 756–772. Springer, Heidelberg (2013). https://doi.org/10.1007/978-3-642-39799-8_53

23. Kaiser, A., Kroening, D., Wahl, T.: Dynamic cutoff detection in parameterized concurrent programs. In: Touili, T., Cook, B., Jackson, P. (eds.) CAV 2010. LNCS, vol. 6174, pp. 645–659. Springer, Heidelberg (2010). https://doi.org/10.1007/978-3-642-14295-6_55

24. Karbyshev, A., Bjørner, N., Itzhaky, S., Rinetzky, N., Shoham, S.: Property-directed inference of universal invariants or proving their absence. J. ACM, 64(1):7:1–7:33 (2017)

25. Klein, G., Andronick, J., Elphinstone, K., Heiser, G., Cock, D., Derrin, P., Elkaduwe, D., Engelhardt, K., Kolanski, R., Norrish, M., Sewell, T., Tuch, H., Winwood, S.: seL4: formal verification of an operating-system Kernel. Commun. ACM 53(6), 107–115 (2010)

26. Konnov, I.V., Lazic, M., Veith, H., Widder, J.: A short counterexample property for safety and liveness verification of fault-tolerant distributed algorithms. In: Proceedings of the 44th ACM SIGPLAN Symposium on Principles of Programming Languages, POPL 2017, Paris, France, 18–20 January 2017, pp. 719–734 (2017)

27. Korovin, K.: iProver - an instantiation-based theorem prover for first-order logic (system description). In: Automated Reasoning, 4th International Joint Conference, IJCAR 2008, Sydney, Australia, 12–15 August 2008, Proceedings, pp. 292–298 (2008)

28. Lamport, L.: The part-time parliament. ACM Trans. Comput. Syst. 16(2), 133–169 (1998)

29. Leino, K.R.M.: Dafny: an automatic program verifier for functional correctness. In: Clarke, E.M., Voronkov, A. (eds.) LPAR 2010. LNCS (LNAI), vol. 6355, pp. 348–370. Springer, Heidelberg (2010). https://doi.org/10.1007/978-3-642-17511-4_20

30. Leino, K.R.M., Pit-Claudel, C.: Trigger selection strategies to stabilize program verifiers. In: Chaudhuri, S., Farzan, A. (eds.) CAV 2016. LNCS, vol. 9779, pp. 361–381. Springer, Cham (2016). https://doi.org/10.1007/978-3-319-41528-4_20

31. Leroy, X.: Formal verification of a realistic compiler. Commun. ACM 52(7), 107–115 (2009)

32. Lewis, H.R.: Complexity results for classes of quantificational formulas. J. Comput. Syst. Sci. 21(3), 317–353 (1980)

33. Madhusudan, P., Qiu, X.: Efficient decision procedures for heaps using STRAND. In: Yahav, E. (ed.) SAS 2011. LNCS, vol. 6887, pp. 43–59. Springer, Heidelberg (2011). https://doi.org/10.1007/978-3-642-23702-7_8

34. Møller, A., Schwartzbach, M.I.: The pointer assertion logic engine. In: Proceedings of the 2001 ACM SIGPLAN Conference on Programming Language Design and Implementation (PLDI), Snowbird, Utah, USA, 20–22 June 2001, pp. 221–231 (2001)

35. Nipkow, T., Wenzel, M., Paulson, L.C.: Isabelle/HOL: A Proof Assistant for Higher-order Logic. Springer, Heidelberg (2002)

36. Padon, O., Losa, G., Sagiv, M., Shoham, S.: Paxos made EPR: decidable reasoning about distributed protocols. Proc. ACM Program. Lang. PACMPL, **1**(OOPSLA), 108:1–108:31 (2017)

37. Padon, O., McMillan, K.L., Panda, A., Sagiv, M., Shoham, S.: Ivy: safety verification by interactive generalization. In: Proceedings of the 37th ACM SIGPLAN Conference on Programming Language Design and Implementation, PLDI 2016, Santa Barbara, CA, USA, 13–17 June 2016, pp. 614–630 (2016)

38. Pnueli, A., Ruah, S., Zuck, L.D.: Automatic deductive verification with invisible invariants. In: Tools and Algorithms for the Construction and Analysis of Systems, 7th International Conference, TACAS 2001 Held as Part of the Joint European Conferences on Theory and Practice of Software, ETAPS 2001 Genova, Italy, 2–6 April 2001, Proceedings, pp. 82–97 (2001)

39. Ramsey, F.: On a problem in formal logic. Proc. London Math. Soc. **30**, 264–286 (1930)

40. Sharygina, N., Veith, H. (eds.) Computer Aided Verification - 25th International Conference, CAV 2013, Saint Petersburg, Russia, 13–19 July 2013, Proceedings. LNCS, vol. 8044. Springer, Heidelberg (2013)

41. Taube, M., et al.: Modularity for decidability of deductive verification with applications to distributed systems. In: Proceedings of the 39th ACM SIGPLAN Conference on Programming Language Design and Implementation, PLDI 2018, Philadelphia, PA, USA, 18–22 June 2018, pp. 662–677 (2018)

42. Wilcox, J.R., Woos, D., Panchekha, P., Tatlock, Z., Wang, X., Ernst, M.D., Anderson, T.E.: Verdi: a framework for implementing and formally verifying distributed systems. In: Proceedings of the 36th ACM SIGPLAN Conference on Programming Language Design and Implementation, Portland, OR, USA, 15–17 June 2015, pp. 357–368 (2015)

43. Woos, D., Wilcox, J.R., Anton, S., Tatlock, Z., Ernst, M.D., Anderson, T.E.: Planning for change in a formal verification of the raft consensus protocol. In: Proceedings of the 5th ACM SIGPLAN Conference on Certified Programs and Proofs, Saint Petersburg, FL, USA, 20–22 January 2016, pp. 154–165 (2016)

Abstract Interpretation of Stateful Networks

Kalev Alpernas[1]([✉]), Roman Manevich[2], Aurojit Panda[3], Mooly Sagiv[1],
Scott Shenker[4], Sharon Shoham[1], and Yaron Velner[5]

[1] Tel Aviv University, Tel Aviv, Israel
kalevalp@post.tau.ac.il
[2] Ben-Gurion University of the Negev, Beer-Sheva, Israel
[3] NYU, New York, USA
[4] UC Berkeley, Berkeley, USA
[5] Hebrew University of Jerusalem, Jerusalem, Israel

Abstract. Modern networks achieve robustness and scalability by maintaining states on their nodes. These nodes are referred to as middleboxes and are essential for network functionality. However, the presence of middleboxes drastically complicates the task of network verification. Previous work showed that the problem is undecidable in general and EXPSPACE-complete when abstracting away the order of packet arrival.

We describe a new algorithm for conservatively checking isolation properties of stateful networks. The asymptotic complexity of the algorithm is polynomial in the size of the network, albeit being exponential in the maximal number of queries of the local state that a middlebox can do, which is often small.

Our algorithm is sound, i.e., it can never miss a violation of safety but may fail to verify some properties. The algorithm performs on-the fly abstract interpretation by (1) abstracting away the order of packet processing and the number of times each packet arrives, (2) abstracting away correlations between states of different middleboxes and channel contents, and (3) representing middlebox states by their effect on each packet separately, rather than taking into account the entire state space. We show that the abstractions do not lose precision when middleboxes may reset in any state. This is encouraging since many real middleboxes reset, e.g., after some session timeout is reached or due to hardware failure.

1 Introduction

Modern computer networks are extremely complex, leading to many bugs and vulnerabilities that affect our daily life. Therefore, network verification is an increasingly important topic addressed by the programming languages and networking communities [5,12,14–17,23,30]. Previous network verification tools leverage a simple network forwarding model, which renders the datapath *immutable*. That is, normal packets going through the network do not change

© Springer Nature Switzerland AG 2018
A. Podelski (Ed.): SAS 2018, LNCS 11002, pp. 86–106, 2018.
https://doi.org/10.1007/978-3-319-99725-4_8

its forwarding behaviour, and the control plane explicitly alters the forwarding state at relatively slow time scales.

While the notion of an immutable datapath supported by an assemblage of routers makes verification tractable, it does not reflect reality. *Middleboxes* are widespread in modern enterprise networks [31]. A simple example of a middlebox is a stateful firewall which permits traffic from untrusted hosts only after they have received a packet from a trusted host. Middleboxes, such as firewalls, WAN optimizers, transcoders, proxies, load-balancers and the like, are the most common way to insert new functionality in the network datapath, and are commonly used to improve network performance and security. Middleboxes maintain a state and may change their state and forwarding behavior in response to packet arrivals. While useful, middleboxes are a common source of errors in the network [27].

As a simple example, consider the middlebox chain described in Fig. 1. In this network, a firewall is used to ensure that low security hosts $(l_1, \ldots, l_m)$ do not receive packets from the S_h server, and a cache and load balancer are used to improve performance. Unfortunately, the configuration of the network is incorrect since the cache may respond with a stored packet, bypassing the security policy enforced by the firewall. Swapping the order of the cache and the firewall results in a correct configuration.

Safety of Stateful Networks. We address the problem of verifying safety of networks with middleboxes, referred to as *stateful networks*. We target verification of *isolation* properties, namely, that packets sent from one host (or class of hosts) can never reach another host (or class of hosts). Yet, our approach is sound for any safety property. For example, it detects the safety violation described in Fig. 1, and verifies the safety of the correct configuration of this network.

Our focus is on verifying the configuration of stateful networks, i.e., addressing errors that arise from the interactions between middleboxes, and not from the complexity of individual middleboxes. Hence, we follow [35] and use an abstraction of middleboxes as finite-state programs. Previous work [32,35] has shown that many kinds of middleboxes, including proxy, cache proxy, NAT, and various kinds of load-balancers can be modeled in this way, sometimes using nondeterminism to over-approximate the behaviour, e.g. to model timers, counters, etc. Since we are interested in safety properties, such an abstraction (overapproximation) is suitable.

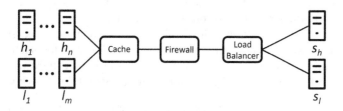

Fig. 1. A middlebox chain with a buggy topology.

As shown in [35], it is undecidable to check safety properties in general and isolation in particular, even for middleboxes with a finite state space, and even when the order of packets pending for each middlebox is abstracted away the complexity is quite high (EXPSPACE-complete). Therefore, in this paper we develop additional abstractions for scaling up the verification.

Our Approach. This paper makes a first attempt to apply abstract interpretation [7] to automatically prove the safety of stateful networks. Our approach combines sound network-level abstractions and middlebox-level abstractions that, together, make the verification task tractable. Roughly speaking, we apply (i) order abstraction [35], abstracting away the order of packets on channels, (ii) counter abstraction [26], abstracting away their cardinality, (iii) network-level Cartesian abstraction [7,11,13], abstracting away the correlation between the states of different middleboxes and different channel contents, and (iv) middlebox-level Cartesian abstraction, abstracting away the correlation between states of different packets within each middlebox.

The network-level abstractions, (i)–(iii), lead to a chaotic iteration algorithm that is polynomial in the state space of the individual middleboxes and packets. However, the number of middlebox states can be exponential in the size of the network. For example, a firewall may record the set of trusted hosts and thus its states are subsets of hosts. Therefore, the resulting analysis is exponential in the number of hosts[1].

The middlebox-level Cartesian abstraction, (iv), is the key to reducing the complexity to polynomial. The crux of this abstraction is the observation that the abstraction of middleboxes as reactive processes that query and update their state in a restricted way (e.g., [35]) allows to represent a middlebox state as a product of loosely-coupled *packet states*, one per potential packet. This lets us define a novel, non-standard, semantics of middlebox programs that we call *packet effect semantics*. The packet effect semantics is equivalent (bisimilar) to the natural semantics. However, while the natural semantics is monolithic, the packet effect semantics decomposes a single middlebox state into the parts that determine the forwarding behavior of different packets, and therefore facilitates the use of Cartesian abstraction to further reduce the complexity.

One of the main challenges for abstract interpretation is evaluating its precision. To address this challenge, we provide sufficient conditions that ensure precision of our analysis. Namely, we show that if the network is safe in the presence of packet reordering and middlebox reverts, where a middelbox may revert to its initial state at any moment, then our analysis is guaranteed to be precise, and will never report false alarms. This is, to a great extent, due to the packet effect semantics, which allows to use a middlebox-level Cartesian abstraction without incurring additional precision loss for such networks. Notice that middlebox reverts enable modelling arbitrary hardware failures, which have not been addressed by previous work on stateful network verification

---

[1] Unfortunately, if the set of hosts is not fixed, the safety problem becomes undecidable (even under the unordered abstraction) [1]. This means that, in general, it is not possible to alleviate the dependency of the complexity on the hosts.

(e.g., in [35]). Surprisingly, verification becomes easier under the assumption that middleboxes may reset at any time. (Recall that for arbitrary unordered networks safety checking is EXPSPACE-complete.).

In summary, the main contributions of this paper are

- We introduce the first abstract interpretation algorithm for verifying safety of stateful networks, whose time complexity is polynomial in the size of the network, albeit exponential in the maximal number of queries of the local state that a middlebox can do, which is often small even for complex middelboxes (up to 5 in our examples).
- We develop *packet effect semantics*, a non-standard semantics of middelbox programs that facilitates middlebox-level Cartesian abstraction, reducing the complexity of the abstract interpretation algorithm from exponential in the size of the network to polynomial without incurring any additional precision loss for unordered reverting networks.
- We provide sufficient conditions for precision of the analysis that have a natural interpretation in the domain of stateful networks: ignoring the order of packet processing and letting middleboxes revert to their initial states at any time.
- We prove lower bounds on the complexity of safety verification in the presence of packet reordering and/or middlebox reverts, showing that our algorithm is essentially optimal.
- We implement our analysis and show that it scales well with the number of hosts and middelboxes in the network.

We defer proofs of key claims to the extended version of this paper [1].

2   Expressing Middlebox Effects

This section defines our programming language for modeling the abstract behavior of middleboxes in the network. Our modeling language is independent of the particular network topology, which is defined in Sect. 3. The proposed language, AMDL (**A**bstract **M**iddlebox **D**efinition **L**anguage), is a restricted form of OCCAM [29], similar to the languages of [32,35].

We first define the syntax and informal semantics of AMDL (Sect. 2.1); we then define a formal "standard" *relation effect semantics* (Sect. 2.2); we continue by defining an alternative *packet effect* semantics (Sect. 2.3), which is bisimilar to the relation effect semantics (Sect. 2.4); and finally we present a localized version of the packet effect semantics (Sect. 2.5), which is suitable for Cartesian abstraction.

Packets. Middlebox behavior in our model is defined with respect to packets that consist of a fixed, finite, number of packet fields, ranging over finite domains. As such, a packet $p \in P$ in our formalism is a tuple of packet fields over predefined finite sorts. In our examples, a packet is a tuple $\langle s, d, t \rangle$, where s, d are the source and destination hosts, respectively, taken from a finite set of hosts H, and t is a packet tag (or type) that ranges over a finite domain T. In this case, $|P|$ is polynomial in $|H|$. (Our approach is also applicable when additional fields are added, e.g., for modeling the packet's payload via an abstract finite domain.).

2.1 Syntax and Informal Semantics

Figure 3 describes the syntax of the AMDL language[2]. Middleboxes are implemented as reactive processes, with events triggered by the arrival of packets. If multiple packets are pending, the AMDL process non-deterministically reads a packet from one of the incoming channels of the process. The packet processing code is a loop-free block of guarded-commands, which may update relations and forward potentially modified packets to some of the output ports. AMDL uses *relations* over finite domains to store the middlebox state. These are the only data structures allowed in AMDL. The only relation operations allowed are inserting a value to a relation, removing a value from a relation, and *membership queries*—checking whether a value is in a relation. For a membership query of the form $\bar{a}$ **in** r, we denote the relation, r, used in the query by $rel(q)$ and denote the tuple of atoms $\bar{a}$ by $atoms(q)$. For example, the code for a session firewall is depicted in Fig. 2.

Middleboxes may enforce safety properties using the **abort** command. For example, an isolation middlebox would abort when a forbidden packet is received.

```
sfirewall = do
  internal_port ? p =>
    if
      p.dst in trusted => external_port ! p
      □
      p.type = 0 => // request packet
        external_port ! p;
        requested(p.dst) := true
    fi
  □
    external_port ? p =>
      if
        p.src in trusted => internal_port ! p
        □
        p.type = 1 and p.src in requested =>
          // response packet with a request
          trusted(p.src) := true
      fi
  od
```

Fig. 2. AMDL code for session firewall.

---

[2] In the code examples, we write p for the triple (src,dst,type) and use access path notation to refer to the fields, e.g., p.src.

$$\langle mbox \rangle \ ::= m = \textbf{do} \ \langle pblock \rangle \ [\square \ \langle pblock \rangle]^* \ \textbf{od}$$

$$\langle pblock \rangle ::= c \ ? \ \overline{pfld} \ \Rightarrow \ \langle gc \rangle$$

$$\langle gc \rangle \quad ::= \langle cond \rangle \Rightarrow \langle action \rangle \mid \textbf{if} \ \langle gc \rangle \ [\square \ \langle gc \rangle]^* \ \textbf{fi}$$

$$\langle action \rangle ::= \langle action \rangle \ ; \ \langle action \rangle \mid c \ ! \ \overline{\langle atom \rangle} \mid r(\overline{\langle atom \rangle}) := \langle cond \rangle \mid \textbf{abort}$$

$$\langle cond \rangle \quad ::= \textbf{true} \mid \langle cond \rangle \ \textbf{and} \ \langle cond \rangle \mid \textbf{not} \ \langle cond \rangle \mid \langle atom \rangle = \langle atom \rangle \mid \overline{\langle atom \rangle} \ \textbf{in} \ r$$

$$\langle atom \rangle \quad ::= pfld \mid const$$

Fig. 3. AMDL syntax. $\bar{e}$ denotes a comma-separated list of elements drawn from the domain e. **abort** imposes a safety condition. $c \ ? \ p$ reads p from a channel c and $c \ ! \ p$ writes p into c. We write m for a middlebox name, r for a relation name, and c for a channel name. We write *const* for a constant symbol and *pfld* for identifiers used to match fields in packets, e.g., `src`. Non-deterministic choice is denoted by $\square$.

2.2   Middlebox Relation Effect Semantics

We now sketch the semantics of AMDL. The definitions below supply a part of the full network semantics, which is given in Sect. 3.

Middlebox States. Each middlebox $m \in M$ maintains its own local state as a set of relations. The domain of a relation r defined over sorts $s_{1..k}$ is $D(r) \overset{\text{def}}{=} D(s_1) \times \ldots \times D(s_k)$, where $D(s_i)$ is the domain of sort s_i. We use $rels(m)$ to denote the set of relations in m, and $D(m)$ to denote the union of $D(r)$ over $r \in rels(m)$.

The *middlebox state* of m is then a function $s \in \Sigma^{R}[m] \overset{\text{def}}{=} rels(m) \to \wp(D(m))$, mapping each $r \in rels(m)$ to $v \subseteq D(r)$. In addition, we introduce a unique *error* middlebox state, denoted *err*. We assume that $err \in \Sigma^{R}[m]$ for every middlebox m.

Middlebox Transitions. Middlebox transitions have the form

$$\xrightarrow{(p,c)/(p_i,c_i)_{i=1..k}}_R \subseteq \Sigma^{R}[m] \times \Sigma^{R}[m]$$

where (p, c) denotes packet-channel at the input, and $(p_i, c_i)_{i=1..k}$ is the sequence of packet-channel pairs that the middlebox outputs.

For example, for $s \overset{\text{def}}{=} [\texttt{requested} \mapsto \emptyset, \texttt{trusted} \mapsto \emptyset]$, the guarded command corresponding to the internal port of the firewall middlebox (Fig. 2) induces a transition $s \xrightarrow{((h_1,h_2,0),\vec{c_{in}})/((h_1,h_2,0),\vec{c_{out}})}_R s'$ where $s' \overset{\text{def}}{=} [\texttt{requested} \mapsto \{h_2\}, \texttt{trusted} \mapsto \emptyset]$.

abort commands induce transitions to the *err* state.

The formal definition of the middlebox transitions appears in the extended version of this paper [1].

2.3   Middlebox Packet Effect Semantics

We now present a semantics that is equivalent to the relation effect semantics. The semantics is based on an alternative (yet isomorphic) representation of middlebox states that reveals a loose coupling between the parts of the state that are relevant for different packets. This loose coupling then facilitates a Cartesian abstraction that abstracts away correlations between packets in the same state.

Packet Effect Representation of Middlebox State. Recall that in Sect. 2.1 we restrict the values that can be used in a middlebox program to either constants or the values of fields of the currently processed packet. We do not allow extracting tuples from the relation (e.g., by having a `get` command, or by iterating over the contents of the relation). Instead, we limit the interaction with the relation to checking whether a tuple (that consists of packet fields or constants) exists in the relation. Consequently, instead of storing the contents of all relations, the state of the middlebox can be represented by mapping all potential packets in the network to their effect on the middlebox. Specifically, we map each packet and membership query in the program to whether that membership query will be evaluated to True when the program is executed on that packet.

For every middlebox m, we denote by $Q(m)$ the set of membership queries in m's program. (We need not distinguish between different instances of the same query.) For example, in Fig. 2, $Q(fw) = \{$p.dst in trusted, p.src in trusted, p.src in requested$\}$.

The *packet effect state* of a middlebox m is a function $s \in \Sigma^P[m] \overset{\text{def}}{=} P \to Q(m) \to \{$True, False$\}$, mapping each packet $p \in P$ to the evaluation of all queries of m when p is the input packet, thus capturing the way in which p traverses m's program. We refer to $s(p) \in Q(m) \to \{$True, False$\}$ as the *packet state* of packet p in middlebox state s. We extend $\Sigma^P[m]$ with an error state $\lambda p \in P.\ err$, which is also denoted *err*.

Middlebox Transition Relation in the Packet Space. The semantics of middlebox m in the packet space is defined via a transition relation $\xrightarrow{(p,c)/(p_i,c_i)_{i=1..k}}_{P,m} \subseteq \Sigma^P[m] \times \Sigma^P[m]$. When m is clear, we omit it from the notation. A transition $\tilde{s} \xrightarrow{(p,c)/(p_i,c_i)_{i=1..k}}_P \tilde{s}'$ exists if (one of) the sequence of operations applied on $\tilde{s}$ when packet p arrives on channel c outputs $(p_i, c_i)_{i=1..k}$ and leads to $\tilde{s}'$.

The semantics of operations is defined similarly to the "standard" relation effect semantics. The semantics of error and output actions (that do not change the middlebox state) is straightforward. Next, we explain the semantics of the operations that depend on or change the middlebox state—membership queries and relation updates.

Consider a membership query q. Let $\tilde{s}$ be the middlebox state before evaluating q, i.e., $\tilde{s}$ is the state that results from executing all previous relation updates, and let p be the packet that invoked the middlebox transition. Then q is evaluated to $\tilde{s}(p)(q)$.

Next, consider a relation update. A relation update $r(\overline{a}) := cond$ updates the packet states of all packets that are affected by the operation. This is done as follows. As before, let $\tilde{s}$ be the intermediate state of m right before executing the operation, and let p be the packet that the middlebox program is operating on.

Consider the case where *cond* evaluates to True in $\tilde{s}$, corresponding to addition of a value. (Removal of a value is symmetric.) We denote by $\bar{a}(p)$ the result of substituting each field name in $\bar{a}$ by its value in p. That is, $\bar{a}(p) \in D(r)$ is the value being added to r. This addition may affect the value of membership queries $q \in Q(m)$ with $rel(q) = r$ (querying the same relation r) for other packets $\tilde{p}$ as well, in case that $atoms(q)(\tilde{p})$, i.e., the value being queried on $\tilde{p}$, is the same as the value $\bar{a}(p)$ being added to r. Therefore, the intermediate state obtained after the relation update operation has been applied is

$$\tilde{s}' = \lambda \tilde{p} \in P. \; \lambda q \in Q(m). \begin{cases} \text{True,} & \text{if } rel(q) = \text{r} \wedge atoms(q)(\tilde{p}) = \bar{a}(p). \\ \tilde{s}(\tilde{p})(q), & \text{otherwise.} \end{cases}$$

Namely, the operation updates to True the value of queries that coincide with the tuple of elements inserted to the relation.

Example 1. Consider the packet effect state $\tilde{s} \stackrel{\text{def}}{=} \lambda p. \; \lambda q.\text{False} \in \Sigma^{P}[fw]$ of the firewall (Fig. 2), where q ranges over the three membership queries in the code. Upon reading the packet $(h_1, h_2, 0)$ from an internal port, the middlebox performs a sequence of internal transitions which includes evaluating the expression "p.type=0" to True, outputting the packet $(h_1, h_2, 0)$ to the output port, and executing the command requested(p.dst) := true, which results in updating the state to:
$$\tilde{s}' \stackrel{\text{def}}{=} \lambda \tilde{p}. \; \lambda q. \begin{cases} \text{True, if } rel(q) = \text{requested} \wedge atoms(q)(\tilde{p}) = h_2 \\ \text{False, otherwise.} \end{cases}$$
That is, $\tilde{s}'((h_2, *, *))(\text{p.src in requested}) = \text{True}$ and all the other values in $\tilde{s}'$ remain False as before. Therefore, $\tilde{s} \xrightarrow{((h_1,h_2,0),\vec{c_{in}})/((h_1,h_2,0),\vec{c_{out}})}_P \tilde{s}'$. □

2.4 Bisimulation of Packet Effect Semantics and Relation Effect Semantics

We continue by showing that the transition systems defining the semantics of middleboxes in the packet effect and in the relation effect representations are bisimilar.

To do so, we first define a mapping $ps: \Sigma^R[m] \to \Sigma^P[m]$ from the relation state representation to the packet effect state representation. Recall that the relation state representation of middlebox states is $s \in \Sigma^R[m] \stackrel{\text{def}}{=} rels(m) \to \wp(D(m))$. Given a state $s \in \Sigma^R[m]$, ps maps it to the packet effect state s^P defined as follows:

$$s^P \stackrel{\text{def}}{=} \lambda \tilde{p} \in P. \; \lambda q \in Q(m). \; atoms(q)(\tilde{p}) \in s(rel(q)).$$

That is, for every input packet $\tilde{p}$, the value in s^P of the query $q \in Q(m)$ is equal to the evaluation of the same query in s based on an input packet $\tilde{p}$.

Definition 1 (Bisimulation Relation). *For a middlebox m, we define the relation $\sim_m \subseteq \Sigma^R[m] \times \Sigma^P[m]$ as the set of all pairs (s, s^P) such that $s = s^P = err$ or $ps(s) = s^P$.*

Lemma 1. *Let $s \in \Sigma^R[m]$ and $\tilde{s} \in \Sigma^P[m]$ and $s \sim_m \tilde{s}$. Then the following holds:*

- *For every state $s' \in \Sigma^R[m]$, if $s \xrightarrow{(p,c)/o}_R s'$ then there exists a state $\tilde{s}' \in \Sigma^P[m]$ s.t. $\tilde{s} \xrightarrow{(p,c)/o}_P \tilde{s}'$ and $s' \sim_m \tilde{s}'$, and*
- *For every state $\tilde{s}' \in \Sigma^P[m]$ if $\hat{s} \xrightarrow{(p,c)/o}_P \tilde{s}'$ then there exists a state $s' \in \Sigma^R[m]$ s.t. $s \xrightarrow{(p,c)/o}_R s'$ and $s' \sim_m \tilde{s}'$.*

2.5   Locality of Packet-Effect Middlebox Transitions

In this section we present a locality property of the packet effect semantics that will allow us to efficiently compute an abstract transformer when applying a Cartesian abstraction. Namely, we observe that an execution of an operation $r(\bar{a}) := cond$, in the context of processing an input packet p, potentially updates the packet states of all packets. However, for each packet $\tilde{p}$, the updated packet state $\tilde{s}'(\tilde{p})$ depends only on its pre-state $\tilde{s}(\tilde{p})$, the input channel c, the input packet p, and $\tilde{s}(p)$, which determines the value of queries; it is completely independent of the packet states of all other packets. Since, in addition, the execution path of the middlebox when processing input packet p depends only on the packet state of p, this form of *locality*, which we formalize next, extends to entire middlebox programs.

Definition 2 (Substate). *Let $\tilde{s} \in P \to Q(m) \to \{\textsf{True}, \textsf{False}\}$ be a packet effect state. We denote by $\tilde{s}|_{\{p,\tilde{p}\}} \in \{p, \tilde{p}\} \to Q(m) \to \{\textsf{True}, \textsf{False}\}$ the substate obtained from $\tilde{s}$ by dropping all packet states other than those of p and $\tilde{p}$. Let $\Sigma^P[m, p, \tilde{p}] \stackrel{\text{def}}{=} \{p, \tilde{p}\} \to Q(m) \to \{\textsf{True}, \textsf{False}\}$ denote the set of substates for p and $\tilde{p}$.*

Definition 3 (Substate transition relation). *We define the substate transition relation $\xrightarrow{(p,c)/(p_i,c_i)_{i=1..k}}_{P[p,\tilde{p}]}: \Sigma^P[m, p, \tilde{p}] \times \Sigma^P[m, p, \tilde{p}]$ as follows. A substate transition $\tilde{s}[p, \tilde{p}] \xrightarrow{(p,c)/(p_i,c_i)_{i=1..k}}_{P[p,\tilde{p}]} \tilde{s}[p, \tilde{p}]'$ holds if there exist $\tilde{s}$ and $\tilde{s}'$ such that $\tilde{s}|_{[p,\tilde{p}]} = \tilde{s}[p, \tilde{p}]$, $\tilde{s}'|_{[p,\tilde{p}]} = \tilde{s}[p, \tilde{p}]'$ and $\tilde{s} \xrightarrow{(p,c)/(p_i,c_i)_{i=1..k}}_P \tilde{s}'$.*

The locality of AMDL programs manifests itself in the ability to compute the substate transition relation, $\xrightarrow{(p,c)/(p_i,c_i)_{i=1..k}}_{P[p,\tilde{p}]}$, directly from the code (without first computing the transition relation and then using projection). This property will be important later to efficiently compute a network-level abstract transformer (Sect. 4.1):

Lemma 2 (2-Locality). *Given $\tilde{s}[p, \tilde{p}]$ and $\tilde{s}[p, \tilde{p}]'$, checking whether*

$$\tilde{s}[p, \tilde{p}] \xrightarrow{(p,c)/(p_i,c_i)_{i=1..k}}_{P[p,\tilde{p}]} \tilde{s}[p, \tilde{p}]'$$

can be done in time linear in the size of the middlebox program.

3   Network Semantics

This section defines the semantics of stateful networks by defining the semantics of packet traversal over communication channels in the network, and the transitions between network configurations. We first define a concrete semantics, followed by two relaxations: unordered semantics and reverting semantics. These relaxations provide sufficient conditions for completeness of the abstract interpretation performed in Sect. 4.

Network Topology. A *network* N is a finite bidirected[3] graph of *hosts* and *middleboxes*, equipped with a *packet domain*. Formally, $N = (H \cup M, E, P)$, where:

- P is a set of packets.
- H is a finite set of *hosts*. A *host* $h \in H$ consists of a unique identifier and a set of packets $P_h \subseteq P$ that it can send.
- M is a finite set of *middleboxes*. A middlebox $m \in M$ is associated with a set of communication channels C_m.
- $E \subseteq \{\langle h, c_m, m \rangle, \langle m, c_m, h \rangle \mid h \in H, m \in M, c_m \in C_m\} \cup \{\langle m_1, c_{m_1}, c_{m_2}, m_2 \rangle \mid m_1, m_2 \in M, c_{m_1} \in C_{m_1}, c_{m_2} \in C_{m_2}\}$ is the set of directed communication channels in the network, each connecting a communication channel $c_{m_1} \in C_{m_1}$ of middlebox m_1 either to a host, or to a communication channel $c_{m_2} \in C_{m_2}$ of middlebox m_2. For e of the form $\langle m, c_m, h \rangle$ or $\langle m, c_m, c_{m_2}, m_2 \rangle$, we say that e is an *egress* channel of middlebox m connected to channel c_m and an *ingress* channel of host h, respectively middlebox m_2, connected to channel c_{m_2}.

The network semantics is parametric in the middlebox semantics. It considers the semantics of a middlebox $m \in M$ to be a transition system with a finite set of states $\Sigma[m]$, an initial state $\sigma_I(m) \in \Sigma[m]$ and a set of transitions $\xrightarrow{(p,c)/(p_i,c_i)_{i=1..k}} \subseteq \Sigma[m] \times \Sigma[m]$. This can be realized with either the relation effect semantics or the packet effect semantics defined in Sects. 2.2 and 2.3, respectively.

3.1   Concrete (Ordered) Network Configurations

All variants of the network semantics defined in this section are defined over the same set of configurations. Let $\Sigma[M] \overset{\text{def}}{=} \bigcup_{m \in M} \Sigma[m]$ denote the set of middlebox states of all middleboxes in a network. An *ordered network configuration* $(\sigma, \pi) \in \Sigma = (M \to \Sigma[M]) \times (E \to P^*)$ assigns middleboxes to their (local) middlebox states and communication channels to sequences of packets. The sequence of packets on each channel represents all packets sent from the source and not yet processed by the destination.

---

[3] A *bidirected graph* is a directed graph in which every edge has a matching edge in the opposite direction. i.e., $(u, v) \in E \iff (v, u) \in E$.

Initial Configuration. We denote the ordered initial configuration by $(\sigma_I, \lambda e \in E \,.\, \epsilon)$, where $\sigma_I \colon M \rightarrow \Sigma[M]$ denotes the initial state of all middleboxes.

Error Configurations. We say that a configuration is an *error configuration* if any of its middleboxes is in the error state. We denote all error configurations by *err*.

3.2 Concrete (FIFO) Network Semantics

We first consider the First-In-First-Out (FIFO) network semantics, under which communication channels retain the order in which packets were sent.

Ordered Network Transitions. The network semantics is defined via *middlebox transitions* and *host transitions*.

A middlebox transition is $(\sigma, \pi) \xrightarrow{p,e,m}_o (\sigma', \pi')$ where the following holds: (i) p is the *first* packet on the channel $e \in E$, (ii) the channel e is an ingress channel of middlebox m connected to channel $c \in C_m$, (iii) $\sigma(m) \xrightarrow{(p,c)/(p_i,c_i)_{i=1..k}} \sigma'(m)$, meaning that $\sigma'(m)$ is the result of updating $\sigma(m)$ according to the middlebox semantics, (iv) the channels e_i are egress channels of middlebox m connected to the channels $c_i \in C_m$, (v) π' is the result of removing packet p from (the head of) channel e and appending p_i to the tails of the appropriate channels e_i, and (vi) the states of all other middleboxes equal their states in σ.

A host transition is $(\sigma, \pi) \xrightarrow{h,e,p}_o (\sigma, \pi')$ where one of the following holds:

Packet Production (i) the channel e is an egress channel of host h, (ii) $p \in P_h$ is a packet sent by h, and (iii) π' is the result of appending p to the tail of e; or

Packet Consumption (i) the channel e is an ingress channel of host h, (ii) p is the first packet on the channel e, and (iii) π' is the result of removing p from the head of e.

We denote the ordered transition relation obtained by the union of all middlebox and host transitions by $\Rightarrow_o$. It is naturally lifted to a concrete transformer $\mathcal{T}^o \colon \wp(\Sigma) \rightarrow \wp(\Sigma)$ defined as:

$$\mathcal{T}^o(X) \stackrel{\text{def}}{=} \{(\sigma', \pi') \mid (\sigma, \pi) \in X \wedge (\sigma, \pi) \Rightarrow_o (\sigma', \pi')\} \,.$$

Collecting Semantics. The ordered collecting semantics of a network N is the set of configurations reachable from the initial configuration.

$$[\![\mathsf{N}]\!]^o \stackrel{\text{def}}{=} LeastFixpoint(\mathcal{T}^o)(\sigma_I, \lambda e \in E \,.\, \epsilon) = \bigcup_{i=1}^{\infty} (\mathcal{T}^o)^i(\sigma_I, \lambda e \in E \,.\, \epsilon) \,.$$

Definition 4 (Safety Verification Problem). *For a network N and initial state σ_I for the middleboxes, the safety verification problem is to determine whether an error configuration is reachable from the initial configuration. That is, whether* $err \in [\![\mathsf{N}]\!]^o$.

Theorem 1   [35].   *The safety verification problem for ordered networks is undecidable.*

In this work, we tackle the undecidability of verification by developing a sound abstract interpretation that can be used to check the safety of networks. Before doing so, we present two relaxed network semantics that motivate the abstractions we employ, and also provide sufficient conditions for their completeness.

3.3   Unordered and Reverting Network Semantics

The "unordered" semantics allows channels to not preserve the packet transmission order. Namely, packets in the same channel may be processed in a different order than the order in which they were received. The "reverting" semantics allows middleboxes to revert to their initial state after every transition. Formally, these relaxed semantics extend the set of network transitions (and consequently, the transformer and the collecting semantics) with reordering transitions and reverting transitions, respectively.

A *reordering transition* has the form $(\sigma, \pi) \stackrel{e}{\Rightarrow} (\sigma, \pi')$ where for the channel $e \in E$, $\pi'(e)$ is a permutation of $\pi(e)$ and for all other channels $e' \neq e$, $\pi'(e') = \pi(e')$.

A *reverting transition* has the form $(\sigma, \pi) \stackrel{m}{\Rightarrow} (\sigma', \pi)$ where for the middlebox $m \in M$, $\sigma'(m) = \sigma_I(m)$ and for all other middleboxes $m' \neq m$, $\sigma'(m) = \sigma(m)$.

The *unordered network transitions* consist of the ordered transitions as well as the reordering transitions; the *ordered reverting transitions* consist of the ordered transitions and the reverting transitions; and the *unordered reverting transitions* consist of all of the above. We denote the corresponding collecting semantics by $[\![N]\!]^u$, $[\![N]\!]^{or}$ and $[\![N]\!]^{ur}$, respectively. Clearly,

$$[\![N]\!]^o \subseteq [\![N]\!]^u \subseteq [\![N]\!]^{ur} \text{ and } [\![N]\!]^o \subseteq [\![N]\!]^{or} \subseteq [\![N]\!]^{ur}$$

By plugging-in the two representations of middleboxes in the definition of the network semantics, we obtain two variants of the network semantics for each of the four variants considered so far. In the sequel, we use a *pa* subscript to refer to the packet effect semantics, and no subscript to refer to the relation effect semantics. The bisimulation between middlebox representations is lifted to a bisimulation between each relation state network semantics and the corresponding packet state network semantics. Therefore, the following holds:

Lemma 3. *For every semantic identifier $i \in \{o, u, or, ur\}$, $err \in [\![N]\!]^i$ iff $err \in [\![N]\!]^i_{pa}$.*

The safety verification problem is adapted for the different variants of the network semantics. The following theorem summarizes the complexity of the obtained problems. (We do not distinguish the packet effect semantics from the relation effect semantics, since due to Lemma 3 they induce the same safety verification problem.)

Theorem 2. *The safety verification problem is*

(i) EXPSACE-complete for unordered networks [35].
(ii) undecidable for ordered reverting networks.
(iii) coNP-hard for unordered reverting networks.

Theorem 2(ii) justifies the need for the unordered abstraction even in reverting networks. Theorem 2(iii) implies that our abstract interpretation algorithm, presented in Sect. 4, which is both sound and complete for the unordered reverting semantics, is essentially optimal since it essentially meets the lower bound stated in the theorem (it is exponential in the number of state queries of any middlebox and polynomial in the number of middleboxes, hosts and packets).

Sticky Properties. Unordered reverting networks have a useful property of *sticky packets*, meaning that if a packet is pending for a middlebox in some run of the network then any run has an extension in which the packet is pending again with multiplicity $> n$, for any $n \in \mathbb{N}$. This property implies a stronger property:

Lemma 4 (Sticky Packet States Property). *For every channel e, packets $p, \tilde{p}$, middlebox m and packet state $\tilde{v}$ of $\tilde{p}$ in m: If, in some reachable configuration, channel e contains p and in some (possibly other) reachable configuration the packet state of $\tilde{p}$ in m is $\tilde{v}$, then there exists a reachable configuration where simultaneously e contains p and the packet state of $\tilde{p}$ in m is $\tilde{v}$.*

Intuitively, Lemma 4 follows from the fact that all middleboxes can revert to their initial state and the unordered semantics enables a scenario where the particular state and packets are reconstructed. It ensures that ignoring the correlation between the packet states of a middlebox for different packets, the packet states across different middleboxes, and the occurrence (and cardinality) of packets on channels does not incur any precision loss w.r.t. safety. This makes the network-level abstraction defined in Sect. 4, which treats channels as sets of packets and ignores correlations between packet states and channels, precise.

4   Abstract Interpretation for Stateful Networks

In this section, we present our algorithm for safety verification of stateful networks based on abstract interpretation of the semantics $[\![N]\!]_{pa}^{o}$, and discuss its guarantees.

4.1   Abstract Interpretation for Packet Space

We apply sound abstractions to different components of the concrete packet state network domain. Due to space constraints, we do not describe the intermediate steps in the construction of the abstract domain, and only present the final domain used by the analysis. Roughly speaking, the obtained domain abstracts away (i) the order and cardinality of packets on channels; (ii) the correlation between the states of different middleboxes and different channel contents; and (iii) the correlation between states of different packets within each middlebox.

Cartesian Packet Effect Abstract Domain. Let $Q \to \{T, F\}$ denote the union of $Q(m) \to \{T, F\}$ over all middleboxes $m \in M$, including the error state *err*. The Cartesian abstract domain of the packet state of the network is given by the lattice $\mathcal{A} \overset{\text{def}}{=} (A, \bot, \sqsubseteq, \sqcup)$, where $A \overset{\text{def}}{=} (M \to P \to \wp(Q \to \{T, F\})) \times (E \to \wp(P))$. That is, an abstract element maps each packet in each middlebox to a set of possible valuations for the queries, and each channel to a set of packets. The bottom element is $\bot \overset{\text{def}}{=} (\lambda m.\ \lambda p.\ \emptyset, \lambda e.\ \emptyset)$, the partial order $a_1 \sqsubseteq a_2$ is defined by pointwise set inclusions per middlebox and channel, and join is defined by pointwise unions $(\omega_1, \omega_2) \sqcup (\omega_1', \omega_2') \overset{\text{def}}{=} (\lambda m.\ \lambda p.\ \omega_1(m)(p) \cup \omega_1'(m)(p), \lambda e.\ \omega_2(p) \cup \omega_2'(p))$.

Let $\mathcal{C} \overset{\text{def}}{=} (\wp(\Sigma^{\mathrm{P}}), \subseteq)$ be the concrete network domain. We define the Galois connection $(\mathcal{C}, \gamma, \alpha, \mathcal{A})$ as follows. The abstraction function $\alpha : \wp(\Sigma^{\mathrm{P}}) \to A$ for a set of packet state configurations $X \subseteq \Sigma^{\mathrm{P}}$ is defined as $\alpha(X) = (\omega_{mboxes}, \omega_{chans})$ where

$$\omega_{mboxes} = \lambda m.\ \lambda p.\ \{\sigma(m)(p) \mid (\sigma, \pi) \in X\} \text{ and } \qquad \omega_{chans} = \lambda e. \bigcup_{(\sigma, \pi) \in X} \pi(e) \ .$$

The concretization function $\gamma : A \to \wp(\Sigma^{\mathrm{P}})$ is induced by α and $\sqsubseteq$. We denote the initial abstract element as $a_I = \alpha(\{(\sigma_I, \lambda e \in E.\emptyset)\})$.

Abstract Transformer. Next, we define the abstract transformer $T^{\sharp} : A \to A$, which soundly abstracts the concrete transformer T° and show that it is efficient, due to the locality property of middlebox transitions. We use the predicate $in(c, e, m)$ to denote that the network channel e is an ingress channel of middlebox m, connected to its c channel. Similarly, $out(c, e, m)$ means that e is an egress channel of m connected to its c channel. Further, let $[x_1 \mapsto y_1, \ldots, x_n \mapsto y_n]$ denote a mapping from each x_i to y_i for $i = 1..n$ and $f[x \mapsto y]$ denote the function f updated by (re-)mapping x to y.

Definition 5. *Let* $(\omega_1, \omega_2) \in (M \to P \to \wp(Q \to \{T, F\})) \times (E \to \wp(P))$ *be an abstract element. Then* $T^{\sharp}(\omega_1, \omega_2) \overset{\text{def}}{=}$

$$\bigsqcup \left\{ \begin{array}{l|l} (\omega_1[m \mapsto \tilde{p}s], \\ \omega_2[e_i \mapsto \omega_2(e_i) \cup \{p_i\}]) \end{array} \middle| \begin{array}{l} (1)\ m \in M, \\ (2)\ p \in \omega_2(e),\ in(c, e, m), \\ (3)\ \tilde{s} \in \omega_1(m),\ \tilde{p} \in P, \\ \qquad \tilde{s}[p, \tilde{p}] = [p \mapsto \tilde{s}(p), \tilde{p} \mapsto \tilde{s}(\tilde{p})], \\ (4)\ \tilde{s}[p, \tilde{p}] \xrightarrow{\ (p,c)/(p_i, c_i)_{i=1..k}\ }_{P[p, \tilde{p}]} \tilde{s}[p, \tilde{p}]', \\ (5)\ \tilde{p}s = \tilde{s}[\tilde{p} \mapsto \{\ \tilde{s}[p, \tilde{p}]'(\tilde{p})\ \}], \\ (6)\ out(c_i, e_i, m),\ i = 1..k \end{array} \right\} .$$

Intuitively, the transformer updates the abstract state by joining the individual effects obtained by: (1) considering each middlebox, (2) considering each input packet to the middlebox, (3) considering every possible substate for the input packet p and every other packet $\tilde{p}$, (4) considering every possible substate transition, (5) adding the new packet state for $\tilde{p}$ to the relevant set, and (6) adding each output packet to the corresponding edge.

Proposition 1. *The running time of* $T^\sharp$ *is* $O((|M|+|E|) \cdot |P|^2 \cdot 2^{2|Q_{max}|})$, *where* Q_{max} *denotes the maximal set of queries* $Q(m)$ *over all middleboxes* $m \in M$.

Our algorithm for safety verification computes $\mu^\sharp \overset{\text{def}}{=} LeastFixpoint(T^\sharp)(a_I) = \bigsqcup_{i=1}^{\infty} T^{\sharp^i}(a_I)$ and checks whether $err \in \mu^\sharp$.

Complexity of Least Fixpoint Computation. The height of the abstract domain lattice is determined by the number of packets that can be added to the channels of the network—$(|P| \cdot |E|)$, multiplied by the number of state changes that can occur in any of the middleboxes—$O(|M| \cdot |P| \cdot 2^{|Q|})$. The time complexity of the abstract interpretation is bounded by the height of the abstract domain lattice multiplied by the time complexity of the abstract transformer:

$$O(|P|^4 \cdot |E| \cdot |M| \cdot 2^{3|Q_{max}|} \cdot (|M| + |E|)) \ .$$

4.2   Soundness and Completeness

Our algorithm is sound in the sense that it never misses an error state. This follows from the use of a sound abstract interpretation:

Theorem 3 (Soundness). $[\![N]\!]_{pa}^o \subseteq [\![N]\!]_{pa}^{ur} \subseteq \gamma(\mu^\sharp)$.

Our algorithm is also complete relative to the reverting unordered semantics.

Theorem 4 (Completeness). $\mu^\sharp \sqsubseteq \alpha([\![N]\!]_{pa}^{ur})$.

The proof of Theorem 4 relies on the sticky property formalized by Lemma 4. The theorem states that for reverting unordered networks $\mu^\sharp$ is at least as precise as applying the abstraction function on the concrete packet state network semantics. In particular, this implies that if $\mu^\sharp$ is an abstract error element then $err \in [\![N]\!]_{pa}^{ur}$. As a result, for such networks our algorithm is a decision procedure. For other networks it may produce false alarms, if safety is not maintained by an unordered reverting abstraction.

Properties. Recall that we express safety properties via middleboxes in the network. Therefore, in unordered reverting networks, the possibility to revert applies to the safety property as well, and may introduce false alarms due to addition of behaviors leading to error. However, for safety properties such as isolation which are suffix-closed (i.e., all the suffixes of a safe run are themselves safe runs), this cannot happen [1].

5   Implementation and Initial Evaluation

In this section, we describe our implementation of the analysis described in Sect. 4, and report our initial experience running the algorithm on a few example networks.

Implementation. We have developed a compiler, `amdlc`, which takes as input a network topology and its initial state (given in `json` format) and AMDL programs for the middleboxes that appear in the topology. The compiler outputs a Datalog program, which can then be efficiently solved by a Datalog solver. Specifically, we use LogicBlox [3].

The generated Datalog programs include three relations: (i) `packetsSeen`, which stores the packets sent over the network channels; (ii) `middleboxState`, which stores the packet state of individual packets in each middlebox (i.e., the possible valuation of each middlebox program's queries for each individual packet); and (iii) `abort`, which stores the middleboxes that have reached an *err* state.

We encode the packets that hosts can send to their neighboring middleboxes and the initial state of the middleboxes as Datalog *facts* (edb), and the effects of the middlebox programs, i.e. relation update actions and packet output actions, as Datalog *rules* (idb).

We then use the datalog engine to compute the fixed point of the datalog program. That fixed point is exactly the least fixed point $\mu^{\sharp} \overset{\text{def}}{=}$ $LeastFixpoint(T^{\sharp})(a_I) = \bigsqcup_{i=1}^{\infty} T^{\sharp^i}(a_I)$

Evaluation. The main challenge in acquiring realistic benchmarks is that middlebox configuration and network topology are considered security sensitive, and as a result enterprises and network operators do not release this information to the public. Consequently, we benchmarked our tool using the synthetic topologies and configurations described by [24].

Our benchmarks focus on datacenter networks and enterprise networks. The set of middleboxes we used in our datacenter benchmarks is based on information provided in [27], and on conversations with datacenter providers. We ran both a simple case where each tenant machine is protected by firewalls and an IPS (Intrusion Prevention System); and a more complex case where we use redundant servers and distribute traffic across them using a load balancer. Our enterprise topology is based on the standard topology used in a variety of university departments including UIUC (reported in [18]), UC Berkeley, Stanford, etc. which employ firewalls and an IP gateway.

We ran two scaling experiments, measuring how well our system scales when the number of hosts or the number of middleboxes in the network increases The experiments were run on Amazon EC2 r4.16 instances with 64-core CPUs and 488 GiB RAM.

Multi Tenant Datacenter Network. Figure 4 illustrates the topology of a multi tenant datacenter. Each rack hosts a different tenant, and the safety property we wish to verify is isolation between the hosts of the two racks. In this

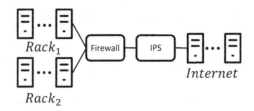

Fig. 4. Topology of the datacenter example.

example the network also employs an IPS to prevent malicious traffic from reaching the datacenter. Actual IPS code is too complex to be accurately modeled in AMDL; instead we over-approximate the behaviour of an IPS by modeling it as a process that non-deterministically drops incoming packets.

Enterprise Network. Figure 5a illustrates the topology of an enterprise network. The enterprise network consists of three subnets, each with a different security policy. The *public* subnet is allowed unrestricted access with the outside network. The *quarantined* subnet is not allowed any communication with the outside network. The *private* subnet can initiate communication with a host in the outside network, but hosts in the outside network cannot initiate communication with the hosts in the *private* subnet.

To evaluate the feasibility of our solution, we ran the analysis of Fig. 5a on networks with varying numbers of hosts ranging from 20 to 2,000. Our implementation successfully verified a network with 2,000 hosts in under four hours, suggesting that the implementation could be used to verify realistic networks. Figure 5b shows the times of the analysis on an enterprise network with 20–2,000 hosts.

Datacenter Middlebox Pipeline. Figure 6a describes a datacenter topology with a pipeline of middleboxes connecting servers to the Internet. The topology contains multiple middlebox pipelines for load-balancing purposes and to ensure resiliency. We use this topology to test the scalability of our approach w.r.t the

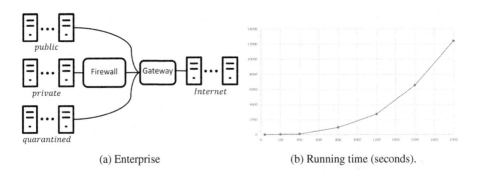

(a) Enterprise   (b) Running time (seconds).

Fig. 5. Topology and running times of the host scalability test.

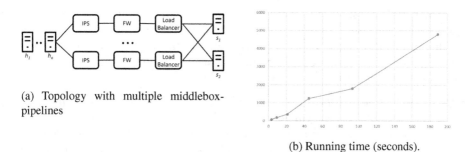

(a) Topology with multiple middlebox-pipelines

(b) Running time (seconds).

Fig. 6. Topology and running times of the network topology scalability test.

size of the network, by adding additional middlebox pipelines and keeping the number of hosts constant.

Figure 6b shows the running times of the analysis of a datacenter with 3–189 middleboxes (1–32 middlebox chains). All topologies contained 1000 hosts.

6   Concluding Remarks and Related Work

In this paper, we applied abstract interpretation for efficient verification of networks with stateful nodes. We now briefly survey closely related works in this area.

Topology Independent Network Verification. Early work in network verification focused on proving correctness of network protocols [6,28]. Subsequent work in the context of software define networking (SDN) including Flowlog [23] and VeriCon [4] looked at verifying the correctness of network applications (implemented as middleboxes or in network controllers) independent of the topology and configuration of the network where these were used. However, since this problem is undecidable, these methods use bounded model checking or user provided inductive invariants, which are hard to specify even in simple network topologies.

Verifying Immutable Network Configurations. Verifying networks with immutable states is an active line of research [2,5,12,14–16,18,30,33]. In the future, we hope to combine our abstraction with the techniques used in these papers. We hope to use similar techniques to Veriflow [16] to handle switches more efficiently, and leverage compact header representation described in NetKat [12].

Stateful Network Verification. Previous works provide useful tools for detecting errors in firewalls [19,20,22]. Buzz [9] and SymNet [34] have looked at how to use symbolic execution and packet generation for testing and verifying the behavior of stateful networks. These works implement testing techniques rather than verifying network behavior and are hence complementary to our approach.

Velner et al. [35] show that checking safety in stateful networks is undecidable, necessitating the use of overapproximations. They provide a general algorithm for checking safety using Petri nets. This algorithm has high complexity and scales poorly. They also provide an efficient algorithm for checking safety in a limited class of networks.

Exploring Network Symmetry. Recent work explored the use of bisimulation to leverage the extensive symmetry found in real network topologies [21] to accelerate stateless [25] and stateful [24] network verification. Both approaches are not automatic. We are encouraged by the fact that our automatic approach achieves performance comparable to VMN [24] on the same examples without requiring human intervention. We attribute this improvement to modularity and to the use of packet state representation.

Extensible Semantics. Previous works have explored ideas similar to the reverting semantics, to obtain complexity and decidability results in different settings.

In [8] the authors analyze the complexity of verifying asynchronous shared-memory systems. They use *copycat* processes that mirror the behaviour of another process to show that executions are extensible, similarly to how our work uses the sticky packet states property (Lemma 4). In their model, when the processes are finite state machines, they obtain coNP-complete complexity for verification.

In [10] the authors explore a more general setting of well-structured transition system, and present the *home-state idea*, which allows the system to return to its initial state (essentially, revert). They obtain decidability results for well-structured transition systems with a home-state, but do not show any tighter complexity results.

Acknowledgments. We thank our anonymous shepherd, and anonymous referees for insightful comments which improved this paper. We thank LogicBlox for providing us with an academic license for their software, and Todd J. Green and Martin Bravenboer for providing technical support and helping with optimization. This publication is part of projects that have received funding from the European Research Council (ERC) under the European Union's Seventh Framework Program (FP7/2007–2013)/ERC grant agreement no. [321174-VSSC], and Horizon 2020 research and innovation programme (grant agreement No. [759102-SVIS]). The research was supported in part by Len Blavatnik and the Blavatnik Family foundation, the Blavatnik Interdisciplinary Cyber Research Center, Tel Aviv University, and the Pazy Foundation. This material is based upon work supported by the United States-Israel Binational Science Foundation (BSF) grants No. 2016260 and 2012259. This research was also supported in part by NSF grants 1704941 and 1420064, and funding provided by Intel Corporation.

References

1. Alpernas, K., et al.: Abstract interpretation of stateful networks. arXiv preprint arXiv:1708.05904 (2018)
2. Anderson, C.J., et al.: NetKAT: semantic foundations for networks. In: POPL (2014)
3. Aref, M., et al.: Design and implementation of the LogicBlox system. In: ACM SIGMOD International Conference on Management of Data, pp. 1371–1382 (2015)
4. Ball, T., et al.: VeriCon: towards verifying controller programs in software-defined networks. In: ACM SIGPLAN Conference on Programming Language Design and Implementation, PLDI, p. 31 (2014)
5. Canini, M., Venzano, D., Peres, P., Kostic, D., Rexford, J.: A NICE way to test OpenFlow applications. In: 9th USENIX Symposium on Networked Systems Design and Implementation (NSDI 2012) (2012)
6. Clarke, E.M., Jha, S., Marrero, W.: Using state space exploration and a natural deduction style message derivation engine to verify security protocols. In: Gries, D., de Roever, W.-P. (eds.) Programming Concepts and Methods PROCOMET 1998. ITIFIP, pp. 87–106. Springer, Boston, MA (1998). https://doi.org/10.1007/978-0-387-35358-6_10
7. Cousot, P., Cousot, R.: Systematic design of program analysis frameworks. In: Proceedings of the 6th ACM SIGACT-SIGPLAN Symposium on Principles of Programming Languages, pp. 269–282. ACM (1979)
8. Esparza, J., Ganty, P., Majumdar, R.: Parameterized verification of asynchronous shared-memory systems. In: Sharygina, N., Veith, H. (eds.) CAV 2013. LNCS, vol. 8044, pp. 124–140. Springer, Heidelberg (2013). https://doi.org/10.1007/978-3-642-39799-8_8
9. Fayaz, S.K., Yu, T., Tobioka, Y., Chaki, S., Sekar, V., Vyas, S.: BUZZ: testing context-dependent policies in stateful networks. In: NSDI (2016)
10. Finkel, A., Schnoebelen, P.: Well-structured transition systems everywhere! Theor. Comput. Sci. **256**(1–2), 63–92 (2001)
11. Flanagan, C., Freund, S.N., Qadeer, S., Seshia, S.A.: Modular verification of multithreaded programs. Theor. Comput. Sci. **338**(1–3), 153–183 (2005)
12. Foster, N., Kozen, D., Milano, M., Silva, A., Thompson, L.: A coalgebraic decision procedure for NetKAT. In: Proceedings of the 42nd Annual ACM SIGPLAN-SIGACT Symposium on Principles of Programming Languages, POPL 2015, Mumbai, India, 15–17 January 2015, pp. 343–355 (2015)
13. Hoenicke, J., Majumdar, R., Podelski, A.: Thread modularity at many levels: a pearl in compositional verification. In: POPL, pp. 473–485 (2017)
14. Kazemian, P., Chang, M., Zeng, H., Varghese, G., McKeown, N., Whyte, S.: Real time network policy checking using header space analysis. In: 10th USENIX Symposium on Networked Systems Design and Implementation (NSDI 2013) (2013)
15. Kazemian, P., Varghese, G., McKeown, N.: Header space analysis: static checking for networks. In: 9th USENIX Symposium on Networked Systems Design and Implementation (NSDI 2012) (2012)
16. Khurshid, A., Zhou, W., Caesar, M., Godfrey, B.: VeriFlow: verifying network-wide invariants in real time. Comput. Commun. Rev. **42**(4), 467–472 (2012)
17. Kuzniar, M., Peresini, P., Canini, M., Venzano, D., Kostic, D.: A SOFT way for OpenFlow switch interoperability testing. In: CoNEXT, pp. 265–276 (2012)
18. Mai, H., Khurshid, A., Agarwal, R., Caesar, M., Godfrey, B., King, S.T.: Debugging the data plane with anteater. In: SIGCOMM (2011)

19. Marmorstein, R.M., Kearns, P.: A tool for automated iptables firewall analysis. In: USENIX Annual Technical Conference, Freenix Track, pp. 71–81 (2005)
20. Mayer, A., Wool, A., Ziskind, E.: Fang: a firewall analysis engine. In: Proceedings of 2000 IEEE Symposium on Security and Privacy, S&P 2000, pp. 177–187. IEEE (2000)
21. Namjoshi, K.S., Trefler, R.J.: Uncovering symmetries in irregular process networks. In: Giacobazzi, R., Berdine, J., Mastroeni, I. (eds.) VMCAI 2013. LNCS, vol. 7737, pp. 496–514. Springer, Heidelberg (2013). https://doi.org/10.1007/978-3-642-35873-9_29
22. Nelson, T., Barratt, C., Dougherty, D.J., Fisler, K., Krishnamurthi, S.: The margrave tool for firewall analysis. In: LISA (2010)
23. Nelson, T., Ferguson, A.D., Scheer, M.J.G., Krishnamurthi, S.: Tierless programming and reasoning for software-defined networks. In: Proceedings of the 11th USENIX Symposium on Networked Systems Design and Implementation, NSDI 2014, Seattle, WA, USA, 2–4 April 2014, pp. 519–531 (2014)
24. Panda, A., Lahav, O., Argyraki, K.J., Sagiv, M., Shenker, S.: Verifying reachability in networks with mutable datapaths. In: 14th USENIX Symposium on Networked Systems Design and Implementation, NSDI 2017, Boston, MA, USA, 27–29 March 2017, pp. 699–718 (2017)
25. Plotkin, G.D., Bjørner, N., Lopes, N.P., Rybalchenko, A., Varghese, G.: Scaling network verification using symmetry and surgery. In: Proceedings of the 43rd Annual ACM SIGPLAN-SIGACT Symposium on Principles of Programming Languages, POPL 2016, St. Petersburg, FL, USA, 20–22 January 2016, pp. 69–83 (2016)
26. Pnueli, A., Xu, J., Zuck, L.: Liveness with $(0, 1, \infty)$-counter abstraction. In: Brinksma, E., Larsen, K.G. (eds.) CAV 2002. LNCS, vol. 2404, pp. 107–122. Springer, Heidelberg (2002). https://doi.org/10.1007/3-540-45657-0_9
27. Potharaju, R., Jain, N.: Demystifying the dark side of the middle: a field study of middlebox failures in datacenters. In: Proceedings of the 2013 Internet Measurement Conference, IMC 2013, Barcelona, Spain, 23–25 October 2013, pp. 9–22 (2013)
28. Ritchey, R.W., Ammann, P.: Using model checking to analyze network vulnerabilities. In: Security and Privacy (2000)
29. Roscoe, A.W., Hoare, C.A.R.: The laws of OCCAM programming. Theor. Comput. Sci. **60**(2), 177–229 (1988)
30. Sethi, D., Narayana, S., Malik, S.: Abstractions for model checking SDN controllers. In: FMCAD (2013)
31. Sherry, J., Hasan, S., Scott, C., Krishnamurthy, A., Ratnasamy, S., Sekar, V.: Making middleboxes someone else's problem: network processing as a cloud service. In: SIGCOMM (2012)
32. Sivaraman, A., et al.: Packet transactions: high-level programming for line-rate switches. In: Proceedings of the ACM SIGCOMM 2016 Conference, Florianopolis, Brazil, 22–26 August 2016, pp. 15–28 (2016)
33. Skowyra, R., Lapets, A., Bestavros, A., Kfoury, A.: A verification platform for SDN-enabled applications. In: HiCoNS (2013)
34. Stoenescu, R., Popovici, M., Negreanu, L., Raiciu, C.: Scalable symbolic execution for modern networks. In: SIGCOMM (2016)
35. Velner, Y., et al.: Some complexity results for stateful network verification. In: Chechik, M., Raskin, J.-F. (eds.) TACAS 2016. LNCS, vol. 9636, pp. 811–830. Springer, Heidelberg (2016). https://doi.org/10.1007/978-3-662-49674-9_51

Block-Size Independence
for GPU Programs

Rajeev Alur, Joseph Devietti, and Nimit Singhania$^{(\boxtimes)}$

University of Pennsylvania, Philadelphia, USA
{alur,devietti}@cis.upenn.edu,
nimits@seas.upenn.edu

Abstract. Optimizing GPU programs by tuning execution parameters is essential to realizing the full performance potential of GPU hardware. However, many of these optimizations do not ensure correctness and subtle errors can enter while optimizing a GPU program. Further, lack of formal models and the presence of non-trivial transformations prevent verification of optimizations.

In this work, we verify transformations involved in tuning the execution parameter, *block-size*. First, we present a formal programming and execution model for GPUs, and then formalize *block-size independence* of GPU programs, which ensures tuning block-size preserves program semantics. Next, we present an inter-procedural analysis to verify block-size independence for synchronization-free GPU programs. Finally, we evaluate the analysis on the Nvidia CUDA SDK samples, where 35 global kernels are verified to be block-size independent.

1 Introduction

Graphics Processing Units (GPUs) have emerged as an important data-parallel compute platform. They are high-throughput, scalable, and useful for a wide variety of data-intensive applications like deep learning, virtual reality, and bioinformatics. However, programmers often struggle with tuning their GPU applications. The programmer has to repeatedly tune various execution parameters and rewrite parts of the program to achieve significant speedups compared to the CPU version. To add to the programmer's burden, performance is often not portable and the application needs to be re-tuned for another GPU.

Tuning GPU applications can introduce subtle errors into the application which can be difficult to debug and resolve. We need tools that can automatically detect such errors and ensure transformations performed while tuning an application are correct. Existing tools for GPU verification help identify correctness issues like data-races and barrier-divergence [2,11,12], but none verify correctness of transformations. Furthermore, synthesizing optimal execution configuration at compile-time is difficult since the optimization space is large and non-convex [21]. Hence, tuning applications by trying out different values for parameters is unavoidable. This makes it essential to have automatic tools to verify the correctness of transformations.

© Springer Nature Switzerland AG 2018
A. Podelski (Ed.): SAS 2018, LNCS 11002, pp. 107–126, 2018.
https://doi.org/10.1007/978-3-319-99725-4_9

In this work, we focus on the correctness of tuning an execution parameter, *block-size*. A GPU program consists of a large number of threads that execute the same sequence of instructions. The threads are organized in a two-level hierarchy where individual threads are grouped into thread-blocks and the thread-blocks together form a thread-grid. The parameter *block-size* represents the number of threads in each thread-block and is specified during program invocation, along with the total number of threads. The block-size determines how resources required by the program are allocated on GPU cores, and is often tuned to maximally utilize each core for performance while balancing performance across cores in a GPU. For instance, a 75% improvement in performance is achieved for a benchmark "SobolQRNG" on tuning block-size from 64 to 256.

We present an analysis to verify *block-size independence* of GPU programs which ensures modifying block-size is a valid transformation and does not introduce errors into the program. In the GPU execution model, sharing of data is permitted between threads of a thread-block, and changing the block-size alters the sets of threads allowed to share data, making program equivalence hard to reason about. Therefore, we only consider *synchronization-free* programs, where each thread executes independently of the other threads, and any sharing of data between threads is prohibited and leads to a data-race.

For synchronization-free programs, the analysis only needs to ensure that the execution of each thread is independent of block-size. Each thread in a GPU program is provided with a block-id, bid, a thread-id within the block, tid, and the block-size, bdim, which helps distinguish its execution from other threads. These values get modified when the block-size is modified, and the analysis tracks the flow of these values through variables in the program. Interestingly, the expression (bid.bdim + tid) identifies a globally unique id for each thread, and remains unchanged when the block-size is modified. Hence, the analysis further tracks the sub-expressions of this expression and whenever a variable is observed to be a function of this expression, it is marked independent of block-size. Further, to gain precision, the analysis also tracks block-size independent *multipliers*, so that expressions of the form (k.bid.bdim + k.tid), where k is a block-size independent value, can be proven block-size independent. Finally, if none of the block-size dependent values flow into the final state of any thread, then the program is block-size independent. The analysis uses a novel abstraction to track these values, where the *symbolic* constants track multipliers while the *abstract* constants track sub-expressions. This combination of abstract interpretation [7,18] with symbolic execution [3,8] helps scale the analysis while retaining good precision.

To understand this further, consider the function cudaProcess() in Fig. 1 from a GPU program 'simpleCUDA2GL'. The function initializes pixels in an image represented by the array g_odata. Each thread initializes a globally unique location (x, y) with a value that is only a function of these coordinates. The coordinates x and y are independent of block-size. Also, the function is synchronization-free and each thread executes independently. Therefore, the function must be block-size independent. To prove this, the analysis tracks the

```
__global__ void cudaProcess(unsigned *g_odata, int imgw) {
    int tx = tid[0]; int ty = tid[1];
    int bw = bdim[0]; int bh = bdim[1];
    int x = bid[0]*bw + tx;
    int y = bid[1]*bh + ty;
    uchar4 c4 = make_uchar4((x & 0x20)?100:0, 0,
                            (y & 0x20)?100:0, 0);
    g_odata[y*imgw+x] = rgbToInt(c4.z, c4.y, c4.x);
}
```

Fig. 1. Example illustrating block-size independence.

flow of block-size dependent values bid, bdim, and tid through program variables. Note that, to mirror the 2-dimensional nature of the image, the threads are organized in a 2-dimensional grid, where the first and second dimensions identify the x and y coordinates, respectively. During the analysis run, *imgw* is first assigned a block-size independent value. Next, tx is assigned tid_0, ty is assigned tid_1 and so on. Importantly, variables x and y are assigned $(bid_0.bdim_0 + tid_0)$ and $(bid_1.bdim_1 + tid_1)$, respectively, both of which are block-size independent. Further, calls to functions make_uchar4 and rgbToInt return block-size independent values. Therefore, writes to array *g_odata* by threads are block-size independent, and the analysis verifies the program to be block-size independent.

We have implemented our tool in the LLVM open-source compiler. We implement an inter-procedural analysis and evaluate it on 34 sample programs from the Nvidia CUDA SDK 8.0 [19] samples. We observe that a large number of programs are synchronization-free and can be proven block-size independent. A few programs were trivially fixed to be block-size independent. Overall, the analysis verifies a total of 35 global kernels in 11 programs to be block-size independent, where a *global kernel* is an independent unit of execution in a GPU application. To summarize, the paper makes the following contributions.

- Identifies and formalizes the problem of *block-size independence* for GPU programs (Sect. 2).
- Presents a *scalable* inter-procedural analysis to verify block-size independence for the class of *synchronization-free* GPU programs (Sect. 3).
- Demonstrates the relevance of the problem through an extensive evaluation on the Nvidia CUDA SDK 8.0 samples (Sect. 4).

Lastly, we present some related work in Sect. 5 and conclude in Sect. 6.

2   Formalization

In this section, we present a formalization for the problem of block-size independence. We first define a formal semantics for the GPU programming model (Sect. 2.1) and the GPU execution model (Sect. 2.2). This establishes a framework under which we can reason about the correctness of transformations. We formalize block-size independence in Sect. 2.3. Finally, we discuss some design choices and limitations for the above formalization (Sect. 2.4).

2.1   GPU Programming Model

GPUs follow a Single Instruction Multiple Threads (SIMT) programming model, where a large number of threads execute the same sequence of instructions, called kernels. The threads are organized in a two-level hierarchy, where a set of threads form a thread-block, and set of blocks forms a thread-grid. The thread-grid can be multi-dimensional, where each thread is assigned a multi-dimensional thread-id and block-id. Further, threads have access to thread-private *local* memory, block-level *shared* memory, and a grid-level *global* memory. Each thread has access to its thread-id (tid), block-id (bid), number of threads per block (bdim) and the total number of threads (gdim). Finally, threads within a block can synchronize via a __syncthreads() barrier.

Formally, a GPU program is the tuple $\langle d, V_L, V_S, V_G, C, K \rangle$, where d represents the number of dimensions in the thread-grid, V_L, V_S, V_G represent the sets of local, shared and global variables in the program, $C = \{\mathsf{tid}, \mathsf{bid}, \mathsf{bdim}, \mathsf{gdim}\}$ represents a set of local constants, and K is the *kernel* or the sequence of instructions executed by each thread. Let $l \in V_L$ be a local variable and $v \in V_S \cup V_G$ be a shared/global array. Let E be a computable expression. The kernel K is defined by the grammar:

$$S := AS \mid \textbf{if } \langle test \rangle \textbf{ then } S_1 \textbf{ else } S_2 \mid \textbf{while } \langle test \rangle \textbf{ do } S \mid \texttt{\_\_syncthreads}() \mid S_1; S_2$$

$$
\begin{aligned}
AS := &[l := E(l_0, \ldots, l_n)] && \text{local assignments} \\
\mid &[l := v[l_0, \ldots, l_n]] && \text{multi-dimensional array reads} \\
\mid &[v[l_0, \ldots, l_n] := l] && \text{multi-dimensional array writes}
\end{aligned}
$$

Thread-Grid. Given the total number of threads (*i.e.* grid-size) and the number of threads per block (*i.e.* block-size), represented by d-dimensional vectors $\boldsymbol{N}$ and $\boldsymbol{B}$ respectively, we define the structure for the thread-grid. The thread-grid is d-dimensional where each dimension i is divided into $\lceil \boldsymbol{N}_i / \boldsymbol{B}_i \rceil$ blocks. The total number of threads along ith dimension is $\boldsymbol{N}_i$, and therefore, the first $(\lceil \boldsymbol{N}_i / \boldsymbol{B}_i \rceil - 1)$ blocks consist of $\boldsymbol{B}_i$ threads, whereas the last block consists of $(\boldsymbol{N}_i - (\lceil \boldsymbol{N}_i / \boldsymbol{B}_i \rceil - 1)\boldsymbol{B}_i)$ threads. The blocks and threads are assigned a d-dimensional block-id $\boldsymbol{b}$ and thread-id $\boldsymbol{t}$. The block-ids range from 0 to $\lceil \boldsymbol{N}_i / \boldsymbol{B}_i \rceil - 1$ for each dimension i, while the thread-ids range from 0 to $\min(\boldsymbol{B}_i, \boldsymbol{N}_i - \boldsymbol{b}_i \boldsymbol{B}) - 1$ and identify the positions of threads within their blocks.

Figure 2 presents an example 2-dimensional thread-grid with 22×10 total threads, with 4×3 threads per block. There are in total 6×4 blocks. Also, the last block along each dimension has fewer threads than the first few blocks to preserve the total number of threads along the dimension.

2.2   GPU Execution Model

We next present the semantics of executing a GPU program. Given a global state σ^G that maps each global variable to a specific value, and a thread-grid configuration, given by the grid-size $\boldsymbol{N}$ and the block-size $\boldsymbol{B}$, let $[\![K]\!]^G(\sigma^G, \boldsymbol{N}, \boldsymbol{B})$

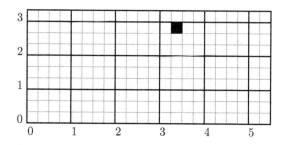

Fig. 2. An example 2-dimensional thread-grid with 22×10 total threads and 4×3 threads per block. Each solid block represents a thread-block, while each cell represents a thread. The darkened cell corresponds to a thread with block-id $(3, 2)$ and thread-id $(1, 2)$.

represent the global state obtained after the execution of kernel K. Let τ represent a thread in the thread-grid. Let $t = \mathsf{tid}(\tau)$ and $b = \mathsf{bid}(\tau)$ be the thread-id and block-id for the thread. Let $\mathcal{G}(N, B)$ represent the set of all threads in the grid. Let $T(b, N, B)$ be the set of all threads with block-id b, i.e. $\{\tau \in \mathcal{G}(N, B) : \mathsf{bid}(\tau) = b\}$. We first present the semantics for executing threads within a block, and then the semantics of composing executions for blocks.

Fine-Grained Execution for Threads. We use a fine-grained semantics to execute threads within a block, where all threads execute instructions in lock-step. Given a block-id b, the threads in the block are $T = T(b, N, B)$. We simultaneously maintain state for all threads. Each thread has access to a private copy of local variables and a common copy of shared and global variables. Therefore, the execution state σ consists of the local state $\sigma^L : V_L \times T \to \mathcal{V}$ that maps local variables in each thread to their values, the shared state $\sigma^S : V_S \to \mathcal{V}$ that maps shared variables to their values, and the global state $\sigma^G : V_G \to \mathcal{V}$ that maps global variables to their values. Further for each thread $\tau \in T$, the local constants $\mathsf{bdim}(\tau)$ and $\mathsf{gdim}(\tau)$ are assigned block-size B and grid-size N, respectively. We now present the semantics. Let $[\![S]\!](\sigma, \Pi)$ represent the execution of a statement S for a set of threads Π starting in state σ. The semantics of executing kernel K for threads with block-id b is given by $[\![K]\!](\sigma, T(b, N, B))$. Note the resulting state consists of all variables and not just global variables. We define semantics by structural induction on S.

Assignments. We first define semantics of executing an assignment statement for a single thread τ. Let $\sigma' \equiv [\![AS]\!](\sigma, \tau)$ represent the semantics. For local computations, $[l := E(l_0, \ldots, l_n)]$, the semantics updates the value of l in state σ' to the value $E(\sigma(l_0, \tau), \ldots, \sigma(l_n, \tau))$. For array reads, $[l := v[l_0, \ldots, l_n]]$, the semantics updates the value of variable l with the value at location $x = (\sigma(l_0, \tau), \sigma(l_1, \tau), \ldots, \sigma(l_n, \tau))$ in array v, i.e. $\sigma'(l, \tau) = \sigma(v)(x)$. Finally, for array writes, $[v[l_0, \ldots, l_n] := v]$, the semantics updates the value at location

$x = (\sigma(l_0, \tau), \sigma(l_1, \tau), \ldots, \sigma(l_n, \tau))$ in array v to the value $\sigma(l, \tau)$:

$$\sigma'(v)(x) = \sigma(l, \tau), \text{ and for all } y \neq x, \sigma'(v)(y) = \sigma(v)(y).$$

Note that the constants tid, bid, bdim, and gdim can also appear on the right-hand side of these assignments. Next, we present the semantics of executing the assignment for a set of threads $\Pi = \{\tau_0, \ldots, \tau_n\}$. The semantics sequentially compose the execution of individual threads, ordered by their thread-ids. Hence, $[\![AS]\!](\sigma, \{\}) = \sigma$, and for all $0 \leq i \leq n$,

$$[\![AS]\!](\sigma, \{\tau_i, \ldots, \tau_n\}) = [\![AS]\!]([\![AS]\!](\sigma, \tau_i), \{\tau_{i+1}, \ldots, \tau_n\}).$$

Sequences. The semantics of executing sequence of statements $S_1; S_2$ consists of executing S_1 for all threads, followed by executing S_2:

$$[\![S_1; S_2]\!](\sigma, \Pi) = [\![S_2]\!]([\![S_1]\!](\sigma, \Pi), \Pi).$$

Conditionals. The semantics for conditionals *serializes* the execution of the two branches. First all threads for which the test, given by a local boolean variable l, is true, execute S_1. Then the remaining threads execute S_2 to produce the desired state. Let $\Pi_1 = \{\tau \in \Pi : \sigma(l, \tau) = \text{true}\}$. The semantics are:

$$[\![\textbf{if } l \textbf{ then } S_1 \textbf{ else } S_2]\!](\sigma, \Pi) = [\![S_2]\!]([\![S_1]\!](\sigma, \Pi_1), \Pi \setminus \Pi_1).$$

Loops. The semantics for loops are similar to that for conditionals, except the execution repeats until the test condition, given by a local boolean variable, becomes false for all threads. Let $\sigma_0, \ldots, \sigma_n$ and $\Pi_0, \ldots, \Pi_n$ be a series of states and sets of threads, such that $\sigma_0 = \sigma$, $\Pi_0 = \{\tau \in \Pi : \sigma(l, \tau) = \text{true}\}$, $\sigma_i = [\![S]\!](\sigma_{i-1}, \Pi_{i-1})$, $\Pi_i = \{\tau \in \Pi_{i-1} : \sigma_i(l, \tau) = \text{true}\}$, and $\Pi_n = \{\}$. If such a series exists, then the final state σ_n is the desired result of executing the loop.

Syncthreads. Due to the lock-step execution of threads, the __syncthreads() barrier does not need special semantics and returns the initial state σ.

Coarse-Grained Execution for Blocks. We next present the semantics of composing executions of individual blocks. We present a coarse-grained semantics where each block executes independently and the final state is obtained by sequentially composing executions of individual blocks, ordered by their block-ids. The blocks share only the global variables, and the local and shared variables are initialized to undefined values before the execution for a block begins and discarded after the execution ends. Let $[\![K]\!]^G(\sigma^G, \Gamma, N, B)$ represent the execution for blocks with block-ids in $\Gamma = \{b_0, \ldots, b_n\}$ starting in initial global state σ^G. We define it as follows. First, $[\![K]\!]^G(\sigma^G, \{\}, N, B) = \sigma^G$. Next, for all $0 \leq i \leq n$,

$$[\![K]\!]^G(\sigma^G, \{b_i, \ldots, b_n\}, N, B) = [\![K]\!]^G(\text{Proj}(\sigma', V_G), \{b_{i+1}, \ldots, b_n\}, N, B),$$
$$\text{where } \sigma' = [\![K]\!](\sigma^G \cup \sigma_\perp^S \cup \sigma_\perp^L, T(b_i, N, B)),$$

and $\sigma_\perp^L$ and $\sigma_\perp^S$ are local and shared states with undefined values, while $\mathsf{Proj}(\sigma, V)$ projects the state σ onto the variables in set V. Note that the final state consists only of the global variables. Now the desired state after the execution of the GPU program, $[\![K]\!]^G(\sigma^G, \boldsymbol{N}, \boldsymbol{B})$, is given by $[\![K]\!]^G(\sigma^G, \mathcal{B}, \boldsymbol{N}, \boldsymbol{B})$ where $\mathcal{B}$ is the set of all block-ids in the thread-grid.

Invalidation Semantics. We next describe scenarios under which the execution of the program is erroneous and produces an error state $\perp$. First, a *data-race* between threads leads to an error state. A data-race occurs when two threads access the same shared/global memory location, and the execution of the accesses is not separated by a __syncthreads() barrier. Second, an execution where only few of the threads within a block reach a __syncthreads() barrier produces an error state, and is called a *barrier divergence*. These semantics help incorporate features of the general GPU execution model into the formalization.

To keep the execution model simple, we discuss the invalidation semantics informally. The focus of the paper is on proving *functional* equivalence of the original and the transformed program. For such a property, precise invalidation semantics are not necessary. We still rely on the data-race freedom of programs to prove the correctness of our analysis. However, the informal nature of the semantics suffices.

2.3 Block-Size Independence

We now define the block-size independence for a GPU program. Let two states σ and σ' be equivalent ($\sigma \equiv \sigma'$), if they consist of the same set of variables and each variable has the same valuation in both states. We state the formal definition here.

Definition 1. *A GPU program* $\langle d, V_L, V_S, V_G, C, K \rangle$ *is block-size independent, iff for all initial global states σ^G and grid-sizes $\boldsymbol{N}$, the execution of the program is independent of the block-size $\boldsymbol{B}$, that is:*

$$\text{for all } \sigma^G, \boldsymbol{N}, \boldsymbol{B}, \boldsymbol{B}', \ [\![K]\!]^G(\sigma^G, \boldsymbol{N}, \boldsymbol{B}) \equiv [\![K]\!]^G(\sigma^G, \boldsymbol{N}, \boldsymbol{B}').$$

2.4 Discussion

We have presented so far a formal programming and execution model for GPU programs and defined block-size independence with respect to this model. The proposed model closely follows popular programming models like CUDA and OpenCL. However, there are few restrictions and limitations in the proposed model that we discuss here:

Lock-Step Execution. We use a simplified execution model where we assume all threads in a block to execute in lock-step. This is not true in practice for performance reasons. However, we are only concerned with the functional behavior of programs and proving functional correctness of block-size transformation.

Also, the simplified execution model is functionally equivalent to the model used in practice when programs are free of data-races.

Data-Race Freedom. Our formalization assumes that the GPU program being transformed is free of data-races and other such correctness issues. These issues have been tackled previously [2,11,12], and therefore, we focus only on the correctness of block-size transformation.

Total Number of Threads. In our formalization, we specify the number of threads N as one of the invocation parameters. Among the popular models, OpenCL [24] closely follows this model. CUDA [17], however, specifies the number of blocks N_b as an invocation parameter and computes the number of threads along ith dimension as $B_i.(N_b)_i$ *i.e.* the product between the number of blocks and the block-size. However, specifying the number of threads N provides more flexibility in defining the total number of threads. Also, the total number of threads remains unchanged when the block-size is modified, which makes proving program equivalence easier. Further, when the new block-size B' is a divisor the number of threads N along each grid-dimension, our model is also applicable to CUDA and the new number of blocks along ith dimension can be computed as $B_i.(N_b)_i/B'_i$.

Structures and Pointers. Our formal model only considers scalars and arrays, while the general models CUDA and OpenCL also support structures and pointers. The key insights for arrays carry over to structures and pointers, and therefore for simplicity, we omit them from our model. We address these, however, in the implementation of our analysis.

3   Analysis for Synchronization-Free GPU Programs

This section presents an analysis to verify block-size independence for *synchronization-free* GPU programs, where the kernel does not consist of __syncthreads() barriers. In a synchronization-free GPU program, each thread must execute independently of the other threads (since any dependence on updates from other threads leads to a data-race). Therefore, the *global* problem of verifying block-size independence of the program reduces to the *local* problem of verifying block-size independence for the execution of each thread in the program (Sect. 3.1).

Next, the execution of a thread is independent of block-size if the writes by the thread to the shared and global variables do not depend on block-size.[1] A write can depend on block-size if either the location accessed, the value written or the condition under which the write is executed is dependent on block-size. The only sources of block-size dependence in a thread are the thread's block-id, $bid(\tau)$, the thread-id, $tid(\tau)$, and the block-size itself, $bdim(\tau) = B$. Further,

---

[1] Reads can be ignored because our __syncthreads()-free and race-free assumptions permit a thread to only read values it has written itself or are part of the initial state.

the expression $\mathsf{gid}(\tau) = (\mathsf{bid}.\mathsf{bdim} + \mathsf{tid})(\tau)$ is independent of block-size. This is because $\mathsf{gid}(\tau)$ identifies a unique global location of the thread in the thread-grid and remains unchanged when the block-size is modified. For example in Fig. 2, the thread with thread-id $(1, 2)$ and block-id $(3, 2)$ has a unique global-id $(3.4 + 1, 2.3 + 2) = (13, 8)$, which remains unchanged for all block-sizes. We incorporate these features into our analysis to check block-size independence for each thread (Sect. 3.2).

3.1 Reduction to Thread-Local Block-Size Independence

We first define *thread-local block-size independence* for GPU programs. A GPU program is thread-local block-size independent if the execution of each thread in the thread-grid is independent of block-size. Given block-sizes $\boldsymbol{B}$ and $\boldsymbol{B}'$, let a thread τ in grid $\mathcal{G}(\boldsymbol{N}, \boldsymbol{B})$ be equivalent to another thread τ' in grid $\mathcal{G}(\boldsymbol{N}, \boldsymbol{B}')$, *i.e.* $\tau \equiv \tau'$, if they have the same unique global location in the thread-grid, namely:

$$\text{for all } 0 \le i < d, \ (\mathsf{bid}_i(\tau).\boldsymbol{B}_i + \mathsf{tid}_i(\tau)) = (\mathsf{bid}_i(\tau').\boldsymbol{B}'_i + \mathsf{tid}_i(\tau'))$$

We observe this to be a one-to-one relation, where each thread τ in the first grid corresponds to a *unique* global thread τ' in the second grid. Now, the program is thread-local block-size independent, if each pair of equivalent global threads has equivalent executions. Recall $[\![S]\!](\sigma, \Pi)$ denotes the execution of statement S for a set of threads Π starting in initial state σ.

Definition 2. *A GPU program $\langle d, V_L, V_S, V_G, C, K \rangle$ is thread-local block-size independent, iff for all initial states σ^G and grid-sizes $\boldsymbol{N}$, the global state after the execution of a thread in the thread-grid is independent of block-size, where the local and shared variables are initialized to undefined values. Formally, the program is thread-local block-size independent iff:*

$$\textit{for all } \sigma^G, \boldsymbol{N}, \boldsymbol{B}, \boldsymbol{B}', \tau \in \mathcal{G}(\boldsymbol{N}, \boldsymbol{B}), \tau' \in \mathcal{G}(\boldsymbol{N}, \boldsymbol{B}'),$$
$$\tau \equiv \tau' \implies \mathsf{Proj}([\![K]\!](\sigma, \{\tau\}), V_G) \equiv \mathsf{Proj}([\![K]\!](\sigma, \{\tau'\}), V_G),$$
$$\textit{where } \sigma \equiv (\sigma_\perp^L \cup \sigma_\perp^S \cup \sigma^G).$$

We show that if a GPU program is synchronization-free, verifying thread-local block-size independence is sufficient to verify block-size independence for the program. We first observe that for a synchronization-free program, the lock-step execution of threads in a block is equivalent to executing threads one after another. This is because, to avoid data-races, each thread must operate independently and not see updates from other threads. Therefore, the order of execution between threads does not matter and a fine-grained interleaving (Fig. 3a) produces the same execution as a coarse-grained interleaving (Fig. 3b).

$t_0\ t_1\ t_2\ t_3\ t_4\ t_5\ \ldots$

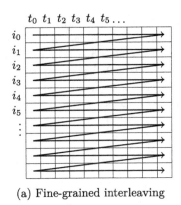

$t_0\ t_1\ t_2\ t_3\ t_4\ t_5\ \ldots$

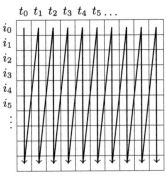

(a) Fine-grained interleaving   (b) Coarse-grained interleaving

Fig. 3. The figure shows fine-grained vs coarse-grained interleaving of threads in a block. The rows represent sequence of instructions to be executed, while the columns represent the threads in a block. The arrows signify the order in which the threads and the instructions are executed.

Lemma 1. *Given a synchronization-free GPU program* $\langle d, V_L, V_S, V_G, C, K\rangle$ *and a set of threads* $\Pi = \{\tau_0, \ldots, \tau_k\}$, *the lock-step execution of threads is equivalent to executing threads sequentially:*

$$for\ all\ \sigma, \Pi,\ [\![K]\!](\sigma, \Pi) \equiv \sigma_{k+1},$$
$$where\ \sigma_0 = \sigma\ and\ \sigma_{i+1} = [\![K]\!](\sigma_i, \{\tau_i\}) for\ all\ 0 \leq i \leq k.$$

By Lemma 1, the lock-step execution of threads in a block can be substituted with sequential execution of threads. Next, we observe that we can execute each thread in a state where the local and shared variables are undefined initially. This is because, the thread must not observe any updates to these variables from the previously executed threads, or we would have a data-race. Also, these variables are discarded at the end of the execution of the block, and we need not retain their values. Remember $[\![K]\!]^G(\sigma^G, \Gamma, N, B)$ represents execution of a set of blocks Γ, where the shared and local variables are undefined initially and the result of the execution consists only of the global state.

Lemma 2. *Given a synchronization-free GPU program* $\langle d, V_L, V_S, V_G, C, K\rangle$ *and a block-id* b, *the lock-step execution for block* b *is equivalent to executing threads sequentially, with local and shared variables initialized to undefined values:*

$$for\ all\ \sigma^G, b, N, B,\ [\![K]\!]^G(\sigma^G, \{b\}, N, B) \equiv \sigma^G_{k+1},$$
$$where\ \sigma^G_0 = \sigma^G\ and\ \sigma^G_{i+1} = \mathsf{Proj}([\![K]\!](\sigma^L_\perp \cup \sigma^S_\perp \cup \sigma^G_i, \{\tau_i\}), V_G),$$
$$for\ all\ \tau_i\ in\ T(b, N, B).$$

Finally from Lemma 2, the execution of each thread in the first grid can be substituted with the execution of equivalent thread in the second grid, and therefore, thread-local block-size independence of a synchronization-free program implies block-size independence for the program. We conclude the following theorem.

Theorem 1. *If a synchronization-free GPU program* $\langle d, V_L, V_S, V_G, C, K \rangle$ *is thread-local block-size independent, then it is also block-size independent.*

3.2 Analysis

We present our analysis to check thread-local block-size independence of GPU programs and to ensure that the execution of each thread is block-size independent. Initially when a thread's execution starts, only constants bid, bdim and tid are block-size dependent and the remaining variables are block-size independent. While bdim is equal to block-size, the thread-id tid and block-id bid of a thread also depend on the block-size and get updated when the block-size is modified. Hence, if any of these values potentially flows into a global variable update, then the final global state after the thread's execution depends on block-size and the program is block-size dependent. The analysis defines an abstraction of state and abstract semantics for kernel instructions to track the flow of block-size dependent values during a thread's execution. Note that we run the analysis and show the block-size independence separately for each dimension of thread-grid. So for the subsequent discussion, consider bid, bdim and tid to be one-dimensional values. This is not too restrictive, since most programs are block-size independent with respect to each grid-dimension. Also, this greatly simplifies the analysis both in its complexity and running time.

Abstraction. The analysis defines an abstraction of program state to track dependence of local scalar variables on block-size. Let $\hat{\sigma}$ be the abstraction of the program state σ, which maps each local variable to an abstract value, *i.e.* $V_L \to \hat{\mathcal{V}}$. Let l, k_0 be local variables. Let f_0 be a function that maps each thread to a block-size independent value. For integer and real variables, the abstraction is defined as:

$$\hat{\sigma}(l) = \begin{cases} \mathsf{c_{ind}}, & \text{for all } \tau, \sigma(l, \tau) = f_0(\tau). \\ k_0 \mathsf{c_{bid}}, & \hat{\sigma}(k_0) = \mathsf{c_{ind}}; \text{for all } \tau, \sigma(l, \tau) = \sigma(k_0, \tau).\mathsf{bid}(\tau). \\ k_0 \mathsf{c_{bdim}}, & \hat{\sigma}(k_0) = \mathsf{c_{ind}}; \text{for all } \tau, \sigma(l, \tau) = \sigma(k_0, \tau).\mathsf{bdim}(\tau). \\ k_0 \mathsf{c_{tid}}, & \hat{\sigma}(k_0) = \mathsf{c_{ind}}; \text{for all } \tau, \sigma(l, \tau) = \sigma(k_0, \tau).\mathsf{tid}(\tau) + f_0(\tau). \\ k_0 \mathsf{c_{bid}} \mathsf{c_{bdim}}, & \hat{\sigma}(k_0) = \mathsf{c_{ind}}; \\ & \text{for all } \tau, \sigma(l, \tau) = \sigma(k_0, \tau).\mathsf{bid}(\tau).\mathsf{bdim}(\tau) + f_0(\tau). \\ \mathsf{c_{bsize}}, & \text{otherwise.} \end{cases}$$

The value $\mathsf{c_{ind}}$ represents all block-size independent values. The abstract value $\mathsf{c_{bsize}}$ represents values with arbitrary dependence on block-size. We observe the expression $(k_0.\mathsf{bid}.\mathsf{bdim} + k_0.\mathsf{tid})$, where k_0 is a block-size independent variable, is independent of block-size. To take this account, our abstraction tracks different sub-expressions of this expression, $k_0 \mathsf{c_{bid}}, k_0 \mathsf{c_{bdim}}, k_0 \mathsf{c_{tid}}$, and $k_0 \mathsf{c_{bid}} \mathsf{c_{bdim}}$, where k_0 is the *multiplier* or a symbolic constant representing a block-size independent

$$\text{Sum1} \frac{l := l_0 + l_1 \quad \hat{\sigma}(l_0) = \mathsf{c_{ind}} \quad \hat{\sigma}(l_1) \in \{k_0 \mathsf{c_{tid}}, k_1 \mathsf{c_{bid}} \mathsf{c_{bdim}}\}}{\hat{\sigma}'(l) := \hat{\sigma}(l_1)}$$

$$\text{Sum2} \frac{l := l_0 + l_1 \quad \hat{\sigma}(l_0) = k_0 \mathsf{c_{tid}} \quad \hat{\sigma}(l_1) = k_1 \mathsf{c_{bid}} \mathsf{c_{bdim}} \quad k_0 \equiv k_1}{\hat{\sigma}'(l) := \mathsf{c_{ind}}}$$

$$\text{Prod1} \frac{l := l_0.l_1 \quad \hat{\sigma}(l_0) = \mathsf{c_{ind}} \quad \hat{\sigma}(l_1) \in \{\mathsf{c_{bid}}, \mathsf{c_{bdim}}, \mathsf{c_{tid}}, \mathsf{c_{bid}} \mathsf{c_{bdim}}\}}{\hat{\sigma}'(l) := l_0 \hat{\sigma}(l_1)}$$

$$\text{Prod2} \frac{l := l_0.l_1 \quad \hat{\sigma}(l_0) = \mathsf{c_{bid}} \quad \hat{\sigma}(l_1) = k_0 \mathsf{c_{bdim}}}{\hat{\sigma}'(l) := k_0 \mathsf{c_{bid}} \mathsf{c_{bdim}}}$$

$$\text{Prod3} \frac{l := l_0.l_1 \quad \hat{\sigma}(l_0) = k_0 \mathsf{c_{bid}} \quad \hat{\sigma}(l_1) = \mathsf{c_{bdim}}}{\hat{\sigma}'(l) := k_0 \mathsf{c_{bid}} \mathsf{c_{bdim}}}$$

$$\text{Read} \frac{l := v[l_0, \ldots, l_n] \quad \hat{\sigma}(l_0) = \mathsf{c_{ind}} \ldots \hat{\sigma}(l_n) = \mathsf{c_{ind}}}{\hat{\sigma}'(l) := \mathsf{c_{ind}}}$$

$$\text{Arith} \frac{l := l_0 \text{ op } l_1 \quad \hat{\sigma}(l_0) = \mathsf{c_{ind}} \quad \hat{\sigma}(l_1) = \mathsf{c_{ind}}}{\hat{\sigma}'(l) := \mathsf{c_{ind}}}$$

$$\text{Rel} \frac{l := l_0 \text{ rel } l_1 \quad \hat{\sigma}(l_0) = \mathsf{c_{ind}} \quad \hat{\sigma}(l_1) = \mathsf{c_{ind}}}{\hat{\sigma}'(l) := \mathsf{b_{ind}}}$$

$$\text{Bool} \frac{l := l_0 \text{ bop } l_1 \quad \hat{\sigma}(l_0) = \mathsf{b_{ind}} \quad \hat{\sigma}(l_1) = \mathsf{b_{ind}}}{\hat{\sigma}'(l) := \mathsf{b_{ind}}}$$

Fig. 4. Abstract semantics for different assignment statements and initial abstract states. State $\hat{\sigma}$ is the incoming abstract state while $\hat{\sigma}'$ is the updated state after the assignment. The rules are valid only when the path-predicate $\hat{\pi}$ is $\mathsf{b_{ind}}$. Lastly, op, rel and bop are arithmetic, relational and boolean operators, respectively.

local variable. We assume each local variable has a unique definition (*e.g.* SSA form), and the variables are not updated after they are first defined. Hence, the symbolic constant truly represents the variable used as multiplier in the abstract value, and we do not differentiate between the variable and the symbolic constant representing the variable.

We similarly define an abstraction for local boolean variables, which tracks dependence of the condition on block-size. Let b_0 be a block-size independent boolean function. The abstraction for boolean variables is:

$$\hat{\sigma}(l) = \begin{cases} \mathsf{b_{ind}}, & \text{for all } \tau, \ \sigma(l, \tau) = b_0(\tau). \\ \mathsf{b_{bsize}}, & \text{otherwise.} \end{cases}$$

Finally, we do not track shared and global variables or arrays in our abstraction. We compensate by tracking each write to these variables and ensuring that the writes are independent of block-size.

We further define a *path-predicate*, $\hat{\pi}$, which is the condition under which a statement is executed. The value of $\hat{\pi}$ is an abstract boolean value, representing whether the condition is dependent on block-size or not.

Abstract Semantics. We now define some abstract semantics for propagating abstract state $\hat{\sigma}$ and path-predicate $\hat{\pi}$ through statements in the kernel. Figure 4 defines updates to abstract states for different assignment statements and initial states. Note the rules in Fig. 4 are only valid if the path-predicate $\hat{\pi}$ is $\mathsf{b_{ind}}$. Also, we only show rules for scenarios where the result is non-trivial and not $\mathsf{c_{bsize}}/\mathsf{b_{bsize}}$. Otherwise, if $\hat{\pi} = \mathsf{b_{bsize}}$ or the rule is not shown, the updated value for arithmetic/boolean variables is $\mathsf{c_{bsize}}/\mathsf{b_{bsize}}$. The path-predicate remains unchanged after each statement, unless specified.

We now briefly describe the rules shown in Fig. 4. Note when the multiplier k for an abstract value is constant 1, we drop the multiplier, *e.g.* c_{bid} in rule PROD1. The rules ensure that the abstraction is preserved. For example, in rule SUM2, abstract values $k_0 c_{tid}$ and $k_1 c_{bid} c_{bdim}$ are added together, where k_0 equals k_1. This is equivalent to the expression $(k_0.\text{tid} + k_0.\text{bid.bdim})$, which we know is block-size independent. Hence, the final result is assigned the value c_{ind}. Similarly, the other rules update the abstract state while preserving the abstraction. An important point to note here is that during the product operation (rules PROD1, PROD2, PROD3), the multiplier for at least one of the operands must be constant 1, so that the multiplier for the other operand is set as the final multiplier. Otherwise, the result is set to c_{bsize}. This ensures that the set of symbolic values for the multiplier is limited to the set of variables in the program and we do not consider complex expressions on variables for the multiplier. While this is imprecise, it is necessary to scale the analysis.

We next consider writes to shared/global arrays $[v[l_0, \ldots, l_n] := l]$, where the analysis checks if the accessed location, the value written and the path-predicate are independent of block-size, *i.e.* the values $\hat{\sigma}(l_0), \ldots, \hat{\sigma}(l_n)$ and $\hat{\sigma}(l)$ must be c_{ind} and the path-predicate $\hat{\pi}$ must be b_{ind}. If this is not the case, the write is potentially a function of block-size and the analysis reports the write, and the kernel itself, to be *block-size dependent*. This also ensures the values in shared/global arrays are always block-size independent, and thus, the array reads return a consistent value in rule READ in Fig. 4.

For conditionals $[\text{if } l \text{ then } S_1 \text{ else } S_2]$, the analysis sets the path-predicates for S_1 and S_2 to $(\hat{\pi} \land \hat{\sigma}(l))$ and $(\hat{\pi} \land \neg \hat{\sigma}(l))$, respectively, and propagates the same initial abstract state $\hat{\sigma}$ to both statements. Further, the final state after the conditional is a *merge* of states after S_1 and S_2. If the values for a variable are identical in both states (*i.e.* the type and the multiplier are equal), then this is set as the merged value for the variable. Otherwise, the merged value is set to c_{bsize}/b_{bsize}. The path-predicate after the conditional is the same as the predicate $\hat{\pi}$ before the conditional.

The semantics for loops are defined similarly to conditionals, but we must additionally ensure that the analysis terminates. We observe that the set of abstract values and the merge operation define a finite upper semi-lattice, with a small number of different value types and the multiplier ranging over the finite set of local variables. Further, the abstract semantics are monotonic over the semi-lattice. Therefore, the fixed point computation on loops must terminate.

Algorithm. The overall algorithm is as follows. We initialize local variables to c_{ind}/b_{ind} in the initial abstract state $\hat{\sigma}$, while the path-predicate $\hat{\pi}$ is initialized to b_{ind}. The constants bid, bdim and tid are assigned values c_{bid}, c_{bdim} and c_{tid}, respectively, while gdim is independent of block-size and assigned c_{ind}. The analysis executes the kernel for the abstract state $\hat{\sigma}$ and the path-predicate $\hat{\pi}$ with the abstract semantics defined above. If it encounters a potentially block-size dependent shared or global write, it terminates with block-size dependence. Otherwise, it reports the kernel to be block-size independent.

Inter-procedural Analysis. Our analysis also supports inter-procedural analysis, where a kernel can call other kernels. We do a bottom-up traversal on the call-graph, where the callees are analyzed before the callers. We analyze each kernel assuming the parameters are set to c_{ind}/b_{ind} initially and reuse this analysis result for all calls to the kernel with call arguments as c_{ind}/b_{ind}. For calls with block-size dependent arguments, we conservatively report the call to be block-size dependent and return c_{bsize}/b_{bsize}. For library calls (where the source code is not linked) and inline assembly instructions, we conservatively assume the function to be block-size dependent and to return value c_{bsize}/b_{bsize}. However, for specific cases, like library calls to Math functions __sinf, __cosf, __sqrtf etc., where the result is a trivial function of inputs, we assume the call to be block-size independent, and also return c_{ind}/b_{ind} if the call-arguments are c_{ind}/b_{ind}. Note that we do not support recursive procedures in our analysis, which are rarely present in GPU programs.

Example. We illustrate our analysis using the example in Fig. 1. We run the analysis separately for the two thread-grid dimensions. For the first thread-grid dimension, the analysis initializes variables as $\hat{\sigma}(bid_0) = c_{bid}, \hat{\sigma}(bdim_0) = c_{bdim}, \hat{\sigma}(tid_0) = c_{tid}, \hat{\sigma}(bid_1) = \hat{\sigma}(bdim_1) = \hat{\sigma}(tid_1) = \hat{\sigma}(imgw) = c_{ind}$. Also, it initializes the path-condition to b_{ind}, which is never modified. Next, it executes the statement $[tx := tid_0]$, and sets $\hat{\sigma}(tx)$ to c_{tid}. It similarly assigns values to variables ty, bw, bh. When computing x, it first computes the product $bid_0.bw$ which is equal to $c_{bid}c_{bdim}$, and then computes x as the sum of values $c_{bid}c_{bdim}$ and c_{tid}, which we know is c_{ind}. The execution for the remaining statements continues similarly. Finally, the global write to image *g_odata* is executed with block-size independent abstract values and path-condition, and hence, the write is block-size independent. Therefore, the analysis declares the program block-size independent along this thread-grid dimension. The analysis repeats a similar process for the other thread-grid dimension and concludes the program to be block-size independent.

Implementation. We have implemented the analysis as a pass in LLVM compiler. We define the abstract domain and the abstract semantics, and rely on an *abstract execution engine* to execute the program using the abstract semantics during the analysis. To handle pointers, we use abstract values to track block-size dependence of the *address* of location represented by a pointer. Hence, when a pointer is dereferenced, we conservatively return c_{ind}/b_{ind} if the pointer is constant, and c_{bsize}/b_{bsize} if the pointer is not a constant. We only update the value of a pointer variable on pointer assignment and pointer updates through indexing. Structures are represented similar to arrays in LLVM and hence no special semantics are necessary.

We represent multipliers in the abstract values as follows. LLVM exposes each variable in the program as a unique Value* pointer. We use this pointer to represent the multiplier and compare it against other pointers. Since LLVM uses the SSA form, the pointer corresponds to a unique definition and the value for the variable is not updated after it is first defined. Note that the program variables which are accessed via load/store instructions, do not appear as operands in regular arithmetic or boolean operations, and vice-versa. Hence, such variables are never used as multipliers in the abstract domain and the value for the multipliers is never updated through indirect store operations.

Correctness. We show the correctness of our analysis. The analysis preserves the abstraction and ensures that each variable gets an abstract value c_{ind}/b_{ind} only if the value is truly block-size independent, *i.e.* the assigned value and the path-predicate are block-size independent. Further, each write to global variables is guarded by a check for block-size independence. Therefore, if the analysis does not report any block-size dependent writes, the updates to the global memory are always block-size independent, and the global state at the end of each thread's execution must also be block-size independent. This implies the program is thread-local block-size independent, and hence, we conclude the following theorem.

Theorem 2. *A synchronization-free GPU program* $\langle d, V_L, V_S, V_G, C, K \rangle$ *is block-size independent, if the analysis reports the program to be block-size independent.*

4   Evaluation

We have implemented the block-size independence analysis in LLVM 7.0, a popular open-source compiler framework, and evaluate it on the Nvidia CUDA SDK 8.0 sample programs. The SDK consists of 62 applications, out of which 28 benchmarks rely on texture memory fetches and the Thrust library and could not be compiled with LLVM. Hence, we analyze the remaining 34 benchmarks. For each benchmark, we analyze *global* kernels which are entry-points into the call-graph and are invoked directly from CPU code. For each global kernel, the analysis reports whether the kernel is block-size independent (BSI), and if not, the potential block-size dependent accesses in the kernel. We run the analysis on an Amazon EC2 machine with 4-core Intel Xeon 2.3 GHz CPU and 16GB memory running Ubuntu 16.04 LTS (OS).

How Many BSI Kernels Are Found by the Analysis? Table 1 shows the results for the analysis. The graph shows the the total number of global kernels and the number of BSI kernels reported by our analysis. Note that in few of the benchmarks, the global kernels are instantiations of templated kernels. The global kernels have similar functionality, and hence, the numbers are slightly bloated. For example, in benchmarks "reduction", "threadFenceReduction", and "alignedTypes", the total number of kernels is 132, 40 and 16, though these are instantiations of 7, 2 and 1 templated kernels, respectively. Yet, the analysis is able to verify a large number of kernels as BSI. It finds 35 BSI kernels in 11 benchmarks, and runs in a few seconds for most benchmarks, rarely taking more than a minute.

Are There Truly Non-BSI Kernels? We manually investigated the benchmarks and found a few non-BSI kernels. These kernels asymmetrically

Table 1. Results of BSI analysis for Nvidia CUDA SDK 8.0 samples. # Kernels represents the total number of global kernels. # BSI represents the number of these kernels that are block-size independent.

Benchmark	# Kernels	# BSI	Benchmark	# Kernels	# BSI
Mandelbrot	6	0	concurrentKernels	2	0
simpleGL	1	0	eigenValues	4	0
convolutionSeparable	2	0	fastWalshTransform	3	2
cudaDecodeGL	2	2	FDTD3dGPU	1	0
dwtHaar1D	2	0	interval	1	0
histogram	4	0	mergeSort	7	3
recursiveGaussian	3	2	newDelete	14	4
simpleCUDA2GL	2	2	reduction	132	0
binomialOptions	1	0	scalarProd	1	0
BlackScholes	1	0	scan	3	0
MonteCarloMultiGPU	2	0	shfl_scan	4	0
quasiRandomGenerator	2	2	SimpleHyperQ	3	0
SobolQRNG	1	1	sortingNetworks	6	0
nbody	2	0	StreamPriorities	1	1
oceanFFT	3	2	threadFenceReduction	40	0
alignedTypes	12	12	threadMigration	1	0
cdpLUDecomposition	2	0	transpose	8	0

distribute computation between blocks and threads, and hence, are block-size dependent. For example, benchmarks "binomialOptions" and "MonteCarloMultiGPU" allocate an 'option' per block while the threads collaborate to compute the value for the option. Similarly, "scalarProd" allocates a vector-pair per block while the threads multiply and add individual elements to get the scalar product.

What Class of Kernels Could Not Be Verified? We could not verify block-size independence for kernels where shared memory and thread-synchronization were used to intricately share data between threads within a block. A common scenario was a parallel reduction operation such as summing elements. The block-size was hard-coded via `#define` constants for few of the kernels, which prevented verification. We observed an interesting pattern in benchmarks "dwtHaar1D" and "reduction" where each thread operated on two locations in a global array: (2bid.bdim + tid) and (2bid.bdim + bdim + tid). The locations individually are block-size dependent. However, cumulatively, the threads operate on all elements, which makes the operation block-size independent. Finally, we could not verify kernels in "simpleGL", "oceanFFT" and "interval" to be BSI, because library calls containing inline assembly calls and addition between integers and booleans were inlined into the kernels, which were falsely reported block-size dependent.

Does Tuning Block-Size for BSI Kernels Improve Performance? We experimented with benchmark "SobolQRNG" to gauge performance improvement via block-size tuning. The benchmark originally used shared memory to cache global constants and was reported non-BSI by our analysis. The block-size was set to 64 threads/block and produced 18.8 Gsamples/s (baseline) on an Nvidia GTX Titan X GPU. We removed caching to obtain a BSI version. Here for 64 threads/block, we lost performance by 40% (11.6 Gsamples/s), but then for 256 threads/block, we regained performance with an improvement of 9% over the baseline (20.5 Gsamples/s). Our analysis helped tune block-size to gain performance while ensuring correctness, unlike the other optimization.

How Many Kernels Could Be Easily Fixed to Become BSI? We fixed 7 kernels to be BSI with our analysis (included in the 35 BSI kernels found by the analysis). In "quasiRandomGenerator" and "fastWalshTransform", the number of blocks for the second grid dimension was set to 1, and thus bid_1 was always set to 0 and dropped from the computation for gid_1. In "cudaDecodeGL", gid was computed as $(bdim).(bid << 1) + (tid << 1)$, where the '$<<$' operator was not supported by our analysis. Finally, in "quasiRandomGenerator", gid was computed as $(mul(bid, bdim) + tid)$, where the 'mul' method was not supported.

5 Related Work

Auto-tuning. A rich body of work exists on automatically tuning GPU applications for specific hardware configurations. Broadly, there are three types of auto-tuning: *empirical tuning* [13,16,20,23,27,28], where different program variants are executed and the best variant is identified via exhaustive search or a hill-climbing approach; *model-based tuning* [4,5], where a hand-crafted model is used to select the best program variant; and *predictive model-based tuning* [1,9,13,14,26], where a predictive model trained via machine learning techniques like decision trees is used to select the best program variant. All these approaches either automatically generate the final GPU program, or transform an existing program to generate the tuned program. A few of these works tune block-size directly [1,13,14,27], but do not verify correctness of the transformation. A few are domain-specific [5,16,20,23,28], often using programs written in a domain-specific languages instead of CUDA and OpenCL. Finally, many recent works focus on data-layout optimization [9,26] and data placement [4]. These works segregate specification of data-layout and data-placement from the actual program by hiding it under a data-abstraction layer. Hence, only the spec for data-layout and placement is modified during auto-tuning and the program remains unchanged. This localizes any errors to the implementation of data-layout specifications, which ensures greater correctness. Tuning block-size is, however, essential to utilize resources on GPUs effectively, and our work on validating block-size independence can enable robust auto-tuning for block-size transformation.

GPU Verification. Several systems exist for verification of GPU programs. GKLEE [12] and KLEE-CL [6] extend KLEE, a popular symbolic execution engine, to verify GPU programs against data-races and barrier divergence. Due to the presence of a large number of threads, these tools do not scale to large programs. GPUVerify [2] and PUG [11] improve upon GKLEE and KLEE-CL, by using *symbolic threads* and SMT-based verification to identify data-races. The underlying SMT solvers have trouble scaling to very large formulae as well. Finally, Leung et al. [10] present an approach where they analyze programs for *input-independence*, verify safety properties of input-independent programs for a small set of inputs and then generalize results to all other inputs. The analysis to verify input-independence is similar to ours, except it tracks the flow of input variables instead of the block-size dependent constants.

Abstract Interpretation + Symbolic Execution. A few works, similar to our work, use symbolic constants to improve precision of an abstract domain, while retaining the scalability of the analysis. Sankaranarayanan et al. [22] and Venet [25] extend the Interval domain with symbolic ranges, where the upper and lower bounds of an interval are a linear combination of symbolic constants representing program variables. Miné [15] presents two generic techniques: *linearization*, which instantiates symbolic variables with abstract constants to obtain a linear expression in symbolic variables, and *symbolic constant propagation*, which propagates symbolic constants across expressions to gain precision.

6   Conclusion

The paper formalizes block-size independence for GPU programs and presents an inter-procedural analysis to verify block-size independence for synchronization-free programs. The analysis relies on tracking the flow of block-size dependent values via an abstraction that combines symbolic multipliers with abstract constants representing different dependencies on block-size. It is very efficient and finds a considerable number of block-size independent global kernels in Nvidia CUDA SDK.

In future, we would like to extend the analysis to GPU programs with restricted synchronization between threads, by either transforming these programs into synchronization-free programs or ensuring that the execution of each thread is independent of the set of threads it synchronizes with, and then the present analysis would suffice to prove block-size independence of the programs.

We would like to thank the anonymous reviewers and our shepherd Sylvie Putot for their valuable feedback. We would also like to thank NSF award XPS-1337174 and hardware donations from Nvidia for supporting this research.

References

1. Bergstra, J., Pinto, N., Cox, D.: Machine learning for predictive auto-tuning with boosted regression trees. In: 2012 Innovative Parallel Computing (InPar), pp. 1–9, May 2012
2. Betts, A., Chong, N., Donaldson, A., Qadeer, S., Thomson, P.: GPUVerify: a verifier for GPU kernels. SIGPLAN Not. **47**(10), 113–132 (2012). https://doi.org/10.1145/2398857.2384625
3. Boyer, R.S., Elspas, B., Levitt, K.N.: SELECT - a formal system for testing and debugging programs by symbolic execution. In: Proceedings of the International Conference on Reliable Software, pp. 234–245. ACM, New York 1975). https://doi.org/10.1145/800027.808445
4. Chen, G., Wu, B., Li, D., Shen, X.: PORPLE: an extensible optimizer for portable data placement on GPU. In: Proceedings of the 47th Annual IEEE/ACM International Symposium on Microarchitecture, pp. 88–100. MICRO-47. IEEE Computer Society, Washington (2014). https://doi.org/10.1109/MICRO.2014.20
5. Choi, J.W., Singh, A., Vuduc, R.W.: Model-driven autotuning of sparse matrix-vector multiply on GPUs. In: Proceedings of the 15th ACM SIGPLAN Symposium on Principles and Practice of Parallel Programming, PPoPP 2010, pp. 115–126. ACM, New York (2010). https://doi.org/10.1145/1693453.1693471
6. Collingbourne, P., Cadar, C., Kelly, P.H.J.: Symbolic testing of OpenCL code. In: Eder, K., Lourenço, J., Shehory, O. (eds.) HVC 2011. LNCS, vol. 7261, pp. 203–218. Springer, Heidelberg (2012). https://doi.org/10.1007/978-3-642-34188-5_18
7. Cousot, P., Cousot, R.: Abstract interpretation: a unified lattice model for static analysis of programs by construction or approximation of fixpoints. In: Proceedings of the 4th ACM SIGACT-SIGPLAN Symposium on Principles of Programming Languages, POPL 1977, pp. 238–252. ACM, New York (1977). https://doi.org/10.1145/512950.512973
8. King, J.C.: A new approach to program testing. In: Proceedings of the International Conference on Reliable Software, pp. 228–233. ACM, New York (1975). https://doi.org/10.1145/800027.808444
9. Kofler, K., Cosenza, B., Fahringer, T.: Automatic data layout optimizations for GPUs. In: Träff, J.L., Hunold, S., Versaci, F. (eds.) Euro-Par 2015. LNCS, vol. 9233, pp. 263–274. Springer, Heidelberg (2015). https://doi.org/10.1007/978-3-662-48096-0_21
10. Leung, A., Gupta, M., Agarwal, Y., Gupta, R., Jhala, R., Lerner, S.: Verifying GPU kernels by test amplification. In: Proceedings of the 33rd ACM SIGPLAN Conference on Programming Language Design and Implementation, PLDI 2012, pp. 383–394. ACM, New York (2012). https://doi.org/10.1145/2254064.2254110
11. Li, G., Gopalakrishnan, G.: Scalable SMT-based verification of GPU kernel functions. In: Proceedings of the Eighteenth ACM SIGSOFT International Symposium on Foundations of Software Engineering, FSE 2010, pp. 187–196. ACM, New York (2010). https://doi.org/10.1145/1882291.1882320
12. Li, G., Li, P., Sawaya, G., Gopalakrishnan, G., Ghosh, I., Rajan, S.P.: GKLEE: concolic verification and test generation for GPUs. In: Proceedings of the 17th ACM SIGPLAN Symposium on Principles and Practice of Parallel Programming, PPoPP 2012, pp. 215–224. ACM, New York (2012). https://doi.org/10.1145/2145816.2145844
13. Liu, Y., Zhang, E.Z., Shen, X.: A cross-input adaptive framework for GPU program optimizations. In: 2009 IEEE International Symposium on Parallel Distributed Processing, pp. 1–10, May 2009

14. Magni, A., Dubach, C., O'Boyle, M.: Automatic optimization of thread-coarsening for graphics processors. In: Proceedings of the 23rd International Conference on Parallel Architectures and Compilation, PACT 2014, pp. 455–466. ACM, New York (2014). https://doi.org/10.1145/2628071.2628087

15. Miné, A.: Symbolic methods to enhance the precision of numerical abstract domains. In: Emerson, E.A., Namjoshi, K.S. (eds.) VMCAI 2006. LNCS, vol. 3855, pp. 348–363. Springer, Heidelberg (2005). https://doi.org/10.1007/11609773_23

16. Monakov, A., Lokhmotov, A., Avetisyan, A.: Automatically tuning sparse matrix-vector multiplication for GPU architectures. In: Patt, Y.N., Foglia, P., Duesterwald, E., Faraboschi, P., Martorell, X. (eds.) HiPEAC 2010. LNCS, vol. 5952, pp. 111–125. Springer, Heidelberg (2010). https://doi.org/10.1007/978-3-642-11515-8_10

17. Nickolls, J., Buck, I., Garland, M., Skadron, K.: Scalable parallel programming with CUDA. Queue 6(2), 40–53 (2008). https://doi.org/10.1145/1365490.1365500

18. Nielson, F., Nielson, H.R., Hankin, C.: Principles of Program Analysis. Springer, Heidelberg (2010)

19. Nvidia: Nvidia CUDA SDK. https://developer.nvidia.com/cuda-code-samples/

20. Ragan-Kelley, J., Barnes, C., Adams, A., Paris, S., Durand, F., Amarasinghe, S.: Halide: a language and compiler for optimizing parallelism, locality, and recomputation in image processing pipelines. In: Proceedings of the 34th ACM SIGPLAN Conference on Programming Language Design and Implementation, PLDI 2013, pp. 519–530. ACM, New York (2013). https://doi.org/10.1145/2491956.2462176

21. Ryoo, S., Rodrigues, C.I., Stone, S.S., Baghsorkhi, S.S., Ueng, S.Z., Stratton, J.A., Hwu, W.m.W.: Program optimization space pruning for a multithreaded GPU. In: Proceedings of the 6th Annual IEEE/ACM International Symposium on Code Generation and Optimization, CGO 2008, pp. 195–204. ACM, New York (2008). https://doi.org/10.1145/1356058.1356084

22. Sankaranarayanan, S., Ivančić, F., Gupta, A.: Program analysis using symbolic ranges. In: Nielson, H.R., Filé, G. (eds.) SAS 2007. LNCS, vol. 4634, pp. 366–383. Springer, Heidelberg (2007). https://doi.org/10.1007/978-3-540-74061-2_23. http://dl.acm.org/citation.cfm?id=2391451.2391476

23. Sørensen, H.H.B.: Auto-tuning dense vector and matrix-vector operations for Fermi GPUs. In: Wyrzykowski, R., Dongarra, J., Karczewski, K., Waśniewski, J. (eds.) PPAM 2011. LNCS, vol. 7203, pp. 619–629. Springer, Heidelberg (2012). https://doi.org/10.1007/978-3-642-31464-3_63

24. Stone, J.E., Gohara, D., Shi, G.: OpenCL: a parallel programming standard for heterogeneous computing systems. IEEE Des. Test 12(3), 66–73 (2010). https://doi.org/10.1109/MCSE.2010.69

25. Venet, A.J.: The gauge domain: scalable analysis of linear inequality invariants. In: Madhusudan, P., Seshia, S.A. (eds.) CAV 2012. LNCS, vol. 7358, pp. 139–154. Springer, Heidelberg (2012). https://doi.org/10.1007/978-3-642-31424-7_15

26. Weber, N., Goesele, M.: MATOG: array layout auto-tuning for CUDA. ACM Trans. Archit. Code Optim. 14(3), 28:1–28:26 (2017). https://doi.org/10.1145/3106341

27. Yang, Y., Xiang, P., Kong, J., Mantor, M., Zhou, H.: A unified optimizing compiler framework for different GPGPU architectures. ACM Trans. Archit. Code Optim. 9(2), 9:1–9:33 (2012). https://doi.org/10.1145/2207222.2207225

28. Zhang, Y., Mueller, F.: Auto-generation and auto-tuning of 3D stencil codes on GPU clusters. In: Proceedings of the Tenth International Symposium on Code Generation and Optimization, CGO 2012, pp. 155–164. ACM, New York (2012). https://doi.org/10.1145/2259016.2259037

Extending Constraint-Only Representation of Polyhedra with Boolean Constraints

Alexey Bakhirkin$^{(\boxtimes)}$ and David Monniaux

Univ. Grenoble Alpes, CNRS, Grenoble INP,
VERIMAG, 38000 Grenoble, France
{alexey.bakhirkin,david.monniaux}@univ-grenoble-alpes.fr

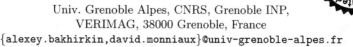

Abstract. We propose a new relational abstract domain for analysing programs with numeric and Boolean variables. The main idea is to represent an abstract state as a set of linear constraints over numeric variables, with every constraint being enabled by a formula over Boolean variables. This allows us, unlike in some existing approaches, to avoid duplicating linear constraints shared by multiple Boolean formulas. To perform domain operations, we adapt algorithms from constraint-only representation of convex polyhedra, most importantly Fourier-Motzkin elimination and projection-based convex hull. We made a prototype implementation of the new domain in our abstract interpreter for Horn clauses. Our initial experiments are, in our opinion, promising and show directions for future improvement.

1 Introduction and Related Work

Static program analysis by abstract interpretation over-approximates the set of reachable states of a program by a set with a simple description, for instance, by attaching one interval to each program variable at every location in the program. Intervals however cannot express relationships between variables, so a richer approach is to attach to every location a set of valid linear inequalities, which geometrically is, a *convex polyhedron* [12,17].

Convex polyhedra are already quite formidable objects to compute with efficiently, yet they are insufficient for expressing certain invariants, and what is often needed is a *disjunction* of convex polyhedra. For instance, the strongest invariant of the following loop: for(int i=0; i < n; i++){ } is $(n < 0) \lor (0 \leq i \leq n)$. Note how the disjunction arises from the partition of executions into those that execute the loop at least once and those that do not. Better analysis precision may often be achieved by partitioning executions according to an abstraction of the control flow [30], or by partitioning abstract states with respect to conditions extracted from the program [11], etc. Some analyses of programs operating over arrays and maps abstract properties over these objects

A. Bakhirkin and D. Monniaux—Institute of Engineering Univ. Grenoble Alpes.

A. Podelski (Ed.): SAS 2018, LNCS 11002, pp. 127–145, 2018.
https://doi.org/10.1007/978-3-319-99725-4_10

onto disjunctive relations between the scalar variables of the program and the values in the array cells [25,27]. For instance, a loop that fills an array `for (int i=0; i < n; i++){ a[i]=42; }` can be proved correct using an invariant $\forall k \ (0 \le i \le n) \wedge (0 \le k < i \rightarrow a[k] = 42)$, with a disjunction between the cases $k < i$ (filled) and $k \ge i$ (unfilled).[1]

In all cases, the analysis needs to efficiently represent sets of convex polyhedra, possibly (but not necessarily [4]) tagged by elements of a finite set T (abstract traces, Boolean vectors, etc.). Earlier works proposed to represent an abstract element by an explicit map from T to convex polyhedra, either as an array of pairs (T_i, P_i) where $T_i \subseteq T$ and P_i are polyhedra, or as a decision tree or DAG with polyhedra at the leaves. Both approaches are implemented in Jeannet's BddApron library [19].

One issue with this approach is that the possible number of abstract partitions is often exponential in some parameter (length of the recorded trace, number of Boolean variables) and thus every operation (post-condition, convex hull) is potentially repeated for each of the exponentially many polyhedra. At the same time, the polyhedra in different abstract partitions often share most of the constraints and only differ in few that are related to the partitioning criterion. Thus, it is tempting to store a set of polyhedra in some structure that does not require duplicating shared constraints, and to use symbolic algorithms that, as much as possible, avoid enumerating abstract partitions individually.

One approach to this is offered by different kinds of decision diagrams over linear constraints. A notable example is Linear Decision Diagrams (LDD) developed by Chaki, Gurfinkel, and Strichman [10]. An LDD is a DAG, where internal nodes are labelled with linear constraints, and the two leaves are *true* and *false*, thus a path through an LDD corresponds to a convex polyhedron. Based on the LDD algorithms, the same authors later developed an abstract domain of boxes [15], that only allows to have a comparison of a variable with a constant in an interior node.

Theoretical Contribution. In this paper, we propose an alternative approach: to represent an abstract state as a set of implications $\{B_i \rightarrow c_i\}_{i=0..k}$, where B_i are arbitrary Boolean formulas, and c_i are linear constraints. This way, an abstract element can still be seen as an implicit map from a partition of $\mathbb{B}^m$ to convex polyhedra (similar to a BddApron element), but we do not have to duplicate storage and computations for constraints shared by multiple partitions. Another appeal of this approach is that some operations on constraint-only polyhedra can be naturally adapted to sets of implications of the form $B_i \rightarrow c_i$. The algorithms in this paper are based on Fourier-Motzkin elimination [28] and the reduction of convex hull to projection of Benoy, King, and Mesnard [7,31]. Whether it is possible to also adapt the more recent algorithms based on parametric linear programming and raytracing by Maréchal, Monniaux, and Périn [21–23] is a question for future work.

---

[1] $\rightarrow$ denotes logical implication.

The Boolean variables occurring in the formulas B_i may be program variables (from small enumerated types) but may also be *observers*, partitioning according to trace history or calling context. This solves one issue with untagged disjunctions of polyhedra: when applying the widening operator to $\bigcup_i P_i$ and $\bigcup_j Q_j$, how does one "match" the P_i's and Q_j's to perform conventional widening over polyhedra [4]? Similarly, for the "join" operation $(\bigcup_i P_i) \sqcup (\bigcup_j Q_j)$, does one simply concatenate the two unions while removing duplicates (thus creating longer and longer lists), or does one "match" some P_i and Q_j for convex hull, and if so under which criteria? In our case, widening and join are guided by the Boolean variables: the polyhedra associated to the same Boolean choice are matched together.

Experimental Evaluation. We made a prototype implementation of the proposed abstract domain in our abstract interpreter for Horn clauses [5,6].

2   Notation

We consider programs with Boolean and rational variables: a concrete program state is a tuple $(\mathbf{b}, \mathbf{x}) \in \mathbb{B}^m \times \mathbb{Q}^n$. We use bold lowercase symbols $\mathbf{b} \in \mathbb{B}^m$ and $\mathbf{x} \in \mathbb{Q}^n$ to denote valuations of Boolean and numeric variables respectively. We use lowercase Italic symbols b and x respectively to denote vectors of Boolean and rational variables. We refer to the j-th variable in x as $x_{(j)}$. We use other lowercase Italic symbols, e.g., a, d, to denote vector and scalar coefficients, and their meaning will be clear within their context.

Without loss of generality, we make a number of assumptions on the syntactic form of linear constraints. We assume that there exists the unique unsatisfiable linear constraint *cfalse*, i.e. we will not distinguish logically equivalent, but syntactically different falsities: $0 < 0$, $1 \geq 2$, etc. We assume that every linear constraint c_i is written as a greater-or-equal constraint with integer coefficients, i.e. $c_i = a_i x \succ d_i$, where $a_i \in \mathbb{N}^n$, $d_i \in \mathbb{N}$, and $\succ \in \{=, \geq, >\}$.

We sometimes write a Boolean or a linear constraint as $B[b]$ or $c[x]$ to emphasize that free variables in B and c come from vectors b and x respectively. We use the $[/]$ notation to denote substitution. For example, $B[b_{(j)}/true]$ denotes the result of substituting in B the variable $b_{(j)}$ with *true*. As a shortcut, we write $B[\mathbf{b}]$ to denote the result of substituting every free variable in B with its valuation given by $\mathbf{b}$.

3   Abstract Domain of Boolean and Linear Constraints

We propose to represent an abstract state as a set of implications:

$$S = \{B_i \to c_i\}_{i=0..k}$$

where B_i is a propositional formula over Boolean variables, and c_i is a linear constraint (equality or inequality) over numeric variables. We do *not* want B_i to be a partition of $\mathbb{B}^m$. Our intention is to never duplicate linear constraints that are shared by multiple valuations of Boolean variables.

An abstract state S represents the set of concrete states:

$$\gamma(S) = \left\{ (\mathbf{b}, \mathbf{x}) \mid \bigwedge_{i=0}^{k} B_i[\mathbf{b}] \rightarrow c_i[\mathbf{x}] \right\}$$

Alternatively, one can see an abstract state as a function that maps every valuation of Boolean variables to a convex polyhedron that describes the possible values of numeric variables. This is captured by the partial concretization γ_b:

$$\gamma_b(S) = \left\{ \mathbf{b} \mapsto \bigwedge_{B_i[\mathbf{b}]} c_i \mid \mathbf{b} \in \mathbb{B}^m \right\}$$

The notion of partial concretization is useful when we want to show that we correctly lift operations on sets of constraints (e.g., projection) from linear constraints to implications $B_i \rightarrow c_i$. We normally want a operation to commute with γ_b, i.e., $\gamma_b(f_{\text{lifted}}(S))(\mathbf{b}) = f_{\text{original}}(\gamma_b(S)(\mathbf{b}))$, which would mean that there is no loss of precision on the Boolean level.

Without loss of generality, we assume that in every abstract state, the 0-th constraint has the form $B_0 \rightarrow \textit{cfalse}$, and no other constraint has $\textit{cfalse}$ on the right-hand side. In particular, the empty polyhedron is represented by $\perp = \{\textit{true} \rightarrow \textit{cfalse}\}$ and the universal polyhedron is represented by $\top = \{\textit{false} \rightarrow \textit{cfalse}\}$.

Example 1. The abstract state where $x_{(0)}$ is always non-negative, and in addition, if $b_{(0)}$ holds, $x_{(0)}$ is not greater than 1 can be represented as

$$\{\textit{false} \rightarrow \textit{cfalse}, \ \textit{true} \rightarrow x_{(0)} \geq 0, \ b_{(0)} \rightarrow x_{(0)} \leq 1\}$$

3.1   Elimination of a Rational Variable

In constraint-only representation, existential quantifier elimination (projection) is the main operation on polyhedra, and most other operations are expressed using projection.

We can naturally adapt Fourier-Motzkin elimination [14,18,28] to our abstract domain in the following way. Let an abstract element S be $\{B_i \rightarrow c_i\}_{i=0..k}$ and let $x_{(j)}$ be the variable to eliminate. First, we split every equality where $x_{(j)}$ appears with nonzero coefficient into a pair of inequalities. Then, we partition the constraints into three sets:

1. E_0, where in the linear part $x_{(j)}$ appears with coefficient 0;
2. E_+, where in the linear part $x_{(j)}$ appears with a positive coefficient;
3. E^-, where in the linear part $x_{(j)}$ appears with a negative coefficient.

The constraints from E_0 we keep as-is, and from every pair of constraints in E_+ and E_-, we produce a positive combination, in which $x_{(j)}$ has coefficient 0. The difference from the original Fourier-Motzkin algorithm is that when we combine two constraints, we conjoin their Boolean parts. This is summarized in Fig. 1.

$$eliminateR(x_{(j)}, S) \equiv E_0 \cup \{ combine(j, B_+ \to c_+, B_- \to c_-) \mid B^+ \to c_+ \in E_+,$$
$$B_- \to c_- \in E_- \},$$

where

$$E_0 = \{B_i \to a_i x > d_i \in S \mid a_i(j) = 0\}$$
$$E_+ = \{B_i \to a_i x > d_i \in S \mid a_i(j) > 0\}$$
$$E_- = \{B_i \to a_i x > d_i \in S \mid a_i(j) < 0\}$$
$$combine(j, B_1 \to c_1, B_2 \to c_2) = B_1 \wedge B_2 \to \lambda_1 c_1 + \lambda_2 c_2, \text{ s.t. } \lambda_1, \lambda_2 > 0, \text{ and}$$
$$\text{in } \lambda_1 c_1 + \lambda_2 c_2, x_{(j)} \text{ appears with coefficient } 0$$

Fig. 1. Elimination of the variable $x_{(j)}$. Assuming that every equality that contains $x_{(j)}$ was replaced by a pair of inequalities.

Example 2. Let

$$S = \{true \to x_{(0)} - x_{(1)} = 0, b_{(0)} \to x_{(0)} \geq 0, \overset{.}{b}_{(1)} \to -x_{(1)} \geq -1\}$$

and let us apply the Fourier-Motzkin-based elimination to the variable $x_{(0)}$. First, we partition the constraints into the three sets:

$$E_0 = \{b_{(1)} \to -x_{(1)} \geq -1\}$$
$$E_+ = \{true \to x_{(0)} - x_{(1)} \geq 0, b_{(0)} \to x_{(0)} \geq 0\}$$
$$E_- = \{true \to -x_{(0)} + x_{(1)} \geq 0\}$$

We keep the elements of E_0 and combine the elements of E_+ and E_-, producing the set

$$\{b_{(1)} \to -x_{(1)} \geq -1, \; true \to 0 \geq 0, \; b_{(0)} \to x_{(1)} \geq 0\} =$$
$$\{b_{(1)} \to -x_{(1)} \geq -1, \; b_{(0)} \to x_{(1)} \geq 0\}$$

In this case, we only need to eliminate the trivially valid constraint $true \to 0 \geq 0$; in general Fourier-Motzkin elimination can produce constraints that are non-trivially redundant.

Lemma 1. *For every abstract state S, rational variable $x_{(j)}$, and $\mathbf{b} \in \mathbb{B}^m$,*

$$\gamma_b(eliminateR(x_{(j)}, S))(\mathbf{b}) \leftrightarrow \exists x_{(j)}. \gamma_b(S)(\mathbf{b})$$

Proof Idea. To prove Lemma 1, we can pick an arbitrary $\mathbf{b} \in \mathbb{B}^m$ and show that the set of linear constraints $\{c_i \mid B_i \to c_i \in eliminateR(j, S) \wedge B_i[\mathbf{b}]\}$ is the same as the set of constraints produced by applying standard Fourier-Motzkin elimination to $\gamma_b(S)(\mathbf{b})$.

To eliminate multiple rational variables, we apply *eliminateR* iteratively. The standard heuristic is to pick and eliminate in every step a variable that minimizes $|E_+||E_-| - |E_+| - |E_-|$, which is the upper bound on the growth of the number of constraints.

Gaussian Elimination. When an abstract element contains an equality $true \to ax = d$, where $a_{(j)} \neq 0$, this equality can be used as a definition of the variable $x_{(j)}$. Then, to eliminate the $x_{(j)}$ from an abstract element, we can replace it with this definition in every remaining constraint, instead of performing Fourier-Motzkin elimination. This is useful for eliminating, e.g., temporary variables that an analysis may introduce when pre-processing the program.

Example 3. Let

$$S = \{ true \to x_{(0)} - x_{(1)} = 0, b_{(0)} \to x_{(0)} \geq 0, b_{(1)} \to -x_{(1)} \geq -1 \}$$

and let us apply the Gaussian elimination to the variable $x_{(0)}$, using the equality $true \to x_{(0)} - x_{(1)} = 0$. That is, we replace $x_{(0)}$ with $x_{(1)}$ in the two remaining constraints, getting

$$\{ b_{(0)} \to x_{(1)} \geq 0, b_{(1)} \to -x_{(1)} \geq -1 \}$$

This can be generalized to the case when the abstract element contains a subset of equalities $\{ B_j \to a_j x = d_j \}_{j=1..m} \subseteq S$, s.t. $\bigvee_{j=1}^{m} B_j = true$, as shown in Fig. 2

$gaussEliminateR(x_{(j)}, S) \equiv \{ combine(j, B_i \to c_i, B_= \to c_=) \mid B_i \to c_i \in S, B_= \to c_= \in E_= \},$

where

$E_= = \{ B_j \to a_j x = d_j \}_{j=1..m} \in S,$ s.t. $a_{j_{(x)}} \neq 0, \bigvee_{j=1}^{m} B_j = true,$

$combine(j, B_1 \to c_1, B_2 \to c_2) = B_1 \wedge B_2 \to \lambda_1 c_1 + \lambda_2 c_2,$ s.t. $\lambda_1 > 0,$ and

in $\lambda_1 c_1 + \lambda_2 c_2, x_{(j)}$ appears with coefficient 0

Fig. 2. Generalization of Gaussian elimination of the variable $x_{(j)}$.

3.2   Equivalent and Redundant Constraints

When working with constraint-only representation of polyhedra, one of the big challenges is eliminating redundant constraints. As shown above, every round of Fourier-Motzkin elimination creates a quadratic number of new constraints, an most of them are usually redundant. When eliminating multiple variables (notably, during join computation, see Sect. 3.3), redundant constraints have to be eliminated regularly, otherwise their number might grow in a double-exponential way (while McMullen's upper bound theorem [24] implies that the number of non-redundant constraints cannot grow more than exponentially with the number of projected dimensions). In his work on constraint-only representation of polyhedra [13], A. Fouilhé argues for redundancy elimination after eliminating every variable. The conventional approach to redundancy elimination in a list of n constraints is to go over every constrain and use linear programming test whether it is redundant with respect to the $n - 1$ other ones (some other criteria [18,20] cannot eliminate all redundancies. "Raytracing" [23] is a fast method to identify redundancies, but it degenerates into the conventional linear programming approach in the worst case). We adapt that approach to the Boolean setting: to check whether a constraint is redundant, we call an SMT solver. We also implement a number of less costly redundancy checks.

Pairwise Redundancy Checks. There is a number of reductions that can be implemented without necessarily calling an SMT solver.

First, we can combine constraints with identical linear part:

$$\{B_1 \rightarrow c, B_2 \rightarrow c\} \equiv \{B_1 \lor B_2 \rightarrow c\}$$

This is an important step that allows to not duplicate linear constraints; duplication would be amplified by Fourier-Motzkin elimination.

Second, we can eliminate a constraint if it is implied by another constraint:

$$\text{if } B_2 \rightarrow B_1 \land c_1 \rightarrow c_2, \text{ then}$$
$$\{B_1 \rightarrow c_1, B_2 \rightarrow c_2\} \equiv \{B_1 \rightarrow c_1\}$$

This requires a procedure to efficiently check implication between Boolean formulas, which is available, e.g., if they are represented as BDDs. Implication between a pair of linear constraints is a straightforward syntactic check.

Pairwise reduction checks reduce the number of SMT calls, which are costly. This is especially important in lower dimensions and when few constraints are relational. In these cases, most of redundant constraints can be eliminated with pairwise checks.

SMT-Based Redundancy Check. Let $S = \{B_i \rightarrow c_i\}_{i=0..k}$. Then the j-th constraint is redundant, if its negation is unsatisfiable with respect to the other constraints:

$$isRedundant(j, S) \equiv B_j \land \neg c_j \land \bigwedge_{i=0..k, i \neq j} (B_i \rightarrow c_i) \text{ is UNSAT}$$

An SMT-based redundancy check is an expensive operation, but it has to be performed regularly to limit the growth of the number of constraints.

In general, for a given abstract state S, there may be no unique smallest set of non-redundant constraints. Currently, we implement a greedy strategy: we successively check every constraint and if it is redundant, immediately eliminate it, before checking other constraints. We can artificially make this procedure deterministic by ordering the constraints; in particular it is beneficial to first attempt to remove constraints with larger absolute values of coefficients, both for human-readable output and for performance of an SMT solver.

Example 4. Let

$$S = \{true \rightarrow x_{(0)} \geq 0, \ b_{(0)} \rightarrow x_{(0)} \geq -1, \ b_{(1)} \rightarrow x_{(1)} \geq 0, \ b_{(1)} \rightarrow x_{(0)} + x_{(1)} \geq 0\}$$

Let us remove redundant constraints from this system. First, we note that $(true \rightarrow x_{(0)} \geq 0) \rightarrow (b_{(0)} \rightarrow x_{(0)} \geq -1)$, since $b_{(0)} \rightarrow true$ and $x_{(0)} \geq 0 \rightarrow x_{(0)} \geq -1$, thus the latter constraint is redundant. Second, we note that:

$$(true \rightarrow x_{(0)} \geq 0) \wedge (b_{(1)} \rightarrow x_{(1)} \geq 0) \wedge b_{(1)} \wedge x_{(0)} + x_{(1)} < 0 \text{ is UNSAT}$$

Thus, the remaining non-redundant constraints are:

$$\{ true \rightarrow x_{(0)} \geq 0, \, b_{(1)} \rightarrow x_{(1)} \geq 0 \}$$

3.3   Join

To perform join of two abstract elements, we adapt the projection-based convex hull computation of Benoy et al. [7,31]. The original algorithm is based on the observation that every point in the convex hull is a convex combination of a pair of points from the original polyhedra. Figure 3 expresses this more formally and adapted to our setting. Given the two abstract elements S_1 and S_2, first we construct the set of constraints S_{12}. The variables λ_1, λ_2 are the scaling coefficients of the two points in S_1 and S_2 respectively, s.t. $\lambda_1, \lambda_2 \geq 0$ and $\lambda_1 + \lambda_2 = 1$; y_1 an y_2 are the vectors of coordinates of the two points, pre-multiplied by scaling coefficients, and thus should satisfy the pre-multiplied constraints of S_1 and S_2; finally x is the vector of coordinates of a point in the convex hull, and thus $x = y_1 + y_2$. Eliminating y_1, y_2, λ_1, and λ_2 from S_{12} produces the closure of the convex hull. With some extra bookkeeping, it is then possible to express the resulting linear constraints in terms of the original constraints [13] and turn some closed constraints back into open (a positive combination a set of constraints, where at least one constraints is open, is also open).

$convexHull(S_1, S_2) \equiv eliminateR(\{y_1, y_2, \lambda_1, \lambda_2\}, S_{12}),$ where

$S_{12} = \{B_i^1 \rightarrow a_i^1 y_1 \geq d_i^1 \lambda_1 \mid B_i^1 \rightarrow a_i^1 x > d_i^1 \in S_1\} \cup$

$\quad \{B_i^2 \rightarrow a_i^2 y_2 \geq d_i^2 \lambda_2 \mid B_i^2 \rightarrow a_i^2 x > d_i^2 \in S_2\} \cup$

$\quad \{true \rightarrow \lambda_1 \geq 0, \, true \rightarrow \lambda_2 \geq 0, \, true \rightarrow \lambda_1 + \lambda_2 = 1\} \cup$

$\quad \{true \rightarrow x_{(j)} = y_1(j) + y_2(j) \mid j = 1..n\} \cup$

$\quad \{B_0^1 \rightarrow \lambda_1 = 0, \, B_0^2 \rightarrow \lambda_2 = 0 \mid B_0^1 \rightarrow cfalse \in S_1, \, B_0^2 \rightarrow cfalse \in S_2\}$

Fig. 3. Convex hull of two abstract states. The sign $\succeq$ stands for the closed version of the corresponding sign $\succ$. When $\succ$ is $>$, $\succeq$ is $\geq$; otherwise $\succeq$ is the same as $\succ$.

Lemma 2. *For every pair of abstract states S_1, S_2 and every $\mathbf{b} \in \mathbb{B}^m$,*

$$\gamma_b(join(S_1, S_2))(\mathbf{b}) = \gamma_b(S_1)(\mathbf{b}) \sqcup \gamma_b(S_2)\mathbf{b}$$

Proof Idea. To prove Lemma 2, similarly to Lemma 1, we can pick an arbitrary $\mathbf{b} \in \mathbb{B}^m$ and show that the set of constraints S_{12} in Fig. 3 is the same as the set of constraints generated by F. Benoy's convex hull applied to $\gamma_b(S_1)(\mathbf{b})$ and $\gamma_b(S_2)\mathbf{b}$.

Join of Elements with Disjoint Pure Boolean Constraints. Let S_1, S_2 be a pair of abstract elements:

$$S_1 = \{B_0^1 \rightarrow \mathit{cfalse}\} \cup \{B_i^1 \dashrightarrow c_i^1\}_{i=1..n} \quad S_2 = \{B_0^2 \rightarrow \mathit{cfalse}\} \cup \{B_j^2 \rightarrow c_j^2\}_{j=1..m},$$

where $\neg B_0^1 \wedge \neg B_0^2 = \mathit{false}$, i.e., their pure Boolean constraints are disjoint, and for a given valuation of Boolean variables $\mathbf{b}$, at least one of the polyhedra $\gamma_\mathbf{b}(S_1)(\mathbf{b})$, $\gamma_\mathbf{b}(S_2)(\mathbf{b})$ is empty. In this case, S_1 and S_2 can be joined exactly and without computing the convex hull as follows:

$$boolDisjointJoin(S_1, S_2) \equiv \{B_i^1 \wedge \neg B_0^1 \rightarrow c_i^1\}_{i=1..n} \cup \{B_j^2 \wedge \neg B_0^2 \rightarrow c_j^2\}_{j=1..m} \cup$$
$$\{B_0^1 \wedge B_0^2 \rightarrow \mathit{cfalse}\}$$

As we later show, this optimization is important for efficient elimination of Boolean variables. Soundness can be shown by writing down the disjunction of logical formulas corresponding to S_1 and S_2, distributing the disjunction over the conjunctions and applying equivalences that follow from $\neg B_0^1 \wedge \neg B_0^2 = \mathit{false}$. Let S_1, S_2 be a pair of abstract elements:

$$S_1 = \{B_0^1 \rightarrow \mathit{cfalse}\} \cup \{B_i^1 \rightarrow c_i^1\}_{i=1..n} \quad S_2 = \{B_0^2 \rightarrow \mathit{cfalse}\} \cup \{B_j^2 \rightarrow c_j^2\}_{j=1..m},$$

where $\neg B_0^1 \wedge \neg B_0^2 = \mathit{false}$. Let us observe the disjunction of their corresponding logical characterizations:

$$((B_0^1 \rightarrow \mathit{cfalse}) \wedge (\bigwedge_{i=1}^{n} B_i^1 \rightarrow c_i^1)) \vee ((B_0^2 \rightarrow \mathit{cfalse}) \wedge (\bigwedge_{j=1}^{m} B_j^2 \rightarrow c_j^2))$$

Conjoining the pure boolean constraints to numeric constraints

$$=((B_0^1 \rightarrow \mathit{cfalse}) \wedge (\bigwedge_{i=1}^{n} B_i^1 \wedge \neg B_0^1 \rightarrow c_i^1)) \vee ((B_0^2 \rightarrow \mathit{cfalse}) \wedge (\bigwedge_{j=1}^{m} B_j^2 \wedge \neg B_0^2 \rightarrow c_j^2)) =$$

Distributing the disjunction

$$= \bigwedge_{i=1..n, j=1..m} (\neg B_i^1 \vee B_0^1 \vee c_i^1 \vee \neg B_j^2 \vee B_0^2 \vee c_j^2) \wedge$$
$$\bigwedge_{i=1}^{n} (\neg B_i^1 \vee B_0^1 \vee c_i^1 \vee \neg B_0^2 \vee \mathit{cfalse}) \wedge$$
$$\bigwedge_{j=1}^{m} (\neg B_j^2 \vee B_0^2 \vee c_j^2 \vee \neg B_0^1 \vee \mathit{cfalse}) \wedge$$
$$(\neg B_0^1 \vee \mathit{cfalse} \vee \neg B_0^2 \vee \mathit{cfalse})$$

From $\neg B_0^1 \wedge \neg B_0^2 = \mathit{false}$ it follows that $B_0^1 \vee B_0^2 = \mathit{true}$, $\neg B_0^1 \rightarrow B_0^2$, and $\neg B_0^2 \rightarrow B_0^1$

$$= \bigwedge_{i=1}^{n} (B_i^1 \wedge \neg B_0^1 \rightarrow c_i^1) \wedge \bigwedge_{j=1}^{m} (B_j^2 \wedge \neg B_0^2 \rightarrow c_j^2) \wedge (B_0^1 \wedge B_0^2 \rightarrow \mathit{cfalse})$$

Which is the logical characterization of $boolDisjointJoin(S_1, S_2)$.

3.4   Other Operations

Intersection with a Constraint. To intersect an abstract state S with a constraint $B \to c$, we add $B \to c$ to S. To intersect an abstract state S with a linear constraint c, we add $true \to c$ to S. To intersect an abstract state S with a Boolean constraint B, we add $\neg B \to cfalse$ to S.

Linear Assignment. The general way to apply a linear assignment $x_{(j)} := ax + d$ is by renaming and elimination. We introduce a fresh variable $x'_{(j)}$ that denotes the value of $x_{(j)}$ after or before the assignment, relate it to $x_{(j)}$, eliminate $x_{(j)}$ and then rename $x'_{(j)}$ into $x_{(j)}$:

$$post(x_{(j)} := ax + d, S) \equiv eliminateR(x_{(j)}, S \cup \{x'_{(j)} = ax + d\})[x'_{(j)}/x_{(j)}]$$
$$pre(x_{(j)} := ax + d, S) \equiv eliminateR(x_{(j)}, S \cup \{x_{(j)} = (ax + d)[x_{(j)}/x'_{(j)}]\})[x'_{(j)}/x_{(j)}]$$

This applies to both invertible (where in $ax + d$, $x_{(j)}$ has a non-zero coefficient) and non-invertible assignments. Invertible assignments (e.g. $a := 2a+1$) can also be implemented by substituting the inverted expressions (e.g. $a \mapsto (a - 1)/2$) into the constraints [12, Sect. 4.2.2.1].

Elimination of a Boolean Variable. We use the equivalence $\exists b \in \mathbb{B}. \varphi = \varphi[b/true] \vee \varphi[b/false]$ over-approximate logical disjunction with the join operation:

$$eliminateB(b_{(j)}, S) \equiv join(S[b_{(j)}/true], S[b_{(j)}/false])$$

Example 5. Let

$$S = \{b_{(0)} \to x_{(0)} = 0, \; b_{(0)} \to x_{(1)} = 0, \; \neg b_{(0)} \to x_{(0)} = 1, \; \neg b_{(0)} \to x_{(0)} = 1\}$$

That is, when $b_{(0)}$ is $true$, $x_{(0)} = x_{(1)} = 0$, and when $b_{(0)}$ is $false$, $x_{(0)} = x_{(1)} = 0$. To eliminate the single Boolean variable $b_{(0)}$, we take the join of the two abstract elements:

$$S[b_{(0)}/true] = \{true \to x_{(0)} = 0, \; true \to x_{(1)} = 0\}$$
$$S[b_{(0)}/false] = \{true \to x_{(0)} = 1, \; true \to x_{(1)} = 1\}$$

One possible representation of the result is

$$eliminateB(b_{(0)}, S) = \{true \to x_{(0)} \geq 0, \; true \to -x_{(0)} \geq -1, \; true \to x_{(0)} - x_{(1)} = 0\}$$

Example 6. For an example of a join of two Boolean-disjoint abstract states, let us consider the abstract state

$$S = \{true \to x_{(0)} \geq 0, \; b_{(0)} \to -x_{(0)} \geq -1, \; b_{(0)} \neq b_{(1)} \to false\}$$

and let us eliminate the variable $b_{(0)}$ from it. Notice that this abstract state asserts that $b_{(0)} = b_{(1)}$, and thus we expect that the elimination will result in substituting $b_{(0)}$ with $b_{(1)}$ in every constraint. First, we compute

$$S[b_{(0)}/true] = \{true \to x_{(0)} \geq 0, \; true \to -x_{(0)} \geq -1, \; \neg b_{(1)} \to false\}$$
$$S[b_{(0)}/false] = \{true \to x_{(0)} \geq 0, \; b_{(1)} \to false\}$$

Then, we observe that these abstract states are Boolean-disjoint, since $\neg\neg b_{(1)} \wedge \neg b_{(1)} = \textit{false}$, i.e., we can apply the specialized version on join and, as expected, get

$$boolDisjointJoin(S[b_{(0)}/true], S[b_{(0)}/false])$$
$$= \{b_{(1)} \to x_{(0)} \geq 0,\ b_{(1)} \to -x_{(0)} \geq -1,\ \neg b_{(1)} \to x_{(0)} \geq 0\}$$
$$= \{true \to x_{(0)} \geq 0,\ b_{(1)} \to -x_{(0)} \geq -1\}$$

This example demonstrates a common scenario when eliminating temporary Boolean variables. The eliminated variable may be introduced using an explicit equality, like in this example, or in some similar way that makes it so that restricting this variable to *true* and *false* respectively produces Boolean-disjoint elements. Having a specialized join operation for Boolean-disjoint abstract states is important when an analysis may transform the input program and introduce such variables.

Boolean Assignment. An assignment of the form $b_{(j)} := B$ we implement, similarly to the linear case, using renaming and elimination:

$$post(b_{(j)} := B, S) \equiv eliminateB(b_{(j)}, S \cup \{\neg(b'_{(j)} \leftrightarrow B) \to cfalse\})[b'_{(j)}/b_{(j)}]$$
$$pre(b_{(j)} := B, S) \equiv eliminateB(b_{(j)}, S \cup \{\neg(b_{(j)} \leftrightarrow B[b_{(j)}/b'_{(j)}]) \to cfalse\})[b'_{(j)}/b_{(j)}]$$

Linear to Boolean Assignment. In some cases, during the analysis we want to introduce an observer variable – a Boolean variable that the stores truth value of some linear constraint at some point of program execution. When c is an inequality (not an equality), the assignment $b_{(j)} := c$ is straightforward to implement, since the equivalence $b \leftrightarrow c$ can be represented as a pair of constraints: $b \to c, \neg b \to \neg c$. That is,

$$post(b_{(j)} := c, S) \equiv eliminateB(b_{(j)}, S \cup \{b'_{(j)} \to c, \neg b'_{(j)} \to \neg c\})[b'_{(j)}/b_{(j)}]$$

and similarly for *pre*. For an equality $ax = d$, though, we cannot assign its truth value to a single Boolean variable. Instead, we have to use two Boolean variables to separately assign to them the truth values of $ax \geq d$ and $-ax \geq -d$.

Widening. Widening in convex polyhedra is based on the idea of keeping the constraints of the previous approximation that are also satisfied by the new approximation [3,17]. In our setting, we want, for every linear constraint from the previous approximation, to find for which values of Boolean variables it is implied by the new approximation. To find for which values of Booleans an inequality c is implied by an abstract state S, we can conjoin $true \to \neg c$ to S and then eliminate all the rational variables. This produces an abstract state of the form $\{B \to cfalse\}$ which is interpreted as: when B holds, $\neg c$ is unsatisfiable in S and thus $B \to c$ is implied by S. Thus, assuming that every equality is first split into a pair of inequalities and that $S_1 \sqsubseteq S_2$, we get:

$$widen(S_1, S_2) \equiv \left\{ B_i^3 \to c_i^1 \middle| \begin{array}{l} B_i^1 \to c_i^1 \in S_1 \wedge \\ eliminateR(x, S_2 \cup \{true \to \neg c_i^1\}) = \{B_i^3 \to cfalse\} \end{array} \right\} \cup$$
$$\{B_0^2 \to cfalse \mid B_0^2 \to cfalse \in S_2\}$$

Inclusion Test. To check for inclusion between abstract states, we currently use an SMT solver. Let $S_1 = \{B_i^1 \to c_i^1\}_{i=0..k_1}$ and $S_2 = \{B_j^2 \to c_j^2\}_{j=0..k_2}$. Then

$$S_1 \sqsubseteq S_2 \equiv \left(\bigwedge_{i=0}^{k_1} B_i^1 \to c_i^1 \right) \wedge \neg \left(\bigwedge_{j=0}^{k_2} B_j^2 \to c_j^2 \right) \text{ is UNSAT}$$

Checking, whether an abstract state S is empty, i.e., whether $S \sqsubseteq \bot$ also requires an SMT solver call.

3.5 Implementation Details

Representing Boolean Formulas. We currently propose to represent Boolean formulas with BDDs, the main reason being that BDDs allow to represent formulas in a canonical way and avoid unbounded syntactic growth, when formulas are repeatedly conjoined (during elimination) and disjoined (when combining constraints with coinciding linear part).

Constraints over Integer Variables. To achieve additional precision, we can rewrite linear constraints when every variable with a non-zero coefficient is integer. In this case, a strict inequality can be rewritten as non-strict:

$$ax > d \equiv ax \geq d + 1$$

For an inequality over integer variables, we can divide the coefficients of a constraint over integer variables by the GCD of the variable coefficients, rounding the free coefficient towards 0:

$$ax \geq d \equiv (a/g)x \geq round(d/g), \text{ where } g = \gcd a$$

For an equality over integer variables, the free coefficient has to be divisible by the GCD of the variable coefficients, otherwise the equality is unsatisfiable.

4 Implementation and Experiments

We implemented the proposed abstract domain in our abstract interpreter for Horn clauses [5,6]. Our tool can find models of systems of constrained Horn clauses [9] with predicates over numeric and Boolean variables. It is based on the technique of path focusing [26] and uses an SMT solver (Z3) to iterate over relevant disjuncts of the direct consequence relation. As the abstract domain, it supports BddApron [19] and now also the abstract domain that we propose in this paper. The tool is implemented in OCaml.

4.1   Example

Figure 4 shows an example of a kind of a program that we are interested in. Figure 4 is a typical result of instrumenting a program with Boolean observer variables that record which branches were taken during an execution. At every step, this program non-deterministically chooses whether to assume a constraint on a numeric variable $x_{(i)}$, and the choice is recorder in a Boolean variable $b_{(i)}$. At this point, we do not care how exactly this program was obtained, and we are interested in efficiently computing invariants in a way that allows to relate Boolean and numeric variables. Our original motivation though comes from using observer variables for trace partitioning in array-manipulating programs [27], where different branches correspond to different relations between array indices.

Figure 5 encodes the example program as a system of Horn clauses that can be processed by our tool. In this system, predicates $P_0, \cdots, P_3$ denote the invariants of the four program locations, and every Horn clause corresponds to one transition (in general, a clause may encode multiple sequences of statements). The smallest model of the system in Fig. 5 is the collecting semantics of the program in Fig. 4.

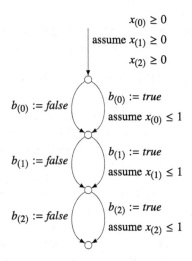

$$x_{(0)} \geq 0$$
$$\text{assume } x_{(1)} \geq 0$$
$$x_{(2)} \geq 0$$

$b_{(0)} := false$ $b_{(0)} := true$
$\quad\quad\quad$ assume $x_{(0)} \leq 1$

$b_{(1)} := false$ $b_{(1)} := true$
$\quad\quad\quad$ assume $x_{(1)} \leq 1$

$b_{(2)} := false$ $b_{(2)} := true$
$\quad\quad\quad$ assume $x_{(2)} \leq 1$

$$x_{(0)} \geq 0 \wedge x_{(1)} \geq 0 \wedge x_{(2)} \geq 0 \rightarrow P_0(x, b)$$
$$P_0(x, b) \wedge \neg b_{(0)} \rightarrow P_1(x, b)$$
$$P_0(x, b) \wedge b_{(0)} \wedge x_{(0)} \leq 1 \rightarrow P_1(x, b)$$
$$P_1(x, b) \wedge \neg b_{(1)} \rightarrow P_2(x, b)$$
$$P_1(x, b) \wedge b_{(1)} \wedge x_{(1)} \leq 1 \rightarrow P_2(x, b)$$
$$P_2(x, b) \wedge \neg b_{(2)} \rightarrow P_3(x, b)$$
$$P_2(x, b) \wedge b_{(2)} \wedge x_{(2)} \leq 1 \rightarrow P_3(x, b)$$

Fig. 4. An example of a program instrumented with observer variables.

Fig. 5. An encoding of the program in Fig. 4 into Horn clauses for our tool.

The original implementation of our tool used the BddApron abstract domain, and the invariant that it infers for the predicate P_3 (the final program location) consists of 8 polyhedra, one for every valuation of Boolean variables:

$$(\neg b_{(0)} \neg b_{(1)} \neg b_{(2)} \wedge x_{(0)} \geq 0 \wedge x_{(1)} \geq 0 \wedge x_{(2)} \geq 0) \vee$$
$$(\neg b_{(0)} \neg b_{(1)} b_{(2)} \wedge x_{(0)} \geq 0 \wedge x_{(1)} \geq 0 \wedge 1 \geq x_{(2)} \geq 0) \vee$$
$$\cdots \vee$$
$$(b_{(0)} b_{(1)} b_{(2)} \wedge 1 \geq x_{(0)} \geq 0 \wedge 1 \geq x_{(1)} \geq 0 \wedge 1 \geq x_{(2)} \geq 0)$$

In a larger program, such an invariant would be propagated further, with every post-condition computation begin essentially repeated for each of the eight polyhedra (i.e., exponentially many times in the number of Boolean variables).

The implementation of the domain that we propose in this paper allows to represent P_3 in a much more compact form:

$$\{\ true \rightarrow x_{(0)} \geq 0,\ true \rightarrow x_{(1)} \geq 0,\ true \rightarrow x_{(2)} \geq 0,$$
$$b_{(0)} \rightarrow -x_{(0)} \geq -1,\ b_{(1)} \rightarrow -x_{(1)} \geq -1,\ b_{(2)} \rightarrow -x_{(2)} \geq -1\ \}$$

4.2 Experiments

We evaluate the performance of the implementation using two sets of programs. For both sets, we measure the total time it took to run on every program a single forward analysis with narrowing. We summarize the results in Table 1. Time figures were obtained on a PC with a Core i7-3630QM CPU and 8GB RAM.

SV-COMP Programs. For the first set of experiments, we selected a number of programs from "loop" and "recursive" categories of the Competition on Software Verification SV-COMP [1] and translated them into Horn clauses (the input language of our tool) with the tool SeaHorn [16] using two different Clang optimization levels -O3 and -O0 (SeaHorn operates on LLVM bytecode). This way we obtained 123 systems of Horn clauses. By default, SeaHorn uses a version of large block encoding [8] and produces programs with relatively few locations, but with complicated transition relations and a large number of temporary Boolean and numeric variables; even a simple C program can produce a good benchmark for the implementation of an abstract domain. In Appendix A, we show an example of a C program and the corresponding system of Horn clauses produced by SeaHorn. On SV-COMP programs, the implementation of the proposed domain is 2–10 times slower than BddApron; about 5 times slower on average.

Hand-Crafted Programs. For the second set, we selected 10 hand-crafted programs coming from different sources: array-manipulating programs encoded using array abstraction of Gonnord and Monniaux [27], other programs that use trace partitioning with observer variables, etc. With hand-crafted examples, we noticed that some of SMT queries that test constraint for redundancy cause the solver (Z3 4.5.0) to reach timeout, which we set at 10 seconds. This does not

Table 1. Experimental results

Program set	#	Total time, s	
		BddApron	This paper
SV-COMP	123	9.2	52
Hand-crafted, no solver timeout	8	0.9	6.8
Hand-crafted, all	10	1.6	113.5

make the analysis unsound; a timeout of a redundancy check only causes the analysis to keep a redundant constraint in an abstract element. We have not yet found a workaround, and we display the hand-crafted programs in two rows: all programs (10) and programs that do not cause solver timeouts (8). On hand-crafted programs without solver timeout, the implementation of the proposed domain is 2–10 times slower than BddApron; about 7 times slower on average.

Conclusion. On average, the current implementation of the proposed abstract domain is about 5–7 times slower than BddApron. We find this result promising (given that this is our initial prototype implementation) and it shows directions for future improvement. In particular, much of the analysis time is spent in SMT solver calls in order to detect redundant constraints. These calls are costly, but have to be performed regularly. We are going to address the performance of eliminating redundant constraints in future work.

5 Conclusion and Future Work

In this paper, we propose a new relational abstract domain for analysing programs with numeric and Boolean variables. The main idea is to represent an abstract state as a set of linear constraints over numeric variables, with every constraint being enabled by a formula over Boolean variables. This allows, unlike in some existing approaches, avoiding the duplication of linear constraints shared by multiple Boolean formulas. Currently, we use the simple formulations of Fourier-Motzkin elimination [28] and projection-based convex hull [7,31], and we rely on an SMT solver for redundancy elimination and inclusion checks (the counterpart of systematically using linear programming). Our experiments have shown that this is a worthy combination, which avoids some of the inefficiencies of earlier works.

The main direction for future work is to improve the performance of eliminating redundant constraints. There may be multiple ways to do this.

First, we may find additional heuristics that will reduce the number calls to a complete elimination procedure (that now calls an SMT solver). For example, Maréchal and Périn propose a fast incomplete procedure to detect non-redundant constraints based on raytracing [23], and there may be a way to adapt it (or a similar heuristic) to our setting.

Second, we may replace the SMT calls with a specialized procedure that combines LP-based and BDD-based reasoning. In particular, the observation is that a constraint is non-redundant, if it is non-redundant for at least one valuation of Boolean variables. While, an abstract element in the worst case describes exponentially many (in the number of constraints) convex polyhedra, there may be a way to not enumerate all of them during the redundancy check, at least in the average case.

Third, we may attempt to adapt to our setting the state-of-the art algorithms for constraint-only polyhedra, but this is not straightforward. For example, we cannot immediately adapt algorithms that require an interior point, such as those on parametric linear programming (for projection and convex hull) and ray-tracing (for redundancy elimination), by Maréchal, Monniaux, and Périn [21–23]: different Boolean assignments may have different interior points (in case of polyhedra with empty interior, we consider the interior relative to the affine span; but again this depends on the affine span). This is unfortunate, since much time is currently spent inside the SMT solver for checking for redundancy, and parametric linear programming is more efficient than Fourier-Motzkin elimination. A possible workaround, to be explored, is to partition the Boolean space according to affine span and point in the relative interior.

Regardless of the issues related to redundancy, presence of Boolean constraints often prevents us from using some standard approaches to representing polyhedra. In computations over convex polyhedra, one usually maintains, in addition to a system of inequalities, a system of linear inequalities that defines the affine span of the polyhedron. Given an ordering over the dimensions, this system of equalities may be echelonized and used to eliminate variables from the system of inequalities. The resulting system of equalities and non-redundant, normalized inequalities is canonical [2]. In our case, the affine span may depend on the Boolean part, thus it is impossible to canonicalize the inequalities uniformly with respect to the Booleans. We intend to investigate partitioning the Boolean space according to the affine span.

```
int main() {
  int x = 0, y = 0;
  while (x <= 99) {
    ++x;
    ++y;
  }
  assert(x == 100 && y == 100);
}
```

Fig. 6. An example of a C program

---

[2] In the case of polyhedra with nonempty interior, an non-redundant system of normalized inequalities canonically describes a polyhedron: each inequality corresponds to a face. This is not true in the general case: both $x \leq y \wedge y \leq x \wedge 0 \leq x \wedge x \leq 1$ and $x \leq y \wedge y \leq x \wedge 0 \leq x \wedge y \leq 1$ are non-redundant systems defining the same polyhedron. Its affine span is defined by $x = y$, then one can rewrite the inequalities using this equality and obtain $x = y \wedge 0 \leq y \wedge y \leq 1$, which is canonical.

A   Input Example

Figure 6 shows an example of a C program. Figure 7 in the next page shows the corresponding system of Horn clauses produced by SeaHorn.

```
(rule (verifier.error false false false))
(rule (verifier.error false true true))
(rule (verifier.error true false true))
(rule (verifier.error true true true))
(rule main@entry)
(rule (=>
  (and main@entry
    true
    (=> main@_bb_0 (and main@_bb_0 main@entry_0))
    main@_bb_0
    (=> (and main@_bb_0 main@entry_0) (= main@%y.0.i2_0 0))
    (=> (and main@_bb_0 main@entry_0) (= main@%x.0.i1_0 0))
    (=> (and main@_bb_0 main@entry_0) (= main@%y.0.i2_1 main@%y.0.i2_0))
    (=> (and main@_bb_0 main@entry_0) (= main@%x.0.i1_1 main@%x.0.i1_0)))
  (main@_bb main@%x.0.i1_1 main@%y.0.i2_1)))
(rule (=>
  (and (main@_bb main@%x.0.i1_0 main@%y.0.i2_0)
    true
    (= main@%_1_0 (+ main@%x.0.i1_0 1))
    (= main@%_2_0 (+ main@%y.0.i2_0 1))
    (= main@%_3_0 (<= main@%_1_0 99))
    (=> main@_bb_1 (and main@_bb_1 main@_bb_0))
    main@_bb_1
    (=> (and main@_bb_1 main@_bb_0) main@%_3_0)
    (=> (and main@_bb_1 main@_bb_0) (= main@%y.0.i2_1 main@%_2_0))
    (=> (and main@_bb_1 main@_bb_0) (= main@%x.0.i1_1 main@%_1_0))
    (=> (and main@_bb_1 main@_bb_0) (= main@%y.0.i2_2 main@%y.0.i2_1))
    (=> (and main@_bb_1 main@_bb_0) (= main@%x.0.i1_2 main@%x.0.i1_1)))
  (main@_bb main@%x.0.i1_2 main@%y.0.i2_2)))
(rule (let ((a!1
  (and
    (main@_bb main@%x.0.i1_0 main@%y.0.i2_0)
    true
    (= main@%_1_0 (+ main@%x.0.i1_0 1))
    (= main@%_2_0 (+ main@%y.0.i2_0 1))
    (= main@%_3_0 (<= main@%_1_0 99))
    (=> main@verifier.error_0
        (and main@verifier.error_0 main@_bb_0))
    (=> (and main@verifier.error_0 main@_bb_0) (not main@%_3_0))
    (=> (and main@verifier.error_0 main@_bb_0)
        (= main@%.lcssa5_0 main@%_2_0))
    (=> (and main@verifier.error_0 main@_bb_0)
        (= main@%.lcssa_0 main@%_1_0))
    (=> (and main@verifier.error_0 main@_bb_0)
        (= main@%.lcssa5_1 main@%.lcssa5_0))
    (=> (and main@verifier.error_0 main@_bb_0)
        (= main@%.lcssa_1 main@%.lcssa_0))
    (=> main@verifier.error_0 (= main@%_4_0 (= main@%.lcssa_1 100)))
    (=> main@verifier.error_0
        (= main@%_5_0 (= main@%.lcssa5_1 100)))
    (=> main@verifier.error_0
        (= main@%or.cond.i_0 (and main@%_4_0 main@%_5_0)))
    (=> main@verifier.error_0 (not main@%or.cond.i_0))
    (=> main@verifier.error.split_0
        (and main@verifier.error.split_0 main@verifier.error_0))
    main@verifier.error.split_0)))
  (=> a!1 main@verifier.error.split)))
(query main@verifier.error.split)
```

Fig. 7. System of Horn clauses produced by SeaHorn for the program in Fig. 6.

References

1. Competition on software verification (SV-COMP). http://sv-comp.sosy-lab.org/. Accessed Apr 2018
2. Proceedings of 9th International Conference on Formal Methods in Computer-Aided Design, FMCAD 2009, 15–18 November 2009, Austin, Texas, USA. IEEE (2009)
3. Bagnara, R., Hill, P.M., Ricci, E., Zaffanella, E.: Precise widening operators for convex polyhedra. Sci. Comput. Program. **58**(1–2), 28–56 (2005)
4. Bagnara, R., Hill, P.M., Zaffanella, E.: Widening operators for powerset domains. STTT **9**(3–4), 413–414 (2007)
5. Bakhirkin, A.: HCAI, a path focusing abstract interpreter for Horn clauses. https://gitlab.com/abakhirkin/hcai. Accessed Apr 2018
6. Bakhirkin, A., Monniaux, D.: Combining forward and backward abstract interpretation of Horn clauses. In: Ranzato [29], pp. 23–45
7. Benoy, F., King, A., Mesnard, F.: Computing convex hulls with a linear solver. TPLP **5**(1–2), 259–271 (2005)
8. Beyer, D., Cimatti, A., Griggio, A., Keremoglu, M.E., Sebastiani, R.: Software model checking via large-block encoding. In: Proceedings of 9th International Conference on Formal Methods in Computer-Aided Design, FMCAD 2009, 15–18 November 2009, Austin, Texas, USA [2], pp. 25–32
9. Bjørner, N., Gurfinkel, A., McMillan, K., Rybalchenko, A.: Horn clause solvers for program verification. In: Beklemishev, L.D., Blass, A., Dershowitz, N., Finkbeiner, B., Schulte, W. (eds.) Fields of Logic and Computation II. LNCS, vol. 9300, pp. 24–51. Springer, Cham (2015). https://doi.org/10.1007/978-3-319-23534-9_2
10. Chaki, S., Gurfinkel, A., Strichman, O.: Decision diagrams for linear arithmetic. In: Proceedings of 9th International Conference on Formal Methods in Computer-Aided Design, FMCAD 2009, 15–18 November 2009, Austin, Texas, USA [2], pp. 53–60
11. Chen, J., Cousot, P.: A binary decision tree abstract domain functor. In: Blazy, S., Jensen, T. (eds.) SAS 2015. LNCS, vol. 9291, pp. 36–53. Springer, Heidelberg (2015). https://doi.org/10.1007/978-3-662-48288-9_3
12. Cousot, P., Halbwachs, N.: Automatic discovery of linear restraints among variables of a program. In: Aho, A.V., Zilles, S.N., Szymanski, T.G. (eds.) Conference Record of the Fifth Annual ACM Symposium on Principles of Programming Languages, Tucson, Arizona, USA, January 1978, pp. 84–96. ACM Press (1978)
13. Fouilhé, A.: Revisiting the abstract domain of polyhedra : constraints-only representation and formal proof. (Le domaine abstrait des polyèdres revisité : représentation par contraintes et preuve formelle). Ph.D. thesis, Université Grenoble Alpes, France (2015)
14. Fourier, J.: Note, second extrait. Histoire de l'Académie pour 1824, p. xlvii, vol. 2, pp. 325–328. Gauthier-Villars, Paris (1890). http://gallica.bnf.fr/ark:/12148/bpt6k33707/f330
15. Gurfinkel, A., Chaki, S.: Boxes: a symbolic abstract domain of boxes. In: Cousot, R., Martel, M. (eds.) SAS 2010. LNCS, vol. 6337, pp. 287–303. Springer, Heidelberg (2010). https://doi.org/10.1007/978-3-642-15769-1_18
16. Gurfinkel, A., Kahsai, T., Komuravelli, A., Navas, J.A.: The seahorn verification framework. In: Kroening, D., Păsăreanu, C.S. (eds.) CAV 2015. LNCS, vol. 9206, pp. 343–361. Springer, Cham (2015). https://doi.org/10.1007/978-3-319-21690-4_20

17. Halbwachs, N.: Détermination automatique de relations linéaires vérifiées par les variables d'un programme. Ph.D. thesis, Université Scientifique et Médicale de Grenoble & Institut National Polytechnique de Grenoble, March 1979. https://tel.archives-ouvertes.fr/tel-00288805

18. Imbert, J.: Fourier's elimination: which to choose? In: PPCP, pp. 117–129 (1993)

19. Jeannet, B.: Bddapron. http://pop-art.inrialpes.fr/~bjeannet/bjeannet-forge/bddapron/. Accessed Apr 2018

20. Kohler, D.: Projections of convex polyhedral sets. Ph.D. thesis, University of California, Berkeley (1967)

21. Maréchal, A.: New Algorithmics for Polyhedral Calculus via Parametric Linear Programming. (Nouvelle Algorithmique pour le Calcul Polyédral via Programmation Linéaire Paramétrique). Ph.D. thesis, Université Grenoble Alpes, France (2017)

22. Maréchal, A., Monniaux, D., Périn, M.: Scalable minimizing-operators on polyhedra via parametric linear programming. In: Ranzato [29], pp. 212–231

23. Maréchal, A., Périn, M.: Efficient elimination of redundancies in polyhedra by ray-tracing. In: Bouajjani, A., Monniaux, D. (eds.) VMCAI 2017. LNCS, vol. 10145, pp. 367–385. Springer, Cham (2017). https://doi.org/10.1007/978-3-319-52234-0_20

24. McMullen, P.: The maximum numbers of faces of a convex polytope. Mathematika **17**, 179–184 (1970)

25. Monniaux, D., Alberti, F.: A Simple abstraction of arrays and maps by program translation. In: Blazy, S., Jensen, T. (eds.) SAS 2015. LNCS, vol. 9291, pp. 217–234. Springer, Heidelberg (2015). https://doi.org/10.1007/978-3-662-48288-9_13

26. Monniaux, D., Gonnord, L.: Using bounded model checking to focus fixpoint iterations. In: Yahav, E. (ed.) SAS 2011. LNCS, vol. 6887, pp. 369–385. Springer, Heidelberg (2011). https://doi.org/10.1007/978-3-642-23702-7_27

27. Monniaux, D., Gonnord, L.: Cell morphing: from array programs to array-free horn clauses. In: Rival, X. (ed.) SAS 2016. LNCS, vol. 9837, pp. 361–382. Springer, Heidelberg (2016). https://doi.org/10.1007/978-3-662-53413-7_18

28. Motzkin, T.S.: Beiträge zur Theorie der Linearen Ungleichungen. Ph.D. thesis, Universität Zürich (1936)

29. Ranzato, F. (ed.): Static Analysis - 24th International Symposium, SAS 2017, New York, NY, USA, August 30 - September 1, 2017, Proceedings, Lecture Notes in Computer Science, vol. 10422. Springer (2017)

30. Rival, X., Mauborgne, L.: The trace partitioning abstract domain. ACM Trans. Program. Lang. Syst. **29**(5), 26 (2007)

31. Simon, A., King, A.: Exploiting sparsity in polyhedral analysis. In: Hankin, C., Siveroni, I. (eds.) SAS 2005. LNCS, vol. 3672, pp. 336–351. Springer, Heidelberg (2005). https://doi.org/10.1007/11547662_23

An Efficient Abstract Domain
for Not Necessarily Closed Polyhedra

Anna Becchi[1] and Enea Zaffanella[2(✉)]

[1] University of Udine, Udine, Italy
becchi.anna@spes.uniud.it
[2] University of Parma, Parma, Italy
enea.zaffanella@unipr.it

Abstract. We present a construction of the abstract domain of NNC (not necessarily topologically closed) polyhedra based on a recently introduced variant of the double description representation and conversion procedure. We describe the implementation of the operators needed to interface the new abstract domain with commonly available static analysis tools, highlighting the efficiency gains enabled by the new representation. We also reconsider the widening operator for NNC polyhedra, proposing a more appropriate specification based on the semantics of the domain elements, rather than their low level representation details. Finally, we provide an experimental evaluation comparing the efficiency of the new abstract domain with respect to more classical implementations.

1 Introduction

When developing or configuring a program analysis or verification tool based on Abstract Interpretation, the choice of the underlying abstract domain is a critical design decision. For numerical properties, many possible alternatives are available, each one characterized by a different tradeoff between the precision of the properties that can be expressed and the corresponding computational cost.

The abstract domain of convex polyhedra [22] is often positively considered as far as precision is concerned, but deemed unfeasible due to well-known results on its worst case exponential complexity. On the other hand, the domain of intervals [20] is definitely one of the most efficient choices, but quite often leads to insufficient precision. Many weakly-relational domains have been proposed (bounded differences [36,42], bounded logahedra [31], octagons [37], octahedra [17], parallelotopes [1], pentagons [35], subpolyhedra [34], template polyhedra [41], two variables per inequality [43], weighted hexagons [23], . . .), each one providing its own contribution to a whole spectrum of options. In many cases, analysis tools are based on a suitable *combination* of several domains [15].

The recent years have witnessed significant progress in the implementation of some of these abstract domains. Sometimes, efficiency gains have been obtained by strictly algorithmic improvements: this is the case, for instance, for the implementation of the octagon domain optimized for dense representations [44], or for

A. Podelski (Ed.): SAS 2018, LNCS 11002, pp. 146–165, 2018.
https://doi.org/10.1007/978-3-319-99725-4_11

the adoption of more efficient adjacency tests [24,47] in the conversion procedures of convex polyhedra. In other cases, the progress resulted from the application of generic techniques that allow for a scalable use of the precise abstract domains, such as the careful adoption of variable packing, either computed statically [15] or dynamically [26,27,45,46]. As a result, analyses that were previously dismissed as unfeasible turn out to be affordable and surprisingly effective.

In this paper, building on a recent result [12,13] on the representation of NNC (not necessarily topologically closed) convex polyhedra in the DD (double description) framework, we describe the development of an alternative implementation for the corresponding abstract domain. We reconsider all of the operators that are needed for the definition of a classical static analysis based on Abstract Interpretation, stressing on the efficiency gains that are triggered by the adoption of the new representation. In particular, by exploiting the availability of an efficiently computable canonical representation for NNC polyhedra, we propose a more appropriate, semantics-based specification for the widening operator.

All the proposed algorithms have been implemented in the PPLite library, a new C++ library derived from the PPL (Parma Polyhedra Library, [8,9]). In order to compare the new domain with respect to some of the available alternatives, we first interface the PPLite library with Apron [32] and then use it in the static analyzer PAGAI [30]. This experimental evaluation allows for comparing both the precision and the efficiency of the analysis, showing significant speedups with respect to the more classical implementations of the domain of NNC polyhedra on a wide range of benchmarks.

The paper is structured as follows: Sect. 2 introduces the required notation and background concepts; Sect. 3 summarizes the new representation for NNC polyhedra [13]; Sect. 4 shows how to implement on the new representation the operators needed for the development of a static analysis tool; Sect. 5 summarizes the results of the experimental evaluation; we conclude in Sect. 6.

2   Preliminaries

We write $\mathbb{R}^n$ to denote the Euclidean topological space of dimension $n > 0$ and $\mathbb{R}_+$ for the set of non-negative reals; for $S \subseteq \mathbb{R}^n$, $\mathrm{cl}(S)$ and $\mathrm{relint}(S)$ denote the topological closure and the relative interior of S, respectively.

A not necessarily topologically closed convex polyhedron (for short, NNC polyhedron) is defined as the set of solutions of a finite system $\mathcal{C} = \langle \mathcal{C}_=, \mathcal{C}_\geq, \mathcal{C}_> \rangle$ of linear equality, non-strict inequality and strict inequality constraints, i.e.,

$$\mathcal{P} = \mathrm{con}(\mathcal{C}) \stackrel{\mathrm{def}}{=} \left\{ \, \boldsymbol{p} \in \mathbb{R}^n \mid \forall \beta = (\boldsymbol{a}^\mathsf{T} \boldsymbol{x} \bowtie b) \in \mathcal{C}, \bowtie \in \{=, \geq, >\} \, . \, \boldsymbol{a}^\mathsf{T} \boldsymbol{p} \bowtie b \, \right\}.$$

The set $\mathbb{P}_n$ of all NNC polyhedra on the vector space $\mathbb{R}^n$, partially ordered by set inclusion, is a lattice[1] $\langle \mathbb{P}_n, \subseteq, \emptyset, \mathbb{R}^n, \cap, \uplus \rangle$, where the emptyset and $\mathbb{R}^n$ are the bottom and top elements, the binary meet operator is set intersection

---

[1] We assume some familiarity with the basic notions of lattice theory [14].

and the binary join operator '$\uplus$' is the convex polyhedral hull. We write $\mathbb{CP}_n$ to denote the lattice of closed polyhedra on $\mathbb{R}^n$, which is a sublattice of $\mathbb{P}_n$.

A constraint $\beta = (\boldsymbol{a}^\mathsf{T}\boldsymbol{x} \bowtie b)$ is said to be *valid* for $\mathcal{P} \in \mathbb{P}_n$ if all the points in $\mathcal{P}$ satisfy β. We write $\mathcal{H}_\beta$ to denote the hyperplane induced by β; the set $F = \mathcal{H}_\beta \cap \mathcal{P}$ is a *face* of $\mathcal{P}$. We write $nncFaces_\mathcal{P}$ to denote the finite set of faces of $\mathcal{P} \in \mathbb{P}_n$. Note that $\mathcal{P} = \bigcup\{\operatorname{relint}(F) \mid F \in nncFaces_\mathcal{P}\}$.

A vector $\boldsymbol{r} \in \mathbb{R}^n$ such that $\boldsymbol{r} \neq \boldsymbol{0}$ is a *ray* of a non-empty polyhedron $\mathcal{P} \subseteq \mathbb{R}^n$ if, $\forall \boldsymbol{p} \in \mathcal{P}$ and $\forall \rho \in \mathbb{R}_+$, it holds $\boldsymbol{p} + \rho\boldsymbol{r} \in \mathcal{P}$. The empty polyhedron has no rays. If both $\boldsymbol{r}$ and $-\boldsymbol{r}$ are rays of $\mathcal{P}$, then $\boldsymbol{r}$ is a *line* of $\mathcal{P}$. A vector $\boldsymbol{c} \in \mathbb{R}^n$ is a *closure point* of a non-empty polyhedron $\mathcal{P} \subseteq \mathbb{R}^n$ if, $\forall \boldsymbol{p} \in \mathcal{P}$ and $\forall \lambda \in \mathbb{R}$ such that $0 < \lambda < 1$, it holds $\lambda\boldsymbol{p} + (1 - \lambda)\boldsymbol{c} \in \mathcal{P}$. The set $\mathcal{P} \subseteq \mathbb{R}^n$ is an NNC polyhedron if there exist finite sets $L, R, C, P \subseteq \mathbb{R}^n$ such that $\boldsymbol{0} \notin (L \cup R)$ and $\mathcal{P} = \operatorname{gen}(\langle L, R, C, P\rangle)$, where

$$\operatorname{gen}(\langle L, R, C, P\rangle) \stackrel{\text{def}}{=} \left\{ L\boldsymbol{\lambda} + R\boldsymbol{\rho} + C\boldsymbol{\gamma} + P\boldsymbol{\pi} \in \mathbb{R}^n \;\middle|\; \begin{array}{l} \boldsymbol{\lambda} \in \mathbb{R}^\ell, \boldsymbol{\rho} \in \mathbb{R}_+^r, \\ \boldsymbol{\gamma} \in \mathbb{R}_+^c, \boldsymbol{\pi} \in \mathbb{R}_+^p, \boldsymbol{\pi} \neq \boldsymbol{0}, \\ \sum_{i=1}^c \gamma_i + \sum_{i=1}^p \pi_i = 1 \end{array} \right\}.$$

We say that $\mathcal{P} \neq \emptyset$ is described by the *generator system* $\mathcal{G} = \langle L, R, C, P\rangle$ [6,11].

For a constraint β and a generator system $\mathcal{G}$, we write $\operatorname{sat}(\beta, \mathcal{G})$ to denote the generator system composed by those elements of $\mathcal{G}$ *saturating* β (i.e., satisfying the corresponding equality constraint). For a constraint system $\mathcal{C}$, we define $\operatorname{sat}(\mathcal{C}, \mathcal{G}) = \bigcap\{\operatorname{sat}(\beta, \mathcal{G}) \mid \beta \in \mathcal{C}\}$.[2] We define $\operatorname{sat}(g, \mathcal{C})$ and $\operatorname{sat}(\mathcal{G}, \mathcal{C})$ similarly.

The DD method [39] combines the constraints and the generators of a polyhedron into a DD pair $(\mathcal{C}, \mathcal{G})$: we write $\mathcal{P} \equiv (\mathcal{C}, \mathcal{G})$ when $\mathcal{P} = \operatorname{con}(\mathcal{C}) = \operatorname{gen}(\mathcal{G})$.

For *topologically closed* polyhedra (i.e., those polyhedra that can be described by a constraint system where $\mathcal{C}_> = \emptyset$ and a generator system where $C = \emptyset$), there exist *conversion procedures* [16] that can compute each description starting from the other one. When converting from constraints to generators,[3] the procedure starts from a DD pair $(\mathcal{C}_0, \mathcal{G}_0)$ representing the whole vector space and adds, one at a time, the elements $\beta_0, \ldots, \beta_m$ of the input constraint system producing a sequence of DD pairs $\{(\mathcal{C}_k, \mathcal{G}_k)\}_{0 \le k \le m+1}$ representing the polyhedra

$$\mathbb{R}^n = \mathcal{P}_0 \xrightarrow{\beta_0} \ldots \xrightarrow{\beta_{k-1}} \mathcal{P}_k \xrightarrow{\beta_k} \mathcal{P}_{k+1} \xrightarrow{\beta_{k+1}} \ldots \xrightarrow{\beta_m} \mathcal{P}_{m+1} = \mathcal{P}.$$

When adding the constraint 'β_k' to polyhedron $\mathcal{P}_k = \operatorname{gen}(\mathcal{G}_k)$, the generator system $\mathcal{G}_k$ is partitioned into the three components $\mathcal{G}_k^+$, $\mathcal{G}_k^0$, $\mathcal{G}_k^-$, according to the sign of the scalar products of the generators with β_k (those in $\mathcal{G}_k^0$ are the saturators of β_k); the new generator system for polyhedron $\mathcal{P}_{k+1}$ is computed as $\mathcal{G}_{k+1} \stackrel{\text{def}}{=} \mathcal{G}_k^+ \cup \mathcal{G}_k^0 \cup \mathcal{G}_k^\star$, where $\mathcal{G}_k^\star = \operatorname{comb\_adj}_{\beta_k}(\mathcal{G}_k^+, \mathcal{G}_k^-)$ and

$$\operatorname{comb\_adj}_{\beta_k}(\mathcal{G}_k^+, \mathcal{G}_k^-) \stackrel{\text{def}}{=} \{\operatorname{comb}_{\beta_k}(g^+, g^-) \mid g^+ \in \mathcal{G}_k^+, g^- \in \mathcal{G}_k^-, \operatorname{adj}_{\mathcal{P}_k}(g^+, g^-)\}.$$

---

[2] Note that we abuse notation by adopting the usual set operator and relation symbols to denote the corresponding component-wise extensions on systems.

[3] The opposite conversion works in the same way, exploiting duality.

Function 'comb$_{\beta_k}$' computes a linear combination of its arguments, yielding a generator that saturates the constraint β_k; predicate 'adj$_{\mathcal{P}_k}$' is used to select only those pairs of generators that are *adjacent* in $\mathcal{P}_k$. The conversion procedure can also simplify systems, putting them in *minimal form*: $\mathcal{C}$ (resp., $\mathcal{G}$) is in minimal form if it contains a maximal set of equalities (resp., lines) and no redundancies.[4]

The classical approach for the extension of the DD method to the case of NNC polyhedra, put forward in [28,29] and studied in more detail in [6,11], is the one adopted in both the NNC_Polyhedra domain of the PPL [9] and the NewPolka domain of the Apron library [32]. It is based on an *indirect representation*, whereby each NNC polyhedron $\mathcal{P} \in \mathbb{P}_n$ is mapped into a closed polyhedron $\mathcal{R} \in \mathbb{CP}_{n+1}$. The mapping encodes the strict inequality constraints by means of an additional space dimension (playing the role of a *slack variable*) usually denoted as ϵ, which needs to be non-negative and bounded from above. While allowing for reusing the same conversion procedures implemented for closed polyhedra, this approach is known to suffer from a few issues (which have been described in full detail in [13]), leading to avoidable inefficiencies.

3 The New Representation for NNC Polyhedra

To the best of our knowledge, the algorithms described in [13] are the first proposals of conversion procedures working on a *direct* DD representation for NNC polyhedra. In this section we summarize the results presented in [13], which lay the foundations for the development of a new implementation of the abstract domain of NNC polyhedra.

The new representation of [13] stems from the observation that some of the constraints and generators describing an NNC polyhedron need not be provided with a fully geometrical description. This can be seen for the polyhedron shown[5] on the left hand side of Fig. 1: there is no need to know the exact slope of the strict inequality constraint β_1, as it can be replaced by any other strict inequality satisfied by all of the points of the polyhedron and saturated by closure point c_0; similarly, there is no need to know the precise position of point p_1, which can be replaced by any other point on the open segment (c_0, c_1).

Hence, the new representation distinguishes between the *skeleton* component, which is described geometrically, and the *non-skeleton* component, which is instead provided with a combinatorial description. For constraints, the non-skeleton component is a collection of strict inequality constraints behaving as *face cutters*: they remove some of the faces from the polyhedron described by the skeleton constraint system. For generators, the non-skeleton consists of generating points behaving as *face fillers*: they add to the polyhedron described by the skeleton generator system (the relative interior of) some of its faces.

---

[4] $\beta \in \mathcal{C}$ is *redundant* in $\mathcal{C}$ if con($\mathcal{C}$) = con($\mathcal{C} \setminus \{\beta\}$); similarly for generators.

[5] In the figures, the (strict) inequality constraints are denoted by (dashed) lines and the (closure) points are denoted by (unfilled) circles.

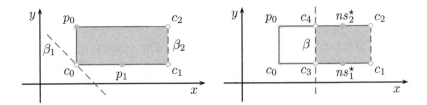

Fig. 1. On the left hand side, an NNC polyhedron having no "canonical" geometric representations; on the right hand side, the same polyhedron, after the strict inequality β has been (incrementally) processed by procedure SKEL-CONV.

For exposition purposes and without loss of generality, in the following we focus on the constraint representation. As usual, by duality arguments, all definitions and results can be extended to the case of generators [13].

A non-empty face can be uniquely identified by the set of skeleton constraints that it saturates: thus, a cutter for such a face can be represented in a combinatorial way using the same set, called its *support*.

Definition 1 (Skeleton and non-skeleton of a constraint system). *Let* $\mathcal{P} = \mathrm{con}(\mathcal{C}) \in \mathbb{P}_n$ *and* $\mathcal{Q} = \mathrm{cl}(\mathcal{P})$, *where* $\mathcal{C} = \langle \mathcal{C}_=, \mathcal{C}_\geq, \mathcal{C}_> \rangle$ *is a constraint system in minimal form; let* $\mathcal{SC} \subseteq \mathcal{C}_>$ *be the set of strict inequalities* $\beta_>$ *whose non-strict version* $\beta_\geq$ *cannot be obtained by a combination of the other constraints in* $\mathcal{C}$. *The skeleton of* $\mathcal{C}$ *is* $\mathcal{SK} = \mathrm{skel}(\mathcal{C}) \overset{\mathrm{def}}{=} \langle \mathcal{C}_=, \mathcal{C}_\geq \cup \mathcal{SC}, \emptyset \rangle$. *The support of a face* F *of* $\mathcal{Q}$ *is* $\mathcal{SK}_F \overset{\mathrm{def}}{=} \{ \beta \in \mathcal{SK} \mid F \subseteq \mathcal{H}_\beta \}$. *The non-skeleton of* $\mathcal{C}$ *is the set* $NS \overset{\mathrm{def}}{=} \uparrow \{ \mathcal{SK}_F \mid \exists \beta \in \mathcal{C}_> . F = \mathcal{H}_\beta \cap \mathcal{Q} \}$.[6]

Note that the skeleton has no strict inequalities, so that $\mathrm{con}(\mathcal{SK}) = \mathrm{cl}(\mathcal{P})$. If $F' \subseteq F$ are two faces of $\mathcal{Q} = \mathrm{cl}(\mathcal{P})$, then $\mathcal{SK}_F \subseteq \mathcal{SK}_{F'}$; also, the set of faces of $\mathcal{Q}$ that are cut (i.e., not included) in $\mathcal{P}$ is downward closed, hence the non-skeleton NS is upward closed. Thus, polyhedron $\mathcal{P}$ can be obtained by removing from its topological closure those faces encoded by the non-skeleton: namely, $\mathcal{P} = \mathrm{con}(\langle \mathcal{SK}, NS \rangle) \overset{\mathrm{def}}{=} \mathrm{con}(\mathcal{SK}) \setminus \bigcup \{ F \mid \mathcal{SK}_F \in NS \}$. Given a support $ns = \mathcal{SK}_F \in NS$, we write $ns \equiv \beta_>$ to denote that $\beta_>$ is a *materialization* of ns, i.e., a geometric cutter for face F, obtained by combining the constraints in ns.

Several optimizations can be applied at the implementation level. Since every $ns \in NS$ always includes all the equalities in $\mathcal{C}_=$, these can be left implicit, i.e., removed from the support. When this is done, the supports that happen to be singletons correspond to the combinatorial encoding of the constraints in $\mathcal{SC}$ (see Definition 1). Since their geometric position is uniquely identified, these can be *promoted*, i.e., removed from the non-skeleton component NS and directly included as strict inequalities in $\mathcal{SK}$; namely, the skeleton $\mathcal{SK} = \langle \mathcal{C}_=, \mathcal{C}_\geq \cup \mathcal{SC}, \emptyset \rangle$ is actually represented as $\mathcal{SK} = \langle \mathcal{C}_=, \mathcal{C}_\geq, \mathcal{SC} \rangle$. Finally, the upward closed set NS is represented by encoding only its minimal elements; a support $ns \in NS$ can

---

[6] $\uparrow S$ denotes the smallest upward closed set containing S.

be identified as redundant (and removed) when $ns \cap SC \neq \emptyset$ or there exists $ns' \in NS$ such that $ns' \sqsubset ns$. In the rest of the paper, when referring to a pair $\langle SK, NS \rangle$, it is assumed that these optimizations are applied.

Example 1. Consider the polyhedron on the left hand side of Fig. 1, defined by constraint system $\mathcal{C} = \{2 \leq x < 7, 1 \leq y \leq 3, x + y > 3\}$. The constraint system is split into the skeleton component

$$SK^{c} = \langle \emptyset, \{2 \leq x, 1 \leq y \leq 3\}, \{x < 7\} \rangle$$

and the non-skeleton component $NS^{c} = \{ns^{c}\}$, where $ns^{c} = \{2 \leq x, 1 \leq y\}$. Note that $\beta_1 = (x + y > 3)$ is one of the materializations of the support ns^{c} and the strict inequality $\beta_2 = (x < 7)$ has been promoted into the skeleton component. Similarly, the generator system is split into $SK^{g} = \langle \emptyset, \emptyset, \{c_0, c_1, c_2\}, \{p_0\} \rangle$ and $NS^{g} = \{ns^{g}\}$, where $ns^{g} = \{c_0, c_1\}$. Point p_0 has been promoted into the skeleton component and point p_1 is a materialization of ns^{g}.

Conversion Algorithm. Consider the conversion from constraints to generators, which incrementally adds a set of geometric constraints SK_{in}^{c} to a DD pair $(\mathcal{C}_{dst}, \mathcal{G}_{dst})$. The new procedure [13], recalled in Pseudocode 1, handles each $\beta \in SK_{in}^{c}$ in two phases, one for each of the components of $\mathcal{G}_{dst} = \langle SK, NS \rangle$.

The skeleton phase follows the same pattern of the conversion procedure for closed polyhedra. Namely, SK is partitioned in SK^{+}, SK^{0}, SK^{-} according to the sign of the scalar products with β, and the set $SK^{\star}$ is computed by combining the generators in SK^{+} with those in SK^{-}. Being restricted to the skeleton, the combination can safely apply the adjacency tests, which are crucial for efficiency.

The non-skeleton phase is where the new algorithm really differs from the classical one. Due to space constraints, we only provide here a high level, intuitive view of this phase, which is described in full detail in [13]. The NS component is partitioned in NS^{+}, NS^{0}, NS^{-} and $NS^{\pm}$, according to the already computed partition for the skeleton. These sets are then processed to produce $NS^{\star}$ by helper procedures MOVE-NS and CREATE-NS. Each support $ns \in NS^{\pm}$ (i.e., those whose materializations lie on both sides of $\mathcal{H}_{\beta}$) is updated by MOVE-NS so as to saturate (resp., satisfy) the non-strict (resp., strict) inequality constraint β. Each other support (i.e., those whose materializations lie on only one of the half-spaces induced by β) is processed by CREATE-NS, which "combines" it with the supports on the other side of β. This combination step includes a partial enumeration of the face lattice (ENUMERATE-FACES). In lines 8 to 12 $NS^{\star}$ is non-redundantly merged (using operator '$\oplus$') with the remaining supports. It should be stressed that the non-skeleton phase of the algorithm only performs set-theoretic operations on supports, i.e., no further linear combinations need to be computed. It uses two basic helper functions, to compute support closure [33] and project it on the correct side of constraint β:

$$\text{supp.cl}(ns) \overset{\text{def}}{=} \text{sat}\big(\text{sat}(ns, \mathcal{SK}^c), \mathcal{SK}^g\big) \setminus L,$$

$$\text{proj}^\beta(ns) \overset{\text{def}}{=} \begin{cases} ns \setminus \mathcal{SK}^-, & \text{if } \beta \text{ is a strict inequality;} \\ ns \cap \mathcal{SK}^0, & \text{otherwise.} \end{cases}$$

Example 2. Consider again the polyhedron $\mathcal{P}$ shown on the left hand side of Fig. 1, already described in Example 1. On the right hand side of the figure, we show the effect of adding to $\mathcal{P}$ the strict inequality $\beta = (4 < x)$.

The skeleton component $\mathcal{SK}^g$ is partitioned in $\mathcal{SK}^+ = \{c_1, c_2\}$, $\mathcal{SK}^0 = \emptyset$ and $\mathcal{SK}^- = \{p_0, c_0\}$; thus, $NS^+ = NS^0 = NS^- = \emptyset$ and $NS^\pm = NS = \{ns^g\}$.[7] In the skeleton phase, the set $\mathcal{SK}^\star = \{c_3, c_4\}$ is obtained combining *adjacent* skeleton generators (c_0 with c_1 and p_0 with c_2, respectively). In the non-skeleton phase, MOVE-NS processes $ns^g \in NS^\pm$, obtaining

$$ns_1^\star = \text{proj}^\beta(\text{supp.cl}(ns^g)) = \{c_0, c_1, c_3\} \setminus \{p_0, c_0\} = \{c_1, c_3\}.$$

We have intuitively *moved* the materializations for ns^g to the correct side of β. Function CREATE-NS processes the skeleton point p_0, which is a filler for (the relative interior of) point p_0 itself, the segments $[p_0, c_2]$, $[p_0, c_0]$ and the whole polyhedron $\mathcal{P}$: ENUMERATE-FACES explores this set of faces and projects them in NS^+, obtaining the new supports $ns_2^\star = \{c_2, c_4\}$ and $ns_3^\star = \{c_1, c_2, c_3, c_4\}$. After removing redundancies (i.e., dropping the non-minimal support $ns_3^\star$), we obtain

$$\mathcal{SK}^g = \langle \emptyset, \emptyset, \{c_1, c_2, c_3, c_4\}, \emptyset \rangle, \quad NS^g = \{ ns_1^\star, ns_2^\star \}.$$

4   Operators on the New Representation

In principle, when adopting the new representation recalled in the previous section, each operator on the abstract domain of NNC polyhedra could be implemented indirectly, by first *materializing* the non-skeleton elements and then applying the operator on the fully geometrical descriptions obtained. In this section we show that such a materialization step (and its computational overhead) is not really needed: all of the classical operators required for static analysis can be *directly* computed on the new representation, by distinguishing their effects on the geometrical and the combinatorial components, also exploiting this division to simplify some of the procedures.

Emptiness, Inclusion and Equality. $\mathcal{P} = \text{gen}(\langle \mathcal{SK}^g, NS^g \rangle)$ is empty if and only if it has no point, i.e., $\mathcal{SK}^g$ contains no point and $NS^g = \emptyset$.

---

[7] Recall that $ns_g = \{c_0, c_1\}$ is the support describing the materialization p_1.

Pseudocode 1. Conversion from geometric constraints to generators.

---

function SKEL-CONVERSION($\mathcal{SK}_{in}^c$, $\langle \mathcal{SK}, NS \rangle$)

2:     **for all** $\beta \in \mathcal{SK}_{in}^c$ **do**

           skel_partition(β, $\mathcal{SK}$);

4:         nonskel_partition($\langle \mathcal{SK}, NS \rangle$);

           $\mathcal{SK}^\star \leftarrow \text{comb\_adj}_\beta(\mathcal{SK}^+, \mathcal{SK}^-)$; $\mathcal{SK}^0 \leftarrow \mathcal{SK}^0 \cup \mathcal{SK}^\star$;

6:         $NS^\star \leftarrow$ MOVE-NS(β, $\langle \mathcal{SK}, NS \rangle$);

           $NS^\star \leftarrow NS^\star \cup$ CREATE-NS(β, $\langle \mathcal{SK}, NS \rangle$);

8:         **if** is_equality(β) **then** $\langle \mathcal{SK}, NS \rangle \leftarrow \langle \mathcal{SK}^0, NS^0 \oplus NS^\star \rangle$;

           else if is_strict_ineq(β) **then**

10:            $\mathcal{SK}^0 \leftarrow$ points_become_closure_points($\mathcal{SK}^0$);

               $\langle \mathcal{SK}, NS \rangle \leftarrow \langle \mathcal{SK}^+ \cup \mathcal{SK}^0, NS^+ \oplus NS^\star \rangle$;

12:        **else** $\langle \mathcal{SK}, NS \rangle \leftarrow \langle \mathcal{SK}^+ \cup \mathcal{SK}^0, (NS^+ \cup NS^0) \oplus NS^\star \rangle$;

           PROMOTE-SINGLETONS($\langle \mathcal{SK}, NS \rangle$);

14:    **return** $\langle \mathcal{SK}, NS \rangle$;

function MOVE-NS(β, $\langle \mathcal{SK}, NS \rangle$)

16:    $NS^\star \leftarrow \emptyset$;

       for all $ns \in NS^\pm$ **do** $NS^\star \leftarrow NS^\star \cup \{\text{proj}^\beta(\text{supp.cl}(ns))\}$;

18:    **return** $NS^\star$;

function CREATE-NS(β, $\langle \mathcal{SK}, NS \rangle$)

20:    $NS^\star \leftarrow \emptyset$;

       let $\mathcal{SK} = \langle L, R, C, SP \rangle$;

22:    **for all** $ns \in NS^- \cup \{\{p\} \mid p \in SP^-\}$ **do**

           $NS^\star \leftarrow NS^\star \cup$ ENUMERATE-FACES(β, ns, $\mathcal{SK}^+$, $\mathcal{SK}$);

24:    **if** is_strict_ineq(β) **then**

           for all $ns \in NS^0 \cup \{\{p\} \mid p \in SP^0\}$ **do**

26:            $NS^\star \leftarrow NS^\star \cup$ ENUMERATE-FACES(β, ns, $\mathcal{SK}^+$, $\mathcal{SK}$);

       else

28:        **for all** $ns \in NS^+ \cup \{\{p\} \mid p \in SP^+\}$ **do**

               $NS^\star \leftarrow NS^\star \cup$ ENUMERATE-FACES(β, ns, $\mathcal{SK}^-$, $\mathcal{SK}$);

30:    **return** $NS^\star$;

function ENUMERATE-FACES(β, ns, $\mathcal{SK}'$, $\mathcal{SK}$)

32:    $NS^\star \leftarrow \emptyset$; **let** $\mathcal{SK}' = \langle L', R', C', SP' \rangle$;

       for all $g \in (R' \cup C')$ **do** $NS^\star \leftarrow NS^\star \cup \{\text{proj}^\beta(\text{supp.cl}(ns \cup \{g\}))\}$;

34:    **return** $NS^\star$;

procedure PROMOTE-SINGLETONS($\langle \mathcal{SK}, NS \rangle$)

36:    **let** $\mathcal{SK} = \langle L, R, C, SP \rangle$;

       for all $ns \in NS$ such that $ns = \langle \emptyset, \emptyset, \{c\}, \emptyset \rangle$ **do**

38:        $NS \leftarrow NS \setminus \{ns\}$; $C \leftarrow C \setminus \{c\}$; $SP \leftarrow SP \cup \{c\}$;

The inclusion $\mathcal{P}_1 \subseteq \mathcal{P}_2$ holds if and only if each generator of $\mathcal{P}_1$ satisfies all of the constraints of $\mathcal{P}_2$. Note that the lines, rays and closure points of $\mathcal{P}_1$ need to be checked only against the *skeleton* constraints of $\mathcal{P}_2$; only the points of $\mathcal{P}_1$ need to be checked against the non-skeleton strict inequalities of $\mathcal{P}_2$. Also, when checking a non-skeleton element, no additional scalar product needs to be computed: the result of the check is derived from the saturation information already computed (and cached) for skeleton elements. For instance, a skeleton point $p_1 \in SK_1^g$ violates a non-skeleton constraint $ns_2 \in NS_2^c$ when $p_1 \in \mathrm{sat}(ns_2, SK_1^g)$.

Equivalence $\mathcal{P}_1 = \mathcal{P}_2$ can be checked by performing two inclusion tests. Since the new representations satisfy a stronger form of normalization,[8] optimizations are possible: for instance, the test can be quickly answered negatively when the cardinalities of the minimized representations do not match.

Conditional and "forget". A conditional test checking an affine predicate on program variables is modeled by adding the corresponding constraint to the polyhedron defining the program state. Similarly, a non-deterministic (or non-linear) assignment can be modeled by "forgetting" all the constraints mentioning the variable assigned to, i.e., by adding the corresponding line as a generator. Hence, these two operators can be directly implemented by a call to the incremental conversion procedure of [13].

Meet and Join. From a high level point of view, when a conversion procedure is available the computation of meets (i.e., set intersections) and joins (i.e., convex polyhedral hulls) on the domain of convex polyhedra is straightforward. Namely, if $\mathcal{P}_1 \equiv (\mathcal{C}_1, \mathcal{G}_1)$ and $\mathcal{P}_2 = (\mathcal{C}_2, \mathcal{G}_2)$, then the DD pair for $\mathcal{P} = \mathcal{P}_1 \cap \mathcal{P}_2$ is obtained by incrementally adding to $(\mathcal{C}_1, \mathcal{G}_1)$ the constraints in $\mathcal{C}_2$; similarly, the DD pair for $\mathcal{P} = \mathcal{P}_1 \uplus \mathcal{P}_2$ is obtained by adding to $(\mathcal{C}_1, \mathcal{G}_1)$ the generators in $\mathcal{G}_2$.

Without loss of generality, consider the case of set intersection. When incrementally adding the constraints in $\mathcal{C}_2 = \langle SK_{in}^c, NS_{in}^c \rangle$ to the DD pair for $\mathcal{P}_1$, we first apply the algorithm in Pseudocode 1 to the skeleton constraints in SK_{in}^c; then, in order to avoid materializations, we process each non-skeleton constraint $ns \in NS_{in}^c$ using the procedure shown in Pseudocode 2 (this extension of the conversion procedure was not considered in [13]).

Note that, in lines 3 to 4, the constraint ns always partitions the generators so that $SK^- = NS^- = NS^\pm = \emptyset$. Hence, we can avoid all the scalar products that would have been computed in the case of a geometric input; also, saturation information is not affected, so that SK^0 (and consequently NS^0) are easily computed by intersecting the generators saturating the support. As a consequence, the non-skeleton conversion procedure can directly call the helper STRICT-ON-EQ-POINTS(ns, SK, NS) defined in [13], which is a tailored version of the CREATE-NS function, also including the final update of SK and NS.[9]

At the implementation level, a little additional care has to be taken when processing the skeleton component: if a geometric constraint $\beta \in SK_{in}^c$ is detected to be redundant, it cannot be eagerly dropped, because it might occur in a

---

[8] It is meant, with respect to those available for ϵ-representations.

[9] The first parameter β of STRICT-ON-EQ-POINTS seems to require a geometrical constraint, but this is not really the case; the parameter is only used to check the constraint kind (equality, non-strict inequality or strict inequality): in the special case of a non-skeleton element ns, we always have a strict inequality.

Pseudocode 2. Conversion from combinatorial constraints to generators.

---

    function NONSKEL-CONVERSION(NS^c_{in}, $\langle SK, NS \rangle$)

2:    **for all** $ns \in NS^c_{in}$ **do**

        $SK^- = \emptyset$; $SK^0 = \text{sat}(ns, SK)$; $SK^+ = SK \setminus SK^0$;

4:        nonskel_partition($\langle SK, NS \rangle$);

        STRICT-ON-EQ-POINTS(ns, $\langle SK, NS \rangle$);

6:    **return** $\langle SK, NS \rangle$;

    procedure STRICT-ON-EQ-POINTS(β, $\langle SK, NS \rangle$)

8:    $NS^\star \leftarrow \emptyset$; let $SK^0 = \langle L^0, R^0, C^0, SP^0 \rangle$;

        for all $ns \in NS^0 \cup \{\{p\} \mid p \in SP^0\}$ **do**

10:       $NS^\star \leftarrow NS^\star \cup \text{ENUMERATE-FACES}(\beta, ns, SK^+, SK)$;

        $SK^0 \leftarrow \text{points-become-closure-points}(SK^0)$;

12:    $\langle SK, NS \rangle \leftarrow \langle SK^+ \cup SK^0, NS^+ \oplus NS^\star \rangle$;

---

support $ns \in NS^c_{in}$ and hence be needed to compute the corresponding partition; thus, the removal of β is delayed till completion of NONSKEL-CONVERSION.

The extension of the conversion procedure that incrementally adds nonskeleton generators (used when computing joins) is similar and can be derived, as usual, by exploiting duality arguments.

Assignment of an Affine Expression. The assignment $x_i := \boldsymbol{a}^\mathsf{T}\boldsymbol{x} + b$ is modeled by computing the image the polyhedron under the affine map $f \colon \mathbb{R}^n \to \mathbb{R}^n$, where $\boldsymbol{q} = f(\boldsymbol{p})$ is such that $q_i = \boldsymbol{a}^\mathsf{T}\boldsymbol{p} + b$ and $q_j = p_j$, when $i \neq j$. If f is *invertible* (i.e., $a_i \neq 0$), then the image and its inverse f^{-1} can be easily applied to the skeleton components of the generator and constraint representations, respectively; the non-skeleton components are not affected at all. If f is not invertible (i.e., $a_i = 0$), then it is computed by first "forgetting" the constraints on x_i, adding the corresponding line, and then adding constraint $\beta = (x_i = \boldsymbol{a}^\mathsf{T}\boldsymbol{x} + b)$. In both cases, the minimal form of the input DD pair is *incrementally* maintained (i.e., there is no need to invoke the full conversion procedure).

4.1 A Semantic Widening for NNC Polyhedra

The design of appropriate widening operators is considered both a key component and a main challenge in the development of abstract domains [5,7,18,19,21], in particular when targeting numerical properties [3,4,40], because their accuracy mostly depends on the particular context of application. For ease of exposition, in the following we will only consider the well known *standard widening* [25].[10]

---

[10] For all widenings '∇', we implicitly specify that $\emptyset \nabla \mathcal{P}_2 = \mathcal{P}_2$.

Definition 2 (Standard widening on $\mathbb{CP}_n$). *Let $\mathcal{P}_1, \mathcal{P}_2 \in \mathbb{CP}_n$ be such that $\mathcal{P}_i = \mathrm{con}(\mathcal{C}_i)$, where $\mathcal{P}_1 \neq \emptyset$ and $\mathcal{C}_1$ is in minimal form. Let also $\mathcal{I}_i = \mathrm{ineqs}(\mathcal{C}_i)$;[11] then $\mathcal{P}_1 \nabla_\mathsf{C} \mathcal{P}_2 \stackrel{\mathrm{def}}{=} \mathrm{con}(\mathcal{I}_1' \cup \mathcal{I}_2')$, where*

$$\mathcal{I}_1' = \left\{ \beta_1 \in \mathcal{I}_1 \mid \mathcal{P}_2 \subseteq \mathrm{con}(\{\beta_1\}) \right\},$$
$$\mathcal{I}_2' = \left\{ \beta_2 \in \mathcal{I}_2 \mid \exists \beta_1 \in \mathcal{I}_1 . \mathcal{P}_1 = \mathrm{con}(\mathcal{I}_1 \setminus \{\beta_1\} \cup \{\beta_2\}) \right\}.$$

When $\mathcal{P}_1 \subseteq \mathcal{P}_2$, the following is an equivalent specification (see [3, Theorem 5]), more appropriate for implementations based on the DD method.

Definition 3. *Let $\mathcal{P}_1, \mathcal{P}_2 \in \mathbb{CP}_n$ be such that $\mathcal{P}_1 \equiv (\mathcal{C}_1, \mathcal{G}_1)$, $\mathcal{P}_2 = \mathrm{con}(\mathcal{C}_2)$, $\emptyset \neq \mathcal{P}_1 \subseteq \mathcal{P}_2$ and $\mathcal{C}_1$ is in minimal form. Then $\mathcal{P}_1 \nabla_\mathsf{C} \mathcal{P}_2 \stackrel{\mathrm{def}}{=} \mathrm{con}(\mathcal{C})$, where*

$$\mathcal{C} = \left\{ \beta_2 \in \mathcal{C}_2 \mid \exists \beta_1 \in \mathcal{C}_1 . \mathrm{sat}(\beta_1, \mathcal{G}_1) = \mathrm{sat}(\beta_2, \mathcal{G}_1) \right\}.$$

More often than desired, the specification of widening operators relies on the "syntactic" representations of the abstract domain elements, rather than their "semantics"; thus, when a canonical representation is missing (or deemed too expensive to compute), the result of the widening depends on low level representation details. This was the case for the original proposal of widening on closed polyhedra [22], which was refined into a "semantic" widening in [25]. Similarly, the widenings defined in [38] for the graph-based representations of bounded differences and octagons were refined into semantic widenings in [2,10]. Available implementations of the domain of NNC polyhedra based on the DD method are affected by the same issue, because they compute the widening of the underlying ϵ-representations, which are not canonical. This happens for all of the widening variants defined on polyhedra, including the one proposed in [3,4], as well as the improved versions that can be obtained by applying generic techniques, such as the *widening up-to* [29].

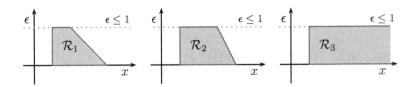

Fig. 2. Widening NNC polyhedra delegating to widening on ϵ-representations.

Example 3. Consider the ϵ-representation polyhedra in Fig. 2. The two polyhedra $\mathcal{R}_1, \mathcal{R}_2 \in \mathbb{CP}_2$ on the left hand side and the middle of the figure are encoding the same NNC polyhedron $\mathcal{P} = \mathrm{con}(\mathcal{C}) \in \mathbb{P}_1$, where $\mathcal{C} = \{0.5 \leq x, x < 2\}$. Both representations encode no redundant constraint; they only differ in the slope of

---

[11] We write $\mathrm{ineqs}(\mathcal{C})$ to denote the constraint system obtained by splitting each equality in $\mathcal{C}$ into a pair of non-strict inequalities.

the facet representing the strict inequality constraint. As a consequence, when computing $\mathcal{R}_3 = \mathcal{R}_1 \nabla_C \mathcal{R}_2$, shown on the right hand side of the figure, the standard widening operator on the ϵ-representations fails to detect the stability of the strict inequality constraint, which is dropped. $\mathcal{R}_3$ represents the NNC polyhedron $\mathcal{P}' = \mathrm{con}(\{0.5 \leq x\})$: even though correct from a theoretical point of view, the widening depends on the syntactic encoding of strict inequalities. As a side note, the user of the abstract domain might reasonably expect that a property such as $\mathcal{P} \nabla_C \mathcal{P} = \mathcal{P}$ always holds, but this is not the case.

When implementing the widening on NNC polyhedra by delegating to the underlying widening on closed polyhedra, some precautions are required too:

- Definition 3 assumes that $\mathcal{P}_1 \subseteq \mathcal{P}_2$; note however that, for NNC polyhedra, $\mathcal{P}_1 \subseteq \mathcal{P}_2$ does not automatically imply that property $\mathcal{R}_1 \subseteq \mathcal{R}_2$ holds for the corresponding ϵ-representations;
- the implementation has to make sure that the result of the widening is still a valid ϵ-representation, i.e., the bounds for ϵ cannot be dropped;
- in order to ensure the finite convergence guarantee, the first argument $\mathcal{P}_1$ should be described by a constraint system encoding no redundant elements; however, a non-redundant description for the ϵ-representation $\mathcal{R}_1$ can still encode many redundant constraints; these have to be removed by applying the *strong minimization* procedures defined in [6,11].

As a consequence, the overall approach may also incur a significant overhead.

In contrast, when adopting the direct encoding of Sect. 3, we can adopt a variant of Definition 3 to obtain a *semantic* widening on NNC polyhedra, because all of the materializations of a non-skeleton strict inequality constraint share the same saturation information, no matter for the variation in their slopes.

Definition 4 (Widening on $\mathbb{P}_n$). *Let $\mathcal{P}_1, \mathcal{P}_2 \in \mathbb{P}_n$ be such that $\mathcal{P}_1 \equiv (\mathcal{C}_1, \mathcal{G}_1)$, $\mathcal{P}_2 = \mathrm{con}(\mathcal{C}_2)$, $\emptyset \neq \mathcal{P}_1 \subseteq \mathcal{P}_2$, each $\mathcal{C}_i = \langle S\mathcal{K}_i^c, NS_i^c \rangle$ is in minimal form and $\mathcal{G}_1 = \langle S\mathcal{K}_1^g, NS_1^g \rangle$. Then $\mathcal{P}_1 \nabla_N \mathcal{P}_2 \overset{\mathrm{def}}{=} \mathrm{con}(\langle S\mathcal{K}^c, NS^c \rangle)$, where*

$$S\mathcal{K}^c = \{\, \beta_2 \in S\mathcal{K}_2^c \mid \exists \beta_1 \in S\mathcal{K}_1^c \, . \, \mathrm{sat}(\beta_1, S\mathcal{K}_1^g) = \mathrm{sat}(\beta_2, S\mathcal{K}_1^g) \,\};$$
$$NS^c = \{\, ns_2 \in NS_2^c \mid ns_2 \subseteq S\mathcal{K}^c \,\}.$$

The next two lemmas show that '∇_N' is a well-defined widening operator on $\mathbb{P}_n$.

Lemma 1. *Definition 4 specifies a binary operator on $\mathbb{P}_n$.*

Proof. We need to show that the result computed by '∇_N' is not affected by a change of representation for the two input arguments.

For $\mathcal{P}_1, \mathcal{P}_2 \in \mathbb{P}_n$, where $\mathcal{P}_1 \neq \emptyset$ and $\mathcal{P}_1 \subseteq \mathcal{P}_2$, let $\mathcal{P}_1 \nabla_N \mathcal{P}_2$ be computed according to Definition 4; in particular, let $\mathcal{P}_1 \equiv (\mathcal{C}_1, \mathcal{G}_1)$ and $\mathcal{P}_2 = \mathrm{con}(\mathcal{C}_2)$, where $\mathcal{C}_i = \langle S\mathcal{K}_i^c, NS_i^c \rangle$ are arbitrary constraint representations for $\mathcal{P}_i$ satisfying the minimality hypothesis and $\mathcal{G}_1 = \langle S\mathcal{K}_1^g, NS_1^g \rangle$.

Note that, due to the inclusion hypothesis $\mathcal{P}_1 \subseteq \mathcal{P}_2$, all of the equality constraints in $\mathcal{SK}_2^c$ are detected as stable. Let $\beta_1 \in \mathcal{SK}_1^c$ be a skeleton (strict or nonstrict) inequality constraint and $\beta_2 \in \mathcal{SK}_2^c$ be a skeleton inequality constraint such that $\mathrm{sat}(\beta_1, \mathcal{SK}_1^g) = \mathrm{sat}(\beta_2, \mathcal{SK}_1^g)$ holds; that is, $\beta_2 \in \mathcal{SK}_2^c$ is detected to be stable due to $\beta_1 \in \mathcal{SK}_1^c$. Being a skeleton constraint and due to the minimality assumption, β_1 identifies a *facet* F_1 of $\mathrm{cl}(\mathcal{P}_1)$; thus, any other constraint system representation for $\mathcal{P}_1$ will always contain a constraint β_1' (identifying the same facet F_1) such that $\mathrm{sat}(\beta_1, \mathcal{SK}_1^g) = \mathrm{sat}(\beta_1', \mathcal{SK}_1^g)$. The same reasoning can be repeated for β_2 and F_2. Hence, the computed skeleton component $\mathcal{SK}^c$ does not depend on the chosen representations for $\mathcal{P}_1$ and $\mathcal{P}_2$. As a side note, if $\mathcal{P}_1 = \mathrm{cl}(\mathcal{P}_1)$ then no strict inequality in $\mathcal{SK}_2^c$ can be detected as stable. When working on closed polyhedra, Definition 4 becomes equivalent to Definition 3 and we have:

$$\mathrm{cl}(\mathcal{P}_1)\nabla_N\mathrm{cl}(\mathcal{P}_2) = \mathrm{cl}(\mathcal{P}_1)\nabla_C\mathrm{cl}(\mathcal{P}_2), \qquad (1)$$

where '∇_C' is known to be well-defined on $\mathbb{CP}_n$ [3, Theorem 5].

Finally, consider the non-skeleton component and let $ns_2 \in NS^c$, so that $ns_2 \in NS_2^c$ and $ns_2 \subseteq \mathcal{SK}^c$. Support ns_2 identifies a *face* (not a facet) F_2 of $\mathrm{cl}(\mathcal{P}_2)$ which is cut from $\mathcal{P}_2$, i.e., $F_2 \cap \mathcal{P}_2 = \emptyset$. Let $\mathcal{F} = \{\, F_\beta \mid \beta \in ns_2 \,\}$ be the set of facets identified by the constraints in ns_2, so that $F_2 = \bigcap \mathcal{F}$. Note that, since ns_2 is non-redundant, all the facets in $\mathcal{F}$ have a non-empty intersection with $\mathcal{P}_2$ (i.e., they correspond to non-strict inequalities); moreover, all the facets in $\mathcal{F}$ are stable and, as observed in the previous paragraph, the set of stable facets does not depend on the chosen constraint representations. Therefore, in any other minimal representation for $\mathcal{P}_2$, there will be a set ns_2' (i.e., a support) of non-strict skeleton constraints that identifies the same set of stable facets $\mathcal{F}$; namely, ns_2' identifies the same cut face F_2 identified by ns_2. Hence, the computed non-skeleton component NS^c does not depend on the chosen representations for $\mathcal{P}_1$ and $\mathcal{P}_2$.   □

Lemma 2. $\nabla_N \colon \mathbb{P}_n \times \mathbb{P}_n \to \mathbb{P}_n$ *is a widening operator.*

Proof. For $\mathcal{P}_1, \mathcal{P}_2 \in \mathbb{P}_n$, where $\mathcal{P}_1 \neq \emptyset$ and $\mathcal{P}_1 \subseteq \mathcal{P}_2$, let $\mathcal{P}' = \mathcal{P}_1\nabla_N\mathcal{P}_2$ be computed according to Definition 4.

First we show that '∇_N' is an upper bound operator, i.e., it satisfies both $\mathcal{P}_1 \subseteq \mathcal{P}'$ and $\mathcal{P}_2 \subseteq \mathcal{P}'$. By Definition 4, it can be seen that $\mathcal{P}' = \mathrm{con}(\mathcal{SK}^c, NS^c)$, $\mathcal{P}_2 = \mathrm{con}(\mathcal{SK}_2^c, NS_2^c)$ and both $\mathcal{SK}^c \subseteq \mathcal{SK}_2^c$ and $NS^c \subseteq NS_2^c$ hold; hence, the inclusion $\mathcal{P}_2 \subseteq \mathcal{P}'$ follows from the anti-monotonicity of function 'con'; the other inclusion $\mathcal{P}_1 \subseteq \mathcal{P}'$ follows from the hypothesis $\mathcal{P}_1 \subseteq \mathcal{P}_2$.

Next we show that the systematic application of '∇_N' forces the upward iteration sequence to stabilize after a finite number of iterates. To this end, we define a ranking function $\mathrm{rank}\colon \mathbb{P}_n \to \mathbb{N}^{2+n}$, mapping a polyhedron into the well-founded set $(\mathbb{N}^{2+n}, \ll)$, where '$\ll$' denotes the strict lexicographic ordering. For each $\mathcal{P} = \mathrm{con}(\mathcal{C}) \in \mathbb{P}_n$ such that $\mathcal{P} \neq \emptyset$ and $\mathcal{C} = \langle \mathcal{SK}^c, NS^c \rangle$ is in minimal form, we define $\mathrm{rank}(\mathcal{P}) \stackrel{\mathrm{def}}{=} (e, s, f_{n-1}, \ldots, f_j, \ldots, f_0)$, where e is the number of equality constraints in $\mathcal{SK}^c$, s is the total number of constraints in $\mathcal{SK}^c$ and, for each $j \in \{0, \ldots, n-1\}$, f_j is the number of strict inequality constraints in $\mathcal{C}$ cutting a face of $\mathrm{cl}(\mathcal{P})$ having affine dimension j.[12] Note that 'rank' is well-defined, because $\mathcal{C}$ is in minimal form.

To complete the proof we have to show that, whenever $\mathcal{P}_1 \subset \mathcal{P}' = \mathcal{P}_1 \nabla_{\mathrm{N}} \mathcal{P}_2$, i.e., when the increasing sequence has not stabilized yet, the ranking function is decreasing, i.e., $\mathrm{rank}(\mathcal{P}') \ll \mathrm{rank}(\mathcal{P}_1)$.

Let $\mathrm{rank}(\mathcal{P}_1) = (e, s, f_{n-1}, \ldots, f_0)$ and $\mathrm{rank}(\mathcal{P}') = (e', s', f'_{n-1}, \ldots, f'_0)$.

Since the constraint systems are in minimal form and '∇_{N}' is an upper bound operator on $\mathbb{P}_n$, for the equality constraints we always have $e' \leq e$. If $e' < e$, then the ranking function is decreasing; thus, in the rest of the proof, we assume that $e' = e$. Namely, we assume that $\mathcal{P}_1$, $\mathcal{P}_2$ and $\mathcal{P}'$ all have the same affine dimension $k = n - e$.

Observe now that, by Definition 4, for the skeleton constraints we have $s' \leq s$. Namely, each skeleton (strict or non-strict) inequality constraint $\beta_2 \in \mathcal{SK}_2^{\mathrm{c}}$ that is selected to enter $\mathcal{SK}^{\mathrm{c}}$ has a unique corresponding skeleton constraint $\beta_1 \in \mathcal{SK}_1^{\mathrm{c}}$, which identifies the same facet of $\mathrm{cl}(\mathcal{P}')$ (recall that $\mathcal{P}_1$ and $\mathcal{P}'$ both have affine dimension k). Again, if $s' < s$, then the ranking function is decreasing; thus, in the rest of the proof, we assume both $e' = e$ and $s' = s$. Under such an assumption, by Definition 4, we obtain a one-to-one correspondence between the facets of $\mathrm{cl}(\mathcal{P}_1)$ and those of $\mathrm{cl}(\mathcal{P}')$: this implies $\mathrm{cl}(\mathcal{P}_1) = \mathrm{cl}(\mathcal{P}_2) = \mathrm{cl}(\mathcal{P}')$.

Consider now the tuples $t = (f_{k-1}, \ldots, f_0)$ and $t' = (f'_{k-1}, \ldots, f'_0)$, where as said above $k = n - e$ is the affine dimension of the polyhedra.[13] By hypothesis, $\mathrm{cl}(\mathcal{P}) = \mathrm{cl}(\mathcal{P}')$ but $\mathcal{P}_1 \subset \mathcal{P}'$; hence we obtain $t \neq t'$. Moreover, we cannot have $t \ll t'$, since this would mean that there exists a strict inequality in $\mathcal{P}'$ cutting a face which is not cut from $\mathcal{P}_1$, contradicting $\mathcal{P}_1 \subset \mathcal{P}'$. Therefore $t' \ll t$, which implies $\mathrm{rank}(\mathcal{P}') \ll \mathrm{rank}(\mathcal{P}_1)$.   □

The new widening satisfies both $\mathcal{P} \nabla_{\mathrm{N}} \mathcal{P} = \mathcal{P}$ and $\mathcal{P} \nabla_{\mathrm{N}} \mathrm{cl}(\mathcal{P}) = \mathrm{cl}(\mathcal{P})$, which is not the case for the widening based on the ϵ-dimension approach. Also, Eq. (1) means that operator '∇_{N}' is indeed an *extension* on the domain $\mathbb{P}_n$ of the standard widening '∇_{C}' defined on $\mathbb{CP}_n$.

Example 4. Reconsider polyhedron $\mathcal{P} = \mathrm{con}(\{0.5 \leq x, x < 2\})$, for which a couple of possible ϵ-representations were shown in Fig. 2. When directly encoding the strict inequalities and applying Definition 4, constraint $\beta = (x < 2)$ is detected to be stable, so that $\mathcal{P} \nabla_{\mathrm{N}} \mathcal{P} = \mathcal{P}$. Moreover, letting $\beta' = (x \leq 2)$, we also have $\mathcal{P} \nabla_{\mathrm{N}} \mathrm{cl}(\mathcal{P}) = \mathrm{cl}(\mathcal{P})$, because $\mathrm{sat}(\beta, \mathcal{SK}_1^{\mathrm{g}}) = \mathrm{sat}(\beta', \mathcal{SK}_1^{\mathrm{g}})$.

In Definition 4, the non-skeleton constraints and generators in NS_1^{c} and NS_1^{g} play no role in the computation of the widening, simplifying its implementation. As shown in Example 4, a *non-strict* inequality in $\beta_2 \in \mathcal{SK}_2^{\mathrm{c}}$ can be detected as stable (i.e., enter the result $\mathcal{SK}^{\mathrm{c}}$) even when it weakens a corresponding *strict* inequality in $\mathcal{SK}_1^{\mathrm{c}}$; this is not the case when blindly extending Definition 2. Also note that a stable non-skeleton constraint $ns \in NS^{\mathrm{c}}$ is only supported by stable skeleton constraints.

---

[12] As an example, f_0 is the number of strict inequality constraints cutting only a vertex from the topological closure of the polyhedron.

[13] Note that for all $k \leq j \leq n - 1$, we have $f_j = f'_j = 0$.

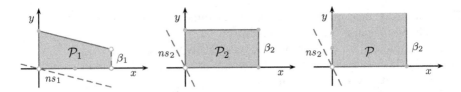

Fig. 3. From left to right: $\mathcal{P}_1$, $\mathcal{P}_2$ and $\mathcal{P} = \mathcal{P}_1 \nabla_N \mathcal{P}_2$.

Example 5. Consider $\mathcal{P}_1 = \mathrm{con}(\{0 \leq x < 4, 0 \leq y, 0 < x + 4y \leq 8\})$ and $\mathcal{P}_2 = \mathrm{con}(\{0 \leq x \leq 4, 0 \leq y \leq 2, 0 < 2x + y\})$, shown on the left and middle of Fig. 3, respectively. Constraint $\beta_2 = (x \leq 4)$ is stable, as it shares on $\mathcal{P}_1$ the same saturation information of $\beta_1 = (x < 4)$. Support $ns_2 = \{x \geq 0, y \geq 0\} \equiv (0 < 2x + y)$ is stable, no matter if the shown materialization differs from the one chosen for $ns_1 \equiv (0 < x + 4y)$, because the skeleton constraints defining it are both stable. Thus, $\mathcal{P}_1 \nabla_N \mathcal{P}_2 = \mathrm{con}(\{0 \leq x \leq 4, 0 \leq y, 0 < 2x + y\})$, shown on the right hand side of the figure. An implementation based on Definition 2 would drop β_2 and, depending on the chosen materializations, maybe also ns_2.

In the next example we show that a blind extension of Definition 3 to the case of NNC polyhedra, where the non-skeleton component NS_2^c is treated the same of the skeleton component $\mathcal{SK}_2^c$, would not result in a proper widening, since the finite convergence guarantee is compromised.

Example 6. For each $i \in \mathbb{N} \setminus \{0\}$, let $\beta_i = (x + iy \leq i)$, $\mathcal{C}_i = \{0 \leq x, 0 \leq y < 1, \beta_i\}$ and $\mathcal{P}_i = \mathrm{con}(\mathcal{C}_i)$; note that $\mathcal{P}_i \subset \mathcal{P}_{i+1}$. Polyhedra $\mathcal{P}_1$ and $\mathcal{P}_2$ are shown on the left hand side and middle of Fig. 4. Note that $\mathcal{C}_i = \langle \mathcal{SK}_i^c, NS_i^c \rangle$, where $\mathcal{SK}_i^c = \{0 \leq x, 0 \leq y, \beta_i\}$, $NS_i^c = \{ns_i\}$ and $ns_i = \{0 \leq x, \beta_i\} \equiv (y < 1)$. By using Definition 3 as is, we would obtain $\mathcal{P}_i \nabla_C \mathcal{P}_{i+1} = \mathcal{P}_{i+1}$; namely, the skeleton constraint β_{i+1} and the non-skeleton constraint ns_{i+1} are detected to be stable, since in $\mathcal{P}_i$ they share the same saturation information of ns_i (they are only saturated by closure point $(0,1)$). Hence, $\{\mathcal{P}_i\}_{i \in \mathbb{N}}$ would form an infinite increasing chain. In contrast, when using Definition 4 to compute $\mathcal{P}_1 \nabla_N \mathcal{P}_2$, shown on the right of the figure, constraints β_2 and ns_2 are both dropped.

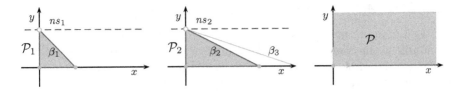

Fig. 4. An increasing chain in $\mathbb{P}_2$ where Definition 3 is not stabilizing; $\mathcal{P} = \mathcal{P}_1 \nabla_N \mathcal{P}_2$ is the result obtained when using Definition 4.

The ranking function defined in the proof of Lemma 2 may be decreasing even though the number of non-redundant constraints is increasing.

Example 7. For $i = 1, 2$, consider $\mathcal{P}_i = \text{con}(\mathcal{C}_i) \in \mathbb{P}_2$, where

$$\mathcal{C}_1 = \{0 < x < 1, 0 < y < 1\},$$
$$\mathcal{C}_2 = \{0 \leq x \leq 1, 0 \leq y \leq 1, 0 < x + y < 2, -1 < x - y < 1\},$$

so that $\mathcal{P}_1$ is a topologically open square and $\mathcal{P}_2$ (which is neither closed nor open) is obtained from $\text{cl}(\mathcal{P}_1)$ by cutting away its four vertices. It is easy to observe that $\mathcal{P}_1 \nabla_N \mathcal{P}_2 = \mathcal{P}_2$, because all of the skeleton constraints are stable. Note that both constraint systems are in minimal form and their cardinalities are increasing: $|\mathcal{C}_2| = 8 > 4 = |\mathcal{C}_1|$. Nonetheless, the ranking function is decreasing:

$$\text{rank}(\mathcal{P}_2) = (e', s', f_1', f_0') = (0, 4, 0, 4) \ll (0, 4, 4, 0) = (e, s, f_1, f_0) = \text{rank}(\mathcal{P}_1).$$

5   Experimental Evaluation

The new representation for NNC polyhedra, the conversion algorithms and the operators presented in the previous sections are implemented in PPLite, a new software library developed at the Department of Mathematical, Physical and Computer Sciences of the University of Parma. Derived from the Parma Polyhedra Library, PPLite is written in modern C++ and has a different goal: to provide a simpler framework for experimenting with new ideas and algorithms in the context of polyhedral computations, for both researchers and students. In particular, it is not aimed at implementing the full range of abstract domains (and operators) made available by the PPL. Other main characteristics are: (a) both closed and NNC rational polyhedra are supported; (b) arithmetic computations are based on FLINT (http://www.flintlib.org/); (c) encapsulation is not fully enforced, so that a knowledgeable user can directly change the contents of data structures, e.g., to experiment with alternative implementations of domain operators; (d) while performance and portability are deemed important, priority is given to ease of implementation and readability.

A preliminary experimental evaluation of the new representation and conversion algorithms for (closed and NNC) polyhedra was reported in [13], showing impressive efficiency gains with respect to the PPL. Those results were obtained inside the PPL framework, hence they were orthogonal with respect to many of the PPLite's implementation choices (e.g., the use of FLINT).[14]

In the following paragraphs we summarize the results of a more thorough experimental evaluation,[15] where the PPLite library is used in a program analysis based on Abstract Interpretation. To this end, we have interfaced the PPLite's NNC polyhedra domain to the Apron library [32], so as to make it available to PAGAI [30], a static analyzer for invariant generation built on top of the LLVM infrastructure. When using PAGAI, it is possible to choose between several abstract domains, including boxes (box), octagons (oct), the native

---

[14] The efficiency gains have been confirmed when adopting the PPLite implementation.
[15] All experiments have been performed on a laptop with an Intel Core i7-3632QM CPU, 16 GB of RAM and running GNU/Linux 4.13.0-36.

Apron domain for polyhedra (pk) and the Apron layer for the PPL's polyhedra (ppl_poly); we added support for the new domain pplite_poly. In Table 1 we report the time spent by PAGAI in calls to the operators of these abstract domains (column 'size' shows the size of the LLVM bitcode file) when analyzing some C source files distributed with PAGAI; most of these are variants of benchmarks taken from the SNU real-time benchmark suite for worst-case execution time analysis.[16]

Table 1. Efficiency comparison for PAGAI's domains.

Test	Size	Apron's time				
	KB	box	oct	pplite	ppl	pk
decompress	549	6.64	41.04	40.83	101.08	211.04
filter	15	1.08	5.77	19.02	88.02	82.32
adpcm	67	0.75	3.12	5.08	14.31	21.78
decompress-opt	71	0.59	9.97	3.02	7.85	13.42
nsichneu	527	0.51	0.49	1.55	3.06	2.33
cover	33	0.35	0.38	1.25	2.09	1.61
fft1	20	0.16	0.51	0.82	1.74	2.02
edn	57	0.17	0.32	0.73	1.57	1.71
compress	30	0.15	0.67	0.69	1.84	2.64
ndes	45	0.17	0.25	0.64	1.27	1.20
minver	30	0.15	0.24	0.52	1.02	1.10

The new domain performs significantly better than the other polyhedra domains, being also competitive with respect to the domain of octagons on the biggest benchmarks. It is worth stressing that these efficiency gains have been obtained even if PAGAI makes a quite limited use of strict inequalities, which are only used to model floating point values: among the tests reported in Table 1, only 'fft1' and 'minver' declare floating point variables. Moreover, the "classic" static analysis implemented in PAGAI applies no variable packing technique at all: hence, all the relational domains incur avoidable overheads [45,47], which are orthogonal with respect to the chosen implementation of NNC polyhedra.

In order to assess correctness, we also performed a different experimental evaluation where, after each and every invocation of an abstract operator, the result computed by the new domain pplite_poly is systematically compared with the result computed by ppl_poly: the only differences were recorded when computing widenings, where the semantic widening '∇_N' used by PPLite was sometimes more precise than the syntactic one used by PPL.

---

[16] We only show those tests where the time spent by pplite_poly is above 0.5 s.

6   Conclusion

By leveraging on a new DD representation and conversion algorithm, we have presented the corresponding implementation of the abstract domain of NNC polyhedra. In particular, we focused our work on the specification of the operators needed for defining a static analysis based on Abstract Interpretation, here included a semantics-based widening operator. The experimental evaluation conducted shows that the new domain systematically outperforms the more classical implementations. As future work, we plan to extend the abstract domain so as to also support operators needed in other contexts. For instance, in the analysis and verification of hybrid systems, strict inequalities usually play a more important role: we reasonably expect that the adoption of our new implementation for the domain of NNC polyhedra may result in even larger efficiency gains.

References

1. Amato, G., Scozzari, F.: The abstract domain of parallelotopes. Electr. Notes Theor. Comput. Sci. **287**, 17–28 (2012)
2. Bagnara, R., Hill, P.M., Mazzi, E., Zaffanella, E.: Widening operators for weakly-relational numeric abstractions. In: Hankin, C., Siveroni, I. (eds.) SAS 2005. LNCS, vol. 3672, pp. 3–18. Springer, Heidelberg (2005). https://doi.org/10.1007/11547662_3
3. Bagnara, R., Hill, P.M., Ricci, E., Zaffanella, E.: Precise widening operators for convex polyhedra. In: Cousot, R. (ed.) SAS 2003. LNCS, vol. 2694, pp. 337–354. Springer, Heidelberg (2003). https://doi.org/10.1007/3-540-44898-5_19
4. Bagnara, R., Hill, P.M., Ricci, E., Zaffanella, E.: Precise widening operators for convex polyhedra. Sci. Comput. Program. **58**(1–2), 28–56 (2005)
5. Bagnara, R., Hill, P.M., Zaffanella, E.: Widening operators for powerset domains. In: Steffen, B., Levi, G. (eds.) VMCAI 2004. LNCS, vol. 2937, pp. 135–148. Springer, Heidelberg (2004). https://doi.org/10.1007/978-3-540-24622-0_13
6. Bagnara, R., Hill, P.M., Zaffanella, E.: Not necessarily closed convex polyhedra and the double description method. Formal Asp. Comput. **17**(2), 222–257 (2005)
7. Bagnara, R., Hill, P.M., Zaffanella, E.: Widening operators for powerset domains. Softw. Tools for Technol. Transf. **8**(4/5), 449–466 (2006)
8. Bagnara, R., Hill, P.M., Zaffanella, E.: The Parma polyhedra library: toward a complete set of numerical abstractions for the analysis and verification of hardware and software systems. Sci. Comput. Program. **72**(1–2), 3–21 (2008)
9. Bagnara, R., Hill, P.M., Zaffanella, E.: Applications of polyhedral computations to the analysis and verification of hardware and software systems. Theor. Comput. Sci. **410**(46), 4672–4691 (2009)
10. Bagnara, R., Hill, P.M., Zaffanella, E.: Weakly-relational shapes for numeric abstractions: improved algorithms and proofs of correctness. Formal Meth. Syst. Des. **35**(3), 279–323 (2009)
11. Bagnara, R., Ricci, E., Zaffanella, E., Hill, P.M.: Possibly not closed convex polyhedra and the parma polyhedra library. In: Hermenegildo, M.V., Puebla, G. (eds.) SAS 2002. LNCS, vol. 2477, pp. 213–229. Springer, Heidelberg (2002). https://doi.org/10.1007/3-540-45789-5_17

12. Becchi, A., Zaffanella, E.: A conversion procedure for NNC polyhedra. CoRR, abs/1711.09593 (2017)
13. Becchi, A., Zaffanella, E.: A direct encoding for NNC polyhedra. In: Chockler, H., Weissenbacher, G. (eds.) Computer Aided Verification, pp. 230–248, Cham, 2018. Springer International Publishing. An extended version with proofs is available as [12]
14. Birkhoff, G.: Lattice Theory, vol. 25. Colloquium Publications. American Mathematical Society, Providence (1967)
15. Blanchet, B., Cousot, P., Cousot, R., Feret, J., Mauborgne, L., Miné, A., Monniaux, D., Rival, X.: A static analyzer for large safety-critical software. In: Proceedings of the ACM SIGPLAN 2003 Conference on Programming Language Design and Implementation (PLDI 2003), pp. 196–207, San Diego, USA (2003)
16. Chernikova, N.V.: Algorithm for finding a general formula for the non-negative solutions of system of linear inequalities. U.S.S.R. Comput. Math. Math. Phys. 5(2), 228–233 (1965)
17. Clarisó, R., Cortadella, J.: The octahedron abstract domain. Sci. Comput. Program. 64(1), 115–139 (2007)
18. Cortesi, A.: Widening operators for abstract interpretation. In: Sixth IEEE International Conference on Software Engineering and Formal Methods (SEFM 2008), pp. 31–40, Cape Town, South Africa (2008)
19. Cortesi, A., Zanioli, M.: Widening and narrowing operators for abstract interpretation. Comput. Lang. Syst. Struct. 37(1), 24–42 (2011)
20. Cousot, P., Cousot, R.: Abstract interpretation: a unified lattice model for static analysis of programs by construction or approximation of fixpoints. In: Proceedings of the Fourth Annual ACM Symposium on Principles of Programming Languages, pp. 238–252, Los Angeles, USA (1977)
21. Cousot, P., Cousot, R.: Comparing the Galois connection and widening/narrowing approaches to abstract interpretation. In: Bruynooghe, M., Wirsing, M. (eds.) PLILP 1992. LNCS, vol. 631, pp. 269–295. Springer, Heidelberg (1992). https://doi.org/10.1007/3-540-55844-6_142
22. Cousot, P., Halbwachs, N.: Automatic discovery of linear restraints among variables of a program. In: Conference Record of the Fifth Annual ACM Symposium on Principles of Programming Languages, pp. 84–96, Tucson, USA (1978)
23. Fulara, J., Durnoga, K., Jakubczyk, K., Schubert, A.: Relational abstract domain of weighted hexagons. Electr. Notes Theor. Comput. Sci. 267(1), 59–72 (2010)
24. Genov, B.: The convex hull problem in practice: improving the running time of the double description method. Ph.D. thesis, University of Bremen, Germany (2014)
25. Halbwachs, N.: Détermination Automatique de Relations Linéaires Vérifiées par les Variables d'un Programme. Thèse de 3ème cycle d'informatique, Université scientifique et médicale de Grenoble, Grenoble, France (1979)
26. Halbwachs, N., Merchat, D., Gonnord, L.: Some ways to reduce the space dimension in polyhedra computations. Formal Meth. Syst. Des. 29(1), 79–95 (2006)
27. Halbwachs, N., Merchat, D., Parent-Vigouroux, C.: Cartesian factoring of polyhedra in linear relation analysis. In: Cousot, R. (ed.) SAS 2003. LNCS, vol. 2694, pp. 355–365. Springer, Heidelberg (2003). https://doi.org/10.1007/3-540-44898-5_20
28. Halbwachs, N., Proy, Y.-E., Raymond, P.: Verification of linear hybrid systems by means of convex approximations. In: Le Charlier, B. (ed.) SAS 1994. LNCS, vol. 864, pp. 223–237. Springer, Heidelberg (1994). https://doi.org/10.1007/3-540-58485-4_43
29. Halbwachs, N., Proy, Y.-E., Roumanoff, P.: Verification of real-time systems using linear relation analysis. Formal Meth. Syst. Des. 11(2), 157–185 (1997)

30. Henry, J., Monniaux, D., Moy, M.: PAGAI: a path sensitive static analyser. Electr. Notes Theor. Comput. Sci. **289**, 15–25 (2012)
31. Howe, J.M., King, A.: Logahedra: a new weakly relational domain. In: Liu, Z., Ravn, A.P. (eds.) ATVA 2009. LNCS, vol. 5799, pp. 306–320. Springer, Heidelberg (2009). https://doi.org/10.1007/978-3-642-04761-9_23
32. Jeannet, B., Miné, A.: APRON: a library of numerical abstract domains for static analysis. In: Bouajjani, A., Maler, O. (eds.) CAV 2009. LNCS, vol. 5643, pp. 661–667. Springer, Heidelberg (2009). https://doi.org/10.1007/978-3-642-02658-4_52
33. Kaibel, V., Pfetsch, M.E.: Computing the face lattice of a polytope from its vertex-facet incidences. Comput. Geom. **23**(3), 281–290 (2002)
34. Laviron, V., Logozzo, F.: SubPolyhedra: a (More) scalable approach to infer linear inequalities. In: Jones, N.D., Müller-Olm, M. (eds.) VMCAI 2009. LNCS, vol. 5403, pp. 229–244. Springer, Heidelberg (2008). https://doi.org/10.1007/978-3-540-93900-9_20
35. Logozzo, F., Fähndrich, M.: Pentagons: a weakly relational abstract domain for the efficient validation of array accesses. In: Proceedings of the 2008 ACM Symposium on Applied Computing, pp. 184–188, Fortaleza, Brazil (2008)
36. Miné, A.: A new numerical abstract domain based on difference-bound matrices. In: Danvy, O., Filinski, A. (eds.) PADO 2001. LNCS, vol. 2053, pp. 155–172. Springer, Heidelberg (2001). https://doi.org/10.1007/3-540-44978-7_10
37. Miné, A.: The octagon abstract domain. In: Proceedings of the Eighth Working Conference on Reverse Engineering, pp. 310–319, Stuttgart, Germany (2001)
38. Miné, A.: Weakly relational numerical abstract domains. Ph.D. thesis, École Polytechnique, Paris, France (2005)
39. Motzkin, T.S., Raiffa, H., Thompson, G.L., Thrall, R.M.: The double description method. In: Contributions to the Theory of Games - Volume II, Number 28 in Annals of Mathematics Studies, pp. 51–73, Princeton, USA (1953)
40. Notani, V., Giacobazzi, R.: Learning based widening. In: 8th Workshop on Tools for Automatic Program Analysis (TAPAS 2017), New York, USA (2017)
41. Sankaranarayanan, S., Sipma, H.B., Manna, Z.: Scalable analysis of linear systems using mathematical programming. In: Cousot, R. (ed.) VMCAI 2005. LNCS, vol. 3385, pp. 25–41. Springer, Heidelberg (2005). https://doi.org/10.1007/978-3-540-30579-8_2
42. Shaham, R., Kolodner, E.K., Sagiv, S.: Heap profiling for space-efficient Java. In: Proceedings of the 2001 ACM SIGPLAN Conference on Programming Language Design and Implementation (PLDI), pp. 104–113, Snowbird, USA (2001)
43. Simon, A., King, A., Howe, J.M.: Two variables per linear inequality as an abstract domain. In: Leuschel, M. (ed.) LOPSTR 2002. LNCS, vol. 2664, pp. 71–89. Springer, Heidelberg (2003). https://doi.org/10.1007/3-540-45013-0_7
44. Singh, G., Püschel, M., Vechev, M.T.: Making numerical program analysis fast. In: Proceedings of the 36th ACM SIGPLAN Conference on Programming Language Design and Implementation, pp. 303–313, Portland, USA (2015)
45. Singh, G., Püschel, M., Vechev, M.T.: Fast polyhedra abstract domain. In: Proceedings of the 44th ACM SIGPLAN Symposium on Principles of Programming Languages, POPL 2017, pp. 46–59, Paris, France (2017)
46. Singh, G., Püschel, M., Vechev, M.T.: A practical construction for decomposing numerical abstract domains. PACMPL, **2**(POPL), 55:1–55:28 (2018)
47. Zaffanella, E.: On the efficiency of convex polyhedra. Electr. Notes Theor. Comput. Sci. **334**, 31–44 (2018)

Modular Software Fault Isolation
as Abstract Interpretation

Frédéric Besson, Thomas Jensen, and Julien Lepiller[⊠]

Inria, Univ Rennes, CNRS, IRISA, Paris, France
julien.lepiller@inria.fr

Abstract. Software Fault Isolation (SFI) consists in transforming untrusted code so that it runs within a specific address space, (called the sandbox) and verifying at load-time that the binary code does indeed stay inside the sandbox. Security is guaranteed solely by the SFI verifier whose correctness therefore becomes crucial. Existing verifiers enforce a very rigid, almost syntactic policy where every memory access and every control-flow transfer must be preceded by a sandboxing instruction sequence, and where calls outside the sandbox must implement a sophisticated protocol based on a shadow stack. We propose to define SFI as a defensive semantics, with the purpose of deriving semantically sound verifiers that admit flexible and efficient implementations of SFI. We derive an executable analyser, that works on a per-function basis, which ensures that the defensive semantics does not go wrong, and hence that the code is well isolated. Experiments show that our analyser exhibits the desired flexibility: it validates correctly sandboxed code, it catches code breaking the SFI policy, and it can validate programs where redundant instrumentations are optimised away.

1 Introduction

A fundamental challenge in system security is to share computing resources and run programs from various level of trusts, some untrusted or even malicious, on the same host machine. In this context, it is desirable to isolate the different programs, limit their interactions and ensure that, whatever the behaviour of imported code, the security of the host machine cannot be compromised. There exist many isolation mechanisms available at the hardware, virtual machine or operating system level. In this paper, we consider Software Fault Isolation (SFI), an isolation mechanism pioneered by Wahbe *et al.* [15] and further developed in Google's Native Client (NaCl) [13,16] and others. SFI is a flexible and lightweight isolation mechanism which does not rely on hardware or operating system support. Instead, it relies on a static, untrusted, program instrumentation that is validated at load-time by a trusted binary verifier. Compared to other isolation mechanisms, SFI allows the safe execution of trusted and untrusted code within the same address space, thus avoiding costly context switches with kernel code.

© Springer Nature Switzerland AG 2018
A. Podelski (Ed.): SAS 2018, LNCS 11002, pp. 166–186, 2018.
https://doi.org/10.1007/978-3-319-99725-4_12

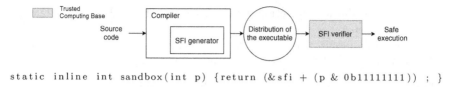

```
static inline int sandbox(int p) {return (&sfi + (p & 0b11111111)) ; }
```

Fig. 1. SFI chain with typical sandboxing code

The general SFI architecture is shown in Fig. 1 together with some typical sandboxing code. The SFI transformation is performed at compile-time. It instruments every memory access so that it is performed inside the memory sandbox. To ensure that a pointer p is within the sandbox variable sfi that is 2^8 bytes aligned and 2^8 bytes wide, the code increments the base address sfi of the sandbox with the 8 least significant bits of the pointer p extracted by masking p using a bitwise &. Control-flow transfers are instrumented so that the code does not jump outside the code sandbox. At load-time, a binary verifier rejects code that is not correctly instrumented. From a security standpoint, only the binary verifier is part of the Trusted Computing Base (TCB). State-of-the-art SFI verifiers trade precision for simplicity and speed, and only perform a linear scan of the binary code. Therefore, the verifiers enforce very strong sufficient conditions for isolation. This has the side-effect that the SFI transformation is performed late in the compiler backend and that the isolated code cannot be optimised. The verifiers perform very local reasoning, and hence cannot verify that function calls, especially between trusted and untrusted code, abide to calling conventions. As a result, trusted code needs to implement a specific protocol for parameter passing and set up its own private run-time stack. This requires low-level platform-specific support and, most notably, increases the run-time overhead of context switches between untrusted and trusted code.

In this paper, we propose a relaxed definition of SFI where trusted and untrusted code may share the same runtime stack but must still respect the isolation properties of the sandbox and abide to calling conventions. Based on this definition, we define an intra-procedural binary verifier which enforces isolation. The verifier implements a static analysis and is using a weakly relational domain in order to verify that calling conventions are satisfied. A difficulty is to ensure that the isolation property holds even in the presence of stack overflow. This is done by ensuring that all stack overflows are caught by so-called *guard zones*, placed at both ends of the stack. The binary verifier is more flexible than state-of-the-art SFI verifiers and, in particular, is able to validate code where redundant sandboxing instrumentations are optimised away by compiler passes. Our contributions can therefore be phrased as follows:

- A defensive semantics which formalises a relaxed Software Fault Isolation property where the runtime stack is safely shared between trusted and untrusted code.

- An intra-procedural abstraction which ensures that the defensive semantics cannot go wrong.
- An executable binary verifier, working on a per-function basis, that is more flexible than state-of-the-art binary verifiers for SFI.

The rest of the paper is organised as follows. In Sect. 2, we define our SFI property by means of a defensive, instrumented semantics. To enable a modular verification, we present in Sect. 3 an intra-procedural abstraction of the defensive semantics. It is further abstracted in Sect. 4 into an executable binary verifier. Section 5 presents our experiments based on the BINCAT [2] binary analysis framework. We present related work in Sect. 6 and conclude in Sect. 7.

2   Software Fault Isolation as a Defensive Semantics

We define SFI and its sandbox property operationally, as a defensive semantics which includes a series of additional (dynamic) verifications. These dynamic checks express what it means for code to be properly sandboxed. Later, we define a static analysis for guaranteeing that the dynamic verifications will not fail at run-time, and hence that the code respects the SFI property.

2.1   Intermediate Language

We define our semantics on an intermediate representation (IR) obtained by disassembling the binary. In this approach, each binary instruction is typically translated into a sequence of instructions of the IR. For instance, for x86, a simple arithmetic operation has the side-effect of setting various flags e.g. the carry or overflow flag. For simplicity, we also assume that the IR only manipulates 32-bits values. The abstract syntax of the instructions is given below:

$$e ::= r \mid n \mid e_1 \bowtie e_2$$
$$i ::= r := e \mid [e_1] = e_2 \mid r = [e] \mid \mathbf{jmpif}\ e_1\ e_2 \mid \mathbf{call}\ e \mid \mathbf{ret}\ e \mid \mathbf{hlt}$$

The language features expressions e made of registers r, numeric constants n and binary operators $\bowtie$. Binary operators range over typical arithmetic operators e.g. $+$, $\times$, bitwise operators e.g. xor and logical operators e.g. $<$. An instruction i consists of assigning an expression to a register ($r = e$); storing in memory the value e_2 at the address e_1 ($[e_1] = e_2$); loading in register r the value stored at address e ($r = [e]$). A conditional jump $\mathbf{jmpif}\ e_1\ e_2$ jumps to the computed address e_2 if the condition e_1 holds ($e_1 \neq 0$). The instruction $\mathbf{call}\ e$ is equivalent to the computed jump $\mathbf{jmpif}\ 1\ e$ but identifies a function call; $\mathbf{ret}\ e$ is also equivalent to a computed jump but identifies a function return. The instruction $\mathbf{halt}$ immediately stops the program.

The operational semantics of the IR operates over a state $\langle \rho, \mu, \iota \rangle$ where ρ is an environment ($Env = Reg \rightarrow \mathbb{B}_{32}$), μ is the whole memory of the process and ι is the current instruction pointer. The memory is divided into regions and each region is granted access rights among **read**, **write** and **execute** that are checked for by the semantics. For instance, before reading in memory, we check that the address has the read permission $\mathbf{r}$. The rules that give the semantics of each instruction are fairly standard and are given in Appendix A.

2.2 Semantic Domains

Our defensive semantics makes use of several semantic domains that we describe below. Our notations are fairly standard: the set $\mathbb{B} = \{0, 1\}$ is the set of booleans and we write $\mathbb{B}_{32}$ for $\mathbb{B}^{32}$ which reads *bitvector of size 32*. A stack frame is a pair $\langle bp, \phi \rangle \in \mathbb{B}_{32} \times \mathbb{B}_{32}^*$ where bp represents the base pointer of the stack frame and ϕ is a list of 32-bits values modelling the content of the stack frame. The semantics is using several architecture-dependent constants. The constant d_0 is the base address of the sandbox, the constant s_0 is the top address of the stack, and the maximum size of a stack frame is f_s.

In order to detect stack overflows at runtime, the runtime stack is surrounded by so-called *guard zones*. The concept of guard zone was already present in the original work on SFI [15]. Semantically, this is modelled as memory regions which have no access rights. As a result, accesses within the guard zones are trapped, by letting the execution enter a specific "crash state" $\blacksquare$ where it stays forever. In the following, $\text{GZ}_\top$ is the size of the guard zone at the top of the stack and $\text{GZ}_\perp$ is the size of the guard zone at the bottom of the stack. The guard zones are part of the stack. A call stack $CS = (\mathbb{B}_{32} \times \mathbb{B}_{32}^*)^*$ is a list of stack frames such that the successive base addresses are decreasing (the stack grows downward). The length of the (intermediate) stack frames is given by the difference between two successive base pointers. A call stack is immutable but the content of the call stack can be read. This is modelled by the following judgement $cs \vdash_a v$ which reads *the call stack cs contains the value v at address a*.

$$\frac{a \le bp \quad \phi(bp - a) = \lfloor v \rfloor}{cs :: \langle bp, \phi \rangle \vdash_a v} \qquad \frac{a > bp \quad cs \vdash_a v}{cs :: \langle bp, \phi \rangle \vdash_a v}.$$

2.3 Defensive Semantics

At binary level, the runtime stack and the code segment are no different from any other part of memory. Our defensive semantics must therefore explicitly enforce a stack discipline and ensure that function boundaries are respected. The program text is located in memory. For this purpose, we identify a set of addresses $Code \subset \mathbb{B}_{32}$ that correspond to the program code. Given an address i, the function $instr(i)$ checks that $i \in Code$ and returns the instruction stored at address i. Moreover, we assume given a set $\mathcal{F} \subseteq Code$ of function entry points, and a set $\mathcal{T} \subseteq \mathbb{B}_{32}$ of trusted functions that form the only authorized entry points of the trusted library.

A semantic derivation occurs in a context $\langle cs, bp, \rho_i \rangle \in CS \times \mathbb{B}_{32} \times Env$ where cs is the call stack, bp is the base pointer of the current frame and ρ_i is the environment at the function entry. A judgement is of the form $\Gamma \vdash s \to s'$ where Γ is an inter-procedural context and s, s' are either intra-procedural states

$s, s' \in State = Env \times \mathbb{B}_{32}^* \times \mathbb{B}_{32}^* \times \mathbb{B} \times \mathbb{B}_{32}$ or the crash state ■. A state $\langle \rho, \delta, \phi^{(\beta)}, \iota \rangle \in State$ is made of an environment ρ mapping registers to values, a public data segment δ i.e. the sandbox, a stack frame ϕ, a boolean β which tells whether a write has occurred in the current frame, and the current instruction pointer ι. (We write ι^+ for the pointer to the next instruction.) The semantics also ensures that there is no overlap between the call stack (including the current stack frame), the code, and the data segment.

The semantics rules are found in Fig. 2. The ASSIGN rule assigns a new value to a register. This is always possible without violating the SFI property and no extra check is needed. The rule STOREDATA describes the execution of the

$$\text{ASSIGN} \frac{instr(\iota) = \lfloor r = e \rfloor}{\Gamma \vdash \langle \rho, \delta, \phi^{(\beta)}, \iota \rangle \longrightarrow \langle \rho[r \mapsto [\![e]\!]_\rho], \delta, \phi^{(\beta)}, \iota^+ \rangle}$$

$$\text{STOREDATA} \frac{instr(\iota) = \lfloor [e_1] = e_2 \rfloor \quad o = [\![e_1]\!]_\rho - d_0 \quad 0 \leq o <| \delta |}{\Gamma \vdash \langle \rho, \delta, \phi^{(\beta)}, \iota \rangle \longrightarrow \langle \rho, \delta[o \mapsto [\![e_2]\!]_\rho], \phi^{(\beta)}, \iota^+ \rangle}$$

$$\text{STOREFRAME} \frac{instr(\iota) = \lfloor [e_1] = e_2 \rfloor \quad o = bp - [\![e_1]\!]_\rho \quad 0 \leq o <| \phi | - \text{GZ}_\perp \quad bp - o \leq s_0 - \text{GZ}_\top}{\langle cs, bp, R \rangle \vdash \langle \rho, \delta, \phi^{(\beta)}, \iota \rangle \longrightarrow \langle \rho, \delta, \phi[o \mapsto [\![e_2]\!]_\rho]^{(1)}, \iota^+ \rangle}$$

$$\text{LDSTCRASH} \frac{instr(\iota) = \lfloor [e_1] = e_2 \rfloor \vee instr(\iota) = \lfloor [r = [e_1]] \rfloor \quad [\![e_1]\!]_\rho = a \quad (s_0 - \text{GZ}_\top < a \leq s_0) \vee (bp - | \phi | < a \leq bp - | \phi | + \text{GZ}_\perp)}{\langle cs, bp, \rho_i \rangle \vdash \langle \rho, \delta, \phi^{(\beta)}, \iota \rangle \longrightarrow ■}$$

$$\text{LOADDATA} \frac{instr(\iota) = \lfloor r = [e] \rfloor \quad [\![e]\!]_\rho = d_0 + o \quad 0 \leq o <| \delta |}{\Gamma \vdash \langle \rho, \delta, \phi^{(\beta)}, \iota \rangle \longrightarrow \langle \rho[r \mapsto \delta(o)], \delta, \phi^{(\beta)}, \iota^+ \rangle}$$

$$\text{LOADSTACK} \frac{instr(\iota) = \lfloor r = [e] \rfloor \quad [\![e]\!]_\rho = a \quad cs :: \langle bp, \phi \rangle \vdash_a v \quad bp - | \phi | + \text{GZ}_\perp < a \leq s_0 - \text{GZ}_\top}{\langle cs, bp, \rho_i \rangle \vdash \langle \rho, \delta, \phi^{(\beta)}, \iota \rangle \longrightarrow \langle \rho[r \mapsto v], \delta, \phi^{(\beta)}, \iota^+ \rangle}$$

$$\text{CALL} \frac{\begin{array}{c} instr(\iota) = \lfloor \mathbf{call}\ e \rfloor \quad [\![e]\!]_\rho = f \quad f \in \mathcal{F} \quad \rho(\mathbf{esp}) = bp - o \quad | \phi_1 |= o \\ o < f_s \quad isret(\iota^+, \rho, \phi_1) \quad \rho \sim \rho' \quad instr(\iota') = \lfloor \mathbf{ret}\ e' \rfloor \quad [\![e']\!]_{\rho'} = \iota^+ \\ \langle cs :: \langle bp, \phi_1 \rangle, bp - o, \rho \rangle \vdash \langle \rho, \delta, \phi_2^{(0)}, f \rangle \longrightarrow^* \langle \rho', \delta', \phi_2'^{(\beta)}, \iota' \rangle \end{array}}{\langle cs, bp, \rho_i \rangle \vdash \langle \rho, \delta, \phi_1 \cdot \phi_2^{(1)}, \iota \rangle \longrightarrow \langle \rho', \delta', \phi_1 \cdot \phi_2'^{(1)}, \iota^+ \rangle}$$

$$\text{CALLTRUST} \frac{\begin{array}{c} instr(\iota) = \lfloor \mathbf{call}\ e \rfloor \quad [\![e]\!]_\rho = f \quad f \in \mathcal{T} \\ \rho(\mathbf{esp}) = bp - o \quad | \phi_1 |= o \quad o < f_s \quad isret(\iota^+, \rho, \phi_1) \quad \rho \sim \rho' \end{array}}{\langle cs, bp, \rho_i \rangle \vdash \langle \rho, \delta, \phi_1 \cdot \phi_2^{(1)}, \iota \rangle \longrightarrow \langle \rho', \delta', \phi_1 \cdot \phi_2'^{(1)}, \iota^+ \rangle}$$

$$\text{CONT} \frac{instr(\iota) = \lfloor \mathbf{jmpif}\ e_1\ e_2 \rfloor \quad [\![e_1]\!]_\rho = 0}{\Gamma \vdash \langle \rho, \delta, \phi^{(\beta)}, \iota \rangle \longrightarrow \langle \rho, \delta, \phi^{(\beta)}, \iota^+ \rangle}$$

$$\text{JUMP} \frac{instr(\iota) = \lfloor \mathbf{jmpif}\ e_1\ e_2 \rfloor \quad [\![e_1]\!]_\rho \neq 0 \quad [\![e_2]\!]_\rho \in Code}{\Gamma \vdash \langle \rho, \delta, \phi^{(\beta)}, \iota \rangle \longrightarrow \langle \rho, \delta, \phi^{(\beta)}, [\![e_2]\!]_\rho \rangle}$$

$$\text{HALT} \frac{instr(\iota) = \lfloor \mathbf{hlt} \rfloor}{\Gamma \vdash \langle \rho, \delta, \phi^{(\beta)}, \iota \rangle \longrightarrow ■} \qquad \text{CRASH} \frac{}{\Gamma \vdash ■ \longrightarrow ■}$$

Fig. 2. Defensive semantics

statement $[e_1] = e_2$ for the case where e_1 evaluates to a memory address within the sandbox. The value of e_1 is computed and the start address of the data segment (the sandbox) d_0 is subtracted from it to obtain an offset o into the data segment. It is then verified that this offset is indeed smaller than the size of the data segment. If this verification succeeds, the location at offset o in the sandbox is updated with the value of e_2.

The rule STOREFRAME similarly makes the checks necessary for storing securely into the run-time stack. Here, the value of e_1 is supposed to be a valid reference into the current stack which starts at the address designated by the base pointer bp. Because the stack grows towards smaller addresses, the relative offset o into the current stack frame is computed as $bp - [\![e_1]\!]_\rho$. In order for the store to proceed normally, this offset must point into that part of the stack frame that is *not* making up the guard zone $(0 \le o <\mid \phi \mid -\text{GZ}_\perp)$. It is also checked that the offset does not point into the guard zone at the beginning of the stack segment $(bp - o \le s_0 - \text{GZ}_\top)$. This rule also sets β to 1, which has the side-effect of ensuring the current base pointer is above the guard zone (there is some space to write to). The rule LDSTCRASH describes what happens on an attempt to write into or read from one of the guard zones. In that case, the program transits to the crash state ■ and stays there forever due to rule CRASH.

The two rules LOADDATA, LOADSTACK describe how data are read from the data segment and the run-time stack. Reading from the data segment uses verification similar to storing into it. Loading from the stack is, however, slightly different in that our version of SFI allow reads from all of the stack frames, and not just the current frame. This allows e.g. functions to read their arguments. It is still verified that the access does not fall in the guard zones, using checks similar to STOREFRAME.

The rule CALL for the function call instruction **call** e first verifies that the value $[\![e]\!]_\rho$ belongs to the set of function entry points $\mathcal{F}$. The current stack frame is divided into two parts $\phi_1 \cdot \phi_2$ where ϕ_1 is local data of the caller and ϕ_2 is the new stack frame for the function call, which starts at the address contained in register **esp**. The offset o between the start of the old stack frame and the new is verified to be smaller than the maximal frame size f_s. Because it is checked that $\beta = 1$, i.e. the frame has already been written to in this function, this check has the side-effect to ensure bp is above the guard zone $\text{GZ}_\perp$ and therefore the new bp is still at least f_s above the bottom of the stack. Note that enforcing a write before calls is not restrictive as writes are generated by compilers before function calls in any architecture. The actual method call is modelled as an execution starting at address f with the same environment ρ, the same data segment δ, and a stack frame $\phi_2^{(0)}$ where the 0 indicates that the frame has not yet been written into. The end of the call is identified by the execution reaching a **ret** e' instruction. The value of $[\![e']\!]_{\rho'}$ is verified to be the return address using the architecture-dependent predicate *isret*. The return address is the next instruction to execute. The semantics verifies that callee-saved registers are restored after the function call. For instance on X86 assembly, registers **esp**, **ebx** etc. are saved. For this same architecture, *isret* checks that the return address has indeed been pushed to the call stack. Calling a trusted function is modelled with the rule CALLTRUST. This rule follows the same pattern as the rule for ordinary calls, except that the trusted call is allowed to modify the sandbox data but should leave the callee's stack frame unchanged. We model this as a non-deterministic rule that can return any δ' in its resulting state.

The rules CONT and JUMP model the instruction **jmpif** e_1 e_2 for conditional jumps to a computed address. If the condition e_1 evaluates to zero, execution continues with the next instruction. Otherwise, the value $[\![e_2]\!]_\rho$ is computed and it is verified that this new jump target is in the code block *Code*. Finally, we use the (secure) crash state ■ to model program termination in the rule HALT. The rule CRASH states that once in a crash state the execution stays in this state forever. This semantic sleight of hand simplifies the statement of the overall security property, which becomes essentially a progress property. Employing a specific error state would be equivalent but slightly more cumbersome.

2.4 The Sandbox Property

The side-conditions of the rules performing memory accesses ensure that the defensive semantics gets stuck when memory accesses do not respect the sandboxing property. This means that we can state our sandbox property as a simple *progress* property of the defensive semantics: as long as the semantics can progress to a new state (possibly the crash state) no security violation has occurred.

There is one obstacle to this, though: due to our *big-step* modelling of function calls, the semantics also gets stuck as soon as a function call does not terminate. In other words, all infinite loops are deemed insecure, which is clearly not what we want. To remedy this, our sandbox property is defined over the set of reachable states induced by the defensive semantics where the transition relation → is extended with a relation ▷ which for each **call** instruction explicitly adds a transition to the callee state.

$$\text{CALLACC} \frac{instr(\iota) = \lfloor \textbf{call } e \rfloor \quad [\![e]\!]_\rho = f \quad f \in \mathcal{F}}{\langle\langle cs, bp, \rho_i\rangle, \langle \rho, \delta, \phi_1 \cdot \phi_2^{(1)}, \iota\rangle\rangle \triangleright \langle\langle cs::\langle bp, \phi_1\rangle, bp-o, \rho\rangle, \langle \rho, \delta, \phi_2^{(1)}, f\rangle\rangle}$$

Dually, we also add a transition stating that, for a **ret** instruction, the return state is not stuck provided that the calling conventions are respected. Since the next step is taken care of by the CALL rule, the resulting state is just a witness that the execution can proceed; we reuse for this purpose the state ■.

$$\text{RETACC} \frac{\rho_i \sim \rho' \quad isret(ret, \phi_1, \rho_i) \quad instr(\iota) = \lfloor \textbf{ret } e' \rfloor \quad [\![e']\!]_{\rho'} = ret}{\langle\langle cs::\langle bp, \phi_1\rangle, bp-o, \rho_i\rangle, \langle \rho', \delta, \phi_2'^{(\beta)}, \iota\rangle\rangle \triangleright \langle\langle cs::\langle bp, \phi_1\rangle, bp-o, \rho_i\rangle, ■\rangle}$$

Definition 1 (Augmented defensive semantics). *The augmented defensive semantics* ⇒ *is given by the union of the relation* → *and* ▷ *such that:*

$$\frac{\Gamma \vdash \Sigma_1 \to \Sigma_2}{\langle \Gamma, \Sigma_1\rangle \Rightarrow \langle \Gamma, \Sigma_2\rangle} \qquad \frac{\langle \Gamma_1, \Sigma_1\rangle \triangleright \langle \Gamma_2, \Sigma_2\rangle}{\langle \Gamma_1, \Sigma_1\rangle \Rightarrow \langle \Gamma_2, \Sigma_2\rangle}$$

The SFI sandbox property can then be expressed as the progress property of the augmented defensive semantics.

Definition 2 (Sandboxing as progress). *Let ι_0 be the entry point of the program and let the initial state be $\langle \Gamma_0, \Sigma_0 \rangle = \langle\langle [\langle s_0, \phi_i \rangle], s_0 - GZ_\top, \rho_0 \rangle, \langle \rho, \delta, \phi^{(0)}, \iota_0 \rangle\rangle$ with $\mid \phi_i \mid = GZ_\top$. The program satisfies the SFI sandbox property if the set of reachable states $Acc = \{s \mid \langle \Gamma_0, \Sigma_0 \rangle \Rightarrow^* s\}$ satisfies $\forall s \in Acc.\exists s'.s \Rightarrow s'$.*

We write $Safe(Acc)$ if this is the case.

3 Intraprocedural Semantics as an Abstract Interpretation

In order to derive a modular static analyser we abstract the defensive semantics into an intra-procedural semantics where the accessible states $I\text{-}Acc$ are computed for each function separately: $I\text{-}Acc = \bigcup_{f \in \mathcal{F}} I\text{-}Acc(f)$. Our intra-procedural semantics abstracts away the data region and all of the call stack, except the frame of the caller. Thus the stack component is abstracted to two small zones of the stack above and below the current base pointer, representing the frames of the caller and the callee (the currently executing function). Both are modelled by memory regions of size f_s where f_s is a chosen maximum size of these abstract stack frames. Figure 3 illustrates the abstraction of the stack segment. The current code can write to its own frame (the W zone) and read from both frames (the R zone). The size of the guard zones are set such that the abstract frames are always contained in the stack, possibly overlapping a guard zone.

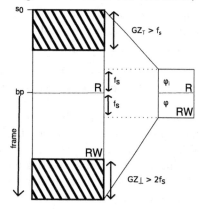

Fig. 3. Abstraction of call stack

The judgement of the intra-procedural semantics is of the form: $\Gamma \vdash s \to s'$ where the context $\Gamma = \langle \phi_i, bp, \rho_i \rangle \in Ctx^\natural$ is constant. Here, ϕ_i is the frame of the caller, bp is the base pointer and ρ_i is the initial environment. The states s and s' are either the crash state $\blacksquare$ or of the form $\langle \rho, \phi^{(\beta)}, \iota \rangle \in State^\natural$.

The intra-procedural semantics has no knowledge about where it is in the stack segment so it cannot detect stack overflows *per se*. We solve this problem by a judicious use of the guard zones. The defensive semantics enforces that a successful memory write occurs within the current stack frame before any call. This entails the semantic invariants that 1. before a function call the base pointer is always inside the stack and outside of the guard zone, 2. at function entry point, the base pointer is always inside the stack or at most f_s bytes inside the guard zone, 3. hence, there are at least f_s bytes left between bp and the end of the stack segment (including the guard zone). These invariants are formally stated by Lemma 3 that is proved in Appendix C.

Similarly, we also guarantee that the call stack is at least of size f_s, possibly overlapping the guard zone GZ$_\top$. Those invariants are enough to detect both stack overflows and underflows using the intra-procedural semantics: if all the stack accesses are proved to be within the bound of f_s above and below the stack pointer bp, the accesses are either defined in the defensive semantics or lead to a crash because the access is performed inside the guard zone.

The intra-procedural and defensive semantics are linked by the concretization function $\gamma : Ctx^\natural \times State^\natural \to \mathcal{P}((Ctx \times State) \cup \{\blacksquare\})$. The data segment is not represented in the intra-procedural semantics, so its concretization is any data segment of size d_s. The concretization constructs the call stack and the current defensive frame in such a way that, once appended to one another, they form a memory region of size s_s and f_i and f are windows of size f_s around the address pointed to by the base pointer. Formally, we have:

$$\gamma(\langle f_i, bp, \rho_i \rangle, \langle \rho, f^{(\beta)}, \iota \rangle) = \{\blacksquare\} \cup \left\{ \langle cs, bp, \rho_i \rangle, \langle \rho, \delta, \phi^{(\beta)}, \iota \rangle \,\middle|\, \begin{array}{l} f = \phi\big|_{[0, f_s - 1]} \\ f_i = \overline{cs}\big|_{[|\overline{cs}| - f_s, |\overline{cs}|]} \end{array} \right\}$$

where $\overline{cs}$ is obtained by concatenating the different stack frames of the call stack and $\phi\big|_{[a,b]}$ extracts the sub-list between the indexes a and b.

$$\overline{cs} = \begin{cases} [] & \text{if } cs = [] \\ \phi \cdot \overline{cs'} & \text{if } cs = \langle bp, \phi \rangle :: cs' \end{cases} \qquad \phi\big|_{[a,b]} = \begin{cases} [] & \text{if } a > b \\ \phi(a) :: \phi\big|_{[a+1,b]} & \text{otherwise} \end{cases}$$

Except for the handling of stack overflows and underflows, the rules for the intra-procedural semantics are fairly standard and can be found in Appendix B. When a memory component is absent from the abstraction i.e. the data region, the intra-procedural semantics non-deterministically picks a value. For the **call** instruction, the rule is similar to the defensive semantics rule CALL with the notable exception that no recursive call is made.

$$\text{FUNCALL} \frac{instr(\iota) = \lfloor \textbf{call } e \rfloor \quad [\![e]\!]_\rho = f \quad f \in \mathcal{F} \cup \mathcal{T} \quad \rho(\textbf{esp}) = bp - o \quad 0 \leq o < f_s \quad |\phi_1| = o \quad isret(\iota^+, \rho, \phi_1) \quad \rho \sim \rho'}{\langle \phi_i, bp, \rho_i \rangle \vdash \langle \rho, \phi_1 \cdot \phi_2^{(1)}, \iota \rangle \to^\natural \langle \rho', \phi_1 \cdot \phi_2^{(1)}, \iota^+ \rangle}$$

The rule FUNLDARG shows how to access the arguments of the function that are placed in the stack frame of the caller modelled by ϕ_i.

$$\text{FUNLDARG} \frac{instr(\iota) = \lfloor r = [e] \rfloor \quad [\![e]\!]_\rho = (bp + f_s) - o \quad 0 \leq o < f_s}{\langle \phi_i, bp, \rho_i \rangle \vdash \langle \rho, \phi^{(\beta)}, \iota \rangle \to^\natural \langle \rho[r \mapsto \phi_i(o)], \phi^{(\beta)}, \iota^+ \rangle}$$

The base address of ϕ_i is obtained by incrementing the base pointer bp by the stack frame size f_s and checking that the offset o is in range $[0; f_s[$. The soundness of this rule exploits the fact that the defensive stack is guarded by GZ$_\top$. As a result, if FUNLDARG succeeds, either the memory access also succeeds in the defensive semantics (rule LOADSTACK) or it accesses the guard zone GZ$_\top$ and triggers a crash (rule LDSTCRASH).

For each function entry $\iota \in \mathcal{F}$, the initial states $Init(f) \subseteq Ctx^{\natural} \times State^{\natural}$ are defined by: $Init(\iota) = \left\{ \langle\langle \phi_i, bp, \rho\rangle, \langle \rho, \phi^{(0)}, \iota\rangle\rangle \,\middle|\, \begin{array}{l} |\phi| = |\phi_i| = f_s \wedge \\ bp > s_0 - s_s + GZ_\perp - f_s \end{array} \right\}$. As we already discussed, the frames ϕ and ϕ_i have length f_s. At the function start, the environments of the caller and the callee are the same; the base pointer is so that there is below it a stack frame of size at least f_s and no memory write has been performed on the current frame ϕ. For a given function entry point $f \in \mathcal{F}$, the reachable states are defined as

$$I\text{-}Acc(f) = \{(\Gamma, s) \mid \Gamma \vdash s_0 \rightarrow^* s \wedge (\Gamma, s_0) \in Init(f)\}.$$

The intra-procedural semantics is also defensive and gets stuck when abstract verification conditions are not met.

Definition 3 (Intra-procedural progress). *The intra-procedural states are safe (written $I\text{-}Safe(I\text{-}Acc)$) iff $\forall f \in \mathcal{F}, \forall (\Gamma, s) \in I\text{-}Acc(f).\exists s'.\Gamma \vdash s \rightarrow s'$.*

The checked conditions are sufficient (but may not be necessary). For instance, the intra-procedural semantics gets stuck when an access is performed outside the bound of the current stack frame ϕ. However, because ϕ only models a prefix of the frame of the defensive semantics, the defensive semantics may not be stuck. As a result, the usual result $Acc \subseteq \gamma(I\text{-}Acc)$ does not hold. Instead, we have Lemma 1 stating that if the intra-procedural semantics is not stuck, it abstracts the defensive semantics and ensures that the accessible states of the defensive semantics are safe.

Lemma 1 (Correctness of the Intra-procedural semantics).

$$I\text{-}Safe(I\text{-}Acc) \Rightarrow Acc \subseteq \gamma(I\text{-}Acc) \wedge Safe(Acc).$$

The proof can be found in Appendix C.

4   A Static SFI Analysis

To get a modular executable verifier, we abstract further the intra-procedural semantics. The verifier needs to track numeric values used as addresses, in order to guarantee that memory accesses are within the sandbox or within the current stack frame, hence we need domains tailored for such uses of numeric values. The verifier also needs to gather some input-output relational information about the registers and verify that, at the end of the functions, callee-saved registers are restored to their initial values.

4.1   Abstract Domains

As pioneered by Balakrishnan and Reps [1], we perform a Value Set Analysis (VSA) where abstract locations (*a-locs*) are DATA for the sandbox region and CODE for the code region. We also introduce an abstract location for the function return RET, the base pointer BP and for each register e.g. EAX, EBX. To model purely numeric data, we have a dedicated *a-locs* ZERO with value 0:

$$\text{a-locs} = \{\text{ZERO}, \text{DATA}, \text{CODE}, \text{RET}, \text{BP}, \text{EAX}, \text{EBX}, \ldots\}.$$

a-locs are equipped with an arbitrary non-relational numeric domain. The abstract value domain $\mathbb{B}_{32}^{\sharp}$ is therefore a pair (L, o) made of an abstract location L and a numeric abstraction $o \in D^{\sharp}$. For each concrete operation $\diamond$ on values, the transfer function on abstract (L, o)-values is using the corresponding operation $\diamond^{\sharp}$ of the abstract domain. For instance, for addition and subtraction, we get:

$$(L, o_1) +^{\sharp} (\text{ZERO}, o_2) = (L, o_1 +^{\sharp} o_2) \quad (\text{ZERO}, o_1) +^{\sharp} (L, o_2) = (L, o_1 +^{\sharp} o_2)$$
$$(L, o_1) -^{\sharp} (\text{ZERO}, o_2) = (L, o_1 -^{\sharp} o_2) \quad (L, o_1) -^{\sharp} (L, o_2) = (\text{ZERO}, o_1 -^{\sharp} o_2)$$

When symbolic computations are not possible, it is always possible to abstract (L, o) by $(\text{ZERO}, \top)$ and use numeric transfer functions. As the usual sandboxing technique consists in masking an address using a bitwise & ($[e_1] := e_2 \rightsquigarrow [d_0 + e_1 \& 1^k] := e_2)^1$ we opt, in our implementation, for the bitfield domain [11].

The abstract machine state at a program point is the product of an abstract environment $Env^{\sharp}$, an abstract frame $Frame^{\sharp}$, and a code pointer $\mathbb{B}_{32}$.

$$Env^{\sharp} = Reg \to \mathbb{B}_{32}^{\sharp} \quad Frame^{\sharp} = (\mathbb{B}_{32}^{\sharp})^{f_s} \times \mathbb{B} \quad State^{\sharp} = Env^{\sharp} \times Frame^{\sharp} \times \mathbb{B}_{32}.$$

The abstract frame is annotated by a boolean indicating whether a memory write has definitively occurred in the stack frame.

The concretization function is parametrised by a mapping $\lambda : \text{a-locs} \to \mathbb{B}_{32}$ assigning a numeric value to abstract locations and the concretization function $\gamma : D^{\sharp} \to \mathcal{P}(\mathbb{B}_{32})$ of the numeric domain. The concretization is then obtained using standard constructions:

$$\begin{aligned}
\gamma_{\lambda}(L, o) &= \{v + \lambda(L) \mid v \in \gamma(o)\} \\
\gamma_{\lambda}(\rho^{\sharp}) &= \{\rho \mid \forall r.\rho(r) \in \gamma_{\lambda}(\rho^{\sharp}(r))\} \\
\gamma_{\lambda}(\phi^{\sharp}) &= \{\phi \mid \forall i \in [0, f_s].\phi(i) \in \gamma_{\lambda}(\phi^{\sharp}(i))\} \\
\gamma_{\lambda}(\langle \rho^{\sharp}, \phi^{\sharp (b)}, \iota \rangle) &= \{\langle \rho, \phi^{(\beta)}, \iota \rangle \mid \beta \geq b \wedge \rho \in \gamma_{\lambda}(\rho^{\sharp}) \wedge \phi \in \gamma_{\lambda}(\phi^{\sharp})\}
\end{aligned}$$

The mapping λ denotes a set of intra-procedural contexts such that a register r in the environment ρ_i has the value $\lambda(r)$ and the return address is constrained by the calling conventions.

$$\gamma(\lambda) = \left\{\langle \phi_i, bp, \rho_i \rangle \,\middle|\, \begin{array}{l} \forall r, \rho(r) = \lambda(r), \\ bp = \lambda(\text{BP}) = \lambda(\text{ESP}), \quad isret(\lambda(\text{RET}), \rho_i, \phi_i) \end{array} \right\}.$$

Finally, the whole concretization $\gamma : State^{\sharp} \to \mathcal{P}(Ctx^{\natural} \times State^{\natural})$ is defined as:

$$\gamma(s^{\sharp}) = \{\langle \Gamma, \blacksquare \rangle\} \cup \{\langle \Gamma, s \rangle \mid \exists \lambda, \Gamma \in \gamma(\lambda) \wedge s \in \gamma_{\lambda}(s^{\sharp})\}.$$

---

[1] This exploits the property that the range of the sandbox is a power of 2.

4.2   Abstract Semantics

The abstract semantics takes the form of a transition system that is presented in Fig. 4. The rule AASSIGN abstracts the assignment to a register and consists in evaluating the expression e using the abstract domain of Sect. 4.1. A memory store is modelled by the rules ASTD and ASTF depending on whether the address is within the sandbox or within the current stack frame. Both rules ensure that the offset is within the bounds of the memory region. A memory load is modelled by the rules ALDD, ALDF or ALDS depending on whether the address is within the sandbox, the current stack frame or the caller stack frame. Each memory access is protected by a verification condition ensuring that the offset is within the relevant bounds. For the ALDF rule, the memory offset off is used to fetch the abstract value from the abstract frame ϕ. As the

$$\text{AAssign} \frac{instr(\iota) = \lfloor r = e \rfloor}{\langle \rho, \phi^{(\beta)}, \iota \rangle \longrightarrow^{\sharp} \langle \rho[r \mapsto \llbracket e \rrbracket_\rho], \phi^{(\beta)}, \iota^+ \rangle}$$

$$\text{AStD} \frac{instr(\iota) = \lfloor [e_1] = e_2 \rfloor \quad \llbracket e_1 \rrbracket_\rho = (\text{DATA}, o) \quad \gamma(o) \subseteq [0; d_s[}{\langle \rho, \phi^{(\beta)}, \iota \rangle \longrightarrow^{\sharp} \langle \rho, \phi^{(\beta)}, \iota^+ \rangle}$$

$$\text{AStF} \frac{instr(\iota) = \lfloor [e_1] = e_2 \rfloor \quad \llbracket e_1 \rrbracket_\rho = (\text{BP}, o) \quad \mathit{off} \in \gamma(o) \quad \gamma(o) \subseteq]-\mid \phi \mid; 0]}{\langle \rho, \phi^{(\beta)}, \iota \rangle \longrightarrow^{\sharp} \langle \rho, \phi[\mathit{off} \mapsto \llbracket e_2 \rrbracket_\rho]^{(1)}, \iota^+ \rangle}$$

$$\text{ALdD} \frac{instr(\iota) = \lfloor r = [e] \rfloor \quad \llbracket e \rrbracket_\rho = (\text{DATA}, o) \quad \gamma(o) \subseteq [0; d_s[}{\langle \rho, \phi^{(\beta)}, \iota \rangle \longrightarrow^{\sharp} \langle \rho[r \mapsto (\text{ZERO}, \top)], \phi^{(\beta)}, \iota^+ \rangle}$$

$$\text{ALdF} \frac{instr(\iota) = \lfloor r = [e] \rfloor \quad \llbracket e \rrbracket_\rho = (\text{BP}, o) \quad \mathit{off} \in \gamma(o) \quad \gamma(o) \subseteq]-\mid \phi \mid; 0]}{\langle \rho, \phi^{(\beta)}, \iota \rangle \longrightarrow^{\sharp} \langle \rho[r \mapsto \phi(\mathit{off})], \phi^{(\beta)}, \iota^+ \rangle}$$

$$\text{ALdS} \frac{instr(\iota) = \lfloor r = [e] \rfloor \quad \llbracket e \rrbracket_\rho = (\text{BP}, o) \quad \gamma(o) \subseteq]0; \mid \phi \mid [}{\langle \rho, \phi^{(\beta)}, \iota \rangle \longrightarrow^{\sharp} \langle \rho[r \mapsto (\text{ZERO}, \top)], \phi^{(\beta)}, \iota^+ \rangle}$$

$$\text{ACall} \frac{\begin{array}{c} instr(\iota) = \lfloor \mathbf{call}\ e \rfloor \quad \gamma(\llbracket e \rrbracket_\rho) \subseteq \mathcal{F} \cup \mathcal{T} \quad \rho(\mathbf{esp}) = (\text{BP}, o) \\ \mathit{off} \in \gamma(o) \quad \mid \phi_1 \mid = -\mathit{off} \quad \gamma(o) \subseteq]-f_s; 0] \\ isret(\iota^+, \rho, \phi_1) \quad \rho \sim \rho' \quad \mid \phi_2 \mid = \mid \phi_2' \mid \end{array}}{\langle \rho, \phi_1 \cdot \phi_2^{(1)}, \iota \rangle \longrightarrow^{\sharp} \langle \rho', \phi_1 \cdot \phi_2'^{(1)}, \iota^+ \rangle}$$

$$\text{ARet} \frac{instr(\iota) = \lfloor \mathbf{ret}\ e \rfloor \quad preserve(\rho) \quad \llbracket e \rrbracket_\rho = (\text{RET}, o) \quad \{0\} = \gamma(o)}{\langle \rho, \phi^{(\beta)}, \iota \rangle \longrightarrow^{\sharp} \blacksquare}$$

$$\text{ACont} \frac{instr(\iota) = \lfloor \mathbf{jmpif}\ e_1\ e_2 \rfloor \quad 0 \in \gamma(\llbracket e_1 \rrbracket_\rho)}{\langle \rho, \phi^{(\beta)}, \iota \rangle \longrightarrow^{\sharp} \langle \rho, \phi^{(\beta)}, \iota^+ \rangle}$$

$$\text{AJump} \frac{instr(\iota) = \lfloor \mathbf{jmpif}\ e_1\ e_2 \rfloor \quad c \in \gamma(\llbracket e_1 \rrbracket_\rho) \quad c \neq 0 \\ \llbracket e_2 \rrbracket_\rho = (\text{CODE}, o) \quad \iota_2 \in \gamma(o) + c_0 \quad \iota_2 \in Code}{\langle \rho, \phi^{(\beta)}, \iota \rangle \longrightarrow^{\sharp} \langle \rho, \phi^{(\beta)}, \iota_2 \rangle}$$

$$\text{AHalt} \frac{instr(\iota) = \lfloor \mathbf{hlt} \rfloor}{\langle \rho, \phi^{(\beta)}, \iota \rangle \longrightarrow \blacksquare} \qquad \text{ACrash} \frac{}{\blacksquare \longrightarrow \blacksquare}$$

Fig. 4. Abstract semantics

sandbox and the caller frame are not represented, we get the top element of the abstract domain i.e. (ZERO, $\top$). The rule ACALL models function calls. It checks whether the target of the call is a trusted ($f \in \mathcal{T}$) or untrusted function ($f \in \mathcal{F}$). For the call to proceed, the stack pointer **esp** must be within the bounds of the current stack frame and the return address ι^+ needs to be stored according to the calling conventions ($isret(\iota^+, \rho, \phi_1)$). After the call, the resulting environment ρ' satisfies that the callee-saved registers are restored to their values in ρ ($\rho \sim \rho'$) and the suffix of the current frame ϕ'_2 is arbitrary i.e. $\phi'_2 = (\text{ZERO}, \top)^{|\phi_2|}$. The rule ARET ensures that the expression e evaluates to the return of the current function ($[\![e]\!]_\rho = (\text{RET}, o)$ $\{0\} = \gamma(o)$), and also that the callee-saved registers are restored to their initial values. For instance, for **ebx**, $preserve(\rho)$ ensures that $\rho(\textbf{ebx}) = (EBX, o)$ with $\gamma(o) = \{0\}$. The rules ACONT and AJUMP model control-flow transfer and check that the obtained code pointer is within the bounds of the code. The last two rules AHALT and ACRASH model the crash state that is produced by the **hlt** instruction and is its own successor.

Like the intra-procedural semantics, the abstract semantics is safe if it is not stuck (Definition 4).

Definition 4 (Abstract progress). *The reachable intra-procedural states are safe (written A-Safe(A-Acc)) iff $\forall f \in \mathcal{F}, \forall s \in A\text{-}Acc(f).\exists s'.s \to s'$.*

The abstract semantics embeds abstract verification conditions that are only sufficient but not necessary for the intra-procedural semantics. As a result, it only computes a safe approximation under the condition that all the reachable abstract states are safe.

Lemma 2 (Correctness of the abstract semantics).

$$A\text{-}Safe(A\text{-}Acc) \Rightarrow I\text{-}Acc \subseteq \gamma(I\text{-}Acc) \wedge I\text{-}Safe(I\text{-}Acc)$$

The proof can be found in Appendix D. By transitivity, using Lemma 2 and Lemma 1, we get Theorem 1.

Theorem 1 (Correctness of SFI Verifier). $A\text{-}Safe(A\text{-}Acc) \Rightarrow Safe(Acc)$

By definition of *Safe*, Theorem 1 means that the defensive semantics is not stuck.

5   Implementation and Experiments

We have implemented the static analysis on top of the BinCAT binary code analysis toolkit [2]. First, our SFI analyser reconstructs the structure of the binary and in particular partitions the code into separate functions and transforms the binary instructions into the REIL [4] intermediate representation. Second, each previously identified function is analysed separately, using the abstraction described in Sect. 4. For each function, the analysis checks that all the intra-procedural jumps stays within the current function and that the abstract semantics never blocks. The analysis also checks that all calls are towards previously identified entry points thus validating *a posteriori* that the initial partition of the code into distinct functions is indeed correct.

The analysis has been tested on three test suites: correctly sandboxed programs, incorrectly sandboxed programs, and optimised, correctly sandboxed programs. The first test suite is built by compiling programs that are part of the CompCert test suite with a modified version of CompCert that includes sandboxing instructions. Because these binaries are correct by construction, the verifier should accept all of them. In our experiments, we have tested 10 programs, composed of 51 functions in total. 41 functions are verified in under 100 ms, 9 functions are verified in less than 300 ms and 1 function is verified in 3.5 s. This last function occurs in sha3.c, and is responsible for the program being verified in 3.5 s. This file is 200LoC long, while another file, aes.c, is 1.5KLoC long, composed of 7 functions and takes only 1s to validate. This suggests that the time complexity depends on the number of nested loops rather than on the size of the code to verify.

The second test suite for catching incorrect programs has been obtained by compiling incorrectly sandboxed programs with gcc and verifying they do not pass our verification. Each test in the suite aims at a different error: returning before the end of a function, writing above and below the frame, stack or sandbox and bypassing the guard zones. Overall, the test suite contains 9 programs and all are correctly identified as violating the sandbox property. Some of these programs can be found in Fig. 5.

```
asm(" sub $5000000 , %esp\n\t"
    " push $1");
```

(a) Attempt to write below the stack

```
data [−5] = 0;
```

(b) Attempt to write outside of the sandbox

```
int f(int *e) {
   int i;
   asm(" push $main\n\t"
       "mov %1, %%ebp\n\t"
       "add %%ebp, (%%esp)\n\t"
       "ret"
       : "=r"(i)
       : "r"(*((int *)(sandbox(e, 4))))
       : "%ebp");
   return i+5;
}
```

(c) Attempt to return before the end

Fig. 5. Violation of sandboxing

We have also evaluated the ability of the analysis to verify programs where redundant sandboxing instructions have been optimised away. For instance, the sandboxing of consecutive accesses to an array can be factorised and implemented by a single sandboxing instruction. In addition to masking the most significant bits, this sandboxing instruction also zeroes out several least significant bits thus aligning the base address of the array. The reasoning is that if an address a of the sandbox is aligned on k bits we have that $a+i$ for $i \in [0, 2^k - 1]$ is also in the sandbox. We have sandboxed the programs manually and compiled them with gcc and verified whether they passed our verification. Our numerical domain is able to model alignment constraints and the analysis accepts programs where consecutive writes are protected by the previous sandboxing operation. Yet, the analysis rejects programs where the sandboxing instruction is factored outside loops because the information inferred about the loop bound is currently not precise enough. More precision could be obtained by using more sophisticated numerical domains. An example program that fails our verification is given in Fig. 6.

```
char *a = (sfi + (t & 0b11111000)
for(char i=0; i<5; i++) {
  a[i] = i;
}
```

Fig. 6. Optimising array accesses in a loop

The use of alloca(size_t size) is another example of a code that respects the security property as defined by the defensive semantics, but cannot be understood by the analyser, unless more work is done by the programmer with the result of that function. Because we limit the maximum size of the stack frame, this function cannot work properly when its argument is bigger than this limit. The result is a pointer outside of the frame, and the module is rejected when a write at this address is detected.

6   Related Work

Software Fault Isolation has been proposed by Wahbe *et al.* [15] as a way to ensure that a binary code runs inside a sandbox. Native Client (NaCl) [13,16] is a state-of-the-art implementation that was part of chromium-based browsers in order to safely run binary plugins. The NaCl binary verifier only performs a linear scan of the code. It is very fast, simple and has a small TCB. As shown by the RockSalt project [12], it is also amenable to formal verification. The NaCl verifier requires setting up trampoline code to share a runtime stack between trusted and untrusted code. Using abstract interpretation, we propose a more flexible binary verifier where redundant sandboxing operations can be optimised away and where the runtime stack is safely shared between trusted and untrusted code. Our TCB is bigger than NaCl but could be reduced using certified abstract interpretation [6].

Kroll *et al.* [8] propose to implement SFI as a CMINOR compiler pass of the CompCert [9] verified compiler. They show that proving both safety and security of the SFI pass is enough to get a secure binary. For their approach, redundant sandboxing operations can be optimised away by the compiler back-end; the runtime stack is managed by the compiler and therefore shared between trusted and untrusted code. A main difference with our work is that we explicitly state, using our defensive semantics, the security property that holds at binary level. Moreover, we propose a flexible binary verifier for this property.

The NaCl technology has recently been replaced by WebAssembly [5]. Webassembly is an intermediate language, similar to CMINOR, that is *just-in-time* compiled into binary code. As the code may be malicious, the just-in-time compiler adds runtime checks to make sure the code runs inside a sandbox. Compared to the previous approaches, the TCB includes the just-in-time compiler and there is no independent binary verifier.

Binary Analysis frameworks e.g. BAP [3] and Angr [14] propose rich APIs to develop static analyses on top of an architecture independent intermediate language. We use BinCAT [2] based on the REIL intermediate representation [4]. Our binary verifier has the rare feature of being intra-procedural. As a result, we have adapted their interprocedural analysis engine and implemented our own analysis domains. Our analysis domain is inspired from the *a-locs* domain of Balakrishnan and Reps [1] which we adapt to a purely intra-procedural setting and where *a-locs* are also used to model the initial values of registers. There are full-fledged, whole-program, binary analysers e.g. Jackstab [7] and Bindead [10]. They both use a sophisticated combination of abstract domains. Our domains are simpler but specialised to prove the sandboxing property. Moreover, our analysis is intra-procedural and finely models the calling conventions.

7 Conclusions

We have shown that the Software Fault Isolation mechanism for safely executing untrusted binaries can be formalised as a defensive semantics of an intermediate representation of binary code. Our semantics generalises existing approaches and defines a relaxed SFI property where the runtime stack is safely shared between trusted and untrusted code. Using abstract interpretation, we derive from the defensive semantics an intra-procedural binary verifier which for each individual function can verify that memory accesses are sandboxed and that the code abides to calling conventions. The verifier is implemented and our tests show that it is able to validate programs even when compiler optimisations are enabled.

Further work will concern improving the robustness of the verifier and ensuring a degree of completeness *w.r.t.* more complex optimisations. To do so, we intend to enrich our abstract domains to cope specifically with program transformations based on code motion where sandboxing instrumentations are factored outside loops. In addition, we intend to extend the verifier to handle multithreaded applications. We expect that the data-local, intra-procedural design of the verifier will greatly facilitate the extension to such a multi-threaded setting.

A   Concrete Operational Semantics

$$\text{ISTR} \frac{instr(\iota) = \lfloor r = e \rfloor}{\langle \rho, \mu, \iota \rangle \longrightarrow \langle \rho[r \mapsto [\![e]\!]_\rho], \mu, \iota^+ \rangle}$$

$$\text{ISTM} \frac{instr(\iota) = \lfloor [m] = e \rfloor \quad Writable([\![m]\!]_\rho)}{\langle \rho, \mu, \iota \rangle \longrightarrow \langle \rho, \mu[[\![m]\!]_\rho \mapsto [\![e]\!]_\rho], \iota^+ \rangle}$$

$$\text{IWCRASH} \frac{instr(\iota) = \lfloor [m] = e \rfloor \quad \neg Writable([\![m]\!]_\rho)}{\langle \rho, \mu, \iota \rangle \longrightarrow \blacksquare}$$

$$\text{ILDM} \frac{instr(\iota) = \lfloor r = [m] \rfloor \quad Readable([\![m]\!]_\rho)}{\langle \rho, \mu, \iota \rangle \longrightarrow \langle \rho[r \mapsto \mu([\![m]\!]_\rho)], \mu, \iota^+ \rangle}$$

$$\text{IRCRASH} \frac{instr(\iota) = \lfloor r = [m] \rfloor \quad \neg Readable([\![m]\!]_\rho)}{\langle \rho, \mu, \iota \rangle \longrightarrow \blacksquare}$$

$$\text{IJCCNO} \frac{instr(\iota) = \lfloor \mathbf{jmpif}\ cond\ addr \rfloor \quad [\![cond]\!]_\rho = 0}{\langle \rho, \mu, \iota \rangle \longrightarrow \langle \rho, \mu, \iota^+ \rangle}$$

$$\text{IJCC} \frac{instr(\iota) = \lfloor \mathbf{jmpif}\ cond\ addr \rfloor \quad [\![cond]\!]_\rho \neq 0)}{\langle \rho, \mu, \iota \rangle \longrightarrow \langle \rho, \mu, [\![addr]\!]_\rho \rangle}$$

$$\text{ICALL} \frac{instr(\iota) = \lfloor \mathbf{call}\ addr \rfloor}{\langle \rho, \mu, \iota \rangle \longrightarrow \langle \rho, \mu, [\![addr]\!]_\rho \rangle}$$

$$\text{IRET} \frac{instr(\iota) = \lfloor \mathbf{ret}\ addr \rfloor}{\langle \rho, \mu, \iota \rangle \longrightarrow \langle \rho, \mu, [\![addr]\!]_\rho \rangle} \qquad \text{IHLT} \frac{instr(\iota) = \lfloor \mathbf{hlt} \rfloor}{\langle \rho, \mu, \iota \rangle \longrightarrow \blacksquare}$$

B   Intra-procedural Semantics

$$\text{FUNASSIGN} \frac{instr(\iota) = \lfloor r = e \rfloor}{\Gamma \vdash \langle \rho, \phi^{(\beta)}, \iota \rangle \rightarrow^\natural \langle \rho[r \mapsto [\![e]\!]_\rho], \phi^{(\beta)}, \iota^+ \rangle}$$

$$\text{FUNSTD} \frac{instr(\iota) = \lfloor [e_1] = e_2 \rfloor \quad [\![e_1]\!]_\rho = d_0 + o \quad 0 \leq o <\mid \delta \mid}{\Gamma \vdash \langle \rho, \phi^{(\beta)}, \iota \rangle \rightarrow^\natural \langle \rho, \phi^{(\beta)}, \iota^+ \rangle}$$

$$\text{FUNSTF} \frac{instr(\iota) = \lfloor [e_1] = e_2 \rfloor \quad [\![e_1]\!]_\rho = bp - o \quad 0 \leq o <\mid \phi \mid}{\langle \phi_i, bp, \rho_i \rangle \vdash \langle \rho, \phi^{(\beta)}, \iota \rangle \rightarrow^\natural \langle \rho, \phi[o \mapsto [\![e_2]\!]_\rho]^{(1)}, \iota^+ \rangle}$$

$$\text{FUNLDD} \frac{instr(\iota) = \lfloor r = [e] \rfloor \quad [\![e]\!]_\rho = d_0 + o \quad 0 \leq o <\mid \delta \mid}{\Gamma \vdash \langle \rho, \phi^{(\beta)}, \iota \rangle \rightarrow^\natural \langle \rho[r \mapsto v], \phi^{(\beta)}, \iota^+ \rangle}$$

$$\text{FUNLDARG} \frac{instr(\iota) = \lfloor r = [e] \rfloor \quad [\![e]\!]_\rho = (bp + f_s) - o \quad 0 \leq o < f_s}{\langle \phi_i, bp, \rho_i \rangle \vdash \langle \rho, \phi^{(\beta)}, \iota \rangle \rightarrow^\natural \langle \rho[r \mapsto \phi_i(o)], \phi^{(\beta)}, \iota^+ \rangle}$$

$$\text{FUNLDFRAME} \frac{instr(\iota) = \lfloor r = [e] \rfloor \quad [\![e]\!]_\rho = bp - o \quad 0 \leq o < f_s}{\langle \phi_i, bp, \rho_i \rangle \vdash \langle \rho, \phi^{(\beta)}, \iota \rangle \rightarrow^\natural \langle \rho[r \mapsto \phi(o)], \phi^{(\beta)}, \iota^+ \rangle}$$

$$\text{FUNCONT} \frac{instr(\iota) = \lfloor \mathbf{jmpif}\ e_1\ e_2 \rfloor \quad [\![e_1]\!]_\rho = 0}{\Gamma \vdash \langle \rho, \phi^{(\beta)}, \iota \rangle \rightarrow^\natural \langle \rho, \phi^{(\beta)}, \iota^+ \rangle}$$

$$\text{FunJump} \frac{instr(\iota) = \lfloor \mathbf{jmpif}\ e_1\ e_2 \rfloor \quad [\![e_1]\!]_\rho \neq 0 [\![e_2]\!]_\rho \in Code}{\Gamma \vdash \langle \rho, \phi^{(\beta)}, \iota \rangle \to^\natural \langle \rho, \phi^{(\beta)}, [\![e_2]\!]_\rho \rangle}$$

$$\text{FunCall} \frac{\begin{array}{c} instr(\iota) = \lfloor \mathbf{call}\ e \rfloor \quad [\![e]\!]_\rho = f \quad f \in \mathcal{F} \cup \mathcal{T} \\ \rho(\mathbf{esp}) = bp - o \quad 0 \leq o < f_s \quad \mid \phi_1 \mid = o \\ isret(\iota^+, \rho, \phi_1) \quad \rho \sim \rho' \end{array}}{\langle \phi_i, bp, \rho_i \rangle \vdash \langle \rho, \phi_1 \cdot \phi_2^{(1)}, \iota \rangle \to^\natural \langle \rho', \phi_1 \cdot \phi_2'^{(1)}, \iota^+ \rangle}$$

$$\text{FunRet} \frac{\begin{array}{c} instr(\iota) = \lfloor \mathbf{ret}\ e \rfloor \quad [\![e]\!]_\rho = ret \\ isret(\iota^+, \rho_i, \phi_i) \quad \rho_i \sim \rho \end{array}}{\langle \phi_i, bp, \rho_i \rangle \vdash \langle \rho, \phi^{(\beta)}, \iota \rangle \to^\natural \blacksquare}$$

$$\text{FunHalt} \frac{instr(\iota) = \lfloor \mathbf{hlt} \rfloor}{\Gamma \vdash \langle \rho, \phi^{(\beta)}, \iota \rangle \to^\natural \blacksquare} \qquad \text{FunCrash} \frac{}{\Gamma \vdash \blacksquare \to^\natural \blacksquare}$$

C   Proof of Lemma 1

First we need an intermediate lemma:

Lemma 3 (Base pointer is contained).

$$\begin{aligned} \forall S = &\ \langle \langle bp, cs, \rho_i \rangle, \langle \rho, \delta, \phi^{(\beta)}, \iota \rangle \rangle \in Acc, \\ if \quad & \beta = 1 \\ then \quad & s_0 - s_s + \text{GZ}_\bot < bp \leq s_0 - \text{GZ}_\top \\ else \quad & s_0 - s_s + \text{GZ}_\bot - f_s < bp \leq s_0 - \text{GZ}_\top \end{aligned}$$

Proof. We reason by induction on $S \in Acc$. In the initial state, we have $bp = s_0 - \text{GZ}_\top$ and $\beta = 0$, so the property is true since $s_s > \text{GZ}_\top + \text{GZ}_\bot$.

In the inductive case, we procede by case analysis on $S \Rightarrow S'$, where S verifies the property. Because the property only depends on the context and β, most cases are trivial: they preserve the context and β. In the case of the StoreFrame rule, the context is preserved, and β is updated to 1. The property is still preserved because the property when $\beta = 0$ implies the property when $\beta = 1$.

The last case is when the extended call rule applies. In that case, $\beta(S) = 1$, $bp(S') = bp(S) - \mid \phi_1 \mid$ with $\mid \phi_1 \mid \leq f_s$ and $\beta(S') = 0$.

Since $s_0 - s_s + \text{GZ}_\bot < bp(S) \leq s_0 - \text{GZ}_\top$, $s_0 - s_s + \text{GZ}_\bot - \mid \phi_1 \mid < bp(S') \leq s_0 - \text{GZ}_\top$, so $s_0 - s_s + \text{GZ}_\bot - f_s < bp(S') \leq s_0 - \text{GZ}_\top$ and the property holds.

Now we can prove the main lemma:

Proof. First, we prove that $Acc \subseteq \gamma(I\text{-}Acc)$.

Let $S \in Acc$. By induction on S, we have the following cases:

- $S = \langle \Gamma_0, \Sigma_0 \rangle = \langle \langle [\langle s_0, \phi_i \rangle], s_0 - \text{GZ}_\top, \rho_0 \rangle, \langle \rho, \delta, \phi^{(0)}, \iota_0 \rangle \rangle$ with $\mid \phi_i \mid = \text{GZ}_\top$. By definition, $\iota_0 \in \mathcal{F}$, so we can construct $Init(\iota_0)$. By construction, $S \in \gamma(Init(\iota_0))$.

- $S = \langle \Gamma_2, \Sigma_2 \rangle$ with $\langle \Gamma_1, \Sigma_1 \rangle \in Acc$ and $\langle \Gamma_1, \Sigma_1 \rangle \Rightarrow \langle \Gamma_2, \Sigma_2 \rangle$. By induction hypothesis, we also have $S^\natural$ such that $\langle \Gamma_1, \Sigma_1 \rangle \in \gamma(S^\natural)$.
  Since $I\text{-}Safe(I\text{-}Acc)$, $S^\natural \rightarrow^\natural S_2^\natural$.
  By case analysis on the rule that allows $\rightarrow^\natural$, we have:
  - *(FunAssign)*   The preconditions are the same as for (Assign), so there is S' such that $S \rightarrow^\natural S'$. Furthermore, $S' \in \gamma(s'^\sharp)$.
  - *(FunStD, FunLdD, FunCont, FunIndirectJump, FunHalt, FunCrash)* Similar reasoning.
  - *(FunStF)*   Here, the preconditions are either true for (StoreFrame) or (StoreCrash) because of Lemma 3, so there is S' such that $S \rightarrow^\natural S'$, with $S' = \blacksquare$ (writing in the guard zone) or $S' = \langle \rho, \delta, \phi^{(\beta)}, \iota \rangle$ (writing in the frame). Furthermore, $S' \in \gamma(s'^\sharp)$.
  - *(FunLdS)*   Here, the preconditions are either true for (LoadStack) or (LoadCrash) because of Lemma 3, so there is S' such that $S \rightarrow^\natural S'$, with $S' = \blacksquare$ (reading in the guard zone) or $S' = \langle \rho, \delta, \phi^{(\beta)}, \iota \rangle$ (reading in the stack). Futhermore, $S' \in \gamma(s'^\sharp)$.
  - *(FunCall)*   Here the preconditions are the same as for (CallAcc) because of Lemma 3, so there is S' such that $S \Rightarrow S'$. Furthermore, $S' \in \gamma_s(Init(f)) \subseteq \gamma_s(S^\sharp)$.
  - *(FunRet)*   Here the preconditions are the same as for (RetAcc), so $S \Rightarrow \blacksquare$. Furthermore, $\blacksquare \in \gamma(s'^\sharp)$.

Hence our intermediate conclusion: $Acc \subseteq \gamma(I\text{-}Acc)$.

Let's now take $S \in Acc$. We use the previous conclusion to also choose $S^\natural \in I\text{-}Acc$ such that $S \in \gamma(S^\natural)$. Because we have $I\text{-}Safe(I\text{-}Acc)$, we can also take $S_2^\natural$ such that $S^\natural \rightarrow S_2^\natural$.

By case analysis with a similar reasoning as the previous property, we get that $S \Rightarrow S'$ with $S' \in \gamma(S_2^\natural)$.

Hence $Safe(Acc)$.

D   Proof of Lemma 2

Proof. First, we prove that $I\text{-}Acc \subseteq \gamma(A\text{-}Acc)$.

Let $S \in I\text{-}Acc$. By induction on S, we have the following cases:

- $S \in Init(f) = \langle \langle \phi_i, bp, \rho \rangle, \langle \rho, \phi^{(f)}, 0 \rangle \rangle$
  We can construct $S^\sharp = \langle \langle \phi_i', bp, \rho' \rangle, \langle \rho', \phi'^{(f)}, 0 \rangle \in AInit(f)$ such that $S \in \gamma(S^\sharp)$.
  $S^\sharp \in A\text{-}Acc$, so the property is true in that case.
- $S = \langle \Gamma, \Sigma_2 \rangle$ with $\langle \Gamma, \Sigma_1 \rangle \in I\text{-}Acc$ and $\Gamma \vdash \Sigma_1 \rightarrow^\natural \Sigma_2$. By induction hypothesis, we also have $S^\sharp$ such that $\langle \Gamma_1, \Sigma_1 \rangle \in \gamma(S^\sharp)$.
  Because we have $A\text{-}Safe(A\text{-}Acc)$, we also have $S_2^\sharp$ such that $S^\sharp \rightarrow S_2^\sharp$.
  By case analysis on $\rightarrow$, we can see as before that the preconditions of the abstract semantics are the same or more restrictive than those of the intra procedural semantics. It is also built in a way that $\langle \Gamma, \Sigma_2 \rangle \in \gamma(S_2^\sharp)$.

Hence our intermediate conclusion: $I\text{-}Acc \subseteq \gamma(A\text{-}Acc)$.

Let's now take $S \in I\text{-}Acc$. We use the previous conclusion to also choose $S^\sharp \in A\text{-}Acc$ such that $S \in \gamma(S^\sharp)$. Because we have $A\text{-}Safe(A\text{-}Acc)$, we can also take $S_2^\sharp$ such that $S^\sharp \to S_2^\sharp$.

By case analysis with a similar reasoning as the previous property, we get that $S \Rightarrow S'$ with $S' \in \gamma(S_2^\sharp)$.

Hence $Safe(I\text{-}Acc)$.

References

1. Balakrishnan, G., Reps, T.: Analyzing memory accesses in x86 executables. In: Duesterwald, E. (ed.) CC 2004. LNCS, vol. 2985, pp. 5–23. Springer, Heidelberg (2004). https://doi.org/10.1007/978-3-540-24723-4_2

2. Biondi, P., Rigo, R., Zennou, S., Mehrenberger, X.: BinCAT: purrfecting binary static analysis. In: Symposium sur la sécurité des technologies de l'information et des communications (2017)

3. Brumley, D., Jager, I., Avgerinos, T., Schwartz, E.J.: BAP: a binary analysis platform. In: Gopalakrishnan, G., Qadeer, S. (eds.) CAV 2011. LNCS, vol. 6806, pp. 463–469. Springer, Heidelberg (2011). https://doi.org/10.1007/978-3-642-22110-1_37

4. Dullien, T., Porst, S.: REIL: a platform-independent intermediate representation of disassembled code for static code analysis. In: CanSecWest 2009 (2009)

5. Haas, A., et al.: Bringing the web up to speed with WebAssembly. In: Proceedings of the 38th Conference on Programming Language Design and Implementation, pp. 185–200. ACM (2017)

6. Jourdan, J.-H., Laporte, V., Blazy, S., Leroy, X., Pichardie, D.: A formally-verified C static analyzer. In: Proceedings of the 42nd Symposium on Principles of Programming Languages, pp. 247–259. ACM (2015)

7. Kinder, J.: Static analysis of x86 executables. Ph.D. thesis, Technische Universität Darmstadt, November 2010

8. Kroll, J.A., Stewart, G., Appel, A.W.: Portable software fault isolation. In: Proceedings of the 27th IEEE Computer Security Foundations Symposium, pp. 18–32. IEEE (2014)

9. Leroy, X.: Formal verification of a realistic compiler. Commun. ACM **52**(7), 107–115 (2009)

10. Mihaila, B.: Adaptable static analysis of executables for proving the absence of vulnerabilities. Ph.D. thesis, Technische Universität München (2015)

11. Miné, A.: Abstract domains for bit-level machine integer and floating-point operations. In: Proceedings of the Workshops on Automated Theory eXploration and on Invariant Generation. EPiC Series in Computing, vol. 17, pp. 55–70. EasyChair (2012)

12. Morrisett, G., Tan, G., Tassarotti, J., Tristan, J.-B., Gan, E.: RockSalt: better, faster, stronger SFI for the x86. SIGPLAN Not. **47**(6), 395–404 (2012)

13. Sehr, D., et al.: Adapting software fault isolation to contemporary CPU architectures. In: Proceedings of the 19th USENIX Conference on Security, pp. 1–12. USENIX (2010)

14. Shoshitaishvili, Y., et al.: SoK: (state of) the art of war: offensive techniques in binary analysis. In: IEEE Symposium on Security and Privacy (2016)

15. Wahbe, R., Lucco, S., Anderson, T.E., Graham, S.L.: Efficient software-based fault isolation. SIGOPS Oper. Syst. Rev. **27**(5), 203–216 (1993)
16. Yee, B., et al.: Native client: a sandbox for portable, untrusted x86 native code. Commun. ACM **53**(1), 91–99 (2010)

Closing the Performance Gap Between Doubles and Rationals for Octagons

Aziem Chawdhary and Andy King[✉]

University of Kent, Canterbury CT2 7NF, UK
a.m.king@kent.ac.uk

Abstract. Octagons have enduring appeal because their domain operations are simple, readily mapping to for-loops which apply max, min and sum to the entries of a Difference Bound Matrix (DBM). In the quest for efficiency, arithmetic is often realised with double-precision floating-point, albeit at the cost of the certainty provided by arbitrary-precision rationals. In this paper we show how Compact DBMs (CoDBMs), which have recently been proposed as a memory refinement for DBMs, enable arithmetic calculation to be short-circuited in various domain operations. We also show how comparisons can be avoided by changing the tables which underpin CoDBMs. From the perspective of implementation, the optimisations are attractive because they too are conceptually simple, following the ethos of Octagons. Yet they can halve the running time on rationals, putting CoDBMs on rationals on a par with DBMs on doubles.

1 Introduction

The dominating arithmetic operations for Difference Bound Matrices (DBMs) are addition and comparison. The speed of these operations for double-precision floating-point arithmetic is comparable with that of long integer arithmetic for modern 64-bit desktop processors, hence the trend to work with floating-point rather than idealised arithmetic, even though the latter is arguably more attractive for verification since it avoids any concerns on rounding. The problem is not just one of speed: arbitrary-precision rational numbers, as supported by the GNU multiple precision (GMP) library, require at least 24 bytes to store each entry of a DBM, whereas an IEEE 754-1983 double occupies exactly 8 bytes.

Recent progress has been made on reducing space requirements by observing the DBM entries are frequently repeated [7]. This leads to a factored representation for a DBM [7] in which the entries in the matrix are identifiers for the rationals rather than the rationals themselves. The idea is to interpret matrix entries using a table which maps each identifier to its corresponding rational; a second table is used for searching for the (unique) identifier for a given rational. The first table is used for reading a matrix and the second is used for writing to a matrix; both tables are shared across all matrices. Since the number of distinct rationals occurring as DBM entries is small, typically thousands over the lifetime of a long-running static analysis, the identifiers can be represented as 16-bit integers. Even with the overhead of the two additional tables, this reduces

© Springer Nature Switzerland AG 2018
A. Podelski (Ed.): SAS 2018, LNCS 11002, pp. 187–204, 2018.
https://doi.org/10.1007/978-3-319-99725-4_13

the space consumption of a matrix, mimicking the space savings which come with hash consing (that incidentally was invented with linear probing [12,13]). The resulting alternative representation for a DBM has been dubbed a Compact DBM (CoDBM) [7] (which is not to be confused with a Coherent DBM [23,24]). The net reduction in space over DBMs, which derives from each rational now being represented exactly once, improves cache behaviour. It also saves repeatedly initialising memory for storing the rationals, an auxiliary operation which matches the frequency of the addition and comparison. For long-running analyses, CoDBMs reduce memory consumption by approximately 30% and improve running-time by approximately 40%, by virtue of the reduction in memory initialisation and improved locality [7].

This paper focuses on the computational, rather than the space-saving aspects of CoDBMs. Our first contribution is in optimising a write to a CoDBM. A CoDBM employs an ordered table (the second table) which maps each rational encountered thus far during analysis to its unique identifier. Whenever an entry is to be written, the table is searched (using binary search) for a rational and its corresponding identifier. We show how hashing and linear probing can avoid the repeated comparisons made by binary search and avoid the need to maintain an ordered table. We report that the number of resulting comparisons (and multiplications) is indeed reduced and demonstrate a commensurate speedup and improved cache behaviour.

Our second contribution relates to join, which is one of the domain operations that occurs with high frequency. Join is computed pairwise on the entries of two DBMs, and likewise for CoDBMs, by comparing each entry point-wise and taking the maximum. Point-wise join can be simplified by checking if the two identifiers align, or if one matches the special identifier which is reserved for infinity. Both operations can be implemented in a lightweight manner using CoDBMs, thus avoiding expensive number comparison operations. These refinements constitute our second contribution.

Our third contribution exploits the infinity identifier in another domain operation: closure. Closure reduces to a sequence of addition and maximum calculations, the results of which will be infinity if either of their arguments are infinity. Thus, if an entry of the CoDBM feeds an addition, and that entry is the infinity identifier, the result of the addition is infinity, irrespective of its other argument. Likewise for maximum. A lightweight check can be introduced to detect when the inner loop of the closure calculation can be bypassed. An analogous refinement carries over to incremental closure [10,24]. These refinements make up the third contribution.

Cumulatively, these refinements close the performance gap between doubles and rationals for octagons, from which we conclude that the role of rationals needs to be reevaluated. The paper feeds into the growing body of work [2,3,7, 17,26,28,29] on how best to realise octagons on stock architectures.

2   Background

An octagonal constraint [1,23,24] is a two-variable inequality of the syntactic form $x_i - x_j \leqslant c$, $x_i + x_j \leqslant c$ or $-x_i - x_j \leqslant c$ where c is a constant, and x_i and x_j are drawn from a finite set of variables $\{x_0, \ldots, x_{n-1}\}$. This class includes unary inequalities $x_i + x_i \leqslant c$ and $-x_i - x_i \leqslant c$ which express interval constraints. An octagon is a set of points satisfying a system of octagonal constraints. The octagon domain is the set of all octagons defined over a given set of variables.

2.1   DBMs

Implementations of the octagon domain reuse machinery developed for solving difference constraints of the form $x_i - x_j \leqslant c$. An octagonal constraint over $\{x_0, \ldots, x_{n-1}\}$ can be translated [24] to a difference constraint over an augmented set of variables $\{x'_0, \ldots, x'_{2n-1}\}$, which are interpreted by $x'_{2i} = x_i$ and $x'_{2i+1} = -x_i$. The translation proceeds as follows:

$$
\begin{aligned}
x_i - x_j \leqslant c &\rightsquigarrow \quad x'_{2i} - x'_{2j} \leqslant c \ \wedge x'_{2j+1} - x'_{2i+1} \leqslant c \\
x_i + x_j \leqslant c &\rightsquigarrow x'_{2i} - x'_{2j+1} \leqslant c \ \wedge \quad x'_{2j} - x'_{2i+1} \leqslant c \\
-x_i - x_j \leqslant c &\rightsquigarrow x'_{2i+1} - x'_{2j} \leqslant c \ \wedge \quad x'_{2j+1} - x'_{2i} \leqslant c \\
x_i \leqslant c &\rightsquigarrow x'_{2i} - x'_{2i+1} \leqslant 2c \\
-x_i \leqslant c &\rightsquigarrow x'_{2i+1} - x'_{2i} \leqslant 2c
\end{aligned}
$$

A difference bound matrix (DBM) [11,22] (denoted **m**) which is a square matrix of dimension $n \times n$, is commonly used to represent a systems of n^2 (syntactically irredundant [21]) difference constraints over n variables. The entry $\mathbf{m}_{i,j}$ represents the constant c of the inequality $x_i - x_j \leqslant c$ where $i, j \in [0, n)$. Since an octagonal constraint system over n variables translates to a difference constraint system over $2n$ variables, a DBM representing an octagon has dimension $2n \times 2n$. Figure 1 illustrates how an octagon translates to a system of differences. The entries of the DBM correspond to the constants in the difference constraints. Note how differences which are (syntactically) absent from the system lead to entries which take a symbolic value of ∞. Observe how the DBM can be viewed as an adjacency matrix for the illustrated graph.

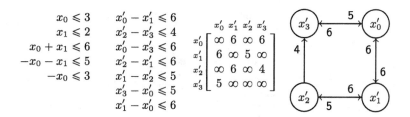

Fig. 1. Example of an octagonal system and its DBM representation

2.2 Closure

Closure properties define canonical representations of DBMs, and can decide satisfiability and support operations such as join and projection. Bellman [4] showed that the satisfiability of a difference system can be decided using shortest path algorithms on a graph representing the differences. If the graph contains a negative cycle (a cycle whose edge weights sum to a negative value) then the difference system is unsatisfiable. The same applies for DBMs representing octagons. Closure propagates all the implicit (entailed) constraints in a system, leaving each entry in the DBM with the sharpest possible constraint entailed between the variables. A DBM $\mathbf{m}$ of dimension $n \times n$ is said to be closed iff $\forall i . \mathbf{m}_{i,i} = 0$ for all $i \in [0, n)$ and $\mathbf{m}_{i,j} \leqslant \mathbf{m}_{i,k} + \mathbf{m}_{k,j}$ for all $i, j, k \in [0, n)$. Zero diagonal elements are enjoyed by octagons which are satisfiable. The DBM is said to be strongly closed iff additionally $\forall i, j . \mathbf{m}_{i,j} \leqslant \mathbf{m}_{i,\bar{i}}/2 + \mathbf{m}_{\bar{j},j}/2$ for all $i, j \in [0, n)$, where $\bar{i}$ is $i + 1$ if i is even, and $i - 1$ otherwise. Strong closure merges a pair of unary constraints into a single binary constraint: the binary constraint $2(x'_i - x'_j) \leqslant \mathbf{m}_{i,\bar{i}} + \mathbf{m}_{\bar{j},j}$ following from the two unary constraints $2x'_i = x'_i - x'_{\bar{i}} \leqslant \mathbf{m}_{i,\bar{i}}$ and $-2x'_j = x'_{\bar{j}} - x'_j \leqslant \mathbf{m}_{\bar{j},j}$. Figure 2 gives a cubic implementation which tightens a DBM to ensure closure and a quadratic pass which enforces strong closure. Satisfiability is checked by merely inspecting the diagonal of the tightened DBM.

2.3 Incremental Closure

Minè introduced incremental closure [24] which reestablishes closure once a small number of constraints are added to a closed DBM. This algorithm was subsequently refined [9,10] to give the quadratic algorithm listed in Fig. 3, presented both with and without loop-invariant code hoisting. The idea is to determine how

```
 1: function CLOSE(m)
 2:     for k ∈ {0, . . . , 2n − 1} do
 3:         for i ∈ {0, . . . , 2n − 1} do
 4:             for j ∈ {0, . . . , 2n − 1} do
 5:                 m_{i,j} ← min(m_{i,j}, m_{i,k} + m_{k,j})
 6:             end for
 7:         end for
 8:     end for
 9:     return m
10: end function
```

```
 1: function STR(m)
 2:     for i ∈ {0, . . . , 2n − 1} do
 3:         for j ∈ {0, . . . , 2n − 1} do
 4:             m_{i,j} ← min(m_{i,j}, (m_{i,ī} + m_{j̄,j})/2)
 5:         end for
 6:     end for
 7:     return m
 8: end function
```

Fig. 2. Non-incremental closure and strengthening

```
1: function INCCLOSE(m, x'ₐ − x'_b ≤ d)
2:     for i ∈ {0, . . . , 2n − 1} do
3:         for j ∈ {0, . . . , 2n − 1} do
```

$$4: \qquad \mathbf{m'}_{i,j} \leftarrow \min \begin{pmatrix} \mathbf{m}_{i,j}, \\ \mathbf{m}_{i,a} + d + \mathbf{m}_{b,j}, \\ \mathbf{m}_{i,\bar{b}} + d + \mathbf{m}_{\bar{a},j}, \\ \mathbf{m}_{i,\bar{b}} + d + \mathbf{m}_{\bar{a},a} + d + \mathbf{m}_{b,j}, \\ \mathbf{m}_{i,a} + d + \mathbf{m}_{b,\bar{b}} + d + \mathbf{m}_{\bar{a},j} \end{pmatrix}$$

```
5:         end for
6:     end for
7: end function
```

```
1: function INCCLOSEHOIST(m, x'ₐ − x'_b ≤ d)
2:     t₁ ← d + m_{ā,a} + d;
3:     t₂ ← d + m_{b,b̄} + d;
4:     for i ∈ {0, . . . , 2n − 1} do
5:         t₃ ← min(m_{i,a} + d, m_{i,b̄} + t₁);
6:         t₄ ← min(m_{i,b̄} + d, m_{i,a} + t₂);
7:         for j ∈ {0, . . . , 2n − 1} do
8:             m_{i,j} ← min(m_{i,j}, t₃ + m_{b,j}, t₄ + m_{ā,j})
9:         end for
10:     end for
11:     return m
12: end function
```

Fig. 3. Incremental Closure (without and with code hoisting)

each DBM entry $\mathbf{m}_{i,j}$ is effected by the addition of a new constraint $x'_a - x'_b \leq d$, independent of every other DBM entry.

The force of (strong) closure, whether incremental or not, is that it gives a canonical representation for DBMs; it also reduces join to the pointwise max of two closed DBMs, to give the quadratic join operation illustrated in Fig. 4.

```
1: function JOIN(m¹, m²)
2:     for i ∈ {0, . . . , 2n − 1} do
3:         for j ∈ {0, . . . , 2n − 1} do
4:             m_{i,j} ← max(m¹_{i,j}, m²_{i,j})
5:         end for
6:     end for
7:     return m
8: end function
```

Fig. 4. Join of two closed DBMs

2.4   Apron

Apron is a widely-used Octagon domain library [18] which is implemented in C, with bindings for C++, Java and OCaml. It supports various number systems. Numbers are represented by a type bound_t, which, depending on compile-time options, will select a specific header file with a specific concrete implementation of numbers extended with symbolic values of $-\infty$ and $+\infty$. Every bound_t object is initialised via a call to bound_init, which in the case of GMP rationals will call a malloc function. Numbers of type bound_t cannot be assigned directly, but instead are assigned via function calls such as bound_set.

DBMs are stored by taking advantage of coherence [24], which can be assumed without loss of generality. A DBM $\mathbf{m}$ is said to be coherent if $\mathbf{m}_{i,j} = \mathbf{m}_{\bar{j},\bar{i}}$ for all $i, j \in [0, n)$. Coherence allows a half-matrix to be represented which, in turn, can then be packed into a (linear) array of bound_t objects as follows: If $i \geqslant j$ or $i = \bar{j}$ then the entry at (i, j) in the DBM is stored at index $j + \lfloor i^2/2 \rfloor$ in the array. Otherwise (i, j) is stored at the index location reserved for entry $(\bar{j}, \bar{i})$. A DBM of dimension $n \times n$ then requires an array of size $2n(n + 1)$.

2.5   CoDBMs

Compact DBMs (CoDBMs) [7] redistribute the cost of memory allocation and initialisation, and do so in a way that is sensitive to the relative frequency of DBM reads to DBM writes (the latter being less frequent than the former). CoDBMs are matrices where the entries are identifiers (short integers), rather than numeric values (rationals), and each identifier references a number in a shared number pool, as illustrated in Fig. 5. The number pool is abstracted by two functions: values : $\mathbb{N} \to \mathbb{Q}$ and search : $\mathbb{Q} \to \mathbb{N}$, which are mutual inverses.

The change from DBMs to CoDBMs requires a new API for reading and writing an entry $\mathbf{c}_{i,j}$ of a CoDBM $\mathbf{c}$. Reading $\mathbf{c}_{i,j}$ amounts to interpreting the index stored in $\mathbf{c}_{i,j}$ using values to obtain a value $v = \text{values}(\mathbf{c}_{i,j})$. Writing a value v to $\mathbf{c}_{i,j}$ involves applying a function $\ell = \text{SEARCH}(v)$ to retrieve the identifier ℓ for v and then assigning $\mathbf{c}_{i,j}$ to ℓ. The function SEARCH, which is listed in Fig. 6, manufactures a unique identifier if v is fresh and extends values and search accordingly. Previous work [7] realised values as an array of rationals and search as an ordered array of rationals, the index of a particular rational defining the identifier. The identifier was found using Bisection search [32]. CoDBMs achieve

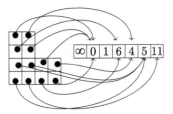

Fig. 5. Example illustrating the difference between DBMs and CoDBMs

```
1: function SEARCH(v)
2:     if v ∈ dom(search) then
3:         return search(v)
4:     else
5:         values ← values ∪ {ℓ ↦ v} where ℓ ∉ dom(values)
6:         search ← search ∪ {v ↦ ℓ}
7:         return ℓ
8:     end if
9: end function
```

Fig. 6. Searching and extending search and values

speedups because they store identifiers which are more compact than rationals (improving locality) and each distinct rational is stored once in the number pool (saving initialisation).

3   Hashing

The GMP manual [15] alludes to the fact that comparisons on rationals are expensive since $p/q \leqslant r/s$ reduces to $sp \leqslant qr$ if the denominators p and s are positive. Comparison thus involves two multiplications in general. Moreover, SEARCH is invoked on every write to the CoDBM and each invocation will compute $\lceil log_2(n) \rceil$ comparisons in the worst case where n is the number of rationals in number pool. Thus, even if the pool contains just 256 rationals, a write can induce 16 multi-precision multiplications. Moreover, to insert a new rational into an ordered table it is necessary to shuffle along other elements. These costs motivate hashing.

A rational r is hashed by converting it to a double-precision floating point number f, an operation which is supported by GMP. If s is the size of the hash table then a multiplicative hash [20] $h(f)$ is computed by calculating $\ell = \lceil fs(1 + \sqrt{5})/2 \rceil$ mod s with floating-point arithmetic and defining $h(f) = \ell$ if $\ell \geqslant 0$ and $h(f) = s - \ell$ otherwise. Hashing with the Golden Ratio helps ensure that the hashes are scattered evenly, reducing the chance of collisions [20, Chap. 6.4]. If a rational does not exist at entry $h(f)$ then r is inserted at this entry and $h(f)$ is returned by SEARCH. If the entry $h(f)$ is already occupied by a rational r', then an equality check $r = r'$ is performed on rationals (which is constant-time by virtue of a canonical representation). If $r = r'$ succeeds then $h(f)$ is returned by SEARCH. If $r = r'$ fails then linear probing is applied to find the next consecutive (modulo s) identifier ℓ' whose entry is empty in the table. The rational r is then inserted at ℓ' and ℓ' is returned by SEARCH. Note if that r is exceptionally large then f can conceivably be NaN in which case a constant hash can be assigned.

Although multiplicative hashes are not renowned for avoiding collisions, they are simple, and it turns out that collisions are incredibly rare because the number of distinct rationals is small and thus the occupancy of the table is low.

4   Optimising Join

DBMs typically contain many symbolic infinity values: a property has sparked an interest in using sparse representations for difference constraints [14]. However, sparse representations complicate the join of octagons [19], the simplicity of which we want to preserve. Nevertheless, the identifiers employed by CoDBMs enable join to bypass vacuous DBM entries, without adding any conceptual complexity to join itself. The idea is to merely fix the identifier for symbolic infinity up-front so that infinity can be intercepted with a lightweight check without inspecting the symbolic value itself.

```
1: function SETDBMMAX(c, (i, j), c¹, c²)
2:      BOUND_INIT(TMP)
3:      TMP ← BOUND_MAX(values(c¹ᵢ,ⱼ), values(c²ᵢ,ⱼ))
4:      cᵢ,ⱼ ← SEARCH(TMP)
5: end function
```

```
1: function SETDBMMAX_OPT(c, (i, j), c¹, c²)
2:      if (c¹ᵢ,ⱼ = ℓ∞ ∨ c²ᵢ,ⱼ = ℓ∞) then
3:          cᵢ,ⱼ ← ℓ∞
4:      else if (c¹ᵢ,ⱼ = c²ᵢ,ⱼ) then
5:          cᵢ,ⱼ ← c¹ᵢ,ⱼ
6:      else
7:          if values(c¹ᵢ,ⱼ) ⩾ values(c²ᵢ,ⱼ) then
8:              cᵢ,ⱼ ← c¹ᵢ,ⱼ
9:          else
10:             cᵢ,ⱼ ← c²ᵢ,ⱼ
11:         end if
12:     end if
13: end function
```

Fig. 7. DBM max operation used in join and widening, and its optimised version

To reflect on the cost of join, consider the implementation of a max operation (SETDBMMAX) used in join, which assigns $c_{i,j}$ to the maximum of $c^1{}_{i,j}$ and $c^2{}_{i,j}$ shown in Fig. 7. Quite apart from the two multi-precision multiplications used in the comparison which underpins BOUND_MAX in line 3, line 2 allocates and initialises memory (which we make explicit to highlight a hidden cost).

Yet if either $c^1{}_{i,j}$ or $c^2{}_{i,j}$ is the identifier for infinity, denoted ℓ_∞, then there is no need to perform any comparison between rationals: the entry $c_{i,j}$ can simple be assigned the identifier ℓ_∞. Moreover, if the identifiers $c^1{}_{i,j}$ and $c^2{}_{i,j}$ align, then again a rational comparison is not needed. In fact, only in exceptional cases do the rationals need to be looked-up at all, which reduces memory pressure. This optimisation can be rolled out for widening which also uses SETDBMMAX. An analogous optimisation applies for meet, using min instead of max (though meet arises relatively infrequently during analysis).

5   Optimising Closure

Figure 8 shows how the identifier ℓ_∞ can be likewise trapped to speed up non-incremental and incremental closure. The observation is that if $c_{i,k} = \ell_\infty$ then sum values($c_{i,k}$) + values($c_{k,j}$) will be infinity irrespective of the identifier stored in $c_{k,j}$. Moreover, the check $c_{i,k} = \ell_\infty$ is performed on identifiers (integers) rather than rationals, so has negligible overhead, yet it potentially enables the entire inner loop of closure to be short-circuited (see CLOSEOPT of Fig. 8). Incremental closure algorithm can also be optimised (see INCCLOSEHOISTOPT of Fig. 8) where both the outer and inner loop can be skipped if certain indices match the fixed identifier ℓ_∞. These optimisations will only really benefit closure calculations on large CoDBMs so it is important that the checks are sufficiently lightweight to not overburden closures operating on small CoDBMs.

```
 1: function CLOSEOPT(c)
 2:     for k ∈ {0, . . . , 2n − 1} do
 3:         for i ∈ {0, . . . , 2n − 1} do
 4:             if c_{i,k} ≠ ℓ_∞ then
 5:                 for j ∈ {0, . . . , 2n − 1} do
 6:                     c_{i,j} ← SEARCH(min(values(c_{i,j}), values(c_{i,k}) + values(c_{k,j})))
 7:                 end for
 8:             end if
 9:         end for
10:     end for
11: end function
12:
13: function INCCLOSEHOISTOPT(c, x'_a − x'_b ≤ d)
14:     t_1 ← d + values(c_{ā,a}) + d;
15:     t_2 ← d + values(c_{b,b̄}) + d;
16:     for i ∈ {0, . . . , 2n − 1} do
17:         if c_{i,a} ≠ ℓ_∞ ∧ c_{i,b̄} ≠ ℓ_∞ then
18:             t_3 ← min(values(c_{i,a}) + d, values(c_{i,b̄}) + t_1);
19:             t_4 ← min(values(c_{i,b̄}) + d, values(c_{i,a}) + t_2);
20:             for j ∈ {0, . . . , 2n − 1} do
21:                 if c_{b,j} ≠ ℓ_∞ ∧ c_{ā,j} ≠ ℓ_∞ then
22:                     c_{i,j} ← SEARCH(min(values(c_{i,j}), t_3 + values(c_{b,j}), t_4 + values(c_{ā,j})))
23:                 end if
24:             end for
25:         end if
26:     end for
27: end function
```

Fig. 8. Optimised versions of closure and incremental closure

6 Experiments

This section compares the performance of CoDBMs over rationals against DBMs over doubles using three abstract interpreters [6,16,30], reporting execution times augmented with memory statistics for the longest running analyses. All statistics were gathered on a Linux machine equipped with 128 GB of RAM and dual 2.0 GHz Intel Xeon E5-2650 processors. Timings were averaged over five runs using multitime (http://tratt.net/laurie/src/multitime/) and include the time required to perform a complete analysis from parsing source to output.

6.1 FuncTion: Timings

Figure 9 presents the running times of the FuncTion termination analyser on all the 58 benchmarks from its repository (https://github.com/caterinaurban/function); timings which are fully detailed in the accompanying technical report [8]. FuncTion [30] applies abstract interpretation to infer piece-wise ranking functions for verifying termination. It is implemented in OCaml and can analyse simple programs in a C-like language. FuncTion has options for intervals, arbitrary polyhedra and octagons. For octagons, the default setting is Apron DBMs instantiated with rationals, reflecting a focus on verification. Doubles and CoDBMs were supported by changing the build system.

The cross marks of the scatter plot compare the running time for Apron DBMs over rationals against the execution time for Apron DBMs over doubles, so

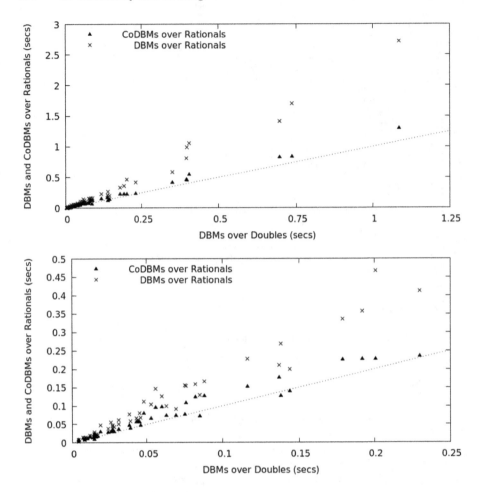

Fig. 9. CoDBMs and DBMs for rationals against DBMs for doubles

as quantify the overhead induced by rationals. The dotted-line has the gradient of one. The triangles illustrate the execution time of CoDBMs over rationals, equipped with the complete set of optimisations, again relative to doubles on DBMs. The top graph illustrates these timing for all benchmarks, whereas the bottom graph zooms in on the cluster of benchmarks around the origin. The proximity of the triangles near to the dotted line suggests that CoDBMs over rationals, when optimised, compare favourably to DBMs over doubles, at least for the benchmarks under test. Figure 10 compares CoDBMs to DBMs using a different perspective: it also compares CoDBMs over rationals to CoDBMs over doubles, showing how CoDBMs, when optimised, reduce the overhead of moving from doubles to rationals relative to the same move on DBMs.

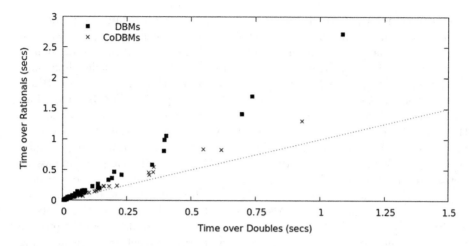

Fig. 10. DBMs for rationals against DBMs for doubles and likewise for CoDBMs

6.2 Crab-LLVM: Timings

To compare rationals against doubles with a state-of-the-art [16] inter-procedural analysis, Crab-LLVM (https://github.com/seahorn/crab-llvm) was built against Apron and CoDBMs and then applied to the 596 benchmarks of product-line SV-COMP series to infer octagonal invariants. This setup also exercised the domain operations from C rather than through OCaml bindings so as to check whether the bindings impact on performance.

The large number of benchmarks make a scatter plot infeasible, hence Fig. 11 plots the cumulative running time for the first n benchmarks against n itself;

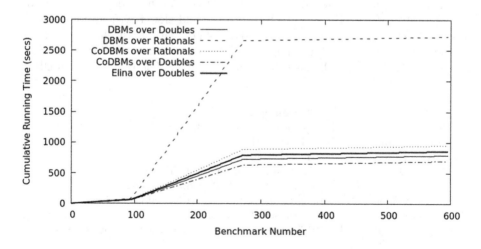

Fig. 11. Cumulative execution times over product-lines SV-COMP benchmarks

the technical report [8] details all these timings. These benchmarks divide into the elevator, email, and minepump sub-series of unreachability problems. Each benchmark in each sub-series has a broadly similar execution time, so the cumulative running time approximates a piece-wise linear function. The headline message is that, again, CoDBMs over rationals approach the performance of DBMS over doubles; moreover CoDBMs provide a modest gain on DBMs for doubles when all the optimisations are in place. Interestingly, Crab-LLVM defaults to the Elina library [29] which partitions a DBM on-the-fly into sub-DBMs that do not share variables, whilst simultaneously applying vectorisation. This invited a comparison. Elina did not perform as well as CoDBMs with the join and closure optimisations or even DBMs. Though unexpected, we include these results nevertheless. (It should be stressed that Elina was built exactly as specified, to the same level of optimisation as DBMs and CoDBMs, with the vector flag correctly set for an E5-2650 which supports vectorisation. Elina currently does not provide OCaml bindings otherwise we would have performed further comparisons using FuncTion and Frama-C.)

6.3   Frama-C: Timings

With an eye towards longer running analyses, EVA [6], the abstract interpretation plugin for Frama-C Sulfur, was used for comparing rationals against doubles for DBMs and CoDBMs. EVA is a prototype analyser for C99 which supports Apron but does not provide state-of-the-art optimisations such as automatic variable clustering [17] or access-based localisation [3]. Nevertheless, Fig. 12 lists the programs used for benchmarking, which represent eight programs from the Frama-C case study repository (https://github.com/Frama-C/open-source-case-studies) that successfully terminate when the EVA plugin is instantiated with octagons.

Figure 13 details the overall execution for DBMs, both for doubles and rationals. Interestingly, teas, mod and bzip are ten-fold slower with rationals than doubles for DBMs. This stems from a high number of DBMs with high dimension so that, cumulatively, the total number of DBMs entries created during analysis for each of these three problems is between 40- and 400-fold the number of DBM

Abbrv	Benchmark	LOC	Description
lev	levenstein	187	Levenstein string distance library
sol	solitaire	334	card cipher
2048	2048	435	2048 game
kh	khash	652	hash code from klib C library
taes	Tiny-AES	813	portable AES-128 implementation
mod	libmodbus	7685	library to interact with Modbus protocol
mgmp	mini-gmp	11787	subset of GMP library
bzip	bzip-single-file	74017	bzip single file for static analysis benchmarking

Fig. 12. Benchmarks

Abbrv	Apron DBM rationals	doubles	Ids	CoDBM rationals Bisect	Hash	Join	Close	CoDBM doubles Bisect	Hash	Join	Close
lev	22.78	4.71	900	12.16	10.66	8.15	7.41	5.87	4.78	4.74	4.30
sol	92.13	42.77	2161	80.22	71.00	51.48	50.61	52.09	44.03	42.89	42.52
2048	37.74	8.28	358	22.36	19.57	14.09	13.31	10.79	8.73	8.26	7.77
kh	3.087	1.92	196	2.44	2.447	2.167	2.131	1.871	2.014	1.928	1.843
taes	1883.50	153.43	140	740.47	663.37	411.72	386.67	261.32	164.85	143.63	129.67
mod	820.88	96.68	3627	558.27	494.12	321.72	293.68	192.63	111.92	102.78	91.70
mgmp	4.33	4.36	126	4.33	4.28	4.18	4.16	4.38	4.28	4.22	4.15
bzip	655.82	54.15	262	232.63	94.98	95.49	94.20	168.90	60.01	59.00	58.99

Fig. 13. Frama-C EVA plugin timings

entries created for any of the other five problems. The Ids column records the total number of identifiers (distinct DBM entries) used over the lifetime of each analysis. These counts are significantly smaller than the total number of DBM entries over the lifetime of each analysis by typically six orders of magnitude larger. (Shorter running analyses typically have smaller Ids counts.)

The Bisect column records the overall running time when bisection search is used to locate an identifier. Hash gives the runtime when hashing and linear probing is used instead. The hash table was allocated to store 10K rationals and collisions were barely discernible (since the Ids count was always low) hence the table was never expanded. Join presents the time when hashing is augmented with join (and meet) optimisation. The Close column additions applies the optimisations on both closure and incremental closure. For the longer running problems, Hash significantly improves on Bisect and Join significantly improves on Bisect (which the notable exception of mgmp where it has little effect). Close makes a less significant improvement on Join, but is useful nevertheless.

As a control, the last four columns of the table repeat the experiments but with CoDBMs instantiated with doubles. Since arithmetic is faster on doubles and doubles are compact, it is surprising to see that CoDBMs sometimes outperform DBMs. We surmise that the speedup comes from reduced memory pressure.

6.4   Frama-C: Memory Usage

Figure 14 records total memory usage as harvested by GNU time, which returns the maximum resident set size of the process during its lifetime. The table contains some surprises. First, memory usage for CoDBMs over rationals gives a net increase on DBMs over rationals for some problems. This increase occurs for the Sulfur version of Frama-C; the previous version gives a consistent reduction in memory usage (which is expressed as a percentage in the same column). The problem in recycling memory seems to relate to GNU multi-precision arithmetic since Sulfur gives a reduction when the same CoDBM code is instantiated with doubles. The second surprise is that Sulfur gives a dramatic overall decrease when CoDBMs are deployed with the join optimisation. This stems from the

		CoDBM			
rationals	Apron DBM	Bisect	Hash	Join	Close
lev	1,498,168	1,457,632	1,452,868	106,072	106,620
sol	6,187,568	10,718,464	10,717,924	246,008	247,044
2048	3,714,408	2,999,468	3,034,068	170,840	170,700
kh	163,840	142,168	142,264	69,696	69,440
taes	20,845,632	119,190,024	119,153,636	591,228	590,700
mod	28,945,580	73,116,452	73,111,892	911,572	901,788
mgmp	89,496	89,992	88,844	89,308	88,508
bzip	9,499,460	1,636,276	1,634,444	551,664	551,516

		CoDBM			
doubles	Apron DBM	Bisect	Hash	Join	Close
lev	191,968	106,264	106,004	106,200	105,756
sol	690,476	284,556	284,068	283,812	283,952
2048	413,916	167,432	165,548	165,712	165,284
kh	73,608	68,780	68,720	68,376	68,696
taes	2,044,832	603,056	604,440	604,416	604,420
mod	2,871,612	921,780	939,056	919,808	922,108
mgmp	89,832	88,092	88,548	88,008	88,628
bzip	1,158,460	555,216	551,884	552,524	552,988

Fig. 14. Memory Usage in kb for Frama-C: rationals above and doubles below

allocation and initialisation space for each maxima. This only occurs for rationals, hence Join offers little improvement for doubles.

Figure 15 records cache statistics for DBMs and CoDBMs which were harvested with Cachegrind [25] (for four representative benchmarks). Refs and Miss respectively denote the number of memory references and last-level cache misses for rationals for both DBMs and CoDBMs, where m denotes millions. A, B, H, J and C abbreviate the column names of Fig. 14. Reading an element from a CoDBM incurs an extra layer of indirection compared to a DBM and writing to

Abbrv		Insts	Refs	Miss	Rate	Abbrv		Insts	Refs	Miss	Rate
2048	A	242190m	99227m	185m	0.187	lev	A	145649m	59428m	72m	0.121
2048	B	125304m	47092m	52m	0.112	lev	B	67952m	25346m	25m	0.101
2048	H	95078m	41082m	52m	0.128	lev	H	52800m	22565m	25m	0.113
2048	J	65529m	30433m	5m	0.016	lev	J	38634m	17472m	3m	0.017
2048	C	56981m	26670m	5m	0.018	lev	C	32925m	14975m	3m	0.020
kh	A	13870m	6545m	5.2m	0.08	bzip	A	52677557m	2166803m	19579m	0.904
kh	B	9228m	4595m	2.7m	0.06	bzip	B	1855916m	410861m	76m	0.019
kh	H	8579m	4465m	2.7m	0.06	bzip	H	533543m	229553m	76m	0.033
kh	J	7840m	4196m	1.3m	0.03	bzip	J	522984m	225737m	57m	0.026
kh	C	7690m	4130m	1.3m	0.03	bzip	C	512926m	221316m	57m	0.026

Fig. 15. Instruction count and cache statistics for Frama-C for rationals

a CoDBM can incur multiple memory references, so one might expect additional memory references. Yet the number of references reduces uniformly between DBMs and CoDBMs for Bisect and then across the CoDBM optimisations. The number of cache misses reduces even faster, indicating that locality is improved too, hence the decreasing cache miss-rate percentage (Rate). Reassuringly, the number of misses does not increase between Bisect and Hash, even though hashing can map a number to any location in the hash table, whereas bisection will only search the portion of the second table which is actually populated. A single (non-local) read into the hash table (which is the norm as collisions are rare) seems to more than offset the multiple reads incurred by bisection, which become progressively more local as search proceeds. Join gives an order of magnitude reduction in the number of misses because it bypasses accessing numbers in the first table as well as avoiding initialising a temporary variable and then storing the maxima. Cachegrind also records the number of instructions executed, which is a reflected in the Insts column, and is a proxy for work. The reduction in instruction count stands independent of the timings which are ultimately dependent on system behaviour.

7 Related Work

The tension between the elegance of octagons and their scalability has motivated a number of imaginative techniques [2,3,5,7,17,26,28,29] for enhancing octagonal analysis. First, variable clustering was proposed [5,23,31] for grouping variables into sets which scope the relationships that are tracked. However, deciding variable groupings is an art, although there has been recent progress made in automating decomposition both before [17] and during [29] analysis.

Second, the domain operations themselves have been refined, notably showing how strengthening (the act of combining pairs of unary octagon constraints to improve binary octagon constraints) need not be applied repeatedly, but instead can be left to a single post-processing step [1]. This led to a significant performance improvement of approximately 20% [1].

Thirdly, and more recently, there has been a move to curb the size of DBMs using sparse analyses [27] and access-based localisation techniques [3]. Access-based localisation uses scoping heuristics to adjust the size of the DBM to those variables that can actually be updated [3]. Sparse analyses generalise access-based localisation techniques, using data dependencies to adjust the size of abstract states propagated to method calls: [27] defines a generic technique to apply sparse techniques to abstract interpretation and combines this with variable packing to scale an octagon-based abstract interpreter for C programs. Access-based localisation and sparse frameworks (and variable clustering too) are orthogonal to our work, and can take advantage of the techniques introduced in this paper. Sparse matrix representations have been proposed for octagons [19] and differences [14] as an alternative to DBMs, but these representations sit at odds with the simplicity of the algorithms originally proposed for the domain. The desirable property of strong closure [24] (the normal form for octagons) does not hold for a sparse representation, motivating the need to rework domain operations [19].

Fourthly, there has been a move to better exploit the underlying architecture, either to harness GPUs [2] or advanced vector extensions (AVX) [29] in closure and strengthening (the latter being the first work to comment on the impact of cache misses in domain engineering).

8   Conclusion Discussions

The paper contributes to the growing body of work on domain engineering, where performance is improved, often in small steps, by devising refinements which relieve the pressure of the most commonly occuring domain operations. We buck the trend towards instantiating octagons with doubles by showing how CoDBMs, which save space over DBMs, can also save on computation if equipped with simple optimisations. These optimisations enable arithmetic to be short-circuited in join and closure, and also avoid repeated comparisons by changing the tables which underpin CoDBMs. The net effect is to put rationals on a par with doubles, so as to simultaneously achieve performance and soundness.

In terms of future work, it would be interesting to apply caching more aggressively and determine whether the hash could preserve the ordering on the rationals. If so, then join (and meet) could be further refined by comparing hashes. Moreover, it would be interesting to investigate temporal locality on rational arithmetic itself and determine if caching could be deployed to further accelerate the domain operations.

Acknowledgements. We thank Colin King at Canonical and Laurie Tratt at Kings for their help with the performance analysis which underpinned this work. We thank Oleg Kiselyov for his help navigating soviet computer science literature. This work was funded by EPSRC EP/K032585/1 and EPSRC EP/N020243/1.

References

1. Bagnara, R., Hill, P.M., Zaffanella, E.: Weakly-relational shapes for numeric abstractions: improved algorithms and proofs of correctness. Formal Methods Syst. Des. **35**(3), 279–323 (2009)
2. Banterle, F., Giacobazzi, R.: A fast implementation of the octagon abstract domain on graphics hardware. In: Nielson, H.R., Filé, G. (eds.) SAS 2007. LNCS, vol. 4634, pp. 315–332. Springer, Heidelberg (2007). https://doi.org/10.1007/978-3-540-74061-2_20
3. Beckschulze, E., Kowalewski, S., Brauer, J.: Access-based localization for octagons. Electron. Notes Theor. Comput. Sci. **287**, 29–40 (2012)
4. Bellman, R.: On a routing problem. Q. Appl. Math. **16**, 87–90 (1958)
5. Blanchet, B., Cousot, P., Cousot, R., Feret, J., Mauborgne, L., Miné, A., Monniaux, D., Rival, X.: A static analyzer for large safety-critical software. In: PLDI, pp. 196–207 (2003)

6. Bühler, D., Cuoq, P., Yakobowski, B., Lemerre, M., Maroneze, A., Perrelle, V., Prevosto, V.: The EVA Plug-in. CEA LIST, Software Reliability Laboratory, Saclay, France (2017). https://frama-c.com/download/frama-c-value-analysis.pdf
7. Chawdhary, A., King, A.: Compact difference bound matrices. In: Chang, B.-Y.E. (ed.) APLAS 2017. LNCS, vol. 10695, pp. 471–490. Springer, Cham (2017). https://doi.org/10.1007/978-3-319-71237-6_23
8. Chawdhary, A., King, A.: Closing the performance gap between doubles and rationals for octagons. Technical report 67227, University of Kent (2018). https://kar.kent.ac.uk/67227/
9. Chawdhary, A., Robbins, E., King, A.: Simple and efficient algorithms for octagons. In: Garrigue, J. (ed.) APLAS 2014. LNCS, vol. 8858, pp. 296–313. Springer, Cham (2014). https://doi.org/10.1007/978-3-319-12736-1_16
10. Chawdhary, A., Robbins, E., King, A.: Incrementally closing octagons. Formal Methods Syst. Des. 1–46 (2018). https://doi.org/10.1007/s10703-017-0314-7
11. Dill, D.L.: Timing assumptions and verification of finite-state concurrent systems. In: Sifakis, J. (ed.) CAV 1989. LNCS, vol. 407, pp. 197–212. Springer, Heidelberg (1990). https://doi.org/10.1007/3-540-52148-8_17
12. Ershov, A.P.: On programming of arithmetic operations. Commun. ACM 1(8), 3–6 (1958). Translated by M. D. Friedman
13. Ershov, A.P.: Programming of arithmetic operations. Doklady Akademii Nauk SSSR 118(3), 427–430 (1958)
14. Gange, G., Navas, J.A., Schachte, P., Søndergaard, H., Stuckey, P.J.: Exploiting sparsity in difference-bound matrices. In: Rival, X. (ed.) SAS 2016. LNCS, vol. 9837, pp. 189–211. Springer, Heidelberg (2016). https://doi.org/10.1007/978-3-662-53413-7_10
15. GNU: GNU MP Manual (2016). https://gmplib.org/manual/
16. Gurfinkel, A., Kahsai, T., Komuravelli, A., Navas, J.A.: The SeaHorn verification framework. In: Kroening, D., Păsăreanu, C.S. (eds.) CAV 2015. LNCS, vol. 9206, pp. 343–361. Springer, Cham (2015). https://doi.org/10.1007/978-3-319-21690-4_20
17. Heo, K., Oh, H., Yang, H.: Learning a variable-clustering strategy for octagon from labeled data generated by a static analysis. In: Rival, X. (ed.) SAS 2016. LNCS, vol. 9837, pp. 237–256. Springer, Heidelberg (2016). https://doi.org/10.1007/978-3-662-53413-7_12
18. Jeannet, B., Miné, A.: APRON: a library of numerical abstract domains for static analysis. In: Bouajjani, A., Maler, O. (eds.) CAV 2009. LNCS, vol. 5643, pp. 661–667. Springer, Heidelberg (2009). https://doi.org/10.1007/978-3-642-02658-4_52
19. Jourdan, J.-H.: Verasco: a formally verified C static analyzer. Ph.D. thesis, Université Paris Diderot (Paris 7) Sorbonne Paris Cité, May 2016
20. Knuth, D.: The Art of Computer Programming, Volume 3: Sorting and Searching, 2nd edn. Addison Wesley, Reading (1998)
21. Lassez, J.-L., Huynh, T., McAloon, K.: Simplication and elimination of redundant linear arithmetic constraints. In: Constraint Logic Programming, pp. 73–87. MIT Press (1993)
22. Measche, M., Berthomieu, B.: Time Petri-nets for analyzing and verifying time dependent communication protocols. In: Rudin, H., West, C. (eds.) Protocol Specification, Testing and Verification III, pp. 161–172. North-Holland, Amsterdam (1983)
23. Miné, A.: Weakly relational numerical abstract domains. Ph.D. thesis, École Polytechnique En Informatique (2004)

24. Miné, A.: The octagon abstract domain. HOSC **19**(1), 31–100 (2006)
25. Nethercote, N.: Dynamic binary analysis and instrumentation. Ph.D. thesis, Trinity College, University of Cambridge (2004)
26. Oh, H., Brutschy, L., Yi, K.: Access analysis-based tight localization of abstract memories. In: Jhala, R., Schmidt, D. (eds.) VMCAI 2011. LNCS, vol. 6538, pp. 356–370. Springer, Heidelberg (2011). https://doi.org/10.1007/978-3-642-18275-4_25
27. Oh, H., Heo, K., Lee, W., Park, D., Kang, J., Yi, K.: Global sparse analysis framework. ACM TOPLAS **36**(3), 8:1–8:44 (2014)
28. Oh, H., Lee, W., Heo, K., Yang, H., Yi, K.: Selective context-sensitivity guided by impact pre-analysis. In: PLDI, pp. 475–484 (2014)
29. Singh, G., Püschel, M., Vechev, M.: Making numerical program analysis fast. In: PLDI, pp. 303–313. ACM Press (2015)
30. Urban, C.: FuncTion: an abstract domain functor for termination. In: Baier, C., Tinelli, C. (eds.) TACAS 2015. LNCS, vol. 9035, pp. 464–466. Springer, Heidelberg (2015). https://doi.org/10.1007/978-3-662-46681-0_46
31. Venet, A., Brat, G.: Precise and efficient static array bound checking for large embedded C programs. In: PLDI, pp. 231–242 (2004)
32. Williams Jr., L.F.: A modification to the half-interval search (binary search) method. In: Proceedings of the 14th ACM Southeast Conference, pp. 95–101 (1976)

Verifying Properties of Differentiable Programs

Jan Hückelheim[1]([✉]) [iD], Ziqing Luo[2], Sri Hari Krishna Narayanan[3],
Stephen Siegel[2], and Paul D. Hovland[3]

[1] Imperial College London, London, UK
j.hueckelheim@imperial.ac.uk
[2] University of Delaware, Newark, DE, USA
[3] Argonne National Laboratory, Argonne, IL, USA

Abstract. There is growing demand for formal verification methods in the scientific and high performance computing communities. For scientific applications, it is not only necessary to verify the absence of violations such as out of bounds access or race conditions, but also to ensure that the results satisfy certain mathematical properties. In this work, we explore the limits of automated bounded verification in the verification of these programs by applying the symbolic execution tool CIVL to some numerical algorithms that are frequently used in scientific programs, namely a conjugate gradient solver, a finite difference stencil, and a mesh quality metric. These algorithms implement differentiable functions, allowing us to use the automatic differentiation tools Tapenade and ADIC in the creation of their specifications.

Keywords: Formal verification · Static analysis · Symbolic execution
Model checking · Algorithmic differentiation · Numerical algorithms

1 Introduction

Numerical algorithms are at the core of many scientific and high performance computing (HPC) applications such as weather forecasting and climate modelling, computational fluid dynamics, or seismic imaging. Other authors have noted that there is a growing need for formal methods or more rigorous testing in scientific computing [10, 15], since errors regularly have costly consequences.

The submitted manuscript has been created by UChicago Argonne, LLC, Operator of Argonne National Laboratory ('Argonne'). Argonne, a U.S. Department of Energy Office of Science laboratory, is operated under Contract No. DE-AC02-06CH11357. The U.S. Government retains for itself, and others acting on its behalf, a paid-up nonexclusive, irrevocable worldwide license in said article to reproduce, prepare derivative works, distribute copies to the public, and perform publicly and display publicly, by or on behalf of the Government. The Department of Energy will provide public access to these results of federally sponsored research in accordance with the DOE Public Access Plan. http://energy.gov/downloads/doe-public-access-plan.

© Springer Nature Switzerland AG 2018
A. Podelski (Ed.): SAS 2018, LNCS 11002, pp. 205–222, 2018.
https://doi.org/10.1007/978-3-319-99725-4_14

A recent report by the U.S. Department of Energy speaks of an ongoing *correctness crisis* [13], and lists a number of reasons for the difficulty in establishing correctness of scientific software. One of them is that bugs do not always lead to a detectable violation of a safety property, and may instead lead to wrong results. At the same time, wrong results may look plausible even to experts [15].

While a full verification of most scientific or HPC applications is beyond the current capabilities of formal verification methods, we present a step towards this goal by using the static analysis, model checking and symbolic execution tool CIVL [30] to verify properties of implementations of some commonly used numerical algorithms.

Each of the algorithms verified in this paper is differentiable. We exploit this fact by applying the algorithmic differentiation (AD) tools Tapenade [14] and ADIC [24] to generate specifications. AD can be viewed as a formal method and has a long history in scientific computing, and is introduced in Sect. 2.2.

The paper is structured as follows. First, we verify that a conjugate gradient solver for systems of linear equations is guaranteed to find a solution under particular circumstances described in Sect. 3, before showing that the derivatives of that CG solver have some expected properties. We then show that a function from the mesh adaptation framework FeasNewt [21] correctly implements the gradients and Hessians of another function in Sect. 4. Finally, we show the correctness of a table of finite difference coefficients in Sect. 5. We conclude with related work in Sect. 6 and a summary in Sect. 7.

For experiments, we used an iMac with a 3.5 GHz Intel Quad Core i7-4771 CPU and 32 GB memory. Java 1.8 and CIVL 1.13 were used. The Java Virtual Machine was permitted to use up to 30 GB for the heap. All experimental artifacts can be downloaded from https://vsl.cis.udel.edu/civl/sas18.

1.1 Contributions

In the paper, we present

- automated verification to prove properties of a conjugate gradient solver,
- algorithmic differentiation as a technique to create program specifications,
- automated verification of the order of accuracy of finite difference stencils,
- verification of a non-trivial part of a mesh adaptation framework, and
- the incorporation of probabilistic techniques into a verification framework to check assertions involving very large symbolic expressions.

1.2 Limitations

Full verification of scientific codes is hard, and we can not claim to have solved this problem. Remaining limitations of our approach include:

- We only perform bounded verification. This can complement traditional testing with larger problem sizes.
- Some of our experiments use probabilistic methods to scale to larger problem sizes. This leaves a small probability of error ($< 10^{-36}$).

- We are verifying simplified implementations.
- We are only showing correctness of the C code, which ignores the possibility of errors in the compiler, runtime environment, or hardware.
- We are ignoring roundoff effects.
- Our approach requires writing code that serves as a specification. The specification codes are very simple, but there is the possibility of human error.

2   Background

This section describes the CIVL tool that we used for verification, and the Tapenade and ADIC algorithmic differentiation tools used to create specifications.

2.1   The CIVL Verification Platform

CIVL is a verification framework for sequential or parallel C programs. The verifier uses static analysis, symbolic execution and model checking techniques. In particular, it explores a set of program states, and within a state, each variable is assigned a symbolic expression. The state includes models of the scoped memory structure of the program, the call stack and the heap. (For a parallel program, there is a call stack for each process.) As usual in symbolic execution, the state also includes a *path condition* variable which records the Boolean condition that must have held in order for an execution path to have been followed.

Arithmetic operations are all interpreted as taking place in the mathematical integers and real numbers. This can be seen as a limitation or a feature. When verifying that an algorithm has been implemented correctly, we show that properties that ought to hold in real arithmetic (but do not usually hold in floating point arithmetic) do in fact hold. In this way we are able to separate discrepancies due to roundoff error from discrepancies due to an incorrect implementation. In this context, symbolic execution with real-valued semantics has advantages.

The CIVL verifier performs a depth-first search of the reachable state space, checking a number of properties along the way. It also uses the Symbolic Algebra and Reasoning Library (SARL, [27]) to manipulate, simplify, and reason about symbolic expressions. SARL's simplification process can resolve many validity queries quickly; for those that it cannot resolve, it invokes one or more automated theorem provers, including CVC4 [3] and Z3 [8].

CIVL is typically used by placing small bounds on the sizes of input data structures. It can then prove, automatically, that assertions hold for all executions and all possible concrete inputs within those bounds.

The input language for CIVL is CIVL-C, an extension of C. The framework also includes a number of translators to convert a C program that uses one or more parallel programming models (such as Pthreads, OpenMP, CUDA, or MPI) to CIVL-C. However, in this work, we wrote in the CIVL-C language directly, and we deal only with sequential programs.

2.2   Algorithmic Differentiation

Algorithmic differentiation (AD), sometimes also called *automatic* differentiation, is a way to compute derivatives of numerical programs. Assuming that a given program implements a differentiable function

$$y = F(x)$$

that computes an output vector y based on some input vector x, one can apply AD to F to obtain the derivative of y with respect to x. One approach in AD is *source transformation*, where a derivative program is created by static analysis and source-to-source compilation [25].

There are two basic modes of AD, namely *forward* and *reverse* mode. In forward mode AD, derivatives are computed in the order of the original computation, while in reverse mode, derivatives are computed in the reverse order. The result $\dot{y}$ of the forward mode is equivalent to the product of the Jacobian matrix J of the function F and a user-provided vector $\dot{x}$ that has the same size as the input vector x, or more formally

$$\dot{y} = J\dot{x} \qquad with \qquad J_{i,j} = \frac{\partial F_i}{\partial x_j}.$$

The vector $\dot{x}$ can be chosen by the user. For example, selecting the i-th Cartesian basis vector for $\dot{x}$ will cause $\dot{y}$ to become the i-th column of the Jacobian matrix. Conversely, the reverse-mode result $\bar{x}$ is the product of the transposed Jacobian matrix J^T with a provided vector $\bar{y}$ of the size of the output vector y, or

$$\bar{x} = J^T \bar{y},$$

where choosing the j-th Cartesian basis vector for $\bar{y}$ will cause $\bar{x}$ to become the j-th row of the Jacobian matrix. While the forward mode is often easier to implement, the reverse mode is a much more efficient way to compute the Jacobian matrix if F has many inputs and few outputs.

In principle, AD can be applied to a program that was created by AD. In this way, higher-order derivatives can be obtained. For example, applying AD to a derivative program will yield a program that computes second-order derivatives. The forward and reverse mode can be combined freely, for example a program generated by reverse mode AD can be differentiated using forward mode AD.

Two source transformation AD tools were used in this work: ADIC, a source transformation tool for automatic differentiation of C and C++ codes [24], and Tapenade, an automatic differentiation Engine for Fortran77, Fortran95 or C codes. [14]. A developer may also choose to perform manual differentiation of some computer program, and can largely follow either of the previous approaches. Often, a human expert can exploit high-level properties to compute derivatives more efficiently than an AD tool.

3   Verifying Properties of Conjugate Gradient Solvers

The conjugate gradient method (CG, Fig. 1) is an algorithm for solving a linear system $Ax = b$, where $A \in \mathbf{R}^{n \times n}$ is a symmetric positive definite matrix and $b \in \mathbf{R}^n$ [4]. CG is widely used in HPC. The algorithm has many extensions, but in this paper we focus on the basic version.

CG can be used as an iterative method, meaning one can start with any "guess" for the solution, and after each iteration of the main loop, this approximation gets closer to the true solution. However, CG was originally developed as a direct solver, as after exactly n iterations, the exact solution will be achieved—assuming all operations are carried out with infinite precision.

In practice, the number of iterations performed is often much smaller than n—control exits the loop as soon as a convergence criterion is met. The number of iterations may also be greater than n because with round-off error the approximation may continue to improve after n iterations. In this paper, we assume that the number of iterations is exactly n, as this allows us to specify the expected output of CG.

Input : right hand side b, initial guess x, matrix **A**, step count n_{steps}
Output: solution x

1 $p, r \leftarrow b - A \cdot x$;
2 $\rho_{old} \leftarrow r^T \cdot r$;
3 **for** $k \leftarrow 0 \ldots n_{steps} - 1$ **do**
4 $\quad$ $p_A \leftarrow A \cdot p$;
5 $\quad$ $\alpha \leftarrow \dfrac{\rho_{old}}{p^T \cdot p_A}$;
6 $\quad$ $x \leftarrow x + \alpha \cdot p$;
7 $\quad$ $r \leftarrow r - \alpha \cdot p_A$;
8 $\quad$ $\rho_{new} \leftarrow r^T \cdot r$;
9 $\quad$ **if** $\rho_{new} = 0$ **then break** ;
10 $\quad$ $p \leftarrow r + \dfrac{\rho_{new}}{\rho_{old}} \cdot p$;
11 $\quad$ $\rho_{old} \leftarrow \rho_{new}$;
12 **end**

Fig. 1. Conjugate gradient solver. The highlighted statements are assumed not to divide by zero. The algorithm is then guaranteed to find the exact solution $x = A^{-1}b$ (where A^{-1} is the inverse of A) if n_{steps} is set to the size of A. Note that x is not only an output but also an input. In practice, a good initial guess for x can speed up CG convergence. In our verification we assume that initially $x = 0$.

We implemented CG as a C function with the following signature:

void cg(int n, double A[n][n], double b[n], double x[n], int nsteps)

Here, A and b are the inputs, and x is the "out" variable that will hold the approximate solution obtained after nsteps iterations. This function definition is in file cg.c and its prototype in cg.h.

3.1   Verification of Exactness of Solution After n Iterations

The implementation of CG in our experiment runs for the number of iterations required to guarantee an exact solution, and only breaks earlier if the exact solution is found. It can easily be shown that $r = b - A \cdot x$ is an invariant for the loop in Fig. 1. Therefore, the break condition in line 9 can only occur if $r = 0$ and therefore if $b - A \cdot x = 0$, meaning that a solution has been found. What is less obvious is that after n iterations, $r = 0$ must hold and x must be a solution. This is known to hold in real arithmetic, and we use CIVL to verify it.

We first verified the following: for any A and b, if cg is called with nsteps $= n$, and the denominators in Fig. 1 are never 0, then the resulting x satisfies $Ax = b$. To do this, we wrote a driver in the CIVL-C language (cg_driver.cvl, Fig. 2). CIVL-C extends C with keywords beginning with \$. The type qualifier \$input (lines 3–5) declares an *input variable*. The value of an input variable may be specified on the command line when invoking the CIVL verifier. If no command line value is specified but an initializer is given—as in line 3—then the initializer is used. If neither command line nor initializer are given, then the variable has an unconstrained value of its type. In the driver, M and b therefore respectively represent an arbitrary $n \times n$ matrix and vector of length n.

```
1 #include "cg.h"
2 #include "vectorutils.h"
3 $input int n = 5; // should be at least 1
4 $input double M[n][n]; // used to construct A; only use upper triangle
5 $input double b[n]; // right-hand side
6 int main() {
7    double A[n][n], x[n], b_test[n];
8    for (int i=0; i<n; i++) { // construct a symmetric matrix A
9      for (int j=0; j<i; j++)
10       A[i][j] = A[j][i] = M[i][j];
11     A[i][i] = M[i][i];
12   }
13   cg(n, A, b, x, n); // invoke conjugate gradient function with nsteps = n
14   matvecprod(n, A, x, b_test); // check that x is a solution
15   $assert($forall (int i : 0..n-1) b_test[i]==b[i]);
16 }
```

Fig. 2. cg_driver.cvl: CIVL driver for verification of cg

Lines 8–12 construct a symmetric matrix A from M. Function cg is then invoked on A and b, with nsteps $= n$, and the result going to x. The function matvecproc (provided in vectorutils) multiplies a matrix and vector—in this case A with the solution x returned by cg. If x is an actual solution, then the result, b_test should equal b. This is asserted in line 15.

Initially, the driver included the assumption (formulated using *Sylvester's criterion* [33]) that A is positive definite, which is a sufficient condition to guarantee existence of a solution and convergence of CG. Later, we discovered that this assumption is unnecessary *in the case that all denominators in CG are non-zero.* We discovered this by removing the assumption and observing that verification still succeeded. In contrast, the assumption that A is symmetric is necessary, and verification will fail if that assumption is removed. Also, instead of using $assume statements that declare the denominators to be non-zero, we use a CIVL verifier option which instructs CIVL to turn off checks that all divisors are non-zero.

The CIVL verifier is invoked, for example, as follows:

```
civl verify -userIncludePath=../shared -checkDivisionByZero=false
-inputn=2 ../shared/cg.c ../shared/vectorutils.c cg_driver.cvl
```

The user include path tells CIVL where to find #include-ed files. The option -inputX=*val* specifies the value of input variable X. The verifier can analyze a program composed of several translation units; in this case three input files are specified. The verifier enumerates the reachable symbolic states of the program, calling on automated theorem provers to check the satisfiability of the path condition or the validity of an assertion as needed. In this example ($n = 2$), CIVL returns in a few seconds with the result "The standard properties hold for all executions", which indicates that the assertions must hold, as well as standard properties including absence of illegal pointer dereferences, memory leaks, deadlocks and out-of-bound array indexes.

When we tried to run the verifier for $n = 3$, it did not return after $2\,h$. We found that most of the time was spent expanding polynomial expressions that are part of the rational expressions occurring in CG. These polynomials are symbolic expressions involving addition, multiplication, powers with concrete natural number exponents, rational number constants, and "variables" of the form A[i][j] and b[i] for $0 \leq i, j < n$. Expansion involves repeated multiplications and additions to transform the expression into a linear combination of monomials. For example, the expression $(x+y)^2$ expands to $x^2+2xy+y^2$. SARL, the symbolic algebra library used by CIVL, expands a polynomial to determine whether it is 0, which is required to check the assertion on line 15.

In CG, the size of these polynomials blows up quickly with n. Figure 4 gives some statistics illustrating this, which we now describe. An expression can be represented as a tree, as in Fig. 3 (left). In SARL, expressions are immutable, and the Flyweight Pattern [12] is used to guarantee that there is at most one instance of each equivalance class of expressions, where two expressions are equivalent if

Fig. 3. Standard tree representation of $2(x+y)^{10} + 3(x+y)+1$ and compressed DAG

they have the exact same form. Figure 3 (right) shows how the expression is actually represented; we refer to this as the compressed form. The compressed form is a directed acyclic graph (DAG).

The table gives some statistics for any one of the n polynomials that must be expanded when verifying CG for size n. It shows the number of variables involved, an upper bound on the total *degree* of the polynomial, the *height* of the tree, the number of *tree nodes* (if it were to be expanded), and the number of nodes in the compressed DAG. The scale of these expressions suggests that, even using the most efficient known polynomial multiplication algorithms, full expansion for $n \geq 3$ is intractable. We also used several other tools to attempt to prove that the polynomial for $n = 3$ is zero. All of these tools, including Mathematica [34], SAGE [31], CVC4, Z3, and Maple [1], either timed out after 2 h or returned immediately with "unknown".

We therefore used a probabilistic approach. The DeMillo-Lipton-Schwartz-Zippel lemma [29,35] provides a randomized method to test the zero-ness of a polynomial with an upper bound on the probability of error. Specifically, let F be a field, and P a non-zero polynomial in m variables over F and with total degree at most d. Let S be a finite subset of F, and let $r_1, \ldots, r_m$ be chosen randomly and with uniform probability from S. Then the probability that P evaluates to 0 at $(r_1, \ldots, r_m)$ is at most $d/|S|$. The method proceeds as follows. Given P, choose m random values from S and evaluate P. If the result is non-zero, then P is not zero, terminate. Otherwise, choose another random point and repeat. If k evaluations are carried out and all return 0, one can conclude that P is zero, with the probability *of being wrong* at most $(d/|S|)^k$.

In our case, the field is the field of rational numbers, and for S we use the set of Java ints, i.e., $[-2^{31}, 2^{31} - 1]$. The Java class Random is used to generate a stream of pseudorandom integers using method nextInt, which guarantees that "[a]ll 2^{32} possible int values are produced with (approximately) equal probability" [26]. Given a polynomial of total degree at most d, the number k of random evaluations is chosen so that the probability of error is at most $2^{-128} \approx 2.9e - 39$. Note that SARL uses exact, unbounded representations of integers and rational numbers. There is no issue of overflows or round-off errors, but the intermediate numbers can grow quite large in the course of an evaluation.

We added a command-line option -prob to CIVL which activates the probabilistic method whenever the size of a polynomial exceeds some threshold. In these cases, CIVL also prints a warning message saying that a probabilistic technique was used. If p polynomials are determined to be 0 in this way, then the probability of an incorrect verification result is at most $1 - (1 - 2^{-128})^p$.

Using this approach, we were able to verify (with an extremely small probability of error) the desired property of CG for all $n \leq 8$. The table shows the number of polynomials that were determined to be zero using the probabilistic approach, and the number of evaluations performed on each. These numbers are quite modest—at most 11 evaluations. Nevertheless, the time visibly explodes for $n \geq 7$. Examination revealed that most of the time involves exact arithmetic on very large integers which arise in the course of the evaluations. For example,

full			probabilistic		
n	states	vars	height	degree	tree	DAG	time (s)	time (s)	evals	prob
1	96	2	2	1	3	2	1.3	-	-	-
2	240	5	20	23	2.0e+3	57	1.5	1.4	5	5.9e−39
3	476	9	29	134	2.7e+5	143	TO	1.4	6	8.8e−39
4	822	14	39	781	6.0e+7	280	TO	1.6	6	1.2e−38
5	1296	20	47	4552	2.1e+10	470	TO	1.9	7	1.5e−38
6	1916	27	57	26531	1.1e+13	723	TO	7.3	8	1.8e−38
7	2700	35	65	154634	7.9e+15	1041	TO	95.8	9	2.1e−38
8	3666	44	75	901273	7.3e+18	1434	TO	1820.2	11	2.4e−38

Fig. 4. CIVL verification of CG: matrix size n; the number of reachable symbolic *states*; the number of *variables* in one of the n polynomials P that is asserted to be 0; the *height* of the tree representation of P; the total *degree* of P; the number of nodes in the *tree*; the number of nodes in the compressed *DAG* representation of P; the *time* for *full* verification; the *time* for *probabilistic* verification with probability of error in checking zero-ness of P less than 2^{-128}; the number of random *evaluations* performed on P. The final upper bound on the *prob*ability of an incorrect verification result is $1 - (1 - 2^{-128})^n$. Time out (TO) occurs after 2 h.

full			probabilistic		
n	states	vars	height	degree	tree	DAG	time (s)	time (s)	evals	prob
2	718	5	29	44	1.2e+4	146	5.6	2.4	5	1.2e−38
3	1987	9	50	266	5.5e+6	547	TO	2.8	6	2.6e−38
4	4426	14	70	1560	5.1e+9	1365	TO	3.4	6	4.7e−38
5	8569	20	90	9102	9.3e+12	2803	TO	13.2	7	7.3e−38
6	15046	27	109	53060	3.1e+16	5095	TO	250.2	8	1.1e−37

Fig. 5. Statistics for CIVL verification of CG derivatives.

for $n = 8$, over 2000 multiplication operations on big integers are carried out while evaluating one polynomial at a random point. The mean size of these big integers is over 27 million bits (or approximately 8 million decimal digits).

3.2   Verification of Derivatives of CG

We prove the equivalence of applying AD to CG and computing the inverse of the matrix. This experiment could be interpretted as verifying the correctness of the AD-generated code, or as verifying the correctness of the mathematical derivation described in the following. We use the Tapenade in forward mode to create a differentiated CG solver with the following signature:

void cg_d(**int** n, **double** A[n][n], **double** b[n], **double** bd[n],
          double x[n], **double** xd[n], **int** steps);

As explained in Sect. 2.2, the resulting function will be an implementation of

$$\dot{x} = J_{CG}\dot{b},$$

where J_{CG} is the Jacobian matrix of a CG solver applied to A. It is also known as explained and verified in Sect. 3.1 that a CG solver applied to a matrix A and right hand side b is equivalent to the matrix vector product

$$x = A^{-1}b,$$

and therefore the Jacobian matrix of the CG solver must be equal to A^{-1}.

We verify this in the following experiment. The forwardmode derivative of CG is called n times, where in each call the vector $\dot{x}$ is set to a different Cartesian basis vector. In this way, the entire Jacobian matrix is constructed, which we expect to be A^{-1}. The obtained matrix is multiplied with A, and we use CIVL to prove that the result of this procedure is the identity matrix, which proves that the code generated by Tapenade did indeed compute the correct derivative. The CIVL driver for this experiment is shown in Fig. 6. Figure 5 shows some statistics from CIVL for this experiment.

```
1 #include "cg_d.h"
2 #include "vectorutils.h"
3 $input int n = 2;
4 $input double b[n], A[n][n];
5
6 int main() {
7     double Ainv[n][n], M[n][n], P[n][n];
8
9     for (int i=0; i<n; i++) {
10         for (int j=0; j<i; j++)
11             M[i][j] = M[j][i] = A[i][j];
12         M[i][i] = A[i][i];
13     }
14     fwdDriver(n, Ainv, M, b, n);   // apply AD to CG to get the inverse
15     matmatprod(A, Ainv, P);        // compute matrix product P=A*Ainv
16     for (int i=0; i<n; i++)        // now show that P == I
17         for (int j=0; j<n; j++)
18             if (i==j) $assert(P[i][j]==1);
19             else $assert(P[i][j]==0);
20 }
```

Fig. 6. cg_d_driver.cvl: CIVL driver for verification of differentiated cg.

4   Verifying the Correctness of Hand-Coded Derivatives

In this section we verify for two given subprograms that one computes the first-order or second-order derivative of the other. As a case study, we use the FeasNewt mesh-adaptation program [21,23]. Computational meshes are an important component in solving partial differential equations (PDEs). The space-time domain in which the solution is computed is split into many discrete elements, for example triangles in two dimensions or tetrahedra in three dimensions, where each element contains a part of the computed solution. Most PDE solvers rely on the elements to be almost unilateral, that is, the ratio between the shortest and longest edge of a given element should be close to 1.

FeasNewt achieves this by optimising the coordinates of individual vertices, thereby changing the distribution of elements and the length of their edges without changing the topology of the mesh. To do this systematically, a differentiable function is implemented that computes the quality of elements based on their vertex positions. By differentiating this function, one obtains the derivative of the mesh quality with respect to the coordinates, which can then be used for a gradient-based optimisation. An optimal vertex distribution can be found faster if not only gradients, but also Hessians of the mesh quality are known. For this reason, FeasNewt contains mesh quality metrics and their gradients and Hessians, which are studied here.

Previous work [28] showed the floating-point equivalence of some of the test cases that we present. We reproduce these verifications in CIVL assuming real arithmetic, and also verify the equivalence in real arithmetic for test cases that are not floating-point equivalent. We investigate the gradients and Hessians of *inverse mean ratio* (IMR) [22], a metric for triangular elements that is implemented in FeasNewt. The two-dimensional coordinates of the three points that make up the triangle are provided in a vector $\boldsymbol{x}$ with

$$\boldsymbol{x} = [x_0 \ x_1 \ x_2 \ y_0 \ y_1 \ y_2] \, .$$

From this input, IMR uses matrices A and W^{-1} as given below to compute the element quality metric O given by

$$O = \frac{\|AW^{-1}\|_F^2}{2|\det(AW^{-1})|} ,$$

where $\| \cdot \|$ denotes the Frobenius norm.

$$A = \begin{bmatrix} x_1 - x_0 & x_2 - x_0 \\ y_1 - y_0 & y_2 - y_0 \end{bmatrix} ; \qquad W^{-1} = \begin{bmatrix} 1 & \frac{-1}{\sqrt{3}} \\ 0 & \frac{2}{\sqrt{3}} \end{bmatrix} ;$$

The implementation of IMR in the C programming language is shown in Fig. 7. Note that the original implementation contained error-handling, function headers, variable declarations etc., which have been left away for brevity.

The FeasNewt function for calculating the gradient of IMR was manually implemented and optimised for performance, and is also shown in Fig. 7. Again we present only the core function without error handling etc. The Hessian calculation was also manually optimised for efficiency. It is not shown here for space reasons. We refer to these hand-crafted gradient and Hessian functions as *manual gradient* and *manual Hessian*.

Tapenade and ADIC are used to differentiate the element function. We use both tools in their forward and reverse modes as explained in Sect. 2.2, and create wrappers that ensure a matching function signature between the manual gradient, Tapenade forward and reverse gradients, and the ADIC forward and reverse

```
1 // 1/sqrt(3)
2 #define sqrt3 .57735026918962579
3 // Calculate M = A*inv(W).
4 matr[0] = x[1] - x[0];
5 matr[1] = (2.0*x[2] - x[1] - x[0])*sqrt3;
6 matr[2] = x[4] - x[3];
7 matr[3] = (2.0*x[5] - x[4] - x[3])*sqrt3;
8 // Calculate det(M).
9 g = matr[0]*matr[3] - matr[1]*matr[2];
10 // Calculate norm(M).
11 f = matr[0]*matr[0] + matr[1]*matr[1] +
12     matr[2]*matr[2] + matr[3]*matr[3];
13 // Calculate objective function.
14 (*obj) = 0.5 * f / g;
```

```
1 // Start with original IMR (left away for brevity),
2 // then compute the derivative:
3 g = -((obj)/g);
4
5 adj_m[0] = 2.0*matr[0]*loc1 + matr[3]*g;
6 adj_m[1] = 2.0*matr[1]*loc1 - matr[2]*g;
7 adj_m[2] = 2.0*matr[2]*loc1 - matr[1]*g;
8 adj_m[3] = 2.0*matr[3]*loc1 + matr[0]*g;
9
10 loc1 = sqrt3*adj_m[1];
11 g_obj[0] = -adj_m[0] - loc1;
12 g_obj[1] = adj_m[0] - loc1;
13 g_obj[2] = 2.0*loc1;
14
15 loc1 = sqrt3*adj_m[3];
16 g_obj[3] = -adj_m[2] - loc1;
17 g_obj[4] = adj_m[2] - loc1;
18 g_obj[5] = 2.0*loc1;
```

Fig. 7. Left: Implementation of IMR from FeasNewt. **Right:** Gradient of IMR. Is this the derivative of the program on the left?

gradients. Similarly, wrapper functions are created to enable the comparison between the manual Hessians, and Hessians obtained from Tapenade.

CIVL can verify the equivalence of manual gradients and Tapenade forward mode gradients. During the verification of Tapenade reverse mode gradients against the forward mode and manual gradients, CIVL discovered a bug in our wrapper program. The verification succeeds after fixing this. CIVL also found a bug in ADIC: constants with a very long mantissa were truncated in an internal transformation, which led to a loss of precision that was never noticed during testing. CIVL performed these verifications in less than 10 s. Note that due to the fixed small problem size, this works without the use of probabilistic techniques.

The Hessians are verified next. We combine Tapenade forward and reverse mode in three different ways (forward over forward, forward over reverse, reverse over forward) and also apply Tapenade forward mode to the manual gradient, and create a wrapper for all of these variants to match the function signature of the manual Hessian to enable a comparison with CIVL. Due to a similar problem in the wrapper as in the gradient case, the verification fails at first, but is successful after fixing the wrapper. Futhermore, CIVL was able to detect a loss of precision in the manual Hessian, caused by inaccurate constants. This bug in FeasNewt was never detected in testing. The wrong constants were 0.57735026919 instead of $5.7735026918962579795942951958 58e - 01$, and 0.33333333333 instead of $3.333333333333333333333333333333e - 01$. CIVL can detect this type of bug, since all operations are assumed to be carried out in exact arithmetic and the truncated constants will result in different outputs. A simple test based on execution in floating point arithmetic might not lead to the detection of this bug, since the slight difference in outputs may be incorrectly blamed on roundoff effects. Once these problems are corrected, Hessians are verifiably identical for any input. Again, the verification took less than 10 s.

5   Verifying the Accuracy of Central Difference Schemes

Finite difference (FD) schemes are used to compute approximations for the derivative of functions, using only the result of the function at a discrete set of points. This is useful in cases where the function is not known analytically and symbolic derivatives and algorithmic differentiation are infeasible. Two of the most widely known examples are the central difference approximations for first and second order derivatives with fixed step size h, given by

$$\left.\frac{df}{dx}\right|_{x=x_0} = \frac{f(x_0+h) - f(x_0-h)}{2h} + \mathcal{O}(h^2) \tag{1}$$

$$\left.\frac{d^2f}{dx^2}\right|_{x=x_0} = \frac{f(x_0+h) - 2f(x_0) + f(x_0-h)}{h^2} + \mathcal{O}(h^2). \tag{2}$$

The unknown analytical derivatives (left) are approximated with a weighted sum of function values (fraction on the right), where the difference between the derivatives and the approximation is called *truncation error*, and is in this case $\mathcal{O}(h^2)$. The exponent of this expression is called *order of accuracy*, and is in this case 2. The order of accuracy is an important measure for the quality of an FD scheme. Note that the truncation error is independent of roundoff errors.

FD schemes can be constructed for arbitrary orders of derivatives d and arbitrary orders of accuracy a. One way of constructing these schemes is to fit a polynomial of order $a + d - 1$ to the available data, and then computing its d-th order derivative, resulting in a scheme with truncation error a [16]. There are more efficient methods to construct the same FD schemes, see [16,19] for an overview. It is common practice in scientific software to use hard-coded FD coefficients taken from the literature, such as the ones shown in Fig. 9, which can also be found in [11] or Wikipedia [1]. Figure 8 shows one way of implementing a second-order accurate scheme for second order derivatives.

A scheme that computes a-th order accurate d-th order derivatives must be exact when it is applied to arbitrary polynomials of order $a + d - 1$. We can use CIVL to verify that this is the case for all schemes shown in Fig. 9 without using probabilistic techniques. This will also guarantee that the scheme has been implemented correctly in C. To do this, we implement the C function `double p(double x, int k, double* c)` that implements a polynomial of order k with coefficients c as

$$res = c_0 + c_1 \cdot x + c_2 \cdot x^2 + \ldots + c_o \cdot x^k. \tag{3}$$

Using CIVL-C, the coefficient vector c and the position x_0 at which the derivatives are evaluated are declared as symbolic inputs, and the step size h is declared as a strictly positive symbolic input. We then create a driver program that uses FD to approximate derivatives of p, and also uses analytical derivatives of p generated by AD to compute exact derivatives of p. For any scheme that claims

---

[1] https://en.wikipedia.org/w/index.php?title=Finite_difference_coefficient&oldid=82 0038001.

```
1 #include "polynomial.h"
2 #include <civlc.cvh>
3 $input double coef[k+1], x0;
4 $input double h; $assume(h>0);
5 int main() {
6     double fd = (1.0*p(x0-h, k, coef)
7                 - 2.0*p(x0 , k, coef)
8                 + 1.0*p(x0+h, k, coef)
9                 ) / (h*h);
10    double ad = p_d_d(x0,k,coef);
11    $assert(fd == ad);
12 }
```

Fig. 8. Driver program for finite difference scheme verification. The external function p(double x, int k, double* c) implements the polynomial $p(x) = c_0 + c_1 x + c_2 x^2 + \ldots + c_k x^k$, and is called by the driver program at the locations $x_0 - h, x_0, x_0 + h$, where x_0 and the polynomial coefficients are arbitrary symbolic inputs, h is an arbitrary strictly positive input, and k is left undefined. The result is asserted as equal that returned by a call to p_d_d, which is the second-order derivative of p produced by AD. The verification succeeds for $k \in \{0, 1, 2, 3\}$, and fails otherwise.

derivative	accuracy	$-4h$	$-3h$	$-2h$	$-h$	0	h	$2h$	$3h$	$4h$
1	2				$-\frac{1}{2}$	0	$\frac{1}{2}$			
	4			$\frac{1}{12}$	$-\frac{2}{3}$	0	$\frac{2}{3}$	$-\frac{1}{12}$		
	6		$-\frac{1}{60}$	$\frac{3}{20}$	$-\frac{3}{4}$	0	$\frac{3}{4}$	$-\frac{3}{20}$	$\frac{1}{60}$	
	8	$\frac{1}{280}$	$-\frac{4}{105}$	$\frac{1}{5}$	$-\frac{4}{5}$	0	$\frac{4}{5}$	$-\frac{1}{5}$	$\frac{4}{105}$	$-\frac{1}{280}$
2	2				1	-2	1			
	4			$-\frac{1}{12}$	$\frac{4}{3}$	$-\frac{5}{2}$	$\frac{4}{3}$	$-\frac{1}{12}$		
	6		$\frac{1}{90}$	$-\frac{3}{20}$	$\frac{3}{2}$	$-\frac{49}{18}$	$\frac{3}{2}$	$-\frac{3}{20}$	$\frac{1}{90}$	
	8	$-\frac{1}{560}$	$\frac{8}{315}$	$-\frac{1}{5}$	$\frac{8}{5}$	$-\frac{205}{72}$	$\frac{8}{5}$	$-\frac{1}{5}$	$\frac{8}{315}$	$-\frac{1}{560}$
3	2			$-\frac{1}{2}$	1	0	-1	$\frac{1}{2}$		
	4		$\frac{1}{8}$	-1	$\frac{13}{8}$	0	$-\frac{13}{8}$	1	$-\frac{1}{8}$	
	6	$-\frac{7}{240}$	$\frac{3}{10}$	$-\frac{169}{120}$	$\frac{61}{30}$	0	$-\frac{61}{30}$	$\frac{169}{120}$	$-\frac{3}{10}$	$\frac{7}{240}$
4	2			1	-4	6	-4	1		
	4		$-\frac{1}{6}$	2	$-\frac{13}{2}$	$\frac{28}{3}$	$-\frac{13}{2}$	2	$-\frac{1}{6}$	
	6	$\frac{7}{240}$	$-\frac{2}{5}$	$\frac{169}{60}$	$-\frac{122}{15}$	$\frac{91}{8}$	$-\frac{122}{15}$	$\frac{169}{60}$	$-\frac{2}{5}$	$\frac{7}{240}$
5	2		$-\frac{1}{2}$	2	$-\frac{5}{2}$	0	$\frac{5}{2}$	-2	$\frac{1}{2}$	
6	2		1	-6	15	-20	15	-6	1	

Fig. 9. Finite difference coefficients for several schemes. Figure 8 implements a second-order accurate second-order derivative scheme using the coefficients highlighted in gray.

order a accuracy for derivatives of order d, the results of FD and AD must match exactly if a polynomial of order a with $a < d + k$ is used. This was confirmed using CIVL, for all coefficients in Fig. 9. An example of this is shown in Fig. 8. The verification for the complete table takes less than $7s$ on our test machine. As should be expected, the verification fails if the polynomial order is increased to $a => d + k$, or if the coefficients are modified.

6   Related Work

While the lack of formal verification in scientific computing has been noted in Sect. 1, there have been previous attempts to address this problem, for example the full mechanised verification of a PDE solver presented in [6]. The authors use Frama-C [7] and Coq to manually create a mechanised correctness proof for a one-dimensional wave equation solver. They note that this process is labour intensive, and cannot be applied to other PDE solvers without repeating some of the manual steps. In [10], the authors advocate a fully automated verification of PDE solvers that is integrated into the development process, but are using testing as opposed to formal methods.

Between those two extremes, previous work has used formal methods to verify selected properties of scientific programs, such as [28], where the authors prove bitwise equivalence of the gradient and Hessian programs shown in Sect. 4. Others showed the correctness of optimisations applied to LU decomposition [2], and [32] use formal methods in their construction. Previous work has also addressed the verification of some properties of CG [20].

Other authors use formal methods to construct linear algebra kernels [5,18], or formally construct a correct CG solver [9]. Other work has looked at the order of accuracy [36] and the verification of finite difference stencil solvers using a trusted reference implementation [17].

7   Summary and Outlook

In Sect. 3, we explored the limit of the capabilities of symbolic execution in an attempt to verify a conjugate gradient solver. Interestingly, the real limiting factor in this test case is the complexity of the expressions, not the number of states. Non-determinism and state space explosion are well known problems for model checking techniques or finite state verification techniques. However in this case, our programs have few states, but complicated mathematical expressions. There may be unexplored performance improvements for this setting.

We are not aware of a way to automatically and exhaustively check the correctness of these properties, but demonstrated that probabilistic methods can be used successfully in this setting. Since the correctness of the CG algorithm was formally proven in the maths literature, it is likely that a mechanised proof can be constructed, but this would probably require the formalisation of high-level math theorems. CG is only one solver of many. One could attempt to verify other linear solvers with known convergence properties such as GMRES.

In Sects. 4 and 5 we verified that some program computes the derivatives of another program by creating an equivalent function using AD. Specification languages could be extended to include a notion of derivatives and integrals, and some AD capabilities could be built into the verification tool to facilitate the verification of programs with these specifications.

Acknowledgements. This work was supported by the U.S. Department of Energy, Office of Science, Office of Advanced Scientific Computing Research, Applied Mathematics and Computer Science programs under contract number DE-AC02-06CH11357 and contract number DE-SC0012566, and by U.S. National Science Foundation Award CCF-1319571. The authors thank Prof. Dan Roche of the U.S. Naval Academy and Prof. David Saunders of the Univ. of Delaware for their assistance with computer algebra and probabilistic approaches.

References

1. Maplesoft: a division of Waterloo Maple Inc., Maple 18 (2014)
2. Kozen, D., Barth, A.: Equational Verification of Cache Blocking in LU Decomposition using Kleene Algebra with Tests. Technical report, 10. http://hdl.handle.net/1813/5848 (2002)
3. Barrett, C., et al.: CVC4. In: Gopalakrishnan, G., Qadeer, S. (eds.) CAV 2011. LNCS, vol. 6806, pp. 171–177. Springer, Heidelberg (2011). https://doi.org/10.1007/978-3-642-22110-1_14
4. Barrett, R., et al.: Templates for the Solution of Linear Systems: Building Blocks for Iterative Methods, vol. 43. SIAM (1994)
5. Bientinesi, P., Gunnels, J.A., Myers, M.E., Quintana-Ortí, E.S., van de Geijn, R.A.: The science of deriving dense linear algebra algorithms. ACM Trans. Math. Softw. **31**(1), 1–26 (2005). https://doi.org/10.1145/1055531.1055532
6. Boldo, S., Clément, F., Filliâtre, J.-C., Mayero, M., Melquiond, G., Weis, P.: Trusting computations: a mechanized proof from partial differential equations to actual program. Comput. Math. Appl. **68**(3), 325–352 (2014). https://doi.org/10.1016/j.camwa.2014.06.004
7. Cuoq, P., Kirchner, F., Kosmatov, N., Prevosto, V., Signoles, J., Yakobowski, B.: Frama-C. In: Eleftherakis, G., Hinchey, M., Holcombe, M. (eds.) SEFM 2012. LNCS, vol. 7504, pp. 233–247. Springer, Heidelberg (2012). https://doi.org/10.1007/978-3-642-33826-7_16
8. de Moura, L., Bjørner, N.: Z3: an efficient SMT solver. In: Ramakrishnan, C.R., Rehof, J. (eds.) TACAS 2008. LNCS, vol. 4963, pp. 337–340. Springer, Heidelberg (2008). https://doi.org/10.1007/978-3-540-78800-3_24
9. Eijkhout, V., Bientinesi, P., van de Geijn, R.: Towards mechanical derivation of krylov solver libraries. Procedia Comput. Sci. **1**(1), 1805–1813 (2010). ICCS 2010. https://doi.org/10.1016/j.procs.2010.04.202
10. Farrell, P.E., Piggott, M.D., Gorman, G.J., Ham, D.A., Wilson, C.R., Bond, T.M.: Automated continuous verification for numerical simulation. Geosci. Model Dev. **4**(2), 435–449 (2011). https://doi.org/10.5194/gmd-4-435-2011
11. Fornberg, B.: Generation of finite difference formulas on arbitrarily spaced grids. Math. Comput. **51**(184), 699–706 (1988)
12. Gamma, E., Helm, R., Johnson, R., Vlissides, J.: Design Patterns: Elements of Reusable Object-oriented Software (1995)
13. Gopalakrishnan, G., et al.: Report of the HPC correctness summit, 25–26 Jan 2017, Washington, DC. Technical report (2017)

14. Hascoët, L., Pascual, V.: The tapenade automatic differentiation tool: principles, model, and specification. ACM Trans. Math. Softw. **39**(3), (2013). https://doi.org/10.1145/2450153.2450158
15. Hatton, L., Roberts, A.: How accurate is scientific software? IEEE Trans. Softw. Eng. **20**(10), 785–797 (1994). https://doi.org/10.1109/32.328993
16. Hoffman, J.D., Frankel, S.: Numerical Methods for Engineers and Scientists. CRC Press (2001)
17. Hückelheim, J., et al.: Towards self-verification in finite difference code generation. In: Proceedings of the First International Workshop on Software Correctness for HPC Applications, Correctness 2017, pp. 42–49 (2017). ACM, New York. https://doi.org/10.1145/3145344.3145488
18. Igual, F.D., et al.: The flame approach: from dense linear algebra algorithms to high-performance multi-accelerator implementations. J. Parallel Distrib. Comput. **72**(9), 1134–1143 (2012). Accelerators for High-Performance Computing. https://doi.org/10.1016/j.jpdc.2011.10.014
19. LeVeque, R.: Finite Difference Methods for Ordinary and Partial Differential Equations. Society for Industrial and Applied Mathematics (2007). https://doi.org/10.1137/1.9780898717839
20. Marcilon, T.B., de Carvalho Junior, F.H.: Derivation and verification of parallel components for the needs of an HPC cloud. In: Iyoda, J., de Moura, L. (eds.) SBMF 2013. LNCS, vol. 8195, pp. 51–66. Springer, Heidelberg (2013). https://doi.org/10.1007/978-3-642-41071-0_5
21. Munson, T.S., Hovland, P.D.: The FeasNewt benchmark. In: IEEE International. 2005 Proceedings of the IEEE Workload Characterization Symposium 2005, pp. 150–154, October 2005. https://doi.org/10.1109/IISWC.2005.1526011
22. Munson, T.: Mesh shape-quality optimization using the inverse mean-ratio metric. Math. Program. **110**(3), 561–590 (2007). https://doi.org/10.1007/s10107-006-0014-3
23. Munson, T.S.: Optimizing the quality of mesh elements. In: SIAG/OPT Views-and-News, p. 27 (2005)
24. Narayanan, S.H.K., Norris, B., Winnicka, B.: Adic2: development of a component source transformation system for differentiating C and C++. Procedia Comput. Sci. **1**(1), 1845–1853 (2010). ICCS 2010. https://doi.org/10.1016/j.procs.2010.04.206
25. Naumann, U.: The Art of Differentiating Computer Programs: An Introduction to Algorithmic Differentiation, vol. 24. SIAM (2012)
26. Oracle. Java8: Class random (2017). https://docs.oracle.com/javase/8/docs/api/java/util/Random.html
27. SARL: The Symbolic Algebra and Reasoning Library. http://vsl.cis.udel.edu/sarl. Accessed 31 Jan 2018
28. Schordan, M., Hückelheim, J., Lin, P.-H., Menon, H.: Verifying the floating-point computation equivalence of manually and automatically differentiated code. In: Proceedings of the First International Workshop on Software Correctness for HPC Applications, Correctness 2017, pp. 34–41. ACM, New York (2017). https://doi.org/10.1145/3145344.3145489
29. Schwartz, J.T.: Fast probabilistic algorithms for verification of polynomial identities. J. ACM **27**(4), 701–717 (1980). https://doi.org/10.1145/322217.322225
30. Siegel, S.F., et al.: CIVL: the concurrency intermediate verification language. In: Proceedings of the International Conference for High Performance Computing, Networking, Storage and Analysis, SC 2015, pp. 61:1–61:12. ACM, New York (2015). https://doi.org/10.1145/2807591.2807635

31. Stein, W., Joyner, D.: SAGE: system for algebra and geometry experimentation. SIGSAM Bull. **39**(2), 61–64 (2005). https://doi.org/10.1145/1101884.1101889
32. van de Vorst, J.G.G.: The formal development of a parallel program performing LU-decomposition. Acta Informatica **26**(1), 1–17 (1988). https://doi.org/10.1007/BF02915443
33. Wikipedia. Sylvester's criterion. Accessed 31 Jan 2018. https://en.wikipedia.org/wiki/Sylvester%27s_criterion
34. Wolfram, S.: The Mathematica Book, 5th Edn. Wolfram Media Inc, Champaign (2003). http://www.wolfram.com/books/profile.cgi?id=4939
35. Zippel, R.: Probabilistic algorithms for sparse polynomials. In: Ng, E.W. (ed.) Symbolic and Algebraic Computation. LNCS, vol. 72, pp. 216–226. Springer, Heidelberg (1979). https://doi.org/10.1007/3-540-09519-5_73
36. Zirkel, T.K., Siegel, S.F., Rossi, L.F.: Using symbolic execution to verify the order of accuracy of numerical approximations. Technical report UD-CIS-2014/002, Department of Computer and Information Sciences, University of Delaware (2014)

A Reduced Product of Absolute and Relative Error Bounds for Floating-Point Analysis

Maxime Jacquemin[1]($\boxtimes$), Sylvie Putot[2], and Franck Védrine[1]

[1] CEA, List, Software Reliability and Security Laboratory, PC 174,
91191 Gif-Sur-Yvette, France
{maxime.jacquemin,franck.vedrine}@cea.fr
[2] LIX, CNRS and École Polytechnique, Palaiseau, France
putot@lix.polytechnique.fr

Abstract. Rigorous estimation of bounds on errors in finite precision computation has become a key point of many formal verification tools. The primary interest of the use of such tools is generally to obtain worst-case bounds on the absolute errors. However, the natural bound on the elementary error committed by each floating-point arithmetic operation is a bound on the relative error, which suggests that relative error bounds could also play a role in the process of computing tight error estimations. In this work, we introduce a very simple interval-based abstraction, combining absolute and relative error propagations. We demonstrate with a prototype implementation how this simple product allows us in many cases to improve absolute error bounds, and even to often favorably compare with state-of-the art tools, that rely on much more costly relational abstractions or optimization-based estimations.

1 Introduction

Computing worst-case bounds on the potential loss of accuracy in numerical programs due to the use of floating-point arithmetic is of utmost importance in many fields of application, such as embedded systems or numerical simulation. Several analyzes for the computation of sound error bounds have been proposed in the last 15 years, and generally implemented in academic prototypes. Most of them rely on abstractions of the value and absolute errors of program variables. An additional output of such analyses is sometimes bounds on the relative errors, but they are mostly computed a posteriori, from the values and absolute errors. Still, the natural bound on the elementary error committed by each floating-point arithmetic operation is a bound on the relative error. This strongly suggests that relative error bounds can also play a role in the process of computing tight error estimates. This is what this work proposes to explore. We indeed note that on some patterns, abstraction relying only on absolute error yields unreasonably conservative error bounds, and that a simple product with relative error bounds can bring a drastic improvement. One such

© Springer Nature Switzerland AG 2018
A. Podelski (Ed.): SAS 2018, LNCS 11002, pp. 223–242, 2018.
https://doi.org/10.1007/978-3-319-99725-4_15

pattern is a conditional statement that tests a quantity subject to a rounding error. We consider the very simple piece of code introduced in Example 1.

Example 1. Variables i, x, y are double precision floating-point numbers, and input i is given without error in range $[1, 100]$: The multiplication x:=i*i results in variable x in $[1, 10000]$ with an elementary absolute rounding error $\mathcal{E}_a(x)$ bounded in $[-9.09e^{-13}, 9.09e^{-13}]$.

```
x = i * i ;
if (x <= 2.0)
    y = x;
else
    y = 2.0;
```

If evaluated directly by using the fact that the elementary error in floating-point arithmetic is bounded in relative error, we obtain a relative error $\mathcal{E}_r(x)$ bounded in $[-1.11e^{-16}, 1.11e^{-16}]$. It is clear that some information is lost if the error is abstracted by bounds on the absolute error only, especially on a non-relational abstraction like intervals (and the wider the intervals, the more so). Take for instance constraint x <= 2.0 on our variable x. Using the relative error bound allows us to compute a much tighter absolute error bound in the **true** branch of the conditional. Indeed, the value of x knowing that the constraint is satisfied can be reduced in $[1,2]$. Thus, a new absolute error bound for x in this branch can be computed by $\mathcal{E}_a(x) = \mathcal{E}_a(x) \cap x\mathcal{E}_r(x) = [-9.09e^{-13}, 9.09e^{-13}] \cap [1, 2][-1.11e^{-16}, 1.11e^{-16}] = [-2.22e^{-16}, 2.22e^{-16}]$. Therefore, the absolute error on variable y will be bounded in $[-2.22e^{-16}, 2.22e^{-16}]$. Whereas if not using this reduced product, the error on x simply propagates as an error on y, and the absolute error bound on y will be $[-9.09e^{-13}, 9.09e^{-13}]$.

Another simple example, that focuses on arithmetic operations, is taken from the introduction of [16]:

Example 2. We consider expression $t/(t + 1)$, where t is a double precision floating-point value in $[0, 999]$. An error is committed when computing $t + 1$: the absolute error of $t + 1$ is bounded by $\mathcal{E}_a(t + 1) = [-5.68e^{-14}, 5.68e^{-14}]$, the relative error by $\mathcal{E}_r(t+1) = [-1.1e^{-16}, 1.1e^{-16}]$. For comparison, the a posteriori evaluation of the relative error bounds from the absolute error bounds is

$$\frac{\mathcal{E}_a(t + 1)}{t + 1} = \frac{[-5.68e^{-14}, 5.68e^{-14}]}{[1, 1000]} = [-5.68e^{-14}, 5.68e^{-14}]$$

thus 500 times larger than the direct estimate $\mathcal{E}_r(t + 1)$. Thus, if the relative error is not explicitly propagated, some information is lost.

And indeed, as we will develop in Sect. 3.2, it is natural to express the absolute error on the division $x \div y$ using the relative error on y. Actually, the bounds on the absolute error of $t/(t + 1)$ using this product are $[-1.67e^{-13}, 1.67e^{-13}]$, 340 times tighter compared to the bounds $[-5.68e^{-11}, 5.68e^{-11}]$ that would be obtained by classical error propagation relying only on absolute error. On this example, the method of [16], that relies on optimisation of the error globally on subexpressions, is more accurate than our improved bounds. This is because we still suffer here from the conservativeness of interval abstraction in the evaluation of our expressions. But their results come at the expense of much more expensive computations.

In both cases, we note that this conjunction of the propagation of the relative error and the absolute error, in the end, helps us improve sometimes dramatically the absolute error bound, while maintaining a very cheap analysis. It is indeed the center idea of this work to observe that the information contained in the absolute and the relative error bounds are complementary, and to propose an interval-based analysis computing an inexpensive reduced product that combines the information for the best final estimations of error bounds. The idea has been experimented here on a reduced set of operators, and ignoring the possibility of control flow divergences between the floating-point and the corresponding real computations, as a proof of concept. But the approach can naturally be extended to more operators, as well as to relational abstractions of values and error, in order to enhance many existing error analyzes. Additionally, using relational abstractions is necessary to handle with reasonable accuracy errors due to control flow divergences.

Contents. After some background on floating-point arithmetic in Sect. 2, we introduce our abstraction in Sect. 3. In Sect. 4, we demonstrate that our analysis, implemented in the Frama-C platform, while being very efficient in time, often also favorably compares in accuracy to the generally much more expensive existing approaches of the state of the art [11,16]. We use for this a set of benchmarks classically used to compare error analyses, extracted from FPBench[1].

Related Work. Abstract interpretation [2] is widely used for the analysis of floating-point computations. Most analyses dedicated to the propagation of error bounds in floating-point computations focus on absolute round off error bounds. Existing abstraction for rounding errors often are based on intervals [8,13], affine forms [1,4,9,10] as implemented in the analyzer Fluctuat [7]. The tool Gappa [6] relies on interval arithmetic and expression rewriting. It additionally generates a proof of the bounds it computes, that can be automatically checked with a proof assistant such as Coq. Some approaches combine these abstractions with some optimization techniques to enhance bounds on values and errors. The tool PRECiSA [17], relies on intervals, combined with branch-and-bound optimization and symbolic error computations using the Bernstein basis. It also generates proof certificates on the error bounds. Rosa [5] combines affine arithmetic with some SMT solving. Real2float [12] also bounds absolute rounding errors using optimization techniques relying on semidefinite programming and sparse sums of squares certificates.

Some of the tools based on these methods provide the user with relative error bounds, but they are often a posteriori bounds, computed from the bounds on the absolute error. Direct relative error bounds are computed by FPTaylor [16], which formulates the problem of bounding errors as an optimization problem, using first-order Taylor approximations of arithmetic expressions. The optimization based approach of FPTaylor has been extended in Daisy [11], which also relies on some of the techniques already present in Rosa [5] for value and absolute

---

[1] http://fpbench.org.

error estimate. In the present work, we propose a much less costly alternative to the direct estimate of relative error, which we show still behaves very well on a number of classical benchmarks, and demonstrate how this error can be used to also improve absolute error bounds. Compared to the related work which uses optimization somewhat blindly, we demonstrate the interplay between the two types of errors.

2   Floating-Point Arithmetic and Rounding Errors

2.1   Floating-Point Numbers and Rounding Errors

The floating-point representation of a real number x is defined by the IEEE 754 standard as the triple (sgn, sig, exp). In this triple, sgn corresponds to the sign of x, the signific and sig has fixed size p, and, for normalized numbers, is such that $1 \leq sig < 2$, and exp is the exponent. This representation is evaluated as $(-1)^{sgn} \times sig \times 2^{exp}$. Denormalized numbers allow gradual underflow to zero. Their exponent is fixed equal to $e_{\min}$, and the signific and is such that $sig < 1$.

Because of the finite size of the signific and, a real value is represented by a rounded value. This rounding can be represented through the operator $\text{rnd} : \mathbb{R} \rightarrow \mathbb{F}$ that returns the closest floating-point number with respect to the rounding mode. Common rounding modes defined by the standard are rounding to nearest (ties to even), toward zero and toward $\pm\infty$. In this work, we consider the classical case of rounding to nearest. The rounding operator is often modeled as:

$$\text{rnd}(x) = x(1 + e_x) + d_x \tag{1}$$

where $|e_x| \leq \epsilon_M$, $|d_x| \leq \delta_M$, $e_x \times d_x = 0$ and (ϵ_M, δ_M) are parameters fixed by the format (simple, double or quad precision). Constant ϵ_M is often called the *machine epsilon* and depends of the precision p of the floating-point numbers used. It is equal to the distance 2^{1-p} between 1 and its floating-point successor, with $p = 24$ for float and $p = 53$ for double numbers. Constant δ_M is the smallest denormalized number, equal to $2^{e_{\min}+1-p}$, with $e_{\min} = -127$ for float and $e_{\min} = -1023$ for double numbers. In this model, d_x represents the absolute error committed when rounding to a denormalized floating-point number while e_x is the relative error committed when rounding to a normalized floating-point number. They cannot be present at the same time, which is expressed by condition $e_x \times d_x = 0$.

This model can be refined. The normalized floating-point rounding error xe_x in (1) is actually bounded by the distance between two consecutive floating-point numbers around x. This distance can be expressed as $\text{ufp}(x)\,\epsilon_M$, using the notion of *unit in the first place* $\text{ufp}()$ introduced in [15] and defined by:

$$\text{ufp}(x) = \begin{cases} 0 & \text{if } x = 0 \\ 2^{\lfloor log_2 |x| \rfloor} & \text{if } x \neq 0 \end{cases} \tag{2}$$

Function $\text{ufp}()$ is piecewise constant: the result of $\text{ufp}(x)$ for $|x| \in [2^n, 2^{n+1})$ is the constant 2^n. Using this definition, the gap xe_x between the real and its floating-point representation can be rewritten as $\mathrm{ufp}(x)\,e_x$ and the rounding operator is now:

$$\mathrm{rnd}(x) = x + \mathrm{ufp}(x)\,e_x + d_x \tag{3}$$

Absolute and Relative Elementary Rounding Errors. We now define $\Gamma_a(x)$ and $\Gamma_r(x)$ the *elementary absolute* and *relative* rounding errors which occur when a real number x is rounded to its floating-point approximation $\widetilde{x} = \mathrm{rnd}(x)$:

$$\Gamma_a(x) = \mathrm{rnd}(x) - x = \mathrm{ufp}(x)\,e_x + d_x \tag{4}$$

The relative error is defined only when $x \neq 0$:

$$\Gamma_r(x) = \frac{\mathrm{rnd}(x) - x}{x} = \frac{\mathrm{ufp}(x)\,e_x + d_x}{x} \tag{5}$$

2.2 Arithmetic Operations

The IEEE-754 norm standardises some operations that are required to be exactly rounded (addition, subtraction, multiplication, division and square root): the result of the floating-point operation on real operands is the same as if the operation was performed in real numbers on the given inputs, then rounded. For every operation $op : \mathbb{R}^k \to \mathbb{R}$ defined as *exactly* rounded, the corresponding floating-point operation $\widetilde{op}$ can be expressed as:

$$\widetilde{op}(x_1, \ldots, x_k) = \mathrm{rnd}(op(x_1, \ldots, x_k)) \tag{6}$$

The IEEE754-2008 revision additionally recommends that fifty additional operators are correctly rounded. We do not handle these operations in this work, but the approach developed here can be extended.

We now consider the propagation of errors through successive operations. We denote by $\widetilde{x}$ the approximation of an idealized computation x. We thus define the absolute error due to the approximation by:

$$\mathcal{E}_a(x) = \widetilde{x} - x$$

and the relative error, for $x \neq 0$, by:

$$\mathcal{E}_r(x) = \frac{\widetilde{x} - x}{x}$$

The absolute error on the result of an operation op on values $\widetilde{x_1}, \ldots, \widetilde{x_k}$ which are already the approximations of some idealized values $x_1, \ldots, x_k$ is defined by:

$$\mathcal{E}_a(op(x_1, \ldots, x_k)) = \widetilde{op}(\widetilde{x_1}, \ldots, \widetilde{x_k}) - op(x_1, \ldots, x_k)$$

where for all $i = 1, \ldots, k$, the approximated value $\widetilde{x}_i$ is such that $\widetilde{x}_i = x_i + \mathcal{E}_a(x_i) = x_i(1 + \mathcal{E}_r(x_i))$.

Using Eqs. (6) and (4), this can be rewritten:

$$\mathcal{E}_a(op(x_1, \ldots, x_k)) = op(\widetilde{x_1}, \ldots, \widetilde{x_k}) + \Gamma_a(op(\widetilde{x_1}, \ldots, \widetilde{x_k})) - op(x_1, \ldots, x_k) \tag{7}$$

The relative error is derived, when $op(x_1, \ldots, x_k) \neq 0$:

$$\mathcal{E}_r(op(x_1, \ldots, x_k)) = \frac{\mathcal{E}_a(op(x_1, \ldots, x_k))}{op(x_1, \ldots, x_k)} \tag{8}$$

2.3   Concrete Semantics

The concrete model is that of traditional numerical error analyzes, and in particular the static analysis [9], which describe the difference of behavior between the
execution of a program in real numbers and in floating-point numbers, *along the
floating-point execution flow*. We consider in this work the analysis of a language
with the operations $\{+, -, \times, \div, \sqrt{}\}$, which are required to be exactly rounded
in the IEEE-754 standard, conditional statements and loops. The concrete value
that we will compute for all program variables and control points of a program
in this language, is $(x, \tilde{x}, \mathcal{E}_a(x), \mathcal{E}_r(x))$, where:

- $\tilde{x}$ is the result of the execution of the program in a floating-point semantics,
  until the control point of interest,
- x is the result of the execution of the same sequence of arithmetic operations
  in a real semantics, ignoring the possibility of a control flow divergence due
  to rounding errors,
- the errors between the real execution and the floating-point executions $\mathcal{E}_a(x)$
  and $\mathcal{E}_r(x)$ are defined by Eqs. (7) and (8).

Conditional Statements and Unstable Tests. In this work, the path conditions are
those of the floating-point executions. We thus ignore the possibility of unstable
tests, when for same input values, the floating-point and the real-valued executions can take different branches of a conditional statement. We simply issue
a warning when this possibility is detected, as in for instance early versions of
Fluctuat [7,9]. In case an unstable test actually occurs, the analysis is possibly
unsound, as the discontinuity error between the computations performed in the
two branches should be considered as an additional error. Relational analyzes are
needed to estimate such discontinuity errors in a not overly conservative way, and
this has been studied and implemented for instance in [5,10]. But the problem is
somewhat orthogonal to the interplay between relative and absolute error considered here, and is also not considered in the most closely related work [11,16],
to which we compare our analysis in the section dedicated to experiments. But
we intend to handle unstable tests in the future, in a relational version of the
present analysis.

3   Interval-Based Abstraction

Intervals [13] are used in many situations to rigorously compute with interval
domains instead of reals. Throughout the paper, intervals are typeset in boldface
letters. Let $\boldsymbol{x} = [\underline{x}, \overline{x}]$ be such an interval, with its bounds $\underline{x} \leq \overline{x}$ where $\underline{x} \in
\mathbb{R} \cup \{-\infty\}$ and $\overline{x} \cup \{+\infty\}$. Interval arithmetic computes a bounding interval for
each elementary operation by $\boldsymbol{x} \circ \boldsymbol{y} = [\min_{x \in \boldsymbol{x}, y \in \boldsymbol{y}}\{x \circ y\}, \max_{x \in \boldsymbol{x}, y \in \boldsymbol{y}}\{x \circ y\}]$,
where $\circ \in \{+, -, \times, \div\}$, and analogously for the square root. Intervals are the
basis of one of the first and most widely used numerical abstract domains, the
lattice of intervals [3].

In what follows, we propose an abstraction which relies on the lattice of intervals: we abstract with intervals $(\widetilde{x}, \mathcal{E}_a(x), \mathcal{E}_r(x))$, the floating-point range, absolute and relative errors. The errors are computed, on each control-flow path, under the assumption for the error estimation that the real and floating-point executions follow the same path. We deduce bounds for the value in real-valued semantics by $x = \widetilde{x} - \mathcal{E}_a(x)$. The abstract domain forms a complete lattice, fully relying on the lattice of intervals, with a join operator performed componentwise on the value and errors using the classical join operator on intervals.

The rounding mode for computing the interval extremities on the intervals bounding the floating-point range will be the rounding mode of the computation we analyse (rounding to the nearest). The other terms, that bound the errors and the real-valued range, will be computed with outward rounding, in order to ensure a sound implementation.

3.1 Abstraction of the Elementary Rounding Errors

In this section, we define the abstraction $\Gamma_a(x)$ and $\Gamma_r(x)$ of the elementary rounding errors defined by (4) and (5). They will be used for the abstraction of transfer functions in Sect. 3.2.

Terms e_x and d_x that appear in the elementary rounding errors are bounded respectively in $[-\epsilon_M, \epsilon_M]$ and $[-\delta_M, \delta_M]$. Additionally, we know that e_x and d_x cannot be both non-zero for the same x. If x is rounded to a normalized number, then $d_x = 0$ and if x is rounded to a denormalized number, then $e_x = 0$. We can thus compute the abstraction of the elementary absolute rounding error over an interval of real numbers as the union of the two cases:

$$\Gamma_a(x) = \mathrm{ufp}(x)\,\epsilon(x) \cup \delta(x) \qquad (9)$$

where ϵ (resp. δ) returns the interval $[-\epsilon_M, \epsilon_M]$ (resp. $[-\delta_M, \delta_M]$) if its parameter contains at least a normalized (resp. denormalized) number and $[0, 0]$ otherwise. Moreover, as $\mathrm{ufp}()$ is increasing in the absolute value of its argument, we can abstract the rounding error on normalized numbers by

$$\mathrm{ufp}(x)\,\epsilon(x) \subseteq \mathrm{ufp}(\max(|\underline{x}|, |\overline{x}|))\,\epsilon(x).$$

Let us define $\mathrm{norm}(x)$ and $\mathrm{denorm}(x)$ that return respectively the subsets of normalized and denormalized numbers from interval x. We can define the abstraction $\Gamma_r(x)$ of the elementary relative error, for any interval x, as:

$$\Gamma_r(x) = \max_{x \in \mathrm{norm}(x), x \neq 0} \left| \frac{\mathrm{ufp}(x)}{x} \right| [-\epsilon_M, \epsilon_M] \cup \max_{x \in \mathrm{denorm}(x)} \frac{[-\delta_M, \delta_M]}{|x|} \qquad (10)$$

Equation (10) will be used to derive in Sect. 3.2 relative error bounds also when interval x possibly contains zero. These error bounds will be valid whenever the relative error is defined, that is for all non zero value in x.

Let us first evaluate in (10) the error due to the rounding of normalized numbers. Consider x strictly positive (the negative case is symmetric), then we can write:

$$\left| \frac{\mathrm{ufp}(x)}{x} \right| = \frac{2^{exp}}{sig \times 2^{exp}} = \frac{1}{sig} \tag{11}$$

Given $sig \in [1, 2)$, a simple abstraction of $\left| \frac{\mathrm{ufp}(x)}{x} \right|$ is the interval $(\frac{1}{2}, 1]$, and its maximum is always bounded by 1. However, we can slightly refine this estimate when there exists n such that $|\boldsymbol{x}| \subseteq [2^n, 2^{n+1})$. This gives, when $\boldsymbol{x}$ does not contain 0:

$$\max_{x \in \boldsymbol{x}} \left| \frac{\mathrm{ufp}(x)}{x} \right| = \begin{cases} 1/sig_{\min(|\underline{x}|, |\overline{x}|)} & \text{if } \exists n \in \mathbb{Z}, |\boldsymbol{x}| \subseteq [2^n, 2^{n+1}) \\ 1 & \text{otherwise} \end{cases} \tag{12}$$

Let us now consider the error due to denormalized numbers if $\boldsymbol{x}$ contains any. Let us consider again x strictly positive. A positive denormalized number can be expressed as a multiple of δ_M, i.e. $x = n\delta_M$ with $n \in \mathbb{Z}$, and an absolute error of magnitude at most δ_M can be committed, we thus abstract the relative error on denormalized numbers by:

$$\max_{x \in \mathrm{denorm}(\boldsymbol{x})} \frac{[-\delta_M, \delta_M]}{|x|} \subseteq [-1, 1] \tag{13}$$

3.2 Transfer Functions for Arithmetic Operations

Let us now study the transfer functions for each operation in $\{+, -, \times, \div, \sqrt{\ }\}$.

First, the floating-point range $\widetilde{\boldsymbol{x}}$ is abstracted classically in interval arithmetic. Then the absolute and relative error bounds are computed as described in this section, by an interval abstraction of (7) and (8). Finally, bounds for the value in real-valued semantics are deduced by $\boldsymbol{x} = \widetilde{\boldsymbol{x}} - \boldsymbol{\mathcal{E}}_a(\boldsymbol{x})$.

Let us first state that after each operation, which yields a result $z = op(\boldsymbol{x}, \boldsymbol{y})$, we perform a reduced product of the absolute and relative errors:

Reduction

$$\begin{cases} \mathcal{E}_a(\boldsymbol{z}) = \mathcal{E}_a(\boldsymbol{z}) \cap \mathcal{E}_r(\boldsymbol{z})\boldsymbol{z} \\ \mathcal{E}_r(\boldsymbol{z}) = \mathcal{E}_r(\boldsymbol{z}) \cap \dfrac{\mathcal{E}_a(\boldsymbol{z})}{\boldsymbol{z}} \quad \text{whenever } 0 \notin \boldsymbol{z} \end{cases} \tag{14}$$

We will see that, in particular for the division and the square root, the two types of errors are more tightly coupled than by the only use of this reduction. Indeed, some formulations which are equivalent on real numbers, yield different levels of conservativeness when computed abstracted. It is thus important to carefully state the precise expression of the propagation of errors through arithmetic operations. We detail below, for each arithmetic operation, propagation rules that provide a sound abstraction, while reducing the wrapping effect due to the use of intervals:

Lemma 1 (Addition and Subtraction)

$$\mathcal{E}_a(x \pm y) = (\mathcal{E}_a(x) \pm \mathcal{E}_a(y)) + \Gamma_a(\tilde{x} \pm \tilde{y}) \tag{15}$$

The relative error is defined only when $0 \notin x \pm y$. *In this case, we have:*

$$\mathcal{E}_r(x \pm y) = \begin{cases} \left(\dfrac{\mathcal{E}_r(x) - \mathcal{E}_r(y)}{1 \pm y/x} + \mathcal{E}_r(y) \right)(1 + \Gamma_r(\tilde{x} \pm \tilde{y})) + \Gamma_r(\tilde{x} \pm \tilde{y}) \; if \; 0 \notin x \\[3mm] \left(\dfrac{\mathcal{E}_r(y) - \mathcal{E}_r(x)}{1 \pm x/y} + \mathcal{E}_r(x) \right)(1 + \Gamma_r(\tilde{x} \pm \tilde{y})) + \Gamma_r(\tilde{x} \pm \tilde{y}) \; if \; 0 \notin y \end{cases} \tag{16}$$

When x *and* y *both do not include zero, then the relative error can be computed as the intersection of the 2 estimates in (16).*

Proof. The propagation of the absolute error corresponds to a classical absolute rounding error analysis, starting from Eq. (7) instantiated for the addition and subtraction: for all $x \in x$, $y \in y$, $\tilde{x} = x + \mathcal{E}_a(x) \in \tilde{x}$, $\tilde{y} = x + \mathcal{E}_a(y) \in \tilde{y}$,

$$\begin{aligned} \mathcal{E}_a(x \pm y) &= (\tilde{x} \pm \tilde{y}) + \Gamma_a(\tilde{x} \pm \tilde{y}) - (x \pm y) \\ &= ((x + \mathcal{E}_a(x)) \pm (y + \mathcal{E}_a(y))) + \Gamma_a(\tilde{x} \pm \tilde{y}) - (x \pm y) \\ &= (\mathcal{E}_a(x) \pm \mathcal{E}_a(y)) + \Gamma_a(\tilde{x} \pm \tilde{y}) \end{aligned}$$

Abstracting this result in intervals, we get Eq. (15), which defines $\mathcal{E}_a(x \pm y)$ as an interval over-approximation of $\{\mathcal{E}_a(x \pm y), x \in x, y \in y\}$.

Note that we would naturally also get a sound over-approximation of $\mathcal{E}_a(x \pm y)$ by directly computing in intervals $(\tilde{x} \pm \tilde{y}) + \Gamma_a(\tilde{x} \pm \tilde{y}) - (x \pm y)$. However, the result would be very conservative in general, because interval arithmetic does not handle correlations. We thus derive, for each arithmetic operation, error formulas in real numbers by reorganizing terms in an equivalent expression but reducing variable repetitions. We then abstract the final expression in intervals.

For any binary operation $\circ$, for all $x \in x$, $y \in y$ such that $x \circ y \neq 0$, for all $\tilde{x} = x + \mathcal{E}_a(x)$, $\tilde{y} = y + Ea(y)$, we can compute the relative error as

$$\begin{aligned} \mathcal{E}_r(x \circ y) &= \frac{(\tilde{x} \circ \tilde{y}) + \Gamma_a(\tilde{x} \circ \tilde{y}) - (x \circ y)}{x \circ y} \\ &= \frac{(\tilde{x} \circ \tilde{y}) + (\tilde{x} \circ \tilde{y})\Gamma_r(\tilde{x} \circ \tilde{y}) - (x \circ y)}{x \circ y} \end{aligned}$$

from which we have:

$$\mathcal{E}_r(x \circ y) = \frac{\tilde{x} \circ \tilde{y}}{x \circ y}(1 + \Gamma_r(\tilde{x} \circ \tilde{y})) - 1 \tag{17}$$

We can deduce:

$$\begin{aligned} \mathcal{E}_r(x \pm y) &= \frac{x(\mathcal{E}_r(x) + 1) \pm y(1 + \mathcal{E}_r(y))}{x \pm y}(1 + \Gamma_r(\tilde{x} \pm \tilde{y})) - 1 \\ &= \frac{x\mathcal{E}_r(x) \pm y\mathcal{E}_r(y)}{x \pm y}(1 + \Gamma_r(\tilde{x} \pm \tilde{y})) + \Gamma_r(\tilde{x} \pm \tilde{y}) \end{aligned}$$

It is interesting to reformulate this expression in order to suppress as much as possible variable repetitions. This will reduce the loss of correlation when the expression will be evaluated in interval arithmetic. For $x \neq 0$, we can write:

$$\mathcal{E}_r(x \pm y) = \left(\frac{x\mathcal{E}_r(x) - x\mathcal{E}_r(y)}{x \pm y} + \frac{x\mathcal{E}_r(y) \pm y\mathcal{E}_r(y)}{x \pm y} \right)(1 + \Gamma_r(\tilde{x} \pm \tilde{y})) + \Gamma_r(\tilde{x} \pm \tilde{y})$$

$$= \left(\frac{\mathcal{E}_r(x) - \mathcal{E}_r(y)}{1 \pm \frac{y}{x}} + \mathcal{E}_r(y) \right)(1 + \Gamma_r(\tilde{x} \pm \tilde{y})) + \Gamma_r(\tilde{x} \pm \tilde{y})$$

A symmetric transformation can be done, exchanging x and y, which allows us to conclude with Eq. (16), after abstraction in intervals.

We note that the addition is the operation for which propagating relative error is less natural, and thus some accuracy loss can be expected.

Lemma 2 (Multiplication)

$$\mathcal{E}_a(x \times y) = x\mathcal{E}_a(y) + y\mathcal{E}_a(x) + \mathcal{E}_a(x)\mathcal{E}_a(y) + \Gamma_a(\tilde{x} \times \tilde{y}) \qquad (18)$$

$$\mathcal{E}_r(x \times y) = (\mathcal{E}_r(x) + 1)(\mathcal{E}_r(y) + 1)(1 + \Gamma_r(\tilde{x} \times \tilde{y})) - 1 \qquad (19)$$

Proof. As for the addition, the expression of the propagated absolute error by the multiplication is quite natural, and corresponds to a classical absolute rounding error analysis: for all $x \in \boldsymbol{x}$, $y \in \boldsymbol{y}$, $\tilde{x} = x + \mathcal{E}_a(x)$, $\tilde{y} = y + \mathcal{E}_a(y)$,

$$\mathcal{E}_a(x \times y) = (\tilde{x} \times \tilde{y}) + \Gamma_a(\tilde{x} \times \tilde{y}) - (x \times y)$$

$$= (x + \mathcal{E}_a(x))(y + \mathcal{E}_a(y)) + \Gamma_a(\tilde{x} \times \tilde{y}) - (x \times y)$$

$$= x\mathcal{E}_a(y) + y\mathcal{E}_a(x) + \mathcal{E}_a(x)\mathcal{E}_a(y) + \Gamma_a(\tilde{x} \times \tilde{y})$$

Starting from Eq. (17), we obtain an expression of the propagated relative error that naturally involves the relative errors on the operands:

$$\mathcal{E}_r(x \times y) = \frac{\tilde{x} \times \tilde{y}}{x \times y}(1 + \Gamma_r(\tilde{x} \times \tilde{y})) - 1$$

$$= \frac{x(\mathcal{E}_r(x) + 1) \times y(\mathcal{E}_r(y) + 1)}{x \times y}(1 + \Gamma_r(\tilde{x} \times \tilde{y})) - 1$$

$$= (\mathcal{E}_r(x) + 1)(\mathcal{E}_r(y) + 1)(1 + \Gamma_r(\tilde{x} \times \tilde{y})) - 1$$

This propagation of relative errors should be quite accurate, as we could remove correlations to values of x and y.

Example 3. We consider a very simple example to exemplify our analysis. We have 4 input floating-point variables a, b, c, d given respectively in the ranges [0,1], [1,2], [0,1], and [1,2]. All these inputs are supposed to be known exactly, with no rounding error, i.e. $\forall \boldsymbol{v} \in \{a, b, c, d\}, \mathcal{E}_a(\boldsymbol{v}) = \mathcal{E}_r(\boldsymbol{v}) = [0,0]$. We now consider the errors committed on the computations that define floating-point variables x, y, z. For the sake of

```
x = a + 3 * b ;

y = c + 3 * d ;

z = x * y ;
```

demonstration, we explicit here the computation of errors in term of the machine epsilon ϵ_M. In order to evaluate the error on variable x, we first evaluate 3b: its range of value is $3b = [3, 6]$, and the errors are $\mathcal{E}_r(3b) = \Gamma_r(3b) = [-\epsilon_M, +\epsilon_M]$ and $\mathcal{E}_a(3b) = \Gamma_a(3b) = [-4\epsilon_M, +4\epsilon_M]$ The errors on x that results from the addition are obtained using (15) and (16):

$$\mathcal{E}_a(x) = \mathcal{E}_a(3b) + \Gamma_a([3, 7]) = [-8\epsilon_M, +8\epsilon_M]$$

$$\mathcal{E}_r(x) = \left(\frac{\mathcal{E}_r(3b) - \mathcal{E}_r(a)}{1 + a/3b} + \mathcal{E}_r(a)\right)(\Gamma_r([3, 7]) + 1) + \Gamma_r([3, 7])$$

$$= \frac{[-\epsilon_M, +\epsilon_M]}{[1, 4/3]}([-\epsilon_M, +\epsilon_M] + 1) + [-\epsilon_M, +\epsilon_M] = [-2\epsilon_M, +2\epsilon_M] + O(\epsilon_M^2)$$

Note that the bounds for the relative errors are $\frac{4}{3}$ times better than the a posteriori estimate $\mathcal{E}_a(x)/x = \left[-\frac{8}{3}\epsilon_M, +\frac{8}{3}\epsilon_M\right]$. The errors on y are computed similarly. Finally, we can deduce absolute error bounds for z using (18):

$$\mathcal{E}_a(z) = x\mathcal{E}_a(y) + y\mathcal{E}_a(x) + \mathcal{E}_a(x)\mathcal{E}_a(y) + \Gamma_a(x \times y)$$

$$= 2 \times [3, 7]\,[-8\epsilon_M, +8\epsilon_M] + [-8\epsilon_M, +8\epsilon_M]\,[-8\epsilon_M, +8\epsilon_M] + \Gamma_a([9, 49])$$

$$= [-144\epsilon_M, +144\epsilon_M] + O(\epsilon_M^2)$$

and relative error bounds using (19):

$$\mathcal{E}_r(z) = (\mathcal{E}_r(x) + 1)(\mathcal{E}_r(y) + 1)(\Gamma_r(x \times y) + 1) - 1$$

$$= ([-2\epsilon_M, +2\epsilon_M] + 1)([-2\epsilon_M, +2\epsilon_M] + 1)(\Gamma_r([9, 49]) + 1) - 1 + O(\epsilon_M^2)$$

$$= [-5\epsilon_M, +5\epsilon_M] + O(\epsilon_M^2)$$

Neglecting here for simplicity the second order errors, the reduced product yields an estimate for the relative error approximately 3.2 times better than the a posteriori estimate $\mathcal{E}_a(z)/[9, 49]$.

Lemma 3 (Division). *The division is defined whenever $0 \notin y$, by:*

$$\mathcal{E}_a(x \div y) = \frac{\mathcal{E}_a(x) - x\mathcal{E}_r(y)}{\tilde{y}} + \Gamma_a(\tilde{x} \div \tilde{y}) \tag{20}$$

$$\mathcal{E}_r(x \div y) = \frac{\mathcal{E}_r(x) + 1}{\mathcal{E}_r(y) + 1}(1 + \Gamma_r(\tilde{x} \div \tilde{y})) - 1 \tag{21}$$

Proof. The division is a case where the coupling between the computation of two errors is integrated: the absolute error on $x \div y$ naturally involves the absolute error on x and the relative error on y:

$$\mathcal{E}_a(x \div y) = (\tilde{x} \div \tilde{y}) + \Gamma_a(\tilde{x} \div \tilde{y}) - (x \div y)$$

$$= \frac{y\tilde{x} - \tilde{y}x}{y\tilde{y}} + \Gamma_a(\tilde{x} \div \tilde{y})$$

$$= \frac{y(x + \mathcal{E}_a(x)) - (y + \mathcal{E}_a(y))x}{y\tilde{y}} + \Gamma_a(\tilde{x} \div \tilde{y})$$

$$= \frac{\mathcal{E}_a(x) - x\mathcal{E}_r(y)}{\tilde{y}} + \Gamma_a(\tilde{x} \div \tilde{y})$$

This is thus an operation where propagating tight relative error bounds on the operands proves useful to tighten the absolute error bounds on the result.

$$\mathcal{E}_r(x \div y) = \frac{\tilde{x} \div \tilde{y}}{x \div y}(1 + \Gamma_r(\tilde{x} \div \tilde{y})) - 1$$

$$= \frac{x(\mathcal{E}_r(x) + 1)}{y(\mathcal{E}_r(y) + 1)} \times \frac{y}{x} \times (1 + \Gamma_r(\tilde{x} \div \tilde{y})) - 1$$

$$= \frac{\mathcal{E}_r(x) + 1}{\mathcal{E}_r(y) + 1}(1 + \Gamma_r(\tilde{x} \div \tilde{y})) - 1$$

As for the multiplication, we note that the propagation of relative errors should be generally quite accurate. Note also that as for the multiplication as well, the relative error bounds are defined even when $0 \in x \div y$, as long as they are defined for x and y. The bound will be valid for all nonzero values in $x \div y$. This is exemplified in Example 4.

Example 4. Let us come back to Example 2 of the introduction. An error is committed when computing $t + 1$, the absolute error of $t + 1$ is bounded by $\mathcal{E}_a(t + 1) = [-5.68e^{-14}, 5.68e^{-14}]$, the relative error by $\mathcal{E}_r(t + 1) = [-1.1e^{-16}, 1.1e^{-16}]$. Using Eq. (20) to bound the absolute error of the division, we obtain:

$$\mathcal{E}_a\left(\frac{t}{t+1}\right) = -\frac{t\mathcal{E}_r(t+1)}{\tilde{t}+1} + \Gamma_a\left(\frac{\tilde{t}}{\tilde{t}+1}\right)$$

$$= \frac{[0, 900][-1.1e^{-16}, 1.1e^{-16}]}{[1, 1000]} + [-5.68e^{-14}, 5.68e^{-14}]$$

$$= [-1.67e^{-13}, 1.67e^{-13}]$$

If only absolute error bounds were available, we would replace $x\mathcal{E}_r(y)$ by $x\mathcal{E}_a(y)/y$ in Eq. (20) and obtain the absolute error analysis used classically. We would then obtain as absolute error bound on $t/(t + 1)$:

$$\frac{[0, 999] \times [-5.68e^{-14}, 5.68e^{-14}]}{[1, 1000]^2} + [-5.68e^{-14}, 5.68e^{-14}] = [-5.68e^{-11}, 5.68e^{-11}]$$

which is 340 times larger than the absolute error bound computed using our reduced product.

The relative error on $t/(t + 1)$ is bounded where it is defined, that if for all $t \neq 0$, by:

$$\mathcal{E}_r\left(\frac{t}{t+1}\right) = \frac{\mathcal{E}_r(t) + 1}{\mathcal{E}_r(t+1) + 1}\left(1 + \Gamma_r\left(\frac{\tilde{t}}{\tilde{t}+1}\right)\right) - 1$$

$$= \frac{1}{[-1.1e^{-16}, 1.1e^{-16}] + 1}\left(1 + \Gamma_r\left(\frac{\tilde{t}}{\tilde{t}+1}\right)\right) - 1$$

For $t = [0, 999]$, t and $t/(t + 1)$ contain zero. As t is an input, its relative error $\mathcal{E}_r(t)$ is zero when it is defined, that is for all $t \neq 0$. The elementary relative error Γ_r is also defined for all $t \neq 0$, and is bounded by the maximum relative error when using denormalized floating-point numbers around 0, given by (13): for all $t \neq 0$, $\Gamma_r(\frac{t}{t+1}) \subseteq [-1,1]$. Thus

$$\mathcal{E}_r\left(\frac{t}{t+1}\right) = \frac{1}{[-1.1e^{-16}, 1.1e^{-16}]+1}(1+[-1,1])-1 \quad \subseteq 1+[-1,1]-1=[-1,1]$$

The square root is an operation where the relative error on the operand naturally appears in the propagation:

Lemma 4 (Square root)

$$\mathcal{E}_a(\sqrt{x}) = \sqrt{x}(\sqrt{1+\mathcal{E}_r(x)}-1) + \Gamma_a(\sqrt{\tilde{x}}) \tag{22}$$
$$\mathcal{E}_r(\sqrt{x}) = \sqrt{1+\mathcal{E}_r(x)}(\Gamma_r(\sqrt{\tilde{x}})+1)-1 \tag{23}$$

Proof. In order to avoid the loss of correlation, it is natural to factorize $\sqrt{x}$:

$$\mathcal{E}_a(\sqrt{x}) = \sqrt{\tilde{x}} + \Gamma_a(\sqrt{\tilde{x}}) - \sqrt{x}$$
$$= \sqrt{x}(\sqrt{1+\mathcal{E}_r(x)}-1) + \Gamma_a(\sqrt{\tilde{x}})$$

The expression of the relative error is deduced immediately.

$$\mathcal{E}_r(\sqrt{x}) = \frac{\sqrt{\tilde{x}}}{\sqrt{x}}(\Gamma_r(\sqrt{\tilde{x}})+1)-1$$
$$= \sqrt{\frac{x(\mathcal{E}_r(x)+1)}{x}}(\Gamma_r(\sqrt{\tilde{x}})+1)-1$$
$$= \sqrt{\mathcal{E}_r(x)+1}(\Gamma_r(\sqrt{\tilde{x}})+1)-1$$

Using similar developments, it is possible to handle more functions. We chose in this work to focus on the main arithmetic operations which error bounds have long been specified by the IEEE 754 norm.

3.3 Handling Conditional Statements

Interpretation of Conditional expressions. Let $\gamma(x_1,\ldots,x_n)$ a conditional expression defined by $f(x_1,\ldots,x_n) \diamond b$, with $\diamond \in \{<,>,=,\leq,\geq\}$. Let us denote by $\tilde{x}_\gamma$ the interval abstraction of the floating-point value of variable x, after transformation by the interpretation of conditional γ. It is computed by the classical backward constraint propagation on intervals which filters out values of $\tilde{x}$ that do not satisfy the constraint. Note that as already discussed in the section devoted to the concrete semantics, we consider the path condition only on the floating-point value. The bound on the relative error is left unchanged by the interpretation of constraints:

$$\mathcal{E}_r(x_\gamma) = \mathcal{E}_r(x) \tag{24}$$

In a classical error analysis, that is, with no information about the relative error, the absolute error bounds are also left unchanged by the interpretation of this conditional: $\mathcal{E}_a(\boldsymbol{x}_\gamma) = \mathcal{E}_a(\boldsymbol{x})$. When available, the relative error bounds can be used to reduce the absolute error in the case the range of values $\boldsymbol{x}_\gamma$ has been reduced compared to $\boldsymbol{x}$ by the constraint propagation:

$$\mathcal{E}_a(\boldsymbol{x}_\gamma) = \mathcal{E}_a(\boldsymbol{x}) \cap \boldsymbol{x}_\gamma \mathcal{E}_r(\boldsymbol{x}). \tag{25}$$

Example 5. In Example 1 of the introduction, the multiplication x:=i*i results in $\boldsymbol{x} = [1, 10000]$ with an elementary absolute rounding error $\mathcal{E}_a(x) = [-9.09e^{-13}, 9.09e^{-13}]$, and a relative error bound $\mathcal{E}_r(x) = [-1.11e^{-16}, 1.11e^{-16}]$. The constraint x <=2 yields $\boldsymbol{x}_{(x \le 2)} = [1, 2]$ in the **true** branch. We can then reduce the absolute error bound on x in this branch (and thus on y), by $\mathcal{E}_a(\boldsymbol{y}) = [1, 2][-1.11e-16, 1.11e^{-16}]$, as already stated in this introductory example.

Join and widening. Joining values coming from different branches of the program analyzed supposes to define a join or upper bound operator on abstract values. The join can be performed componentwise on the value, relative and absolute errors, relying on the classical join on intervals. Naturally, this relies on the hypothesis that there is no unstable test. Similarly, a widening can be defined componentwise relying on any widening operator on intervals.

4   Implementation and Experimental Evaluation

We have implemented this approach as a new abstract domain called Numerors in the Abstract Interpretation plug-in Eva of the verification platform Frama-C[2]. Frama-C provides a collection of plug-ins that perform static analysis, deductive verification, and testing, for safety- and security-critical software. Those plug-ins can cooperate thanks to their integration on top of a shared kernel and data structures along with their compliance to a common specification language.

   In what follows, we evaluate our approach by comparing the error bounds obtained by our tool against the state of the art tools Fluctuat [9], Daisy [11] and FPTaylor [16], on a set of representative benchmark examples.

Selection and Description of the Benchmarks. The examples are mostly extracted from the FPBench[3] suite for comparing verification tools on floating-point programs, to which we have added 4 examples of our own. Our selection has been guided by the will to keep a reasonably small set of examples, while including most classes of examples which were previously studied with the tools of the related work, Daisy and FPTaylor. We excluded the examples containing calls to mathematical functions like transcendentals that we do not handle, variations of the same examples that did not show a different behavior, and examples

---

[2] Our abstract domain should be included in an upcoming release of Frama-C/Eva (https://frama-c.com/value.html).
[3] http://fpbench.org.

for which the inputs were not fully specified. Finally, we modified[4] the inputs of some examples so that all tools compute a non trivial relative error bounds.

The first four examples were written to highlight some features that were not well represented in FPBench, and in particular programs that include some conditional statements (the first three examples), and a program with square roots (the fourth). Benchmark *log_approx* computes an approximation of the logarithm of the square of its input, using a loop and a Taylor expansion. Benchmark *conditional_ex* is Example 1, and *conditional_1* is similar but with more computation. Finally, *sqrt_1* computes the function $\sqrt{2x+3}/(2\sqrt{x}+3)$. The remaining examples come from the FPbench suite. Example *complex_sqrt* belongs to the Herbie [14] suite. Examples from *intro_example* to *test05_nonlin1_test2* come from the FPTaylor test suite, and *intro_example* and *sec4_example* are specifically used in [16] to introduce their technique. The remaining examples come either from the Rosa [5] or the FPTaylor test suites, and have already been used as benchmarks for both absolute and relative errors [11,16].

Table 1. Tools comparison on the absolute errors

Name	Under-Appprox	Numerors	Fluctuat Intervals	Fluctuat Affine	Daisy 1	Daisy 2	FPTaylor
log_approx	–	**6.25e−14**	*3.56e−11*	*3.56e−11*	–	–	–
conditional_ex	–	**2.22e−16**	*9.09e−13*	*9.09e−13*	–	–	*9.09e−13*
conditional_1	–	**8.43e−13**	*6.82e−12*	*6.82e−12*	–	–	*2.09e−11*
sqrt_1	2.11e−16	5.51e−15	3.72e−14	3.38e−14	3.72e−14	*4.52e−16*	**2.75e−16**
complex_sqrt	5.00e−16	*1.29e−15*	3.93e−15	2.52e−15	3.92e−15	1.89e−15	**5.70e−16**
kepler0	2.42e−13	*3.63e−13*	*3.63e−13*	*3.63e−13*	*3.63e−13*	7.15e−13	**3.18e−13**
intro_example	1.65e−16	1.68e−13	5.68e−11	5.67e−11	5.68e−11	*2.52e−16*	**1.67e−16**
sec4_example	3.25e−15	6.35e−11	1.16e−09	1.16e−09	1.16e−09	**7.00e−14**	*3.73e−13*
test01_sum3	8.88e−16	*3.33e−15*	*3.33e−15*	**2.89e−15**	*3.33e−15*	4.11e−15	**2.89e−15**
test02_sum8	4.00e−15	**6.22e−15**	**6.22e−15**	**6.22e−15**	**6.22e−15**	*9.55e−15*	**6.22e−15**
test03_nonlin2	1.64e−16	3.11e−15	2.42e−14	2.28e−14	2.42e−14	*4.45e−16*	**3.47e−16**
test04_dqmom9	5.87e−12	8.64e−05	8.64e−05	8.64e−05	8.64e−05	**1.78e−09**	*1.85e−05*
test05_nonlin1_r4	1.32e−12	2.78e−07	1.67e−06	1.67e−06	1.67e−06	**5.93e−11**	*2.21e−09*
test05_nonlin1_test2	8.29e−17	**8.33e−17**	**8.33e−17**	**8.33e−17**	**8.33e−17**	*1.39e−16*	**8.33e−17**
doppler1	6.13e−14	*1.62e−13*	3.45e−13	3.45e−13	3.91e−13	1.74e−13	**9.91e−14**
doppler2	1.14e−13	3.27e−13	8.78e−13	8.78e−13	9.78e−13	*3.18e−13*	**1.84e−13**
doppler3	4.16e−14	*8.50e−14*	1.36e−13	1.36e−13	1.60e−13	9.13e−14	**5.70e−14**
rigidBody1	1.79e−13	*2.40e−13*	*2.40e−13*	*2.40e−13*	*2.40e−13*	5.08e−13	**2.13e−13**
rigidBody2	1.81e−11	*2.31e−11*	*2.31e−11*	*2.31e−11*	*2.31e−11*	6.32e−11	**2.27e−11**
turbine1	4.30e−15	4.73e−14	6.04e−14	5.76e−14	6.04e−14	*2.80e−14*	**1.24e−14**
turbine2	4.41e−15	8.57e−15	8.57e−15	*8.54e−15*	8.57e−15	1.71e−14	**7.38e−15**
turbine3	3.22e−15	3.85e−14	4.72e−14	4.54e−14	4.72e−14	*1.65e−14*	**7.15e−15**
verhulst	1.70e−16	3.77e−16	3.77e−16	*3.00e−16*	3.80e−16	4.21e−16	**1.79e−16**
predatorPrey	8.79e−17	1.40e−16	1.40e−16	*1.38e−16*	1.41e−16	2.27e−16	**1.01e−16**
carbonGas	3.13e−09	2.00e−08	2.00e−08	1.58e−08	2.06e−08	*1.03e−08*	**4.96e−09**
sine	2.71e−16	*5.18e−16*	*5.18e−16*	*5.18e−16*	*5.18e−16*	6.55e−16	**4.38e−16**
sqroot	4.41e−16	*5.62e−16*	*5.62e−16*	*5.62e−16*	*5.62e−16*	7.89e−16	**4.86e−16**
sineOrder3	3.11e−16	5.91e−16	5.96e−16	*5.86e−16*	7.84e−16	7.99e−16	**5.28e−16**

---

[4] http://www.lix.polytechnique.fr/Labo/Maxime.Jacquemin/numerors.c for the examples.

Table 2. Tools comparison on the relative errors

Name	Under-Approx	Numerors	Posteriori	Daisy 1	Daisy 2	Daisy 3	FPTaylor
log_approx	–	∞	∞	–	–	–	–
conditional_ex	–	**1.11e−16**	9.09e−13	–	–	–	*1.13e−16*
conditional_1	–	*8.94e−16*	3.41e−12	–	–	–	**7.22e−16**
sqrt_1	3.42e−16	*6.61e−16*	6.83e−12	1.10e−12	1.02e−15	∞	**4.26e−16**
complex_sqrt	2.04e−16	*4.98e−16*	8.64e−14	4.01e−15	1.94e−15	∞	**2.64e−16**
kepler0	3.65e−16	1.20e−15	1.20e−15	1.20e−15	2.13e−15	*1.06e−15*	**5.71e−16**
intro_example	1.87e−16	**1.00**	∞	∞	∞	∞	∞
sec4_example	6.52e−15	**1.40e−13**	8.71e−06	8.71e−06	3.60e−13	*2.34e−13*	6.65e−12
test01_sum3	2.78e−16	∞	∞	∞	*1.37e−15*	∞	**5.05e−16**
test02_sum8	3.42e−16	*5.94e−16*	7.77e−16	7.77e−16	1.19e−15	7.73e−16	**4.82e−16**
test03_nonlin2	2.17e−16	∞	∞	∞	∞	∞	∞
test04_dqmom9	1.46e−12	∞	∞	∞	∞	∞	∞
test05_nonlin1_r4	2.63e−12	**5.55e−12**	5.00e−01	5.00e−01	*2.07e−10*	1.68e−05	3.46e−06
test05_nonlin1_test2	1.66e−16	*2.26e−16*	2.50e−16	2.50e−16	4.17e−16	2.96e−16	**1.69e−16**
doppler1	6.70e−16	*1.10e−15*	1.17e−11	1.33e−11	5.91e−12	1.26e−15	**9.69e−16**
doppler2	7.17e−16	*1.21e−15*	4.62e−11	5.14e−11	1.67e−11	1.37e−15	**9.13e−16**
doppler3	5.63e−16	*9.75e−16*	3.11e−13	3.65e−13	1.82e−13	1.14e−15	**7.36e−16**
rigidBody1	3.44e−16	*7.79e−16*	1.04e−12	1.04e−12	2.21e−12	9.76e−16	**4.39e−16**
rigidBody2	4.84e−16	*9.65e−16*	1.32e−15	1.32e−15	3.50e−15	1.17e−15	**6.27e−16**
turbine1	4.21e−16	3.05e−14	3.90e−14	3.90e−14	1.41e−14	*1.75e−15*	**7.95e−16**
turbine2	2.30e−16	*4.98e−16*	*4.98e−16*	*4.98e−16*	9.23e−16	6.92e−16	**3.97e−16**
turbine3	3.53e−16	7.50e−14	1.01e−13	1.01e−13	2.91e−14	*6.51e−15*	**2.40e−15**
verhulst	2.26e−16	*3.75e−16*	1.20e−15	1.21e−15	1.16e−15	4.59e−16	**2.41e−16**
predatorPrey	3.12e−16	*4.82e−16*	3.76e−15	3.77e−15	6.09e−15	6.87e−16	**3.58e−16**
carbonGas	3.39e−16	**7.16e−16**	9.52e−15	9.80e−15	2.40e−15	8.11e−16	*7.67e−16*
sine	2.71e−16	1.75e−15	2.27e−15	2.27e−15	8.56e−16	*6.31e−16*	**4.41e−16**
sqroot	3.99e−16	6.72e−16	6.72e−16	6.72e−16	7.91e−16	*5.66e−16*	**4.44e−16**
sineOrder3	3.53e−16	1.13e−14	1.41e−14	1.86e−14	9.11e−16	*8.94e−16*	**6.06e−16**

Methodology of Comparison. For each example, absolute error bounds on the output of interest are presented in Table 1, relative error bounds in Table 2. Table 3 presents the running times for each tool, on the complete set of benchmarks.

In Tables 1 and 2, underestimates of the errors are given in the first column denoted Under-Approx. They are obtained with Daisy, computing the maximum of errors obtained for runs on 100000 random input values. The second column denoted Numerors in all result tables presents the results of the approach presented in our work. Fluctuat in its Intervals mode is used in third column of Table 1 as a witness of the results obtained with a classical interval absolute error analysis. The results of the corresponding a posteriori computation of the relative error are presented in third column of Table 2. This also corresponds to the results of our tool Numerors on absolute error, without the reduced product. In the fourth column of Table 1, we give the results of Fluctuat in its affine arithmetic based relational mode. We do not report results in Table 2, as the error is only computed a posteriori, and does not bring much new information. Finally, Daisy and FPTaylor are state on the art references for the computation of relative error bounds, relying on optimisation techniques. Daisy provides many possible options, with different evaluation modes both for values and errors, that combine interval and affine arithmetic based estimates with SMT. We included a representative set, providing different trade-offs between efficiency and accuracy. Mode Daisy 1 is:

```
daisy --analysis=dataflow --rangeMethod=intervals --errorMethod=interval
```

Mode Daisy 2 is

```
daisy --analysis=opt --rangeMethod=smt --errorMethod=affine.
```

Finally, mode Daisy 3, which is dedicated to relative error (and provides to absolute error bound, hence is not included in Table 1), is:

```
daisy --analysis=relative --rel-rangeMethod=smtcomplete.
```

Our understanding is that Daisy 3 corresponds to [11]. Note that Daisy does not currently handle conditional statements, so that we give no estimate for these examples. We can specify conditionals as constraints to FPTaylor, however this is inconvenient for loops, so that we do not give any estimate for *log_approx*.

Results. Let us first comment the timings results presented in Table 3, that correspond, for each tool, to the sum of times spent for each of the examples that could be analyzed. Fluctuat, which is dedicated to error analysis, is the fastest, even in its affine mode: the examples here being all quite simple, affine forms scale well. While our abstract domain should theoretically be comparable to Fluctuat Intervals, it is here 10 times slower, partially due to the less specialization of the frama-C core on which we rely. Finally and most importantly, we want to stress that Numerors is drastically more efficient than Daisy in any of its modes or than FPTaylor, which rely on SMT or optimization. We compare ourselves to the results given by these tools, not because we aim at being more accurate, but in order to demonstrate that we manage to often come close, or even beat in precision these more costly approaches, while keeping very low analysis costs.

Table 3. Times comparison

Numerors	Fluctuat Intervals	Fluctuat Affine	Daisy 1	Daisy 2	Daisy 3	FPTaylor
0.271	0.059	0.049	4.220	652.062	16056.987	197.774

On each line, the result in boldface letters corresponds to the best estimate, the one in italic one corresponds to the second best one.

Numerors does not manage to bound the relative error on four examples: (*log_approx*, *test01_sum3*, *test03_nonlin2* and *test04_dqmom9*. The reason is that it finds that the range of the variable of interest includes zero for all these examples, and some addition and subtraction where involved with a result including zero. Daisy and FPTaylor also cannot bound the relative error on three of these examples, for the same reason. On the fourth (*test01_sum3*), Daisy and FPTaylor get finite bounds. This is because the actual range does not include zero, but a relational analysis is needed to infer this. Note that the reduced product would allow us to compute again relative error bounds on further computations (if they do not include zero in their result range). Finally, on example *intro_example*, which corresponds to Example 2, the range of the result also contains zero, and Numerors produces an error bound of 1 while Daisy and FPTaylor do not produce relative error bounds. This bound of 1 is valid for all non-zero values of the range, and corresponds to the maximum error bounds on denormalized numbers, as detailed in Example 4.

One obvious strength of our analysis concerns the interpretation of conditional statements. This is highlighted by the first three examples, where we are much better on absolute errors than FPTaylor, and comparable in relative error.

On the remaining benchmarks, our experiments often demonstrate that FPTaylor obtains the most accurate results, both in absolute and relative errors. However, for the absolute error, Numerors is still the best for 2 cases out of 25, and it is second best in more 10 cases. For the relative error, considering only the 23 examples for which at least one tool finds a finite bound, it is best on 4 examples, and sometimes even spectacularly so, and second best in 12 examples. Naturally, it is also always at least - and often considerably - better than Fluctuat in its interval mode. But it is also often better also than Fluctuat in its affine mode, when the loss of correlation due to intervals is not too important.

5   Conclusion and Future Work

We have demonstrated how a simple interval-based reduced product of absolute and relative error bounds greatly enhanced the absolute error bounds, at a very low additional cost. A possible additional interest of such analysis, is to further valorize these relative error bounds: indeed, some undesired phenomena of floating-point arithmetic, such as catastrophic cancellation, are best detected using relative error bounds.

Another possibility offered by this analysis is to refine error bounds by local subdivisions of the range of variables. Partitioning the range of some well chosen program variables is an approach used in most tools, that often allows them to considerably narrow value and error estimation. But this approach is costly, and it usually has to be performed globally on the program. We believe that relative error bounds can be used to enhance the quality of results using much cheaper local subdivisions, using an idea similar to the interpretation of conditional: the relative error bounds can be used to reduce the absolute error bounds, given some additional constraint on the value that corresponds to a local subdivision of the range. This refinement can be used to improve locally an error estimation, on demand. An additional advantage of the local compared to the global subdivision is that it can be realized on any quantity and not only on input variables.

Finally, a natural extension of this work, that we intend to investigate in the future, is its combination with relational abstractions such as affine forms.

A simple way to do this is to simply adapt the analysis presented here, using a relational abstraction to bound the values and errors. But we expect that more refined interactions would improve the strength of the analysis. Using a relational abstraction will also allow us to accurately compute discontinuity errors between branches, and thus handle possible control flow divergences.

Acknowledgments. The work was partially supported by ANR project ANR-15-CE25-0002. We also gratefully acknowledge the help of the anonymous reviewers and Jérôme Féret, in improving the presentation of this work.

References

1. Comba, J.L.D., Stolfi, J.: Affine arithmetic and its applications to computer graphics. In: SEBGRAPI 1993 (1993)
2. Cousot, P., Cousot, R.: Static determination of dynamic properties of programs. In: Proceedings of the Second International Symposium on Programming, pp. 106–130. Dunod, Paris (1976)
3. Cousot, P., Cousot, R.: Static determination of dynamic properties of programs. In: Proceedings of ISOP 1976, pp. 106–130. Dunod, Paris (1976)
4. Darulova, E., Kuncak, V.: Trustworthy numerical computation in Scala. In: OOPSLA (2011)
5. Darulova, E., Kuncak, V.: Sound compilation of reals. In: POPL 2014, pp. 235–248, New York, NY, USA. ACM (2014)
6. Daumas, M., Melquiond, G.: Certification of bounds on expressions involving rounded operators. ACM Trans. Math. Softw. **37**(1), 2:1–2:20 (2010)
7. Delmas, D., Goubault, E., Putot, S., Souyris, J., Tekkal, K., Védrine, F.: Towards an industrial use of FLUCTUAT on safety-critical avionics software. In: Alpuente, M., Cook, B., Joubert, C. (eds.) FMICS 2009. LNCS, vol. 5825, pp. 53–69. Springer, Heidelberg (2009). https://doi.org/10.1007/978-3-642-04570-7_6
8. Goubault, E.: Static analyses of the precision of floating-point operations. In: Cousot, P. (ed.) SAS 2001. LNCS, vol. 2126, pp. 234–259. Springer, Heidelberg (2001). https://doi.org/10.1007/3-540-47764-0_14
9. Goubault, E., Putot, S.: Static analysis of finite precision computations. In: Jhala, R., Schmidt, D. (eds.) VMCAI 2011. LNCS, vol. 6538, pp. 232–247. Springer, Heidelberg (2011). https://doi.org/10.1007/978-3-642-18275-4_17
10. Goubault, E., Putot, S.: Robustness analysis of finite precision implementations. In: APLAS, pp. 50–57 (2013)
11. Izycheva, A., Darulova, E.: On sound relative error bounds for floating-point arithmetic. In: Proceedings of the 17th Conference on Formal Methods in Computer-Aided Design, FMCAD 2017, pp. 15–22 (2017)
12. Magron, V., Constantinides, G., Donaldson, A.: Certified roundoff error bounds using semidefinite programming. Submitted
13. Moore, R.E., Kearfott, R.B., Cloud, M.J.: Introduction to Interval Analysis (2009)
14. Wilcox, J.-R., Panchekha, P., Sanchez-Stern, A., Tatlock, Z.: Automatically improving accuracy for floating point expressions. In: Grove, D., Blackburn, S. (eds.) PLDI 2015, pp. 1–11. ACM (2015)
15. Rump, S.M., Ogita, T., Oishi, S.: Accurate floating-point summation part i: faithful rounding. SIAM J. Sci. Comput. **31**(1), 189–224 (2008)

16. Solovyev, A., Jacobsen, C., Rakamarić, Z., Gopalakrishnan, G.: Rigorous estimation of floating-point round-off errors with symbolic taylor expansions. In: Bjørner, N., de Boer, F. (eds.) FM 2015. LNCS, vol. 9109, pp. 532–550. Springer, Cham (2015). https://doi.org/10.1007/978-3-319-19249-9_33

17. Titolo, L., Feliú, M.A., Moscato, M., Muñoz, C.A.: An abstract interpretation framework for the round-off error analysis of floating-point programs. Verification, Model Checking, and Abstract Interpretation. LNCS, vol. 10747, pp. 516–537. Springer, Cham (2018). https://doi.org/10.1007/978-3-319-73721-8_24

Modular Static Analysis of String Manipulations in C Programs

Matthieu Journault[✉], Antoine Miné, and Abdelraouf Ouadjaout

Sorbonne Université, CNRS, Laboratoire d'Informatique de Paris 6,
LIP6, 75005 Paris, France
{matthieu.journault,antoine.mine,abdelraouf.ouadjaout}@lip6.fr

Abstract. We present a modular analysis able to tackle out-of-bounds accesses in C strings. This analyzer is modular in the sense that it infers and tabulates (for reuse) input/output relations, automatically partitioned according to the shape of the input state. We show how the inter-procedural iterator discovers and generalizes contracts in order to improve their reusability for further analysis. This analyzer was implemented and was able to successfully analyze and infer relational contracts for functions such as strcpy, strcat.

1 Introduction

Abstract interpretation [9] enables the development of sound static analyzers that infer and prove invariants on the set of states reachable in a program. Consider for instance the strcpy function in C, shown in Program 1.1. This function is often called and may cause out-of-bounds errors. Therefore the implementation of

```
while (*q != '\0') {    1
    *p = *q;            2
    p ++;               3
    q ++;               4
};                      5
*p = *q;                6
```

Program 1.1. strcpy

a modular static analyzer able to infer and prove contracts on such functions without losing precision would yield a scalable analyzer able to prove the absence of buffer overruns in C projects manipulating strings.

In a C string, a '\0' character designates the end of the string. Henceforth the length of a string is defined to be the index of the first '\0' character appearing in the string. As emphasized in Program 1.1, the correctness of a string manipulating program (in the sense that it does not yield an out of memory access) depends upon the length and the allocated size of the buffer in which it is contained. Therefore in the fashion of [24] we summarize strings by two values: the position of the first '\0' character and the buffer size.

The fragment of C on which we want to perform modular analysis supports string manipulations, unions, structures, arrays, memory allocations (static and dynamic), pointer casts, function calls, ... Accordingly we need to build our analyzer, that manipulates predicates and can perform modular analysis, upon an existing analyzer able to deal with low level features of C.

This work is supported by the European Research Council under Consolidator Grant Agreement 681393 – MOPSA.

A. Podelski (Ed.): SAS 2018, LNCS 11002, pp. 243–262, 2018.
https://doi.org/10.1007/978-3-319-99725-4_16

An analyzer computing invariants by induction on the syntax of programs requires abstract transformers for function calls. A straightforward way to achieve this, provided that there is no recursivity, is to analyze the body of the function at each call site. Therefore a way to improve scalability is to design modular analyzers able to reuse previous analysis results so that reanalysis is not always needed (as emphasized in [11]). As an example, in a project containing an incrementation function, we want to be able to express and to infer that $\forall x, \mathtt{incr}(x) = x + 1$. Once this relation discovered, no further analysis of the body of $\mathtt{incr}$ is required. Abstract interpretation is always sound and inferred invariants describe an over-approximation of the reachable set of states. Therefore the use of input/output relations discovered on statements must yield an over-approximation. Nonetheless we do not want to give up too much precision to achieve scalability. This was done by using classical techniques to express input/output relations on numerical variables as performed in [11], partitioning these relations according to symbolic conditions in the abstract state as proposed by Bourdoncle [4], and generalizing them using widening operations.

By mixing the idea of representing a string as its length using a numeric abstraction and input/output relations, our analyzer is able to handle the $\mathtt{strcpy}$ example. More precisely, consider that $\mathtt{char*}$ $\mathtt{p}$ points to some $\mathtt{char[10]}$ $\mathtt{dest}$ string and $\mathtt{char*}$ $\mathtt{q}$ points to some $\mathtt{char[20]}$ $\mathtt{src}$ string with $\mathtt{dest} \neq \mathtt{src}$, furthermore let variables o_q, o_p denote the initial offset of $\mathtt{p}$ and $\mathtt{q}$, variable l_{src} codes for the length of $\mathtt{src}$, and variable a_{dest} denotes the size of the allocated memory of the string pointed to by $\mathtt{dest}$. Our analyzer is able to prove that if $l_{\mathrm{src}} < a_{\mathrm{src}}$ and $l_{\mathrm{src}} - o_q < a_{\mathrm{dest}} - o_p$ then no out of bounds access are performed. Moreover enabling modular analysis would yield that $l_{\mathrm{src}} = l'_{\mathrm{src}}$ and $l_{\mathrm{dest}} = l'_{\mathrm{src}}$ where primed variables (resp. unprimed variables) denote the state at the beginning (resp. at the end) of the analysis of the body of the function. Therefore these two relations state that the length of $\mathtt{src}$ was not modified by the call to $\mathtt{strcpy}$, while the length of $\mathtt{dest}$ is now that of $\mathtt{src}$.

Outline. Section 2 describes the subset of $\mathtt{C}$ we wish to analyze, Sect. 3 defines a low-level $\mathtt{C}$ abstraction upon which our analyzer is based, Sect. 4 details the String abstract domain, Sect. 5 outlines the lifting of our analyzer to a modular analysis, Sect. 6 contains a few remarks on the implementation of the analyzer. Finally Sect. 7 gives an overview of related works, while Sect. 8 concludes.

Contributions. The main contributions of this article are: (1) The development of a static analyzer able to reason on low level $\mathtt{C}$, while performing higher level abstractions (such as the String domain that will be presented thereafter) (2) The lifting of this analyzer to a precise modular framework based on numerical input/output relations [11], partitioning [4] and input generalizations.

2   Syntax and Concrete Semantics

Syntax. We will thereafter call $\mathtt{C--}$ the language defined in Fig. 1 and denote by $\mathcal{V}$ a set of variables. The description of Fig. 1 omits some classical statements but make precise some low-level features of the language. Note moreover that *int-types* are denoted by their signededness (**s** for signed integers, **u** for unsigned integers) and their length in bits, instead of char or unsigned long. This transformation is made before the analysis, and depends on the platform. Moreover, in order to simplify the presentation we will consider strings as arrays of **u8** (or **unsigned char**), results can be easily extended to arrays of **s8** (**char**).

$$int\text{-}type \quad \triangleq \textbf{s8} \mid \textbf{s16} \mid \textbf{s32} \mid \textbf{s64}$$
$$\mid \textbf{u8} \mid \textbf{u16} \mid \textbf{u32} \mid \textbf{u64}$$
$$scalar\text{-}type \triangleq int\text{-}type \mid \textbf{ptr}$$
$$type \quad \triangleq scalar\text{-}type$$
$$\mid type[n] \quad n \in \mathbb{N}$$
$$\mid \textbf{struct}\{u_0 : type, \dots, u_{n-1} : type\}$$
$$\mid \textbf{union}\{u_0 : type, \dots, u_{n-1} : type\}$$

$$lval \triangleq *_{scalar\text{-}type} expr \mid v \in \mathcal{V}$$
$$expr \triangleq cst \quad cst \in \mathbb{N}$$
$$\mid \&lval$$
$$\mid expr \diamond expr \quad \diamond \in \{+, \leq, \dots\}$$
$$stmt \triangleq v = \texttt{malloc}(e)$$
$$v \in \mathcal{V}, e \in expr$$
$$\mid type\ v \quad v \in \mathcal{V}$$
$$\mid \dots$$

Fig. 1. The syntax of the C-- subset of C.

Cells. Our C-like language features a rich type system. In a classic way, we will present the semantics of operations on scalar data-types: integers of various size and pointers, and reduce structured data-types, such as arrays, struct and unions, malloced blocks, to collections of scalar objects, we call *cells*. A simple solution would be to use the type of a structured variable and decompose it statically into such collections; left-values thus become access paths. Unfortunately, this static view does not hold for programs that abuse the type system and access some block of memory with various types, which is possible (and even common) in C using union types and pointer casts. One solution would be to model the memory as arrays of bytes or even bits, and synthesize non-byte access (for instance, reading a 16-bit integer a would be expressed as a[0]+256*a[1]), but such a complex modeling would put a great strain on numeric abstract domains and cause huge precision losses. We thus rely on previous work [18], that proposes to model memory blocks as collections of (possibly multi-byte) scalar cells, that are inferred and maintained dynamically during the analysis, according to the memory access pattern effectively employed by the program at run-time. For our purpose, we can assume that all memory accesses have the form $*_\tau e$, where τ is a scalar type and e is a pointer expression using pointer arithmetic at the byte level (this reduction can be performed statically as a pre-processing).

Remark 1. In addition to the definitions of Fig. 1, we assume that we are given a function $typeof \in (\mathcal{V} \rightarrow type)$. The type of a variable is given by its declaration in a C-- program. Moreover we assume given a *sizeof* function from *type* to $\mathbb{N}$ that gives the size in bytes of each type (e.g. $sizeof(\textbf{int}) = 4$).

A cell denotes an addressable group of bytes to store a scalar value, it is represented by a base variable (V), an integer coding for the offset of the cell

(o), and the type of the cell (t). Therefore we define the following set of cells: $Cell \triangleq \{\langle V, o, t\rangle \mid V \in \mathcal{V}, \ t \in scalar\text{-}type, \ 0 \leq o \leq sizeof(typeof(V)) - sizeof(t)\}$. By construction $Cell$ represents the set of all addressable memory locations. The abstract states we will build contain a subset of those cells. Cells might denote overlapping portions of the memory. In such cases the underlying state satisfies every constraint implied by a cell: cells are understood conjunctively. Therefore removing cells induces a loss of information. A key aspect of [18] we reuse is that new cells from $Cell$ are added to the current environment dynamically to account for the access patterns encountered during the analysis, in a flow-sensitive way. As we do not rely on static type information, which can be misleading in C, we can handle union types, type-punning, and untyped allocated blocks transparently.

Concrete semantic. We will not detail here the complete concrete semantic of the C-- language, however we give a definition of the set of concrete environments using cells, noted $\mathcal{E}$. An environment is a set of cells C and a function ρ mapping each cell to a value. A value can be either a numerical value or a pointer. A pointer is represented by: the base variable towards which it points and its offset. The set of pointer $\mathcal{P}tr$ is augmented with two special values: the **NULL** pointer and the **invalid** pointer : $\mathcal{P}tr \triangleq (\mathcal{V} \times \mathbb{Z}) \cup \{\mathbf{NULL}, \mathbf{invalid}\}$

$$\mathcal{E} \triangleq \bigcup_{C \subseteq Cell} \{\langle C, \rho\rangle \mid \rho \in R \triangleq C \to (\mathbb{N} \cup \mathcal{P}tr)\}$$

3   Cell Abstract Domain

Let us consider the Cell abstraction [18], an abstract domain able to abstract the semantic of C programs manipulating pointers. This abstract domain comes with an abstract interpreter that can successfully analyze C programs with no recursion and no dynamic memory allocation. The abstraction we propose here is built upon the cell abstract domain, it extends this domain so as to handle dynamic allocations and higher level string manipulations.

Pointers bases. When $C \subseteq Cell$ is a set of cells, we define $\overline{C}$ to be the set of cells denoting pointers : $\overline{C} \triangleq \{\langle V, o, t\rangle \in C \mid t = \mathbf{ptr}\}$. Upon this we define $\mathcal{P}_C = \overline{C} \to \wp(\mathcal{V} \cup \{\mathbf{NULL}, \mathbf{invalid}\})$. $\mathcal{P}_C$ represents the possible memory locations pointed to by cells representing pointers (note that $\mathcal{P}_C$ only accounts for the base variable that is pointed to and not for the offset).

Numerical domain. We assume that for any set of variables $\mathcal{V}$ we are given a numerical domain $N_{\mathcal{V}}^{\sharp}$ abstracting $\wp(\mathcal{V} \to \mathbb{N})$ with concretization function $\gamma_{\mathcal{V}} \in N_{\mathcal{V}}^{\sharp} \to \wp(\mathcal{V} \to \mathbb{N})$. For example we can use the polyhedra domain [15] or the interval domain [10]. These domains come with an environment change operator $\square_{|\mathcal{V}}$ such that: $\forall \mathcal{V}'$, if $S^{\sharp} \in N_{\mathcal{V}}^{\sharp}$, then $S^{\sharp}_{|\mathcal{V}} \in N_{\mathcal{V}}^{\sharp}$. $S^{\sharp}_{|\mathcal{V}}$ is obtained by removing all variables not in $\mathcal{V}$ and adding all variables in $\mathcal{V}$ but not in $\mathcal{V}'$ (with unconstrained value), so that the result is defined exactly over the variable set $\mathcal{V}$. Furthermore we assume given a function $\mathbf{range}(x, S^\sharp_\mathcal{V})$, yielding an interval of $\mathbb{N}$ containing all concrete values associated to variable x in $N^\sharp_\mathcal{V}$. For any subset $C \subseteq \mathcal{C}ell$ we can therefore rely on a numerical abstraction $N^\sharp_C$ abstracting $\wp(C \to \mathbb{N})$. We give the numerical domain of our abstraction a double role:

- For a cell containing a pointer, the variable (from the numerical domain) assigned to this cell codes for possible offsets of the pointer (thus paired with information from $\mathcal{P}_C$ we will describe completely the pointer contained in the cell)
- For other cells (containing e.g. a **u8**, a **s32**) the variable (from the numerical domain) codes for values contained in the cell.

Abstract states. We define the domain $\mathcal{D}^\sharp_m$ with concretization $\gamma_m \in \mathcal{D}^\sharp_m \to \mathcal{E}$ as:

$$\mathcal{D}^\sharp_m \triangleq \{\langle C, R^\sharp, P\rangle \mid C \subseteq \mathcal{C}ell,\ R^\sharp \in N^\sharp_C,\ P \in \mathcal{P}_C\}$$

$$\gamma_m \langle C, R^\sharp, P\rangle \triangleq \langle C, \{\rho' \in R, \exists \rho \in \gamma_C(R^\sharp),\ \forall c = \langle V, o, t\rangle \in C,$$
$$\begin{cases} \rho'(c) = \rho(c) & \text{if } t \neq \mathbf{ptr} \\ \rho'(c) = \langle p, \rho(c)\rangle & \text{if } t = \mathbf{ptr} \wedge p \in P(c) \cap \mathcal{V} \\ \rho'(c) = p & \text{if } t = \mathbf{ptr} \wedge p \in P(c) \setminus \mathcal{V} \end{cases} \}\rangle$$

Example 1. Consider the abstract state: $S^\sharp = \langle\{\langle \mathsf{a}, 0, \mathbf{u64}\rangle\}, \{\langle \mathsf{a}, 0, \mathbf{u64}\rangle = 2^{32} + 2\}, \emptyset\rangle$. Moreover we assume that due to some cast operations, cells $\{\langle \mathsf{a}, 0, \mathbf{u32}\rangle\}$ and $\{\langle \mathsf{a}, 4, \mathbf{u32}\rangle\}$ are needed (imagine for example the encoding in little-endian of a pair of **u32** as a **u64**). $S^\sharp$ is equivalent to: $\langle\{\langle \mathsf{a}, 0, \mathbf{u64}\rangle, \langle \mathsf{a}, 0, \mathbf{u32}\rangle, \langle \mathsf{a}, 4, \mathbf{u32}\rangle\}, \{\langle \mathsf{a}, 0, \mathbf{u64}\rangle = 2^{32} + 2, \langle \mathsf{a}, 0, \mathbf{u32}\rangle = 2\ (= (2^{32} + 2) \mod 2^{32})), \langle \mathsf{a}, 4, \mathbf{u32}\rangle = 1\ (= (2^{32} + 2)\ /2^{32})\}, \emptyset\rangle$.

Abstract operators and abstract transformers. Abstract operators (join, meet, widening) are defined by first unifying the operands, and then performing the operation in the underlying unified numerical domain and pointer map. The unification operator transforms two abstract elements into abstract

```
int a = 1;        1
int p = &a;       2
*p = *p + 1;      3
```

Program 1.2. Dereferencing

elements with the same set of cells. This is done by adding cells in both elements so that the resulting set of cells in both elements is the union of the initial sets of cells. We do not give here the definition of all the abstract transformers operating on our abstract states, however the following example emphasizes how an abstract state is modified by expressions and statements of the C language. In particular, we note that when cells are available, most expressions are treated as expressions on a language where cells are the variables. When cells mentioned in the expressions are not available, they are added to the set of cells of the abstract state, by collecting information available in the overlapping cells, such as joining two byte-cells to synthesize the initial value of a new **u16**-cell at the same position.

Example 2. Consider Program 1.2, starting from $\top = \langle \emptyset, \emptyset, \emptyset \rangle$. The first statement requires the existence of the cell $\mathbf{a} = \langle \mathbf{a}, 0, \mathbf{s32} \rangle$. The set of cells constrained by our abstract state is dynamically updated to mention $\mathbf{a}$, yielding: $\langle \{\mathbf{a}\}, \emptyset, \emptyset \rangle$, then we rewrite the statement in the following manner: $\mathbf{a} = 1$. We execute this statement in the underlying numerical domain, and get: $\langle \{\mathbf{a}\}, \{\mathbf{a} = 1\}, \emptyset \rangle$. The second statement adds a new cell $\mathbf{p} = \langle \mathbf{p}, 0, \mathbf{ptr} \rangle$ and an element to the pointer map: $\langle \{\mathbf{a}, \mathbf{p}\}, \{\mathbf{a} = 1, \mathbf{p} = 0\}, \{\mathbf{p} \mapsto \{\mathbf{a}\}\} \rangle$. Note that $\mathbf{p} = 0$ codes for the value of the offset of pointer $\mathbf{p}$. Finally the expression $*\mathbf{p}$ of the third statement is evaluated by following the P component of the abstract state, therefore the statement is transformed into $\mathbf{a} = \mathbf{a} + 1$. Thus yielding: $\langle \{\mathbf{a}, \mathbf{p}\}, \{\mathbf{a} = 2, \mathbf{p} = 0\}, \{\mathbf{p} \mapsto \{\mathbf{a}\}\} \rangle$. Henceforth, in order to clarify the presentation, $\mathbf{a}$ denotes $\langle a, 0, \tau \rangle$ when τ is the declared type of variable $\mathbf{a}$.

4   String Abstract Domain

4.1   Domain Definition

The introductory example shows that describing a string by a set of cells (one cell per character of the string) was usually not necessary to prove the absence of buffer overrun in string manipulations. Therefore we propose to add to our existing low-level abstraction of C--, an abstraction of strings that sums up all of its characters into two variables, one coding for the length of the string and the other for the allocated size of the buffer in which it is contained. Memory blocks will therefore be abstracted either by the cell abstract domain or by the string abstract domain. In order to simplify the presentation we assume given a set of memory locations $\mathfrak{V}$ for which we will use a string summary, however this set can be dynamically modified and reductions could be proposed in order to store information on some memory locations in both the String domain and the Cell domain. We assume that for each memory location $s \in \mathfrak{V}$, we are given two variables denoted s_l and s_a. Those variables code for the length and the allocated size of the string, they will be added to the numerical domain of the cell abstract domain so that we are able to describe relations between length of variables and offsets of pointers. In the following $\mathfrak{V}^\star$ denotes $\bigcup_{s \in \mathfrak{V}} \{s_a, s_l\}$, this is the set of all numerical variables needed to describe strings in $\mathfrak{V}$.

Definition of the String abstract domain. We define the String abstract domain to be: $\mathcal{S}_m^\sharp \triangleq \{\langle C, R^\sharp, P \rangle \mid C \subseteq \mathcal{C}ell \setminus \{\langle V, \_, \_ \rangle \mid V \in \mathfrak{V}\}, R^\sharp \in N_{C \cup \mathfrak{V}^\star}^\sharp, P \in \mathcal{P}_C\}$. This abstract domain is ordered by the same relation as the cell abstract domain: $\sqsubseteq_{\mathcal{S}_m^\sharp} \triangleq \sqsubseteq_{D_m^\sharp}$. We recall that $\sqsubseteq_{\mathcal{D}_m}$ will test the inclusion of the two numerical domains once cell sets have been unified, therefore our definition of $S^\sharp \sqsubseteq_{\mathcal{S}_m^\sharp} S^{\sharp\prime}$ amounts to verifying that the constraints on the string variables (s_l and s_a) are stronger in the left member of the inequality.

Galois connection with the Cell abstract domain. The String abstract domain is an abstraction of the Cell abstract domain. Indeed we forget information that do not help us track the position of the first '\0' character. We define the Galois connection between the Cell domain and the String domain using two functions : **to_cell** and **from_cell**. The **to_cell**$(s, S^\sharp)$ function computes the range of s_l in the numeric abstract domain, for each possible length value we set the cells placed before (resp. at) the length to $[1; 255]$ (resp. 0), this yields an abstract element per possible value in the range, those are then joined. Conversely **from_cell**$(s, S^\sharp)$ computes the minimum length value (the index of the first cell whose range contains 0), and the maximum length value (the index of the first cell whose range is exactly $\{0\}$), finally those constraints are added to the numerical domain. If a string does not contain any '\0' character, we define its length to be the allocated size of the buffer it is contained in. Both functions can be found in Appendix A.1. With $\mathfrak{V} = \{s_0, \ldots, s_{n-1}\}$, we can define:

$$\gamma_{S_m^\sharp, D_m^\sharp}(S^\sharp) = \mathbf{to\_cell}(s_0, \ldots, (\mathbf{to\_cell}(s_{n-1}, S^\sharp)) \ldots)$$

$$\alpha_{S_m^\sharp, D_m^\sharp}(S^\sharp) = \mathbf{from\_cell}(s_0, \ldots, (\mathbf{from\_cell}(s_{n-1}, S^\sharp)) \ldots)$$

Example 3. Consider the string abstract elements $\langle \emptyset, \{s_l = 2, s_a = 4\}, \emptyset \rangle$ when $sizeof(type(s)) = 4$. We have: $\gamma_{S_m^\sharp, D_m^\sharp} = \langle \{\langle s, 0, \mathbf{u8}\rangle, \langle s, 1, \mathbf{u8}\rangle, \langle s, 2, \mathbf{u8}\rangle\},$ $\{\langle s, 2, \mathbf{u8}\rangle = 0, \langle s, 0, \mathbf{u8}\rangle \neq 0, \langle s, 1, \mathbf{u8}\rangle \neq 0\}, \emptyset\rangle$. The corresponding concrete state is the set of states in which there is a memory location where the first two bytes are non zero bytes, the third byte is set to zero and the fourth byte is unconstrained.

Remark 2. The interest of the definition of $\gamma_{S_m^\sharp, D_m^\sharp}$ and $\alpha_{S_m^\sharp, D_m^\sharp}$ is twofold: it enables us to define the semantic of the String abstract domain, but we also note that both functions **to_cell** and **from_cell** are computable. Therefore the set of memory locations dealt with by each domain can easily evolve during the analysis. Moreover with $\gamma_{S_m^\sharp, D_m^\sharp}$ and $\alpha_{S_m^\sharp, D_m^\sharp}$ being both computable, we can define a reduction operator between the String abstract domain and the Cell abstract domain. For efficiency reasons we can remove some information from the Cell domain, knowing that information from the String domain can be brought back to the Cell domain. This situation is similar to a reduction between octagons and the, strictly less expressive, interval domain as proposed in [12].

4.2   Operators and Transformers

Operators. As for the definition of the $\sqsubseteq_{S_m^\sharp}$ operator, the join $(\sqcup_{S_m^\sharp})$, meet $(\sqcap_{S_m^\sharp})$ and widening $(\nabla_{S_m^\sharp})$ of two abstract elements is defined by applying the according operator in the underlying numerical abstract domain (after the addition on both sides of potentially missing variables and the unification of the set of cells).

Example 4. Consider Program 1.1 of the introductory example where $typeof(\mathbf{p}) = typeof(\mathbf{q}) = \mathbf{u8*}$, if $S_1^\sharp = \langle\{\mathbf{p}, \mathbf{q}\}, \{\mathbf{p} = 0, \mathbf{q} = 0, src_l \geq 0, src_a \geq src_l, dest_l \geq 0, dest_a \geq dest_l\}, \{\mathbf{p} \mapsto \{dest\}, \mathbf{q} \mapsto \{src\}\}\rangle$ is the abstract state from which we start the analysis then $S_2^\sharp = \langle\{\mathbf{p}, \mathbf{q}\}, \{\mathbf{p} = 1, \mathbf{q} = 1, src_l \geq 1, src_a \geq dest_l, dest_l \geq 1, dest_a \geq dest_l\}, \{\mathbf{p} \mapsto \{dest\},$

$q \mapsto \{\texttt{src}\}\}\rangle$ is the abstract state after one analysis of the body of the $\texttt{while}$ loop (constraint $\texttt{src}_a \geq \texttt{dest}_l$ comes from the fact that we collect error free executions). Therefore our analyzer has to perform the join of those two abstract states before reanalyzing the body of the loop. $S_1^\sharp \sqcup_{S_m^\sharp} S_2^\sharp = \langle\{\mathbf{p}, \mathbf{q}\}, \{\mathbf{p} = \mathbf{q}, \mathbf{p} \leq 1, \mathbf{p} \geq 0, \mathbf{p} \leq \texttt{dest}_l, \texttt{dest}_a \geq \texttt{dest}_l, \mathbf{p} \leq \texttt{src}_l, \mathbf{p} \leq \texttt{src}_a\}, \{\mathbf{p} \mapsto \{\texttt{dest}\}, \mathbf{q} \mapsto \{\texttt{src}\}\}\rangle$.

The state transformations induced on our abstract state by the semantic of the C language is mainly dealt with by the Cell abstraction. In order to ease the presentation of the relation between the Cell abstraction and the String abstraction, we add expressions of the form $@[v, e]$ with $e \in expr$ and $v \in \mathcal{V}$ to the C-- language. Such expressions denote pointers to variable v, with offset e: $((\texttt{char} \ *) \ \&v) + e$.

Example 5. We want to perform the analysis of the statement

$$\texttt{stmt} = *_{\mathbf{u8}}\texttt{t} = *_{\mathbf{u8}}(\texttt{p} + *_{\mathbf{s32}}(\&\texttt{u} + 2))$$

(where $typeof(p) = typeof(t) = \mathbf{u8}*$) in the following abstract state: $S^\sharp = \langle\{\mathbf{p}, \langle \mathbf{u}, 2, \mathbf{s32}\rangle, \mathbf{t}\}, R^\sharp, \{\mathbf{p} \mapsto s', \mathbf{t} \mapsto s\}\rangle$ where $R^\sharp$ is a numerical abstract state built from the set of constraints we do not need to explicit for this example.

The Cell abstraction rewrites $\texttt{stmt}$ into: $*_{\mathbf{u8}}@[s, \mathbf{t}] = *_{\mathbf{u8}}(@[s', \mathbf{p} + \langle \mathbf{u}, 2, \mathbf{s32}\rangle])$. The operations that remain to be defined are therefore:

$\mathbb{S}^\sharp[\![*_\tau@[s, e_1] = e_2]\!](S^\sharp)$ where $s \in \mathfrak{V}, e_1 \in expr, e_2 \in expr, \tau \in scalar\text{-}type$
$\mathbb{E}^\sharp[\![*_\tau@[s, e]]\!](S^\sharp)$ where $s \in \mathfrak{V}, e \in expr, \tau \in scalar\text{-}type$

Abstract evaluation. Let us first consider the evaluation of the dereferencing of a pointer to a string. The analyzer we want to define performs partitioning on the abstract state during the evaluation of expressions, therefore evaluation results are pairs (evaluated expression × abstract state). This set is understood disjunctively and greatly improves the precision of the analyzer. The result of an evaluation is therefore a finite element of $\wp(exp \times S_m^\sharp)$. Five cases can be distinguished during the evaluation of $*_\tau@[s, e]$:

- **before:** $\tau = \mathbf{u8}$ and $@[s, e]$ points before the first '$\backslash 0$' character. In this case the evaluation can yield any character that is not '$\backslash 0$'.
- **at:** $\tau = \mathbf{u8}$ and $@[s, e]$ points at the first '$\backslash 0$' character. In this case the evaluation yields '$\backslash 0$'.
- **after:** $\tau = \mathbf{u8}$ and $@[s, e]$ points after the first '$\backslash 0$' character. In this case the evaluation can yield any character.
- **eerror:** $\tau = \mathbf{u8}$ and $@[s, e]$ points after the end of the allocated memory. In such a case we generate an **out_of_bounds** error.
- $\tau \neq \mathbf{u8}$, in this case we over-approximate the evaluation by the range of the type τ.

$$\textbf{before}(e, s, S^\sharp) =$$
$$\{([1; 255],$$
$$\langle C, R^\sharp \sqcap \{0 \le e, e < s_l, e < s_a\}, P\rangle\}$$

function	tests on offset	evaluation
before	$0 \le o \wedge o < l \wedge o < a$	$[1; 255]$
at	$0 \le o \wedge o = l \wedge o < a$	0
after	$0 \le o \wedge o > l \wedge o < a$	$[0; 255]$
eerror	$o > a \vee o < 0$	$\emptyset$

Fig. 2. Evaluation of a dereferencing.

Figure 2 summarizes those cases and gives the example of the **before** function. In this table o is the offset of the pointer, l and a are the length and the allocated size of the string. The definition of these functions can be found in Appendix A.2. We can now define $\mathbb{E}^\sharp[\![*_{\tau=\textbf{u8}}@[s,e]]\!](S^\sharp) = \bigcup\{\textbf{before}(e', s, S^\sharp) \cup \textbf{at}(e', s, S^\sharp) \cup \textbf{after}(e', s, S^\sharp) \cup \textbf{eerror}(e', s, S^\sharp) \mid (e', S^\sharp) \in \mathbb{E}^\sharp[\![e]\!](S^\sharp)\}$ and $\mathbb{E}^\sharp[\![*_{\tau\ne\textbf{u8}}@[s,e]]\!](S^\sharp) = \{(range(\tau), S^\sharp)\}$.

Abstract transformations. In order to complete the definition of our abstract interpreter, we need to provide the abstract semantic of an assignment in a string $*_\tau@[s,e_1] = e_2$. We can distinguish 6 cases in such an assignment:

- **set0:** $\tau = \textbf{u8}$ and a character that appears before the first '\0' is assigned to '\0', in which case we need to set the variable coding for the length of the string to its new value (the offset of the pointer to the string).
- **setnon0:** $\tau = \textbf{u8}$ and the first '\0' is replaced with a non-'\0' character, in which case we need to set the variable coding for the length of the string to its new value (it can be anything greater than the offset of the pointer to the string).
- **unchanged:** $\tau = \textbf{u8}$ and we are performing an assignment that does not change the position of the first '\0' character.
  Either because we are replacing a character placed before the first '\0' character by a non-'\0' character,
  or because we are assigning a character after the position of the first '\0' character.
- **l_unchanged:** $\tau \ne \textbf{u8}$ and we are performing an assignment that does not change the position of the first '\0' character: the only modified characters are placed after the first '\0' character.
- **forget:** $\tau \ne \textbf{u8}$ and the offset of the pointer is less than the length of the string, in this case the position of the first '\0' character is greater than the offset of the pointer.
- **serror:** The writing generates an out of bounds, in which cases we generate an **out_of_bounds** warning.

Figure 3 summarizes these cases. In this table l and a denote respectively the length and the allocated size of string s, o denotes the offset of the pointer, c denotes the evaluated right-hand side of the assignment, and finally r denotes $sizeof(\tau)$. The definitions of all these functions can be found in Appendix A.3 and

function	tests on offsets	tests on rhs	transformation
set0	$o \geq 0 \wedge o \leq l \wedge o < a$	$c = 0$	$l \leftarrow o$
setnon0	$o \geq 0 \wedge o = l \wedge o < a$	$c \neq 0$	$l \leftarrow [o+1;a]$
unchanged	$o \geq 0 \wedge o < l \wedge o < a$	$c \neq 0$	
unchanged	$o \geq 0 \wedge o > l \wedge o < a$	$\top$	
l_unchanged	$o \geq 0 \wedge o > l \wedge o + r \leq a$	$\top$	
forget	$o \geq 0 \wedge o \leq l \wedge o + r \leq a$	$\top$	$l \leftarrow [o;a]$
serror	$o + r > a \vee o < 0$	$\top$	out_of_bounds

Fig. 3. Summary of transformations.

they are similar to the definition of **before** in Fig. 2. Using the 6 transformations aforementioned we can now define:

$$S^\sharp [\![*_\tau @ [s \in \mathfrak{V}, e_1] = e_2]\!] (S^\sharp) =$$

- $\bigsqcup \{ \mathbf{set0}(s, e_1', e_2', S^{\sharp\prime\prime}) \sqcup \mathbf{serror}(s, e_1', 1, S^{\sharp\prime\prime}) \sqcup \mathbf{unchanged}(s, e_1', e_2', S^{\sharp\prime\prime})$

  $\sqcup \mathbf{setnon0}(s, e_1', e_2', S^{\sharp\prime\prime}) \mid (e_1', S^{\sharp\prime}) \in \mathbb{E}^\sharp [\![e_1]\!] (S^\sharp), (e_2', S^{\sharp\prime\prime}) \in \mathbb{E}^\sharp [\![e_2]\!] (S^{\sharp\prime}) \}$

  if $\tau = \mathbf{u8}$

- $\bigsqcup \{ \mathbf{l\_unchanged}(s, e_1', \textit{sizeof}(\tau), S^{\sharp\prime}) \sqcup \mathbf{forget}(s, e_1', \textit{sizeof}(\tau), S^{\sharp\prime}) \sqcup$

  $\mathbf{serror}(s, e_1', \textit{sizeof}(\tau), S^{\sharp\prime}) \mid (e_1', S^{\sharp\prime}) \in \mathbb{E}^\sharp [\![e_1]\!] (S^\sharp) \}$ if $\tau \neq \mathbf{u8}$

Example 6. Going back to Example 5, we now assume that $R^\sharp$ is a numerical abstract state built from the constraint set: $\{ \mathbf{t} < s_a, \mathbf{t} = s_l, \mathbf{p} + \langle \mathbf{u}, 2, \mathbf{s32} \rangle < s_l', s_l' < s_a' \}$. Moreover in the following $S^\sharp[E]$ denotes the abstract state $S^\sharp$ in which the numerical component has been extended with the constraints set E, and e denotes the expression $\mathbf{p} + \langle \mathbf{u}, 2, \mathbf{s32} \rangle$. $\mathbb{E}^\sharp [\![*(@[s', e])]\!] (S^\sharp) = \{ ([1; 255], S^\sharp [\{ e \geq 0, e < s_l', e < s_a' \}]), (0, S^\sharp [\{ e \geq 0, e = s_l', e < s_a' \}]), ([0; 255], S^\sharp [\{ e \geq 0, e > s_l', e < s_a' \}]) \}$. With a precise enough numerical domain (e.g. polyhedra), $S^\sharp [\{ e \geq 0, e = s_l', e < s_a' \}]$, $S^\sharp [\{ e \geq 0, e > s_l', e < s_a' \}]$ and $S^\sharp [\{ e < 0 \vee e \geq s_a' \}]$ form empty partitions, meaning that in this example, they represent impossible cases. For similar reasons $S^\sharp [\![\mathbf{stmt}]\!] (S^\sharp)$ will compute abstract elements that are reduced to $\bot$ for functions **set0, unchanged** and **serror**. Therefore: $S^\sharp [\![\mathbf{stmt}]\!] (S^\sharp) = \langle \{ \mathbf{p}, \langle \mathbf{u}, 2, \mathbf{s32} \rangle, \mathbf{t} \}, R^{\sharp\prime}, \{ \mathbf{p} \mapsto s', \mathbf{t} \mapsto s \} \rangle$ with $R^{\sharp\prime} = \{ \mathbf{t} < s_a, \mathbf{t} + 1 \leq s_l, \mathbf{p} + \langle \mathbf{u}, 2, \mathbf{s32} \rangle < s_l', s_l' < s_a' \}$. This assignment made our abstraction lose the position of the first '\0' character, as it wrote a non-'\0' character in its place.

String declaration. When encountering a local variable declaration ($\mathbf{u8}$ $\mathbf{s}[n]$ with $n \in \mathbb{N}_{\geq 0}$ and $\mathbf{s} \in \mathfrak{V}$) we can set the allocated size of the string to n, and set the length to the range $[0, n]$ as shown in the following example: $S^\sharp [\![\mathbf{u8} \ \mathbf{s} [27]]\!] (\langle \emptyset, \emptyset, \emptyset \rangle) = \langle \emptyset, \{ s_l \geq 0, s_l \leq 27, s_a = 27 \}, \emptyset \rangle$. The formal definition is straightforward (see Appendix A.4).

Example 7. Consider again Program 1.1 from the introductory example, analyzed starting from an abstract state $S^\sharp = \langle \{\mathbf{p}, \mathbf{q}\}, \{\mathbf{p} = 0, \mathbf{q} = 0, 0 \leq s_l < s_a, 0 \leq s'_l < s'_a\}, \{\mathbf{p} \mapsto s, \mathbf{q} \mapsto s'\}\rangle$. Note that the input state contains the information that $\mathbf{p}$ and $\mathbf{q}$ do not alias. The numerical invariant (the rest of the abstract state is not modified by the analysis) found at the beginning of line 2 is: $\{-\mathbf{p} + \mathbf{q} = 0, s'_l \geq \mathbf{p} + 1, s'_a - s'_l \geq 0, \mathbf{p} \geq 0, s_l \geq \mathbf{p}\}$. An **out_of_bounds** error is generated at line 3, indeed in the starting abstract state, no hypothesis is made on the relation between s'_l and s_a therefore there might be a buffer overrun at line 3. Finally the numerical invariant discovered at the end of line 6 is: $\{s'_l = s_l, \mathbf{q} = s_l, \mathbf{p} = s_l, s'_a \geq s_l + 1, s_l \geq 0, s_a \geq s_l + 1\}$, thus showing that we were able to infer that the two strings pointed to by $\mathbf{p}$ and $\mathbf{q}$ have the same size at the end of the analysis.

Dynamic memory allocation. As mentioned in Fig. 1, we allow dynamic memory allocations. The Cell abstract domain as presented in Sect. 3 is not able to handle those. To model dynamic memory allocation, we consider a finite set $\mathcal{A}$ of heap addresses, derived from the allocation site using recency abstraction [2]: for each allocation site $\mathfrak{a}$, one abstract address, $\mathfrak{a}^s$, is used to model the last block allocated at $\mathfrak{a}$, and another one, $\mathfrak{a}^w$, to summarize the blocks allocated previously at $\mathfrak{a}$.

```
void aux1(char** x,int e) {    1
  ●¹*x = malloc(e);            2
}                              3
void aux2(char** x,int e) {    4
  ●²*x = malloc(e);            5
}                              6
int main() {                   7
  char* x;                     8
  aux1(&x,10); aux1(&x,20);    9
  aux1(&x,30); aux2(&x,40);   10
  *x = '\0';                  11
}                             12
```

Program   1.3.   Dynamic memory allocation

While we perform weak updates on the later, we can perform strong updates on the former, which ensures a gain in precision.

Example 8. Consider now Program 1.3, and assume that $\mathfrak{a}^s$ and $\mathfrak{a}^w$ (resp. $\mathfrak{b}^s$ and $\mathfrak{b}^w$) are addresses for which we perform strong and weak update at program point $●^1$ (resp. $●^2$). Starting from $\top$ the analysis of the body of function `main`, we get: $\langle \{\mathbf{x}\}, \{0 \leq \mathfrak{a}^w_l \leq \mathfrak{a}^w_a, 10 \leq \mathfrak{a}^w_a \leq 20, 0 \leq \mathfrak{a}^s_l \leq \mathfrak{a}^s_a, \mathfrak{a}^s_a = 30, \mathfrak{b}^s_a = 40, \mathfrak{b}^s_l = 0, \mathbf{x} = 0\}, \{\mathbf{x} \mapsto \mathfrak{b}^s\}\rangle$ This state gives us that $\mathbf{x}$ points to a memory location starting from a '\0' character. We also note that information about the two first allocations made at program point $\mathfrak{a}$ have been collapsed into the $\mathfrak{a}^w$ address.

5   Modular Analysis

In a C project that manipulates strings, calls to functions such as `strcpy`, `strcat` are performed many times and at many different call sites. Performing a modular analysis of such functions and inferring a summary that is reusable at subsequent calls has poten-

```
void strcat(char* dest, char* src)  1
{                                    2
  int i; int j;                      3
  for (i=0; dest[i]!='\0';i++) ;     4
  for (j=0; src[j]!='\0';j++)        5
    dest[i+j] = src[j];              6
  dest[i+j] = '\0';                  7
}                                    8
```

Program 1.4. strcat

tial to greatly improve scalability. We chose to perform our modular analysis in a classic top-down fashion. This ensures that when a function is analyzed, we already have some information on its context (in particular, the possible pointer aliasing and variable range), which helps maintaining the precision of the function analysis. Therefore we would like to be able to infer a partial function that, given an input abstract state and a statement, can produce an output abstract state that is an over approximation of the abstract state we would have obtained by performing the analysis of the statement. Such a function will be called a *summary*. Note that substituting some of the statement analysis by a call to a summary is sound.

Example 9. Given $\mathtt{stmt} \in stmt$, $(I^\sharp, O^\sharp) \in (\mathcal{S}_m^\sharp \times \mathcal{S}_m^\sharp)$ such that $\mathbb{S}^\sharp[\![\mathtt{stmt}]\!](I^\sharp) \sqsubseteq O^\sharp$, let us define $\mathbf{R}^\sharp = \lambda(\mathtt{stmt}', S^\sharp), \text{if } \mathtt{stmt}' = \mathtt{stmt} \wedge S^\sharp \sqsubseteq I^\sharp \text{ then } O^\sharp \text{ else } \mathtt{undefined}$. $\mathbf{R}^\sharp$ is a summary function, built using an input/output relation. This can be easily generalized using a set of input/output relations. Moreover we can remove constraints on $I^\sharp$ before the analysis of the body of the function in order to improve the reusability of the input/output relation obtained, the drawback being that the corresponding output abstract value will be greater thus losing precision. Furthermore computing and storing new $(I^\sharp, O^\sharp)$ relations whenever no existing summary could be used can cause the computation of input/output relations that will never be reused, hence the importance of generalizing $I^\sharp$ in the direction of newly discovered call contexts, so as to tailor summaries to actual call sites abstract values.

Remark 3. Consider the statement $\mathtt{stmt} = \mathtt{x} = \mathtt{x} + \mathtt{1}$, and assume our abstract domain to be the interval domain [6]. For every input state of the form $\{x \mapsto [\alpha, \beta]\}$, the output state will be of the form $\{x \mapsto [\alpha + 1, \beta + 1]\}$. A summary function $\mathbf{R}^\sharp$ defined on $\{\mathtt{stmt}\} \times \mathcal{S}_m^\sharp$ in the manner of Example 9 (with a finite list of input/output relations) will never yield an analyzer able to express that for every input $[\gamma, \delta]$ the output is $[\gamma+1, \delta+1]$. Indeed the interval domain would produce a set of input/output relations $\{[\alpha_i, \beta_i] \mapsto [\alpha_i + 1, \beta_i + 1]\}$, and for an input $[\gamma, \delta] \subsetneq [\alpha_0, \beta_0]$ we could only use as output abstract state $[\alpha_0 + 1, \beta_0 + 1]$, thus losing information compared to $[\gamma + 1, \delta + 1]$.

Using relational domains. Relational domains are able to express relations of the form $y = x+1$. Such a relation can grasp the semantic of $\mathtt{stmt}$ from the previous remark. We use the relational aspect of the numerical domain to express relations not only between the values of variables, but also between their values and their input values. This idea was introduced in [7] and is also used in [11]. Consider two sets of variables $\mathcal{V} = \{x, y\}$ and $\mathcal{V}' = \{x', y'\}$ and the abstract element: $S^\sharp = \{x = y', y = x'\}$. Moreover assume at input that $\{x = 3, y = 5\}$, then using the meet provided by the numerical domain in order to instantiate $S^\sharp$ with input constraints: $\{x = 3, y = 5\}_{|\{x',y',\ x,y\}} \sqcap \{x = y', y = x'\} = \{x = 3, y = 5, x' = 5, y' = 3\}$, and finally $\{x = 3, y = 5, x' = 5, y' = 3\}_{|\{x,y\}} = \{x' = 5, y' = 3\}$. This example emphasized how relational domains are used to express precise input/output relations between numerical variables.

Building the summary function. We feel that two analyses starting from different aliasing patterns should be kept separated in order to improve precision.

Indeed, analyzing strcat(p,q) (see Program 1.4) without any hypothesis on the possible aliasing of p and q would result in a huge loss of precision and in false alarms being raised at every call (p and q might be aliased, which would raise a segmentation fault). Therefore we must use partitioning of the abstract domain, performing an analysis for every possible aliasing scheme would result in a combinatorial blow up, moreover we might perform analysis for partitions that will never occur at any call site. For these reasons we will only analyze partitions on demand. Our goal is therefore to build a summary that is a set of numerical relations such as defined above. The decision to extend a partition or to build a new one will be based on the "symbolic" part of the abstract domain. The heuristic we chose was to separate abstract states with different aliasing, but also those where the unification of the cell or string sets would induce major differences in the numerical domain set. Moreover the summary function is extended on demand, meaning that when the analyzer encounters a function call, it tries to use an existing relation and if none can be found it builds a new relation or it generalizes an existing one. Generalization of a relation is done in the following way: assume known a relation with input $I^\sharp$ and an abstract state $S^\sharp$, such that $S^\sharp \not\sqsubseteq I^\sharp$. If the analyzer deems that $S^\sharp$ and $I^\sharp$ should be in the same relation (e.g. because they have the same aliasing), we perform a new analysis of the function starting from $I^\sharp \triangledown (S^\sharp \sqcup I^\sharp)$, that is a generalization, of $I^\sharp$, by the mean of the widening operator. This ensures that, given an aliasing, a function will be analyzed only a finite number of times and that the input of the obtained relation is tailored to the actual values at call site. Building numerical relations does not require a transformation of the intra-procedural iterator. Indeed variables are added to the numerical domain with equality constraints between primed and unprimed variables. Analysis is then performed as if primed variables were not present in the numerical domain and they are removed after storing the summary.

Example 10. Consider the statement s32 x = a + 1 (with *typeof*(a) = s32), from input state: $\langle\{a'\}, \{a' = a, a \geq 0\}, \emptyset\rangle$. The output state is then $\langle\{a', x'\}, \{a' = a, x' = a + 1, a \geq 0\}, \emptyset\rangle$. From this we deduce the relation: let $I_\alpha^\sharp$ be some input state, if the set of cells of $I_\alpha^\sharp$ is precisely $\{a\}$ and if the numerical domain of $I_\alpha^\sharp$ satisfies the condition $a = \alpha$ and if the pointer map is empty, then the best possible output state is $\langle\{a, x\}, \{a = \alpha, x = \alpha + 1\}, \emptyset\rangle$.

Example 11. Consider now the function strcat of Program 1.4. The modular analysis of this function yields a relation stating that:

if dest points (at offset 0) to some memory location s, with length s_l and allocated size s_a, and if src points (at offset 0) to some memory location t with equivalent length and allocated size definition and $t \neq s$
then $\{s'_l = t_l + s_l, s'_a = s_a, t'_a = t_a, t'_l = t_l, t'_l \geq 0, t'_l \leq t'_a - 1, t'_l \leq s'_l, s'_l \leq s'_a - 1\}$

Therefore thanks to the $s'_l = t_l + s_l$ relation, if another call to strcat is performed in a state where $s_l = \alpha$ and $t_l = \beta$ for some α and β, our analyzer, can conclude (without reanalysis) that the length of the string t_l at the end of the analysis is $\alpha + \beta$.

Remark 4. The following improvements were added:

- in order to improve reusability, we increase the input state by removing some memory blocks (meaning we leave out constraints on these regions) from the input state. This plays the role of the framing rule in separation logic. Note that this improvement does not induce any precision loss.
- when a summary is created, some memory blocks are quantified universally, therefore when trying to apply a summary we try to unify the memory blocks from the actual input state with those of the summary input state.

6   Implementation

The analyzer was implemented in OCaml in the novel and still in development MOPSA framework. MOPSA enables a modular development of static analyzers defined by abstract interpretation. An analyzer is built by choosing abstract domains, and combining them according to the user specification. Abstract domains are either predefined (e.g. Cell abstract domain, loop iterators, ...) or user-defined (e.g. String abstract domain). The String abstract domain was added to the library of existing domains, and a new inter-procedural iterator was added to implement the modular analysis presented in Sect. 5. The current analyzer is in development, it is able to analyze all C code fragments presented in this article, but can not tackle complete realist C projects yet. To test our modular string analysis, we thus considered the examples and benchmarks used in previous works on string analysis [1,16].

In related works, Allamigeon et al. mentioned in [1], Sect. 5, that the most difficult example they had to deal with were calls to strcpy performed on string placed in a structure, itself placed in a matrix, and accessed via pointer manipulations (see Program 1.6, in Appendix B). This example was successfully analyzed with the version of strcpy defined in Program 1.1 and with an alternate implementation found in Qmail (see Program 1.7), the second case was more complex and required the use of partitioning. Our ability to easily deal with such manipulations comes from the use of the Cell domain to deal with low-level features of C.

We are able to tackle most of the programs from web2c mentioned in [16] (7 out of 9, programs that could not be analyzed are due to the fact that we do not have yet implemented all the features of the C language). The precision of this analysis (number of errors and false alarms) is similar to that of [16] and the execution time of the analyzer was always below 2 s. As an example consider Program 1.5, starting the analysis under the conditions that: cp points to buf, a buffer of size

```
char * insert_long (cp)        1
    char *cp;                  2
{                              3
    char tbuf[BUFSIZ];         4
    int i;                     5
    for (i=0;&buf[i]<cp;++i)   6
        tbuf[i] = buf[i];      7
    strcpy(&tbuf[i],"(long)"); 8
    strcpy(&tbuf[i + 6], cp);  9
    strcpy(buf, tbuf);        10
    return cp + 6;            11
}                             12
```

Program 1.5. insert_long from web2c

BUFSIZ before the first '\0' character produces alarms at line 9 and 10. Indeed under such hypothesis strcpy tries to write outside of tbuf. Note moreover that both [1,16] defined special abstract transformations for `strcpy`, whereas we perform a modular analysis of the function.

7   Related Works

Modular Static Analysis. Cousot and Cousot mentioned in [11] the importance of performing modular analyses and described several methods to design them. An efficient way is to use user-provided contracts as in [17]. Our goal was to infer contracts, as in [14], therefore works closest to ours would be the input/output inference performed by Bourdoncle in [4], however this method was limited to non-relational (interval) domains, unlike our method, which is thus more expressive (see Remark 3). In [11], numerical relations are used to represent the semantic of a set of statements, however this is limited to numerical programs whereas we extend the method to consider both numbers and pointers, including pointer arithmetic. The analyzer proposed by Sotin and Jeannet in [23] is able to infer input/output relations of the form proposed in Sect. 5. Nevertheless they consider a subset of C that does not contain pointer arithmetic, union types nor pointer casts. Müller-Olm and Seidl [19] and Sharma and Reps [20] proposed domains specialized in the discovery of numerical input/output relations on statements, in both cases the relations discovery is performed during the analysis of the statement by a special domain. In Sect. 5 we mentioned that we implemented a mechanism to infer framing in order to improve analysis reusability, framing mechanisms are fundamentals in tools base on separation logic such as Smallfoot [3] or Infer [5].

String analysis. One popular technique to avoid buffer overflows is dynamic analysis. There is a long history of such technique (see [25] for some examples). These methods induce an overhead cost and do not prevent program failures. By contrast we employ static analysis. String are arrays of characters, therefore analysis methods proposed in [8,13] could be used to design static analyzers handling strings. The three following works are the closest to ours and all follow the idea introduced in [24] to track the length of strings. Dor et al. [16] tackled the problem by rewriting string manipulating statements into statements over a numerical variable language, however this transformation induced the usage of a number of variables quadratic in the number of strings present in the analysis, in order to account for pointer aliasing. Simon and King [22] proposed an analyzer for a sub-C language manipulating strings, and allowing dynamic memory allocation, but some pointer manipulations could not be handled. They improved their results in [21], the string domain presented here is a combination of results from [21] and the cell abstract domain, moreover we provided a way to dynamically balance strings dealt with by the string abstract domain and by the cell domain. Additionally string length and allocated size are bound to pointers (whereas we bind them to the actual memory location containing the string), and this approach seems to prevent the modular integration of this domain in a full C language analyzer. Allamigeon et al. [1] also proposed an analyzer that keeps track of the position of the first '\0' character, however their analysis is non-relational, can not handle arbitrary pointer cast, and uses static information on string length, therefore preventing the domain reusability for dynamically allocated strings. We believe that our analysis is the first one that is both modular, able to reason both on the C at a low-level (including pointer casts and unions), and at a higher-level (on strings using dedicated abstractions).

8   Conclusion

In this article we proposed an abstract domain able to tackle C string of parametric size, built as an add-on to an existing domain [18] capable of dealing with most of the features of the C language. We have shown how our analyzer can be tuned dynamically (by choosing whether the String or Cell domain should deal with certain memory regions, by changing the partitioning heuristics in the inter-procedural iterator or by changing the underlying numerical domain) so as to adjust its precision. Upon the aforementioned analyzer we defined an inter-procedural iterator designed to increase statement analysis reusability without having to lose precision.

A   Tool functions

A.1   Definition of the Galois Connection

In the following st denotes $sizeof \circ typeof$.

$\mathbf{to\_cell}(s, S^\sharp) =$

$\quad$ let $\langle C, R^\sharp, P \rangle = \mathbf{add\_cells}(\{\langle s, 0, \mathbf{u8} \rangle, \ldots, \langle s, st(s), \mathbf{u8} \rangle\}, S^\sharp)$ in

$\quad$ let $[a; b] = \mathbf{range}(s_l, R^\sharp) \cap [0; st(s)]$ in

$\quad$ let $(R_i^\sharp)_{i \in [a;b]} = R^\sharp \sqcap \{\langle s, 0, \mathbf{u8} \rangle \neq 0, \ldots, \langle s, i-1, \mathbf{u8} \rangle \neq 0, \langle s, i, \mathbf{u8} \rangle = 0\}$ in

$$\bigsqcup_{j=0}^{b} \langle C', R_j^\sharp, P \rangle$$

$\mathbf{from\_cell}(s, S^\sharp) =$

$\quad$ let $\langle C, R^\sharp, P \rangle = \mathbf{add\_cells}(\{\langle s, 0, \mathbf{u8} \rangle, \ldots, \langle s, st(s), \mathbf{u8} \rangle\}, S^\sharp)$ in

$\quad$ let $c_\geq = \min(\{i \mid 0 \in \mathbf{range}(\langle s, i, \mathbf{u8} \rangle, R^\sharp)\} \cup \{st(s)\})$ in

$\quad$ let $c_\leq = \min(\{i \mid \{0\} = \mathbf{range}(\langle s, i, \mathbf{u8} \rangle, R^\sharp)\} \cup \{st(s)\})$ in

$\quad$ let $C^\star = \{\langle s', i, \tau \rangle \in C \mid s \neq s'\}$ in

$\quad$ let $R^\star = R \sqcap \{s_l \geq c_\geq, s_l \leq c_\leq, s_a = st(s)\}$ in

$\quad$ $\langle C^\star, R^\star, P \rangle$

Using functions $\mathbf{to\_cells}$ and $\mathbf{from\_cells}$, and under the hypothesis that $\mathfrak{V} = \{s_0, \ldots, s_{n-1}\}$, we can define the Galois connection between the Cell abstract domain and the String abstract domain:

$$\gamma_{S_m^\sharp, D_m^\sharp}(S^\sharp) = \mathbf{to\_cell}(s_0, \dots, (\mathbf{to\_cell}(s_{n-1}, S^\sharp)) \dots)$$
$$\alpha_{S_m^\sharp, D_m^\sharp}(S^\sharp) = \mathbf{from\_cell}(s_0, \dots, (\mathbf{from\_cell}(s_{n-1}, S^\sharp)) \dots)$$

A.2   Definition of the Evaluation of a Dereferencing

$$\mathbf{before}(e, s, S^\sharp) =$$
$$\{([1; 255], \langle C, R^\sharp \sqcap \{0 \le e, e < s_l, e < s_a\}, P\rangle)\}$$
$$\mathbf{at}(e, s, S^\sharp) =$$
$$\{(0, \langle C, R^\sharp \sqcap \{0 \le e, e = s_l, e < s_a\}, P\rangle)\}$$
$$\mathbf{after}(e, s, S^\sharp) =$$
$$\{([0; 255], \langle C, R^\sharp \sqcap \{0 \le e, e > s_l, e < s_a\}, P\rangle)\}$$
$$\mathbf{eerror}(e, s, S^\sharp) =$$
$$\text{let } R_1^\sharp = R^\sharp \sqcap \{e \ge s_a\} \sqcup R^\sharp \sqcap \{e < 0\} \text{ in}$$
$$\textit{test for } \mathbf{out\_of\_bounds} \ (R_1^\sharp \sqsubseteq_{S_m^\sharp} \bot)?$$
$$\emptyset$$

A.3   Definition of the Abstract Postcondition of an Assignment

$$\mathbf{set0}(s, e_1, e_2, \langle C, R^\sharp, P\rangle) =$$
$$\text{let } R_1^\sharp = R^\sharp \sqcap \{e_1 \ge 0, e_1 \le s_l, e_1 < s_a, e_2 = 0\} \text{ in}$$
$$\text{let } R_2^\sharp = \mathbb{S}^\sharp[\![s_l \leftarrow e_1]\!](R_1^\sharp) \text{ in}$$
$$\langle C, R_2^\sharp, P\rangle$$
$$\mathbf{setnon0}(s, e_1, e_2, \langle C, R^\sharp, P\rangle) =$$
$$\text{let } R_1^\sharp = R^\sharp \sqcap \{e_1 \ge 0, e_1 = s_l, e_1 < s_a, e_2 \ne 0\} \text{ in}$$
$$\text{let } R_2^\sharp = \mathbb{S}^\sharp[\![s_l \leftarrow [e_1 + 1; s_a]]\!](R_1^\sharp) \text{ in}$$
$$\langle C, R_2^\sharp, P\rangle$$
$$\mathbf{unchanged}(s, e_1, e_2, \langle C, R^\sharp, P\rangle) =$$
$$\text{let } R_1^\sharp = (R^\sharp \sqcap \{e_1 \ge 0, e_1 < s_l, e_1 < s_a, e_2 \ne 0\})$$
$$\sqcup (R^\sharp \sqcap \{e_1 \ge 0, e_1 > s_l, e_1 < s_a\}) \text{ in}$$
$$\langle C, R_1^\sharp, P\rangle$$

$$\textbf{l\_unchanged}(s, e_1, r, \langle C, R^{\sharp}, P \rangle) =$$
$$\textbf{let } R_1^{\sharp} = (R^{\sharp} \sqcap \{e_1 \geq 0, e_1 > s_l, e_1 + r \leq s_a\}) \textbf{ in}$$
$$\langle C, R_1^{\sharp}, P \rangle$$

$$\textbf{forget}(s, e_1, r, \langle C, R^{\sharp}, P \rangle) =$$
$$\textbf{let } R_1^{\sharp} = R^{\sharp} \sqcap \{e_1 \geq 0, e_1 \leq s_l, e_1 + r \leq s_a\} \textbf{ in}$$
$$\textbf{let } R_2^{\sharp} = \mathbb{S}^{\sharp}[\![s_l \leftarrow [e_1; s_a]]\!](R_1^{\sharp}) \textbf{ in}$$
$$\langle C, R_2^{\sharp}, P \rangle$$

$$\textbf{serror}(s, e_1, r, \langle C, R^{\sharp}, P \rangle) =$$
$$\textbf{let } R_1^{\sharp} = R^{\sharp} \sqcap \{e_1 \geq s_a\} \textbf{ in}$$
$$\textbf{let } R_2^{\sharp} = R^{\sharp} \sqcap \{e_1 < 0\} \textbf{ in}$$
$$test \; for \; \textbf{out\_of\_bounds}((R_2^{\sharp} \sqcup_{S_m^{\sharp}} R_1^{\sharp}) \sqsubseteq_{S_m^{\sharp}} \bot)?$$
$$\bot$$

A.4   String Declaration

$$\mathbb{S}^{\sharp}[\![\texttt{u8 } s \in \mathfrak{V}[n \in \mathbb{N}_{\geq 0}]]\!](\langle C, N^{\sharp}, P \rangle) = \langle C, \mathbb{S}^{\sharp}[\![s_l \leftarrow [0, n]]\!](\mathbb{S}^{\sharp}[\![s_a \leftarrow n]\!](N^{\sharp})), P \rangle$$

B   C Programs

```
1 typedef struct {
2    char* f;
3 } s;
4 char buf[10];
5
6 void init(s* x) {
7    x[1].f = buf;
8 }
9 int main () {
10   s a[2][2];
11   s* ptr = (s*) &(a[1]);
12   init(ptr);
13   ptr = (s*) &(a[0]);
14   strcpy(a[1][1].f,"strcpy ok");
15   strcpy(a[1][1].f,"strcpy not ok");
16 }
```

Program 1.6. Program from [1]

```
void strcpy(char* s, char* t)          1
{                                      2
   for (;;) {                          3
      if (!(*s = *t)) return ; ++s; ++t; 4
      if (!(*s = *t)) return ; ++s; ++t; 5
      if (!(*s = *t)) return ; ++s; ++t; 6
      if (!(*s = *t)) return ; ++s; ++t; 7
   }                                   8
}                                      9
```

Program 1.7. Strcpy from Qmail

References

1. Allamigeon, X., Godard, W., Hymans, C.: Static analysis of string manipulations in critical embedded C programs. In: Yi, K. (ed.) SAS 2006. LNCS, vol. 4134, pp. 35–51. Springer, Heidelberg (2006). https://doi.org/10.1007/11823230_4
2. Balakrishnan, G., Reps, T.: Recency-abstraction for heap-allocated storage. In: Yi, K. (ed.) SAS 2006. LNCS, vol. 4134, pp. 221–239. Springer, Heidelberg (2006). https://doi.org/10.1007/11823230_15
3. Berdine, J., Calcagno, C., O'Hearn, P.W.: Smallfoot: modular automatic assertion checking with separation logic. In: de Boer, F.S., Bonsangue, M.M., Graf, S., de Roever, W.-P. (eds.) FMCO 2005. LNCS, vol. 4111, pp. 115–137. Springer, Heidelberg (2006). https://doi.org/10.1007/11804192_6
4. Bourdoncle, F.: Abstract interpretation by dynamic partitioning. J. Funct. Prog. 2(4), 407–423 (1992)
5. Calcagno, C., et al.: Moving fast with software verification. In: Havelund, K., Holzmann, G., Joshi, R. (eds.) NFM 2015. LNCS, vol. 9058, pp. 3–11. Springer, Cham (2015). https://doi.org/10.1007/978-3-319-17524-9_1
6. Cousot, P., Cousot, R.: Static determination of dynamic properties of programs. In: Proceedings of the Second International Symposium on Programming, pp. 106–130. Dunod, Paris (1976)
7. Cousot, P., Cousot, R.: Static determination of dynamic properties of recursive procedures. In: Neuhold, E.J. (ed.) IFIP Conference on Formal Description of Programming Concepts, St-Andrews, N.B., CA, pp. 237–277, North-Holland (1977)
8. Cousot, P.: Verification by abstract interpretation. In: Dershowitz, N. (ed.) Verification: Theory and Practice. LNCS, vol. 2772, pp. 243–268. Springer, Heidelberg (2003). https://doi.org/10.1007/978-3-540-39910-0_11
9. Cousot, P., Cousot, R.: Abstract interpretation: a unified lattice model for static analysis of programs by construction or approximation of fixpoints. In: Graham, R.M., Harrison, M.A., Sethi, R. (eds.) Conference Record of the Fourth ACM Symposium on Principles of Programming Languages, Los Angeles, California, USA, January 1977, pp. 238–252. ACM (1977)
10. Cousot, P., Cousot, R.: Static determination of dynamic properties of generalized type unions. In: Language Design for Reliable Software, pp. 77–94 (1977)
11. Cousot, P., Cousot, R.: Modular static program analysis. In: Horspool, R.N. (ed.) CC 2002. LNCS, vol. 2304, pp. 159–179. Springer, Heidelberg (2002). https://doi.org/10.1007/3-540-45937-5_13
12. Cousot, P., et al.: Combination of abstractions in the ASTRÉE static analyzer. In: Okada, M., Satoh, I. (eds.) ASIAN 2006. LNCS, vol. 4435, pp. 272–300. Springer, Heidelberg (2007). https://doi.org/10.1007/978-3-540-77505-8_23
13. Cousot, P., Cousot, R., Logozzo, F.: A parametric segmentation functor for fully automatic and scalable array content analysis. In: Ball, T., Sagiv, M. (eds.) Proceedings of the 38th ACM SIGPLAN-SIGACT Symposium on Principles of Programming Languages, POPL 2011, Austin, TX, USA, 26–28 January 2011, pp. 105–118. ACM (2011)
14. Cousot, P., Cousot, R., Logozzo, F.: Precondition inference from intermittent assertions and application to contracts on collections. In: Jhala, R., Schmidt, D. (eds.) VMCAI 2011. LNCS, vol. 6538, pp. 150–168. Springer, Heidelberg (2011). https://doi.org/10.1007/978-3-642-18275-4_12

15. Cousot, P., Halbwachs, N.: Automatic discovery of linear restraints among variables of a program. In: Aho, A.V., Zilles, S.N., Szymanski, T.G. (eds.) Conference Record of the Fifth Annual ACM Symposium on Principles of Programming Languages, Tucson, Arizona, USA, January 1978, pp. 84–96. ACM Press (1978)
16. Dor, N., Rodeh, M., Sagiv, M.: Cleanness checking of string manipulations in C programs via integer analysis. In: Cousot, P. (ed.) SAS 2001. LNCS, vol. 2126, pp. 194–212. Springer, Heidelberg (2001). https://doi.org/10.1007/3-540-47764-0_12
17. Fähndrich, M., Logozzo, F.: Static contract checking with abstract interpretation. In: Beckert, B., Marché, C. (eds.) FoVeOOS 2010. LNCS, vol. 6528, pp. 10–30. Springer, Heidelberg (2011). https://doi.org/10.1007/978-3-642-18070-5_2
18. Miné, A.: Field-sensitive value analysis of embedded C programs with union types and pointer arithmetics. In: Irwin, M.J., De Bosschere, K. (eds.) Proceedings of the 2006 ACM SIGPLAN/SIGBED Conference on Languages, Compilers, and Tools for Embedded Systems (LCTES 2006), Ottawa, Ontario, Canada, 14–16 June 2006, pp. 54–63. ACM (2006)
19. Müller-Olm, M., Seidl, H.: Analysis of modular arithmetic. ACM Trans. Program. Lang. Syst. **29**(5), 29 (2007)
20. Sharma, T., Reps, T.: A new abstraction framework for affine transformers. In: Ranzato, F. (ed.) SAS 2017. LNCS, vol. 10422, pp. 342–363. Springer, Cham (2017). https://doi.org/10.1007/978-3-319-66706-5_17
21. Simon, A.: Value-Range Analysis of C Programs: Towards Proving the Absence of Buffer Overflow Vulnerabilities. Springer, London (2008)
22. Simon, A., King, A.: Analyzing string buffers in C. In: Kirchner, H., Ringeissen, C. (eds.) AMAST 2002. LNCS, vol. 2422, pp. 365–380. Springer, Heidelberg (2002). https://doi.org/10.1007/3-540-45719-4_25
23. Sotin, P., Jeannet, B.: Precise interprocedural analysis in the presence of pointers to the stack. In: Barthe, G. (ed.) ESOP 2011. LNCS, vol. 6602, pp. 459–479. Springer, Heidelberg (2011). https://doi.org/10.1007/978-3-642-19718-5_24
24. Wagner, D.A., Foster, J.S., Brewer, E.A., Aiken, A.: A first step towards automated detection of buffer overrun vulnerabilities. In: Proceedings of the Network and Distributed System Security Symposium, NDSS 2000, San Diego, California, USA. The Internet Society (2000)
25. Wilander, J., Kamkar, M.: A comparison of publicly available tools for dynamic buffer overflow prevention. In: Proceedings of the Network and Distributed System Security Symposium, NDSS 2003, San Diego, California, USA. The Internet Society (2003)

Verifying Bounded Subset-Closed Hyperproperties

Isabella Mastroeni and Michele Pasqua$^{(\boxtimes)}$

Dipartimento di Informatica, University of Verona,
Strada le Grazie 15, 37134 Verona, Italy
{isabella.mastroeni,michele.pasqua}@univr.it

Abstract. Hyperproperties are quickly becoming very popular in the context of systems security, due to their expressive power. They differ from classic trace properties since they are represented by sets of sets of executions instead of sets of executions. This allows us, for instance, to capture information flow security specifications, which cannot be expressed as trace properties, namely as predicates over single executions. In this work, we reason about how it is possible to move standard abstract interpretation-based static analysis methods, designed for trace properties, towards the verification of hyperproperties. In particular, we focus on the verification of *bounded subset-closed hyperproperties* which are easier to verify than generic hyperproperties. It turns out that a lot of interesting specifications (e.g., Non-Interference) lie in this category.

1 Introduction

When reasoning about systems executions, a key point is the degree of approximation given by the choice of the semantics used to represent computations. Since its origin in 1977, abstract interpretation [12] has been widely used to describe and formalize approximate systems computations in many different areas of computer science and, in particular, in program verification. In this direction, comparative semantics consists in comparing semantics at different levels of abstraction, always by abstract interpretation [11,17]. The choice of the semantics is a key point, not only for finding the desirable trade-off between precision and decidability of program analysis in terms, for instance, of verification expressiveness, but also because not all the semantics are suitable for proving any possible specification of interest. In other words, the semantics must describe at least the program features involved by the specification of interest. For instance, in the security context, there are specifications that can be expressed as trace properties, like Access Control, and others which cannot, like Non-Interference[1]. In this latter case, it is necessary to specify it as an *hyperproperty*. Intuitively, a trace property is defined exclusively in terms of individual executions and, in general, do not specify any relation between different executions of a system.

---

[1] Access Control is defined over systems (reachable) states. Non-Interference, instead, is defined over systems input/output (I/O) traces.

© Springer Nature Switzerland AG 2018
A. Podelski (Ed.): SAS 2018, LNCS 11002, pp. 263–283, 2018.
https://doi.org/10.1007/978-3-319-99725-4_17

Instead, an hyperproperty specifies the set of sets of system executions allowed by the specification, therefore expressing relations between executions. In [9] it is stated that hyperproperties are able to define every possible specification concerning systems modeled as sets of traces (of states).

Unfortunately, hyperproperties are not, in general, precisely verifiable with standard methods, e.g., with standard abstract interpretation-based static analyses. In [25] we face the problem of formally verifying hyperproperties from a very general point of view, by providing several ingredients necessary for tackling the problem of verifying hyperproperties. We introduce a classification of hyperproperties distinguishing between those that can be "precisely" analyzed with standard program analysis (*trace* hyperproperties), those that technically could be analyzed with standard methods (with potentially unsatisfactory results) but for which an analysis at hyperlevel could gain precision (*subset-closed* hyperproperties) and those for which standard static analyses cannot work properly (all other hyperproperties). Then we formally describe the hyperlevel of semantics by integrating the hyperlevel in the hierarchy of semantics [11], providing a formal framework for reasoning about hyperproperties of systems.

Contribution. In the present work, program verification of hyperproperties, which was the main motivation of [25], becomes the central focus. First of all, we deepen the verification problem of a restriction of subset-closed hyperproperties, i.e., *bounded subset-closed hyperproperties*. These hyperproperties are expressive enough to capture lots of interesting specifications (such as information flow) but their verification is made easier. In particular, verification of these hyperproperties is bounded to a fixed input cardinality, restricting the search space for confutation. Nevertheless, also for this kind of hyperproperties, the analysis has to move to the hyperlevel for reducing the loss of precision, which, at the standard level, could make the analysis useless (even if it is still possible).

At this point, we wonder how we can lift, not the whole concrete semantics (as in [25]), but the interpreter computing the collecting semantics. We propose a general technique for lifting collecting semantics and we observe that the semantics proposed in [9] is a particular instance of our general approach. The added value of tackling the problem from a general and formal point of view is that it allows us to discuss and prove soundness and completeness properties.

Finally, as it happens in standard analysis where the collecting semantics is approximated in a domain of observations, we aim at defining hyper abstract domains, in order to approximate the collecting hypersemantics. With this aim in mind, we propose a methodology for lifting abstract domains to the hyperlevel.

Structure of the Paper. In Sect. 2, we briefly recall the concept of hyperproperty and the issue of its verification. Then we introduce the new notion of bounded subset-closed hyperproperty. In Sect. 3, we deal with the problem of lifting the collecting semantics of a given static analysis at the level of sets of sets. In Sect. 4, we describe general patterns for building (hyper) domains, suitable for the verification of hyperproperties. In Sect. 5, we show how to instantiate the methodologies introduced, in order to obtain sound and complete static analyses for bounded subset-closed hyperproperties. Finally, in the last two sections, we have related works, future research directions and conclusions.

2 Concerning Hyperproperties Verification

Let $\mathbb{D}\textsc{en}$ be the set of all possible denotations for systems executions (e.g., reachable states, pairs of input and output states, finite sequences of states, etc.). We recall that while a trace property $\mathfrak{P}$, i.e., a property whose satisfaction depends on single executions, is modeled as the set of all executions satisfying it (hence $\mathfrak{P} \in \wp(\mathbb{D}\textsc{en})$), an hyperproperty $\mathfrak{Hp}$, verifiable on sets of executions, is modeled as the set of all sets of executions satisfying it (hence $\mathfrak{Hp} \in \wp(\wp(\mathbb{D}\textsc{en}))$).

2.1 Bounded Subset-Closed Hyperproperties

In [25], we define the following hyperproperties classification:

$$\textsc{trc}^{\text{H}} \triangleq \{\mathfrak{Hp} \in \wp(\wp(\mathbb{D}\textsc{en})) \mid \wp(\bigcup \mathfrak{Hp}) = \mathfrak{Hp}\}$$

$$\textsc{ssc}^{\text{H}} \triangleq \{\mathfrak{Hp} \in \wp(\wp(\mathbb{D}\textsc{en})) \mid X \in \mathfrak{Hp} \Rightarrow (\forall Y \subseteq X . Y \in \mathfrak{Hp})\}$$

The first are called *trace hyperproperties* and the second *subset-closed hyperproperties*. Trace hyperproperties are isomorphic to trace properties, namely they corresponds to all and only the hyperproperties verifiable on single executions, i.e., they do not need the comparison of different executions. Subset-closed hyperproperties are those hyperproperties that can be refuted just by showing an arbitrary subset of the semantics that does not satisfies the hyperproperty (witness of refutation).

In this paper, we introduce a stronger notion of subset-closed hyperproperty, allowing us to further restrict the search space for possible refuting witnesses.

Definition 1 (k-Bounded Subset-Closed Hyperproperty)

$$\textsc{ssc}^{\text{H}}_k \triangleq \{\mathfrak{Hp} \in \wp(\wp(\mathbb{D}\textsc{en})) \mid X \notin \mathfrak{Hp} \Leftrightarrow (\exists T_k \subseteq X . (|T_k| \leq k \wedge T_k \notin \mathfrak{Hp}))\}$$

The set T_k is the *witness of refutation*, namely a set of traces of cardinality at most $k \in \mathbb{N}$ violating the property. In other words, in a k-bounded subset-closed hyperproperty, every set of traces not satisfying the hyperproperty has a refuting witness with at most k traces. This means that, in order to refute the hyperproperty, we need to exhibit a counterexample consisting in at most k traces. Formally, suppose $\mathfrak{Hp} \in \textsc{ssc}^{\text{H}}_k$, if we find $\{\eth^1, \eth^2, \ldots \eth^k\} \subseteq X$ such that $\{\eth^1, \eth^2, \ldots \eth^k\} \notin \mathfrak{Hp}$, then we can imply that $X \notin \mathfrak{Hp}$. Hence $X \models \mathfrak{Hp}$, meaning X satisfies $\mathfrak{Hp}$, iff $\{\{\eth^1, \eth^2, \ldots \eth^k\} \mid \eth^1, \eth^2, \ldots \eth^k \in X\} \subseteq \mathfrak{Hp}$. Clearly, it turns out that a trace hyperproperty is 1-bounded, namely $\textsc{trc}^{\text{H}} = \textsc{ssc}^{\text{H}}_1$.

It is also clear that the union of all the k-bounded subset-closed hyperproperties and the unbounded subset-closed hyperproperties (i.e., those with $k = \omega$) is precisely the set of all the subset-closed hyperproperties.

Proposition 1. *It holds that* $\textsc{ssc}^{\text{H}} = \bigcup_{k \leq \omega} \textsc{ssc}^{\text{H}}_k$.

For every $\mathfrak{H}\mathfrak{p} \in \mathsf{SSC}^{\mathsf{H}}$ we can define a refuting set $R_{\mathfrak{H}\mathfrak{p}}$, namely a set of sets of traces representing the witnesses for refuting the hyperproperty. These sets are inspired by the prefixes representing the "bad thing" in safety properties. It is possible to define different refuting sets for a given hyperproperty, since when a set $X \notin \mathfrak{H}\mathfrak{p}$ then we have that $X \cup Y \notin \mathfrak{H}\mathfrak{p}$, by subset-closure. A $\mathsf{SSC}^{\mathsf{H}}$ hyperproperty $\mathfrak{H}\mathfrak{p}$ is violated iff the given set of traces is a superset of an element in $R_{\mathfrak{H}\mathfrak{p}}$. So $\mathfrak{H}\mathfrak{p}$ can be characterized as:

$$\forall X \in \wp(\mathbb{D}\textsc{en}) . (\exists T_r \in R_{\mathfrak{H}\mathfrak{p}} . T_r \subseteq X) \Leftrightarrow X \notin \mathfrak{H}\mathfrak{p} \tag{1}$$

If $\mathfrak{H}\mathfrak{p} \in \mathsf{SSC}_k^{\mathsf{H}}$ (i.e., it is bounded) then we can define the *minimal* refuting set $R_{\mathfrak{H}\mathfrak{p}}^{\min}$ (i.e., the one containing the sets with minimal cardinality) characterizing the hyperproperty. This means that for every set violating the hyperproperty, $R_{\mathfrak{H}\mathfrak{p}}^{\min}$ contains only its minimal representative (w.r.t. $\subseteq$). In particular, every element in $R_{\mathfrak{H}\mathfrak{p}}^{\min}$ has cardinality k.

Example 1. Let $\mathsf{St} = \mathsf{Var} \to \mathbb{Z}$ and $\mathbb{D}\textsc{en} = \mathsf{St} \times \mathsf{St}$. Non-Interference [10,21], parametric on a security variables typing $\Gamma \in \mathsf{Var} \to \{\mathsf{L}, \mathsf{H}\}$, is:

$$\mathsf{NI} \triangleq \{X \in \wp(\mathbb{D}\textsc{en}) \mid \forall \eth, \eth' \in X . (\eth_{\vdash} =_{\mathsf{L}} \eth'_{\vdash} \Rightarrow \eth_{\dashv} =_{\mathsf{L}} \eth'_{\dashv})\}$$

where $\eth_{\vdash}$ and $\eth_{\dashv}$ are the projections on the first and last element of the pair $\eth$, respectively. The equivalence $=_{\mathsf{L}}$ holds for memories agreeing on the values of public (L) variables. NI is in $\mathsf{SSC}_2^{\mathsf{H}}$, namely $X \models \mathsf{NI}$ iff $\{\{\eth, \eth'\} \mid \eth, \eth' \in X\} \subseteq \mathsf{NI}$. Hence, if we find a pair of interfering executions, i.e., $\{\eth, \eth'\} \notin \mathsf{NI}$, then we prove that $X \not\models \mathsf{NI}$. Indeed, the minimal refuting set for Non-Interference is:

$$R_{\mathsf{NI}}^{\min} \triangleq \{\{\eth, \eth'\} \in \wp(\mathbb{D}\textsc{en}) \mid \eth_{\vdash} =_{\mathsf{L}} \eth'_{\vdash} \wedge \eth_{\dashv} \neq_{\mathsf{L}} \eth'_{\dashv}\}$$

End example.

Note that substituting $\subseteq$ with the prefix-set relation $\leqslant^2$ in (1) we obtain the minimal refuting set for an hypersafety.

2.2 The Safety/Liveness Dichotomy

In the context of trace properties, a particular kind of properties are the *safety* ones [2], expressing the fact that "nothing bad happens". These properties are interesting because they depend only on the history of single executions, meaning that safety properties are dynamically monitorable [2]. Similarly, *safety hyperproperties* (or hypersafety) are the lift to sets of safety properties. This means that, for each set of executions that is not in a safety hyperproperty, there exists a finite prefix-set of finite executions (the "bad thing") which cannot be extended for satisfying the property. Dually, liveness (trace) properties express the fact that "something good eventually happens", namely the systems satisfying a liveness property are those that, eventually, exhibit a good behavior. Again, *liveness*

---

[2] Here $X \leqslant Y$ iff for every $d \in X$ exists $d' \in Y$ such that d is a prefix of d' [9].

hyperproperties (or hyperliveness) are the lift to sets of liveness properties. This means that a set of finite traces can be extended to a set of infinite traces satisfying the property. An interesting aspect of the safety/liveness dichotomy is that every trace property can be expressed as the intersection of a safety and a liveness one. This also holds for hyperproperties, i.e., every hyperproperty can be expressed as the intersection of a hypersafety and a hyperliveness one [9,28].

Another particular class of hyperproperties are the *k-safety hyperproperties* (or *k*-hypersafety). They are safety hyperproperties in which the "bad thing" never involves more than *k* executions [9]. This means that it is possible to check the violation of a *k*-hypersafety just observing a set of *k* executions (note that 1-hypersafeties are exactly safety properties). This is important for verification, in fact, it is possible to reduce the verification of a *k*-hypersafety on a system S to the verification of a safety on the self-composed system S^k [9].

It turns out that all hypersafety are subset-closed [9]. But also some hyperliveness are subset-closed, in fact every trace hyperproperty is subset-closed and hence every liveness property, which is an hyperliveness, is in SSC^H. Every *k*-hypersafety is *k*-bounded and every liveness is a 1-bounded subset-closed hyperproperty. But there are also other hyperliveness which are bounded, as we can see in the following example.

Example 2. Suppose now that executions denotations are infinite sequences of states, namely $\mathbb{D}\text{EN} = \mathsf{St}^\omega$. Suppose also that the systems of interest can receive requests and can provide responses to these requests. We denote with the predicate $\text{Req}(\eth, i)$ the fact that a system, in the execution $\eth$, has received a request at time i, namely in the state $\eth_i$. Analogously, we denote with the predicate $\text{Resp}(\eth, i, j)$ the fact that the system has provided a response at time j to the request received at time i. Then we can define a policy saying that if the executions of a system receive a request at time i then they have to provide a response at time j, meaning that if they receive a request at the same time then they have to respond at the same time. Formally:

$$\mathsf{SyncR} \triangleq \left\{ X \subseteq \mathsf{St}^\omega \;\middle|\; \forall \eth, \eth' \in X \, \forall i \in \mathbb{N} \, . \, \begin{array}{l} (\text{Req}(\eth, i) \wedge \text{Req}(\eth', i)) \Rightarrow \\ \exists j \in \mathbb{N} \, . \, (\text{Resp}(\eth, i, j) \wedge \text{Resp}(\eth', i, j)) \end{array} \right\}$$

It is easy to note that SyncR is subset-closed but it is not an hypersafety. Indeed it is an hyperliveness, but it is also a bounded subset-closed hyperproperty. In particular, it is in $\mathsf{SSC}^\mathsf{H}_2$: In order to refute it, it is sufficient to look for sets of (infinite) sequences with cardinality 2.   *End example.*

Example 2 proves that there are hyperproperties which are not *k*-hypersafety but are *k*-bounded subset-closed (other than the trivial liveness properties). In Fig. 1 we have a graphical representation of how we can classify hyperproperties, w.r.t. the safety/liveness dichotomy and subset-closure.

2.3   Exploring the Hyperproperties Verification Issue

Let us now consider as systems the programs P written in a given imperative deterministic programming language, with assignments, conditionals and while

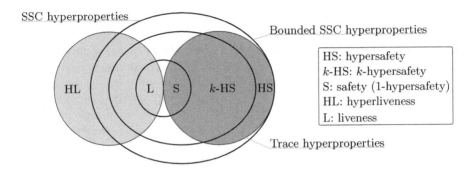

Fig. 1. Classification of hyperproperties.

loops. Let $\mathbb{D}\text{EN}$ be the domain of denotations for program behaviors, then $\mathcal{S}[\mathsf{P}] \in \wp(\mathbb{D}\text{EN})$ denotes the semantics of P, intended as the strongest trace property of P. In this case properties of P are those in $\wp(\mathbb{D}\text{EN})$, while hyperproperties of P are those in $\wp(\wp(\mathbb{D}\text{EN}))$. For instance, if $\mathbb{D}\text{EN} = \text{St} \triangleq \text{Var} \to \mathbb{Z}$, i.e., states are represented as mappings from variables to values, we cannot express Non-Interference (comparing traces of executions sharing the same low inputs) but we can express Access Control (checking whether in a program point an access has been granted or not). For defining Non-Interference we need, at least, denotations representing the programs input/output (I/O) relation, e.g., $\mathbb{D}\text{EN} = \text{St} \times \text{St}$.

In the context of program verification of (trace) properties, the satisfaction is given by set inclusion, i.e., a program P satisfies a property $\mathfrak{P} \in \wp(\mathbb{D}\text{EN})$, written $\mathsf{P} \models \mathfrak{P}$, iff $\mathcal{S}[\mathsf{P}] \subseteq \mathfrak{P}$. For hyperproperties, $\mathsf{P} \models \mathfrak{H}\mathfrak{p}$ iff $\mathcal{S}[\mathsf{P}] \in \mathfrak{H}\mathfrak{p}$ iff $\{\mathcal{S}[\mathsf{P}]\} \subseteq \mathfrak{H}\mathfrak{p}$. In particular, $\{\mathcal{S}[\mathsf{P}]\} \in \wp(\wp(\mathbb{D}\text{EN}))$ is the strongest hyperproperty of P [25].

In general, the semantics of a program is not computable, hence practical verification methods rely on approximations. In standard trace properties verification, we compute an over-approximation, e.g., by abstract interpretation, $O \supseteq \mathcal{S}[\mathsf{P}]$ which is such that, if $O \subseteq \mathfrak{P}$, then we can soundly imply $\mathsf{P} \models \mathfrak{P}$. Unfortunately, over-approximations on $\wp(\mathbb{D}\text{EN})$ do not always work properly with hyperproperties. In particular, it formally does work for $\mathfrak{H}\mathfrak{p} \in \text{SSC}^{\text{H}}$, in fact if we prove that $O \supseteq \mathcal{S}[\mathsf{P}]$ and $O \in \mathfrak{H}\mathfrak{p}$, then by subset-closure of $\mathfrak{H}\mathfrak{p}$ we also have that $\mathcal{S}[\mathsf{P}] \in \mathfrak{H}\mathfrak{p}$. Hence, we can conclude that standard approaches for semantic approximation may work also for hyperproperties, clearly taking into account the imprecision due to the semantics approximation. For instance, suppose $\mathbb{D}\text{EN} = \text{St}$, and suppose to be interested in verifying the hyperproperty

$$\text{PP} \triangleq \{X \in \wp(\mathbb{Z}) \mid \forall \eth_1, \eth_2 \in X . \text{Par}(\eth_1) = \text{Par}(\eth_2) \Rightarrow \text{Pos}(\eth_1) = \text{Pos}(\eth_2)\}$$

where $\texttt{Par}$ is the parity while $\texttt{Pos}$ is the sign of numerical values, respectively.

Then, suppose $\mathcal{S}[\mathsf{P}_1] = \{1, 3, 4\}^3$, in this case it is clear that $\mathsf{P}_1 \models \text{PP}$, but also the abstract computation of P_1 computing the sign of the set (in this case

---

[3] For the sake of simplicity, we suppose the programs P_i have only one variable and the state is denoted by the set of its possible values.

positive) would allow to verify the hyperproperty for P_1 (if all computed values have the same sign, PP is trivially verified). It is anyway clear that, as usual in abstraction, we lose precision since, for example, the program P_2 such that $\mathcal{S}[P_2] = \{-1, -3, 4\}$ satisfies PP, but the sign abstraction of the semantics would return $\top$, not allowing to verify PP.

Moreover, real problems of precision arise, also for SSC^H, when, due to the approximation, we move verification on domains less expressive than $\mathbb{DEN}$. For instance, when $\mathbb{DEN}$ is defined on traces of states (e.g., I/O traces St^2 or partial traces St^*) and the verification method deals with states only. Indeed, if the abstract computation could approximate sets of traces as sets of traces, then still we could reason as before, but sets of traces are usually approximated as a trace of sets, computing the trace of reachable states. This approximation completely loses the trace information necessary for verifying a hyperproperty defined on a trace domain of denotations. In Fig. 2 it is graphically provided the intuition that, by approximating the collecting semantics at the hyperlevel, we obtain a more precise approximation, since we can keep distinctions among reachable states allowing us to verify hyperproperties, with sufficient precision, even in presence of approximation.

Example 3. Consider, for instance, Non-Interference of Example 1, where states in St are denoted as tuples of values, namely a state $[h/_h, l/_l]$ is denoted as $\langle h, l \rangle$. Let $P \triangleq h := 0 \; ; \; l := 2l$ and $\Gamma(h) \triangleq H, \Gamma(l) \triangleq L$. Now consider $\mathfrak{J} \triangleq \{\langle h, l \rangle \mid l \in \{1, 2, 3, 4\}, h \in \mathbb{Z}\}$, then the resulting semantics of the program, starting from $\mathfrak{J}$, is $\{\langle h, l \rangle \langle 0, 2l \rangle \mid l \in \{1, 2, 3, 4\}, h \in \mathbb{Z}\}$. Any over-approximation of this set in $\wp(\mathbb{DEN})$ allows us to soundly verify NI, e.g., if we abstractly compute, in output, the set $\{\langle h, l \rangle \langle 0, 2l \rangle \mid h, l \in \mathbb{Z}\}$ then we can still soundly verify NI. But, any approximation on traces of sets (i.e., on $\wp(St)^2$), e.g., the trace of sets $\{\langle h, l \rangle \mid l \in \{1, 2, 3, 4\}, h \in \mathbb{Z}\}\{\langle 0, l \rangle \mid l \in \{2, 4, 6, 8\}\}$, losing the I/O relation of traces, becomes useless for NI verification. In this case, we need to move towards the hyperlevel of semantics, in order to not lose too much information, necessary to verify the hyperproperty. In the example, the possibility to compute the trace of (hyper)sets $\{\{\langle h, l \rangle \mid h \in \mathbb{Z}\} \mid l \in \{1, 2, 3, 4\}\}\{\{\langle 0, l \rangle\} \mid l \in \{2, 4, 6, 8\}\}$ would allow us to verify NI observing that, independently from a fixed low input and from any high input, the low output is always a constant, being the output of the resulting trace a set of sets of states sharing the same low value. Graphically:

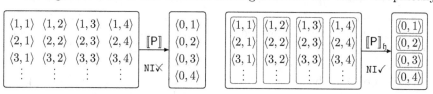

End example.

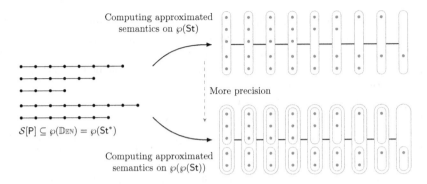

Computing approximated
semantics on $\wp(\mathsf{St})$

More precision

$\mathcal{S}[\mathsf{P}] \subseteq \wp(\mathbb{D}\text{EN}) = \wp(\mathsf{St}^*)$

Computing approximated
semantics on $\wp(\wp(\mathsf{St}))$

Fig. 2. The intuition: Why computing approximation on $\wp(\wp(\mathsf{St}))$ is more precise.

3 Lifting the Collecting Semantics

In this section, we describe how we can move the computation of a semantics into the hyperlevel, in order to be able to approximate the verification of hyperproperties, still keeping as much precision as possible, together with analysis feasibility. We provide the lifting framework parametric on the domain of denotations of the collecting semantics to lift, namely we consider a collecting semantics defined in $\wp(\mathbb{D}\text{EN})$ and we show how to lift it on $\wp(\wp(\mathbb{D}\text{EN}))$. Independently from the domain of the hyperproperty to verify, it is the verification and approximation process that fixes the relation between denotations domains, as shown in Fig. 2. In the figure, the semantics and the hyperproperty to verify are defined on $\wp(\mathsf{St}^*)$, while we lift into the hyperlevel a collecting semantics computed on $\wp(\mathsf{St})$, moving the computation at the hyperlevel, i.e., on $\wp(\wp(\mathsf{St}))$.

As we have observed, in order to verify hyperproperties, we may need to move program semantics into the hyperlevel. In [25], we describe the links between standard and hypersemantics of a transition system. In this section, we show how to *lift* a given collecting semantics[4], defined on sets, in order to obtain a corresponding *collecting hypersemantics*, defined on sets of sets, suitable for hyperproperties verification. In this work, we consider big-step semantics, but the whole framework can be generalized to other types of semantics.

Let $\mathfrak{L}$ be a deterministic imperative language whose set of statements is $Stm_{\mathfrak{L}}$ (single statements without composition). Given the domain of denotations $\mathbb{D}\text{EN}$, the semantic computation is defined by a semantic operator inductively defined on the syntax of $\mathfrak{L}$, i.e., $f^{\mathfrak{L}} \in Stm_{\mathfrak{L}} \times \mathbb{D}\text{EN} \to \mathbb{D}\text{EN}$. Let $\mathsf{P} \in \mathfrak{L}$ be a program written in $\mathfrak{L}$, its concrete (big-step) semantics is a function $\langle\!|\mathsf{P}|\!\rangle \in \mathbb{D}\text{EN} \to \mathbb{D}\text{EN}$ defined compositionally on the statements of P, i.e., it is computed by composing the application of $f^{\mathfrak{L}}$ to the program statements. For instance, let $\mathsf{P} = \mathsf{h} := 0 \, ; \, \mathsf{l} := 2\mathsf{l}$, the concrete semantics is $\langle\!|\mathsf{P}|\!\rangle \eth = f^{\mathfrak{L}}(\mathsf{l} := 2\mathsf{l}, f^{\mathfrak{L}}(\mathsf{h} := 0, \eth))$. In particular, $\langle\!|\mathsf{P}|\!\rangle$ is defined also in terms of the semantics of arithmetic expressions, denoted $\langle\!|\mathsf{a}|\!\rangle \in \mathbb{D}\text{EN} \to \mathbb{Z}$, and of boolean expressions, denoted $\langle\!|\mathsf{b}|\!\rangle \in \mathbb{D}\text{EN} \to \mathbb{B}$.

---

[4] Namely a semantics function, defined on a program P syntax, computing $\mathcal{S}[\mathsf{P}]$.

3.1   Lifting the (Collecting) Interpreter

The collecting semantics $[\![P]\!] \in \wp(\mathbb{D}\textsc{en}) \to \wp(\mathbb{D}\textsc{en})$ is the additive lift (i.e., the set of the direct images of the elements in input) to sets of denotations, namely $[\![P]\!]X = \{(\![P]\!)\eth \mid \eth \in X\}$. As far as expression semantics is concerned, for boolean expressions $[\![b]\!] \in \wp(\mathbb{D}\textsc{en}) \to \wp(\mathbb{D}\textsc{en})$ is a filtering function, namely $[\![b]\!]X \triangleq \{\eth \in X \mid (\![b]\!)\eth = \mathtt{tt}\}$, while for arithmetic expressions it is the additive lift of the concrete semantics. The collecting semantics is computed by composing a new operator $F^{\mathcal{L}} \in Stm_{\mathcal{L}} \times \wp(\mathbb{D}\textsc{en}) \to \wp(\mathbb{D}\textsc{en})$, which is the additive lift of $f^{\mathcal{L}}$. For example, the semantics for assignments is $[\![x := a]\!]X = F^{\mathcal{L}}(x := a, X) \triangleq \{f^{\mathcal{L}}(x := a, \eth) \mid \eth \in X\}$. The while statement operator is defined as $F^{\mathcal{L}}(\mathtt{while}\ b\ \{\,P\,\}, X) \triangleq [\![\neg b]\!](lfp_{\varnothing}^{\subseteq}\mathcal{W})$, where $\mathcal{W} \triangleq \lambda T . X \cup [\![P]\!][\![b]\!]T$. It can be shown that $\mathcal{W}$ is a monotone function over the complete lattice $\langle \wp(\mathbb{D}\textsc{en}), \subseteq, \cup, \cap, \mathbb{D}\textsc{en}, \varnothing \rangle$ hence its least fixpoint exists and it can be computed as $\bigcup_{n \geq 0} \mathcal{W}^n(\varnothing)$, with $\mathcal{W}^0 \triangleq \lambda X . \varnothing$ and $\mathcal{W}^{n+1} \triangleq \lambda X . \mathcal{W} \circ \mathcal{W}^n(X)$. In this case, this least fixpoint is precisely the additive lift of $f^{\mathcal{L}}$, namely $F^{\mathcal{L}}(\mathtt{while}\ b\ \{\,P\,\}, X) = \{f^{\mathcal{L}}(\mathtt{while}\ b\ \{\,P\,\}, \eth) \mid \eth \in X\}$. Note that, if $\mathfrak{I} \subseteq \mathbb{D}\textsc{en}$ is the set of *all* possible inputs of the program, the collecting semantics $[\![P]\!]$ from $\mathfrak{I}$ computes the strongest program property $\mathcal{S}[P] \in \wp(\mathbb{D}\textsc{en})$, i.e., $\mathcal{S}[P] = [\![P]\!]\mathfrak{I}$.

At this point, we have to move semantics towards the hyperlevel, namely on $\wp(\wp(\mathbb{D}\textsc{en}))$, since, when we are interested in hyperproperties, we may need to define a *collecting hypersemantics* $[\![P]\!]_{\mathfrak{h}} \in \wp(\wp(\mathbb{D}\textsc{en})) \to \wp(\wp(\mathbb{D}\textsc{en}))$. In this case, we need to lift the semantic operator $F^{\mathcal{L}}$, and we can show several ways for doing it. Suppose to have the filtering function $[\![b]\!]_{\mathfrak{h}} \in \wp(\wp(\mathbb{D}\textsc{en})) \to \wp(\wp(\mathbb{D}\textsc{en}))$ for boolean expressions, defined as $[\![b]\!]_{\mathfrak{h}}\mathcal{X} \triangleq \{[\![b]\!]X \mid X \in \mathcal{X}\}$. The definition of the collecting hypersemantics is just the additive lift (to sets of sets) of $F^{\mathcal{L}}$ for every statement, except for the while case. Indeed, we can observe that, at hyperlevel, the semantic operator $F_{\mathfrak{h}}^{\mathcal{L}}$ for the while statements does not coincide with the additive lift of $F^{\mathcal{L}}$, which would be $F_{\mathfrak{h}}^{\mathcal{L}}(\mathtt{while}\ b\ \{\,P\,\}, \mathcal{X}) \triangleq [\![\neg b]\!]_{\mathfrak{h}}(lfp_{\varnothing}^{\subseteq}\mathcal{W}_{\mathfrak{h}})$ with $\mathcal{W}_{\mathfrak{h}} \triangleq \lambda T . \mathcal{X} \cup [\![P]\!]_{\mathfrak{h}}[\![b]\!]_{\mathfrak{h}}T$. Unfortunately, this semantics is not sound being such that $[\![P]\!]X \notin [\![P]\!]_{\mathfrak{h}}\{X\}$. This is a problem, since when $[\![P]\!]\mathfrak{I} \notin [\![P]\!]_{\mathfrak{h}}\{\mathfrak{I}\}$, from $[\![P]\!]_{\mathfrak{h}}\{\mathfrak{I}\} \subseteq \mathfrak{H}\mathfrak{p}$ we cannot infer anything about the property validation.

Example 4. Let $\mathbb{D}\textsc{en} = \mathsf{Var} \to \mathbb{Z}$ and $P = \mathtt{while}\ (x < 4)\ \{x := x + 1\}$. Since P has only one variable, we simplify the notation by denoting $[x/v]$ just by v and the set of functions $\{[x/v_1], \ldots [x/v_n]\}$ by $\{v_1, \ldots v_n\}$. The collecting semantics, from $\mathfrak{I} = \{2, 5\}$, is $[\![P]\!]\{2, 5\} = \{4, 5\}$, computed as $\{2, 5\} \xrightarrow{w} \{4, 5\}$ where

$$\mathcal{W}^0 = \varnothing;\ \mathcal{W}^1 = \{2, 5\};\ \mathcal{W}^2 = \{2, 3, 5\};\ \mathcal{W}^3 = \{2, 3, 4, 5\}$$

The trivial additive lift of the while collecting semantics would be $[\![P]\!]_{\mathfrak{h}}\{\{2, 5\}\} = \{\varnothing, \{4\}, \{5\}\}$, computed as $\{\{2, 5\}\} \xrightarrow{w_{\mathfrak{h}}} \{\varnothing, \{4\}, \{5\}\}$ where

$$\mathcal{W}_{\mathfrak{h}}^0 = \varnothing;\ \mathcal{W}_{\mathfrak{h}}^1 = \{\{2, 5\}\};\ \mathcal{W}_{\mathfrak{h}}^2 = \{\{3\}, \{2, 5\}\};\ \mathcal{W}_{\mathfrak{h}}^3 = \{\{3\}, \{4\}, \{2, 5\}\};$$
$$\mathcal{W}_{\mathfrak{h}}^4 = \{\varnothing, \{3\}, \{4\}, \{2, 5\}\}$$

From the iterates of $\mathcal{W}^i$ and $\mathcal{W_\hbar}^i$ we can observe the monotonicity (and the extensivity) of $\mathcal{W}$ and $\mathcal{W_\hbar}$, but the hypersemantics is not sound, because $[\![P]\!]\{2,5\} = \{4,5\} \notin \{\varnothing, \{4\}, \{5\}\} = [\![P]\!]_\hbar \{\{2,5\}\}$. *End example.*

In order to lift the while semantics, we propose the following three possibilities. We define the collecting hypersemantics operator for while statements as $F_\hbar^\mathcal{L}(\text{while } b \ \{P\}, \mathcal{X}) \triangleq [\![\neg b]\!]_\hbar(lfp_\varnothing^\subseteq \mathcal{W_\hbar})$ where:

1. *(Bcc lift)* $\mathcal{W_\hbar} \triangleq \lambda \mathcal{T}.\wp(\bigcup \mathcal{X} \cup [\![P]\!][\![b]\!]\bigcup \mathcal{T})$
2. *(Inner lift)* $\mathcal{W_\hbar} \triangleq \lambda \mathcal{T}.\{\varnothing\} \cup (\mathcal{X} \uplus [\![P]\!]_\hbar[\![b]\!]_\hbar \mathcal{T})$
3. *(Mixed lift)* $\mathcal{W_\hbar} \triangleq \lambda \mathcal{T}.\mathcal{X} \cup \{[\![P]\!][\![b]\!]T \cup [\![\neg b]\!]T \mid T \in \mathcal{T}\}$

The *Bcc lift* defines the collecting hypersemantics as the best complete concretization [25] of the while semantics. The *Inner lift* combines by union, at each step of computation, all the possible results. In particular, the binary operator $\uplus \in \wp(\wp(\mathbb{DEN})) \times \wp(\wp(\mathbb{DEN})) \to \wp(\wp(\mathbb{DEN}))$, defined as $\mathcal{X} \uplus \mathcal{Y} \triangleq \{X \cup Y \mid X \in \mathcal{X} \wedge Y \in \mathcal{Y}\}$, is a slight modification of $\uplus$, introduced in [25] and it is an instance of the construction presented in [14] (Page 4, example 1). Moreover, the resulting semantics corresponds to the one proposed in [20] for analyzing analyses. Finally, the *Mixed lift* is the instantiation of the hypercollecting semantics of [4] to a generic trace denotations domain $\mathbb{DEN}$. Each while operator $\mathcal{W_\hbar}$ is a monotone function over the complete lattice $\langle \wp(\wp(\mathbb{DEN})), \subseteq, \cup, \cap, \wp(\mathbb{DEN}), \varnothing \rangle$, hence its least fixpoint exists and it can be computed as shown before.

Unfortunately, none of the previous definitions computes the additive lift of $F^\mathcal{L}$, namely $\{F^\mathcal{L}(\text{while } b \ \{P\}, X) \mid X \in \mathcal{X}\} \neq F_\hbar^\mathcal{L}(\text{while } b \ \{P\}, \mathcal{X})$, as we can observe in the next example.

Example 5. Consider P of Example 4. The *Bcc lift* collecting hypersemantics is $[\![P]\!]_\hbar \{\{2,5\}\} = \wp(\{4,5\})$, computed as $\{\{2,5\}\} \xrightarrow{\mathcal{W_\hbar}} \wp(\{4,5\})\}$ where

$$\mathcal{W_\hbar}^0 = \varnothing; \ \mathcal{W_\hbar}^1 = \wp(\{2,5\}); \ \mathcal{W_\hbar}^2 = \wp(\{2,3,5\}); \ \mathcal{W_\hbar}^3 = \wp(\{2,3,4,5\})$$

The *Inner lift* collecting hypersemantics is $[\![P]\!]_\hbar \{\{2,5\}\} = \{\varnothing, \{5\}, \{4,5\}\}$, computed as $\{\{2,5\}\} \xrightarrow{\mathcal{W_\hbar}} \{\varnothing, \{5\}, \{4,5\}\}$ where

$$\mathcal{W_\hbar}^0 = \varnothing; \ \mathcal{W_\hbar}^1 = \{\varnothing, \{2,5\}\}; \ \mathcal{W_\hbar}^2 = \{\varnothing, \{2,5\}, \{2,3,5\}\};$$
$$\mathcal{W_\hbar}^3 = \{\varnothing, \{2,5\}, \{2,3,5\}, \{2,3,4,5\}\}$$

The *Mixed lift* collecting hypersemantics is $[\![P]\!]_\hbar \{\{2,5\}\} = \{\{5\}, \{4,5\}\}$, computed as $\{\{2,5\}\} \xrightarrow{\mathcal{W_\hbar}} \{\{5\}, \{4,5\}\}$ where

$$\mathcal{W_\hbar}^0 = \varnothing; \ \mathcal{W_\hbar}^1 = \{\{2,5\}\}; \ \mathcal{W_\hbar}^2 = \{\{2,5\}, \{3,5\}\}; \ \mathcal{W_\hbar}^3 = \{\{2,5\}, \{3,5\}, \{4,5\}\}$$

From the iterates $\mathcal{W_\hbar}^i$ we observe the monotonicity (extensivity) of $\mathcal{W_\hbar}$. All the semantics are sound, because $[\![P]\!]\{2,5\} \in [\![P]\!]_\hbar \{\{2,5\}\}$. *End example.*

3.2 Soundness and Completeness Issues

Let $[\![P]\!]_\mathfrak{h}^\mathfrak{b}$, $[\![P]\!]_\mathfrak{h}^\mathfrak{i}$ and $[\![P]\!]_\mathfrak{h}^\mathfrak{m}$ be the collecting hypersemantics defined in terms of the *Bcc*, *Inner* and *Mixed* lifts, respectively, for the while case of $F_\mathfrak{h}^\mathcal{L}$, and defined as the additive lift to $\wp(\wp(\mathbb{D}\textsc{en}))$ of $F^\mathcal{L}$ for all the other statements. Then, all these collecting hypersemantics are sound.

Theorem 1 (Soundness). *For every* $X \in \wp(\mathbb{D}\textsc{en})$ *we have*

$$[\![P]\!]X \in [\![P]\!]_\mathfrak{h}^\mathfrak{b}\{X\} \quad and \quad [\![P]\!]X \in [\![P]\!]_\mathfrak{h}^\mathfrak{i}\{X\} \quad and \quad [\![P]\!]X \in [\![P]\!]_\mathfrak{h}^\mathfrak{m}\{X\}$$

This results tells us that these hypersemantics can be soundly used for the verification of hyperproperties of P, unfortunately adding some further spurious information not directly due to approximation, i.e., spurious elements of $\wp(\wp(\mathbb{D}\textsc{en}))$. This is somewhat new: Usually the source of incompleteness is the abstraction process (of an abstract semantics), not the collecting semantics itself. Luckily, for subset-closed hyperproperties this is not a real concern. In fact when $\mathfrak{Hp} \in \textsc{SSC}^\textsf{H}$, we have that $P \models \mathfrak{Hp}$ iff $\wp([\![P]\!]\mathfrak{I}) \subseteq \mathfrak{Hp}$. Furthermore, the three collecting hypersemantics introduced above, are related as follows.

Proposition 2. $\forall \mathcal{X} \in \wp(\wp(\mathbb{D}\textsc{en}))$: $[\![P]\!]_\mathfrak{h}^\mathfrak{m}\mathcal{X} \subseteq [\![P]\!]_\mathfrak{h}^\mathfrak{b}\mathcal{X}$ *and* $[\![P]\!]_\mathfrak{h}^\mathfrak{i}\mathcal{X} \subseteq [\![P]\!]_\mathfrak{h}^\mathfrak{b}\mathcal{X}$.

Hence we can state that all the proposed collecting hypersemantics are complete verification methods for bounded subset-closed hyperproperties.

Theorem 2 (Completeness). *Let* $\mathfrak{Hp} \in \textsc{SSC}_k^\textsf{H}$ *(for some* $k \in \mathbb{N}$*), then:*

$$P \models \mathfrak{Hp} \Leftrightarrow [\![P]\!]_\mathfrak{h}^\mathfrak{b}\{\mathfrak{I}\} \subseteq \mathfrak{Hp} \Leftrightarrow [\![P]\!]_\mathfrak{h}^\mathfrak{i}\{\mathfrak{I}\} \subseteq \mathfrak{Hp} \Leftrightarrow [\![P]\!]_\mathfrak{h}^\mathfrak{m}\{\mathfrak{I}\} \subseteq \mathfrak{Hp}$$

The theorem follows from the fact that all three semantics, computed from $\mathfrak{I}$, are contained in $\wp([\![P]\!]\mathfrak{I})$. So, even if the collecting hypersemantics inserts spurious information, this information does not lower the precision of the analysis, when we deal with bounded subset-closed hyperproperties. Note that the Theorem 2 also holds with $k = \omega$, i.e., it also holds for unbounded subset-closed hyperproperties.

4 Lifting Abstract Domains

Once we have lifted the semantics, in order to perform verification we need to compute the semantics on an abstract domain[5], namely we have to compute an abstract semantics. In the classic framework of abstract interpretation [12,13] we compute an over-approximation $O \supseteq [\![P]\!]\mathfrak{I}$ of a program semantics, allowing us to soundly verify trace properties. This is obtained by means of an abstraction of the concrete domain, where the abstract semantics plays the role of the over-approximation. Let P be a program, $\mathcal{A}$ an abstract domain of $\wp(\mathbb{D}\textsc{en})$, forming

---

[5] $\mathcal{A}$ is an abstract domain of $\mathcal{C}$ if there exists a Galois connection $(\langle \mathcal{C}, \preccurlyeq \rangle, \alpha, \gamma, \langle \mathcal{A}, \preceq \rangle)$, where α, γ are monotone maps such that: $\forall c \in \mathcal{C}, a \in \mathcal{A} . \alpha(c) \preceq a \Leftrightarrow c \preccurlyeq \gamma(a)$.

the Galois connection $(\langle \wp(\mathbb{DEN}), \subseteq \rangle, \alpha, \gamma, \langle \mathcal{A}, \preceq \rangle)$, $\mathfrak{P}$ a trace property in $\wp(\mathbb{DEN})$ and $[\![P]\!]^{\mathcal{A}}$ an abstract interpretation of $[\![P]\!]$ on $\mathcal{A}$, i.e., $[\![P]\!]X \subseteq \gamma \circ [\![P]\!]^{\mathcal{A}} \circ \alpha(X)$. Then $\gamma \circ [\![P]\!]^{\mathcal{A}} \circ \alpha(\mathfrak{I}) \subseteq \mathfrak{P}$ implies $P \models \mathfrak{P}$. Similarly, an over-approximation $\mathcal{O} \supseteq [\![P]\!]_{\mathfrak{h}}\{\mathfrak{I}\}$ leads to a sound verification mechanism for hyperproperties. Let $\mathcal{A}\mathfrak{h}$ be an abstract domain of $\wp(\wp(\mathbb{DEN}))$, forming the Galois connection $(\langle \wp(\wp(\mathbb{DEN})), \subseteq \rangle, \alpha_{\mathfrak{h}}, \gamma_{\mathfrak{h}}, \langle \mathcal{A}\mathfrak{h}, \preceq_{\mathfrak{h}} \rangle)$, $\mathfrak{H}\mathfrak{p} \in \wp(\wp(\mathbb{DEN}))$ an hyperproperty, $[\![P]\!]_{\mathfrak{h}}$ a sound collecting hypersemantics, i.e., $[\![P]\!]\mathfrak{I} \in [\![P]\!]_{\mathfrak{h}}\{\mathfrak{I}\}$, and $[\![P]\!]_{\mathfrak{h}}^{\mathcal{A}\mathfrak{h}}$ an abstract interpretation of $[\![P]\!]_{\mathfrak{h}}$ on $\mathcal{A}\mathfrak{h}$, i.e., $[\![P]\!]_{\mathfrak{h}}\mathcal{X} \subseteq \gamma_{\mathfrak{h}} \circ [\![P]\!]_{\mathfrak{h}}^{\mathcal{A}\mathfrak{h}} \circ \alpha_{\mathfrak{h}}(\mathcal{X})$. Then:

$$\gamma_{\mathfrak{h}} \circ [\![P]\!]_{\mathfrak{h}}^{\mathcal{A}\mathfrak{h}} \circ \alpha_{\mathfrak{h}}(\{\mathfrak{I}\}) \subseteq \mathfrak{H}\mathfrak{p} \quad \text{implies} \quad P \models \mathfrak{H}\mathfrak{p}$$

Hence, at this point we wonder how we can define/lift abstract domains at the hyperlevel, i.e., on sets of sets, in order to approximate hypersemantics, i.e., semantics lifted to the hyperlevel.

4.1   The Compositional Nature of Hyper Abstract Domains

An hyper abstract domain, or *hyperdomain*, can be decomposed basically into two parts: an inner abstraction and an outer abstraction. Note that we are not talking about a generic abstract domain on sets of sets: Our focus is on the verification of hyperproperties, hence we need domains, on sets of sets, which *represent* information concerning programs, whose concrete semantics is on sets. Let us consider Non-Interference (NI) as running example, for providing the intuition beyond these concepts. NI requires that, for each set of computations agreeing on the the same low input, the low output is constant.

The *inner abstraction* approximates sets of denotations in $\mathbb{DEN}$, namely it says which information about program executions should be observed. In NI, for each set of computations we are interested in the constant analysis on low variables, i.e., each set of computations (starting from states agreeing on the low variables) should be contained in a set of the form $\mathsf{C}_l \triangleq \{\langle h, l \rangle \mid h \in \mathbb{Z}\}, l \in \mathbb{Z}$.

The *outer abstraction* approximates sets of sets of denotations, namely it says which information about programs semantics is interesting, in other words, which is the desired invariant among all the sets of computations collected. In the example, we require that all the possible resulting sets are constants in the low variable, hence they are a set in $\wp(\{\mathsf{C}_l \mid l \in \mathbb{Z}\})$.

It should be clear that, the outer abstraction is defined at the hyperlevel and therefore in order to compose it with the inner one, defined at the standard level $\wp(\mathbb{DEN})$, we need to lift the inner abstraction to $\wp(\wp(\mathbb{DEN}))$. In this case, the *lifting function* just leverages the domain at the level of sets of sets. In the case of hyperdomains lifting a domain does not introduce computability problems, hence we can always use the additive lift. Formally, suppose the *inner abstraction* $\mathcal{A}$ is given by the Galois connection

$$\langle \wp(\mathbb{DEN}), \subseteq \rangle \xleftarrow[\alpha_i]{\gamma_i} \langle \mathcal{A}, \preceq \rangle$$

The *lifting transformer* $\mathcal{L} \in (\wp(\mathbb{D}\mathrm{EN}) \rightarrow \mathcal{A}) \rightarrow (\wp(\wp(\mathbb{D}\mathrm{EN})) \rightarrow \wp(\mathcal{A}))$ is the transformer addively lifting functions, namely $\mathcal{L} \triangleq \lambda f . \lambda \mathcal{X} . \{f(X) \mid X \in \mathcal{X}\}$ [11]. Let us consider the transformer $\mathcal{G} \in (\wp(\mathbb{D}\mathrm{EN}) \rightarrow \mathcal{A}) \rightarrow (\wp(\mathcal{A}) \rightarrow \wp(\wp(\mathbb{D}\mathrm{EN})))$ [11] defined as $\mathcal{G} \triangleq \lambda f . \lambda Y . \{X \mid f(X) \in Y\}$. Due to elementwise set abstraction, we have that $\mathcal{L}(\alpha_i)$ and $\mathcal{G}(\alpha_i)$ form a Galois connection [11], in particular we have

$$\langle \wp(\wp(\mathbb{D}\mathrm{EN})), \subseteq \rangle \xleftarrow[\mathcal{L}(\alpha_i)]{\mathcal{G}(\alpha_i)} \langle \wp(\mathcal{A}), \subseteq \rangle$$

We obtained so far, starting form the inner abstraction defined on the standard level and applying the additive lift, the hyper domain on which we can define the outer abstraction. In other words, the *outer abstraction* is a further abstraction of $\wp(\mathcal{A})$ given by the Galois connection

$$\langle \wp(\mathcal{A}), \subseteq \rangle \xleftarrow[\alpha_o]{\gamma_o} \langle \mathcal{A}_\mathfrak{h}, \preccurlyeq_\mathfrak{h} \rangle$$

This outer abstraction captures the information that must be invariant among all the collected sets of executions (abstracted in $\mathcal{A}$), looking, by construction, for invariants among elements of $\mathcal{A}$. Finally, by composition, we have that

$$\langle \wp(\wp(\mathbb{D}\mathrm{EN})), \subseteq \rangle \xleftarrow[\alpha_o \circ \mathcal{L}(\alpha_i)]{\mathcal{G}(\alpha_i) \circ \gamma_o} \langle \mathcal{A}_\mathfrak{h}, \preccurlyeq_\mathfrak{h} \rangle$$

Note that, it is not mandatory, for the inner abstraction $\mathcal{A}$, to form a Galois connection. Indeed, in order to apply the lifting transformer, the abstraction function α_i may also fail additivity [11]. Note that, the abstract domains defined in [4] are instances of the pattern proposed here. For instance, cardinality abstraction $\mathtt{crdval} \in \wp(\mathbb{Z}) \rightarrow [0, \infty]$ (which is not additive) corresponds to our inner abstraction, while $\alpha_{\max} \in \wp([0, \infty]) \rightarrow [0, \infty]$ computing the least upper bound, i.e., $\alpha_{\max}(X) \triangleq \max(X)$, is the outer abstraction. The resulting abstraction is obtained by lifting the inner one and composing it with outer one, i.e., $\alpha_{\mathtt{crdval}} \in \wp(\wp(\mathbb{Z})) \rightarrow [0, \infty]$ coincides with $\alpha_{\max} \circ \mathcal{L}(\mathtt{crdval})$, which is the process we have generalized above. In the following, we give some examples of hyper abstract domains obtained starting from initial known abstractions on sets.

4.2   Dealing with Constants Propagation

Suppose to define an hyperanalysis on the concrete domain $\wp(\wp(\mathbb{Z}))$, and to be interested in constants propagation at the hyperlevel, namely we aim at verifying whether all the sets of computations provide constant results. This corresponds intuitively to an inner abstraction which is the hyperlevel constant propagation (lifted as shown before), and an outer abstraction retrieving information about the constant analysis at standard level. The standard domain of constants $C \triangleq \mathbb{Z} \cup \{\bot, \top\}$ is defined by the Galois insertion[6] $(\langle \wp(\mathbb{Z}), \subseteq \rangle, \alpha_c, \gamma_c, \langle C, \preceq \rangle)$ where $c_1 \preceq c_2 \triangleq (c_1 = \bot \vee c_1 = c_2 \vee c_2 = \top)$ and

$$\alpha_c \triangleq \lambda X . \begin{cases} \bot & \text{if } X = \varnothing \\ n & \text{if } X = \{n\} \\ \top & \text{otherwise} \end{cases} \qquad \gamma_c \triangleq \lambda c . \begin{cases} \varnothing & \text{if } c = \bot \\ \{n\} & \text{if } c = n \\ \mathbb{Z} & \text{otherwise} \end{cases}$$

In order to get an abstract domain on sets of sets we rely on the lifting transformer, obtaining the following Galois insertion

$$\langle \wp(\wp(\mathbb{Z})), \subseteq \rangle \xleftarrow[\mathcal{L}(\alpha_c)]{\mathcal{G}(\alpha_c)} \langle \wp(C), \subseteq \rangle$$

At this point, to look for constant invariants at the hyperlevel, namely in the outer abstraction, means to check whether all the collected sets of values are constants. Hence, we need to retrieve information about what there is inside the analysis at standard level. This is obtained by using the Galois insertion

$$\langle \wp(C), \subseteq \rangle \xleftarrow[\alpha_{cc}]{\gamma_{cc}} \langle \wp(\mathbb{Z}) \cup \{C\}, \subseteq \rangle \quad \text{where} \quad \alpha_{cc}(X) \triangleq \begin{cases} X & \text{if } X \subseteq \mathbb{Z} \\ C & \text{otherwise} \end{cases} \quad \gamma_{cc} \triangleq id$$

Obtaining, by composition, the insertion

$$\langle \wp(\wp(\mathbb{Z})), \subseteq \rangle \xleftarrow[\alpha_{cc} \circ \mathcal{L}(\alpha_c)]{\mathcal{G}(\alpha_c) \circ \gamma_{cc}} \langle \wp(\mathbb{Z}) \cup \{C\}, \subseteq \rangle \tag{2}$$

In this example, we have an outer abstraction that simply checks whether all the collected sets of computations satisfy the constant property for numerical variables, namely all the sets of computations produce constant values. We can generalize the same idea to any inner abstraction, namely we can build an outer abstraction checking whether all the collected sets of computations constantly satisfy an abstract property, fixed by the inner abstraction. We call this hyper abstract domain *hyperlevel (abstract) constants* of an inner abstraction.

Hyperlevel (Abstract) Constants. Consider a lattice $\langle \mathcal{A}, \preccurlyeq, \curlyvee, \curlywedge, \top_{\mathcal{A}}, \bot_{\mathcal{A}} \rangle$, forming the Galois connection $(\langle \wp(C), \subseteq \rangle, \alpha, \gamma, \langle \mathcal{A}, \preccurlyeq \rangle)$. The set of *atoms* $\text{Atm}^{\mathcal{A}}$ of $\mathcal{A}$ is the set of its elements covering the bottom, i.e., $\text{Atm}^{\mathcal{A}} \triangleq \{a \in \mathcal{A} \mid \forall a' \in \mathcal{A} . a' \preccurlyeq a \Rightarrow (a' = \bot^{\mathcal{A}} \vee a' = a)\}$. Suppose $\mathcal{A}$ is *partitioning*[7] [22,29], which in particular implies that $\text{Atm}^{\mathcal{A}}$ induces, by means of α, a partition of C, namely for each element $c \in C$ we have that $\alpha(c) \in \text{Atm}^{\mathcal{A}}$. For instance, consider the abstract domain $\text{Pos} \triangleq \{\varnothing, \mathbb{Z}_{<0}, \{0\}, \mathbb{Z}_{>0}, \mathbb{Z}_{\geq 0}, \mathbb{Z}_{\leq 0}, \mathbb{Z}_{\neq 0}, \mathbb{Z}\}^{8} \subseteq \wp(\mathbb{Z})$. The set of its atoms is $\text{Atm}^{\text{Pos}} = \{\mathbb{Z}_{<0}, \{0\}, \mathbb{Z}_{>0}\}$. In order to perform hyperlevel constants

---

[6] It is a Galois connection with surjective abstraction function.

[7] We recall that any abstract domain can be made partitioning [22].

[8] Where $\mathbb{Z}_{<0} \triangleq \{n \in \mathbb{Z} \mid n < 0\}$ and the others are similarly defined.

on $\mathcal{A}$ we consider the set of its atoms, which precisely identify the properties of concrete values observed in $\mathcal{A}$ (in Pos the sign of any value). The idea is to check whether these abstract values remain constant during computations. For instance, we aim at checking whether all the computations starting from inputs with the same sign, keep constant the value sign during execution. At this point, we can define the hyperlevel (abstract) constants domain for $\mathcal{A}$ as $\mathcal{A}_{\mathfrak{h}c} \triangleq \wp(\mathrm{Atm}^{\mathcal{A}}) \cup \{\mathcal{A}\}$, forming the following insertion:

$$\langle \wp(\mathcal{A}), \subseteq \rangle \xleftrightarrow[\alpha_{\mathfrak{h}c}]{\gamma_{\mathfrak{h}c}} \langle \mathcal{A}_{\mathfrak{h}c}, \subseteq \rangle \text{ where } \alpha_{\mathfrak{h}c}(X) \triangleq \begin{cases} X & \text{if } X \subseteq \mathrm{Atm}^{\mathcal{A}} \\ \mathcal{A} & \text{otherwise} \end{cases} \quad \gamma_{\mathfrak{h}c} \triangleq id$$

Then, applying the lifting transformer and composing, we have

$$\langle \wp(\wp(\mathcal{C})), \subseteq \rangle \xleftrightarrow[\mathcal{L}(\alpha)]{\mathcal{G}(\alpha)} \langle \wp(\mathcal{A}), \subseteq \rangle \qquad \langle \wp(\wp(\mathcal{C})), \subseteq \rangle \xleftrightarrow[\alpha_{\mathfrak{h}c} \circ \mathcal{L}(\alpha)]{\mathcal{G}(\alpha) \circ \gamma_{\mathfrak{h}c}} \langle \mathcal{A}_{\mathfrak{h}c}, \subseteq \rangle \quad (3)$$

For instance, if $\mathcal{C} = \mathbb{Z}$ and $\mathcal{A} = \mathrm{Pos}$ then $\mathrm{Pos}_{\mathfrak{h}c} \triangleq \wp(\{\varnothing, \mathbb{Z}_{<0}, \{0\}, \mathbb{Z}_{>0}\}) \cup \{\mathrm{Pos}\}$ is the hyperdomain, abstraction of $\wp(\wp(\mathbb{Z}))$, for hyperlevel (abstract) Pos-constants.

4.3   Dealing with Intervals

Suppose now to be interested in a hyper intervals analysis. The classic abstract domain of intervals is defined over numerical values, but the interval construction can be easily generalized [13]. Given a complete lattice $\langle \mathcal{C}, \leqslant, \vee, \wedge, \top, \bot \rangle$, we can define its interval domain as:

$$\mathcal{I} = \{[a, b] \mid a \in \mathcal{C} \smallsetminus \{\top\}, b \in \mathcal{C} \smallsetminus \{\bot\}, a \leqslant b\} \cup \{\bot_{\imath}\}$$

We have that $\langle \mathcal{I}, \sqsubseteq, \sqcup, \sqcap, [\bot, \top], \bot_{\imath} \rangle$ is a complete lattice where: $\forall I \in \mathcal{I}. \bot_{\imath} \sqsubseteq I \sqsubseteq [\bot, \top]$ and $[a, b] \sqsubseteq [c, d]$ iff $c \leqslant a$ and $b \leqslant d$; $[a, b] \sqcup [c, d] \triangleq [a \wedge c, b \vee d]$; $[a, b] \sqcap [c, d] \triangleq [a \vee c, b \wedge d]$ if $a \vee c \leqslant b \wedge d$ and $[a, b] \sqcap [c, d] \triangleq \bot_{\imath}$ if $a \vee c \not\leqslant b \wedge d$. An instance of this pattern is the classic domain of intervals over integers, where the initial domain is the lattice $\langle \mathbb{Z} \cup \{-\infty, +\infty\}, \leqslant, \max, \min, +\infty, -\infty \rangle$ [13].

The corresponding Galois connection between (the powerset of) the concrete domain $\mathcal{C}$ and its intervals domain is

$$\langle \wp(\mathcal{C}), \subseteq \rangle \xleftrightarrow[\alpha_{\imath}]{\gamma_{\imath}} \langle \mathcal{I}, \sqsubseteq \rangle$$

$$\text{where } \alpha_{\imath}(X) \triangleq [\bigwedge X, \bigvee X] \quad \gamma_{\imath}([a, b]) \triangleq \{c \in \mathcal{C} \mid a \leqslant c \leqslant b\}$$

We can use this construction for an inner abstraction when we aim at characterizing invariants of intervals of computations. In this case we use the lift $\mathcal{L}$ and then we compose it with an outer abstraction determining the desired invariants. But, we can use this construction also for an outer abstraction by defining it on a domain $\mathcal{A}$ already obtained by an inner abstraction. In this case we characterize interval invariants of an inner abstract domain, abstraction of $\wp(\mathcal{A})$. For instance, if the inner is Pos, then we would characterize the sign properties of interval bounds.

5   Verifying Bounded Subset-Closed Hyperproperties

As we have seen in Sect. 2, for bounded subset-closed hyperproperties the verification process is simplified. Instead of checking the hyperproperty for the set
of all inputs $\mathfrak{I}$, or for all its subsets, it is sufficient to check the hyperproperty
for a set of *finite* subsets of $\mathfrak{I}$. Namely, if $\mathfrak{Hp} \in \mathrm{SSC}_k^{\mathrm{H}}$, we need to check the sets
in $\mathfrak{I}^{|k} \triangleq \{X \subseteq \mathfrak{I} \mid |X| = k\}$. Then with a sound collecting hypersemantics $[\![\mathsf{P}]\!]_{\mathfrak{h}}$
(Sect. 3), we can verify the hyperproperty just approximating $[\![\mathsf{P}]\!]_{\mathfrak{h}} \mathfrak{I}^{|k}$.

Theorem 3. *Given $\mathfrak{Hp} \in \mathrm{SSC}_k^{\mathrm{H}}$, we have that $[\![\mathsf{P}]\!]_{\mathfrak{h}} \mathfrak{I}^{|k} \subseteq \mathfrak{Hp}$ iff $\mathsf{P} \models \mathfrak{Hp}$.*

Proof. By soundness and completeness (for $\mathrm{SSC}^{\mathrm{H}}$) of the collecting hyperseman-
tics, stated in Sect. 3, we have that $\{[\![P]\!]X \mid X \in \mathfrak{I}^{|k}\} \subseteq [\![\mathsf{P}]\!]_{\mathfrak{h}} \mathfrak{I}^{|k}$. Then, recalling
that we are in a deterministic setting, we have that $\{[\![P]\!]X \mid X \in \mathfrak{I}^{|k}\} = \{X \subseteq$
$[\![P]\!]\mathfrak{I} \mid |X| = k\}$. Then, the theorem follows from the results of Sect. 2.   □

Theorem 3 allows us to simplify the design of hyperanalyses for bounded subset-
closed hyperproperties. It justifies also the methodology used in [4] in order
to verify information flow. In fact, despite their analysis starts from $\{\mathfrak{I}\}$, the
(abstract) semantics indeed decomposes $\mathfrak{I}$ in all its subsets, in order to apply
approximations at the level of sets of sets. Theorem 3 confirms the correctness
of the approach used in [4] and states that the "decomposition" can be made
explicit, splitting the input set from which we start the hyperanalysis.

5.1   Non-Interference

Information flows control is one of the primary motivations that has led
researchers to develop a theory about hyperproperties. A well-known information flow property is Non-Interference [10, 21], introduced in Example 1. As we
have seen in the example, NI is defined over I/O traces, i.e., $\mathbb{D}\mathrm{EN} \triangleq \mathsf{St} \times \mathsf{St} =$
$(\mathsf{Var} \to \mathbb{Z}) \times (\mathsf{Var} \to \mathbb{Z})$, and a program P satisfies NI iff $[\![\mathsf{P}]\!]\mathfrak{I} \in$ NI. It is
trivial to show that NI $\in \mathrm{SSC}_2^{\mathrm{H}}$, hence $\mathsf{P} \models$ NI iff $\forall X \in \mathfrak{I}^{|2}.[\![\mathsf{P}]\!]X \in$ NI. In
particular, we only need to check the sets $\{\eth, \eth'\}$ such that $\eth_{\vdash} =_{\mathsf{L}} \eth'_{\vdash}$. Let
$\mathfrak{I}_{\mathsf{L}}^{|2} = \{\{\eth, \eth'\} \in \mathfrak{I}^{|2} \mid \eth_{\vdash} =_{\mathsf{L}} \eth'_{\vdash}\}$. Suppose to have a sound collecting hyperseman-
tics $[\![\mathsf{P}]\!]_{\mathfrak{h}} \in \wp(\wp(\mathbb{D}\mathrm{EN})) \to \wp(\wp(\mathbb{D}\mathrm{EN}))$. Then we have that $\mathsf{P} \models$ NI iff $[\![\mathsf{P}]\!]_{\mathfrak{h}} \mathfrak{I}_{\mathsf{L}}^{|2} \subseteq$ NI.
Now we look for a hyper abstract domain allowing us to verify NI. First of all,
we abstract sets of sets of traces in sets of traces of sets, namely sets of traces of
"abstract memories" $\mathsf{St}^{\natural} \triangleq \mathsf{Var} \to \wp(\mathbb{Z})^9$. Hence, consider the following Galois
connection $(\langle \wp(\wp(\mathbb{D}\mathrm{EN})), \subseteq \rangle, \alpha_{\mathrm{tr}}, \gamma_{\mathrm{tr}}, \langle \wp(\mathsf{St}^{\natural}), \subseteq \rangle)$ with

$$\alpha_{\mathrm{tr}}(\mathcal{X}) = \{\lambda \mathsf{x} \in \mathsf{Var}_{\mathsf{L}} . \{\eth_{\dashv}(\mathsf{x}) \mid \eth \in X\} \mid X \in \mathcal{X}\} \quad \gamma_{\mathrm{tr}}(\mathcal{Y}) = \bigcup \{\mathcal{X} \mid \alpha_{\mathrm{tr}}(\mathcal{X}) \subseteq \mathcal{Y}\}$$

and where $\mathsf{Var}_{\mathsf{L}} \triangleq \{\mathsf{x} \in \mathsf{Var} \mid \Gamma(\mathsf{x}) = \mathsf{L}\}$. This abstraction keeps only the abstract
memories collecting values of the low variables, moving from sets of sets of traces
to sets of abstract memories. This means that, for all computations starting from

---

[9] Here we implicitly apply a non-relational variables abstraction.

sets (of cardinality 2) which agree on low input variables, NI requires that the resulting sets of values for low variables are constant. Hence, in order to verify NI we compose this connection with the one defined in Eq. 2. Let $\alpha_{\mathtt{NI}} \triangleq \alpha_{cc} \circ \mathcal{L}(\alpha_c) \circ \alpha_{tr}$ where we abuse notation by defining $\forall X \in \wp(\mathtt{St}^\natural)$, $\alpha_{cc} \circ \mathcal{L}(\alpha_c)(X) \triangleq \lambda x \in \mathsf{Var_L} . \alpha_{cc} \circ \mathcal{L}(\alpha_c)(\{\eth^\natural(x) \mid \eth^\natural \in X\})$, and $\gamma_{\mathtt{NI}}$ is the corresponding concretization. Then we have $(\langle \wp(\wp(\mathbb{D}\textsc{en})), \subseteq \rangle, \alpha_{\mathtt{NI}}, \gamma_{\mathtt{NI}}, \langle \mathsf{Var} \to \wp(\mathbb{Z}) \cup \{\mathtt{C}\}, \dot{\subseteq} \rangle)^{10}$.

Proposition 3. $\mathsf{P} \models \mathtt{NI}$ *iff* $\forall x \in \mathsf{Var_L} . \alpha_{\mathtt{NI}}(\llbracket \mathsf{P} \rrbracket_\mathfrak{h} \mathfrak{I}_\mathsf{L}^{|2})(x) \neq \mathtt{C}$.

So, we can soundly approximate NI verification by computing the approximated hypersemantics on the hyper abstract domain $\wp(\mathbb{Z}) \cup \{\mathtt{C}\}$, for all low variables.

5.2   Abstract Non-Interference

Abstract Non-Interference [18,19] is a weakening of Non-Interference by abstract interpretation. The idea is to model flows of *properties* of data, modeled as abstractions of data. In particular, let us consider a simplified form of the notion given in [19]. Let $(\langle \wp(\mathbb{Z}), \subseteq \rangle, \alpha_\phi, \gamma_\phi, \langle \Phi, \preccurlyeq_\phi \rangle)$ be an abstraction on input values, fixing what is observable/not-observable of the input. For instance, in the standard case of Non-Interference it is the abstraction observing $\top$ (nothing) of H variables, and the identity of L variables. But it possible to weaken the policy by observing other properties of input variables, where the input property fixed for H variables represents the information we allow to flow, while the property of L ones represents a weakening of what an observer may observe of low inputs. Consider also an output abstraction $(\langle \wp(\mathbb{Z}), \subseteq \rangle, \alpha_\vartheta, \gamma_\vartheta, \langle \Theta, \preccurlyeq_\vartheta \rangle)$, which represents what can be observed in output, in the standard case the identity on L variables and $\top$, i.e., nothing, on H variables. Also in this case, the framework allows us to weaken the policy by fixing a more abstract observable property of L variables. Formally, Abstract Non-Interference is:

$$\mathtt{ANI} = \{X \in \wp(\mathbb{D}\textsc{en}) \mid \forall \eth, \eth' \in X . (\alpha_\phi(\eth_\vdash) = \alpha_\phi(\eth'_\vdash) \Rightarrow \alpha_\vartheta(\eth_\dashv) = \alpha_\vartheta(\eth'_\dashv))\}$$

As it happens for Non-Interference, we only need to check ANI for the sets $\{\eth, \eth'\}$ such that $\alpha_\phi(\eth_\vdash) = \alpha_\phi(\eth'_\vdash)$. Let $\mathfrak{I}_\phi^{|2} \triangleq \{\{\eth, \eth'\} \in \mathfrak{I}^{|2} \mid \alpha_\phi(\eth_\vdash) = \alpha_\phi(\eth'_\vdash)\}$, then we have that $\mathsf{P} \models \mathtt{ANI}$ iff $\llbracket \mathsf{P} \rrbracket_\mathfrak{h} \mathfrak{I}_\phi^{|2} \subseteq \mathtt{ANI}$. Consider the Galois insertion of Eq. 3 instantiated on $\mathcal{A} = \Theta$ and $\mathcal{C} = \mathbb{Z}$, and consider the abstraction α_{tr} defined before for NI. Let us define then $\alpha_{\mathtt{ANI}} = \alpha_{\mathfrak{h}c} \circ \mathcal{L}(\alpha_\vartheta) \circ \alpha_{tr}$. As before, we abuse notation by defining $\forall X \in \wp(\mathtt{St}^\natural)$, $\alpha_{\mathfrak{h}c} \circ \mathcal{L}(\alpha_\vartheta)(X) \triangleq \lambda x \in \mathsf{Var_L} . \alpha_{\mathfrak{h}c} \circ \mathcal{L}(\alpha_\vartheta)(\{\eth^\natural(x) \mid \eth^\natural \in X\})$, and $\gamma_{\mathtt{ANI}}$ the corresponding concretization. By composition, we have $(\langle \wp(\wp(\mathbb{D}\textsc{en})) \subseteq \rangle, \alpha_{\mathtt{ANI}}, \gamma_{\mathtt{ANI}}, \langle \Theta_{\mathfrak{h}c}, \dot{\subseteq} \rangle)$.

Proposition 4. $\mathsf{P} \models \mathtt{ANI}$ *iff* $\forall x \in \mathsf{Var_L} . \alpha_{\mathtt{ANI}}(\llbracket \mathsf{P} \rrbracket_\mathfrak{h} \mathfrak{I}_\phi^{|2})(x) \neq \Theta$.

Hence, we can soundly approximate the verification of ANI by computing the approximated hyper semantics on the hyper domain $\Theta_{\mathfrak{h}c}$ of abstract stores, checking whether all the computations have constant values in Θ for all the low variables.

---

[10] Here $\dot{\subseteq}$ denotes the pointwise set inclusion.

6   Related Works

The topic of hyperproperties verification is relatively new. In [9], the authors state that it is possible to reduce the verification of a k-hypersafety on a system S to the verification of a safety property on the self-composed system S^k. The self-composition can be sequential, parallel or in an interleaving manner and a lot of works applied this methodology [6,27,30,31]. All these approaches only deal with hypersafety, but we believe that self-composition methods could be extended to the more general bounded subset-closed hyperproperties, in order to verify also non-safety hyperproperties. A very recent work [3] proposes a new methodology for proving the absence of timing channels. This work is based on the idea of "decomposition instead of self-composition" [3]. The authors claim that self-composition is computationally to expensive to be used in practice, so they propose a different approach. The idea is to partition the program semantics and to analyze each partition with standard methods. All previous approaches are proven to be sound and complete for k-hypersafety, but our methodology is sound and complete for the more general subset-closed hyperproperties.

Besides the reduction to safety, in [1] the authors introduce a runtime refutation methods for k-safety, based on a three-valued logic. Similarly, [8,15] define hyperlogics (HyperLTL and HyperCTL/CTL*), i.e., extensions of temporal logic able to quantify over multiple traces. Some algorithms for model-checking in these extended temporal logics exist, but only for particular decidable fragments, since the model-checking problem for these logics is, in general, undecidable.

The use of abstract interpretation in hyperproperties verification is limited to [4,25,32]. In [4], the authors deal with information flow specifications and they focus on the definition of the abstract domains over sets of sets needed for the analysis. They proposed an hyper collecting semantics computed denotationally on the code of the program to analyze. We already highlighted (Sects. 4.1 and 5) the links between the present work and [4]. Our approach is a generalization of the methodologies of [4], since their hypercollecting semantics is an instance of our semantics lift and the abstract domains they use follow our inner/outer abstractions pattern. In [25] we extend the hierarchy of semantics of a transition system [11], in order to cope with hyperproperties verification. Furthermore, we introduce the notion of subset-closed hyperproperties. Our present work follows this latter, but it is focused on how it is possible to construct a collecting hypersemantic, for computer programs, lifting a given collecting semantics (Sect. 3). Furthermore, our work aims at the verification of particular subset-closed hyperproperties. Finally, in [32] the authors use abstract interpretation in order to define an ad-hoc semantics at the level of sets of sets suitable for the verification of a particular hyperproperty called "data input usage". This latter is not subset-closed, hence it is beyond the scope of the present work. Furthermore, their goal is not to give a general methodology for defining new verification methods for hyperproperties, as we do for subset-closed hyperproperties. Indeed, despite the interesting approach, their work can be applied only to the particular hyperproperty they introduced.

7   Conclusion and Future Works

In this work, we made another little step into the understanding of hyperproperties. In particular, we reasoned about particular subset-closed hyperproperties, which are more suitable for verification. Subset-closed hyperproperties are those allowing to disprove program hyperproperties by finding a subset of its semantics which do not satisfy the hyperproperty. If we can limit the cardinality of these refuting witnesses we obtain the bounded subset-closed hyperproperties. These latter generalize k-hypersafety and some hyperliveness, so they capture a lot of interesting systems specifications. In this work, we described how it is possible to leverage the standard abstract interpretation based static analysis framework in order to verify bounded subset-closed hyperproperties. In particular, we showed how to lift a collecting semantics to sets of sets and how to build hyper abstract domains. Putting all the ingredients together, we specified the general recipe for defining an hyperanalysis (i.e., a static analysis at the level of sets of sets) for bounded subset-closed hyperproperties. It is clear that, such an analysis would be useful, not only for checking (abstract) non-interference in its different forms (e.g., declassified) [5,19,23], but also in other contexts related to information flow such as abstract slicing [24,26] or injection vulnerability analysis [7].

As future works, we want to investigate whether it is possible to compute a collecting hypersemantics reducing as much as possible the spurious information added by lifting semantics at the hyperlevel. We already observed that this is not a problem for $\mathrm{SSC}^{\mathbb{H}}$ hyperproperties, we wonder whether we can improve the proposed framework by enriching the information represented by states, in order to reduce the noise added by collecting at the hyperlevel. Moreover, we want to deepen the link between hyperproperties and the problem of analyzing analyzers, aiming at systematically analyzing static analyses [16]. In particular, we believe that the hyperdomains, introduced in Sect. 4, can be used not only for hyperproperties verification but also for this latter purpose.

Acknowledgments. We thank Roberto Giacobazzi and Francesco Ranzato for sharing with us their preliminary work on analyzing analyses [20], which has many connections with the present work and may create interesting future collaborations. Finally, we would like to thank the anonymous reviewers for the useful suggestions and comments, helping us in improving the presentation of our work.

References

1. Agrawal, S., Bonakdarpour, B.: Runtime verification of k-safety hyperproperties in HyperLTL. In: IEEE 29th Computer Security Foundations Symposium, pp. 239–252 (2016)
2. Alpern, B., Schneider, F.B.: Defining liveness. Inf. Process. Lett. **21**(4), 181–185 (1985)
3. Antonopoulos, T., Gazzillo, P., Hicks, M., Koskinen, E., Terauchi, T., Wei, S.: Decomposition instead of self-composition for proving the absence of timing channels. In: Proceedings of PLDI, pp. 362–375 (2017)

4. Assaf, M., Naumann, D.A., Signoles, J., Totel, E., Tronel, F.: Hypercollecting semantics and its application to static analysis of information flow. In: Proceedings of POPL, pp. 874–887 (2017)
5. Banerjee, A., Giacobazzi, R., Mastroeni, I.: What you lose is what you leak: Information leakage in declassification policies. ENTCS **173**, 47–66 (2007)
6. Barthe, G., D'Argenio, P.R., Rezk, T.: Secure information flow by self-composition. In: Proceedings of 17th IEEE Computer Security Foundations Workshop, pp. 100–114 (2004)
7. Buro, S., Mastroeni, I.: Abstract code injection - A semantic approach based on abstract non-interference. In: Dillig, I., Palsberg, J. (eds.) VMCAI 2018. LNCS, vol. 10747, pp. 116–137. Springer, Cham (2018). https://doi.org/10.1007/978-3-319-73721-8_6
8. Clarkson, M.R., Finkbeiner, B., Koleini, M., Micinski, K.K., Rabe, M.N., Sánchez, C.: Temporal logics for hyperproperties. In: Proceedings of POST (2014)
9. Clarkson, M.R., Schneider, F.B.: Hyperproperties. J. Comput. Secur. **18**(6), 1157–1210 (2010)
10. Cohen, E.: Information transmission in computational systems. SIGOPS Oper. Syst. Rev. **11**(5), 133–139 (1977)
11. Cousot, P.: Constructive design of a hierarchy of semantics of a transition system by abstract interpretation. Theor. Comput. Sci. **277**(1–2), 47–103 (2002)
12. Cousot, P., Cousot, R.: Abstract interpretation: a unified lattice model for static analysis of programs by construction or approximation of fixpoints. In: Proceedings of POPL, pp. 238–252 (1977)
13. Cousot, P., Cousot, R.: Systematic design of program analysis frameworks. In: Proceedings of POPL, pp. 269–282 (1979)
14. Cousot, P., Cousot, R.: Higher-order abstract interpretation (and application to comportment analysis generalizing strictness, termination, projection and PER analysis of functional languages). In: Proceedings of ICCL, pp. 95–112 (1994)
15. Finkbeiner, B., Rabe, M.N., Sánchez, C.: Algorithms for model checking HyperLTL and HyperCTL*. In: Kroening, D., Păsăreanu, C.S. (eds.) CAV 2015. LNCS, vol. 9206, pp. 30–48. Springer, Cham (2015). https://doi.org/10.1007/978-3-319-21690-4_3
16. Giacobazzi, R., Logozzo, F., Ranzato, F.: Analyzing program analyses. In: Proceedings of POPL, pp. 261–273 (2015)
17. Giacobazzi, R., Mastroeni, I.: Transforming semantics by abstract interpretation. Theor. Comput. Sci. **337**(1–3), 1–50 (2005)
18. Giacobazzi, R., Mastroeni, I.: Abstract non-interference: parameterizing non-interference by abstract interpretation. In: Proceedings of POPL, pp. 186–197 (2004)
19. Giacobazzi, R., Mastroeni, I.: Abstract non-interference: a unifying framework for weakening information-flow. ACM Trans. Priv. Secur **21**(2), 9:1–9:31 (2018)
20. Giacobazzi, R., Ranzato, F.: Personal communication (2017)
21. Goguen, J.A., Meseguer, J.: Security policies and security models. In: IEEE Symposium on Security and Privacy, pp. 11–20 (1982)
22. Hunt, S., Mastroeni, I.: The PER model of abstract non-interference. In: Proceedings of 12th International Symposium on Static Analysis, pp. 171–185 (2005)
23. Mastroeni, I., Banerjee, A.: Modelling declassification policies using abstract domain completeness. MSCS **21**(6), 1253–1299 (2011)
24. Mastroeni, I., Nikolić, Đ.: Abstract program slicing: from theory towards an implementation. In: Dong, J.S., Zhu, H. (eds.) ICFEM 2010. LNCS, vol. 6447, pp. 452–467. Springer, Heidelberg (2010). https://doi.org/10.1007/978-3-642-16901-4_30

25. Mastroeni, I., Pasqua, M.: Hyperhierarchy of semantics - A formal framework for hyperproperties verification. In: Ranzato, F. (ed.) SAS 2017. LNCS, vol. 10422, pp. 232–252. Springer, Cham (2017). https://doi.org/10.1007/978-3-319-66706-5_12
26. Mastroeni, I., Zanardini, D.: Abstract program slicing: An abstract interpretation-based approach to program slicing. ACM TOCL **18**(1), 7:1–7:58 (2017)
27. Naumann, D.A.: From coupling relations to mated invariants for checking information flow. In: Proceedings of ESORICS, pp. 279–296 (2006)
28. Pasqua, M., Mastroeni, I.: On topologies for (hyper)properties. In: Proceedings of ICTCS, pp. 1–12 (2017). http://ceur-ws.org/Vol-1949/ICTCSpaper13.pdf
29. Ranzato, F., Tapparo, F.: Strong preservation as completeness in abstract interpretation. In: Schmidt, D. (ed.) ESOP 2004. LNCS, vol. 2986, pp. 18–32. Springer, Heidelberg (2004). https://doi.org/10.1007/978-3-540-24725-8_3
30. Sousa, M., Dillig, I.: Cartesian hoare logic for verifying k-safety properties. In: Proceedings of PLDI, pp. 57–69 (2016)
31. Terauchi, T., Aiken, A.: Secure information flow as a safety problem. In: Hankin, C., Siveroni, I. (eds.) SAS 2005. LNCS, vol. 3672, pp. 352–367. Springer, Heidelberg (2005). https://doi.org/10.1007/11547662_24
32. Urban, C., Müller, P.: An abstract interpretation framework for input data usage. In: ESOP, pp. 683–710 (2018)

Process-Local Static Analysis
of Synchronous Processes

Jan Midtgaard[1(✉)], Flemming Nielson[2], and Hanne Riis Nielson[2]

[1] The Maersk Mc-Kinney Moller Institute,
University of Southern Denmark, Odense, Denmark
mail@janmidtgaard.dk
[2] DTU Compute, Technical University of Denmark, Kongens Lyngby, Denmark

Abstract. We develop a modular approach to statically analyse imperative processes communicating by synchronous message passing. The approach is modular in that it only needs to analyze one process at a time, but will in general have to do so repeatedly. The approach combines lattice-valued regular expressions to capture network communication with a dedicated shuffle operator for composing individual process analysis results. We present both a soundness proof and a prototype implementation of the approach for a synchronous subset of the Go programming language. Overall our approach tackles the combinatorial explosion of concurrent programs by suitable static analysis approximations, thereby lifting traditional sequential analysis techniques to a concurrent setting.

1 Introduction

Concurrent software surrounds us: whether as an *app* on a mobile phone communicating with a server, in the software business where a system has been structured as a service-oriented architecture, or at the data center where processes spread on many processors to collectively solve a computational query, they are all structured as software processes communicating by some form of message passing. The past decades contain a line of work towards ensuring correctness of such software: The model checking community has developed techniques for validating such distributive designs and the types community has developed *session types* for checking the overall communication structure. Within the static analysis community a line of work has pursued static analysis of process calculi (which may themselves be viewed as suitable process abstractions).

In this work we develop a static analysis approach that works directly at the source code level and addresses how safety properties of a distributed program may depend on intricate details involving both the order and content of the network communication. Rather than risk a combinatorial explosion by computing a collective state of all involved processes, our approach captures the network communication between a number of synchronous, message-passing processes with a dedicated abstract domain. This approach allows us to analyze each

© Springer Nature Switzerland AG 2018
A. Podelski (Ed.): SAS 2018, LNCS 11002, pp. 284–305, 2018.
https://doi.org/10.1007/978-3-319-99725-4_18

process separately. We then combine the analysis results of individual processes with a dedicated shuffle operator for the domain. We prove soundness of the analysis with respect to an operational semantics for a subset of Go and discuss a prototype implementation of the approach.

```
1     package main
2
3     func main() {
4             ch1 := make(chan int);
5             ch2 := make(chan int);
6             go func() { ch1 <-1; ch2 <-2; }()
7             go func() { var x int;
8                         x = <-ch1; ch2 <- x+1; }()
9             var y int;
10            y = <- ch2;
11    }
```

Fig. 1. An example Go program

Consider the Go program in Fig. 1. It declares two common channels ch1 and ch2, spawns off two processes (*go-routines*), and proceeds to the main read-statement at the bottom. The first process in line 6 attempts to send 1 on channel ch1 and 2 on channel ch2. The second process in line 7 reads a value (1) from channel ch1 into variable x and sends the value of x+1 (2) on channel ch2. Finally the read statement in line 10 reads a value from ch2. Under worst-case intra-process analysis assumptions this read could receive any value and bind it to y. This is also the result of a first iteration of our intra-process analysis. From this first intra-process analysis result we can read off that the three processes perform (the prefix-closure of) the network actions ch1!$[1; 1]$ · ch2!$[2; 2]$, ch1?$[-\infty; +\infty]$ · ch2!$[-\infty; +\infty]$, and ch2?$[-\infty; +\infty]$ respectively, here expressed as *lattice-valued regular expressions* with channel-tagged intervals. By *shuffling* the first and third result and performing intra-process reanalysis of the second process under this stronger assumption, we learn that it actually performs (the prefix-closure of) the network actions ch1?$[1; 1]$ · ch2!$[2; 2]$. Finally we shuffle this result with the result from the first process and run a third round of intra-process reanalysis to learn that the value read from ch2 and assigned to y is constant $[2; 2]$.

2   Language

We consider an imperative core language extended with primitives for synchronous message passing between individual processes, as illustrated by the above example. The core language is designed to be a genuine subset of Go (restricted to synchronous message passing), which we term *nano-Go*. Because of our restrictions, programs in nano-Go consist of a fixed number of top-level processes communicating through a fixed number of channels:

```
func main() {
        ch₁ := make(chan int)  ...  ch_k := make(chan int)
        go func() { s₁    }()
        ...
        go func() { s_{n-1} }()
        s_n
    }
```

As such, the programs spawn off n processes and can thereby conveniently be described by their process bodies $s_1, \ldots, s_n$ from an abstract syntax point of view. We provide a BNF grammar of the process language in Fig. 2. Each process is defined by a composite statement (ending in a blocking **select** { } statement) and has access to a process-local environment of pre-declared variables.

The statements of the language are mostly self-explanatory. **select** { $a_1 \ldots a_n$ } non-deterministically chooses between a list of read and write cases $a_1, \ldots, a_n$. The case **case** x = <- ch : s reads a value from channel ch, stores it in the variable x, and proceeds to execute s. The case **case** ch <- e : s writes the value of the expression e to channel ch and proceeds to execute s. Reading and writing messages is synchronous: a writing process blocks without an available receiver. Similarly a reading process cannot proceed until a writing process is ready to supply an input.

We assume that all statements and cases have been uniquely labeled. To be able to refer to specific labels occurring in a given statement or case we define the three functions *first*, *last*, and *labels* in Fig. 3. Each of these

$$e ::= n \mid x \mid e + e \mid e - e \mid \cdots$$

$$b ::= \mathbf{tt} \mid \mathbf{ff} \mid x < x \mid \cdots$$

$$s ::= \mathbf{skip}^\ell \mid x =^\ell e \mid s \, ; \, s \mid \mathbf{if}\ b^\ell\ \{\, s \,\}\ \mathbf{else}\ \{\, s \,\} \mid \mathbf{for}\ b^\ell\ \{\, s \,\} \mid \mathbf{select}^\ell\ \{\, a \ldots a \,\}$$

$$a ::= \mathbf{case}\ x =\ <\!-^\ell ch : s \mid \mathbf{case}\ ch <\!-^\ell e : s$$

$$p ::= (s \, ; \, \mathbf{select}^\ell\ \{\ \}) : \cdots : (s \, ; \, \mathbf{select}^\ell\ \{\ \})$$

Fig. 2. BNF grammar of nano-Go

$s \, / \, a$	*first*	*last*	*labels*
$\mathbf{skip}^\ell$	ℓ	$\{\ell\}$	$\{\ell\}$
$x =^\ell e$	ℓ	$\{\ell\}$	$\{\ell\}$
$s_1 \, ; \, s_2$	*first*(s_1)	*last*(s_2)	*labels*$(s_1) \cup$ *labels*(s_2)
$\mathbf{if}\ b^\ell\ \{\, s_1 \,\}\ \mathbf{else}\ \{\, s_2 \,\}$	ℓ	*last*$(s_1) \cup$ *last*(s_2)	$\{\ell\} \cup$ *labels*$(s_1) \cup$ *labels*(s_2)
$\mathbf{for}\ b^\ell\ \{\, s \,\}$	ℓ	$\{\ell\}$	$\{\ell\} \cup$ *labels*(s)
$\mathbf{select}^\ell\ \{\, a_1 \ldots a_n \,\}$	ℓ	*last*$(a_1) \cup \cdots \cup$ *last*(a_n)	$\{\ell\} \cup$ *labels*$(a_1) \cup \cdots \cup$ *labels*(a_n)
$\mathbf{case}\ x =\ <\!-^\ell ch : s$	ℓ	*last*(s)	$\{\ell\} \cup$ *labels*(s)
$\mathbf{case}\ ch <\!-^\ell e : s$	ℓ	*last*(s)	$\{\ell\} \cup$ *labels*(s)

Fig. 3. Definitions of *first*, *last*, and *labels*

accept a labeled statement or case as input, *first* returns a label, whereas *last* and *labels* return a set of labels. For example, for the statement $s =$ if $\mathtt{tt}^{\ell_0}\;\{\,x =^{\ell_1} 1\,\}$ else $\{\,\mathtt{skip}^{\ell_2}\,\}$ we get $first(s) = \ell_0$ while $last(s) = \{\ell_1, \ell_2\}$

$$\frac{}{\rho \vdash_A n \Downarrow n} \text{ Lit} \qquad \frac{}{\rho \vdash_A x \Downarrow \rho(x)} \text{ Var} \qquad \frac{\rho \vdash_A e_1 \Downarrow v_1 \quad \rho \vdash_A e_2 \Downarrow v_2}{\rho \vdash_A e_1 + e_2 \Downarrow v_1 + v_2} \text{ Add}$$

$$\frac{\rho \vdash_A e_1 \Downarrow v_1 \quad \rho \vdash_A e_2 \Downarrow v_2}{\rho \vdash_A e_1 - e_2 \Downarrow v_1 - v_2} \text{ Sub} \qquad \frac{}{\rho \vdash_B \mathtt{tt} \Downarrow \mathtt{tt}} \text{ True} \qquad \frac{}{\rho \vdash_B \mathtt{ff} \Downarrow \mathtt{ff}} \text{ False}$$

$$\frac{\rho(x_1) < \rho(x_2)}{\rho \vdash_B x_1 < x_2 \Downarrow \mathtt{tt}} \text{ LessThan1} \qquad \frac{\rho(x_1) \geq \rho(x_2)}{\rho \vdash_B x_1 < x_2 \Downarrow \mathtt{ff}} \text{ LessThan2}$$

$$\frac{}{\langle \mathtt{skip}^\ell, \rho \rangle \xrightarrow{\tau} \rho} \text{ Skip} \qquad \frac{\rho \vdash_A e \Downarrow v}{\langle x =^\ell e, \rho \rangle \xrightarrow{\tau} \rho[x \mapsto v]} \text{ Assign}$$

$$\frac{\langle s_1, \rho \rangle \xrightarrow{\alpha} \langle s_3, \rho' \rangle}{\langle s_1 \,;\, s_2, \rho \rangle \xrightarrow{\alpha} \langle s_3 \,;\, s_2, \rho' \rangle} \text{ Seq1} \qquad \frac{\langle s_1, \rho \rangle \xrightarrow{\alpha} \rho'}{\langle s_1 \,;\, s_2, \rho \rangle \xrightarrow{\alpha} \langle s_2, \rho' \rangle} \text{ Seq2}$$

$$\frac{\rho \vdash_B b \Downarrow \mathtt{tt}}{\langle \mathtt{if}\ b^\ell\ \{\,s_1\,\}\ \mathtt{else}\ \{\,s_2\,\}, \rho \rangle \xrightarrow{\tau} \langle s_1, \rho \rangle} \text{ If1}$$

$$\frac{\rho \vdash_B b \Downarrow \mathtt{ff}}{\langle \mathtt{if}\ b^\ell\ \{\,s_1\,\}\ \mathtt{else}\ \{\,s_2\,\}, \rho \rangle \xrightarrow{\tau} \langle s_2, \rho \rangle} \text{ If2}$$

$$\frac{\rho \vdash_B b \Downarrow \mathtt{tt}}{\langle \mathtt{for}\ b^\ell\ \{\,s_1\,\}, \rho \rangle \xrightarrow{\tau} \langle s_1 \,;\, \mathtt{for}\ b^\ell\ \{\,s_1\,\}, \rho \rangle} \text{ For1} \qquad \frac{\rho \vdash_B b \Downarrow \mathtt{ff}}{\langle \mathtt{for}\ b^\ell\ \{\,s_1\,\}, \rho \rangle \xrightarrow{\tau} \rho} \text{ For2}$$

$$\frac{\langle a_i, \rho \rangle \xrightarrow{\alpha} \langle s_i, \rho' \rangle}{\langle \mathtt{select}^\ell\ \{\,a_1 \ldots a_n\,\}, \rho \rangle \xrightarrow{\alpha} \langle s_i, \rho' \rangle} \text{ Select}$$

$$\frac{}{\langle \mathtt{case}\ x = \texttt{<-}^\ell ch : s, \rho \rangle \xrightarrow{ch?v} \langle s, \rho[x \mapsto v] \rangle} \text{ Read}$$

$$\frac{\rho \vdash_A e \Downarrow v}{\langle \mathtt{case}\ ch \texttt{<-}^\ell e : s, \rho \rangle \xrightarrow{ch!v} \langle s, \rho \rangle} \text{ Write}$$

$$\frac{c_i \xrightarrow{\tau} c_i'}{c_1 \ldots c_i \ldots c_n \xRightarrow{i,\tau} c_1 \ldots c_i' \ldots c_n} \text{ SysTau}$$

$$\frac{c_i \xrightarrow{ch!v} c_i' \quad c_j \xrightarrow{ch?v} c_j' \quad i \neq j}{c_1 \ldots c_i \ldots c_j \ldots c_n \xRightarrow{i,ch,v,j} c_1 \ldots c_i' \ldots c_j' \ldots c_n} \text{ SysComm}$$

Fig. 4. Operational semantics of nano-Go

and $labels(s) = \{\ell_0, \ell_1, \ell_2\}$. Technically skip^ℓ is not a valid statement in concrete Go syntax, but we include it nevertheless as it is convenient (as the identity) in translating valid Go statement sequences into abstract syntax trees (ASTs) with only binary statement composition.

We provide an operational semantics of nano-Go in Fig. 4. In the semantics a system configuration consists of an ordered sequence of process configurations $c_1 \ldots c_n$. This setup can capture execution from the point just after all go-routines have been started. Each process configuration is a pair $c_i = \langle s_i, \rho_i \rangle$ where the store ρ_i captures the values of the ith process's variables and s_i is either a statement or a case (also denoted a_i) that captures the program point of the ith process. As traditional we express message-passing communication with annotation labels, writing $ch!v$ and $ch?v$ for a message write and a message read, respectively. Synchronization is expressed in rule SYSCOMM by pairing a read with a write, whereas the rule SYSTAU expresses a non-communicating action. We label the system-level transitions with the indices of the involved processes, writing i, τ for the ith process performing a non-communicating action and i, ch, v, j for process i writing a value v on channel ch which is read by process j. Following the (informal) semantics of Go, a process cannot send a message on a channel to itself. We model this restriction by testing the sender's index i against the receiver's index j. Because two senders can write to the same channel, in a given trace the semantics non-deterministically puts the message of one sender before another.

Nano-Go embodies two simplifying assumptions: there is no dynamic channel or process creation and message passing is synchronous. We are well aware of the limitations induced by these assumptions but find them orthogonal to the topic of this paper: process-local static analysis. As such we plan to address them in future work.

3   Background

We assume the reader is familiar with lattice theory [8,11] and abstract interpretation [5,6], and only recall the more specialized and recent material on the abstract domain of lattice-valued regular expressions [21].

3.1   Lattice Theory and Abstract Interpretation

An *atom* $a \in L$ is a lattice element such that if $\bot \sqsubseteq s \sqsubseteq a$ for some other $s \in L$ then $s = \bot$ or $s = a$. We write $Atoms(L)$ for L's set of atoms and let a, a' range over this set. An *atomic lattice* requires that for all non-bottom elements $s \in L$ there exists $a \in Atoms(L)$ such that $a \sqsubseteq s$. An *atomistic lattice* requires that each non-bottom element $s \in L$ is expressible as a join of atoms $s = \sqcup S$ for some $S \subseteq Atoms(L)$. An *atomistic Galois insertion* $\langle C; \sqsubseteq \rangle \xleftrightarrow[\alpha]{\gamma} \langle A; \leq \rangle$ requires that α, γ connect two atomistic lattices such that $\alpha : Atoms(C) \longrightarrow Atoms(A)$ is surjective (α maps atoms to atoms and for all $a \in Atoms(A)$ there exists an $c \in Atoms(C)$ such that $\alpha(c) = a$).

3.2   Lattice-Valued Regular Expressions

To analyze the network communication and content we will use the domain of *lattice-valued regular expressions* (LVREs) [18,21]. We recall here the basics of LVREs (sans complement as it is irrelevant for the problem at hand). Syntactically LVREs are regular expressions with its characters drawn from a lattice $\langle A; \sqsubseteq \rangle$:

$$\widehat{R}_A ::= \emptyset \mid \epsilon \mid \ell \mid \widehat{R}_A^* \mid \widehat{R}_A \cdot \widehat{R}_A \mid \widehat{R}_A + \widehat{R}_A \mid \widehat{R}_A \& \widehat{R}_A \quad \text{where } \ell \in A \setminus \{\bot\}$$

We assume that the meaning of the *lattice literals* (A's elements) are given by a Galois insertion $\langle \wp(C); \subseteq \rangle \xleftrightarrow[\alpha]{\gamma} \langle A; \sqsubseteq \rangle$ and that α maps atoms to atoms: $\alpha : Atoms(\wp(C)) \longrightarrow Atoms(A)$. These assumptions are liberal enough to allow many standard domains from the Galois connection framework (signs, parity, constant propagation, intervals, etc.). A number of consequences follow from these basic assumptions: A is a complete lattice, A is atomic, and A is atomistic. They also have the consequence that γ is strict ($\gamma(\bot) = \emptyset$), that $\alpha : Atoms(\wp(C)) \longrightarrow Atoms(A)$ is surjective (we have an atomistic Galois insertion), and that A's atoms have no overlapping meaning ($\forall a, a'. \ a \neq a' \implies \gamma(a) \cap \gamma(a') = \emptyset$) [21].

We give meaning to the LVREs relative to the γ of the given Galois insertion. The denotation is given in Fig. 5. Based on this denotation two LVREs r, r' are ordered language-wise: $r \sqsubseteq_{\mathcal{L}} r' \iff \mathcal{L}(r) \subseteq \mathcal{L}(r')$. This ordering constitutes only a pre-order as it fails anti-symmetry. To regain a partial order we consider LVREs up to language equivalence $\widehat{R}_A/_{\approx}$. The resulting quotient domain constitutes a lattice with binary least upper bounds $+$ and greatest lower bounds $\&$. It follows from the definition of $\mathcal{L}$ that, e.g., concatenation $\cdot$ is monotone in both arguments.

LVREs provide a number of domain operations: *nullable* $: \widehat{R}_A \longrightarrow \mathbb{B}$ determines whether the empty string is accepted by the language of a LVRE r ($nullable(r) \iff \epsilon \in \mathcal{L}(r)$). We omit the straight-forward, structural definition here for brevity. *The Brzozowski derivative* [2] $\widehat{\mathcal{D}} : Atoms(A) \times \widehat{R}_A \longrightarrow \widehat{R}_a$ defined in Fig. 6 represents the language of a LVRE r remaining after having matched some $a \in Atoms(A)$ as the first character. One can prove that $\mathcal{L}(\widehat{\mathcal{D}}_a(r)) = \{w \mid \forall c \in \gamma(a). \ cw \in \mathcal{L}(r)\}$ for all $a \in Atoms(A)$ and $r \in \widehat{R}_A$. The definition of Brzozowski derivatives over LVREs extends structurally to strings: $\widehat{\mathcal{D}}_\epsilon(r) = r$ and $\widehat{\mathcal{D}}_{aw}(r) = \widehat{\mathcal{D}}_w(\widehat{\mathcal{D}}_a(r))$. Following Brzozowski [2] derivatives can be used for translating LVREs to lattice-valued automata. One can thus view *LVREs as automata states* and the *derivatives as transitions*. A LVRE r is

$$\mathcal{L}(\emptyset) = \emptyset \qquad\qquad \mathcal{L}(r^*) = \cup_{i \geq 0} \mathcal{L}(r)^i \qquad \mathcal{L}(r_1 + r_2) = \mathcal{L}(r_1) \cup \mathcal{L}(r_2)$$
$$\mathcal{L}(\epsilon) = \{\epsilon\} \qquad\quad \mathcal{L}(r_1 \cdot r_2) = \mathcal{L}(r_1) \cdot \mathcal{L}(r_2) \qquad \mathcal{L}(r_1 \& r_2) = \mathcal{L}(r_1) \cap \mathcal{L}(r_2)$$
$$\mathcal{L}(\ell) = \{c \mid c \in \gamma(\ell)\}$$

Fig. 5. The denotation of lattice-valued regular expressions

$$\widehat{\mathcal{D}}_a(\emptyset) = \emptyset$$

$$\widehat{\mathcal{D}}_a(\epsilon) = \emptyset \qquad\qquad \widehat{\mathcal{D}}_a(r_1 \cdot r_2) = \begin{cases} \widehat{\mathcal{D}}_a(r_1) \cdot r_2 + \widehat{\mathcal{D}}_a(r_2) & \epsilon \sqsubseteq r_1 \\ \widehat{\mathcal{D}}_a(r_1) \cdot r_2 & \epsilon \not\sqsubseteq r_1 \end{cases}$$

$$\widehat{\mathcal{D}}_a(\ell) = \begin{cases} \epsilon & a \sqsubseteq \ell \\ \emptyset & a \not\sqsubseteq \ell \end{cases}$$

$$\widehat{\mathcal{D}}_a(r_1 + r_2) = \widehat{\mathcal{D}}_a(r_1) + \widehat{\mathcal{D}}_a(r_2)$$

$$\widehat{\mathcal{D}}_a(r^*) = \widehat{\mathcal{D}}_a(r) \cdot r^* \qquad \widehat{\mathcal{D}}_a(r_1 \,\&\, r_2) = \widehat{\mathcal{D}}_a(r_1) \,\&\, \widehat{\mathcal{D}}_a(r_2)$$

Fig. 6. The Brzozowski derivative of lattice-valued regular expressions

considered an accept state iff *nullable*(r). This view is underlined by the fact that there are only a finite number of syntactically different LVRE derivatives (*corresponding to individual states*) up to associativity, commutativity, and idempotency (ACI) of $+$ when $Atoms(A)$ is finite.

In practice many derivatives are syntactically identical, e.g., over LVREs with intervals $\widehat{\mathcal{D}}_{[0;0]}([0;100] \cdot [1;2]^*) = \ldots = \widehat{\mathcal{D}}_{[100;100]}([0;100] \cdot [1;2]^*) = \epsilon \cdot [1;2]^*$ which motivated to group atoms with identical derivatives together in equivalence classes. For this purpose $\widehat{range}(r) : \widehat{R}_A \longrightarrow \widehat{equiv}_A$ computes a partition of $Atoms(A)$ such that two atoms a, a' are placed in the same equivalence class $a, a' \in [a''] \in \widehat{range}(r)$ if $\widehat{\mathcal{D}}_a(r) = \widehat{\mathcal{D}}_{a'}(r)$. Similarly $\widehat{overlay} : \widehat{equiv}_A \times \widehat{equiv}_A \longrightarrow \widehat{equiv}_A$ refines two partitions into a new partition coarser than both. $\widehat{overlay}$ is thus monotone over the lattice of partitions ordered under refinement [11]. Finally we require an operation $\widehat{repr} : (\wp(Atoms(A)) \setminus \{\emptyset\}) \longrightarrow Atoms(A)$ that returns a representative atom $a \in \widehat{repr}([a'])$ of a given equivalence class $[a']$ in a partition, and a second operation $\widehat{project} : (\wp(Atoms(A)) \setminus \{\emptyset\}) \longrightarrow A$ that returns a lattice element greater than all atoms in a given equivalence class: $\forall a \in [a']. \, a \sqsubseteq \widehat{project}([a'])$.

4   Shuffling Lattice-Valued Regular Expressions

To support analysis of arbitrary combinations of processes we extend LVREs with a symbolic shuffle operator. Formally we extend the grammar of LVREs with an additional production: $\widehat{R}_A ::= \ldots \mid \widehat{R}_A \parallel \widehat{R}_A$

Next we consider how to extend the various auxiliary operations to support the shuffle operator. First we define single string shuffling over the concrete domain C as follows:

$$\epsilon \parallel w = \{w\} \qquad\qquad w \parallel \epsilon = \{w\}$$
$$c_1 w_1 \parallel c_2 w_2 = \{c_1 w \mid w \in w_1 \parallel c_2 w_2\} \cup \{c_2 w \mid w \in c_1 w_1 \parallel w_2\}$$

This definition is taken from Sulzmann and Thiemann [31]. For example, for $C = \{a, b, c\}$ we have $ab \parallel bc = \{abbc, abcb, babc, bacb, bcab\}$. The single string operation is commutative: for any strings w, w' we have $w \parallel w' = w' \parallel w$. We can lift the single string shuffling definition (elementwise) to languages (also from Sulzmann and Thiemann [31]):

$$L_1 \parallel L_2 = \{w \mid w \in w_1 \parallel w_2 \wedge w_1 \in L_1 \wedge w_2 \in L_2\}$$

Before we continue we establish a number of properties. Interestingly, the language shuffling operation is not idempotent. For example: $\{a\} \parallel \{a\} = \{aa\} \neq \{a\}$. We believe the following four properties are well known [31] but nevertheless include them for completeness.

Lemma 1 (Shuffling of prefixed languages)

$$c_1 \cdot L_1 \parallel c_2 \cdot L_2 = c_1 \cdot (L_1 \parallel c_2 \cdot L_2) \ \cup \ c_2 \cdot (c_1 \cdot L_1 \parallel L_2)$$

Lemma 2 (Shuffling is commutative, distributive, associative)

$$L_1 \parallel L_2 = L_2 \parallel L_1 \qquad \text{(commutative)}$$

$$L \parallel (L_1 \cup L_2) = (L \parallel L_1) \cup (L \parallel L_2) \qquad \text{(distributive)}$$

$$L_1 \parallel (L_2 \parallel L_3) = (L_1 \parallel L_2) \parallel L_3 \qquad \text{(associative)}$$

We can prove a general shuffle property, that says that the shuffle of two arbitrary strings accounts for all possible splits of them: both the recursive shuffling of their first halves and their second halves are taken into consideration.

Lemma 3 (Generalized shuffle property)

$$\forall w_1, w_2, w_3, w_4 \in C^*. \ (w_1 \parallel w_2) \cdot (w_3 \parallel w_4) \subseteq (w_1 \cdot w_3) \parallel (w_2 \cdot w_4)$$

For example, by choosing $w_3 = \epsilon$ and $w_4 = c$ we obtain $\forall c \in C, w_1, w_2 \in C^*. \ (w_1 \parallel w_2) \cdot c \subseteq w_1 \parallel (w_2 \cdot c)$ which says that choosing c last is one possibility. Similarly in an alphabet with $\{rd, wr\} \subseteq C$ by choosing $w_3 = rd$ and $w_4 = wr$ as a corollary we obtain $\forall c \in C, w_1, w_2 \in C^*. \ (w_1 \parallel w_2) \cdot \{rd \cdot wr, wr \cdot rd\} \subseteq (w_1 \cdot rd) \parallel (w_2 \cdot wr)$.

Shuffling LVREs. We can now give meaning to symbolic shuffling of LVREs as language shuffling of their meanings: $\mathcal{L}(r_1 \parallel r_2) = \mathcal{L}(r_1) \parallel \mathcal{L}(r_2)$. Consequently the symbolic operation is commutative and associative under language equality: $r_1 \parallel r_2 \approx r_2 \parallel r_1$ and $r_1 \parallel (r_2 \parallel r_3) \approx (r_1 \parallel r_2) \parallel r_3$. It is also monotone by definition: $r_1 \sqsubseteq r_1' \implies r_1 \parallel r_2 \sqsubseteq r_1' \parallel r_2$ (and similarly in the second argument by commutativity).

Derivatives and the nullable predicate. Under the view of *expressions-as-states* and *derivatives-as-transitions*, the combined, synchronized automaton can take an a-step if either the first automaton can take an a-step or the second automaton can take an a-step. This leads to the following definition: $\widehat{\mathcal{D}}_a(r_1 \parallel r_2) = \widehat{\mathcal{D}}_a(r_1) \parallel r_2 + r_1 \parallel \widehat{\mathcal{D}}_a(r_2)$. Similarly the combined, shuffling automaton is in an acceptance state if both automata are in acceptance states. This leads to the following definition: $nullable(r_1 \parallel r_2) = nullable(r_1) \wedge nullable(r_2)$.

Our previous work established the Brzozowski equation for LVREs. We extend this result by showing how it also holds for LVREs with shuffle expressions:

Theorem 4 (Brzozowski's equation)

$$r \approx \sum_{a \in Atoms(A)} a \, \widehat{\mathcal{D}}_a(r) \; + \; \delta(r) \quad where \;\; \delta(r) = \begin{cases} \epsilon & \epsilon \subsetneq r \\ \emptyset & \epsilon \not\subsetneq r \end{cases}$$

Based on this we can now extend the following lemmas to hold for LVREs with shuffle.

Lemma 5 (Meaning of derivatives).

$$\mathcal{L}(\widehat{\mathcal{D}}_a(r)) = \{w \mid \forall c \in \gamma(a). \, c \cdot w \in \mathcal{L}(r)\}$$

Lemma 6 ($\widehat{\mathcal{D}}$ monotone in second argument). $r \subsetneq r' \implies \widehat{\mathcal{D}}_a(r) \subsetneq \widehat{\mathcal{D}}_a(r')$

Lemma 7 (Correctness of *nullable*). $nullable(r_1 \parallel r_2) \iff \epsilon \in \mathcal{L}(r_1 \parallel r_2)$

Finitely many derivatives. We argue that for all r, there exists at most d_r different derivatives up to ACI of $+$. We first prove a syntactic characterization of all derivatives as a sum of derived shuffle pairs. There are only as many different derivatives (up to ACI of $+$) as there are different sets of such pairs. For each of the d_{r_1} different first components in such pairs there are at most d_{r_2} different second components and hence at most $d_{r_1} * d_{r_2}$ different pairs. This gives an upper bound of $2^{d_{r_1} * d_{r_2}}$ different sets of pairs. To reduce the number of derivatives further, we can utilize that $\parallel$ is commutative, meaning there are only as many unique derivative pairs as there are unique first and second components. This reduction is however not required to upper-bound the number of different derivatives.

The $\widehat{range}$ operator We extend the $\widehat{range}$ operator to shuffled expressions:

$$\widehat{range}(r_1 \parallel r_2) = \widehat{overlay}(\widehat{range}(r_1), \widehat{range}(r_2))$$

and we subsequently verify that this definition satisfies our formal requirements:

Lemma 8 ($\widehat{range}$ partitions atoms). $\forall r_1, r_2, [a_i] \in \widehat{range}(r_1 \parallel r_2), a, a' \in Atoms(A)$.

$$a, a' \in [a_i] \implies \widehat{\mathcal{D}}_a(r_1 \parallel r_2) = \widehat{\mathcal{D}}_{a'}(r_1 \parallel r_2)$$

5   Analysis

Our core analysis is a standard imperative analysis over abstract stores $\widehat{\rho} \in \widehat{Store}$, e.g., with intervals. It requires auxiliary, monotone functions $\widehat{assign}$, $\widehat{\mathcal{A}}$, $\widehat{true}$, and

$\widehat{false}$ which are standard and omitted for space reasons. We assume they satisfy the following:

Lemma 9 (Soundness of $\widehat{A}$, $\widehat{assign}$, $\widehat{true}$, $\widehat{false}$ [20]).

$$\forall e \in E, \widehat{\rho} \in \widehat{Store}. \; \alpha_v(\{v \mid \rho \in \gamma_{st}(\widehat{\rho}) \; \wedge \; \rho \vdash_A e \Downarrow v\}) \sqsubseteq \widehat{A}(e, \widehat{\rho})$$

$$\forall \widehat{\rho}, x, \widehat{v}. \; \alpha_{st}(\{\rho[x \mapsto v] \mid v \in \gamma_v(\widehat{v}) \; \wedge \; \rho \in \gamma_{st}(\widehat{\rho})\}) \dot{\sqsubseteq} \widehat{assign}(\widehat{\rho}, x, \widehat{v})$$

$$\forall b, \widehat{\rho}. \; \alpha_{st}(\{\rho \in \gamma_{st}(\widehat{\rho}) \mid \rho \vdash_B b \Downarrow \mathtt{tt}\}) \dot{\sqsubseteq} \widehat{true}(b, \widehat{\rho})$$

$$\forall b, \widehat{\rho}. \; \alpha_{st}(\{\rho \in \gamma_{st}(\widehat{\rho}) \mid \rho \vdash_B b \Downarrow \mathtt{ff}\}) \dot{\sqsubseteq} \widehat{false}(b, \widehat{\rho})$$

where $\dot{\sqsubseteq}$ is the pointwise lifting of the value ordering $\sqsubseteq$ and where the definitions of α_v, γ_v and α_{st}, γ_{st} are postponed to Sec. 6.

Rather than try to track the state of each individual process simultaneously which would lead to a combinatorial explosion, each process is approximated by its network interaction and analyzed in isolation against a given environment of network communication behaviour. We thus let LVREs of futures track *writes* and *reads* over a given channel when analyzing an individual process and set up a product $\widehat{Ch}(\widehat{Val})$ of a write domain ($\widehat{Write}(\widehat{Val})$ in Fig. 7 captures approximate write characters) and a read domain ($\widehat{Read}(\widehat{Val})$ in Fig. 7 captures approximate read characters). [1] We use an interval in both to capture channel numbers. The analysis future $\widehat{f} \in \widehat{R}_{\widehat{Ch}(\widehat{Val})}$ represents the network communication the surrounding environment may offer. Finally the analysis specification is expressed as two global analysis caches $\widehat{\mathcal{E}}$, $\widehat{\mathcal{X}}$ where $\widehat{\mathcal{E}}(\ell) = (\widehat{\rho}, \widehat{f})$ capture the store and future upon entry to the statement labeled ℓ and $\widehat{\mathcal{X}}(\ell)$ capture a corresponding pair upon completion of the statement. The caches are naturally partitioned into process-individual parts $\widehat{\mathcal{E}}^1, \ldots, \widehat{\mathcal{E}}^n$ with $dom(\widehat{\mathcal{E}}^i) = labels(s_i)$ such that $\widehat{\mathcal{E}}^i$ accounts for the labels in process i's body s_i (and similarly for $\widehat{\mathcal{X}}^i$). Collectively these are non-overlapping and span *Labels* for an entire program. Notationally we write $\widehat{\mathcal{E}}^i_\rho(\ell)$ and $\widehat{\mathcal{E}}^i_f(\ell)$ to refer to the two components of $\widehat{\mathcal{E}}^i(\ell)$ (and similarly for $\widehat{\mathcal{X}}^i$).

$$ch!\widehat{v} \in \widehat{Write}(\widehat{Val}) = Interval \times \{!\} \times \widehat{Val} \qquad \widehat{\rho} \in \widehat{Store} = (Var \longrightarrow \widehat{Val})_\perp$$

$$ch?\widehat{v} \in \widehat{Read}(\widehat{Val}) = Interval \times \{?\} \times \widehat{Val} \qquad \widehat{h}, \widehat{f} \in \widehat{R}_{\widehat{Ch}(\widehat{Val})}$$

$$\widehat{Ch}(\widehat{Val}) = \widehat{Write}(\widehat{Val}) \times \widehat{Read}(\widehat{Val}) \qquad \widehat{\mathcal{E}}, \widehat{\mathcal{X}} \in \widehat{Cache} = Labels \longrightarrow \widehat{Store} \times \widehat{R}_{\widehat{Ch}(\widehat{Val})}$$

Fig. 7. Analysis domains

---

[1] The product with singleton sets $\{!\}$ and $\{?\}$ is just presentational: one component denotes writes and another component denotes reads.

5.1 Analysis Algorithm

The analysis is structured in two parts: an intra-process part (in Figs. 8 and 9) for analyzing each individual process in isolation and an inter-process part (in Fig. 10) for analyzing a system of processes with the latter depending on the former.

The intra-process analysis specification in Fig. 8 is standard [25] modulo the cases for network interaction. Here a read action involves a suitable derivative of the future wrt. a write action (and vice versa). The specification is slightly complicated by our partitioning of atoms into equivalence classes with identical derivatives. Algorithmically we use this intra-process analysis to infer process-local caches $\widehat{\mathcal{E}^i}$ and $\widehat{\mathcal{X}^i}$ for a given initial future $\widehat{f}$ and statement s_i.

$\widehat{\mathcal{E}^i}, \widehat{\mathcal{X}^i} \vDash \texttt{skip}^\ell$ iff $\widehat{\mathcal{E}^i}(\ell) \sqsubseteq \widehat{\mathcal{X}^i}(\ell)$

$\widehat{\mathcal{E}^i}, \widehat{\mathcal{X}^i} \vDash x =^\ell e$ iff $(\widehat{assign}(\widehat{\rho}, x, \widehat{\mathcal{A}}(e, \widehat{\rho})), \widehat{f}) \sqsubseteq \widehat{\mathcal{X}^i}(\ell)$ where $(\widehat{\rho}, \widehat{f}) = \widehat{\mathcal{E}^i}(\ell)$

$\widehat{\mathcal{E}^i}, \widehat{\mathcal{X}^i} \vDash s_1 \,;\, s_2$ iff $\widehat{\mathcal{E}^i}, \widehat{\mathcal{X}^i} \vDash s_1 \wedge \widehat{\mathcal{E}^i}, \widehat{\mathcal{X}^i} \vDash s_2 \wedge \forall \ell_1 \in last(s_1). \widehat{\mathcal{X}^i}(\ell_1) \sqsubseteq \widehat{\mathcal{E}^i}(first(s_2))$

$\widehat{\mathcal{E}^i}, \widehat{\mathcal{X}^i} \vDash \texttt{if } b^\ell \,\{\, s_1 \,\} \texttt{ else } \{\, s_2 \,\}$ iff $\widehat{\mathcal{E}^i}, \widehat{\mathcal{X}^i} \vDash s_1 \wedge \widehat{\mathcal{E}^i}, \widehat{\mathcal{X}^i} \vDash s_2 \wedge$

$\qquad (\widehat{true}(b, \widehat{\rho}), \widehat{f}) \sqsubseteq \widehat{\mathcal{E}^i}(first(s_1)) \wedge (\widehat{false}(b, \widehat{\rho}), \widehat{f}) \sqsubseteq \widehat{\mathcal{E}^i}(first(s_2)) \wedge$

$\qquad \forall \ell_1 \in last(s_1), \widehat{\mathcal{X}^i}(\ell_1) \sqsubseteq \widehat{\mathcal{X}^i}(\ell) \wedge \forall \ell_2 \in last(s_2). \widehat{\mathcal{X}^i}(\ell_2) \sqsubseteq \widehat{\mathcal{X}^i}(\ell)$

$\qquad$ where $(\widehat{\rho}, \widehat{f}) = \widehat{\mathcal{E}^i}(\ell)$

$\widehat{\mathcal{E}^i}, \widehat{\mathcal{X}^i} \vDash \texttt{for } b^\ell \,\{\, s_1 \,\}$ iff $\widehat{\mathcal{E}^i}, \widehat{\mathcal{X}^i} \vDash s_1 \wedge$

$\qquad (\widehat{true}(b, \widehat{\rho}), \widehat{f}) \sqsubseteq \widehat{\mathcal{E}^i}(first(s_1)) \wedge (\widehat{false}(b, \widehat{\rho}), \widehat{f}) \sqsubseteq \widehat{\mathcal{X}^i}(\ell) \wedge$

$\qquad \forall \ell_1 \in last(s_1). \widehat{\mathcal{X}^i}(\ell_1) \sqsubseteq \widehat{\mathcal{E}^i}(\ell)$ where $(\widehat{\rho}, \widehat{f}) = \widehat{\mathcal{E}^i}(\ell)$

$\widehat{\mathcal{E}^i}, \widehat{\mathcal{X}^i} \vDash \texttt{select}^\ell \,\{\, a_1 \ldots a_n \,\}$ iff $\widehat{\mathcal{E}^i}, \widehat{\mathcal{X}^i} \vDash a_1 \wedge \ldots \wedge \widehat{\mathcal{E}^i}, \widehat{\mathcal{X}^i} \vDash a_n \wedge$

$\qquad \widehat{\mathcal{E}^i}(\ell) \sqsubseteq \widehat{\mathcal{E}^i}(first(a_1)) \wedge \ldots \wedge \widehat{\mathcal{E}^i}(\ell) \sqsubseteq \widehat{\mathcal{E}^i}(first(a_n)) \wedge$

$\qquad \forall \ell_1 \in last(a_1). \widehat{\mathcal{X}^i}(\ell_1) \sqsubseteq \widehat{\mathcal{X}^i}(\ell) \wedge \ldots \wedge \forall \ell_n \in last(a_n). \widehat{\mathcal{X}^i}(\ell_n) \sqsubseteq \widehat{\mathcal{X}^i}(\ell)$

$\widehat{\mathcal{E}^i}, \widehat{\mathcal{X}^i} \vDash \texttt{case } x = \texttt{<-}^\ell ch : s$ iff $\widehat{\mathcal{E}^i}, \widehat{\mathcal{X}^i} \vDash s \wedge$

$\qquad \forall [ch!\widehat{v}_a] \in \widehat{range}(\widehat{f}).$

$\qquad\qquad (ch!\widehat{v} = \widehat{project}([ch!\widehat{v}_a]) \wedge \widehat{\mathcal{D}}_{\widehat{repr}([ch!\widehat{v}_a])}(\widehat{f}) \not\sqsubseteq \emptyset$

$\qquad\qquad \implies (\widehat{assign}(\widehat{\rho}, x, \widehat{v}), \widehat{\mathcal{D}}_{\widehat{repr}([ch!\widehat{v}_a])}(\widehat{f})) \sqsubseteq \widehat{\mathcal{X}^i}(\ell) \sqsubseteq \widehat{\mathcal{E}^i}(first(s)))$

$\qquad$ where $(\widehat{\rho}, \widehat{f}) = \widehat{\mathcal{E}^i}(\ell)$

$\widehat{\mathcal{E}^i}, \widehat{\mathcal{X}^i} \vDash \texttt{case } ch \texttt{<-}^\ell e : s$ iff $\widehat{\mathcal{E}^i}, \widehat{\mathcal{X}^i} \vDash s \wedge$

$\qquad \forall [ch?\widehat{v}_a] \in \widehat{range}(\widehat{f}).$

$\qquad\qquad (ch?\widehat{v} = \widehat{project}([ch?\widehat{v}_a]) \wedge \widehat{v} \sqcap \widehat{v}' \neq \bot \wedge \widehat{\mathcal{D}}_{\widehat{repr}([ch?\widehat{v}_a])}(\widehat{f}) \not\sqsubseteq \emptyset$

$\qquad\qquad \implies (\widehat{\rho}, \widehat{\mathcal{D}}_{\widehat{repr}([ch?\widehat{v}_a])}(\widehat{f})) \sqsubseteq \widehat{\mathcal{X}^i}(\ell) \sqsubseteq \widehat{\mathcal{E}^i}(first(s))$

$\qquad$ where $(\widehat{\rho}, \widehat{f}) = \widehat{\mathcal{E}^i}(\ell) \wedge \widehat{v}' = \widehat{\mathcal{A}}(e, \widehat{\rho})$

Fig. 8. Intra-process analysis specification

$$\mathcal{H}(\widehat{\mathcal{E}^i}, \widehat{\mathcal{X}^i}, \mathtt{skip}^\ell) = \langle \epsilon, \epsilon \rangle$$

$$\mathcal{H}(\widehat{\mathcal{E}^i}, \widehat{\mathcal{X}^i}, x =^\ell e) = \langle \epsilon, \epsilon \rangle$$

$$\mathcal{H}(\widehat{\mathcal{E}^i}, \widehat{\mathcal{X}^i}, s_1 \ ; \ s_2) = \langle p_1 + (c_1 \cdot p_2), c_1 \cdot c_2 \rangle$$

$$\text{where } \langle p_1, c_1 \rangle = \mathcal{H}(\widehat{\mathcal{E}^i}, \widehat{\mathcal{X}^i}, s_1) \text{ and } \langle p_1, c_2 \rangle = \mathcal{H}(\widehat{\mathcal{E}^i}, \widehat{\mathcal{X}^i}, s_2)$$

$$\mathcal{H}(\widehat{\mathcal{E}^i}, \widehat{\mathcal{X}^i}, \mathtt{if} \ b^\ell \ \{ \ s_1 \ \} \ \mathtt{else} \ \{ \ s_2 \ \}) = \langle p_1 + p_2, c_1 + c_2 \rangle$$

$$\text{where } \langle p_1, c_1 \rangle = \mathcal{H}(\widehat{\mathcal{E}^i}, \widehat{\mathcal{X}^i}, s_1) \text{ and } \langle p_1, c_2 \rangle = \mathcal{H}(\widehat{\mathcal{E}^i}, \widehat{\mathcal{X}^i}, s_2)$$

$$\mathcal{H}(\widehat{\mathcal{E}^i}, \widehat{\mathcal{X}^i}, \mathtt{for} \ b^\ell \ \{ \ s \ \}) = \langle c^* \cdot p, c^* \rangle \text{ where } \langle p, c \rangle = \mathcal{H}(\widehat{\mathcal{E}^i}, \widehat{\mathcal{X}^i}, s)$$

$$\mathcal{H}(\widehat{\mathcal{E}^i}, \widehat{\mathcal{X}^i}, \mathtt{select}^\ell \ \{ \ a_1 \ldots a_n \ \}) = \langle \epsilon + \sum_i p_i, \sum_i c_i \rangle$$

$$\text{where } \langle p_i, c_i \rangle = \mathcal{H}(\widehat{\mathcal{E}^i}, \widehat{\mathcal{X}^i}, a_i) \text{ and } 1 \le i \le n$$

$$\mathcal{H}(\widehat{\mathcal{E}^i}, \widehat{\mathcal{X}^i}, \mathtt{case} \ x = \ \texttt{<-}^\ell \ ch : s) = \langle \epsilon + ch?\widehat{v} + ch?\widehat{v} \cdot p, ch?\widehat{v} \cdot c \rangle$$

$$\text{where } \widehat{v} = \widehat{\mathcal{E}}^i_\rho(first(s))(x) \text{ and } \langle p, c \rangle = \mathcal{H}(\widehat{\mathcal{E}^i}, \widehat{\mathcal{X}^i}, s)$$

$$\mathcal{H}(\widehat{\mathcal{E}^i}, \widehat{\mathcal{X}^i}, \mathtt{case} \ ch \ \texttt{<-}^\ell \ e : s) = \langle \epsilon + ch!\widehat{v} + ch!\widehat{v} \cdot p, ch!\widehat{v} \cdot c \rangle$$

$$\text{where } \widehat{v} = \widehat{\mathcal{A}}(e, \widehat{\mathcal{E}}^i_\rho(\ell)) \text{ and } \langle p, c \rangle = \mathcal{H}(\widehat{\mathcal{E}^i}, \widehat{\mathcal{X}^i}, s)$$

Fig. 9. Reading off a collective trace history

$$\widehat{\mathcal{E}}, \widehat{\mathcal{X}} \vDash s_1 : \cdots : s_n \text{ iff } \forall i. \ \widehat{\mathcal{E}^i}, \widehat{\mathcal{X}^i} \vDash s_i \ \wedge$$

$$\forall i, \ell, [ch!\widehat{v}] \in \widehat{overlay}(\{\pi_1(\widehat{range}(\widehat{\mathcal{E}}^i_f(\ell)))\} \cup \bigcup_{[ch'!\widehat{v}'] \in \widehat{range}(\widehat{\mathcal{E}}^i_f(\ell))} \pi_2(\widehat{range}(\widehat{\mathcal{D}}_{\widehat{repr}([ch'!\widehat{v}'])}(\widehat{\mathcal{E}}^i_f(\ell))))).$$

$$\widehat{\mathcal{D}}_{\widehat{repr}([ch!\widehat{v}])\widehat{repr}([ch?\widehat{v}])}(\widehat{\mathcal{E}}^i_f(\ell)) \sqsubseteq \widehat{\mathcal{E}}^i_f(\ell) \ \wedge$$

$$\forall i, \ell, [ch?\widehat{v}] \in \widehat{overlay}(\{\pi_2(\widehat{range}(\widehat{\mathcal{E}}^i_f(\ell)))\} \cup \bigcup_{[ch'?\widehat{v}'] \in \widehat{range}(\widehat{\mathcal{E}}^i_f(\ell))} \pi_1(\widehat{range}(\widehat{\mathcal{D}}_{\widehat{repr}([ch'?\widehat{v}'])}(\widehat{\mathcal{E}}^i_f(\ell))))).$$

$$\widehat{\mathcal{D}}_{\widehat{repr}([ch?\widehat{v}])\widehat{repr}([ch!\widehat{v}])}(\widehat{\mathcal{E}}^i_f(\ell)) \sqsubseteq \widehat{\mathcal{E}}^i_f(\ell)$$

Fig. 10. Inter-process analysis specification

Given an acceptable analysis result $\widehat{\mathcal{E}}^i$ and $\widehat{\mathcal{X}}^i$ of a process s_i we subsequently use $\mathcal{H}(\widehat{\mathcal{E}}^i, \widehat{\mathcal{X}}^i, s_i)$ in Fig. 9 to read off the collective network communication history of this process's writes and reads. $\mathcal{H}$ returns a pair of two languages: The first component denotes the *prefix* p of network communication strings that may arise from a statement s_i, whereas the second component denotes the *complete* language c of network communication strings that may arise from an end-to-end execution of statement s_i. Collectively $p + c$ represents all prefixes of s_i's network communication. For a less structured language we expect Tarjan's algorithm [33] could be adapted.

We can now combine intra-process communication histories $\langle p_i, c_i \rangle = \mathcal{H}(\widehat{\mathcal{E}}^i, \widehat{\mathcal{X}}^i, s_i)$ via the shuffle operator to obtain a better approximation of futures and repeat the intra-process analysis from this new starting point. For example, for an analysis of three processes s_1, s_2, s_3 we reanalyze s_1 under the future $\widehat{\mathcal{E}}_f^1(first(s_1))$ & $(p_2 + c_2) \parallel (p_3 + c_3)$. To soundly model how a third party process may interfere or communicate with either party before or after a message synchronization the inter-process analysis specification in Fig. 10 imposes a closure requirement. In this setup a future *write* followed by a matching *read* (and vice versa) may match up and thereby cancel each other out. We express this requirement with derivatives: a *write* requires a derivative with respect to a suitable *read* (and vice versa). Since $\widehat{range}$ groups into equivalence classes atoms with identical derivatives, a little extra care is needed to find equivalence classes for which two consecutive derivatives are guaranteed to yield the same. This is the purpose of the bottom requirement in Fig. 10, which utilizes that the atoms of $\widehat{Ch}(\widehat{Val})$ can be partitioned with a pair (the first projection π_1 partitions the atoms $Atoms(\widehat{Write}(\widehat{Val})) \times \{\bot\}$ and the second projection π_2 the atoms $\{\bot\} \times Atoms(\widehat{Read}(\widehat{Val}))$).

6   Soundness

The soundness proof is complicated by the fact that we relate two concepts of inherently different shape: we approximate a property expressible as a set of (prefix) traces, albeit where a single computation step in the trace itself may require a *derivation tree* in the structural operational semantics of the corresponding process, whereas we specify the static analysis as a syntax-directed *acceptability relation* over the program text of each participating process. We proceed by first proving local statement-level soundness and then use this to prove system-level soundness. As these assume some over-approximate futures, we finally prove how an acceptable analysis result may be combined into a better over-approximation.

The analysis is parametric in the value abstraction, assuming it is given as an atomistic Galois insertion $\wp(Val) \xleftrightarrow[\alpha_v]{\gamma_v} \widehat{Val}$. The value abstraction is straightforwardly lifted to a Galois insertion over stores: $\wp(Var \hookrightarrow Val) \xleftrightarrow[\alpha_{st}]{\gamma_{st}} \widehat{Store}$. Finally the channel abstraction $\wp(Action) \xleftrightarrow[\alpha_{ch}]{\gamma_{ch}} \widehat{Ch}(\widehat{Val})$ is a standard Cartesian abstraction with $Action = WrAction \cup RdAction$, $\alpha_{ch}(S) = (\alpha_{wr}(\{ch!v \in S\}), \alpha_{rd}(\{ch?v \in S\}))$ and $\gamma_{ch}(\widehat{v}_w, \widehat{v}_r) = \gamma_{wr}(\widehat{v}_w) \cup \gamma_{rd}(\widehat{v}_r)$. We sometimes abbreviate $\alpha_{ch}(S)$ as $\widehat{S}$. The channel abstraction itself utilizes two atomistic Galois insertions $\wp(WrAction) \xleftrightarrow[\alpha_{wr}]{\gamma_{wr}} \widehat{Write}(\widehat{Val})$ with $\alpha_{wr}(S) = \bigsqcup_{ch!v \in S}(\alpha_{Int}(\{ch\}), \alpha_v(\{v\}))$ and $\gamma_{wr}([l; u], \widehat{v}) = \bigcup_{ch \in \gamma_{Int}([l;u]) v \in \gamma_v(\widehat{v})}\{ch!v\}$ and similarly for α_{rd}, γ_{rd} [20].

6.1   Statement-Level Soundness

The following two lemmas express soundness at the statement level for both SOS steps leading to a terminal and a non-terminal configuration. Properties related to how futures propagate across processes are handled at the system level. The two lemmas are reminiscent of lemmas 7.9, 7.10 in our previous work [20] with the key difference that those were expressed in terms of an instrumented semantics. Both of these lemmas express soundness of a network action α against the environment using a derivative of the converse action $\overline{\alpha}$ defined as $\overline{\tau} = \epsilon \quad \overline{ch?v} = ch!v \quad \overline{ch!v} = ch?v$.

Lemma 10 (One step statement soundness, terminal). *If* $\langle s, \rho \rangle \xrightarrow{\alpha} \rho'$, $\widehat{\mathcal{E}^i}, \widehat{\mathcal{X}^i} \models s$, *and* $\rho \in \gamma_{st}(\widehat{\mathcal{E}^i_\rho}(\mathit{first}(s)))$ *then* $\forall \ell \in \mathit{last}(s).$ $\rho' \in \gamma_{st}(\widehat{\mathcal{X}^i_\rho}(\ell)) \wedge \widehat{\mathcal{D}_{\widehat{\alpha}}}(\widehat{\mathcal{E}^i_f}(\mathit{first}(s))) \sqsubseteq \widehat{\mathcal{X}^i_f}(\ell)$

Lemma 11 (One step statement soundness, non-terminal). *If* $\langle s, \rho \rangle \xrightarrow{\alpha} \langle s', \rho' \rangle$, $\widehat{\mathcal{E}^i}, \widehat{\mathcal{X}^i} \models s$, $\rho \in \gamma_{st}(\widehat{\mathcal{E}^i_\rho}(\mathit{first}(s)))$, *and* $\widehat{\mathcal{D}_{\widehat{\alpha}}}(\widehat{\mathcal{E}^i_f}(\mathit{first}(s))) \not\sqsubseteq \emptyset$ *then* $\widehat{\mathcal{E}^i}, \widehat{\mathcal{X}^i} \models s' \wedge \rho' \in \gamma_{st}(\widehat{\mathcal{E}^i_\rho}(\mathit{first}(s'))) \wedge \widehat{\mathcal{D}_{\widehat{\alpha}}}(\widehat{\mathcal{E}^i_f}(\mathit{first}(s))) \sqsubseteq \widehat{\mathcal{E}^i_f}(\mathit{first}(s'))$

6.2   System-Level Soundness

To express system-level soundness we introduce two homomorphisms over the labels of the semantics's system-level transitions:

$$\hbar_k(i, \tau) = \epsilon \qquad\qquad f_k(i, \tau) = \epsilon$$

$$\hbar_k(i, ch, v, j) = \begin{cases} ch!v & k = i \\ ch?v & k = j \\ \epsilon & k \notin \{i, j\} \end{cases} \qquad f_k(i, ch, v, j) = \begin{cases} ch?v & k = i \\ ch!v & k = j \\ ch!v \cdot ch?v & k \notin \{i,j\}, i < j \\ ch?v \cdot ch!v & k \notin \{i,j\}, i > j \end{cases}$$

Note how in two cases f_k maps a single communication to a string of two characters: write-read or read-write, depending on the index of the participant (we have chosen somewhat arbitrarily to let the lowest process index go first).

Theorem 12 (Analysis soundness). *For all programs* $s_1 : \cdots : s_n$, *initial stores* ρ_{init}, *acceptable analysis answers* $\widehat{\mathcal{E}}, \widehat{\mathcal{X}}$ *such that* $\widehat{\mathcal{E}}, \widehat{\mathcal{X}} \models s_1 : \cdots : s_n$ *and the initial store is soundly account for* $\forall i.$ $\rho_{init} \in \gamma_{st}(\widehat{\mathcal{E}^i_\rho}(\mathit{first}(s_i)))$, *and arbitrary traces* $\langle s_1, \rho_{init} \rangle \ldots \langle s_n, \rho_{init} \rangle \xrightarrow{\alpha_1} \ldots \xrightarrow{\alpha_k} c'_1 \ldots c'_n$ *with futures soundly accounted for* $\forall i.$ $f_i(\alpha_1 \ldots \alpha_k) \in \mathcal{L}(\widehat{\mathcal{E}^i_f}(\mathit{first}(s_i)))$ *then for any* i *such that* $1 \le i \le n$ *and* $c'_i = \langle s'_i, \rho'_i \rangle$ *we have* $\rho'_i \in \gamma_{st}(\widehat{\mathcal{E}^i_\rho}(\mathit{first}(s'_i))) \wedge \widehat{\mathcal{D}}_{\overline{f_i(\alpha_1 \ldots \alpha_k)}}(\widehat{\mathcal{E}^i_f}(\mathit{first}(s_i))) \sqsubseteq \widehat{\mathcal{E}^i_f}(\mathit{first}(s'_i))$

Intuitively, the analysis accounts for all execution traces in the program such that the abstract store associated to each entry accounts for the reachable concrete stores and the abstract future associated to each entry accounts for the network communication of the surrounding process environment. We prove the generalization that concludes $\widehat{\mathcal{E}^i}, \widehat{\mathcal{X}^i} \models s'_i$ in addition to the above.

6.3 Soundness of Iterative Approach

The above proves soundness of the process analysis assuming that all futures are soundly accounted for in the initial statements of the individual processes, e.g., from worst-case assumptions $\forall i.\ \widehat{\mathcal{E}_f^i}(\mathit{first}(s_i)) = \top^*$. To do better, we first express futures as a suitable shuffling of histories:

Lemma 13 (Futures as histories, sans sum). *For all programs* $s_1 : \cdots : s_n$, *initial stores* ρ_{init}, *and traces* $\langle s_1, \rho_{init} \rangle \ldots \langle s_n, \rho_{init} \rangle \stackrel{\alpha_1}{\Longrightarrow} \ldots \stackrel{\alpha_k}{\Longrightarrow} c'_1 \ldots c'_n$ *such that for all* $1 \le i \le n$ *and* $c'_i = \langle s'_i, \rho'_i \rangle$ *we have* $f_i(\alpha_1 \ldots \alpha_k) \in \left\| \right._{j \ne i} \hbar_j(\alpha_1 \ldots \alpha_k)$

As a corollary by monotonicity of $\|$ we obtain the following:

Corollary 14 (Futures as histories, with sum). *For all programs* $s_1 : \cdots :$ s_n, *initial stores* ρ_{init}, *and traces* $\langle s_1, \rho_{init} \rangle \ldots \langle s_n, \rho_{init} \rangle \stackrel{\alpha_1}{\Longrightarrow} \ldots \stackrel{\alpha_k}{\Longrightarrow} c'_1 \ldots c'_n$ *such that for all* $1 \le i \le n$ *and* $c'_i = \langle s'_i, \rho'_i \rangle$ *we have* $f_i(\alpha_1 \ldots \alpha_k) \in$ $\left\| \right._{j \ne i} \left(\sum_{k' \le k} \hbar_j(\alpha_1 \ldots \alpha_{k'}) \right)$

Finally we can prove soundness of $\mathcal{H}$ from an acceptable analysis result:

Lemma 15 (History soundness). *For all programs* $s_1 : \cdots : s_n$, *initial stores* ρ_{init}, *and traces* $\langle s_1, \rho_{init} \rangle \ldots \langle s_n, \rho_{init} \rangle \stackrel{\alpha_1}{\Longrightarrow} \ldots \stackrel{\alpha_k}{\Longrightarrow} c'_1 \ldots c'_n$ *such that for all* $1 \le i \le n$ *and* $c'_i = \langle s'_i, \rho'_i \rangle$ *and analysis answers* $\widehat{\mathcal{E}}, \widehat{\mathcal{X}}$ *such that* $\rho_{init} \in \gamma_{st}(\widehat{\mathcal{E}_\rho^i}(\mathit{first}(s_i)))$, $f_i(\alpha_1 \ldots \alpha_k) \in \mathcal{L}(\widehat{\mathcal{E}_f^i}(\mathit{first}(s_i)))$, *and* $\widehat{\mathcal{E}}, \widehat{\mathcal{X}} \models s_i$. *we have* $\hbar_i(\alpha_1 \ldots \alpha_k) \in \mathcal{L}(p + c)$ *where* $\langle p, c \rangle = \mathcal{H}(\widehat{\mathcal{E}^i}, \widehat{\mathcal{X}^i}, s)$

From a sound analysis result we utilize Corollary 14, Theorem 15, and monotonicity of $\|$ to obtain a (potentially better) approximation of the futures which proves the soundness of the inter-process analysis result shuffling:

$$f_i(\alpha_1 \ldots \alpha_k) \in \left\| \right._{\substack{j \ne i}} \left(\sum_{k' \le k} \hbar_j(\alpha_1 \ldots \alpha_{k'}) \right) \subseteq \left\| \right._{\substack{j \ne i \\ \langle p_j, c_j \rangle = \mathcal{H}(\widehat{\mathcal{E}^i}, \widehat{\mathcal{X}^i}, s)}} \mathcal{L}(p_j + c_j)$$

7   Implementation

To illustrate feasibility of our approach we have implemented a proof-of-concept prototype in OCaml. The prototype takes roughly 4200 lines of code and is available for download at https://github.com/jmid/nano-go. It is structured as a traditional front end with a lexer and a parser. The input is subsequently translated and labeled into an internal AST representation. The analysis walks this AST repeatedly until stabilization. As the shuffling operator over LVREs is commutative and associative we represent a sequence of shuffles $r_1 \| (r_2 \| (\cdots \| r_n))$ internally as a sorted sequence, since the element order does not matter.

Since $\mathcal{L}(\emptyset \parallel r) = \mathcal{L}(\emptyset)$ and $\mathcal{L}(\epsilon \parallel r) = \mathcal{L}(r)$ we furthermore simplify LVREs internally from the former to the latter. Such meaning-preserving simplifications are common in derivative-based language processors [26]. We have implemented the closure requirement from the inter-process analysis specification in Fig. 10 as a local iteration, that repeats an inclusion of consecutive reads-and-writes (and vice versa) until stabilization. As there are only finitely many derivatives of a given future this iteration is bound to terminate. We only trigger the closure iteration on newly formed entries. Internally in the intra-process analysis the prototype widens on loop headers to ensure termination. Seen as a black box, the intra-process analysis is a deterministic function expecting a future $\widehat{f}$ as input. Since there are only finitely many derivatives of a given $\widehat{f}$ we do not need to widen over futures. Finally we widen over abstract stores by pointwise lifting of a traditional interval widening operator [4]. In the outer inter-process analysis the prototype starts from a safe $\top^*$ approximation of futures and runs at most 100 iterations of the inter-process analysis to improve on this worst case assumption.

We have used the js_of_ocaml compiler to create a client-side web-interface for the prototype, available at https://jmid.github.io/nano-go/. To illustrate the applicability of the analysis we have implemented two kinds of warnings based on the analysis results: We mark a statement s^ℓ with $\widehat{\mathcal{E}}_\rho^i(\ell) = \bot$ as *unreachable* and read and write actions with an empty derivative over futures as *unable to succeed*. Both of these are safety properties compatible with the analysis output. Figure 11 illustrates these warnings in the web-interface on a simple deadlock example with two processes both attempting to read before writing, thereby mutually blocking each other. In the example, the prototype highlights the read statements in lines 7 and 12 as unable to succeed and the subsequent lines as unreachable.

For a more elaborate example, consider the nano-Go program in Fig. 12 ported from Stadtmüller et al. [30]. The program declares two channels ch and done and consists of 5 processes. The first process (Send) in line 6 sends an integer over channel ch and thereby triggers one of two competing receiver processes (Recv1 and Recv2) in lines 7 and 12. The successful receiver acknowledges reception by subsequently writing the received value on channel done. A fourth process (Work) in line 17 simply runs an infinite loop, while the main process at the end expects to receive two acknowledgments. In the first inter-process iteration the intra-process analysis infers the history $\epsilon + \mathtt{ch}![42; 42]$ for Send, $\epsilon + \mathtt{ch}?[-\infty; +\infty] + \mathtt{ch}?[-\infty; +\infty] \cdot \mathtt{done}![-\infty; +\infty]$ for Recv1 and Recv2, ϵ for Work, and $\epsilon + \mathtt{done}?[-\infty; +\infty] + \mathtt{done}?[-\infty; +\infty] \cdot \mathtt{done}?[-\infty; +\infty]$ for the final process. Each of these are obtained from the worst case assumption $\top^*$ about futures. Throughout the remaining inter-process iterations the results for Send and Work are unchanged. In the second inter-process iteration when the above histories are shuffled and fed to an intra-process re-analysis, Recv1's and Recv2's histories are both improved to $\epsilon + \mathtt{ch}?[42; 42] + \mathtt{ch}?[42; 42] \cdot \mathtt{done}![42; 42]$ and the final process's history is improved to $\epsilon + \mathtt{done}?[-\infty; +\infty]$. In the third iteration Recv1's and Recv2's histories remain unchanged while the final process's history is improved to $\epsilon + \mathtt{done}?$ [42; 42]. The fourth and final iteration confirms inter-process stabilization. The analysis prototype thereby discovers that the second read statement in line 17 is unable to succeed.

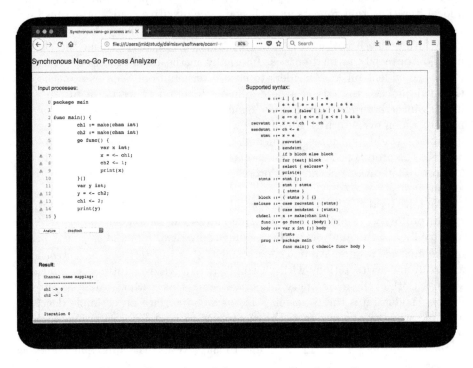

Fig. 11. Screenshot of the prototype's web-interface

```
1   package main
2
3   func main() {
4       ch := make(chan int)
5       done := make(chan int)
6       go func() { ch <- 42 }() // Send
7       go func() {              // Recv1
8           var val int;
9           val = <-ch; done <- val;
10      }()
11      go func() {              // Recv2
12          var val int;
13          val = <-ch; done <- val;
14      }()
15      go func() { for {} }()   // Work
16      <-done;
17      <-done
18  }
```

Fig. 12. A deadlock example ported from Stadtmüller et al. [30]

Table 1. Preliminary performance measurement (all reported times are in seconds)

program	# proc	# chan	# interproc. iter	min time	max time	avg.time
initial example, Fig. 1	3	2	4	0.014	0.018	0.0158
simple deadlock, Fig. 11	2	2	3	0.010	0.012	0.0110
deadlock, Fig. 12	5	2	4	0.055	0.058	0.0572
fanIn	4	3	4	0.896	0.938	0.9140
philo	4	1	3	0.770	0.793	0.7822

Table 1 lists performance of the command-line prototype on a number of examples, including two additional example programs ported from Stadtmüller et al. [30]. The reported timings were measured using the `time` tool for the natively compiled prototype running on a lightly loaded 3.1Ghz MacBook Pro laptop. For each program we list the number of processes and channels, the number of inter-process analysis iterations, and the minimum, maximum, and average analysis time across five analysis runs. Whereas these numbers are promising they are also preliminary and included here only to demonstrate feasibility of the approach. The deadlock examples from Figs. 11 and 12 illustrate how it is possible to catch some deadlocks despite analyzing a safety property over-approximately. In contrast, our tool raises no warnings when analyzing the `philo` dining philosophers program listed in Table 1 as it *may* execute successfully. In Sect. 8 we further compare our approach with that of Stadtmüller et al. [30].

In order to meet our long term goal of scalable inter-process analysis, we expect a number of optimizations to be relevant. For one, an alternative implementation based on extracting constraints would only need to traverse the AST once to eliminate the repeated interpretive overhead. For another, one could consider caching (or dependencies between) the intra-process analysis results to avoid needless intra-process reanalysis. Finally, our division into repeated intra-process analysis lends itself to parallelization.

8   Related Work

Historically, channel-based concurrency in the style of Hoare's CSP has influenced programming languages such as Concurrent ML (CML) [27] and more recently Google's Go programming language. Static analysis of CSP-like programs dates back to an early application of abstract interpretation [7], a *whole program* analysis. Since the nineties various forms of static analysis of concurrent programs have been investigated. In an early contribution Mercouroff [19] developed an abstract interpretation-based, polynomial-time analysis of CSP-like programs. It could infer the communication count on each channel connecting two processes. Nielson and Nielson [24] developed a type and effect system for CML with dynamic process and channel creation that could predict, e.g., the number of processes and channels created during a program's execution. Compared to our analysis it did not characterize the content of the messages sent.

Colby [3] subsequently developed an abstract interpretation of CML, including dynamic process creation. Akin to Nielson and Nielson [24] he analyzed the communication topology of a given program, to answer questions of the form *'which occurrences of receive can a transmit occurrence reach'*? In subsequent work various analyses for process calculi were investigated. For example, Venet [34] developed a framework for static analysis of π-calculus programs, Rydhof Hansen et al. [28] developed a static analyses for control flow and occurrence counting of mobile ambients, and Feret [9] developed control-flow and occurrence counting analyses of π-calculus programs.

Kobayashi and co-authors have since developed a range of type-based static analyses for π-calculus: Igarashi and Kobayashi [12] developed a type-based analysis of channel communication count, Kobayashi [13] developed an type-based information flow analysis including a type inference algorithm, Kobayashi [14] developed a type system that guarantees deadlock-freedom including an type inference algorithm, and Kobayashi and Sangiorgi [15] developed a hybrid *lock-freedom analysis* guaranteeing that certain communications will succeed while itself relying on deadlock-freedom and termination analyses. Most recently Giachino et al. [10] have developed a refinement of Kobayashi's earlier deadlock-freedom analysis that can precisely detect deadlocks in value-passing CCS (and *pi*-calculus) programs with arbitrary numbers of processes while still permitting type inference. Since many of the process analyses can themselves be viewed as operating over a program abstraction (a process calculus term), they are inherently limited by the precision of this abstraction. Our work instead builds on a reduced product, in which information about program variables can influence the knowledge of network communication content and vice versa.

One may view our analysis analysis as an effect system specialized to inferring histories of synchronous network communication akin to Skalka et al. [29] with the LVREs representing sets of traces of such events. In comparison to Skalka et al. [29] our approach however also infers more precise information about the value of individual events: in that sense it refines the primitive notion of an event to a lattice value.

A number of recent papers develop static analyses for various subsets of Go. Ng and Yoshida [23] first developed a static deadlock detection system for a subset of Go with a fixed number of processes and synchronous communication. Stadtmüller et al. [30] then developed a trace-based deadlock analysis of *Synchronous Mini-Go*, a syntactically slightly bigger language than nano-Go. It built on earlier work by Sulzmann and Thiemann [32] by first extracting regular expressions extended with *forkable behaviours* and subsequently analyzing these for deadlocks. Technically this involved both shuffling for the denotation of forkable behaviours and Brzozowski derivatives for the subsequent analysis. Recently Lange et al. [16] have developed a verification framework for a bigger subset of Go, supporting both asynchronous message passing and recursion. It works by approximating program behaviours by *behavioural types* and a subsequent *bounded verification* of these. The above are primarily analyses for detecting potential deadlocks which our approach is not particularly geared for.

However our value analysis is more precise since it utilizes a finer value abstraction than types. Botbol et al. [1] develop a whole-program approach based on *lattice automata* [17] and *symbolic transducers* to analyze synchronous processes communicating via message passing and illustrate it with an application to MPI in C.

Miné [22] developed a thread-modular analysis approach to the different setting of shared variable concurrency, building on the idea of an *interference domain* that capture relations between globally mutable variables. Like our approach it may need to reanalyze each thread repeatedly. In previous work we developed LVREs, including an ordering algorithm and a widening operator [21] and illustrated the domain with an intra-process analysis over LVRE futures. In a follow-up paper [20] we refined this idea to an inter-process analysis with LVREs for both histories and futures, albeit *limited to two synchronous processes*. The current paper generalizes from 2 to n processes by means a shuffle operator and reads off a history with $\mathcal{H}$ in favor of computing it within a fixed-point computation. Logozzo [18] previously suggested LVREs as an abstract domain but his formulation did not fit our purpose. For one, he defines $\mathcal{L}(\epsilon) = \emptyset$ which is algebraically controversial. For another, his structural widening operator was too sensitive to syntactic variations and did not satisfy the classical widening definition [21].

9   Conclusion and Perspectives

We have presented a modular approach to analyzing processes communicating by synchronous message passing. It combines the analysis results of individual processes by a dedicated shuffle operator. The approach has been formalized and proven sound for a subset of the Go programming language. We see a number of advantages to the approach: Since each analysis iteration result is sound, one can run the analysis in the background and warn of, e.g., an unsuccessful read or write, as soon as it is discovered. It also opens for algorithmic improvements to save intra-process reanalysis when futures are unchanged. Finally the analysis cache naturally falls into separate per process caches which opens up for parallelization.

A full version including proofs is available from
http://janmidtgaard.dk/papers/Midtgaard-Nielson-Nielson%3aSAS18-full.pdf

References

1. Botbol, V., Chailloux, E., Le Gall, T.: Static analysis of communicating processes using symbolic transducers. In: Bouajjani, A., Monniaux, D. (eds.) VMCAI 2017. LNCS, vol. 10145, pp. 73–90. Springer, Cham (2017). https://doi.org/10.1007/978-3-319-52234-0_5
2. Brzozowski, J.A.: Derivatives of regular expressions. J. ACM **11**(4), 481–494 (1964)
3. Colby, C.: Analyzing the communication topology of concurrent programs. In: Proceedings of the ACM SIGPLAN Symposium on Partial Evaluation and Semantics-Based Program Manipulation, pp. 202–213 (1995)

4. Cousot, P., Cousot, R.: Static determination of dynamic properties of programs. In: Proceedings of the Second International Symposium on Programming, pp. 106–130. Dunod, France (1976)

5. Cousot, P., Cousot, R.: Abstract interpretation: a unified lattice model for static analysis of programs by construction or approximation of fixpoints. In: Proceedings of the Fourth Annual ACM Symposium on Principles of Programming Languages, pp. 238–252 (1977)

6. Cousot, P., Cousot, R.: Systematic design of program analysis frameworks. In: Proceedings of the Sixth Annual ACM Symposium on Principles of Programming Languages, pp. 269–282 (1979)

7. Cousot, P., Cousot, R.: Semantic analysis of communicating sequential processes. In: de Bakker, J., van Leeuwen, J. (eds.) ICALP 1980. LNCS, vol. 85, pp. 119–133. Springer, Heidelberg (1980). https://doi.org/10.1007/3-540-10003-2_65

8. Davey, B.A., Priestley, H.A.: Introduction to Lattices and Order, 2nd edn. Cambridge University Press, Cambridge (2002)

9. Feret, J.: Confidentiality analysis of mobile systems. In: Palsberg, J. (ed.) SAS 2000. LNCS, vol. 1824, pp. 135–154. Springer, Heidelberg (2000). https://doi.org/10.1007/978-3-540-45099-3_8

10. Giachino, E., Kobayashi, N., Laneve, C.: Deadlock analysis of unbounded process networks. In: Baldan, P., Gorla, D. (eds.) CONCUR 2014. LNCS, vol. 8704, pp. 63–77. Springer, Heidelberg (2014). https://doi.org/10.1007/978-3-662-44584-6_6

11. Grätzer, G.: General Lattice Theory. Pure and Applied Mathematics. Academic Press, New York (1978)

12. Igarashi, A., Kobayashi, N.: Type-based analysis of communication for concurrent programming languages. In: Van Hentenryck, P. (ed.) SAS 1997. LNCS, vol. 1302, pp. 187–201. Springer, Heidelberg (1997). https://doi.org/10.1007/BFb0032742

13. Kobayashi, N.: Type-based information flow analysis for the pi-calculus. Acta Informatica 42(4–5), 291–347 (2005)

14. Kobayashi, N.: A new type system for deadlock-free processes. In: Baier, C., Hermanns, H. (eds.) CONCUR 2006. LNCS, vol. 4137, pp. 233–247. Springer, Heidelberg (2006). https://doi.org/10.1007/11817949_16

15. Kobayashi, N., Sangiorgi, D.: A hybrid type system for lock-freedom of mobile processes. In: Gupta, A., Malik, S. (eds.) CAV 2008. LNCS, vol. 5123, pp. 80–93. Springer, Heidelberg (2008). https://doi.org/10.1007/978-3-540-70545-1_10

16. Lange, J., Ng, N., Toninho, B., Yoshida, N.: Fencing off go: liveness and safety for channel-based programming. In: Proceedings of the 44th Annual ACM Symposium on Principles of Programming Languages, pp. 748–761 (2017)

17. Le Gall, T., Jeannet, B.: Lattice automata: a representation for languages on infinite alphabets, and some applications to verification. In: Nielson, H.R., Filé, G. (eds.) SAS 2007. LNCS, vol. 4634, pp. 52–68. Springer, Heidelberg (2007). https://doi.org/10.1007/978-3-540-74061-2_4

18. Logozzo, F.: Separate compositional analysis of class-based object-oriented languages. In: Rattray, C., Maharaj, S., Shankland, C. (eds.) AMAST 2004. LNCS, vol. 3116, pp. 334–348. Springer, Heidelberg (2004). https://doi.org/10.1007/978-3-540-27815-3_27

19. Mercouroff, N.: An algorithm for analyzing communicating processes. In: Brookes, S., Main, M., Melton, A., Mislove, M., Schmidt, D. (eds.) MFPS 1991. LNCS, vol. 598, pp. 312–325. Springer, Heidelberg (1992). https://doi.org/10.1007/3-540-55511-0_16

20. Midtgaard, J., Nielson, F., Nielson, H.R.: Iterated process analysis over lattice-valued regular expressions. In: PPDP 2016: Proceedings of the 18th International Symposium on Principles and Practice of Declarative Programming, pp. 132–145 (2016)

21. Midtgaard, J., Nielson, F., Nielson, H.R.: A parametric abstract domain for lattice-valued regular expressions. In: Rival, X. (ed.) SAS 2016. LNCS, vol. 9837, pp. 338–360. Springer, Heidelberg (2016). https://doi.org/10.1007/978-3-662-53413-7_17

22. Miné, A.: Relational thread-modular static value analysis by abstract interpretation. In: McMillan, K.L., Rival, X. (eds.) VMCAI 2014. LNCS, vol. 8318, pp. 39–58. Springer, Heidelberg (2014). https://doi.org/10.1007/978-3-642-54013-4_3

23. Ng, N., Yoshida, N.: Static deadlock detection for concurrent go by global session graph synthesis. In: Proceedings of the 25th International Conference on Compiler Construction, CC 2016, pp. 174–184. ACM (2016)

24. Nielson, F., Nielson, H.R.: Higher-order concurrent programs with finite communication topology. In: Proceedings of the 21st Annual ACM Symposium on Principles of Programming Languages, pp. 84–97 (1994)

25. Nielson, F., Nielson, H.R., Hankin, C.: Principles of Program Analysis. Springer, Heidelberg (1999). https://doi.org/10.1007/978-3-662-03811-6

26. Owens, S., Reppy, J., Turon, A.: Regular-expression derivatives re-examined. J. Funct. Program. **19**(2), 173–190 (2009)

27. Reppy, J.: Concurrent Programming in ML. Cambridge University Press, Cambridge (1999)

28. Rydhof Hansen, R., Jensen, J.G., Nielson, F., Nielson, H.R.: Abstract interpretation of mobile ambients. In: Cortesi, A., Filé, G. (eds.) SAS 1999. LNCS, vol. 1694, pp. 134–148. Springer, Heidelberg (1999). https://doi.org/10.1007/3-540-48294-6_9

29. Skalka, C., Smith, S., Van Horn, D.: Types and trace effects of higher order programs. J. Funct. Program. **18**(2), 179–249 (2008)

30. Stadtmüller, K., Sulzmann, M., Thiemann, P.: Static trace-based deadlock analysis for synchronous mini-go. In: Igarashi, A. (ed.) APLAS 2016. LNCS, vol. 10017, pp. 116–136. Springer, Cham (2016). https://doi.org/10.1007/978-3-319-47958-3_7

31. Sulzmann, M., Thiemann, P.: Derivatives for regular shuffle expressions. In: Dediu, A.-H., Formenti, E., Martín-Vide, C., Truthe, B. (eds.) LATA 2015. LNCS, vol. 8977, pp. 275–286. Springer, Cham (2015). https://doi.org/10.1007/978-3-319-15579-1_21

32. Sulzmann, M., Thiemann, P.: Forkable regular expressions. In: Dediu, A.-H., Janoušek, J., Martín-Vide, C., Truthe, B. (eds.) LATA 2016. LNCS, vol. 9618, pp. 194–206. Springer, Cham (2016). https://doi.org/10.1007/978-3-319-30000-9_15

33. Tarjan, R.E.: Fast algorithms for solving path problems. J. ACM **28**(3), 594–614 (1981)

34. Venet, A.: Automatic determination of communication topologies in mobile systems. In: Levi, G. (ed.) SAS 1998. LNCS, vol. 1503, pp. 152–167. Springer, Heidelberg (1998). https://doi.org/10.1007/3-540-49727-7_9

The Impact of Program Transformations on Static Program Analysis

Kedar S. Namjoshi[1] and Zvonimir Pavlinovic[2](✉)

[1] Bell Laboratories, Nokia, Murray Hill, USA
kedar.namjoshi@nokia-bell-labs.com
[2] New York University, New York City, USA
zvonimir@cs.nyu.edu

Abstract. Semantics-preserving program transformations, such as those carried out by an optimizing compiler, can affect the results of static program analyses. In the best cases, a transformation increases precision or allows a simpler analysis to replace a complex one. In other cases, transformations have the opposite effect, reducing precision. This work constructs a theoretical framework to analyze this intriguing phenomenon. The framework provides a simple, uniform explanation for precision changes, linking them to bisimulation relations that justify the correctness of a transformation. It offers a mechanism for recovering lost precision through the systematic construction of a new, bisimulating analysis. Furthermore, it is shown that program analyses defined over a class of composite domains can be factored into a program transformation followed by simpler, equally precise analyses of the target program.

1 Introduction

It has been empirically observed that a semantics-preserving program transformation may alter the outcome of a static analysis, making the results more or less precise. Consider, for instance, the program on the left in Fig. 1. A standard odd-even parity analysis will deduce that x is odd and y is even at the end of the program; but the parity of z is unknown, as the value of y div x could have either parity (consider $y = 10, x = 5$ and $y = 10, x = 3$). An application of constant propagation and folding, a standard compiler optimization that replaces expressions with equivalent constant values, produces the program on the right. Parity analysis on that program will deduce that z is even.

In this instance, the transformation enhances precision. Several tools (e.g., SMACK [4] and SeaHorn [17]) use transformations for this purpose. But not all transformations enhance precision: as pointed out in [22], a translation to 3-address code can render certain relational analyses imprecise. Program analyses are, therefore, not robust under semantics-preserving transformations.

This observation raises three central questions: (1) How does an (arbitrary) transformation affect the results of an (arbitrary) analysis? (2) Is there a mechanism to recover lost precision? and (3) Are there systematic ways to simplify

© Springer Nature Switzerland AG 2018
A. Podelski (Ed.): SAS 2018, LNCS 11002, pp. 306–325, 2018.
https://doi.org/10.1007/978-3-319-99725-4_19

```
x := 3;                          x := 3;
y := x * 4;                      y := 12;
z := (y div x)*z;                z := 4*z;
```

Fig. 1. A constant propagation transformation: source on left, target on right.

analysis through program transformation? In this work, we set up a mathematical framework to analyze these questions, and provide some answers.

The framework is built as follows. Static program analyses are modeled with standard concepts from abstract interpretation [7,8]. Crucially, a semantics-preserving transformation is modeled as a proof-generator. In transforming a source program S to a program T, we suppose that a transformation also provides a bisimulation relation, B, which justifies the semantic equivalence between the two programs. The bisimulation links the state spaces of S and T, making it possible to transfer invariants (in particular, static analysis results) from one side to the other, allowing their relative precision to be compared. Using this framework, we establish general results that explain why precision is gained or lost, and how it may be regained.

We show that an analysis with domain D on program T can be converted to a *bisimulating analysis* on S, producing results that are (near-)equivalent – after transferring through the bisimulation – to the results on T. The bisimulating analysis is defined over a new abstract domain, D', constructed in terms of B and D. One can explain the effect of a transformation on precision by comparing the relative strengths of D and D'. This provides a uniform explanation of precision changes observed in different settings, including the ones discussed above.

Moreover, the analysis designed in [22] to counteract the loss of precision is essentially the analysis induced by the new domain D'. The construction of D' thus provides a systematic, general method to form a new domain and its associated analysis to recover from a loss of precision.

Finally, we establish that any analysis over a one-way reduced product of domains C and D can be factored into a program transformation defined using C, followed by an analysis of the resulting program over domain D, with equally precise results. This provides a systematic method to design transformations which simplify analysis without losing precision.

Together, these results provide a firmer understanding of how transformations influence precision. This should help in practice to choose (or construct) the right set of transformations to simplify an analysis task.

2 Overview

In this section we provide a high-level overview of how we model the effect of program transformations on static analyses. Table 1 summarizes the transformation and parity analysis for the introductory constant propagation example. Parity domain elements E and O represent even and odd numbers, respectively, and $\top$ represents all integers. The analysis maintains an *abstract state* for every

Table 1. (a) the results of the parity analysis for the optimized program, (b) the optimized program, (c) the bisimulation relation witnessing the correctness of the optimization, (d) the original program, (e) the results of the parity analysis on the original program, (f) the results of the bisimulating parity analysis.

$x'{:}O$	$x'{:}= 3$	$x'{=}x{=}3 \land y'{=}y \land z'{=}z$	$x := 3$	$x{:}O$	$x{:}O$
$y'{:}E$	$y' := 12$	$x'{=}x{=}3 \land y'{=}y{=}12 \land z'{=}z$	$y := x * 4$	$y{:}E$	$y{:}E$
$z'{:}E$	$z' := 4{*}z'$	$x'{=}x{=}3 \land y'{=}y{=}12 \land z'{=}z$	$z := (y/x){*}z$	$z{:}\top$	$z{:}E$
a)	b)	c)	d)	e)	f)

location, a map from variables to elements of the parity domain. To avoid clutter, we show only the changes to the abstract state.

Bisimulation Relation. The relation is symbolically presented in Table 1(c). The bisimulation relates corresponding program states iff (1) they share the same location and (2) their variable valuations satisfy the predicates appearing on the horizontal line connecting identical program locations.

Bisimulating Analysis. The new *bisimulating analysis* combines the parity domain and the bisimulation relation. It operates on the original program as follows. In each step, the analysis uses the bisimulation to move from the source to the transformed program, transforming the current abstract state through the bisimulation. Parity analysis on the optimized program with the transformed state produces a new abstract state, which is back-propagated to the source, again using the bisimulation (technically, its inverse). In effect, this process refines abstract states using bisimulation information.

Consider the point just before the last line of the source. The current abstract state, $[x : O, y : E, z : \top]$, is transferred to the same location in the transformed program using the middle horizontal line. This results in the abstract state $[x' : O, y' : E, z' : \top]$, which parity analysis uses to analyze the last command. This produces $[x' : O, y' : E, z' : E]$, which is back-propagated using the bottom horizontal line, resulting in the state $[x : O, y : E, z : E]$, as shown in Table 1(f).

Precision. One can view the bisimulating analysis, roughly speaking, as operating on a domain that is a product of the parity domain and the domain used for constant analysis. That is, to obtain the same precision as on the transformed program, one must analyze the source with a domain that combines constants and parity. This explains the gain in precision provided by the transformation. One can reverse this view, and consider that a source analysis with a product domain (constants × parity) is factored into a transformation based only on the constants domain, and analysis based only on parity. These intuitions are made precise in the rest of the paper.

3   Preliminaries

For convenience, we abstract from programming syntax and represent programs by their induced transition systems and program transformations as transition system transformations. Representing program transformations semantically is uncommon, but was also followed in, e.g. [9], for similar reasons. We represent static analyses formally using the framework of abstract interpretation [7].

3.1   On Notation

We follow the notation of Dijkstra and Scholten from [12] for algebraic calculations. Sets are identified with predicates, Boolean operators stand for set operations, e.g., $A \cap B$ is written as $A \wedge B$, and the "boxed" form $[\varphi]$ represents that the predicate φ is true (equivalently, that the set φ is universal). Thus, $[X \rightarrow Y]$ expresses that set X is a subset of set Y. A calculational proof is a sequence of proof steps, each one being a weakening (indicated by $\rightarrow$) or an equivalence (indicated by $\equiv$). A proof step establishing $[f \rightarrow g]$, say, is displayed as follows.

$$f$$
$$\rightarrow g \qquad\qquad \{\text{hint why } f \text{ is stronger than } g\}$$

3.2   Programs and Program Transformations

Transition Systems. A program is represented by its induced transition system [3]. A transition system is defined by a tuple (S, I, Σ, δ), where S is a set of *states*, I is a non-empty subset of *initial* states, Σ is a set of *actions*, and $\delta \subseteq S \times \Sigma \times S$ is the *transition relation*. For a triple $(s, a, s') \in \delta$, we say that s' is a *successor to s on a*. We use the notation $\delta(Y)$, for a set of states Y, to denote the successors of Y by δ, i.e., $s' \in \delta(Y)$ if, and only if, there is a state s in Y such that $\delta(s, a, s')$ holds for some action label a. An *execution* of the transition system from state s is a sequence of alternating states and actions, of the form $s = s_0, a_0, s_1, a_1, \ldots$, where for each i, (s_i, a_i, s_{i+1}) is a transition in δ. Its trace is the sequence $a_0, a_1, \ldots$. A *computation* is an execution from some initial state. A state is *reachable* if it appears along some computation. The *language* of a transition system T, denoted as $\mathcal{L}(T)$, is the set of traces of its finite and infinite computations.

Program Transformations and Correctness. A program transformation, viewed semantically, is a function mapping one transition system to another with the same action set. A transformation from S to T is correct if $\mathcal{L}(T) \subseteq \mathcal{L}(S)$. I.e., for every computation x of T, there is a computation y of S such that x and y have the same[1] trace.

---

[1] To allow stuttering, one may define a subset of actions to be observable, and let the trace of an execution be the sequence of observable actions on it.

Simulation and Bisimulation. A relation R connecting states of transition system T to states of transition system S is a *simulation* (of T by S) – also called a "refinement mapping" – if:

- For states t, s such that $(t, s) \in R$, for every action a, and every successor t' of t on a, there is a successor s' of s on a such that $(t', s') \in R$, and
- For every initial state t of T, there is an initial state s of S where $(t, s) \in R$.

Relation R is a *bisimulation* if both R and its inverse relation, R^{-1} are simulations. Establishing (bi)simulation is a standard proof technique for showing correctness, thanks to the following standard results.

Theorem 1. *Let S, T be transition systems, and let R be a relation connecting states of T to those of S. If R is a simulation, then $\mathcal{L}(T) \subseteq \mathcal{L}(S)$. If R is a bisimulation, then $\mathcal{L}(T) = \mathcal{L}(S)$.*

Relational Operators. For any relation R on any domain, the modal operators pre_R and post_R, are defined as follows. For any set S,

$$u \in \mathsf{pre}_R(S) = (\exists v : uRv \,\wedge\, v \in S) \qquad \mathsf{post}_R(S) = \mathsf{pre}_{R^{-1}}(S)$$

I.e., $\mathsf{pre}_R(S)$ is the pre-image of S under R; it is the set of all elements that are related by R to some element of S. Likewise, $\mathsf{post}_R(S)$ is the image of S by R; it consists of all elements that are connected to elements in S by R.

A set of states, X, is an inductive invariant of a transition system (S, I, Σ, δ) if it includes all initial states, i.e., $[I \rightarrow X]$, and is closed under the transition relation, i.e., $[\mathsf{post}_\delta(X) \rightarrow X]$. Invariants of S can be transformed into invariants of T through a simulation B, as follows.

Theorem 2 *(cf. [27]).* *Let R be a simulation from T to S. For any inductive invariant φ of S, the set $\mathsf{pre}_R(\varphi)$ is an inductive invariant of T.*

Transformation Witnesses. We assume that every semantic-preserving program transformation has an associated bisimulation relation which acts as a "witness" (i.e., a proof) for correctness. Common compiler transformations, e.g., constant propagation, dead store removal, static single assignment (SSA) conversion and loop invariant code motion have simple witnesses [2,28]. Abadi and Lamport's result [1] shows that every language inclusion has a simulation witness (after adding auxiliary history and prophecy information).

3.3   Static Program Analysis

We briefly review standard notions. A static program analysis is usually defined by specifying (1) a concrete domain as a partial order $(C, \leq_C)$, (2) an abstract domain as a partial order $(A, \leq_A)$, and (3) a pair of functions (α, γ), called a Galois connection, between the two domains where $[\alpha(c) \leq_A a \equiv c \leq_C \gamma(a)]$. The concrete semantics of a program is defined as the least fixpoint of a *transformer* $\tau : C \to C$. The Galois connection induces a transformer $\alpha \circ \tau \circ \gamma$ whose least fixpoint over A defines the most precise abstract semantics, which is an over-approximation of the concrete one [7].

In this work, the concrete domain consists of sets of states ordered by subset inclusion. As we combine aspects of static analysis with those of invariants and (bi)simulation, it is convenient to work entirely within the concrete domain instead of carrying around an abstract domain and a Galois connection. We use an equivalent formulation of abstract domains in terms of closure operators on the concrete domain. An operator cl is a (up-)closure if it is monotonic, i.e., $[X \to Y]$ implies that $[\mathsf{cl}(X) \to \mathsf{cl}(Y)]$; increasing, i.e., $[X \to \mathsf{cl}(X)]$; and idempotent, i.e., $[\mathsf{cl}(\mathsf{cl}(X)) \equiv \mathsf{cl}(X)]$. Given a Galois connection (α, γ), the operator $\gamma \circ \alpha$ is a closure, with closed sets corresponding to abstract elements.

The set of *reachable states* of a transition system (S, I, Σ, δ) is the least fixpoint of the concrete transformer $\delta^+(X) = X \vee \delta(X)$ that includes the initial states, I. Following [8], we write this as lfp (δ^+, I). The general form lfp (f, a) denotes the least fixpoint of f above a, which exists if $a \le f(a)$ for monotone f, cf. [5]. The reachable states can also be expressed as lfp $((\lambda X : I \vee \delta(X)), \emptyset)$. In the abstract setting, we look for closed sets as solutions. Thus, we construct lfp $(\mathsf{cl} \circ \delta^+, I)$ or, equivalently, lfp $((\lambda X : \mathsf{cl}(I \vee \delta(X))), \emptyset)$.

Theorem 3. lfp $(\mathsf{cl} \circ \delta^+, I)$ *is well defined. It is the least closed set that is an inductive invariant of the transition system.*

Proof. As both cl and δ^+ are increasing, $[I \to \mathsf{cl} \circ \delta^+(I)]$. Thus, the least fixpoint exists. Let $L = $ lfp $(\mathsf{cl} \circ \delta^+, I)$. Then $[I \to L]$ by definition of L. Moreover, $[\mathsf{cl}(\delta^+(L)) \equiv L]$ by the fixpoint property; hence, L is closed, and $[\delta(L) \to L]$. Thus, L is a closed inductive invariant.

To show the minimality of L, let Y be any closed set that is also an inductive invariant. From inductiveness, $[I \to Y]$ and $[\delta(Y) \to Y]$ holds. Hence, $[\delta^+(Y) \equiv Y]$; since Y is closed, $[\mathsf{cl}(\delta^+(Y)) \equiv Y]$ holds. Thus, Y includes I and is a fixpoint of $\mathsf{cl} \circ \delta^+$. As L is the least such set, $[L \to Y]$. □

More approximate closed invariants are provided by lfp (η, I), where η is monotone, $[I \to \eta(I)]$, and η maps to closed sets of cl. To be *sound*, lfp (η, I) must be a superset of the reachable states. That is guaranteed if $\eta(X)$ is a superset of $\delta^+(X)$ for all X. We say that such η are *adequate*.

One mechanism to achieve finite convergence of the fixpoint computation is widening [6,7,9]. Let $\mathbb{D}$ be an abstract domain with elements denoted by D. A widening operator is a function $\nabla : \mathbb{D} \times \mathbb{D} \to \mathbb{D}$ such that:

- $[D_2 \subseteq D_1 \nabla D_2]$
- $[D_2 \subseteq D_1 \to D_1 \nabla D_2 = D_1]$
- Let $D_0, D_1, \ldots$ be an increasing chain of abstract elements. Let $D_0', D_1', \ldots$ be a chain of elements such that $D_i \subseteq D_i'$ for every i. Then there exists $n \in \mathbb{N}$ such that $\forall k \ge n : D_k \nabla D_k' = D_n$.

Given an adequate transformer η and a widening ∇, the new transformer $\eta_\nabla(X) \triangleq X \nabla \eta(X)$ is adequate and for every initial approximation $D \in \mathbb{D}$

the sequence $\langle \eta_\nabla^i(D), i \in \mathbb{N} \rangle$ becomes stationary [6]. The least fixpoint of η_∇ is an over-approximation, sacrificing precision for guaranteed eventual termination.

4   Relating Analyses Under Bisimulation

In this section, we formulate a framework for analyzing the effect of transformations on static analysis results. For the remainder of this paper, we assume a source program S, a transformed program T, and a bisimulation B between T and S semantically modeling a semantic-preserving program transformation. We further assume an abstract domain underlying the desired analysis in terms of closures cl_S and cl_T for the source and transformed program, respectively, and corresponding widening operators ∇_S and ∇_T.

The above assumptions fit the setting in which program verification tools such as SMACK [4] and SeaHorn [17] operate. Programs S and T are available in practice as the mentioned tools anyhow run the transformations. Also, tools performing semantic-preserving transformations implicitly have all of the information necessary to generate the underlying bisimulation information [18,28,33]. Lastly, the assumed closure and widening operators are essentially program-specific lifts of corresponding operators defined over readily available program-agnostic domains such as intervals, octagons [25], polyhedra [11], etc.

4.1   Comparing Invariants of S and T

Let G denote the invariant on S computed with cl_S, and let H denote the invariant on T computed with cl_T. In order to compare the relative strengths of the two invariants, we have to transform them from one state space to the other, as the state spaces of S and T may, in general, be different. The bisimulation B is used to perform this transformation, using Theorem 2.

Informally, we would consider H to be stronger than G if, after transferring H from T to S via B^{-1}, the resulting invariant in S is stronger than G, i.e., if $[\mathsf{post}_B(H) \rightarrow G]$. By the symmetry of bisimulation, we should also require that the invariant obtained by transferring G in the other direction, from S to T, is weaker than H. I.e., we want $[H \rightarrow \mathsf{pre}_B(G)]$ to also hold.

Thus, we take the two conditions (a) $[\mathsf{post}_B(H) \rightarrow G]$ and (b) $[H \rightarrow \mathsf{pre}_B(G)]$ as the definition of the property "H is stronger than G". Condition (a) is equivalent to $[\mathsf{cl}_S \circ \mathsf{post}_B(H) \rightarrow G]$, a form that is used in the proofs below.

4.2   Induced Closure for S

Suppose that H is stronger than G. In order to explain the precision gain T exhibits compared to S (equivalently, the precision loss of S subject to T), we formulate a new abstract domain on S (via a new closure operator) such that an analysis on S with this operator produces an invariant that is at least as strong as the transferred invariant $\mathsf{post}_B(H)$.

A natural way to reflect the computation from T into S is as follows: given a subset X of the states of S, its closure is computed by mapping X to its image Y in T through the relation B^{-1}; forming Y', the closure of Y in T through cl_T; and finally, mapping Y' back to a set X' in S through B. The new operator $\mathsf{cl}^{B,H}$ is formulated using this intuition. It is defined as a least fixpoint, $(\lambda X.\, \mathsf{lfp}\,(g, X))$, where the function g is given below. The key to g is the composition $\mathsf{post}_B \circ \mathsf{pre}_B$ (ignoring the intervening closures); this composition formalizes the intuition of moving from S to T and back again.

$$g(Z) \triangleq Z \vee \mathsf{post}_B \circ \mathsf{cl}_T(H \cap \mathsf{pre}_B \circ \mathsf{cl}_S(Z)) \tag{1}$$

The function g is increasing by its first term and monotone as all operators are monotone. It follows from standard arguments that

Lemma 1. $\mathsf{cl}^{B,H} = (\lambda Z.\, \mathsf{lfp}\,(g, Z))$ *is a closure operator on* S.

4.3 Induced Static Analysis

We now turn to the invariants computed with static analysis using the new closure operator on S and the best abstract transformer, $\mathsf{cl}_S^{B,H} \circ \delta_S^+$. We show that the resulting inductive invariant is *at least as precise* as the invariant $\mathsf{post}_B(H)$ obtained by transferring the analysis result H from T to S.

Theorem 4. *Let* $G = \mathsf{lfp}\,(\mathsf{cl}_S \circ \delta_S^+, I_S)$ *be the result of the static analysis on* S. *Let* $H = \mathsf{lfp}\,(\eta_T, I_T)$ *be the result of a sound static analysis on* T *with closure* cl_T. *Let* $G^{B,H} = \mathsf{lfp}\,(\mathsf{cl}_S^{B,H} \circ \delta_S^+, I_S)$ *be the invariant computed on* S *with the newly defined closure operator. If* H *is stronger than* G, *then* $[G^{B,H} \longrightarrow \mathsf{post}_B(H)]$.

Proof. We prove the claim by showing that $\mathsf{post}_B(H)$ is a superset of I_S, and a pre-fixpoint of the function $\mathsf{cl}_S^{B,H} \circ \delta_S^+$.

As $\mathsf{post}_B(H)$ is an inductive invariant of S, it includes the initial states; hence, $[I_S \longrightarrow \mathsf{post}_B(H)]$.

Next, we establish that $[\mathsf{cl}_S^{B,H} \circ \delta_S^+(\mathsf{post}_B(H)) \longrightarrow \mathsf{post}_B(H)]$. As $\mathsf{post}_B(H)$ is inductive for S, this is equivalent to $[\mathsf{cl}_S^{B,H}(\mathsf{post}_B(H)) \longrightarrow \mathsf{post}_B(H)]$, which holds if $\mathsf{post}_B(H)$ is a pre-fixpoint of the function g used to define $\mathsf{cl}_S^{B,H}$ (in Eq. 1). By the form of g, we only need to consider its second term:

$\mathsf{post}_B \circ \mathsf{cl}_T(H \cap \mathsf{pre}_B \circ \mathsf{cl}_S(\mathsf{post}_B(H)))$
$\longrightarrow \mathsf{post}_B \circ \mathsf{cl}_T(H \cap \mathsf{pre}_B(G))$ \hfill $\{H$ is stronger than G, condition (a)$\}$
$\equiv \mathsf{post}_B \circ \mathsf{cl}_T(H)$ \hfill $\{H$ is stronger than G, condition (b)$\}$
$\equiv \mathsf{post}_B(H)$ \hfill $\{H$ is closed under cl_T by property of $\eta_T\}$

$\square$

Discussion. This theorem shows how to construct a new domain on S that matches (or improves) the gain of precision obtained by transforming S to T. The new domain is constructed from the bisimulation B, the abstract domain of T, as well as its invariant H. The structure of $\mathsf{cl}_S^{B,H}$ shows how a transformation, in the form of its bisimulation relation, influences the precision of an analysis. This is a somewhat indirect demonstration: an intriguing open question is whether it is possible to determine directly from B and cl_T if precision is lost or gained.

As bisimulation is symmetric, a loss of precision in a transformation from S to T is a gain of precision when viewed from T towards S. Therefore, if precision is lost, this theorem can be applied to construct a new domain in T which recovers the greater precision of analysis in S – for instance, in the introductory 3-address code translation example.

The reason why the new analysis in S can be strictly more precise than the back-propagated invariant of T is that some transformations can introduce complexity in the transformed program. For instance, envision a transformation that replaces a constant in the program with, say, a binary expression that provably always evaluates to that constant. The induced analysis reaps the benefits of the bisimulation and the simplicity of the original program for such transformations.

5 Practicality Extensions

If verification tools were to implement the induced analysis, the only new operation they are required to implement is refinement of an abstract domain element with the bisimulation information $\mathsf{post}_B \circ \mathsf{pre}_B$ (modulo intervening closures). This operation is often feasible as the bisimulation for many common transformations is essentially a conjunction of equalities between the variables and expressions of T and S at corresponding points in the two programs [18,22,28]. However, the induced analysis has several shortcomings that hinder its usability.

First, the results of Sect. 4.3 hold for the best transformer δ_S^+ of the source program, which might not be easily computable. In fact, the abstract transformer for the source program might not be even available in some cases. Several verification frameworks translate programs written in higher-level source languages to a bytecode representation to support multitude of different programming languages [13,22]. In that case, only the transformer for program T is available. Second, the analysis operates and produces results over the new (induced) abstract domain. The widening operators for this domain are not immediate. Third, the closure operator $\mathsf{cl}_S^{B,H}$ is defined as a fixpoint which might be expensive to compute in practice. Lastly, the new domain relies on the precomputed invariant H of T. We now address these practical limitations of the induced analysis.

5.1 Bisimulating Analysis

The results in Sect. 4.3 show that the least fixpoint of the best transformer induced by $\mathsf{cl}_S^{B,H}$ is at least as strong as the back-propagated invariant from T. In this part, we exhibit a simpler *bisimulating* analysis with a similar property. In essence, the new transformer η_S uses the bisimulation to jump to the transformed program, makes an analysis step there, and then comes back to the source program.

$$\eta_S(X) \triangleq \mathsf{cl}_S \circ \mathsf{post}_B \circ \eta_T \circ \mathsf{cl}_T(H \cap \mathsf{pre}_B(X)) \tag{2}$$

An important property of η_S is that, although it is defined over the source program, the analysis uses only the provided adequate transformer η_T for the transformed program. Hence, it does not depend on the source transformer that, as pointed our earlier, sometimes might not be even available in practice. We also remind the reader that this is the analysis we used in our example of Sect. 2. Furthermore, this analysis avoids the fixpoint calculation in the closure operator $\mathsf{cl}_S^{B,H}$.

The new analysis is step-wise more precise than the provided analysis on the transformed program. That is, in each iteration the bisimulating analysis does not lose precision. The following results formalize this intuition.

Lemma 2. *The new bisimulating analysis operator η_S is sound for S.*

Proof. The operator η_S is monotonic, as all operations in its defining expression are monotonic. We show that $\mathsf{lfp}\ (\eta_S, I_S)$ is well-defined and that the result over-approximates the reachable states.

We first establish that $[I_S \rightarrow \eta_S(I_S)]$, to ensure that $\mathsf{lfp}\ (\eta_S, I_S)$ is defined. As H is an invariant of T and B is a bisimulation, I_T is a subset of $(H \cap \mathsf{pre}_B(I_S))$. By adequacy of η_T, it follows that I_T is a subset of $\eta_T \circ \mathsf{cl}_T(H \cap \mathsf{pre}_B(I_S))$. As B is a bisimulation, I_S is a subset of $\mathsf{post}_B \circ \eta_T \circ \mathsf{cl}_T(H \cap \mathsf{pre}_B(I_S))$, and therefore of $\eta_S(I_S)$.

Next, we establish that $[R^{k+1} \rightarrow \eta_S(R^k)]$ for all k, which establishes that $\mathsf{lfp}\ (\eta_S, I_S)$ includes all reachable states. Consider a state s' in $R^{k+1} = \delta_S^+(R^k)$. There are two cases.

(i) s' is in R^k. Then s' is also in $\mathsf{post}_B(H)$, as that is an invariant of S. Hence, there is a state t' in T such that $t'Bs'$ holds, and $t' \in H$. Therefore, t' is in $H \cap \mathsf{pre}_B(R^k)$ and thus in the closure of that set under cl_T. By adequacy of η_T, the state t' is in $\eta_T \circ \mathsf{cl}_T(H \cap \mathsf{pre}_B(R^k))$. As t' is related to s' by B, s' is in $\mathsf{cl}_S \circ \mathsf{post}_B \circ \eta_T \circ \mathsf{cl}_T(H \cap \mathsf{pre}_B(R^k))$, i.e., s' is in $\eta_S(R^k)$.

(ii) s' is a successor of a state s in R^k. As s is in $\mathsf{post}_B(H)$, there is a state t of T such that tBs and t is in $H \cap \mathsf{pre}_B(R^k)$. As B is a simulation relation, this state has a successor, t', such that $t'Bs'$ holds. By adequacy of η_T, t' is in $\eta_T \circ \mathsf{cl}_T(H \cap \mathsf{pre}_B(R^k))$. As t' is related to s' by B, s' is in $\mathsf{cl}_S \circ \mathsf{post}_B \circ \eta_T \circ \mathsf{cl}_T(H \cap \mathsf{pre}_B(R^k))$, i.e., s' is in $\eta_S(R^k)$. □

We now show that the result of analyzing program S with η_S is as precise as the transferred invariant $\mathsf{post}_B(H)$, when expressed as a closed set using cl_S. Note that as H is presumed to be stronger than G, by condition (a) of that definition, $\mathsf{cl}_S \circ \mathsf{post}_B(H)$ is stronger than G.

Theorem 5. *Let $G = \mathsf{lfp}\ (\mathsf{cl}_S \circ \delta_S^+, I_S)$ be the result of the original analysis on S, and $\hat{G} = \mathsf{lfp}\ (\eta_S, I_S)$ be the result of the analysis on S using the new η_S. Let $H = \mathsf{lfp}\ (\eta_T, I_T)$ be the result of the static analysis on T using an adequate transformer η_T. If H is stronger than G, then $[\hat{G} \rightarrow \mathsf{cl}_S \circ \mathsf{post}_B(H)]$.*

Proof. We prove this by showing that $\mathsf{cl}_S \circ \mathsf{post}_B(H)$ is a pre-fixpoint of η_S and that it includes I_S. As $\mathsf{post}_B(H)$ is an invariant of S, we have that $[I_S \rightarrow \mathsf{post}_B(H)]$. Hence, $[I_S \rightarrow \mathsf{cl}_S \circ \mathsf{post}_B(H)]$. Now consider the pre-fixpoint claim.

$$\eta_S(\mathsf{cl}_S \circ \mathsf{post}_B(H))$$
$$\equiv \mathit{cl}_S \circ \mathsf{post}_B \circ \eta_T \circ \mathsf{cl}_T(H \cap \mathsf{pre}_B(\mathsf{cl}_S(\mathsf{post}_B(H)))) \qquad \{\text{definition}\}$$
$$\rightarrow \mathit{cl}_S \circ \mathsf{post}_B \circ \eta_T \circ \mathsf{cl}_T(H \cap \mathsf{pre}_B(G)) \qquad \{H \text{ is stronger than } G \text{ (a)}\}$$
$$\rightarrow \mathit{cl}_S \circ \mathsf{post}_B \circ \eta_T \circ \mathsf{cl}_T(H) \qquad \{H \text{ is stronger than } G \text{ (b)}\}$$
$$\equiv \mathit{cl}_S \circ \mathsf{post}_B(H) \qquad \{H \text{ } \mathsf{cl}_T\text{-closed, fixpoint of } \eta_T\}$$

$\square$

Widenings. By relying on the abstract domain and transformer of T, we can also use the widening operator for T to ensure finite convergence of the bisimulating analysis. We assume the abstract transformer on T is $\eta_T^{\triangledown}(Y) \triangleq Y \triangledown_T \eta_T(Y)$, where η_T is an adequate monotone function as usual. We therefore use η_T to define η_S, as shown above, and then define the widened bisimulating transformer as $\eta_S^{\triangledown}(X) \triangleq X \triangledown_S \eta_S(X)$. The analysis based on this transformer is guaranteed to converge in a finite number of steps but it may be less precise than the propagated invariant computed by $\eta_T^{\triangledown}$. The reason for this is that, although η_S is more precise than the back-propagated η_T, the widening operators are not necessarily monotone [6]. We leave for future work the investigation of the actual ramifications of this imprecision in practice as well as the construction of more precise bisimulating widening operators.

5.2   Optimizing Domain Calculations Under Bisimulation Closure

The formulations of the new closure operator (Sect. 4.3) and the bisimulating analysis (Sect. 5.1) rely on the invariant H on T. We show below that this dependence can be removed if H is known to be closed under bisimulation within T – i.e., if state s is in H, so is any other state s' that is bisimular to s. This is guaranteed if all closed sets in T are closed under bisimulation, as H is one such. Intuitively, bisimulation-closure asserts that indistinguishable concrete states do not negatively effect the precision of an abstract domain. Formally, we define

Assumption 1 (Bisimulation closure). $[\mathsf{pre}_B \circ \mathsf{post}_B(Y) \rightarrow Y]$ *holds for all closed sets* Y *of* cl_T.

Assuming bisimulation-closure, the definitions can be simplified by eliminating H, as shown below, while retaining the properties shown previously.

$$\mathsf{cl}^{B,H}(X) \triangleq \mathsf{lfp}\,(g, X)), \text{ where } g(Z) \triangleq Z \vee \mathsf{post}_B \circ \mathsf{cl}_T \circ \mathsf{pre}_B \circ \mathsf{cl}_S(Z) \text{ and}$$

$$\eta_S(X) \triangleq \mathsf{cl}_S \circ \mathsf{post}_B \circ \eta_T \circ \mathsf{cl}_T \circ \mathsf{pre}_B(X)$$

Bisimulation-closure holds if B has a functional form, as shown below. Several common program optimizations have functional bisimulation relations. Examples include constant propagation, dead-code removal, and loop unrolling. Even transformations that reorder execution, such as loop inverse, induce a bisimulation relation that maps every source state to a single target state.

Lemma 3. *If B is functional, i.e., $[tBs \land t'Bs \rightarrow t = t']$, then bisimulation-closure holds.*

Proof. Consider any subset Y of T. State t' is in $\text{pre}_B \circ \text{post}_B(Y)$ iff there are states s in S and t in Y such that tBs and $t'Bs$. As B is functional, $t = t'$; thus, t' is in Y.   □

Transformations that can potentially invalidate the bisimulation closure are those that break-up the computation. For instance, 3-address code translation will break a single source statement into several target ones. Consider a source statement `assume (x - y ≤ 7)` and its 3-address translation `t1' := x' - y'; t2' := t1' ≤ 7; assume t2'`. A source state just before the original statement maps to several target states corresponding to the intermediate computation of the starting two statements in the target program. However, these statements only refine the relationship between the variables. That is, at the beginning of the target program no relationship between target variables `t1'`, `x'`, `y'` and `t2'` is known. Each consecutive statement does not invalidate existing relationships between other variables, yet it only refines the ones between the above mentioned target variables, satisfying the bisimulation closure assumption.

5.3   Counteracting Precision Loss in 3-Address Code Transformation

We now exemplify how verification tools can use the new bisimulating analysis to counteract precision loss due to a transformation. Consider a relational static analysis that computes bounds on the difference between the values of pairs of variables. In other words, an abstract state is the conjunction of difference-bounds constraints of the form $x - y \leq c$ and $\pm x \leq c$, where x and y are program variables and c is an integer or real constant [23,24]. For the example of three-address code transformation from [22], shown in Fig. 2, the analysis will infer that $(x - y) \leq 7$ holds at the end of the source program (on the left). The same analysis, however, fails to infer any useful relation between x and y on the transformed program (on the right). As explained in [22], for an accurate result, it is necessary to track a relationship between *three* variables (e.g., $t_1' = x' - y'$), which cannot be done precisely in the given analysis domain.

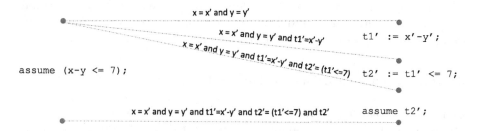

Fig. 2. A 3-address code translation (from [22]) and accompanying bisimulation relation

Bisimulation Relation. The bisimulation is symbolically illustrated in Fig. 2 using the horizontal lines and the attached predicates defined over program variables. The relation also contains "history" information connecting t_1' and t_2' to x' and y'. The bisimulation allows stuttering steps on T. The transformation engine can generate the bisimulation relation while performing the actual transformation [20, 21]. That is, the information about equality of live expressions can be extracted directly from the generated 3-address code.

Bisimulating Analysis. Initially, the invariant approximant for the source program maps the top and bottom difference-bounds abstract element to the first and last source location, respectively. This approximant is then transformed into an approximant for the transformed program using $\mathsf{cl}_T \circ \mathsf{pre}_B$. The resulting approximant assigns the top abstract element to the first three locations of T since the corresponding bisimulation information does not imply any useful difference-bounds of variables in T. The last location of T is assigned the bottom element as that is the element being forward propagated from S. As explained earlier, applying η_T results in the top element being assigned to every location of T. However, the resulting approximant can now be refined using the bisimulation information when propagating the information back to S using $\mathsf{cl}_S \circ \mathsf{post}_B$. That is, the information on the last horizontal line of Fig. 2 implies $x - y \le 7$.

Although the analysis technically works over the source program, the inference step is in fact made on the transformed program. The resulting invariant can again be converted into an invariant for T using the result of Theorem 2. The new operation verification tools are required to implement is refinement/strengthening of abstract elements with the bisimulation information. One possible way to implement this operation is to rely on known techniques for strengthening branch results with guard information when analyzing guard statements [7].

Precision. Logozzo and Fähndrich [22] show how the precision lost by the transformation can be restored if information about available program expressions, and equalities between them, are preserved at each location in T. But this is precisely the information provided by the bisimulation relation. To see this, one has to switch the roles of S and T, which is possible as B^{-1} is a bisimulation from S to T. The domain of the induced bisimulating analysis on T combines information about program expressions, such as the definition of t1, with the original difference domain. One can therefore derive the analysis of [22] systematically from the bisimulating analysis definition, and view their specific implementation as a particular form of the bisimulating analysis.

6   Transformations as Static Analyses

Consider, once again, the transformation shown in Fig. 1. Parity analysis is less precise for variable z in the source program as it does not observe the actual values of variables y and x. That can be done with a second domain to track constant values, combining its information with the parity analysis to obtain a precise parity value for z. This is the role of the standard *reduced product* construction of [8]. Applied to the product domain $C \times D$ of domains C and D, a reduction operation transforms an abstract value (c, d) – where $c \in C$ and $d \in D$ – into a more precise abstract value (c', d') with the same concretization. Reduction is carried out by using the information in c to refine d to d', and the information in d to refine c to c'. In our example, the information flow is one-way: the constants domain is used to refine the parity result. The program transformation shown in Fig. 1 is also based on the constants domain. One might conjecture from this that the transformation plays a role analogous to a one-way reduced product.

In this section, we establish a precise form of this conjecture. We show that an analysis based on a one-way reduced product of domains C with D, where information flows only from C to D, can be "factored" into a program transformation based on an analysis of the source program with domain C, followed by an analysis of the transformed program with D, obtaining results on D that are at least as precise as the original. Thus, an analysis expressed as a chain of one-way products of $C_1, C_2, C_3, \ldots, C_n = D$ where C_i is used to refine C_{i+1}, can be broken down into a chain of transformations, one for each C_i, ending with a program that is analyzed with D. (For a similar reduction over domains but without program transformations, see [15]).

The (simple) transformation eliminates the need to compute with a reduction operator, which can be a significant advantage in practice. It also shows that new program transformations may be designed solely for the purpose of simplifying program analysis, in addition to the use of standard compiler transformations, which are designed primarily to improve run-time performance.

One-Way Reduced Product. Consider abstract domains C and D, specified by their closure functions, cl_C and cl_D. The Cartesian product of C and D is the domain formed by the closure function given by $\mathsf{cl}(X) = \mathsf{cl}_C(X) \cap \mathsf{cl}_D(X)$. For convenience, elements in this domain may be represented by a pair of sets (X, Y), where X is closed for C and Y is closed for D, with the interpretation that (X, Y) denotes the set $X \cap Y$.

A *one-way reduction* function ρ maps a pair (X, Y) of the form above to a set Y' that is closed for D, such that the interpretation of (X, Y) and (X, Y') is the same. (A two-way reduced product, in addition, reduces X to some X'.) The best one-way reduction of (X, Y) is given by $\mathsf{cl}_D(X \cap Y)$. This shows clearly that the reduction transfers information from the X component to the Y component, producing $Y' = \mathsf{cl}_D(X \cap Y)$ which, by its definition, is at least as precise as Y.

Fixpoint Analysis. The standard construction of the best abstract transformer adds reduction as the final step. I.e., to obtain the best abstract representation from a starting point (X, Y), one computes $X' = \mathsf{cl}_C \circ \delta_S^+(X \cap Y)$ and $Y' = \mathsf{cl}_D \circ \delta_S^+(X \cap Y)$ and reduces (X', Y') to $(X', \rho(X', Y'))$. We relax this construction using the common simplification which applies the transformers for C and D individually, i.e., letting $X' = \mathsf{cl}_C \circ \delta_S^+(X)$ and $Y' = \mathsf{cl}_D \circ \delta_S^+(Y)$.

Theorem 6 (Factoring). *Consider the least fixpoint analysis of program S with a one-way reduced product of domains C and D and the relaxed best transformer. Equally or even more precise result can be obtained by transforming S to a program T, based on the analysis of S over domain C, followed by analysis of T over domain D.*

Proof. The proof outline is as follows. We first establish that the least fixpoint analysis can be sequentialized. We use the fixpoint over C to define the transformation from S to T, and prove that analysis of T over D produces the same result as the original fixpoint.

Let $(\bar{c}, \bar{d})$ be the least fixpoint of the relaxed transformer defined earlier that includes the initial states of S. This is a simultaneous fixpoint definition over the vector (X, Y).

We simplify this to a different, but equivalent form, starting from the empty set instead of from I_S. Let functions f_C and g_D be defined on a pair (X, Y) by $f_C(X) = \mathsf{cl}_C(I_S \vee \delta_S(X))$ and $g_D(X, Y) = \rho(f_C(X), \mathsf{cl}_D(I_S \vee \delta_S(Y)))$. Then the original fixpoint can be re-expressed as

$$(\bar{c}, \bar{d}) = \mathsf{lfp}\left((\lambda(X, Y).(f_C(X), g_D(X, Y))), (\emptyset, \emptyset)\right)$$

By a well-known result from Bekič (sometimes called the Scott-Bekič theorem), the fixpoint value for domain D can also be obtained with the "flattened" nested fixpoint defined below, where the outer fixpoint is over the closed sets Y of D, and the inner fixpoint over the closed sets X of C.

$$\text{let } \bar{d} = \mathsf{lfp}\left((\lambda Y. g_D(\mathsf{lfp}((\lambda X : f_C(X)), \emptyset), Y)), \emptyset\right)$$

As f_C is independent of Y, the inner fixpoint can be extracted to form the equivalent, simpler definition:

$$\text{let } \bar{c} = \mathsf{lfp}\left((\lambda X. f_C(X)), \emptyset\right)$$
$$\text{let } \bar{d} = \mathsf{lfp}\left((\lambda Y. g_D(\bar{c}, Y)), \emptyset\right)$$

That is, the computation of the original fixpoint can be sequentialized, by first computing $\bar{c}$, and only then computing $\bar{d}$ in terms of $\bar{c}$. By Theorem 3, $\bar{c}$ is an inductive invariant of S.

We now use the value $\bar{c}$ to define a simple transformation from S to T. The program T has the same state space and the same set of initial states as S, but its transition relation is a restriction of that of S, defined by $[\delta_T(t, t') \equiv \bar{c}(t) \wedge \delta_S(t, t')]$. I.e., transitions are allowed only from states satisfying $\bar{c}$. As $\bar{c}$ is inductive for δ_S, the expression for $\delta_T(t, t')$ is equivalent to $\bar{c}(t) \wedge \delta_S(t, t') \wedge \bar{c}(t')$. Hence, for a set Y of states, $[\delta_T(Y) \equiv \bar{c} \wedge \delta_S(Y \cap \bar{c})]$.

Define the relation B from T to S by $B(t, s) \equiv (t = s) \wedge \bar{c}(s)$. The fact that $\bar{c}$ is an inductive invariant of S helps establish that B is a bisimulation, we omit the simple proof.

The standard analysis with D on T results in $d^\sharp = \mathsf{lfp}\,((\lambda Y.\mathsf{cl}_D(I_T \lor \delta_T(Y))), \emptyset)$. We show that this is at least as precise as $\bar{d}$, i.e., $[d^\sharp \to \bar{d}]$. This follows if $\bar{d}$ is a pre-fixpoint of the function used to define $d^\sharp$.

$$\mathsf{cl}_D(I_T \lor \delta_T(\bar{d}))$$
$$\equiv \mathsf{cl}_D(I_S \lor \delta_T(\bar{d})) \qquad\qquad\qquad \{\text{as } [I_T \equiv I_S]\}$$
$$\equiv \mathsf{cl}_D(I_S \lor (\bar{c} \land \delta_S(\bar{d} \cap \bar{c}))) \qquad \{\text{by the relationship between } \delta_T \text{ and } \delta_S\}$$
$$\equiv \mathsf{cl}_D(\bar{c} \land (I_S \lor \delta_S(\bar{d} \cap \bar{c}))) \qquad \{[I_S \to \bar{c}] \text{ by inductiveness of } \bar{c} \text{ for } S\}$$
$$\to \mathsf{cl}_D(\bar{c} \land \mathsf{cl}_D(I_S \lor \delta_S(\bar{d}))) \qquad\qquad\qquad \{\text{monotonicity}\}$$
$$\to \rho(\bar{c}, \mathsf{cl}_D(I_S \lor \delta_S(\bar{d}))) \qquad\qquad \{\text{by definition of the best reduction}\}$$
$$\equiv g_D(\bar{c}, \bar{d}) \qquad\qquad\qquad\qquad \{\text{by definition of } g_D\}$$
$$\equiv \bar{d} \qquad\qquad\qquad\qquad\qquad\qquad \{\text{by fixpoint}\}$$

$\square$

From the careful examination of the above proof, it becomes clear that the transformation plays the role of the one-way reduction; as noted, the result obtained on the transformed program may even be stronger than that obtained by the one-way reduced product.

7   Related Work and Conclusion

In this work, we introduced a formal account of the impact program transformations can have on static analyses. By modeling transformations semantically using bisimulations and static analyses using abstract interpretation, we show how the improved/decreased precision of an analysis on the transformed program can be explained in terms of the bisimulation. We assemble the bisimulation and a given abstract domain to form a new abstract domain. The newly constructed domain induces an analysis on the source program that is more precise than the given analysis for the transformed program. We also present a weaker but more practical *bisimulating* analysis that utilizes information already present in verification frameworks, allowing the transfer of theoretical results almost directly to practice. We also show, in the opposite direction, how 1-way reduced product static analyses can be broken into a transformation followed by a simpler analysis. Our framework thus provides a formal understanding and theoretical machinery for a more systematic design of program analysis tools that combine program transformations and static analyses. We now discuss related work.

The work most closely related to ours is the one by Logozzo and Fähndrich [22]. The authors exemplify how 3-address code transformation can introduce imprecision for static analyses working over relational abstract domains. They also show how the lost precision can be recovered by additionally tracking available expressions, a technique introduced by Miné [26]. We already overviewed the mentioned imprecision phenomena and the recovering technique in Sect. 5.1. Our work is a substantial generalization. The framework supports any transformation whose correctness can be witnessed by a common general class of bisimulations. Furthermore, there is a general technique for recovering from precision, which specializes to the use of symbolic expressions in their setting. Our work also paves the way for implementing static analyses using transformations.

Cousot and Cousot introduce a general and language-independent framework for designing program transformations [9]. By adopting the view that syntax is an abstraction of semantics, the authors use abstract interpretation to formalize and argue the idea that syntactic transformations are an abstraction of possibly incomputable semantic transformations. Their formalization allows for a more systematic design of syntactic transformations and simpler arguments of their correctness. Our work, on the other hand, is concerned with formal understanding of how program transformations affect static analyses, how the negative effects can be remedied, and how to design static analyses using program transformations. The common theme of the two papers is the semantic view of program transformations. As their work shows, syntactic transformations overapproximate the semantic ones; we use bisimulations to recover the loss of information stemming from the (proper) overapproximation.

Ranzato and Tapparo show in [29,30,32] how strong preservation in abstract model checking, witnessed by a bisimulation, can be characterized and generalized by the notion of completeness in abstract interpretation [8,16]. In effect, the authors show how bisimulations are a particular case of abstract interpretation. As a consequence, abstract models can be refined using domain refinement techniques of abstract interpretation in order to achieve preservation of properties from the concrete model [31]. This body of work and our paper are related by using bisimulations in the context of abstract interpretation, specifically domain refinement [15]. Cousot et al. devise an abstract interpretation framework for inferring invariants over arbitrary abstract domains for refactored code fragments [10]. Focusing on the method extraction refactoring, the authors show how to reuse the invariants computed for the original program to infer the most general correct pre- and post-conditions for the extracted method that are compatible with the method use in the program and do not violate any assertions of the method body. Our work focuses on transformations that can be modeled semantically using bisimulations and is concerned with remedying potential precision loss caused by transformations. Their work has the objective of inferring *good* annotations for the refactored piece of code by utilizing the information provided by the prior analysis of the original program. Fedyukovich et al. present techniques that infer simulation relations that in turn allow transfer of safe inductive invariants from (an abstraction) of a source program P to its arbitrarily modified version Q [14]. Our work assumes a bisimulation relation but is concerned with designing new abstract domains that capture how semantic-preserving program transformations affect static analyses.

SeaHorn is a fully automated framework for verifying safety properties of software [17]. Built on top of LLVM [19], the framework uses sophisticated SMT-based model checking techniques together with abstract interpretation to perform inter-procedural static analysis. As a preprocessing step, SeaHorn performs several known program transformations, such as static single assignment (SSA), function inlining, dead-code elimination, etc. This preprocessing step, as reported, is introduced to simplify the verification task. SMACK is a verification toolchain which is also based on LLVM [4]. As a pre-processing step, SMACK runs common program optimizations provided by LLVM since they, as reported, *improve the performance and accuracy of verification* [4].

Acknowledgments. This work was supported, in part, by NSF grant CCF-1563393 from the National Science Foundation. We would like to thank Patrick Cousot, Thomas Wies, and Siddharth Krishna for helpful discussions.

References

1. Abadi, M., Lamport, L.: The existence of refinement mappings. Theor. Comput. Sci. **82**(2), 253–284 (1991)
2. Aho, A.V., Sethi, R., Ullman, J.D.: Compilers: Principles, Techniques, and Tools. Addison-Wesley series in Computer Science/World Student Series Edition. Addison-Wesley, Reading (1986)
3. Baier, C., Katoen, J.-P.: Principles of Model Checking. MIT Press, Cambridge (2008)
4. Carter, M., He, S., Whitaker, J., Rakamaric, Z., Emmi, M.: SMACK software verification toolchain. In: Proceedings of the 38th International Conference on Software Engineering - Companion Volume, ICSE 2016, Austin, TX, USA, 14–22 May 2016, pp. 589–592 (2016)
5. Cousot, P., Cousot, R.: Constructive versions of Tarski's fixed point theorems. Pac. J. Math. **81**(1), 43–57 (1979)
6. Cousot, P.: Abstracting induction by extrapolation and interpolation. In: D'Souza, D., Lal, A., Larsen, K.G. (eds.) VMCAI 2015. LNCS, vol. 8931, pp. 19–42. Springer, Heidelberg (2015). https://doi.org/10.1007/978-3-662-46081-8_2
7. Cousot, P., Cousot, R.: Abstract interpretation: a unified lattice model for static analysis of programs by construction or approximation of fixpoints. In: Conference Record of the Fourth ACM Symposium on Principles of Programming Languages, Los Angeles, California, USA, January 1977, pp. 238–252 (1977)
8. Cousot, P., Cousot, R.: Systematic design of program analysis frameworks. In: Conference Record of the Sixth Annual ACM Symposium on Principles of Programming Languages, San Antonio, Texas, USA, January 1979, pp. 269–282 (1979)
9. Cousot, P., Cousot, R.: Systematic design of program transformation frameworks by abstract interpretation. In: Launchbury, J., Mitchell, J.C. (eds.) Conference Record of POPL 2002: The 29th SIGPLAN-SIGACT Symposium on Principles of Programming Languages, Portland, OR, USA, 16–18 January 2002, pp. 178–190. ACM (2002)
10. Cousot, P., Cousot, R., Logozzo, F., Barnett, M.: An abstract interpretation framework for refactoring with application to extract methods with contracts. In: Proceedings of the 27th Annual ACM SIGPLAN Conference on Object-Oriented Programming, Systems, Languages, and Applications, OOPSLA 2012, Part of SPLASH 2012, Tucson, AZ, USA, 21–25 October 2012, pp. 213–232 (2012)
11. Cousot, P., Halbwachs, N.: Automatic discovery of linear restraints among variables of a program. In: Conference Record of the Fifth Annual ACM Symposium on Principles of Programming Languages, Tucson, Arizona, USA, January 1978, pp. 84–96 (1978)

12. Dijkstra, E.W., Scholten, C.S.: Predicate Calculus and Program Semantics. Springer, New York (1990). https://doi.org/10.1007/978-1-4612-3228-5
13. Fähndrich, M., Logozzo, F.: Static contract checking with abstract interpretation. In: Beckert, B., Marché, C. (eds.) FoVeOOS 2010. LNCS, vol. 6528, pp. 10–30. Springer, Heidelberg (2011). https://doi.org/10.1007/978-3-642-18070-5_2
14. Fedyukovich, G., Gurfinkel, A., Sharygina, N.: Property directed equivalence via abstract simulation. In: Chaudhuri, S., Farzan, A. (eds.) CAV 2016, Part II. LNCS, vol. 9780, pp. 433–453. Springer, Cham (2016). https://doi.org/10.1007/978-3-319-41540-6_24
15. Giacobazzi, R., Ranzato, F.: Refining and compressing abstract domains. In: Degano, P., Gorrieri, R., Marchetti-Spaccamela, A. (eds.) ICALP 1997. LNCS, vol. 1256, pp. 771–781. Springer, Heidelberg (1997). https://doi.org/10.1007/3-540-63165-8_230
16. Giacobazzi, R., Ranzato, F., Scozzari, F.: Making abstract interpretations complete. J. ACM **47**(2), 361–416 (2000)
17. Gurfinkel, A., Kahsai, T., Komuravelli, A., Navas, J.A.: The SeaHorn verification framework. In: Kroening, D., Pǎsǎreanu, C.S. (eds.) CAV 2015. LNCS, vol. 9206, pp. 343–361. Springer, Cham (2015). https://doi.org/10.1007/978-3-319-21690-4_20
18. Kang, J., Kim, Y., Song, Y., Lee, J., Park, S., Shin, M.D., Kim, Y., Cho, S., Choi, J., Hur, C.-K., Yi, K.: CRELLVM: verified credible compilation for LLVM. In Proceedings of the 39th ACM SIGPLAN Conference on Programming Language Design and Implementation, PLDI 2018, Philadelphia, PA, USA, 18–22 June 2018, pp. 631–645 (2018)
19. Lattner, C., Adve, V.S.: LLVM: a compilation framework for lifelong program analysis & transformation. In: 2nd IEEE/ACM International Symposium on Code Generation and Optimization (CGO 2004), San Jose, CA, USA, 20–24 March 2004, pp. 75–88 (2004)
20. Leroy, X.: Formal certification of a compiler back-end or: programming a compiler with a proof assistant. In: Proceedings of the 33rd ACM SIGPLAN-SIGACT Symposium on Principles of Programming Languages, POPL 2006, Charleston, South Carolina, USA, 11–13 January 2006, pp. 42–54 (2006)
21. Leroy, X.: Formal verification of a realistic compiler. Commun. ACM **52**(7), 107–115 (2009)
22. Logozzo, F., Fähndrich, M.: On the relative completeness of bytecode analysis versus source code analysis. In: Hendren, L. (ed.) CC 2008. LNCS, vol. 4959, pp. 197–212. Springer, Heidelberg (2008). https://doi.org/10.1007/978-3-540-78791-4_14
23. Miné, A.: A new numerical abstract domain based on difference-bound matrices. In: Danvy, O., Filinski, A. (eds.) PADO 2001. LNCS, vol. 2053, pp. 155–172. Springer, Heidelberg (2001). https://doi.org/10.1007/3-540-44978-7_10
24. Miné, A.: A few graph-based relational numerical abstract domains. In: Hermenegildo, M.V., Puebla, G. (eds.) SAS 2002. LNCS, vol. 2477, pp. 117–132. Springer, Heidelberg (2002). https://doi.org/10.1007/3-540-45789-5_11
25. Miné, A.: The octagon abstract domain. High. Order Symb. Comput. **19**(1), 31–100 (2006)
26. Miné, A.: Symbolic methods to enhance the precision of numerical abstract domains. In: Emerson, E.A., Namjoshi, K.S. (eds.) VMCAI 2006. LNCS, vol. 3855, pp. 348–363. Springer, Heidelberg (2005). https://doi.org/10.1007/11609773_23

27. Namjoshi, K.S.: Lifting temporal proofs through abstractions. In: Zuck, L.D., Attie, P.C., Cortesi, A., Mukhopadhyay, S. (eds.) VMCAI 2003. LNCS, vol. 2575, pp. 174–188. Springer, Heidelberg (2003). https://doi.org/10.1007/3-540-36384-X_16
28. Namjoshi, K.S., Zuck, L.D.: Witnessing program transformations. In: Logozzo, F., Fähndrich, M. (eds.) SAS 2013. LNCS, vol. 7935, pp. 304–323. Springer, Heidelberg (2013). https://doi.org/10.1007/978-3-642-38856-9_17
29. Ranzato, F., Tapparo, F.: Making abstract model checking strongly preserving. In: Hermenegildo, M.V., Puebla, G. (eds.) SAS 2002. LNCS, vol. 2477, pp. 411–427. Springer, Heidelberg (2002). https://doi.org/10.1007/3-540-45789-5_29
30. Ranzato, F., Tapparo, F.: Strong preservation as completeness in abstract interpretation. In: Schmidt, D. (ed.) ESOP 2004. LNCS, vol. 2986, pp. 18–32. Springer, Heidelberg (2004). https://doi.org/10.1007/978-3-540-24725-8_3
31. Ranzato, F., Tapparo, F.: An abstract interpretation-based refinement algorithm for strong preservation. In: Halbwachs, N., Zuck, L.D. (eds.) TACAS 2005. LNCS, vol. 3440, pp. 140–156. Springer, Heidelberg (2005). https://doi.org/10.1007/978-3-540-31980-1_10
32. Ranzato, F., Tapparo, F.: Generalized strong preservation by abstract interpretation. J. Log. Comput. **17**(1), 157–197 (2007)
33. Rinard, M.: Credible compilation. Technical report (1999). In: Proceedings of CC 2001: International Conference on Compiler Construction

Efficiently Learning Safety Proofs
from Appearance as well as Behaviours

Sumanth Prabhu[✉], Kumar Madhukar, and R. Venkatesh

TCS Research, Pune, India
sumanth.prabhu@tcs.com

Abstract. Proving safety of programs relies principally on discovering invariants that are inductive and adequate. Obtaining such invariants, therefore, has been studied widely from diverse perspectives, including even mining them from the input program's source in a *guess-and-check* manner [13]. However, guessing candidates based on syntactical constructions of the source code has its limitations. For one, a required invariant may not manifest on the syntactic surface of the program. Secondly, a poor *guess* may give rise to a series of expensive *checks*. Furthermore, unlike conjunctions, refining disjunctive invariant candidates is unobvious and may frequently cause the proof search to diverge. This paper attempts to overcome these limitations, by learning from both – appearance and behaviours of a program. We present an algorithm that (i) infers useful invariants by observing a program's syntactic source as well as its semantics, and (ii) looks for conditional invariants, in the form of implications, that are guided by counterexamples to inductiveness. Our experiments demonstrate its benefits on several benchmarks taken from SV-COMP and the literature.

1 Introduction

Arguing for program correctness is a challenging task. But it is non-optional, especially as software has permeated our lives, in forms that are many times even safety- or business-critical. Not surprisingly, this subject has been the focus of a lot of research in the last several decades, and there is a vast amount of literature covering different facets of this problem. The issue that is central to all of this is that of discovering *inductive invariants*, that are sufficient to discharge the property in question. Invariants help in over-approximating the reachable states, which can then be shown to be disjoint with the set of *bad* states to establish safety, whereas precisely computing what is reachable may be infeasible.

Numerous techniques have been proposed for inferring program invariants automatically, and even semi-automatically with human assistance. Broadly speaking, these techniques learn meaningful information about the input program from its semantics, using approaches based on abstract interpretation [5–7], constraint solving [4,16], counterexample-guided abstraction refinement [3], property directed reachability [2,17], interpolation [1,8], user-assistance [19], etc. In contrast, Fedyukovich et al. [13] recently demonstrated that invariants can

© Springer Nature Switzerland AG 2018
A. Podelski (Ed.): SAS 2018, LNCS 11002, pp. 326–343, 2018.
https://doi.org/10.1007/978-3-319-99725-4_20

```
                                   int LRG = nondet();
                                   assume(LRG > 0);

     int n;
     assume(1 <= n <= 1000);       int x = 0, y = LRG;

     int sum = 0, i = 1;           while(x < 2*LRG) {
                                     if (x < LRG) {
     while(i<=n) {                      y = y;
       sum = sum + i;              } else {
       i = i + 1;                      y = y + 1;
     }                             }
                                     x = x + 1;
     assert(2*sum == n*(n+1));     }

                                   assert(y == 2*LRG);

              (a)
                                              (b)
```

Fig. 1. Motivating examples

often be caught on the surface, i.e. the invariants many times imitate the syntactical constructions appearing in the source code. Their tool, FREQHORN, works in a *guess-and-check* manner, by sampling candidates from an appearance-guided search space built automatically from ingredients found in the program source. A follow-up work [12], and the corresponding tool FREQHORN-2, accelerates this process by computing additional candidates as interpolants from proofs of bounded safety. These candidates likely reflect the nature of the error unreachability, and thus have a semantic value. While this justifies the idea of supplementing syntactic search with behavioural[1] facts about the program, interpolants obtained from bounded proofs may not fully capture these facts. Nevertheless, an important contribution of this technique is the automatic construction of sampling space, which is particular to the input program. This can even assist template-based methods, e.g. Daikon [11], in selecting the templates carefully, instead of working with a generic one that may be needlessly more expressive.

Consider the example shown in Fig. 1a. It computes the sum of first n natural numbers, and asserts that twice the computed sum equals n times $(n+1)$. Since this is an arithmetic fact, the program is safe. The sum is computed by iterating over the numbers from 1 to n in a loop, and by adding each number to the variable sum, which is 0 initially. One way to prove this program correct is to obtain the following inductive invariants for the while loop: $2*sum = (i-1)*i$, and $i \leq (n+1)$. Along with the exit condition of the loop, $(i > n)$, these are sufficient to derive that $2*sum = n*(n+1)$.

---

[1] *behaviour* refers to facts derivable from the program's meaning, not necessarily limited to its concrete runs; we use the terms *behaviours* and *semantics* interchangeably.

A merely syntactic exploration would find the invariant $i \leq (n+1)$ (it is a mutation of the loop condition), but it would fail[2] to deduce that $2 * sum = (i-1) * i$ is a loop invariant. While the latter is quite similar to an expression appearing in the program, namely the property, FREQHORN-2 does not consider mutations that alter variables. And even if it did, that would result in a number of mutants which are poor candidates. I.e. they would fail the inductiveness check, which is an expensive operation in this case because of the non-linear template. On the other hand, if we look to obtain algebraic invariants behaviourally, e.g. as proposed by Sharma et al. [24], we can get that inductive invariant almost immediately.

It is noteworthy that an execution-based approach, similar to the one stated above, would be able to verify this example even when n is replaced by a concrete value, say 239, and the property becomes $2 * sum = 57360$. The desired invariant, $2 * sum = (i-1) * i$, is no longer available as a mutation of the property. But it is still a valid algebraic relation between sum, i and i^2, that can easily be drawn from program executions. In other words, information available from concrete runs complements the syntactic search for invariants, especially when the property does not entirely manifest at the program surface, but also lies deeper in its behaviours.

For another limitation of the existing technique, let us consider the program shown in Fig. 1b, chosen from the benchmarks used in [12]. The program has a positive constant LRG, denoting a large value perhaps, and two variables, x and y. The while loop in the program has two distinct *phases* – first in which only x gets incremented, till it becomes LRG (and equal to y's initial value), and the second where both x and y are incremented as long as x is less than twice the large constant. The assertion holds because x and y are equal after every iteration in the second phase. A formal proof of correctness can be derived from the following inductive invariants: $(((x < \text{LRG}) \Rightarrow (y = \text{LRG})) \wedge ((x \geq \text{LRG}) \Rightarrow (y = x)))$, and $(x \leq 2*\text{LRG})$.

FREQHORN-2 rarely converges to a proof for this program (only once in 20 runs in our experiments, with a timeout of 600 s); the reason being lack of structured search, particularly for disjunctive invariant candidates. For example, in order to get $((x \geq \text{LRG}) \vee (y = \text{LRG}))$, FREQHORN-2 has to choose the candidate's arity as 2, and then sample the parts $(x \geq \text{LRG})$ and $(y = \text{LRG})$ separately. If any of the choices turn out to be bad, the inductiveness check fails, and a subsequent refinement may even replace disjuncts that are useful or necessary. Analyzing behaviours may not work for such programs either. There must be enough runs representing all the *phases* in order to deduce the algebraic relations, even if they exist.

We propose a method to solve this problem by extracting conditional invariants, which are implications with antecedents that are derived from conditions appearing in the program. Whether a conditional invariant needs to be sampled or not is decided by inspecting the counterexamples to inductiveness, or CTIs, of the candidates explored thus far. We check if the counterexamples can be

---

[2] FREQHORN-2 times out after 600 s, in an experimental set-up similar to [12,13].

made to fit into a polynomial over program variables, to determine if they are of the same *kind*. Intuitively, if there are different kinds of counterexamples, it may be worthwhile to look for an invariant for each kind. I.e. implications of the form $cond_i \Rightarrow inv_i$, where $cond_i$ qualifies the kind of CTIs, and inv_i denotes the invariant that gets rid of those.

Given the invariants that are needed to prove safety of the example in Fig. 1b, it is evident that this enhancement allows us to get them quickly. Note that the restriction to sample the antecedents from a very small space (of conditions appearing in the program, and their mutations) prevents us from divergence in many cases. However, at the same time, it is expressive enough to work in a number of cases. In particular, it enables our approach to solve examples with multi-phase loops that require phase-specific invariants [23].

The core contributions of this paper are summarized as follows:

- A technique that combines learning from a program's behaviours, with that from its syntactic source, for inferring useful invariants.
- A heuristic to determine whether conditional invariants could be useful, and a method to obtain them by analyzing implications whose antecedents are chosen to be (possibly, conjunctions and/or mutations of) conditions appearing in the program, or negations thereof.
- An implementation that extends FREQHORN-2[3] – the tool used for evaluation in [12], which forms the basis of this work.
- Experimental evaluation that illustrates the usefulness of our approach on several benchmarks from SV-COMP and the literature.

Outline of the Paper. We start with a survey of the related work in the next section (Sect. 2), before moving over to some of the closely related ones in details, seeing that they serve as the necessary background (Sect. 3). Section 4 describes the core contributions of this work, and is followed by a discussion of the experimental results (Sect. 5). Section 6 concludes the paper, and includes our thoughts on several interesting directions of pursuing this further.

2   Related Work

Invariant synthesis is an essential step in program verification. Abstract interpretation [5,6] is a prominent technique which iteratively computes approximations until a fix point is reached. The assertion generated at fix point is an inductive invariant. In order to overcome the difficulty of choosing widening heuristics in abstract interpretation, template-based techniques were proposed. For example, [4] assumes the invariants to be in a fixed template over program variables. Inductiveness conditions are translated to nonlinear constraints such that the solutions of constraints are invariants. However, this technique relies on the efficiency of nonlinear constraint solving.

---

[3] Thanks to Grigory Fedyukovich, the sources of FREQHORN-2 are available at https://github.com/grigoryfedyukovich/aeval/tree/rnd.

A somewhat related technique for invariant discovery is that of *guess-and-check*, which repeatedly guesses candidate invariants from a known language represented by a grammar, and checks them for invariance. Automatic construction of an adequate grammar, tractable search among candidates, and inductiveness check of candidates are the main challenges of this technique. In general, an SMT solver that can decide the underlying theory is used for the inductiveness check. The other two challenges are addressed using data computed through static and dynamic analysis techniques. For instance, the technique presented in [24] uses concrete program runs as data to discover invariants. Invariants are assumed to have the form of a fixed-degree polynomial equation over program variables. The execution traces are used to solve for coefficients of the polynomial. It uses an SMT solver to check inductiveness of the solutions. A similar dynamic analysis technique to discover polynomial and array invariants has been proposed in [18]. The drawbacks of these techniques are high computational complexity for discovering invariants with inequality [18], and inability to derive disjunctions that are not polynomial equations.

Counterexamples to consecution, along with the information available on unreachable and reachable states (referred to as ICE), are used for guiding the search for invariant candidates in [15]. An invariant is assumed to be boolean combinations of atomic formulas of a particular form, e.g. an octagon. The problem of guessing a candidate is modeled as problem of generating a formula that separates reachable and unreachable states. Techniques from learning theory are used on the available data to solve this problem.

In [22], the invariant candidates are sampled as boolean combinations of linear inequalities, whose coefficients and constants are taken from a data set that is populated from constants occurring in the source code, and their sums and differences. It also incorporates those counterexamples in the data that disqualify a candidate as an invariant. The entire program source may also be considered as data, e.g. [13]. A frequency distribution obtained from the input program's source guides the automatic construction of grammar. Moreover, failed candidates are used to prune the search space of candidates. This technique was found to be competitive to other machine-learning techniques. However, pruning can cause divergence in the algorithm. This problem is partially addressed in [12], which performs consecution checks in batches, and uses the counterexamples to induction effectively. It also supplements the method with candidates of semantic values, obtained as interpolants from bounded proofs. Our work further enhances this by mining candidates from program behaviours, and enabling discovery of conditional invariants.

3   Notations and Background

We begin with a description of the notations that are used in Fedyukovich et al. [12,13], which we also follow.

Definition 1. *A program P is defined as a transition system, or a tuple $\langle V \cup V', Init, Tr \rangle$, where*

- V denotes the set of variables, and the corresponding primed set V' represents their next-state copies,
- $Init$ is a set of initial states encoded as a formula over V, and
- $Tr(V, V')$ is a transition relation encoded as a formula over V and V'.

We assume that the formulas belong to a fixed first order language $\mathcal{L}$. A *state* is an assignment of values to all variables in V or V'. For a formula ϕ over V, a state s satisfies it, $s \models \phi$, when the assignment of values to all variables as per s satisfies the formula ϕ. A state s_k is *reachable* if either $s_k \models Init$ or $\exists s_{k-1}, (s_{k-1}, s'_k) \models Tr$, where s_{k-1} is a reachable state and s'_k assigns same values as V for corresponding primed set V'.

Given $\langle P, Bad \rangle$, where Bad is an undesirable set of states encoded as a formula over V, verification of P is the task of deciding whether a state from Bad is reachable or not. An $\mathcal{L}$-formula Inv which is disjoint from Bad and includes all the reachable states is called a safe inductive invariant, or henceforth simply an invariant. If we assume that an invariant exists in $\mathcal{L}$, then verification of P reduces to finding an invariant Inv, such that the following hold:

$$Init(V) \Rightarrow Inv(V) \qquad \text{initiation}$$
$$Inv(V) \wedge Tr(V, V') \Rightarrow Inv(V') \qquad \text{consecution}$$
$$Inv(V) \wedge Bad(V) \Rightarrow \bot \qquad \text{safety}$$

Note that $\bot$ denotes *false*. These validity checks can be transformed into equivalent unsatisfiability checks, to be discharged by an SMT solver e.g. Z3 [9]. The models corresponding to the consecution check failure are referred to as *CTIs*. More formally, CTIs is a set of pair of states (s_k, s'_{k+1}), such that $s_k \models Inv$ and $(s_k, s'_{k+1}) \models Tr$, but $s'_{k+1} \not\models Inv'$.

We also recall a few basic definitions from linear algebra that we use.

Given a vector space $\mathbf{V}$, over a field $\mathbf{F}$ with its additive identity denoted as 0, its *basis* $\mathbf{B} = \{\mathbf{v}_1, \ldots, \mathbf{v}_n\}$ is a minimal subset of $\mathbf{V}$ satisfying:

1. $\forall\, a_1, \ldots, a_n \in \mathbf{F}$, if $a_1\mathbf{v}_1 + \cdots + a_n\mathbf{v}_n = 0$, then $a_1 = 0, \ldots, a_n = 0$.
2. $\forall\, \mathbf{v} \in \mathbf{V}, \exists\, a_1, \ldots, a_n \in \mathbf{F}$ such that $\mathbf{v} = a_1\mathbf{v}_1 + \cdots + a_n\mathbf{v}_n$.

The cardinality of $\mathbf{B}$ is called *dimension* of $\mathbf{V}$. For a matrix $\mathbf{A}$, the dimension of the vector space generated by its columns is called its *rank*. The *nullspace* of a matrix $\mathbf{A}$ is a set of all vectors $\mathbf{v}$ such that $\mathbf{A}\mathbf{v} = 0$. The dimension of a matrix's nullspace is also called its *nullity*.

3.1 Syntax-Guided Invariant Synthesis

An important contribution of [13] is the automatic generation of production rules for the sampling grammar G, guided by the structure of encoding of $Init$, Tr and Bad. Candidate invariants are guessed using these production rules, and then checked for invariance and safety using an SMT solver. The candidates sampled from G are disjunctions of linear inequalities. The final invariant is assumed to be

---

Algorithm 1. FREQHORN: Syntax-guided invariant generation

    Input: *Init*, *Tr*, *Bad* and *V*
    Output: *lemmas*
1: $\mathcal{P} \leftarrow$ COMPUTEDISTRIBUTION(*Init*, *Tr*, *Bad*)
2: $G \leftarrow$ CONSTRUCTGRAMMAR($\mathcal{P}$)
3: $L \leftarrow \emptyset$ ▷ the set of lemmas
4: **while** $\bigwedge_{l \in L} l \wedge Bad(V)$ is SAT **do**
5:     *init* $\leftarrow$ *false*, *consec* $\leftarrow$ *false*
6:     *cand* $\leftarrow$ NEWCANDIDATE(G)
7:     **if** $Init(V) \wedge \neg cand(V)$ is UNSAT **then** *init* $\leftarrow$ *true*
8:     **if** $cand(V) \bigwedge_{l \in L} l(V) \wedge Tr(V, V') \wedge \neg cand(V')$ is UNSAT **then** *consec* $\leftarrow$ *true*
9:     **if** *init* $\wedge$ *consec* **then** $L \leftarrow L \cup cand$
10:    ADJUST(*cand*, G, $\mathcal{P}$)
11: **return** L

---

a conjunction of these candidates, also called *lemmas*. I.e. $Inv \Leftrightarrow l_0 \wedge l_1 \wedge \cdots \wedge l_n$, where the lemmas $l_i \in G$.

A high level description of their technique is presented in Algorithm 1. The procedure COMPUTEDISTRIBUTION computes a frequency distribution of arities of operations, program variables and constants used, from the *Init*, *Tr* and *Bad*. This distribution is used to construct production rules for the sampling grammar resulting in an initial grammar G in the second step. After this step the algorithm enters a loop where candidate lemmas, as per the grammar G, are guessed and checked until a safe invariant is found. The SAT checks in lines 4, 7, and 8 are, respectively, the checks for safety, initiation, and consecution. If a candidate fails one of the last two checks, the grammar G is adjusted so that syntactically similar candidates are not sampled immediately. Otherwise the candidate is added to the set of lemmas.

3.2 Bootstrapping and Batch Checking

The tool FREQHORN that implements Algorithm 1 outperforms other data-based tools. However, in a follow-up paper [12], Fedyukovich et al. mitigate two downsides of this technique, namely (i) the candidates being ignorant to the program semantics, and (ii) a useful candidate failing the inductiveness check, even though it is inductive relative to some other candidates that may get sampled in due course. They propose an improved algorithm (shown as Algorithm 2) that works in two phases: *bootstrapping* and *sampling*. During bootstrapping they add additional candidates obtained as interpolants, from proofs of bounded safety, as *seeds* (line 1). This adds semantically valuable candidates, unlike its predecessor where candidate sampling was purely syntactic. The seeds themselves may be safe invariants, or they may assist in constructing safe invariants in the sampling phase. The sampling phase works in a similar manner as before, except that the consecution check is done for a batch of candidates at once, instead of a single candidate (line 12). This is to address the latter issue, i.e. to avoid rejecting candidates that are relatively inductive to other lemmas. This check is similar to the algorithm used in HOUDINI tool [14].

Algorithm 2. FREQHORN-2: Bootstrapping and Batch Checking

Input: $Init$, Tr, Bad and V
Output: $lemmas$

1: $candidates \leftarrow$ BOOTSTRAPINTERPOLANTS($Init$, Tr, Bad)
2: $\mathcal{P} \leftarrow$ COMPUTEDISTRIBUTION($Init$, Tr, Bad)
3: $G \leftarrow$ CONSTRUCTGRAMMAR($\mathcal{P}$)
4: $L \leftarrow \emptyset$
5: **while** $\bigwedge_{l \in L} l \wedge Bad(V)$ is SAT **do**
6:     **while** $|candidates| < BatchSize$ **do**   ▷ for a pre-decided $BatchSize$
7:         $cand \leftarrow$ NEWCANDIDATE(G)
8:         **if** $Init(V) \wedge \neg cand(V)$ is UNSAT **then**
9:             $candidates \leftarrow candidates \cup \{cand\}$
10:         **else** ADJUST($cand$, G, $\mathcal{P}$)
11:     **for** $cand \in candidates$ **do**
12:         **if** $\bigwedge_{c \in candidates} c \wedge \bigwedge_{l \in L} l \wedge Tr(V, V') \wedge \neg cand(V')$ is SAT **then**
13:             $candidates \leftarrow candidates \setminus \{cand\}$
14:             ADJUST($cand$, G, $\mathcal{P}$)
15:             $candidates.reset$ ▷ start the loop afresh
16:     **for** $cand \in candidates$ **do**
17:         $L \leftarrow L \cup \{cand\}$
18: **return** L

---

4 Combining Syntax and Behaviours

The semantic information added by interpolants in the bootstrapping phase of [12] certainly accelerates the task. However, we have seen that interpolants from bounded proofs may fail to capture certain behavioural facts. Making the sampling grammar richer is one solution, but without any guidance irrelevant candidates will become a bottleneck during the checking phase. We propose an enhancement to the semantic guidance – from candidates that are not available on surface, but can be discovered by analyzing behaviours. We also show how CTIs may be used to detect the need for conditional invariants and how this can be useful for a certain class of programs.

4.1 Behaviours

Recall the example in Fig. 1a, which needed, along with the inequality $(i \leq n+1)$, an algebraic invariant $(2 * sum = i^2 - i)$ which was not available from syntax.

We aim to discover lemmas such as these, by sampling candidates that have the following fixed degree polynomial equation form:

$$c_1 * m_1 + c_2 * m_2 + \cdots + c_n * m_n = 0$$

where $m_i = x_1^{k_1} \ldots x_l^{k_l}$ are *monomials* and $c_i \in \mathbb{Q}$ are *coefficients*. The *degree* of a monomial is the sum $\sum_i k_i$, and the degree of a polynomial equation is the highest degree among its monomials. In our technique, we consider that x_i's come from the set of variables V. For instance, $2 * sum - i^2 + i = 0$ is a polynomial equation of degree 2 for the program in the variables sum and i, with the monomials sum, i^2 and i. One may sample such candidate lemmas by guessing the monomials and their coefficients. However, the probability of obtaining a poor candidate is very high, resulting in a number of expensive checks. Instead, we rely on the following theorem from [24] to discover them.

Theorem 1. *If an invariant is a conjunction of k polynomial equations each of degree d and nullity of A is k, where A is a data matrix, then any basis for nullspace of A forms an invariant.*

A *data matrix* is a matrix of values of monomials up to degree d. Each row of the data matrix corresponds to values of monomials computed by using concrete values of corresponding variables from V. The concrete values of variables are obtained from behaviours. For example, Table 1 shows a data matrix computed with $d = 2$ for the program in Fig. 1a. The first three columns shows the values of variables i, n and sum at loop head for five iterations of the loop. The value of n is a non-deterministic assignment as it is not initialized in the program.

Table 1. Monomials up to degree 2 for the program in Fig. 1a

i	n	sum	i^2	$i*n$	$i*sum$	n^2	$n*sum$	sum^2	$const$
1	36	0	1	36	0	1296	0	0	1
2	36	1	4	72	2	1296	36	1	1
3	36	3	9	108	9	1296	108	9	1
4	36	6	16	144	24	1296	216	36	1
5	36	10	25	180	50	1296	360	100	1

The central idea of Theorem 1 is that if invariants are assumed to be polynomial equations of degree d over V, then one can obtain coefficients of these equations using the data matrix. This is because the values from data matrix, when substituted for monomials, gives us a system of linear equations in $c_1 \ldots c_n$. The solutions to these equations form a vector space, and the basis of this vector space gives coefficients of polynomial equations. The basis of a system of linear equations can be computed by the well-known Gauss-Jordan elimination algorithm. The computational complexity of this algorithm is $\mathcal{O}(m^2 n)$ for an $m \times n$ matrix.

Algorithm 3. GETALGEBRAICCANDIDATES: Learning algebraic invariants from behaviours

---

1: **procedure** GETALGEBRAICCANDIDATES(*behaviours*)
2:     $candidates \leftarrow \emptyset$
3:     $M \leftarrow$ COMPUTEMONOMIALS(*behaviours*, d_{poly})
4:     $B \leftarrow$ GAUSSJORDAN(M)
5:     **for** *coefficients* $\in B$ **do**
6:         $candidates \leftarrow candidates \cup$ CONSTRUCTPOLYNOMIAL(*coefficients*, d_{poly})
7:     **return** *candidates*

Algorithm 3 presents the procedure GETALGEBRAICCANDIDATES, which takes behaviours as input, provided either by user or computed using an SMT solver, and returns a set of candidates. It starts with computing the values of all monomials up to pre-decided degree d_{poly} using behaviours, and stores them in a data matrix M. The basis of nullspace of this data matrix B is computed using Gauss-Jordan algorithm in the next step. Each vector of the basis is used as coefficients $c_1 \ldots c_n$ to construct a polynomial equation following Theorem 1. Thus computed polynomial equations are returned as candidates. For instance, if we use the values from Table 1 we get basis $B = \{(0\,1\,0\,0\,0\,0\,0\,0\,0\,-36), (-1\,0\,-2\,1\,0\,0\,0\,0\,0\,0), (-36\,0\,0\,0\,1\,0\,0\,0\,0\,0),$ $(0\,0\,0\,0\,0\,1\,0\,0\,-1296), (0\,0\,-36\,0\,0\,0\,0\,1\,0\,0)\}$. When they are substituted as coefficients we get the following polynomials as candidates: $n - 36 = 0$, $-i - 2*sum + i^2 = 0$, $-36*i + i*n = 0$, $n*n - 1296 = 0$ and $-36*sum + sum*n = 0$. Among these candidates $-i - 2*sum + i^2 = 0$ passes both initiation and consecution checks.

4.2 Counterexamples to Induction (CTIs)

In this subsection we present a heuristic to solve programs like Fig. 1b. We observe that invariants of such programs may have different lemmas that hold in different blocks of the loop, i.e. the lemmas may only be conditional. Hence, the technique presented in previous section will not be able to generate necessary invariants. To address this, we first need to check whether a given program requires conditional invariants. A naive solution is to traverse the transition relation Tr and look for *if* conditions in loops. However, this will not work always and may even miss simple invariants. Consider the program shown in Fig. 2 which is taken from the benchmarks of FREQHORN-2. Even though this program has an *if* condition, a simple assertion $i + j = n$ itself is a safe invariant. This invariant can be discovered from the technique mentioned in Sect. 4.1.

We call Tr, a *polynomial relation* if it is possible to represent all variables from V' in a fixed degree polynomial equation over V. This polynomial is of the form:

$$f(x_i') = c_1 * m_1 + c_2 * m_2 + \cdots + c_n * m_n$$

where $x_i' \in V'$, m_i are all possible monomials over V up to a certain degree d and $c_i \in \mathbb{Q}$ are coefficients.

```
main() {
    int i=0,j=0,k=100,n=0,b;
    assume(b == 0 || b == 1);
    while(n < 2*k) {
        if (b == 0) {
            i++; b = 1;
        } else {
            j++; b = 0;
        }
        n++;
    }
    assert(i+j == n);
}
```

Fig. 2. A benchmark program from [12]

Our idea is that if Tr is not a polynomial relation then the loop requires conditional invariants. For example, consider the program in Fig. 1b. Both x' and y' are getting modified by two relations: $y' = y, x' = x + 1, \text{LRG}' = \text{LRG}$ and $y' = y + 1, x' = x + 1, \text{LRG}' = \text{LRG}$, which are from *if* and *else* blocks respectively. It is not possible to find a polynomial function for y'. Hence, we need an implication. Whereas if we consider the example from Fig. 2, all the variables in V' can be represented by the following polynomial equations over V: $n' = n + 1$, $b' = 1 - b$, $i' = i + 1 - b$ and $j' = j + b$. Hence, this program does not require conditional invariant.

One approach to check if Tr is a polynomial relation is to encode a constraint whose satisfiability implies that V' can be represented by V. However, this approach will not scale with larger degrees and variables. We propose an efficient technique by using concepts of linear algebra and CTIs. Recall that the models corresponding to the consecution check failure are referred to as CTIs. In a nutshell, we try to look for coefficients $c_1 \ldots c_n$ that are consistent with CTIs. We substitute values for $f(x_i')$ and m_i in polynomial equations by using values of V' and V respectively from CTIs. If there are l CTIs this results in l linear equations over $c_1 \ldots c_n$. These equations can be represented in matrix form as $\mathbf{M}c = \boldsymbol{f}_{x_i'}$, where $\mathbf{M}$ is the matrix of values for m_i, $\boldsymbol{c}^T = (c_1 \ldots c_n)$ and $\boldsymbol{f}_{x_i'}^T = (x_{i_1}' \ldots x_{i_l}')$. The following standard theorem from linear algebra [21] helps to determine if these equations have a solution for the c_i's or not.

Theorem 2. *A system of linear equations is consistent if and only if the rank of the matrix of the system is equal to the rank of its augmented matrix.*

In our case the matrix of the system is $\mathbf{M}$ and the augmented matrix is $\mathbf{M}|\boldsymbol{f}_{x_i'}$, i.e. $\mathbf{M}$ augmented with $\boldsymbol{f}_{x_i'}$. As per Theorem 2 if $rank(\mathbf{M})$ and $rank((\mathbf{M}|\boldsymbol{f}_{x_i'}))$ are not equal then it is not possible to have a solution for c_i.

The procedure CHECKFORIMPL is presented in Algorithm 4. It takes the *CTIs* as input. In the first step, it computes $\mathbf{M}$ using *CTIs* up to degree d_{poly}. It then checks for each variable x_i' in V' whether the rank of its augmented matrix

Algorithm 4. CHECKFORIMPL: Deciding the need for implications from CTIs

```
1: procedure CHECKFORIMPL(CTIs)
2:     M ← COMPUTEMONOMIALS(CTIs, d_poly)
3:     for x'_i ∈ V' do
4:         f_{x'_i} ← CTIs[x_i']
5:         M_aug ← AUGMENT(M, f_{x'_i})
6:         if RANK(M) ≠ RANK(M_aug) then
7:             return true
```

is equal to rank of the matrix M. If this is not the case for any of the variables, the procedure returns with the decision that implications will be sampled as candidates. The complexity of computing the rank of a $m \times n$ matrix is $\mathcal{O}(m^2 n)$.

We get the candidates for implication by sampling antecedents and consequents from different sampling grammar. The sampling grammar for antecedent is constructed by considering only conditions of *if* statements in Tr. This consideration ensures that candidates for antecedents are sampled from the syntax that is causing implications. For consequent, the *Init*, Tr and *Bad* is considered, like in the FREQHORN algorithm.

A class of programs that this technique can successfully address is the one with *multi-phase* loops, as mentioned in [23]. *Splitter-predicates* are used to identify the different phases of the loop, based on when these predicates, or their negations hold. A loop may start its iteration in one of the phases and then move to new phases as it progresses. Owing to these, such programs require disjunctive invariants. The solution presented in [23] is to compute invariants for each phase separately. The splitter-predicates are either conditions of *if* statements, or their weakest preconditions w.r.t. statements in the loop. Similarly, we derive antecedents from a grammar constructed using the encoding of conditions. In principle, this enables our technique to work for programs where splitter-predicates helps in discovering disjunctive invariants; in fact, even in cases when the phases are not syntactically evident.

4.3 Combining Behaviours and CTIs

Algorithm 5 shows the complete algorithm, which combines the techniques illustrated above. We skip the description of steps that are already explained in Sects. 3.1 and 3.2. The algorithm begins by generating behaviours using an SMT solver, if they are not provided as input. This is done by unwinding Tr to a certain bound and then computing models for V at each unwinding. These behaviours are used to compute algebraic candidate lemmas as described earlier. The next two steps create a frequency distribution $\mathcal{P}$ using *Init*, Tr and *Bad*, and a grammar G using $\mathcal{P}$. The grammar G is used to get candidates when algebraic lemmas are not found, or are insufficient to prove the property. We create a new frequency distribution $\mathcal{P}_a$ based on conditions in loop body and its negations, and a grammar G_a using $\mathcal{P}_a$. These are used to sample antecedents, if required.

Algorithm 5. ELABOR: Learning from Behaviours and CTIs

Input: *Init, Tr, Bad* and *V*
Output: *lemmas*

1: *behaviours* ← EXECUTE(*Init, Tr, Bad*)
2: *candidates* ← GETALGEBRAICCANDIDATES(*behaviours*)
3: $\mathcal{P}$ ← COMPUTEDISTRIBUTION(*Init, Tr, Bad*)
4: *G* ← CONSTRUCTGRAMMAR($\mathcal{P}$)
5: $\mathcal{P}_a$ ← COMPUTEDISTRIBUTION(*Tr$_{conds}$*)
6: G_a ← CONSTRUCTGRAMMAR($\mathcal{P}_a$)
7: $L \leftarrow \emptyset$ ▷ the set of lemmas
8: *disjunct* ← *false*
9: **while** $\bigwedge_{l \in L} l(V) \wedge Bad(V)$ is SAT **do**
10:     **if** ¬*disjunct* **then** *disjunct* ← CHECKFORIMPL(*CTIs*)
11:     **if** *disjunct* **then** *antecedent* ← NEWCANDIDATE(G_a)
12:     **while** |*candidates*| < *BatchSize* **do**   ▷ for a pre-decided *BatchSize*
13:         *cand* ← NEWCANDIDATE(*G*)
14:         **if** *init* ← *Init(V)* ∧ ¬*cand(V)* is UNSAT **then**
15:             **if** *disjunct* **then** *candidates* ← *candidates* ∪ {*antecedent* ⇒ *cand*}
16:             **else** *candidates* ← *candidates* ∪ {*cand*}
17:         **else** ADJUST(*cand, G, $\mathcal{P}$*)
18:     **for** *cand* ∈ *candidates* **do**
19:         **if** $\bigwedge_{c \in candidates} c(V) \bigwedge_{l \in L} l(V) \wedge Tr(V, V') \wedge \neg cand(V')$ is SAT **then**
20:             *candidates* ← *candidates* \ {*cand*}
21:             ADJUST(*cand, G, $\mathcal{P}$*)
22:             *CTIs* ← *CTIs* ∪ {GETMODEL(*V*)} ∪ {GETMODEL(*V'*)}
23:             *candidates.reset*   ▷ start the loop afresh
24:     **if** *disjunct* ∧ |*candidates*| > 0 **then** ADJUST(*antecedent, $G_a, \mathcal{P}_a$*)
25:     **for** *cand* ∈ *candidates* **do** $L \leftarrow L \cup \{cand\}$
26: **return** *L*

The algorithm proceeds to sample and check candidates in a loop, similar to FREQHORN-2. This loop is modified to check if sampling implications is necessary. In the beginning of each iteration, the procedure CHECKFORIMPL is called. If it suggests that an implication is needed then we get them by sampling antecedents from G_a, and consequents from G. This is followed by a check for inductiveness and safety. If the consecution check fails, we store the corresponding models (CTIs) in a matrix. This check is unmodified from FREQHORN-2. The grammar G_a is adjusted when the inductiveness check passes for candidates with existing antecedents, to ensure different antecedents for new candidates. In our experiments, we unwound the transition relation up to bound of 10 for getting the behaviours. We also put a threshold on the number of CTIs collected before checking the need for implications, and bounded the degree of polynomials to 2.

5   Experiments

The aim of our experiments was to evaluate the effectiveness of our ideas. In particular, we were looking to answer the following questions:

1. Does the proposed strategy, of adding behaviours and implications, help improve the performance of FREQHORN-2 - (a) w.r.t. the number of benchmarks solved, and (b) w.r.t. the average time taken to solve a benchmark?
2. Does our CTI-based heuristic hamper the tool's performance in cases when a conditional invariant may not necessarily be required?

Implementation and Set-Up. We have implemented our ideas as an extension of FREQHORN-2. We have named it as ELABOR, which stands for Efficiently Learning from Appearance and Behaviour. Like its predecessors, the input program and the property are assumed to be in the form of linear constrained Horn clauses. Additionally, loop head states observed from behaviours may be provided as input. If that is missing, ELABOR automatically generates behavioural data by unrolling the input program to a certain bound and evaluating models for program variables at loop head using Z3. Candidate lemmas are computed from loop head states using the Gauss-Jordan algorithm. For matrix operations, we use Armadillo [20], a C++ library for linear algebra.

Table 2. Comparison on programs for which FREQHORN-2 timed out in more than half of the runs; the values show the mean execution time taken (in *seconds*)

Program	FREQHORN-2	ELABOR	Reason
exact_iters_5	∞	0.7	B
s_mutants_22	∞	24.6	B
s_mutants_21	∞	0.7	B
dillig22-6	∞	229	I
dillig22-4	∞	7.2	B
dillig22-3	∞	13.6	B
nonlin_gauss_sum	∞	49.9	B
abdu_03	312.3	0.9	B
exact_iters_4	272.2	0.7	B
menlo_park_term_orig	373.2	188.1	B
s_mutants_20	252.6	2.2	B
dillig18	344.4	45.8	I
dillig22-5	224.7	13.1	B
phases_true-unreach-call1	445.7	256.9	I
gj2007_true-unreach-call	342.8	150.1	I
half_true_modif	476.6	0.7	B

We experimented with the benchmarks that are provided with FREQHORN-2. These benchmarks have been taken from SV-COMP and the literature. There were a total of 172 safe programs, of which we excluded 6 programs that had nested conditions and function call which our tool does not support. We only compare ELABOR with its predecessor FREQHORN-2, as the latter has been shown to outperform other data-driven tools on these benchmarks [12]. Our experiments were performed by running 4 tasks in parallel, on a system with 16 cores of 2.40 GHz speed each, and total memory of 20 GB. We used a timeout of 600 s for each task. The tasks were run 10 times each, on both the tools, to handle the stochastic nature of the tools. We ran FREQHORN-2 with the interpolants option and a bound of 3. ELABOR, on the other hand, was run without the interpolants option (it is turned off by default), as it might be unnecessary to employ multiple ways of getting behavioural candidates. The artifact submitted with this paper contains both the tools, the benchmarks, and the instructions and scripts to reproduce the results.

Results. Of the 166 benchmarks that we used, FREQHORN-2 could not generate safe invariants for 13 programs in any of the runs. Apart from these, there were 11 programs which FREQHORN-2 missed on more than half of the runs. Of these 24 programs in total, ELABOR worked for 16 programs almost always (it solved 14 in all 10 runs and for 2 more in 8 runs out of 10). Table 2 lists these programs, along with the mean execution time (over successful runs) of the tools. The symbol ∞ indicates a time out in all runs. The last column shows the reason behind ELABOR discovering a safe invariant: 'B' indicates the enhancement of combining behaviours, and 'I' indicates the one of mining implications.

W.r.t. the average execution time, we say that one of the tool did better than the other only if (i) the faster tool took less than half the time that the other one, or (ii) the time difference was more than 100 s. ELABOR outperformed its predecessor on 31 programs, while for 8 programs it is FREQHORN-2 that worked better. The scatter plot on the left in Fig. 3 compares the time taken

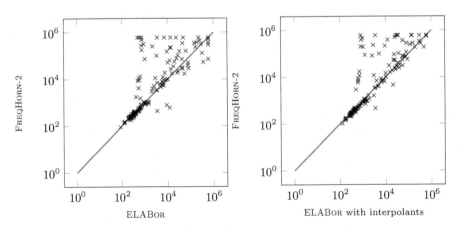

Fig. 3. Scatter plots comparing execution time (in ms) of the tools

(in *milliseconds*) by ELABOR (along the x-axis) and FREQHORN-2 (along the y-axis). The slack for those 8 programs was mostly due to lemmas that the interpolation engine provided upfront to FREQHORN-2, while we took a bit longer in discovering them. We confirmed this by running ELABOR with the interpolants option—now there were only 3 programs for which FREQHORN-2 outperformed us. However, the additional time taken by the interpolation engine gets reflected as points that were above the line, drifting closer to the line in the scatter plot on the right in Fig. 3.

6 Conclusion and Future Work

This work builds upon a recently proposed idea of inferring inductive invariants using a guess-and-check method, by sampling predicates, and its mutants, from the input program source [13]. In addition to obtaining a seed set of candidates from interpolation proofs of bounded safety [12], we show that a similar seed set can be obtained by analyzing behaviours of the program. We also propose a method to overcome a limitation of this guess-and-check method w.r.t. disjunctive invariants, by looking for conditional invariants in the form of implications.

There are a number of interesting directions in which this work may be extended. In particular, it would be worthwhile to explore the following:

- *Guidance from counterexamples to adequacy.* The current approach to deal with the inadequacy of discovered lemmas is to simply look for more. It would be useful to see how the property and the lemmas may together guide the search for additional facts, e.g. using ideas from abductive inference [10].
- *Refining candidates with disjunctions.* In the present algorithm, a disjunctive invariant candidate is either inductive, or is entirely useless. A method to find out which disjunct needs refinement, and how may it be refined, would certainly be helpful.
- *Choosing between syntax and behaviours.* Can there be some guidance in deciding, at every stage of the algorithm, whether the missing lemmas are more likely to be found through a syntactic search, or a behavioural one?
- *Machine learning to refine sampling.* Can machine learning technique be helpful in deciding when and how to nudge the probability distribution of candidates sampling?

We plan to investigate some of these research directions as we go ahead.

References

1. Albarghouthi, A., McMillan, K.L.: Beautiful interpolants. In: Sharygina, N., Veith, H. (eds.) CAV 2013. LNCS, vol. 8044, pp. 313–329. Springer, Heidelberg (2013). https://doi.org/10.1007/978-3-642-39799-8_22
2. Bradley, A.R.: SAT-based model checking without unrolling. In: Jhala, R., Schmidt, D. (eds.) VMCAI 2011. LNCS, vol. 6538, pp. 70–87. Springer, Heidelberg (2011). https://doi.org/10.1007/978-3-642-18275-4_7

3. Clarke, E., Grumberg, O., Jha, S., Lu, Y., Veith, H.: Counterexample-guided abstraction refinement. In: Emerson, E.A., Sistla, A.P. (eds.) CAV 2000. LNCS, vol. 1855, pp. 154–169. Springer, Heidelberg (2000). https://doi.org/10.1007/10722167_15

4. Colón, M.A., Sankaranarayanan, S., Sipma, H.B.: Linear invariant generation using non-linear constraint solving. In: Hunt, W.A., Somenzi, F. (eds.) CAV 2003. LNCS, vol. 2725, pp. 420–432. Springer, Heidelberg (2003). https://doi.org/10.1007/978-3-540-45069-6_39

5. Cousot, P., Cousot, R.: Abstract interpretation: a unified lattice model for static analysis of programs by construction or approximation of fixpoints. In: Proceedings of the 4th ACM SIGACT-SIGPLAN Symposium on Principles of Programming Languages, pp. 238–252. ACM (1977)

6. Cousot, P., Cousot, R.: Systematic design of program analysis frameworks. In: Proceedings of the 6th ACM SIGACT-SIGPLAN Symposium on Principles of Programming Languages, POPL 1979, pp. 269–282. ACM, New York (1979). https://doi.org/10.1145/567752.567778

7. Cousot, P., Halbwachs, N.: Automatic discovery of linear restraints among variables of a program. In: Proceedings of the 5th ACM SIGACT-SIGPLAN Symposium on Principles of Programming Languages, POPL 1978, pp. 84–96. ACM, New York (1978). http://doi.acm.org/10.1145/512760.512770

8. Craig, W.: Three uses of the Herbrand-Gentzen theorem in relating model theory and proof theory. J. Symbolic Logic **22**(3), 269–285 (1957). https://projecteuclid.org:443/euclid.jsl/1183732824

9. de Moura, L., Bjørner, N.: Z3: an efficient SMT solver. In: Ramakrishnan, C.R., Rehof, J. (eds.) TACAS 2008. LNCS, vol. 4963, pp. 337–340. Springer, Heidelberg (2008). https://doi.org/10.1007/978-3-540-78800-3_24

10. Dillig, I.: Abductive inference and its applications in program analysis, verification, and synthesis. In: Formal Methods in Computer-Aided Design, FMCAD 2015, Austin, Texas, USA, 27–30 September 2015, p. 4 (2015)

11. Ernst, M.D., Czeisler, A., Griswold, W.G., Notkin, D.: Quickly detecting relevant program invariants. In: Proceedings of the 22nd International Conference on Software Engineering, pp. 449–458. ACM (2000)

12. Fedyukovich, G., Bodík, R.: Accelerating syntax-guided invariant synthesis. In: Beyer, D., Huisman, M. (eds.) TACAS 2018. LNCS, vol. 10805, pp. 251–269. Springer, Cham (2018). https://doi.org/10.1007/978-3-319-89960-2_14

13. Fedyukovich, G., Kaufman, S.J., Bodík, R.: Sampling invariants from frequency distributions. In: 2017 Formal Methods in Computer Aided Design, FMCAD 2017, Vienna, Austria, 2–6 October 2017, pp. 100–107 (2017)

14. Flanagan, C., Leino, K.R.M.: Houdini, an annotation assistant for ESC/Java. In: Oliveira, J.N., Zave, P. (eds.) FME 2001. LNCS, vol. 2021, pp. 500–517. Springer, Heidelberg (2001). https://doi.org/10.1007/3-540-45251-6_29

15. Garg, P., Neider, D., Madhusudan, P., Roth, D.: Learning invariants using decision trees and implication counterexamples. In: Proceedings of the 43rd Annual ACM SIGPLAN-SIGACT Symposium on Principles of Programming Languages, POPL 2016, pp. 499–512. ACM, New York (2016)

16. Gupta, A., Rybalchenko, A.: InvGen: an efficient invariant generator. In: Bouajjani, A., Maler, O. (eds.) CAV 2009. LNCS, vol. 5643, pp. 634–640. Springer, Heidelberg (2009). https://doi.org/10.1007/978-3-642-02658-4_48

17. Hoder, K., Bjørner, N.: Generalized property directed reachability. In: Cimatti, A., Sebastiani, R. (eds.) SAT 2012. LNCS, vol. 7317, pp. 157–171. Springer, Heidelberg (2012). https://doi.org/10.1007/978-3-642-31612-8_13

18. Nguyen, T., Kapur, D., Weimer, W., Forrest, S.: Using dynamic analysis to discover polynomial and array invariants. In: Proceedings of the 34th International Conference on Software Engineering, pp. 683–693. IEEE Press (2012)
19. Padon, O., McMillan, K.L., Panda, A., Sagiv, M., Shoham, S.: Ivy: safety verification by interactive generalization. In: Proceedings of the 37th ACM SIGPLAN Conference on Programming Language Design and Implementation, PLDI 2016, pp. 614–630. ACM, New York (2016)
20. Sanderson, C., Curtin, R.: Armadillo: a template-based C++ library for linear algebra. J. Open Source Softw. (2016)
21. Shafarevich, I.R., Remizov, A.O.: Linear Algebra and Geometry. Springer, Heidelberg (2013). https://doi.org/10.1007/978-3-642-30994-6
22. Sharma, R., Aiken, A.: From invariant checking to invariant inference using randomized search. Form. Methods Syst Des. **48**(3), 235–256 (2016)
23. Sharma, R., Dillig, I., Dillig, T., Aiken, A.: Simplifying loop invariant generation using splitter predicates. In: Gopalakrishnan, G., Qadeer, S. (eds.) CAV 2011. LNCS, vol. 6806, pp. 703–719. Springer, Heidelberg (2011). https://doi.org/10.1007/978-3-642-22110-1_57
24. Sharma, R., Gupta, S., Hariharan, B., Aiken, A., Liang, P., Nori, A.V.: A data driven approach for algebraic loop invariants. In: Felleisen, M., Gardner, P. (eds.) ESOP 2013. LNCS, vol. 7792, pp. 574–592. Springer, Heidelberg (2013). https://doi.org/10.1007/978-3-642-37036-6_31

Invertible Linear Transforms
of Numerical Abstract Domains

Francesco Ranzato$^{(\boxtimes)}$ and Marco Zanella

Dipartimento di Matematica, University of Padova, Padova, Italy
`ranzato@math.unipd.it`

Abstract. We study systematic changes of numerical domains in abstract interpretation through invertible linear transforms of the Euclidean vector space, namely, through invertible real square matrices. We provide a full generalization, including abstract transfer functions, of the parallelotopes abstract domain, which turns out to be an instantiation of an invertible linear transform to the interval abstraction. Given an invertible square matrix M and a numerical abstraction A, we show that for a linear program P (i.e., using linear assignments and linear tests only), the analysis using the linearly transformed domain $M(A)$ can be obtained by analysing on the original domain A a linearly transformed program P^M. We also investigate completeness of abstract domains for invertible linear transforms. In particular, we show that, perhaps counterintuitively, octagons are not complete for 45° rotations and, additionally, cannot be derived as a complete refinement of intervals for some family of invertible linear transforms.

1 Introduction

In abstract interpretation [6,7], the choice of an abstract domain determines which program properties will be analysed as well as the precision and efficiency of the corresponding program analysis. A vast array of abstract domains for analysing properties of numerical program variables is available as well as a number of operators for their combination, refinement and transformation which have been defined since the beginning of abstract interpretation [6,7,9–12]—see [18] for a recent and comprehensive tutorial on numerical abstract domains. The abstract domain of parallelotopes has been introduced and studied in [1–4] as a linear transform of the standard interval abstract domain [6]. Any invertible $n \times n$ real matrix M defines a domain of M-parallelotopes which consists of (vectors of) intervals $\langle [l_i, u_i] \rangle_{i=1}^n$, for $\mathbf{l}, \mathbf{u} \in (\mathbb{R} \cup \{\pm\infty\})^n$, whose concrete meaning is recast as the set of vectors $\mathbf{x} \in \mathbb{R}^n$ such that $\mathbf{l} \leq M\mathbf{x} \leq \mathbf{u}$. The basic idea is that the matrix M represents a change of basis of the Euclidean vector space $\mathbb{R}^n$, which can be always converted back through its inverse matrix M^{-1}. Hence, $\langle [l_i, u_i] \rangle_{i=1}^n$ is a symbolic representation of the vectors $\{\mathbf{x} \in \mathbb{R}^n \mid \mathbf{l} \leq M\mathbf{x} \leq \mathbf{u}\}$ in the new coordinate system based on M, which is therefore its concretization for the parallelotopes domain.

© Springer Nature Switzerland AG 2018
A. Podelski (Ed.): SAS 2018, LNCS 11002, pp. 344–363, 2018.
https://doi.org/10.1007/978-3-319-99725-4_21

Parallelotopes can be used in program analysis in two different ways. In the first approach described in [1,2], the matrix M is fixed and is purposely synthesized for a program P through some statistical inference of the data gathered by a dynamic analysis of P, typically a variation of principal component analysis. On the other hand, [3,4] put forward a program analysis where the abstract values are pairs consisting of an interval together with a matrix M, so that here the matrix is not computed a priori but rather the abstract transfer functions may change it during program analysis (as happens for convex polyhedra).

We study here a generalization of the first approach to the abstract domain of parallelotopes. An invertible square matrix M can be applied for systematically transforming any numerical abstract domain $\mathcal{A}$ together with all its abstract transfer functions. This is called an invertible linear transform of $\mathcal{A}$ and denoted by $\mathcal{A}^M$. This linear transform M preserves the whole structure of the abstract domain $\mathcal{A}$, meaning that if $\mathcal{A}$ is defined by a Galois connection/insertion then this also holds for $\mathcal{A}^M$, although this M-transform may also preserve domains defined through a concretization map only. Furthermore, it turns out that M systematically transforms the abstract transfer functions available in $\mathcal{A}$. More precisely, for the standard abstract transfer functions and operators used in abstract interpretation, namely lub and glb, (single, parallel and backward) assignment, Boolean test, widening and narrowing, we provide a simple technique for designing the abstract transfer functions in the transformed domain $\mathcal{A}^M$ in terms of the abstract transfer functions in the original domain $\mathcal{A}$. Moreover, this transform of abstract functions preserves all their significant properties: soundness, best correct approximation, completeness and exactness. As a consequence, we show that an analysis with the transformed abstraction $\mathcal{A}^M$ of a program P consisting of linear assignments and tests can be obtained by analysing with the original abstraction $\mathcal{A}$ a transformed program P^M which is obtained from P by transforming all its linear assignments and tests while maintaining the same control flow graph. It should be remarked that this program change may transform single linear assignments of P into parallel linear assignments in P^M. If the analysis in $\mathcal{A}$ of the transformed program P^M relies on abstract transfer functions which are best correct approximations then this technique computes at each program point of P^M precisely the best abstract value for $\mathcal{A}^M$ at the same program point of P. This technique is illustrated through a couple of examples different from parallelotopes, namely linear transforms of constant propagation and octagon analysis.

As an example, a linear transform of Kildall's [15] standard constant propagation domain Const for three program variables through the invertible matrix $M = \begin{pmatrix} 1 & 0 & 0 \\ -1 & 1 & 0 \\ -1 & 0 & 1 \end{pmatrix}$ results in a transformed domain Const^M which is able to represent program invariants of type $x_1 = k_1$, $x_1 + x_2 = k_2$, $x_1 + x_3 = k_3$, where x_i's are variables and k_i's range in Const and therefore represent either a constant value or unreachability or no information. For instance, an analysis based on Const^M of the following program:

$x_1 := 2;\ x_2 := 3;\ x_3 := 6;$
while $(x_2 < x_3)$ **do**
    $\{\ x_1 := x_1 - 2;\ x_3 := x_1 + x_2 + x_3 - 1;\ x_2 := x_2 + 2;\ \}$

is able to compute the abstract loop invariant $\langle \top, 5, 8 \rangle$ meaning that the additions $x_1 + x_2$ and $x_1 + x_3$ are always equal to, respectively, 5 and 8.

We also investigate completeness and exactness [7,13] of abstract domains for invertible linear transforms. Firstly, we show that a linearly transformed domain $\mathcal{A}^M$ is useless—meaning that it is equivalent to $\mathcal{A}$ itself—precisely when $\mathcal{A}$ is both complete and exact for the linear transform M. In particular, as expected, it turns out that any linear transform of Karr's [14], templates [19] and convex polyhedra [8] abstract domains is ineffective. Instead, we prove that a linear transform M of intervals and octagons [17] is useless exactly when M is a monomial matrix, namely each row and column of M has exactly one nonzero entry. This characterization is expected since monomial matrices intuitively encode nonrelational linear transforms. Finally, we show that octagons cannot be obtained from intervals as the minimal refinement which is complete for some family of invertible linear transforms (this is called complete shell in [13]). This is somehow against the graphical intuition that octagons are complete for rotations of $\frac{\pi}{4}$ radians and therefore could be designed through a complete shell of intervals for this family of rotations. Rather, this intuition holds just in 2D, namely for two variables only. What we instead prove is that octagons can be synthesized through a suitable reduced product of $\frac{\pi}{4}$ rotations of intervals.

Due to lack of space all the proofs are omitted.

2   Background

Linear Transformations. We denote by $\overline{\mathbb{R}}$ the set of real numbers $\mathbb{R}$ augmented with $+\infty$ and $-\infty$, where ordering and numeric operations are extended from $\mathbb{R}$ to $\overline{\mathbb{R}}$ in the standard way. Vectors $\mathbf{x} \in \mathbb{R}^n$ (or $\mathbf{x} \in \overline{\mathbb{R}}^n$) are usually intended as column vectors, while $\mathbf{x}^T$ denotes the corresponding (transpose) row vector and $\mathbf{x}_i \in \mathbb{R}$, with $i \in [1, n]$, denotes its i-th component. If $\mathbf{x}, \mathbf{y} \in \mathbb{R}^n$ and $a \in \mathbb{R}$ then $\mathbf{x} \cdot \mathbf{y}$, $\mathbf{x} + \mathbf{y}$ and $a\mathbf{x}$ denote, respectively, scalar product, addition of vectors and scalar multiplication in $\mathbb{R}^n$. The canonical orthonormal basis of $\mathbb{R}^n$ is denoted by $\langle \mathbf{e_1}, ..., \mathbf{e_n} \rangle$, where $\mathbf{e}_{ii} = 1$ and, for any $j \neq i$, $\mathbf{e}_{ij} = 0$. $\mathbb{R}^{m \times n}$ denotes the set of all $m \times n$ matrices with entries in $\mathbb{R}$, while $\mathrm{GL}(n)$ denotes the general linear group of $n \times n$ invertible square matrices with entries in $\mathbb{R}$. $\mathbf{0}_n \in \mathbb{R}^{n \times n}$ denotes the square zero matrix, $I_n \in \mathrm{GL}(n)$ denotes the identity matrix and A^{-1} and A^T denote, respectively, the inverse and transpose of A. A $1 \times n$ matrix is also used as a row vector, while a $n \times 1$ matrix as a column vector. A linear transformation of the n-dimensional Euclidean space $\mathbb{R}^n$ is a function in $\mathbb{R}^n \to \mathbb{R}^n$ of the form $\mathbf{x} \mapsto M\mathbf{x}$, where $M \in \mathbb{R}^{n \times n}$, which is simply denoted by $M : \mathbb{R}^n \to \mathbb{R}^n$. Given any set $X \in \wp(\mathbb{R}^n)$, we use the notation $M \cdot X \triangleq \{M\mathbf{x} \in \mathbb{R}^n \mid \mathbf{x} \in X\}$ to denote the pointwise extension of M, and we also use $T_M : \wp(\mathbb{R}^n) \to \wp(\mathbb{R}^n)$ to denote the corresponding function on sets of vectors. Noteworthy examples of linear transformations include scalings, rotations, shearings and projections. Linear transformations M are partitioned between noninvertible and invertible: for example, (orthogonal or oblique) projections are noninvertible while rotations are always invertible. The set of invertible linear transformations of $\mathbb{R}^n$ endowed with function composition forms the well-known (noncommutative) general linear group GL(n). Let us also recall that $M \cdot X \subseteq Y \Leftrightarrow X \subseteq M^{-1} \cdot Y$ always holds for any $M \in$ GL(n).

An affine transformation of $\mathbb{R}^n$ is a composition of a linear transformation with a transalation, i.e., it is a function in $\mathbb{R}^n \to \mathbb{R}^n$ of the form $\mathbf{x} \mapsto N\mathbf{x} + \mathbf{t}$, where $N \in \mathbb{R}^{n \times n}$ and $\mathbf{t} \in \mathbb{R}^n$. A pure translation $\mathrm{Tr}_{\mathbf{t}}(\mathbf{x}) \triangleq \mathbf{x} + \mathbf{t}$, for some vector $\mathbf{t} \in \mathbb{R}^n$, is the simplest example of (invertible) affine transformation.

Notable Linear Transformations. A *scaling* by a vector $\mathbf{s} \in \mathbb{R}^n$ is the linear transformation $\mathbf{x} \mapsto D^{\mathbf{s}}\mathbf{x}$, where $D^{\mathbf{s}} \in \mathbb{R}^{n \times n}$ is the diagonal matrix defined by $(D^{\mathbf{s}})_{ii} \triangleq \mathbf{s}_i$ and for $i \neq j$, $(D^{\mathbf{s}})_{ij} \triangleq 0$. A scaling transform is invertible iff for any i, $\mathbf{s}_i \neq 0$.

Let $n \geq 2$. Given some $\lambda \in \mathbb{R}$ and $a, b \in [1, n]$ with $a \neq b$, the invertible shear matrix $Sh^{a,b,\lambda} \in$ GL(n) is defined as follows: $(Sh^{a,b,\lambda})_{ii} = 1$, $(Sh^{a,b,\lambda})_{ab} = \lambda$, otherwise $(Sh^{a,b,\lambda})_{ij} = 0$. This defines an invertible linear transformation called *shearing* (often used in computer graphics) which preserves the area of geometric figures and the alignment and relative distances of collinear points (a 2D example is in Fig. 1). The inverse of $Sh^{a,b,\lambda}$ is simply the shearing $Sh^{a,b,-\lambda}$ and, in general, shearings are not closed w.r.t. composition and their composition is not commutative.

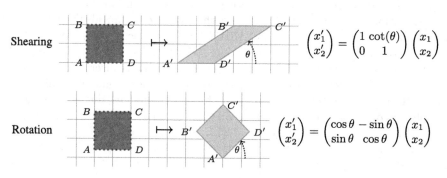

Fig. 1. An example of shearing and rotation transforms for two variables.

A *Givens rotation* (or principal rotation) is the linear transformation which maps $\mathbf{x} \in \mathbb{R}^n$ into the point $\mathbf{x}' \in \mathbb{R}^n$ obtained by rotating $\mathbf{x}$ counterclockwise in a (a, b) plane of $\mathbb{R}^n$ (i.e., generated by $\mathbf{e_a}$ and $\mathbf{e_a}$), where $a, b \in [1, n]$ with $a \neq b$, by an angle of $\theta \in \mathbb{R}$ radians around the origin (a 2D example is in Fig. 1). This transformation is represented by an invertible Givens rotation matrix $R^{a,b,\theta} \in$ GL(n) which is defined as follows: $R^{a,b,\theta}$ differs from the identity matrix I_n in the four entries (a, a), (a, b), (b, a), (b, b), where it assumes, respectively, the values $\cos\theta$, $-\sin\theta$, $\sin\theta$, $\cos\theta$. Clearly, $R^{a,b,-\theta}$ is the inverse of $R^{a,b,\theta}$. Givens rotations are closed by composition and When the rotation angle is $\theta = (2\pi)/m$ for some $m \in \mathbb{N} \setminus \{0\}$, it turns out that $R^{a,b,\theta}$ is cyclic, namely $(R^{a,b,\theta})^k = I_n$ for some integer $k > 0$.

Numerical Abstract Domains. According to the most general definition, a numerical abstract domain is a tuple $\langle A, \leq, \gamma \rangle$ where $\langle A, \leq \rangle$ is at least a preordered set and the concretization function $\gamma : A \to \wp(\mathbb{R}^n)$, where $n \geq 1$, preserves the relation $\leq$, i.e., $a \leq a'$ implies $\gamma(a) \subseteq \gamma(a')$. Thus, A plays the usual role of set of symbolic representations for sets of vectors of $\mathbb{R}^n$. If the base field of real numbers $\mathbb{R}$ is replaced by the field of rationals $\mathbb{Q}$, which is a possible choice for an abstract interpretation framework (see [18]), then completeness of the lattice $\langle \mathbb{R}, \leq \rangle$ is lost (i.e., $\langle \mathbb{Q}, \leq \rangle$ is not a complete lattice) so that some linear transformations cannot be taken into account, e.g., a Givens rotation of $\pi/4$. Also, linear transformations preserving integer vectors in $\mathbb{Z}^n$ (the n-dimensional integer lattice) have a narrow scope (they are studied in lattice geometry) and are not considered here (see [2, Sect. 7.5] for a discussion). Well-known examples of numerical abstract domains include signs, constants, intervals, affine equalities, zones, pentagons, octagons, parallelotopes, templates, convex polyhedra (the interested reader is referred to the recent tutorial [18]). Some numerical domains just form preorders (e.g., standard representations of octagons by DBMs allow multiple representations) while other domains give rise to posets (e.g., signs, constants and intervals). Of course, any preordered abstract domain $\langle A, \leq, \gamma \rangle$ can be canonically quotiented to a poset $\langle A_{/\cong}, \leq, \gamma \rangle$ where $a \cong a'$ iff $a \leq a'$ and $a' \leq a$. While a monotone concretization γ is enough for reasoning about soundness of static analysis on numerical domains, the notions of best correct approximation and completeness rely on the existence of an abstraction function $\alpha : \wp(\mathbb{R}^n) \to A$ which requires that $\langle A, \leq \rangle$ is (at least) a poset and that the pair (α, γ) forms a Galois connection (GC), i.e. for any $X \subseteq \mathbb{R}^n, a \in A$, $\alpha(X) \leq a \Leftrightarrow X \subseteq \gamma(a)$ holds, which becomes a Galois insertion when γ is injective (or, equivalently, α is surjective). Most numerical domains admit a definition through Galois connections, while for some domains this is impossible, notably for convex polyhedra. Let us recall that the nonrelational interval domain $Int = \langle \text{Int}, \leq, \gamma, \alpha \rangle$ is defined by: $\text{Int} \triangleq \{ \langle [l_i, u_i] \rangle_{i \in [1,n]} \mid l_i, u_i \in \overline{\mathbb{R}}, l_i \leq u_i \} \cup \bot$, $\gamma(\langle [l_i, u_i] \rangle_{i \in [1,n]}) = \{ \mathbf{x} \in \mathbb{R}^n \mid \forall i \in [1,n]. \ l_i \leq \mathbf{x}_i \leq u_i \}$, $\gamma(\bot) = \varnothing$, and $\alpha(X) \triangleq \langle \inf_{\mathbf{x} \in X} \mathbf{x}_i, \sup_{\mathbf{x} \in X} \mathbf{x}_i \rangle_{i \in [1,n]}$.

A function $f^\sharp : A \to A$ is a sound approximation of a concrete (transfer) function $f : \wp(\mathbb{R}^n) \to \wp(\mathbb{R}^n)$ when, for any $a \in A$, $f(\gamma(a)) \subseteq \gamma(f^\sharp(a))$ holds, while $f^\sharp$ is forward-complete (or f-complete or exact) when $f \circ \gamma = \gamma \circ f^\sharp$ holds. Assume that a Galois connection (α, γ) for A exists. The abstract function $f^A \triangleq \alpha \circ f \circ \gamma$ is called the best correct approximation (bca) of f on A. Also, soundness of $f^\sharp$ can be equivalently stated by $\alpha(f(X)) \leq f^\sharp(\alpha(X))$, for any $X \in \wp(\mathbb{R}^n)$, while $f^\sharp$ is defined to be backward-complete (or b-complete or just complete) when $\alpha \circ f = f^\sharp \circ \alpha$ holds.

3   Linear Transforms of Abstract Domains

Linear transformations can be used to recast any existing numerical abstract domains: an invertible linear transformation performs a change of basis of the n-dimensional Euclidean space $\mathbb{R}^n$ and the transformed abstract domain is accordingly interpreted with this transformed coordinate system.

Definition 3.1 (Linear Transform of Abstractions). Consider any invertible matrix $M \in \mathrm{GL}(n)$ and a numerical abstract domain $\mathcal{A} = \langle A, \leq, \gamma \rangle$. The M-*transform* of $\mathcal{A}$ is given by $\mathcal{A}^M \triangleq \langle A, \leq, \gamma^M \rangle$, also denoted by $M(\mathcal{A})$, where the concretization map $\gamma^M : A \to \wp(\mathbb{R}^n)$ is defined by $\gamma^M(a) \triangleq M^{-1} \cdot \gamma(a)$. If $\mathcal{A}$ admits an abstraction map $\alpha : \wp(\mathbb{R}^n) \to A$ then $\mathcal{A}^M$ is also endowed with a function $\alpha^M : \wp(\mathbb{R}^n) \to A$ defined by $\alpha^M(X) \triangleq \alpha(M \cdot X)$.   □

Equivalently, we have that $\gamma^M = T_{M^{-1}} \circ \gamma$ and $\alpha^M = \alpha \circ T_M$. The basic idea is that the invertible matrix M represents a change of basis for $\mathbb{R}^n$, which can be always converted back through its inverse matrix M^{-1}. According to this view, an abstract value $a \in A$ becomes a symbolic representation of the set of vectors $\gamma(a) \in \wp(\mathbb{R}^n)$ in the new coordinate system based on M, so that the concretization γ^M of a in the original coordinate system of $\mathbb{R}^n$ is given by the conversion of $\gamma(a)$ through M^{-1} back to the original basis of $\mathbb{R}^n$, namely $\gamma^M(a) = M^{-1} \cdot \gamma(a) \in \wp(\mathbb{R}^n)$. Dually, if $\mathcal{A}$ admits an abstraction function α, so that $\langle A, \leq \rangle$ is (at least) partially ordered, then $\mathcal{A}^M$ also has an abstraction map α^M which provides the best approximation of some $X \in \wp(\mathbb{R}^n)$ in A when interpreted w.r.t. the new coordinate system based on M, namely $\alpha^M(X) = \alpha(M \cdot X)$. Hence, Definition 3.1 is a straightforward generalization of the parallelotope domain defined in [2, Definition 2], since a parallelotope domain indexed by $M \in \mathrm{GL}(n)$ boils down to the M-transform of the interval abstraction $\mathcal{I}nt$.

If $\mathcal{A}$ is a numerical domain equipped with a concretization map γ only, then $\mathcal{A}^M$ is clearly a sound numerical domain, since we just need to check that γ^M still preserves the relation $\leq$ on A: if $a \leq a'$ then $\gamma(a) \subseteq \gamma(a')$, so that $\gamma^M(a) = M^{-1} \cdot \gamma(a) \subseteq M^{-1} \cdot \gamma(a') = \gamma^M(a')$. Moreover, any order-theoretic property of the abstract domain A is obviously preserved when interpreted in its M-transform, e.g., bottom and top elements, lub's and glb's, chains, etc. It is also easy to observe that linear transforms of numerical domains also preserve the existence of abstraction maps.

Lemma 3.2. *If $\mathcal{A} = \langle A, \leq, \gamma, \alpha \rangle$ is a Galois connection (insertion) then its M-transform $\mathcal{A}^M = \langle A, \leq, \gamma^M, \alpha^M \rangle$ is a Galois connection (insertion).*

Example 3.3 (Linear Transform of Constant Propagation). Constant propagation is a well-known and simple abstract interpretation used in compiler optimization for detecting whether a variable at some program point always stores a single constant value for all possible program executions (see, e.g., [18, Sect. 4.3]). Constant propagation relies on the nonrelational constant abstract domain, which is here given for variables assuming real values: Const $\triangleq \mathbb{R} \cup \{\bot, \top\}$. Const is endowed with the usual flat partial order: for any $x \in$ Const, $\bot \leq x \leq \top$ (and $x \leq x$), which makes it an infinite complete lattice with height 2. Const is easily defined by a Galois insertion with its standard abstraction and concretization maps $\alpha : \wp(\mathbb{R}) \to$ Const and $\gamma :$ Const $\to \wp(\mathbb{R})$.

$$\alpha(X) \triangleq \begin{cases} \bot & \text{if } X = \varnothing \\ z & \text{if } X = \{z\} \\ \top & \text{otherwise} \end{cases} \qquad \gamma(a) \triangleq \begin{cases} \varnothing & \text{if } a = \bot \\ \{a\} & \text{if } a \in \mathbb{R} \\ \mathbb{R} & \text{if } a = \top \end{cases}$$

Let us consider 3 variables and the invertible matrix

$$S = \begin{pmatrix} 1 & 0 & 0 \\ -1 & 1 & 0 \\ 0 & 0 & 1 \end{pmatrix} \begin{pmatrix} 1 & 0 & 0 \\ 0 & 1 & 0 \\ -1 & 0 & 1 \end{pmatrix} = \begin{pmatrix} 1 & 0 & 0 \\ -1 & 1 & 0 \\ -1 & 0 & 1 \end{pmatrix}$$ which is obtained as composition of the

two shearing matrices $Sh^{2,1,-1}$ and $Sh^{3,1,-1}$. Its inverse is $S^{-1} = \begin{pmatrix} 1 & 0 & 0 \\ 1 & 1 & 0 \\ 1 & 0 & 1 \end{pmatrix}$.

Let us consider Const for three variables, namely as an abstraction of $\wp(\mathbb{R}^3)$. The matrix S thus induces the transformed domain Const^S, where a vector $\langle a_1, a_2, a_3 \rangle \in \mathrm{Const}^S$, by Definition 3.1, has the following meaning:

$$\gamma^S(\langle a_1, a_2, a_3 \rangle) = S^{-1}\gamma(\langle a_1, a_2, a_3 \rangle) =$$
$$\{\langle z_1, z_1 + z_2, z_1 + z_3 \rangle \in \mathbb{R}^3 \mid z_1 \in \gamma(a_1), z_2 \in \gamma(a_2), z_3 \in \gamma(a_3)\}.$$

Moreover, if $k_i \in \mathbb{R}$ then $\alpha^S(\{\langle k_1, k_2, k_3 \rangle\}) = \alpha(S\langle k_1, k_2, k_3 \rangle) = \alpha(\{\langle k_1, k_2 - k_1, k_3 - k_1 \rangle\}) = \langle k_1, k_2 - k_1, k_3 - k_1 \rangle$. For instance, if $k_i \in \mathbb{R}$ then $\gamma^S(\langle \top, k_2, k_3 \rangle) = \{\langle z, z + k_2, z + k_3 \rangle \mid z \in \mathbb{R}\}$, $\gamma^S(\langle k_1, \top, k_3 \rangle) = \{\langle k_1, z, k_1 + k_3 \rangle \mid z \in \mathbb{R}\}$, while $\alpha^S(\{\langle -1, 0, 1 \rangle, \langle 1, 1, 3 \rangle\}) = \langle \top, \top, 2 \rangle$ and $\alpha^S(\{\langle -1, 0, 1 \rangle, \langle 1, 2, 3 \rangle\}) = \langle \top, 1, 2 \rangle$. This abstraction Const^S is therefore able to represent invariants for program variables x_i of type $x_1 \in \gamma(a_1) \wedge x_1 + x_2 \in \gamma(a_2) \wedge x_1 + x_3 \in \gamma(a_3)$, where $a_i \in \mathrm{Const}$. For instance, for the following program P already considered in Sect. 1 and here decorated with program points:

(1) $x_1 := 2; \; x_2 := 3; \; x_3 := 6;$ (2)
while (3) $(x_2 < x_3)$ **do**
    (4) $x_1 := x_1 - 2;$
    (5) $x_3 := x_1 + x_2 + x_3 - 1;$
    (6) $x_2 := x_2 + 2;$
od (7)

while a constant analysis with Const derives no information at program point (3), namely the abstract value $\langle \top, \top, \top \rangle$, we expect that an analysis based on Const^S is able to compute the abstract value $\langle \top, 5, 8 \rangle$ which represents that at program point (3) the additions $x_1 + x_2$ and $x_1 + x_3$ are always equal to, respectively, 5 and 8. □

4   Linear Transforms of Abstract Functions

Background. An abstract interpretation-based static analysis of programs with numeric variables relies on sound approximations of the standard transfer functions on the concrete domain $\wp(\mathbb{R}^n)$ used by the collecting program semantics (see, e.g., [18]): binary set unions and intersections, variable assignments, Boolean tests, widening and narrowing operators. Let us briefly recall the definitions for assignments and tests.

The most general form of variable assignment is given by a parallel (or simultaneous) assignment $[\mathbf{x}_i := f_i(\mathbf{x})]_{i \in [1,n]}$ (as in Python and JavaScript), with generic (possibly nonlinear) functions $f_i : \mathbb{R}^n \to \mathbb{R}$ which define a n-dimensional transform $f : \mathbb{R}^n \to \mathbb{R}^n$ by $f(\mathbf{x}) \triangleq \langle f_1(\mathbf{x}), ..., f_n(\mathbf{x}) \rangle$. The transfer function $\mathbf{assign}(f) : \wp(\mathbb{R}^n) \to \wp(\mathbb{R}^n)$ is the corresponding pointwise extension of f defined by $\mathbf{assign}(f)(X) \triangleq \{f(\mathbf{x}) \mid \mathbf{x} \in X\}$. If $i \in [1, n]$ and $f : \mathbb{R}^n \to \mathbb{R}$ then a single assignment $\mathbf{x}_i := f(\mathbf{x})$ for the i-th variable is defined by $\mathbf{assign}(i, f) : \wp(\mathbb{R}^n) \to \wp(\mathbb{R}^n)$ as the following specific instance: $\mathbf{assign}(i, f)(X) \triangleq \{\langle \mathbf{x}_1, ..., \mathbf{x}_{i-1}, f(\mathbf{x}), \mathbf{x}_{i+1}, ..., \mathbf{x}_n \rangle \mid \mathbf{x} \in X\}$. Linear parallel assignments rely on a square matrix $N \in \mathbb{R}^{n \times n}$ and a vector $\mathbf{b} \in \mathbb{R}^n$ which define the transfer function $\mathbf{assign}(N, \mathbf{b}) : \wp(\mathbb{R}^n) \to \wp(\mathbb{R}^n)$ as follows: $\mathbf{assign}(N, \mathbf{b})(X) \triangleq \{N\mathbf{x} + \mathbf{b} \mid \mathbf{x} \in X\}$. As a particular case, linear (single) assignments for the i-th variable consider a vector $\mathbf{a} \in \mathbb{R}^n$ and a constant $b \in \mathbb{R}$ which define the affine transformation $\mathbf{x} \mapsto (\mathbf{e_i a}^T)\mathbf{x} + b\mathbf{e_i}$ whose corresponding transfer function is $\mathbf{assign}(i, \mathbf{a}, b) \triangleq \mathbf{assign}(\mathbf{e_i}(\mathbf{a} - \mathbf{e_i})^T + I, b\mathbf{e_i})$, namely,

$$\mathbf{assign}(i, \mathbf{a}, b)(X) = \{\langle \mathbf{x}_1, ..., \mathbf{x}_{i-1}, \mathbf{a} \cdot \mathbf{x} + b, \mathbf{x}_{i+1}, ..., \mathbf{x}_n \rangle \mid \mathbf{x} \in X\}.$$

Let us also recall backward assignment, namely the adjoint of a (forward) assignment, which is typically used in backward abstract interpretation [5] for refining the output of a forward abstract interpretation. In general, the transfer function $\mathbf{assign}^-(f) : \wp(\mathbb{R}^n) \to \wp(\mathbb{R}^n)$ of the backward parallel assignment for $[\mathbf{x} := f(\mathbf{x})]$ is simply given by the inverse image $\mathbf{assign}^-(f)(Y) \triangleq f^{-1}(Y) = \{\mathbf{x} \in \mathbb{R}^n \mid f(\mathbf{x}) \in Y\}$, so that for a single assignment $\mathbf{x}_i := f(\mathbf{x})$, we have that $\mathbf{assign}^-(i, f)(Y) \triangleq \{\mathbf{x} \in \mathbb{R}^n \mid \langle \mathbf{x}_1, ..., f(\mathbf{x}), ..., \mathbf{x}_n \rangle \in Y\}$. In turn, the transfer function of the backward linear parallel assignment for $N \in \mathbb{R}^{n \times n}$ and $\mathbf{b} \in \mathbb{R}^n$ is $\mathbf{assign}^-(N, \mathbf{b}) : \wp(\mathbb{R}^n) \to \wp(\mathbb{R}^n)$ defined by $\mathbf{assign}^-(N, \mathbf{b})(Y) \triangleq \{\mathbf{x} \in \mathbb{R}^n \mid N\mathbf{x} + \mathbf{b} \in Y\}$.

A nondeterministic assignment for the i-th variable $x_i := ?$ is modeled by the transfer function $\mathbf{forget}(i) : \wp(\mathbb{R}^n) \to \wp(\mathbb{R}^n)$ defined as follows: $\mathbf{forget}(i)(X) \triangleq \{\langle \mathbf{x}_1, ..., \mathbf{x}_{i-1}, z, \mathbf{x}_{i+1}, ..., \mathbf{x}_n \rangle \mid \mathbf{x} \in X, z \in \mathbb{R}\}$. This can be viewed as an instance of a more general function $\mathbf{forget}(\mathbf{v}) : \wp(\mathbb{R}^n) \to \wp(\mathbb{R}^n)$ indexed by a vector $\mathbf{v} \in \mathbb{R}^n$ and defined by $\mathbf{forget}(\mathbf{v})(X) \triangleq \{\mathbf{x} + z\mathbf{v} \mid \mathbf{x} \in X, z \in \mathbb{R}\}$. Thus, it turns out that $\mathbf{forget}(i)$ can be retrieved by considering $\mathbf{v} = \mathbf{e_i}$, that is, $\mathbf{forget}(i) = \mathbf{forget}(\mathbf{e_i})$.

The most general form of Boolean test considers any predicate $p : \mathbb{R}^n \to \{\mathsf{t}, \mathsf{f}\}$ and selects those program states that make the predicate p true. This is modeled by a transfer function $\mathbf{test}(p) : \wp(\mathbb{R}^n) \to \wp(\mathbb{R}^n)$ defined by $\mathbf{test}(p)(X) \triangleq X \cap \{\mathbf{x} \in \mathbb{R}^n \mid p(\mathbf{x}) = \mathsf{t}\}$. A linear Boolean test is defined by a matrix $N \in \mathbb{R}^{m \times n}$, a vector $\mathbf{b} \in \mathbb{R}^m$ and some comparison relation $\bowtie \subseteq \mathbb{R}^m \times \mathbb{R}^m$, here used in infix notation, which define a transfer function $\mathbf{test}(N, \mathbf{b}, \bowtie) : \wp(\mathbb{R}^n) \to \wp(\mathbb{R}^n)$ as follows: $\mathbf{test}(N, \mathbf{b}, \bowtie)(X) \triangleq X \cap \{\mathbf{x} \in \mathbb{R}^n \mid N\mathbf{x} \bowtie \mathbf{b}\}$. As a particular case, we have that if $\mathbf{a} \in \mathbb{R}^n$ and $b \in \mathbb{R}$ then $\mathbf{test}(\mathbf{a}, b, \bowtie)(X) \triangleq X \cap \{\mathbf{x} \in \mathbb{R}^n \mid \mathbf{a} \cdot \mathbf{x} \bowtie b\}$.

Linear Transforms. Let us consider how abstract operations can be defined on a linear transform of a numerical abstract domain. Consider a numerical abstract domain $\mathcal{A} = \langle A, \leq, \gamma \rangle$, possibly endowed with an abstraction function α. Consider any concrete transfer function $f : \wp(\mathbb{R}^n) \to \wp(\mathbb{R}^n)$ and a corresponding abstract transfer function $f^\sharp : A \to A$, which may be sound, bca, b-/f-complete w.r.t. f. The following result provides a precise guideline in order to design an abstract transfer function on a transformed domain $\mathcal{A}^M$, with $M \in \mathrm{GL}(n)$.

Lemma 4.1. $f^\sharp : A \to A$ *is sound (bca, b-complete, f-complete) w.r.t.* f *for the abstract domain* $\mathcal{A}^M$ *iff* $f^\sharp : A \to A$ *is sound (bca, b-complete, f-complete) w.r.t. the concrete function* $T_M \circ f \circ T_{M^{-1}} : \wp(\mathbb{R}^n) \to \wp(\mathbb{R}^n)$ *for the abstract domain* $\mathcal{A}$.

By analogy with the standard notion of matrix conjugation, the transformed concrete transfer function $T_M \circ f \circ T_{M^{-1}} : \wp(\mathbb{R}^n) \to \wp(\mathbb{R}^n)$ in Lemma 4.1 may be called M-conjugation of the original function f. Indeed, if f is a transfer function for a linear map N then its conjugation $T_M \circ f \circ T_{M^{-1}}$ involves the standard matrix conjugation of N. Lemma 4.1 allows us to design abstract transfer functions for f on the transformed abstraction $\mathcal{A}^M$ by considering the abstract transfer functions on the original abstraction $\mathcal{A}$ but w.r.t. the M-conjugation of f. Hence, if the family of abstract transfer functions handled by some numerical abstract interpretation $\mathcal{A}$ is closed under conjugation then Lemma 4.1 yields a straight and practical technique for designing a full abstract interpretation on the transformed abstraction $\mathcal{A}^M$. The following result provides the linear transformations of abstract functions for $\mathcal{A}^M$ for all the standard operators and linear transfer functions.

Theorem 4.2. *Let* $\mathcal{A} = \langle A, \leq, \gamma \rangle$ *be a numerical abstract domain, possibly with abstraction map* α*, and let* $M \in \mathrm{GL}(n)$.

(1) *Let* $\mathbf{assign}_A(N, \mathbf{b})$ *be a sound abstract transfer function in* $\mathcal{A}$ *of a linear parallel assignment* $\mathbf{assign}(N, \mathbf{b})$. *Then,* $\mathbf{assign}_A(MNM^{-1}, M\mathbf{b})$ *is the corresponding sound transfer function in* $\mathcal{A}^M$.

(2) *Let* $\mathbf{assign}^\leftarrow_A(N, \mathbf{b})$ *be a sound abstract transfer function in* $\mathcal{A}$ *of a backward linear parallel assignment* $\mathbf{assign}^\leftarrow(N, \mathbf{b})$. *Then,* $\mathbf{assign}^\leftarrow_A(MNM^{-1}, M\mathbf{b})$ *is the corresponding sound transfer function in* $\mathcal{A}^M$.

(3) *Let* $\mathbf{forget}_A(\mathbf{v})$ *be a sound abstract transfer function in* $\mathcal{A}$ *of a nondeterministic assignment* $\mathbf{forget}(\mathbf{v})$. *Then,* $\mathbf{forget}_A(M\mathbf{v})$ *is the corresponding sound transfer function in* $\mathcal{A}^M$.

(4) *Let* $\mathbf{test}_A(N, \mathbf{b}, \bowtie)$ *be a sound abstract transfer function in* $\mathcal{A}$ *of a linear Boolean* $\mathbf{test}(N, \mathbf{b}, \bowtie)$. *Then,* $\mathbf{test}_A(NM^{-1}, \mathbf{b}, \bowtie)$ *is the corresponding sound transfer function in* $\mathcal{A}^M$.

(5) *If* $\sqcup$ *and* $\sqcap$ *are sound abstract lub and glb in* $\mathcal{A}$ *then* $\sqcup$ *and* $\sqcap$ *are also sound in* $\mathcal{A}^M$.

(6) *If* ∇ *and* Δ *are correct widening and narrowing operators in* $\mathcal{A}$ *then* ∇ *and* Δ *are also widening and narrowing in* $\mathcal{A}^M$.

As an instance of Theorem 4.2 (1)–(4) to single assignments and tests, we obtain:

Corollary 4.3

(1) *Let* $\mathbf{assign}_A(i, \mathbf{a}, b)$ *be a sound abstract transfer function in* $\mathcal{A}$ *for a linear single assignment* $x_i := \mathbf{a} \cdot \mathbf{x} + b$. *Then,* $\mathbf{assign}_A(M(\mathbf{e_i}(\mathbf{a} - \mathbf{e_i})^T + I)M^{-1}, M(b\mathbf{e_i}))$ *is the corresponding sound transfer function in* $\mathcal{A}^M$.

(2) Let $\mathbf{assign}^{\leftarrow}_A(i, \mathbf{a}, b)$ be a sound abstract transfer function in $\mathcal{A}$ for a backward linear single assignment $x_i := \mathbf{a} \cdot \mathbf{x} + b$. Then, $\mathbf{assign}^{\leftarrow}_A(M(\mathbf{e_i}(\mathbf{a} - \mathbf{e_i})^T + I)M^{-1}, M(b\mathbf{e_i}))$ is the corresponding sound transfer function in $\mathcal{A}^M$.

(3) Let $\mathbf{forget}_A(i)$ be a sound abstract transfer function in $\mathcal{A}$ of a nondeterministic assignment $x_i := ?$. Then, $\mathbf{forget}_A(M\mathbf{e_i})$ is the corresponding sound transfer function in $\mathcal{A}^M$.

(4) Let $\mathbf{test}_A(\mathbf{a}, b, \bowtie)$ be a sound abstract transfer function in $\mathcal{A}$ of a linear Boolean test $\mathbf{a} \cdot \mathbf{x} \bowtie b$. Then, $\mathbf{test}_A(\mathbf{a}^T M^{-1}, b, \bowtie)$ is the corresponding sound transfer function in $\mathcal{A}^M$.

It is important to remark that since Lemma 4.1 goes beyond soundness and also holds for best correct approximations, and backward- and forward-completeness, we also obtain the following consequence of Theorem 4.2 (1)–(5).

Corollary 4.4. *In Theorem 4.2 (1)–(5) and in Corollary 4.3, sound can be replaced with bca, b-complete and f-complete.*

Hence, this allows us to retrieve as an instance to the transformed interval domain $\mathcal{Int}^M$ all the corresponding results by Amato et al. [2, Theorems 3, 4, 5 and 6] on the best correct approximations of, respectively, lub/glb, linear single assignments, nondeterministic assignments and single Boolean tests for parallelotopes. In particular, Corollary 4.3 holds for best correct approximations, so that once the abstraction $\mathcal{A}$ provides definitions of abstract tests $\mathbf{test}_A(\mathbf{a}, b, \bowtie)$ which are bca's and closed by the matrix multiplications then this same abstraction $\mathcal{A}$ also gives the corresponding bca's in $\mathcal{A}^M$, which are thus given by $\mathbf{test}_A(\mathbf{a}^T M^{-1}, b, \bowtie)$. For linear assignments, it is important to remark that the linear transform of abstract single assignments may well lead to abstract parallel assignments, as shown by the following example for the parallelotope domain.

Example 4.5. Let $M = \begin{pmatrix} 1 & -1 \\ 1 & 1 \end{pmatrix} \in GL(2)$, as considered in [2, Example 1] and obtained by composing a scaling with a Givens rotation, namely $M = D^{(\sqrt{2},\sqrt{2})}R^{1,2,\frac{\pi}{4}}$. Consider two program variables and a single assignment such as $x_1 := k$, for some constant $k \in \mathbb{R}$, whose best correct approximation for the interval domain Int for two variables is given by $\mathbf{assign}_{\mathrm{Int}}(1, (0,0), k)$. Then, by Corollary 4.4, the best correct approximation of $x_1 := k$ for the parallelotope $\mathcal{Int}^M$ is given by the parallel assignment $\mathbf{assign}_{\mathrm{Int}}(M \begin{pmatrix} 0 & 0 \\ 0 & 1 \end{pmatrix} M^{-1}, M(k,0)) = $

$\mathbf{assign}_{\mathrm{Int}}(\begin{pmatrix} 0.5 & -0.5 \\ -0.5 & 0.5 \end{pmatrix}, (k,k))$, namely it coincides with the best correct approximation in Int of the following linear parallel assignment: $[x_1 := 0.5x_1 - 0.5x_2 + k; \quad x_2 := -0.5x_1 + 0.5x_2 + k;]$.   □

5 Transforming Linear Programs

We observe that in the proof of Theorem 4.2, and in turn in Corollary 4.3, the implications from sound (bca, b-complete, f-complete) abstract transfer functions in $\mathcal{A}$ to corresponding sound (bca, b-complete, f-complete) abstract transfer functions in $\mathcal{A}^M$ are indeed *equivalences*. This is a straight consequence of Lemma 4.1, which indeed shows an equivalence between the abstract transfer functions for $\mathcal{A}$ and $\mathcal{A}^M$. Thus, since best correct approximations are always unique, as well as (backward or forward) complete abstract functions, when they exist, are unique, we obtain the following characterizations of linear single assignments and tests.

Theorem 5.1

(1) *The bca in $\mathcal{A}^M$ of a linear single assignment $x_i := \mathbf{a} \cdot \mathbf{x} + b$ coincides with the bca in $\mathcal{A}$ of the linear (possibly) parallel assignment $[\mathbf{x} := M(\mathbf{e}_i(\mathbf{a} - \mathbf{e}_i)^T + I)M^{-1}\mathbf{x} + M(b\mathbf{e}_i);]$.*

(2) *The bca in $\mathcal{A}^M$ of a linear Boolean test $\mathbf{a} \cdot \mathbf{x} \bowtie b$ coincides with the bca in $\mathcal{A}$ of the linear Boolean test $\mathbf{a}^T M^{-1}\mathbf{x} \bowtie b$.*

Moreover, both in (1) and (2), the bca in $\mathcal{A}^M$ is b-complete (f-complete) iff the bca in $\mathcal{A}$ is b-complete (f-complete), and in this case they coincide.

This means that existence of the bca in either domain $\mathcal{A}$ or $\mathcal{A}^M$ implies the existence of the bca in the other domain. This also hints that an analysis with the transformed abstraction $\mathcal{A}^M$ of a program P consisting of linear assignments and tests only can be obtained by analysing with the original abstraction $\mathcal{A}$ a program P^M which is obtained from P by transforming all its linear assignments and tests by exploiting Theorem 5.1, so as to maintain the same program points (i.e., the control flow graphs of P and P^M coincide). In particular, if the analysis in $\mathcal{A}$ of the assignments and tests occurring in the transformed program P^M relies on abstract transfer functions which are the best correct approximations in $\mathcal{A}$ then Theorem 5.1 guarantees that at each program point of P^M we obtain *exactly* the same (best) abstract value that we would have obtained at the same program point by analysing P in $\mathcal{A}^M$. Instead, if the analysis of P^M in $\mathcal{A}$ exploits some abstract transfer functions which are not bca's in $\mathcal{A}$, then we achieve abstract values for P which are still sound in $\mathcal{A}^M$, although, of course, they are not guaranteed to be the best possible abstract values in $\mathcal{A}^M$, since possible losses of precision in $\mathcal{A}$ are shifted to $\mathcal{A}^M$.

As shown in Example 4.5, it should be noted that even if P does not contain parallel assignments, the transformed program P^M may well include parallel assignments. Thus, the program analysis design in $\mathcal{A}$ should also include abstract transfer functions for parallel linear assignments. Of course, this program transformation has a cost. The computational time complexity of the transform $P \mapsto P^M$ of Theorem 5.1 is $O(n^2)$ for each linear assignment and test occurring in P, as argued in [2, Sect. 5] for the case of parallelotopes (the transforms are exactly the same). We envision that this program transform can be implemented as a preprocessing step of the analysis in $\mathcal{A}^M$. Let us consider a first example with parallelotopes.

Example 5.2 (Parallelotopes). Consider the following program P taken from [2]:

$$x_1 := 4; \ x_2 := -4;$$
$$\mathbf{while} \ (x_1 > x_2) \ \mathbf{do}$$
$$x_1 := x_1 - 1;$$
$$x_2 := x_2 + 1;$$

As argued in [2, Sect. 1] and [20], a statistical dynamic analysis such as orthogonal simple component analysis may determine that the analysis of P using the parallelotope instance Int^M may provide precise results when the matrix is $M = \begin{pmatrix} 1 & -1 \\ 1 & 1 \end{pmatrix}$, namely when M is the matrix of Example 4.5 obtained by first applying a $\frac{\pi}{4}$ clockwise rotation matrix followed by a $\sqrt{2}$ scaling for both x_1 and x_2. Let us also recall that $M^{-1} = \begin{pmatrix} 0.5 & 0.5 \\ -0.5 & 0.5 \end{pmatrix}$. Any vector $\langle x_1, x_2 \rangle \in \mathbb{R}^2$ is thus transformed into $M \begin{pmatrix} x_1 \\ x_2 \end{pmatrix} = \begin{pmatrix} x_1 - x_2 \\ x_1 + x_2 \end{pmatrix}$, namely Int^M is able to represent the program invariants: $\{l_1 \leq x_1 - x_2 \leq u_1, l_2 \leq x_1 + x_2 \leq u_2\}$, with $l_i, u_i \in \overline{\mathbb{R}}$. Conversely, any vector of intervals $\langle [l_1, u_1], [l_2, u_2] \rangle \in \mathit{Int}^M$ represents the set of stores $M^{-1} \cdot \gamma_{\mathit{Int}}(\langle [l_1, u_1], [l_2, u_2] \rangle) = \{\langle 0.5z_1 + 0.5z_2, -0.5z_1 + 0.5z_2 \rangle \in \mathbb{R}^2 \mid l_1 \leq z_1 \leq u_1, l_2 \leq z_2 \leq u_2\}$. By Theorem 5.1, P is transformed into the following program P^M, where, for the sake of clarity, we use variables y_i:

$$y_1 := 8; \ y_2 := 0;$$
$$\mathbf{while} \ (y_1 > 0) \ \mathbf{do}$$
$$y_1 := y_1 - 2;$$

This transformed program P^M is obtained as follows. The initializations $\{x_1 := 4; x_2 := -4;\}$ coincide with the parallel assignment $[\mathbf{x} := \mathbf{0}_2\mathbf{x} + \begin{pmatrix} 4 \\ -4 \end{pmatrix}]$ whose M-transform is $[\mathbf{y} := (M\mathbf{0}_2 M^{-1})\mathbf{y} + M \begin{pmatrix} 4 \\ -4 \end{pmatrix}] = [\mathbf{y} := \mathbf{0}_2\mathbf{y} + \begin{pmatrix} 8 \\ 0 \end{pmatrix}]$, namely $[y_1 := 8; \ y_2 := 0;]$. The guard $(x_1 > x_2)$ corresponds to the Boolean test $(1 \ -1)\mathbf{x} > 0$, whose M-transform is $((1 \ -1)M^{-1})\mathbf{y} > 0$, namely $(1 \ 0)\mathbf{y} > 0$, which is the guard $(y_1 > 0)$. Finally, the assignments $\{x_1 := x_1 - 1; x_2 := x_2 + 1;\}$ correspond to the parallel assignment $[\mathbf{x} = I_2\mathbf{x} + \begin{pmatrix} -1 \\ 1 \end{pmatrix}]$, which is M-transformed to $[\mathbf{y} = (MI_2 M^{-1})\mathbf{y} + M \begin{pmatrix} 1 \\ -1 \end{pmatrix}]$, that is, $[y_1 := y_1 - 2; \ y_2 := y_2;]$.

Since the interval abstraction Int provides best correct approximations for all the transfer functions of the statements occurring in the transformed program P_M, by Theorem 5.1, it turns out that the analysis of P_M using Int gives exactly the most precise program invariants for P in Int^M. The analysis of P_M using Int with widening provides $\{y_1 \leq 8, y_2 = 0\}$ as loop invariant, so that at the exit point we obtain $\{y_1 \leq 0, y_2 = 0\}$. Hence, the concrete interpretation of the output of this analysis states that at the exit point of the original program P the invariant $x_1 - x_2 \leq 0 \wedge x_1 + x_2 = 0$ holds, whose abstraction in Int is $\{x_1 \leq 0, x_2 \geq 0\}$. The analysis of P using $\mathcal{I}nt$ with widening is much less precise, since it yields the interval $\{x_1 \leq 4, x_2 \geq -4\}$ both as loop invariant and at the exit point. $\qquad\qquad\qquad\qquad\qquad\qquad\qquad\qquad\qquad\qquad\qquad\qquad\qquad\qquad$ □

In the following we consider a couple of examples different from parallelotopes, namely linear transforms of constant propagation and octagon analysis.

5.1 Linear Transform of Constant Propagation

Let us carry on Example 3.3 on the linear transform Const^S of the constant propagation domain, which is able to represent invariants of type $\{x_1 = a_1, x_1 + x_2 = a_2, x_1 + x_3 = a_3\}$, where $a_i \in \mathrm{Const}$. In order to analyze the program P in Example 3.3 using the abstraction Const^S, we compute its transform P^S by exploiting Theorem 5.1.

The initializations within the program points (1)–(2) correspond to the parallel assignment $[\mathbf{x} = \mathbf{0}_3\mathbf{x} + \begin{pmatrix} 2 \\ 3 \\ 6 \end{pmatrix}]$, whose S-transform is: $[\mathbf{y} = (S\mathbf{0}_3 S^{-1})\mathbf{y} + S\begin{pmatrix} 2 \\ 3 \\ 6 \end{pmatrix}]$, which is $[y_1 := 2; \ y_2 := 5; \ y_3 := 8;]$. The guard $(x_2 < x_3)$ corresponds to the Boolean test $(0\ 1\ -1)\mathbf{x} < 0$, which is transformed into $((0\ 1\ -1)S^{-1})\mathbf{y} < 0$, which leaves it unchanged, i.e. $(y_2 < y_3)$. The S-transforms, denoted by $\Rightarrow^S$, of the three assignments in the body of the while-loop at program points (4)–(5)–(6) are computed in Fig. 2. We obtain the following transformed program P^S:

> (1) $y_1 := 2; \ y_2 := 5 \ y_3 := 8;$ (2)
> **while** (3) $(y_2 < y_3)$ **do**
> > (4) $y_1 := y_1 - 2; \ y_2 := y_2 - 2; \ y_3 := y_3 - 2;$
> > (5) $y_3 := y_2 + y_3 - 1;$
> > (6) $y_2 := y_2 + 2;$
> **od** (7)

All the abstract transfer functions for linear assignments and tests in the constant propagation abstraction Const are best correct approximations. Hence, the optimal analysis of P with Const^S is achieved by analysing P^S with Const, where widening is obviously not needed. The analysis of P^S at program point (3) computes the invariant $\langle y_1 = \top, y_2 = 5, y_3 = 8\rangle \in \mathrm{Const}$. Thus, at the exit point (7), we obtain $\mathbf{test}_{\mathrm{Const}}(\neg(y_2 < y_3))\langle y_1 = \top, y_2 = 5, y_3 = 8\rangle = \bot_{\mathrm{Const}}$, which allows us to derive that the exit point (7) is unreachable. By contrast, constant propagation analysis of the original program P gives no information in (3), namely it computes the invariant $\langle x_1 = \top, x_2 = \top, x_3 = \top\rangle$, so that nothing can be derived at the exit point (7).

(4) $x_1 := x_1 - 2;$ $\Leftrightarrow$ $[\mathbf{x} = I_3\mathbf{x} + \begin{pmatrix} -2 \\ 0 \\ 0 \end{pmatrix}] \Rightarrow^S$

$$[\mathbf{y} = (SI_3S^{-1})\mathbf{y} + S\begin{pmatrix} -2 \\ 0 \\ 0 \end{pmatrix}] = [\mathbf{y} = I_3\mathbf{y} + \begin{pmatrix} -2 \\ -2 \\ -2 \end{pmatrix}] \Leftrightarrow$$

$$[y_1 := y_1 - 2;\ y_2 := y_2 - 2;\ y_3 := y_3 - 2;]$$

(5) $x_3 := x_1 + x_2 + x_3 - 1;$ $\Leftrightarrow$ $[\mathbf{x} = \begin{pmatrix} 1 & 0 & 0 \\ 0 & 1 & 0 \\ 1 & 1 & 1 \end{pmatrix}\mathbf{x} + \begin{pmatrix} 0 \\ 0 \\ -1 \end{pmatrix}] \Rightarrow^S$

$$[\mathbf{y} = (S\begin{pmatrix} 1 & 0 & 0 \\ 0 & 1 & 0 \\ 1 & 1 & 1 \end{pmatrix}S^{-1})\mathbf{y} + S\begin{pmatrix} 0 \\ 0 \\ -1 \end{pmatrix}] =$$

$$[\mathbf{y} = \begin{pmatrix} 1 & 0 & 0 \\ 0 & 1 & 0 \\ 0 & 1 & 1 \end{pmatrix}\mathbf{y} + \begin{pmatrix} 0 \\ 0 \\ -1 \end{pmatrix}] \Leftrightarrow$$

$$[y_1 := y_1;\ y_2 := y_2;\ y_3 := y_2 + y_3 - 1;]$$

(6) $x_2 := x_2 + 2;$ $\Leftrightarrow$ $[\mathbf{x} = I_3\mathbf{x} + \begin{pmatrix} 0 \\ 2 \\ 0 \end{pmatrix}] \Rightarrow^S$

$$[\mathbf{y} = (SI_3S^{-1})\mathbf{y} + S\begin{pmatrix} 0 \\ 2 \\ 0 \end{pmatrix}] = [\mathbf{y} = I_3\mathbf{y} + \begin{pmatrix} 0 \\ 2 \\ 0 \end{pmatrix}] \Leftrightarrow$$

$$[y_1 := y_1;\ y_2 := y_2 + 2;\ y_3 := y_3;]$$

Fig. 2. Linear transforms of assignments.

(1) $x_1 := 2;\ x_2 := 4;$
while (2) $(x_2 > 0)$ **do**
    (3) $x_1 := x_1 - 1;\ x_2 := x_2 - 2;$
od
if (4) $(x_1 > 0)$ **then** (5) $\ldots$

(1) $[y_1 := 2;\ y_2 := 2;]$
while (2) $(y_1 + y_2 > 0)$ **do**
    (3) $[y_1 := y_1 - 1;\ y_2 := y_2 - 1;]$
od
if (4) $(y_1 > 0)$ **then** (5) $\ldots$

Fig. 3. The program P, on the left, and its M-transform P^M, on the right.

5.2 Linear Transform of Octagons

Recall that the weakly-relational octagon abstract domain $\mathcal{O}ct = \langle \text{Oct}, \leq, \gamma_{\text{Oct}}, \alpha_{\text{Oct}} \rangle$ represents program invariants of type $l \leq \pm x_i \pm x_j \leq u$ and $l \leq x_i \leq u$ for $l, u \in \overline{\mathbb{R}}$ [16,17]. Assume that we want to infer that program point (5) of program P in Fig. 3 is unreachable. The analysis of P using $\mathcal{O}ct$ with its standard widening operator computes the invariant $\{x_1 \leq 2, x_2 \leq 4, x_2 - x_1 \leq 2\}$ at program point (2), so that at program point (4) we get $\{x_1 \leq 2, x_2 \leq 0, x_2 - x_1 \leq 2\}$, and, in turn, $\{0 < x_1 \leq 2, x_2 \leq 0, x_2 - x_1 \leq 2\} = \{0 < x_1 \leq 2, x_2 \leq 0\}$ at program point (5), which does not allow us to detect that (5) is an unreachable program point.

Let us consider the matrix $M = \begin{pmatrix} 1 & 0 \\ -1 & 1 \end{pmatrix} \in GL(2)$, which is the shearing matrix $Sh^{2,1,-1}$ and whose inverse is $M^{-1} = \begin{pmatrix} 1 & 0 \\ 1 & 1 \end{pmatrix}$. A vector $\langle x_1, x_2 \rangle \in \mathbb{R}^2$ is transformed into $M\begin{pmatrix} x_1 \\ x_2 \end{pmatrix} = \begin{pmatrix} x_1 \\ -x_1 + x_2 \end{pmatrix}$, so that Oct^M is able to represent the program invariants: $\{l \leq x_1 \leq u, l \leq x_2 \leq u, l \leq x_1 - x_2 \leq u, l \leq 2x_1 - x_2 \leq u\}$.

(1) $x_1 := 2; \; x_2 := 4; \quad \Leftrightarrow \quad [\mathbf{x} = 0_2\mathbf{x} + \binom{2}{4}] \; \Rightarrow^M \; [\mathbf{y} = (M0_2M^{-1})\mathbf{y} + M\binom{2}{4}] =$
$$[\mathbf{y} = 0_2\mathbf{y} + \binom{2}{2}] \; \Leftrightarrow \; [y_1 := 2; \; y_2 := 2;]$$

(2) $(x_2 > 0) \; \Leftrightarrow \; (0 \; 1)\mathbf{x} > 0 \; \Rightarrow^M \; ((0 \; 1)M^{-1})\mathbf{y} > 0 =$
$$(1 \; 1)\mathbf{y} > 0 \; \Leftrightarrow \; (y_1 + y_2 > 0)$$

(3) $x_1 := x_1 - 1; \; x_2 := x_2 - 2; \quad \Leftrightarrow \quad [\mathbf{x} = I_2\mathbf{x} + \binom{-1}{-2}] \; \Rightarrow^M \; [\mathbf{y} = (MI_3M^{-1})\mathbf{y} + M\binom{-1}{-2}] =$
$$[\mathbf{y} = I_3\mathbf{y} + \binom{-1}{-1}] \; \Leftrightarrow \; [y_1 := y_1 - 1; \; y_2 := y_2 - 1;]$$

(4) $(x_1 > 0) \; \Leftrightarrow \; (1 \; 0)\mathbf{x} > 0 \; \Rightarrow^M \; ((1 \; 0)M^{-1})\mathbf{y} > 0 =$
$$(1 \; 0)\mathbf{y} > 0 \; \Leftrightarrow \; (y_1 > 0)$$

Fig. 4. M-transform of statements occurring in P.

On the other hand, an octagon $oct \in \mathrm{Oct}^M$ represents the set of vectors $M^{-1} \cdot$ $\gamma_{\mathrm{Oct}}(oct) = \{\langle z_1, z_1 + z_2 \rangle \in \mathbb{R}^2 \mid \langle z_1, z_2 \rangle \in \gamma_{\mathrm{Oct}}(oct)\}\}$. The computations of the M-transform P^M are given in Fig. 4 by exploiting Theorem 5.1. The assignments (which are single assignments) and tests occurring in P^M are of type $y_i := u_i + k$, $(y_i + y_j \leq k)$ and $(y_i \leq k)$, and Oct provides best correct approximations for them [17, Sects. 4.4 and 4.5]. Hence, the analysis of P^M using the original octagon abstraction $\mathcal{O}ct$ with widening operator is optimal. This analysis computes the invariant $\{y_1 \leq 2, y_2 \leq 2, y_1 - y_2 = 0\}$ at program point (2), so that we obtain $\{y_1 \leq 2, y_2 \leq 2, y_1 - y_2 = 0, y_1 + y_2 \leq 0\} = \{y_1 \leq 0, y_2 \leq 0, y_1 - y_2 = 0\}$ at program point (4). Hence, this analysis infers the invariant $\{y_1 \leq 0, y_2 \leq 0, y_1 - y_2 = 0, y_1 > 0\}$ at program point (5). The reduction of this octagonal constraint shows that (5) is an unreachable program point in P_M, thus proving that (5) is an unreachable program point in the original program P.

```
(1) x₁ := 2; x₂ := 4;              (1) y₁ := 2; y₂ := 2;
while (2) (x₂ > 0) do              while (2) (y₁ + y₂ > 0) do
      (3) x₁ := x₁ - 1;                  (3) [y₁ := y₁ - 1; y₂ := y₂ + 1;]
      if (rnd > 0) x₂ := x₂ - 2;         if (rnd > 0) y₂ := y₂ - 2;
      else x₂ := x₂ - 1;                 else y₂ := y₂ - 1;
od                                 od
if (4) (x₁ > 0) then (5) ...       if (4) (y₁ > 0) then (5) ...
```

Fig. 5. The program Q, on the left, and its M-transform Q^M, on the right.

Consider now the program Q in Fig. 5, where **rnd** outputs a random value. Here again, the goal is to check that (5) is an unreachable program point. By comparison, let us first consider the analysis of Q using parallelotopes. A dynamic analysis of Q typically derives from the partial traces at program point (2) (e.g., $\langle 2, 4 \rangle \to \langle 1, 3 \rangle \to \langle 0, 2 \rangle \to \langle -1, 1 \rangle \to \langle -2, 0 \rangle; \langle 2, 4 \rangle \to \langle 1, 2 \rangle \to \langle 0, 0 \rangle; \langle 2, 4 \rangle \to \langle 1, 3 \rangle \to \langle 0, 1 \rangle \to \langle -1, 0 \rangle)$ that an analysis based on parallelotopes should represent precisely the program invariants $l \leq x_1 - x_2 \leq u$ and $l \leq 2x_1 - x_2 \leq u$, corresponding to the matrix $N = \begin{pmatrix} 1 & -1 \\ 2 & -1 \end{pmatrix} \in GL(2)$. The analysis of Q using these N-parallelotopes with widening computes the loop invariant $prl \triangleq \{-2 \leq x_1 - x_2, 2x_1 - x_2 \leq 0\}$ at program point (2). Consequently, the most precise parallelotope approximating $prl \cap \{x_2 \leq 0\}$ at program point (4) still is prl itself. In turn, at program point (5) the best possible approximation of $prl \cap \{x_1 > 0\}$ is given again by prl, and prl does not allow to infer that (5) is unreachable. By contrast, let us consider the M-transform Q^M in Fig. 5, which is obtained simply by adding the transform of $x_2 := x_2 - 1$ to the transforms in Fig. 4. The analysis of Q^M using the original octagon abstraction Oct with widening computes the invariant $\{y_1 \leq 2, y_2 \leq 2, y_1 - y_2 \leq 0\}$ at program point (2), and $\{y_1 \leq 2, y_2 \leq 2, y_1 - y_2 \leq 0, y_1 + y_2 \leq 0\}$ at program point (4). Hence, after a reduction of this latter octagon, one obtains $\{y_1 \leq 0, y_2 \leq 2, y_1 - y_2 \leq 0, y_1 + y_2 \leq 0\}$ at program point (4). In turn, $\{y_1 \leq 0, y_2 \leq 2, y_1 - y_2 \leq 0, y_1 + y_2 \leq 0\} \cap \{y_1 > 0\}$ allows us to derive that that (5) is an unreachable program point in P_M. Hence, the analysis of P with Oct^M is able to infer that the program point (5) in P is unreachable. Finally, let us observe that even the analysis of Q using M-parallelotopes, which represent invariants of type $l \leq x_1 \leq u$ and $l \leq x_2 - x_1 \leq u$, remains inconclusive: here the loop invariant computed at (2) is $\{x_1 \leq 2, x_2 - x_1 \leq 2\}$, which is also the best invariant at (4), and therefore does not allow to infer that (5) is unreachable.

6   Completeness for Linear Transforms

Let us recall [13] that if $\mathcal{A} = \langle A, \leq, \gamma, \alpha \rangle$ is a Galois Connection and an abstract function $f^\sharp : A \to A$ is f-complete or b-complete for a concrete function $f : C \to C$ then $f^\sharp = f^A$ holds, so that the property of being f- or b-complete for $f^\sharp$ actually depends on the domain A only, i.e., it is an abstract domain property. Hence, by defining the closure operator $\rho \triangleq \gamma \circ \alpha : C \to C$, which encodes an abstraction independently of the representation of its elements, an abstract domain A is defined to be f-complete for f when $\rho \circ f \circ \rho = f \circ \rho$ holds and b-complete for f when $\rho \circ f \circ \rho = \rho \circ f$ holds. It is shown in [13, Sect. 5] that any abstract domain can be refined to its so-called *complete shell* to attain b-completeness, namely, for any domain A and any set of concrete functions $F \subseteq C \to C$ there exists the least refinement $\mathrm{Shell}_F(A)$ of A which is b-complete for F, provided that C is a complete lattice and the functions in F are Scott-continuous.

The following result shows that a linear transform $M(\mathcal{A})$ is equivalent to its input abstract domain $\mathcal{A}$ exactly when $\mathcal{A}$ is backward and forward complete for the linear transformation T_M. This formalizes the intuition that in order to be beneficially used in program analysis, a linear transform $M(\mathcal{A})$ must be applied to abstractions $\mathcal{A}$ which are either backward or forward *incomplete* for M. Recall that two abstract domains $\mathcal{A}_i = \langle A_i, \leq_i, \gamma_i \rangle$, $i = 1, 2$, are equivalent, denoted by $\mathcal{A}_1 \cong \mathcal{A}_2$, when they represent the same concrete sets, i.e., when $\gamma_1(A_1) = \gamma_2(A_2)$ holds.

Theorem 6.1. *Let $\mathcal{A} = \langle A, \leq, \gamma, \alpha \rangle$ be a numerical abstract domain defined by a GC and let $M \in \mathrm{GL}(n)$. Then, $M(\mathcal{A}) \cong \mathcal{A}$ iff A is b- and f-complete for T_M.*

Let $\mathcal{K}$, $\mathcal{T}_X$ and $\mathcal{P}$ denote, respectively, the relational abstract domains of affine equalities, also called Karr's domain [14], templates for some $m \times n$ matrix X [19] and convex polyhedra [8]. As expected, it turns out that any linear transform of these numerical domains is ineffective.

Lemma 6.2. *For any $M \in \mathrm{GL}(n)$, $M(\mathcal{K}) \cong \mathcal{K}$, $M(\mathcal{T}_X) \cong \mathcal{T}_X$ and $M(\mathcal{P}) \cong \mathcal{P}$.*

As a consequence of Theorem 6.1 and Lemma 6.2, since both abstract domains $\mathcal{K}$ and $\mathcal{T}$ can be defined through a Galois connection (see, e.g., [18, Sect. 5]), we derive that for any $M \in \mathrm{GL}(n)$, Karr's $\mathcal{K}$ and template $\mathcal{T}$ abstract domains are backward and forward complete for T_M, as hinted by the intuition. Convex polyhedra do not have an abstraction map, so that completeness does not play a role.

Let us now focus on intervals $\mathcal{I}nt$ and octagons $\mathcal{O}ct$. Recall (see e.g. [21]) that $M \in \mathrm{GL}(n)$ is a *monomial matrix* (or generalized permutation matrix) if each row and column of M has exactly one nonzero entry and all other entries are 0. It turns out that $M \in \mathrm{GL}(n)$ is a monomial matrix if and only if M can be written as a product of an invertible diagonal matrix and a permutation matrix (i.e., each row and column has exactly one 1 and all other entries are 0). We denote by $\mathrm{Mon}(n) \subseteq \mathrm{GL}(n)$ the subset of monomial matrices, which is actually a subgroup (for matrix multiplication). It turns out that monomial matrices characterize precisely the linear transforms which are ineffective for intervals and octagons, where the intuition is that a monomial matrix represents a nonrelational linear transform.

Lemma 6.3. *Let $M \in \mathrm{GL}(n)$. If $n \geq 3$ then $M \in \mathrm{Mon}(n)$ iff $M(\mathcal{I}nt) \cong \mathcal{I}nt$ iff $M(\mathcal{O}ct) \cong \mathcal{O}ct$. If $n = 2$ then $M \in \mathrm{Mon}(n)$ iff $M(\mathcal{I}nt) \cong \mathcal{I}nt$.*

By combining Theorem 6.1 and Lemma 6.3, we derive the following noteworthy consequence: octagons cannot be obtained as a completeness shell from intervals for some family of invertible linear transforms in $\mathrm{GL}(n)$.

Theorem 6.4. *For all $n \geq 3$ and $\mathcal{T} \subseteq \{T_M \mid M \in \mathrm{GL}(n)\}$, $\mathrm{Shell}_{\mathcal{T}}(\mathrm{Int}) \not\cong \mathrm{Oct}$.*

This result is somehow against the intuition that octagons are (backward and forward) complete for $\frac{\pi}{4}$ rotations and therefore could be designed through a complete shell of intervals for this family of rotations. Instead, this intuition holds just in 2D, namely for two variables only.

Lemma 6.5. *Let $\mathcal{R}_{1,2,\frac{\pi}{4}} : \wp(\mathbb{R}^2) \to \wp(\mathbb{R}^2)$ be transformation function for the $\frac{\pi}{4}$ rotation matrix in $\mathrm{GL}(2)$. Then, $\mathrm{Shell}_{\mathcal{R}_{1,2,\frac{\pi}{4}}}(\mathrm{Int}) \cong \mathrm{Oct}$.*

While octagons cannot be obtained from intervals through a complete shell for $\frac{\pi}{4}$ rotations when $n \geq 3$, they can still be synthesized through a suitable reduced (or Cartesian) product [7], here denoted by Π and $\sqcap$, of $\frac{\pi}{4}$ rotations of intervals.

Lemma 6.6. *For all* $n \geq 3$, $\mathcal{O}ct \cong \Pi^n_{i,j=1,i<j} R^{i,j,\frac{\pi}{4}}(\mathcal{I}nt)$. *Furthermore,* $\mathcal{O}ct \cong \Pi^n_{i,j=1,i<j} \left(Sh^{i,j,1}(\mathcal{I}nt) \sqcap Sh^{i,j,-1}(\mathcal{I}nt)\right)$.

The intuition is quite simple. Octagons can be viewed as the product of all the $\frac{\pi}{4}$ rotational transforms of intervals because any such transform $R^{i,j,\frac{\pi}{4}}(\mathcal{I}nt)$, with $i < j$, is able to represent the program invariants $l \leq x_i + x_j \leq u$, $l \leq x_i - x_j \leq u$ and $l \leq x_k \leq u$, for any $k \in [1, n] \setminus \{i, j\}$, so that their reduced product precisely expresses all the octagonal constraints in Oct. Similarly, a reduced product $Sh^{i,j,1}(\mathcal{I}nt) \sqcap Sh^{i,j,-1}(\mathcal{I}nt)$ of two shearing transforms represents $l \leq x_i + x_j \leq u$, $l \leq x_i - x_j \leq u$ and $l \leq x_k \leq u$, for any $k \neq i$, so that their reduced product still gets back all the octagons.

7   Further Work

We have shown how the idea behind the definition of the abstract domain of parallelotopes can be generalized and pushed forward to the class of numerical abstract domains which are not complete for invertible linear transforms. We proved how linear transforms of abstract domains closely correspond to linear transforms of programs, since the analysis of a program P on a linearly transformed domain $M(\mathcal{A})$ can be designed as the analysis of a linearly transformed program $M(P)$ on the original abstract domain $\mathcal{A}$.

As argued in [1,2] for parallelotopes, a good linear transformation matrix M to be used for analyzing a program P with an abstraction $\mathcal{A}$ can be derived by resorting to some statistical technique applied to the data obtained by a dynamic analysis of P. This approach appears to be promising for parallelotopes [2] and therefore it is worth to pursue an investigation of it for linear transforms of octagons by exploiting the general framework of this article. In particular, this would be appealing since octagons have a cubic time complexity, while the cost of applying a linear transform to octagons is quadratic for any assignment and Boolean test occurring in the program to analyze. Moreover, one could also investigate how to adapt and generalize the dynamic approach studied in [3,4] where the linear transform M is part of the abstract value and therefore may be changed by the abstract transfer functions during the analysis of a program. Finally, let us observe that a broad perspective of our analysis technique with a linearly transformed abstraction $M(\mathcal{A})$ is that in order to analyze a program P with some abstraction $\mathcal{A}$, P is first transformed into P', then P' is analyzed with a different but related abstraction $\mathcal{A}'$, and the output of this latter analysis is projected back into $\mathcal{A}$ for the program P. In a sense, this can be seen as a proof-of-concept of a more general problem in program analysis. It is known that the precision of program analyses is an extensional property (analogously to computational complexity of programs), namely the precision of an analysis of P depends upon the way the code of P is written. The possibility of increasing or reducing the precision of the analysis of a program P by transforming the code of P has not been investigated and our transformational approach can be viewed as a step towards this goal.

Acknowledgments.. We are grateful to the anonymous referees for their helpful remarks. The doctoral fellowship of Marco Zanella is funded by Fondazione Bruno Kessler (FBK), Trento, Italy.

References

1. Amato, G., Parton, M., Scozzari, F.: Deriving numerical abstract domains via principal component analysis. In: Cousot, R., Martel, M. (eds.) SAS 2010. LNCS, vol. 6337, pp. 134–150. Springer, Heidelberg (2010). https://doi.org/10.1007/978-3-642-15769-1_9

2. Amato, G., Parton, M., Scozzari, F.: Discovering invariants via simple component analysis. J. Symb. Comput. **47**, 1533–1560 (2012)

3. Amato, G., Rubino, M., Scozzari, F.: Inferring linear invariants with parallelotopes. Sci. Comput. Program. **148**, 161–188 (2017)

4. Amato, G., Scozzari, F.: The abstract domain of parallelotopes. In: Proceedings of 4th International Workshop on Numerical and Symbolic Abstract Domains (NSAD 2012) (2012). ENTCS **287**, 17–28

5. Bourdoncle, F.: Abstract debugging of higher-order imperative languages. In: Proceedings ACM Internationl Conference on Programming Languages Design and Implementation (PLDI 1993), pp. 46–55. ACM Press (1993)

6. Cousot, P., Cousot, R.: Abstract interpretation: a unified lattice model for static analysis of programs by construction or approximation of fixed points. In: Proceedings of the 4th ACM Symposium on Principles of Programming Languages (POPL 1977), pp. 238–252. ACM Press (1977)

7. Cousot, P., Cousot, R.: Systematic design of program analysis frameworks. In: Proceedings of the 6th ACM SIGACT-SIGPLAN Symposium on Principles of programming languages, pp. 269–282. ACM (1979)

8. Cousot, P., Halbwachs, N.: Automatic discovery of linear restraints among variables of a program. In: Proceedings of the 5th ACM Symposium on Principles of Programming Languages (POPL 1978), pp. 84–97. ACM (1978)

9. Filé, G., Giacobazzi, R., Ranzato, F.: A unifying view of abstract domain design. ACM Comput. Surv. **28**(2), 333–336 (1996)

10. Filé, G., Ranzato, F.: The powerset operator on abstract interpretations. Theor. Comput. Sci. **222**(1), 77–111 (1999)

11. Giacobazzi, R., Ranzato, F.: Refining and compressing abstract domains. In: Degano, P., Gorrieri, R., Marchetti-Spaccamela, A. (eds.) ICALP 1997. LNCS, vol. 1256, pp. 771–781. Springer, Heidelberg (1997). https://doi.org/10.1007/3-540-63165-8_230

12. Giacobazzi, R., Ranzato, F.: The reduced relative power operation on abstract domains. Theor. Comput. Sci. **216**(1–2), 159–211 (1999)

13. Giacobazzi, R., Ranzato, F., Scozzari, F.: Making abstract interpretations complete. J. ACM **47**(2), 361–416 (2000)

14. Karr, M.: Affine relationships among variables of a program. Acta Informatica **6**, 133–151 (1976)

15. Kildall, G.A.: A unified approach to global program optimization. In: Proceedings of the 1st ACM Symposium on Principles of Programming Languages (POPL 1973), pp. 194–206. ACM (1973)

16. Miné, A.: Weakly relational numerical abstract domains. Ph.D. thesis, École Normale Supérieure, Paris, France (2004)

17. Miné, A.: The octagon abstract domain. High. Order Symb. Comput. **19**(1), 31–100 (2006)
18. Miné, A.: Tutorial on static inference of numeric invariants by abstract interpretation. Found. Trends Program. Lang. **4**(3–4), 120–372 (2017)
19. Sankaranarayanan, S., Sipma, H.B., Manna, Z.: Scalable analysis of linear systems using mathematical programming. In: Cousot, R. (ed.) VMCAI 2005. LNCS, vol. 3385, pp. 25–41. Springer, Heidelberg (2005). https://doi.org/10.1007/978-3-540-30579-8_2
20. Seladji, Y.: Finding relevant templates via the principal component analysis. In: Bouajjani, A., Monniaux, D. (eds.) VMCAI 2017. LNCS, vol. 10145, pp. 483–499. Springer, Cham (2017). https://doi.org/10.1007/978-3-319-52234-0_26
21. Zhan, X.: Matrix Theory. American Mathematical Society, Providence (2013)

Incremental Verification Using Trace Abstraction

Bat-Chen Rothenberg[1]($\boxtimes$), Daniel Dietsch[2], and Matthias Heizmann[2]

[1] Technion - Israel Institute of Technology, Haifa, Israel
`batg@cs.technion.ac.il`
[2] University of Freiburg, Freiburg, Germany
`{dietsch,heizmann}@informatik.uni-freiburg.de`

Abstract. Despite the increasing effectiveness of model checking tools, automatically re-verifying a program whenever a new revision of it is created is often not feasible using existing tools. Incremental verification aims at facilitating this re-verification, by reusing partial results. In this paper, we propose a novel approach for incremental verification that is based on trace abstraction. Trace abstraction is an automata-based verification technique in which the program is proved correct using a sequence of automata. We present two algorithms that reuse this sequence across different revisions, one eagerly and one lazily. We demonstrate their effectiveness in an extensive experimental evaluation on a previously established benchmark set for incremental verification based on different revisions of device drivers from the Linux kernel. Our algorithm is able to achieve significant speedups on this set, compared to both stand-alone verification and previous approaches.

1 Introduction

Manual detection of bugs in software is extremely time consuming and requires expertise and close acquaintance with the code. Yet, for some applications, delivering a bug-free product is crucial. Using automated program verification tools is a useful means to ease the burden. Despite the increasing effectiveness of such tools, advancements in technology of the past decade have given rise to new challenges. Modern software consists of thousands of lines of code and is developed by dozens of developers at a time. As a result, the software update rate is extremely high and dozens or even hundreds of successive program versions (also called revisions) are created every day. Automatically re-verifying the entire program whenever a new revision is created is often not feasible using existing tools.

Incremental verification is a methodology designed to make re-verification realistic. When a program revision undergoes incremental verification, changes made from the previous revision are taken into account in an attempt to limit

---

This research was partially supported by the Technion Hiroshi Fujiwara cyber security research center and the Israel cyber bureau.

A. Podelski (Ed.): SAS 2018, LNCS 11002, pp. 364–382, 2018.
https://doi.org/10.1007/978-3-319-99725-4_22

the analysis to only the parts of the program that need to be reanalyzed. Partial verification results obtained from previous revisions can help accomplish this task and can also be used to make analysis more effective.

The development of incremental verification techniques is a long-standing research topic (e.g., see [6,8,15,19,20,22,23]). The main challenge these techniques face is deciding which information to pass on from the verification of one revision to another, and to find effective ways to reuse this information. The proposed solutions vary, based on the underlying non-incremental verification technique used. For example, the technique proposed by He, Mao, and Wang [15] is based on assume-guarantee reasoning, and thus suggests reusing contextual assumptions, whereas the technique by Sery, Fedyukovich, and Sharygina [23] is based on bounded model checking using function summaries, and thus suggests reusing these summaries.

In this paper, we propose a new technique for incremental verification, which is based on the verification method of Heizmann, Hoenicke and Podelski [16, 17]. At the basis of this verification method is the idea of looking at the basic statements of the program, i.e., its assignments and conditions, as letters of a finite alphabet. Following this point of view, the paths of the program can be seen as words over this alphabet; the program itself can be seen as a finite automaton whose states are the program locations, and whose language is a set of paths. The way the method works is by constructing an abstraction of the set of infeasible program paths, called a *trace abstraction*, which is a sequence of automata over the alphabet of statements. Our suggestion is to use this trace abstraction for incremental verification. We believe that some of its properties, which we will present in later sections, make it an ideal candidate for reuse.

The paper is organized as follows: In Sect. 2 we will provide notations and formal definitions. Then, in Sect. 3, we will briefly review the work of [16,17] on which our incremental approach is based. Next, in Sect. 4, we will present our approach, and in Sect. 5 we will discuss our implementation details, and present extensive experimental results. Finally, in Sect. 6 we will survey related work, and in Sect. 7 we will conclude.

2   Preliminaries

In this section we will present the formal setting of our work. Basic concepts from the world of verification, such as a program and program correctness, will be defined in terms of formal languages and automata.

Traces. Throughout the paper, we assume the existence of a fixed set of statements, ST. The reader should think of this set as the set of all possible statements one can compose in a given programming language. An *alphabet* is a finite non-empty subset of ST. A *trace* over the alphabet Σ, denoted π, is an arbitrary word over Σ (i.e., $\pi \in \Sigma^*$).

Programs. It is common to represent a program using its control flow graph (CFG). The set of vertices of the CFG is the set of program locations L, which contains a distinguished initial location, l_i, and a subset of distinguished error locations, L_e. Edges of the CFG are labeled with statements of the program. An edge (l_j, s, l_k) appears in the graph iff the control of the program reaches location l_j, i.e., iff it is possible to continue to location l_k if the statement s executes successfully. A trace is an *error trace* of the program if it labels a path from l_i to some error location $l_e \in L_e$ in this graph.

In our setting, we prefer to view the program as an automaton over the alphabet of statements, instead of a graph. Formally, we define a *program* $\mathcal{P}$ as an automaton $(Q, \Sigma, q_0, \delta, F)$, called a *control-flow automaton*, where:

1. Q, the (finite) set of automaton states, is the set of all program locations L.
2. Σ, the alphabet of the automaton, is the set of all statements that appear in the program. Note that this set is indeed an alphabet according to our previous definition (i.e., $\Sigma \subseteq ST$).
3. q_0, the initial state of the automaton, is the initial location l_i.
4. δ, the transition relation, is a subset of $L \times \Sigma \times L$ containing exactly those triples that are edges of the CFG.
5. F, the set of final states, is the set of error locations, L_e.

By construction, the language of this automaton, $\mathcal{L}(\mathcal{P})$, is the set of error traces of the program.

Example 1. Figure 1 presents the pseudo-code of a program $\mathcal{P}_{ex1}$, along with its control-flow automaton, $\mathcal{A}_{\mathcal{P}_{ex1}}$. The correctness of this program is specified via the assert statement at location ℓ_2: every time this location is reached, the value of the variable p must not equal 0. Thus, modeling of the assert statement is done using an edge labeled with the negation of the assertion (here, `p==0`) to a fresh error location, ℓ_e. The initial state of the automaton is the entering point of the program, ℓ_0, and the only accepting state is ℓ_e.

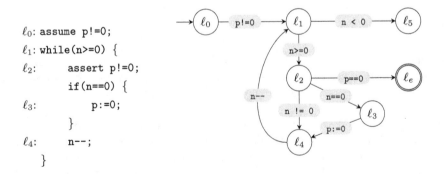

Fig. 1. Pseudo-code of a program $\mathcal{P}_{ex1}$ and its control-flow automaton $\mathcal{A}_{\mathcal{P}_{ex1}}$.

Correctness. We assume a fixed set of predicates Φ, which comes with a binary entailment relation. If the pair (φ_1, φ_2) belongs to the entailment relation, we say that φ_1 *entails* φ_2 and we write $\varphi_1 \models \varphi_2$. We also assume a fixed set HT of triples of the form $(\varphi_1, s, \varphi_2)$, where $\varphi_1, \varphi_2 \in \Phi$ and $s \in ST$. A triple $(\varphi_1, s, \varphi_2)$ is said to be a *valid Hoare triple* if it belongs to HT. In this case, we write $\{\varphi_1\}s\{\varphi_2\}$. The set of valid Hoare triples with $s \in \Sigma$ is denoted HT_Σ. Given a set $S \subseteq HT$, we denote by Φ_S the set of predicates that appear in S (i.e., all predicates that are the first or the last element of some triple in S).

Next, we extend the notion of validity from statements to traces. Given a trace $\pi = s_1 \cdots s_n$, where $n \geq 1$, the triple $(\varphi_1, \pi, \varphi_{n+1})$ is *valid* (and we write $\{\varphi_1\}\pi\{\varphi_{n+1}\}$), iff there exists a sequence of predicates $\varphi_2 \cdots \varphi_n$ s.t. $\{\varphi_i\}s_i\{\varphi_{i+1}\}$ for all $1 \leq i \leq n$. For an empty trace π (a trace of length 0), the triple (φ, π, φ') is *valid* iff φ entails φ'.

In order to define correctness, we also assume the existence of a pair of specific predicates from Φ, *true* and *false*. A trace π is *infeasible* if $\{true\}\pi\{false\}$. The set of all infeasible traces over the alphabet Σ is denoted INFEASIBLE$_\Sigma$. Finally, a program $\mathcal{P}$ is said to be *correct* if all error traces of it are infeasible. That is, if $\mathcal{L}(\mathcal{P}) \subseteq$ INFEASIBLE$_\Sigma$, where Σ is the alphabet of the program.

3   Verification Using Trace Abstraction

In this section we will review the work of [16] and [17], which presents an automata-based approach for verification, upon which our incremental verification scheme is based. Even though some of the notions had to be adapted to our setting, all relevant theorems remain valid.

3.1   Floyd-Hoare Automata

We begin by introducing the notion of a Floyd-Hoare automaton, presented in [17], and describing some of its key properties. Intuitively, a Floyd-Hoare automaton is an automaton over an alphabet Σ whose states can be mapped to predicates from Φ and whose transitions can be mapped to valid Hoare triples. The motivation behind this definition is that we want Floyd-Hoare automata to accept only infeasible traces, by construction. Formally, we use the following definition:

Definition 1 (Floyd-Hoare automaton). *A Floyd-Hoare automaton is a tuple*

$$\mathcal{A} = (Q, \Sigma, q_0, \delta, F, \theta)$$

where Q is a finite set of states, Σ is an alphabet, $q_0 \in Q$ is the initial state, $\delta \subseteq Q \times \Sigma \times Q$ is the transition relation, $F \subseteq Q$ is the set of final states, and

$\theta : Q \to \Phi$ *is a mapping from states to predicates s.t. the following conditions hold:*

1. $\theta(q_0) = true$.
2. *For every* $q \in F$, $\theta(q) = false$.
3. *For every triple* $(q_i, s, q_j) \in \delta$, $\{\theta(q_i)\}s\{\theta(q_j)\}$.

The function θ is called the *annotation* of $\mathcal{A}$. The image of θ (i.e., the set of all predicates $\varphi \in \Phi$ s.t. there exists a $q \in Q$ for which $\theta(q) = \varphi$) is called the *predicate set* of $\mathcal{A}$ and is denoted $\Phi_{\mathcal{A}}$.

Theorem 1 (*[17, p. 12]*). *Every trace accepted by a Floyd-Hoare automaton $\mathcal{A}$ is infeasible. That is, for every Floyd-Hoare automaton $\mathcal{A}$ over Σ,*

$$L(\mathcal{A}) \subseteq \text{INFEASIBLE}_{\Sigma}$$

In what follows, we define a mapping from Floyd-Hoare automata to sets of valid Hoare triples, and vice versa, using a pair of functions, α and β. The function α is a function from sets of valid Hoare triples to Floyd-Hoare automata. A set S of valid Hoare triples over Σ is mapped by α to the Floyd-Hoare automaton $\mathcal{A}_S = (Q_S, \Sigma, q_{0S}, \delta_S, F_S, \theta_S)$ where:

- $Q_S = \{q_\varphi | \varphi \in \Phi_S\} \cup \{q_{true}, q_{false}\}$.
- $q_{0S} = q_{true}$
- $\delta_S = \{(q_{\varphi_1}, s, q_{\varphi_2}) | (\varphi_1, s, \varphi_2) \in S\}$
- $F_S = \{q_{false}\}$
- $\forall q_\varphi \in Q_S \quad \theta_S(q_\varphi) = \varphi$.

Note that this is indeed a Floyd-Hoare automaton according to Definition 1, since S contains only valid Hoare triples.

The function β is a function from Floyd-Hoare automata to sets of valid Hoare triples. Given a Floyd-Hoare automaton $\mathcal{A} = (Q, \Sigma, q_0, \delta, F, \theta)$, β maps $\mathcal{A}$ to the set $\{(\theta(q_i), s, \theta(q_j)) | (q_i, s, q_j) \in \delta\}$. By Definition 1 (specifically, by requirement number 1 of θ), this set contains only valid Hoare triples.

3.2 Automata-Based Verification

Next, we describe how Floyd-Hoare automata can be used to verify programs via trace abstraction [16]. Formally, a *trace abstraction* is a tuple of Floyd-Hoare automata $(\mathcal{A}_1, \dots, \mathcal{A}_n)$ over the same alphabet Σ. The alphabet Σ is referred to as *the alphabet of the trace abstraction*. We say that a program $\mathcal{P}$ *is covered by* $(\mathcal{A}_1, \dots, \mathcal{A}_n)$ if $\mathcal{P}$ and $(\mathcal{A}_1, \dots, \mathcal{A}_n)$ are over the same alphabet and $\mathcal{L}(\mathcal{P}) \subseteq \mathcal{L}(\mathcal{A}_1) \cup \dots \cup \mathcal{L}(\mathcal{A}_n)$.

Theorem 2 (*[16, p. 7]*). *Given a program $\mathcal{P}$, if there exists a trace abstraction $(\mathcal{A}_1, \dots, \mathcal{A}_n)$ s.t. $\mathcal{P}$ is covered by $(\mathcal{A}_1, \dots, \mathcal{A}_n)$, then $\mathcal{P}$ is correct.*

Theorem 2 implies a way to verify a program $\mathcal{P}$, namely, by constructing a trace abstraction $(\mathcal{A}_1, \ldots, \mathcal{A}_n)$ s.t. $\mathcal{P}$ is covered by $(\mathcal{A}_1, \ldots, \mathcal{A}_n)$. This is realized in [16] in an algorithm that is based on the counter-example guided abstraction refinement (CEGAR) paradigm (Fig. 2). Initially, the trace abstraction is an empty sequence of automata, and then it is iteratively refined by adding automata, until the program is covered by the trace abstraction

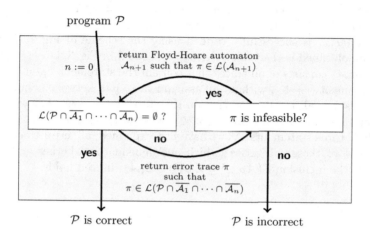

Fig. 2. [16] CEGAR-based scheme for non-incremental verification using trace abstraction.

Each iteration consists of two phases: validation and refinement. During the validation phase, we check whether the equation $\mathcal{L}(\mathcal{P} \cap \overline{\mathcal{A}_1} \cap \cdots \cap \overline{\mathcal{A}_n}) = \emptyset$ holds. The overline notation stands for computing automata complementation and the $\cap$ notation stands for computing automata intersection. Note that complementation, intersection and emptiness checking, can all be done efficiently for finite automata. Checking whether this equation holds is semantically equivalent to checking whether $\mathcal{L}(\mathcal{P}) \subseteq \mathcal{L}(\mathcal{A}_1) \cup \ldots \cup \mathcal{L}(\mathcal{A}_n)$, so if the answer is "yes", we can state that the program is correct (Theorem 2). If the answer is "no", then we get a witness in the form of a trace π s.t. $\pi \in \mathcal{L}(\mathcal{P} \cap \overline{\mathcal{A}_1} \cap \cdots \cap \overline{\mathcal{A}_n})$, which is passed on to the refinement phase.

During the refinement phase, π is semantically analyzed to decide whether it is infeasible or not. If it is not, we can state that the program is incorrect, since π is a feasible error trace of $\mathcal{P}$, i.e., an execution of $\mathcal{P}$ that leads to an error. If it is, then the proof of its infeasibility can be used to construct a Floyd-Hoare automaton $\mathcal{A}_{n+1}$ that accepts π (in particular, the way this is done in [17], is by obtaining a set of valid Hoare triples from the proof and applying α on it). This automaton is then added to the produced trace abstraction, and the process is repeated.

Example 2. Recall program P_{ex1} from Fig. 1. We claim that an assertion violation is not possible in this program. A convincing argument for this claim can be
made by considering separately those executions that visit ℓ_3 at least once and
those who do not. For the later, p is never assigned during the execution, and
the assume statement makes sure that initially p does not equal 0, so every time
the assertion is reached the condition p!=0 must hold. For the former, since ℓ_3
is reached, the true branch of the if statement was taken during that iteration,
so n equals 0 at ℓ_4. Therefore, after the execution of n--, n will equal -1, and
thus the loop will be exited and the assertion will not be reached.

Program P_{ex1} is successfully verified using the scheme of Fig. 2. The trace
abstraction obtained is the tuple $(\mathcal{A}_1, \mathcal{A}_2)$, presented in Fig. 3. Observe that the
language of $\mathcal{A}_1$ consists of all traces that contain the statement p!=0 followed
by the statement p==0 , without an assignment to p in between. The language
of $\mathcal{A}_2$ consists of all traces that contain the statement n==0 followed by the
statement n-- and the statement n>=0 , without an assignment to n between
any of these three statements. As we have just explained, all error traces of P_{ex1}
fall into one of these categories (which one depends on whether or not ℓ_3 is
visited), so the inclusion $\mathcal{L}(\mathcal{A}_{P_{ex1}}) \subseteq \mathcal{L}(\mathcal{A}_1) \cup \mathcal{L}(\mathcal{A}_2)$ indeed holds.

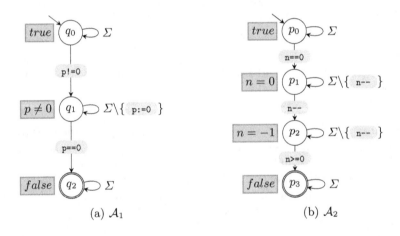

(a) $\mathcal{A}_1$ (b) $\mathcal{A}_2$

Fig. 3. Floyd-Hoare automata $\mathcal{A}_1$ and $\mathcal{A}_2$ with their respective accepting states q_2
and p_3. The gray frames labeling transitions represent letters from Σ, where an edge
labeled with $G \subseteq \Sigma$ means a transition reading any letter from G. The green frames
labeling states represent predicates assigned to states by the annotation θ.

4   Incremental Verification Using Trace Abstraction

In the previous section we saw a CEGAR-based algorithm for verification that
constructed a new trace abstraction. In this section, we show how incremental
verification can be done by reusing a given trace abstraction. For this incremental setting, in addition to the program $\mathcal{P}$, the algorithm also gets as input a trace

abstraction TA^R, which we call the *reused trace abstraction*. We call the trace abstraction TA^C that is constructed by the algorithm the *current trace abstraction*. In addition to the verification result, the algorithm also returns TA^C which might be reused in subsequent verification tasks. The alphabet of the TA^R, which we call *reused alphabet* and denote by Σ^R, may be different from the alphabet of the program $\mathcal{P}$. We call the alphabet of the program *current alphabet* and denote it by Σ^C. While there is no restriction on the reused alphabet Σ^R, the performance of the algorithm is expected to improve the more similar it is to the current alphabet Σ^C (i.e., the larger the set $\Sigma^R \cap \Sigma^C$ is).

4.1   Translation of Floyd-Hoare Automata

The rationale for reusing a trace abstraction TA^R is that each Floyd-Hoare automaton in it forms a proof that the set of traces it accepts is infeasible (see Theorem 1), and therefore we do not need to analyze any trace in this set. The organization of the information in the form of an automaton, gives us a convenient way to get rid of all error traces of $\mathcal{P}$ that belong to this set: simply by subtracting the automaton from the program (which is also an automaton). Still, the above subtraction can not be done straight away, since the program $\mathcal{P}$ and the reused trace abstraction TA^R are not necessarily over the same alphabet.

Traces of the reused trace abstraction TA^R that contain statements that are not from the current alphabet Σ^C are definitely not error traces of our program and hence rather useless for us. Therefore, we would like to "translate" the reused trace abstraction from the reused Σ^R to the current alphabet Σ^C. We first define our notion of such a "translation" for valid Hoare triples and lift the translation to Floyd-Hoare automaton afterwards.

Definition 2 (Translation of a set of valid Hoare triples). *Given a set of valid Hoare triples $S_{\Sigma^R} \subseteq HT_{\Sigma^R}$ over the reused alphabet, we call a set of valid Hoare triples $S_{\Sigma^C} \subseteq HT_{\Sigma^C}$ over the current alphabet a* translation *of S_{Σ^R} to the current alphabet Σ^C, if all valid Hoare triples in S_{Σ^R} are also in S_{Σ^C}. In other words, $S_{\Sigma^C} \subseteq HT_{\Sigma^C}$ is a translation if the following inclusion holds.*

$$S_{\Sigma^R} \cap HT_{\Sigma^R \cap \Sigma^C} \subseteq S_{\Sigma^C}$$

In order to lift our notion of "translation" to Floyd-Hoare automata we use function β which was defined in the previous chapter and maps a Floyd-Hoare automata to a set of valid Hoare triples.

Definition 3 (Translation of a Floyd-Hoare automaton). *Given a Floyd-Hoare automaton A_{Σ^R} over the reused alphabet Σ^R, we call a Floyd-Hoare automaton A_{Σ^C} over the alphabet Σ^C a* translation *of A_{Σ^R} to Σ^C, if the set of valid Hoare triples $\beta(A_{\Sigma^C})$ is a translation of $\beta(A_{\Sigma^R})$ to Σ^C.*

Given a Floyd-Hoare automaton A_{Σ^R} over the reused alphabet Σ^R and a set S_{Σ^C} of valid Hoare triples over the current alphabet Σ^C, we use the procedure depicted in Fig. 4 to translate A_{Σ^R} to a Floyd-Hoare automaton A_{Σ^C} over the current alphabet Σ^C.

Input: A Floyd-Hoare automaton A_{Σ^R} over Σ^R and
a set of valid Hoare triples $S_{\Sigma^C} \subseteq HT_{\Sigma^C}$
Output: A Floyd-Hoare automaton A_{Σ^C} over Σ^C

1. Construct the set of valid Hoare triples $S_1 = \beta(A_{\Sigma^R})$.
2. Construct the set of valid Hoare triples $S_2 = (S_1 \setminus HT_{\Sigma^R \setminus \Sigma^C}) \cup S_{\Sigma^C}$.
3. Return the Floyd-Hoare automaton $A_{\Sigma^C} = \alpha(S_2)$.

Fig. 4. Procedure TRANSLATEAUTOMATON.

Proposition 1. *Every Floyd-Hoare automaton A_{Σ^C} that is constructed using the procedure* TRANSLATEAUTOMATON, *is a translation of the reused Floyd-Hoare automaton A_{Σ^R} to the current alphabet Σ^C.*

Proof. Since all valid Hoare triples removed from S_1 when creating S_2 were over $\Sigma^R \setminus \Sigma^C$, then $S_1 \cap HT_{\Sigma^R \cap \Sigma^C} \subseteq S_2$. Therefore, by Definition 2, S_2 is a translation of S_1 to Σ^C. Now, $S_1 = \beta(A_{\Sigma^R})$, so we conclude that S_2 is a translation of $\beta(A_{\Sigma^R})$ to Σ^C. Next, we want to claim that $\beta(A_{\Sigma^C}) = S_2$. This is correct because, according to the definitions of β and α, for every set S, $\beta(\alpha(S)) = S$, so in particular $\beta(\alpha(S_2)) = S_2$. Thus, we conclude that $\beta(A_{\Sigma^C})$ is a translation of $\beta(A_{\Sigma^R})$ to Σ^C. By Definition 3, this means that A_{Σ^C} is a translation of A_{Σ^R} to Σ^C.   □

The procedure TRANSLATEAUTOMATON enables us to translate the reused trace abstraction TA^R into the alphabet of the program, but the question that remains is the choice of S_{Σ^C}. I.e., the question how many and which valid Hoare triples we should add in addition to the valid Hoare triples that are obtained from TA^R. The set S_{Σ^C} can be any subset of HT_{Σ^C} and obviously the larger S_{Σ^C} is, the more error traces of $\mathcal{P}$ (and other programs that occur in subsequent verification tasks) are proven infeasible.

We note that we do not only have the costs for the construction S_{Σ^C} itself. If S_{Σ^C} is larger, the automaton A_{Σ^C} will have more transitions and the costs for automata operations (e.g., complementation and intersection) and translations in future verification tasks will be higher.

Thus, the choice of S_{Σ^C} is a trade-off between how much effort we are willing to spend on building the translated automata and using them, and how useful they will be for proving the new program correct.

In our implementation we considered the following three options for S_{Σ^C}:

$$S_{\Sigma^C}^{\text{empty}} = \emptyset$$
$$S_{\Sigma^C}^{\text{unseen}} = \{\{\varphi_1\}s\{\varphi_2\} \mid s \in \Sigma^C \setminus \Sigma^R, \; \varphi_1, \varphi_2 \in \Phi_{A_{\Sigma^R}}\} \tag{1}$$
$$S_{\Sigma^C}^{\text{all}} = \{\{\varphi_1\}s\{\varphi_2\} \mid s \in \Sigma^C, \; \varphi_1, \varphi_2 \in \Phi_{A_{\Sigma^R}}\}$$

Note that all three sets are indeed subsets of HT_{Σ^C}, and all of them only use predicates from $\Phi_{A_{\Sigma^R}}$. As a result, the procedure TRANSLATEAUTOMATON with either of these sets as S_{Σ^C} yields an Floyd-Hoare automaton A_{Σ^C} whose states were also states of the input A_{Σ^R} (i.e., states are only removed and not added). Also, in all three cases, transitions with irrelevant letters (i.e., letters in $\Sigma^R \setminus \Sigma^C$) are removed, while transitions with relevant letters (i.e., letters in Σ^C) remain.

The difference between the three options for S_{Σ^C} lies in the transitions that are added to A_{Σ^R}. In the case of $S_{\Sigma^C}^{empty}$, no transitions are added at all. In this case, translated automata are only useful to prove infeasibility of error traces that remained unchanged from the previous version of the program $\mathcal{P}$, but we do not have any costs for the construction of S_{Σ^C}. On the other end of the spectrum there is $S_{\Sigma^C}^{all}$, in which all valid Hoare triples over Σ^C are added as transitions to A_{Σ^C}. Here, any error trace that can be proved infeasible using predicates from $\Phi_{A_{\Sigma^R}}$ will be accepted by A_{Σ^C}. However, in this case the construction of S_{Σ^C} is expensive and the resulting automata are often rather large.

The option $S_{\Sigma^C}^{unseen}$ suggests an intermediate solution, by considering only valid Hoare triples over the difference $\Sigma^C \setminus \Sigma^R$. The rationale is that most valid Hoare triples over the intersection $\Sigma^C \cap \Sigma^R$ that are relevant to prove infeasibility of error traces were already added when the reused Floyd-Hoare automaton A_{Σ^R} was constructed. In pracitice, there are only error traces whose infeasibility can be shown with option $S_{\Sigma^C}^{all}$ but not with option $S_{\Sigma^C}^{unseen}$ if statements in the program $\mathcal{P}$ have been reordered or existing statements were also added at other positions of the program.

We have performed experiments with all three of these options. The set that gave the best overall results on average, was $S_{\Sigma^C}^{all}$ and hence we used as $S_{\Sigma^C} := S_{\Sigma^C}^{all}$ in our experimental evaluation (see Sect. 5.1). The fact that $S_{\Sigma^C}^{all}$ outperforms $S_{\Sigma^C}^{unseen}$ suggests, perhaps, that changes such as reordering code and adding preexisting code (i.e., copy-pasting), on which $S_{\Sigma^C}^{unseen}$ has bad results, are frequent in software evolution.

4.2   Reuse Algorithms

We now present two schemes for incremental verification, that differ in the strategy they use for subtraction of Floyd-Hoare automata from the program. In both schemes, any subtraction $\mathcal{P} - \mathcal{A}$ is replaced with $\mathcal{P} \cap \overline{\mathcal{A}}$, which results in the same language but uses different automata operations that more faithfully represent our implementation.

Eager Reuse. The first scheme, presented in Fig. 5, suggests an eager approach for the reuse of Floyd-Hoare automata. Here, subtraction of Floyd-Hoare automata is done straight away, and entirely (all Floyd-Hoare automata in the trace abstraction are subtracted). Then, the CEGAR-based algorithm continues as in the non-incremental case. The current trace abstraction, TA^C, contains all automata translated from the reused trace abstraction TA^R along with all other automata obtained during the CEGAR loop.

An advantage of this scheme is that all traces whose infeasibility is shown by a Floyd-Hoare automaton from TA^R are excluded right at the beginning. On the other hand, we may have done some subtractions (or, in fact, intersections) that did not change the language at all and hence were not useful.

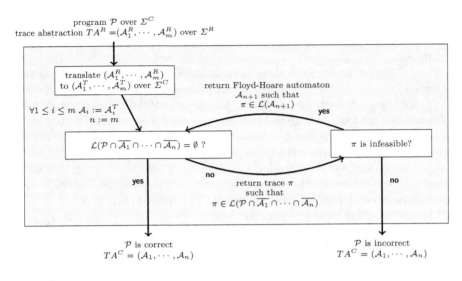

Fig. 5. Scheme for incremental verification using an **eager** approach.

For example, it is possible that for some automaton $\mathcal{A}_i^T$ translated from TA^R, $\mathcal{L}(\mathcal{P} \cap \overline{\mathcal{A}_1^T} \cap \cdots \cap \overline{\mathcal{A}_i^T}) = \mathcal{L}(\mathcal{P} \cap \overline{\mathcal{A}_1^T} \cap \cdots \cap \overline{\mathcal{A}_{i-1}^T})$ and so the computation of the intersection with $\overline{\mathcal{A}_i^T}$ was done in vain. Note that all Floyd-Hoare automata are added to TA^C, regardless of whether they were useful or not, since retrieving this information is prohibitively expensive due to technical reasons.

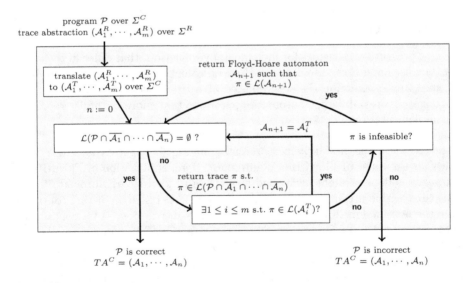

Fig. 6. Scheme for incremental verification using a **lazy** approach.

Lazy Reuse. The second scheme, presented in Fig. 6, suggests a lazy approach for the reuse of Floyd-Hoare automata. A Floyd-Hoare automaton is only subtracted once we know that it is useful, i.e., that its subtraction will remove at least one trace from the set of traces we have not yet proven infeasible.

In this scheme, the current trace abstraction is initially the empty sequence, as in the non-incremental case. Then the CEGAR loop begins, but with an additional phase, which we call the *reuse phase*, inserted between the validation and refinement phases (which themselves are not changed). If the validation phase finds a trace π in $\mathcal{L}(\mathcal{P} \cap \overline{\mathcal{A}_1} \cap \cdots \cap \overline{\mathcal{A}_n})$, then the reuse phase first checks whether this trace is accepted by some automaton $\mathcal{A}_i^T$ which was translated from the reused TA^R. If it is, then $\mathcal{A}_i^T$ is added to the current trace abstraction and we return to the validation phase again. If it is not, then we pass π to the refinement phase and proceed as before. The current trace abstraction in this case includes only those automata translated from the reused TA^R that were added to it during the reuse phase, in addition to all those created during the refinement phase.

Example 3. Figure 7 presents the source code and the control-flow automaton of a program P_{ex2}. This program is an updated version of P_{ex1} (see Fig. 1), where instead of assuming that p is initially different than 0, the variables n is set to -2 if p equals 0. The alphabet Σ^C of the control-flow automaton $\mathcal{A}_{P_{ex2}}$ is the set of P_{ex2}'s statements (i.e., $\Sigma^C = \Sigma^R \cup \{\ \texttt{n:=-2}\ \}$, where the reused alphabet Σ^R is the alphabet of $\mathcal{A}_{P_{ex1}}$).

You will notice that despite the changes made, the assertion still can not be violated. For executions who visit ℓ_4 (formerly ℓ_3) at least once, we can make the same argument as we did in Example 2. For executions who do not visit ℓ_4, the argument we used in Example 2 relied on p being initially different than 0, so now it only applies to those executions beginning in a transition from ℓ_0 to

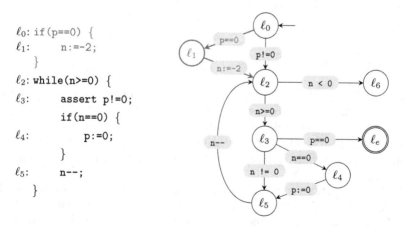

```
ℓ0: if(p==0) {
ℓ1:     n:=-2;
    }
ℓ2: while(n>=0) {
ℓ3:     assert p!=0;
        if(n==0) {
ℓ4:         p:=0;
        }
ℓ5:     n--;
    }
```

Fig. 7. Program P_{ex2}, which is a modified version of program P_{ex1}. Changes from P_{ex1} appear in red. (Color figure online)

ℓ_2. For executions going from ℓ_0 to ℓ_1, we need a new argument. For them, we can say that the visit in ℓ_1 guarantees $\mathbf{n}$ will be equal to -2 upon reaching ℓ_2, and thus the loop will not be entered and the assertion will not be reached.

Figure 8 presents the current trace abstraction $TA^C = (\mathcal{A}_1^C, \mathcal{A}_2^C, \mathcal{A}_3^C)$ produced by our algorithm, in both the Eager and the Lazy variants, when using the tuple $(\mathcal{A}_1, \mathcal{A}_2)$ from Fig. 3 as the reused trace abstraction TA^R. The first two automata, $\mathcal{A}_1^C$ and $\mathcal{A}_2^C$, are the translations of automata $\mathcal{A}_1$ and $\mathcal{A}_2$ to the current alphabet Σ^C, resp. The translation of the trace abstraction, in this case, amounts to adding transitions with the new letter, $\mathbf{n:=-2}$, where appropriate. Specifically, $\mathbf{n:=-2}$ was added to the 3 self-loops in $\mathcal{A}_1$, and to the self loops from p_0 and p_3 in $\mathcal{A}_2$. The third automaton, $\mathcal{A}_3^C$, is a new Floyd-Hoare automaton, obtained during the refinement phase.

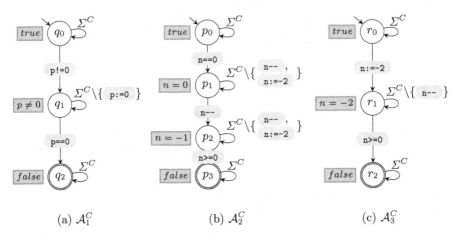

(a) $\mathcal{A}_1^C$ (b) $\mathcal{A}_2^C$ (c) $\mathcal{A}_3^C$

Fig. 8. Trace abstraction $(\mathcal{A}_1^C, \mathcal{A}_2^C, \mathcal{A}_3^C)$, which is the output of our algorithm for P_{ex2}, when using the tuple $(\mathcal{A}_1, \mathcal{A}_2)$ from Fig. 3 as TA^R.

5   Evaluation

We have implemented our incremental verification algorithms on top of the ULTIMATE AUTOMIZER software verification tool, which is part of the ULTIMATE program analysis framework[1]. The source code is available on Github[2]. We currently support incremental verification of C and Boogie programs with respect to safety properties (e.g., validity of assertions or memory-access safety).

On-the-fly Computation. For simplicity of presentation, schemes of our algorithms in Figs. 5 and 6 show a stand-alone translation phase that precedes the CEGAR loop. According to these schemes, each automaton $\mathcal{A}_j^R$ in the reused

---

[1] https://ultimate.informatik.uni-freiburg.de.
[2] https://github.com/ultimate-pa.

trace abstraction is first translated into an automaton $\mathcal{A}_j^T$ over the current alphabet Σ^C. In practice, computing $\mathcal{A}_j^T$ entirely can be quite expensive, depending on the set of valid Hoare triples S_{Σ^C}, as previously discussed. Also, the computation of many transitions may turn out to be redundant, as we may not need these transitions at any point during the CEGAR loop. Therefore, our implementation translates automata on-the-fly, adding transitions only as soon as the need for them emerges. On-the-fly translation may happen during the reuse phase in the Lazy reuse algorithm, and during the validation phase in both algorithms. Additionally, creation of Floyd-Hoare automaton $\mathcal{A}_{n+1}$ in case a trace is found infeasible during the refinement phase is already done on-the-fly in the preexisting implementation of Ultimate Automizer. That is, transitions are added to $\mathcal{A}_{n+1}$ only if they are needed during the following validation phase.

5.1   Experimental Results

We have performed an extensive experimental evaluation of our approach on a set of benchmarks previously established in [4], available on-line[3]. This benchmark set is based on industrial source code from the Linux kernel, and contains 4,193 verification tasks from 1,119 revisions of 62 device drivers. A verification task is a combination of driver name, revision number, and specification, where the specification is one of six different rules for correct Linux kernel core API usage (more details can be found in [4]). We excluded those tasks where ULTIMATE AUTOMIZER was unable to parse the input program successfully, and were left with a total of 2,660 verification tasks.

Our experiments were made on a machine with a 4 GHz CPU (Intel Core i7-6700K). We used ULTIMATE AUTOMIZER version 0.1.23-bb20188 with the default configuration, which was also used in SV-COMP'18[4], [18]. In this configuration ULTIMATE AUTOMIZER first uses SMTINTERPOL[5] with Craig interpolation for the analysis of error traces during the refinement phase, and if this fails, falls back on Z3[6] with trace interpolation [11]. Validity of Hoare triples is also checked with Z3. A timeout of 90s was set to all verification tasks and the Java heap size was limited to 6 GB.

For each verification task we verified the revision against the specification three times: first, without any reuse, and then with reuse, using both the Eager and the Lazy algorithms. The output trace abstraction of each revision was used as the input trace abstraction of the next revision. The results of these experiments are summarized in Table 1.

These results clearly show that our method, both when used with the Eager algorithm and with the Lazy one, manages to save the user a considerable amount of time, for the vast majority of these benchmarks. The difference in performance

---

[3] https://www.sosy-lab.org/research/cpa-reuse/regression-benchmarks.

[4] https://sv-comp.sosy-lab.org/2018/.

[5] https://ultimate.informatik.uni-freiburg.de/smtinterpol, version 2.1-441-gf99e49f.

[6] https://github.com/Z3Prover/z3, version master 450f3c9b.

Table 1. The results of our evaluation. Each row contains the results for a series of revisions of a driver and one type of specification. The table only shows those series where we could parse all files, allowing for a comparison in speedup with [4]. We also limited the display to the best 15 and the worst 10 series in terms of speedup. The number of tasks specifies the number of files including the first revision. The settings "Eager" and "Lazy" are divided in overall and analysis time, where analysis time is the overall time without the time it took writing the output trace abstraction to file. As the "Default" setting does not write an output trace abstraction, its analysis time is the same as its overall time. All times are given as seconds of wall time and do not include the time for the first revision. The speedup colums compare the relative speedup between the Default setting and the Lazy setting. The rows "Sum" and "Mean" show the sum and mean of all the series where we were able to parse all the tasks, whereas the rows "Sum (All)" and "Mean (All)" show the sum and the mean of all the tasks we could parse. We adjusted the mean speedup of [4] for our subset by recomputing their speedup relative to our shared subset, but their mean speedup in the "Mean (All)" row refers to the original 4,193 tasks.

Driver	Spec	Tasks	Default Overall	Eager Overall	Eager Analysis	Lazy Overall	Lazy Analysis	Speedup Overall	Speedup Analysis	[4] Speedup
dvb-usb-rtl28xxu	08_1a	10	20.509	0.352	0.187	0.416	0.257	49.30	79.80	3.6
dvb-usb-rtl28xxu	39_7a	10	110.893	4.081	1.992	4.059	2.546	27.32	43.55	6.3
dvb-usb-rtl28xxu	32_7a	10	35.551	1.306	0.725	1.550	0.844	22.93	42.12	4.9
dvb-usb-az6007	08_1a	5	4.620	0.173	0.118	0.187	0.132	24.70	35.00	3.5
dvb-usb-az6007	39_7a	5	17.952	1.378	0.862	1.425	0.989	12.59	18.15	4.9
cx231xx-dvb	08_1a	13	3.330	0.303	0.206	0.323	0.228	10.30	14.60	1.8
panasonic-laptop	08_1a	16	3.466	0.337	0.222	0.384	0.257	9.02	13.48	2.4
spcp8x5	43_1a	13	5.531	0.632	0.437	0.618	0.432	8.94	12.80	1.6
panasonic-laptop	32_1	4	0.623	0.100	0.061	0.072	0.051	8.65	12.21	3.4
panasonic-laptop	39_7a	16	18.961	2.377	1.654	2.617	1.906	7.24	9.94	3.6
leds-bd2802	68_1	4	1.039	0.180	0.112	0.191	0.123	5.43	8.44	4.4
leds-bd2802	32_1	4	0.484	0.089	0.057	0.097	0.064	4.98	7.56	3.9
wm831x-dcdc	32_1	3	0.330	0.063	0.044	0.066	0.047	5.00	7.02	2.1
cx231xx-dvb	39_7a	13	17.536	3.389	2.425	3.464	2.517	5.06	6.96	3.2
ems_usb	08_1a	21	2.334	0.502	0.327	0.543	0.362	4.29	6.44	2.9
...(for full results cf. http://batg.cswp.cs.technion.ac.il/publications/)										
ar7part	32_7a	6	0.071	0.067	0.056	0.074	0.063	0.95	1.12	1.3
metro-usb	08_1a	25	0.394	0.497	0.330	0.518	0.356	0.76	1.10	2.1
rtc-max6902	32_7a	9	0.133	0.124	0.106	0.147	0.126	0.90	1.05	1.1
i2c-algo-pca	43_1a	7	0.012	0.018	0.018	0.019	0.019	1.00	1.00	1.0
dvb-usb-vp7045	43_1a	2	0.001	0.002	0.002	0.027	0.027	1.00	1.00	2.6
cfag12864b	43_1a	2	0.036	0.039	0.036	0.040	0.037	0.90	0.97	1.0
rtc-max6902	43_1a	5	0.278	0.273	0.262	0.303	0.291	0.91	0.95	1.1
magellan	32_7a	2	0.015	0.018	0.016	0.018	0.016	0.83	0.93	0.93
vsxxxaa	43_1a	2	0.030	0.037	0.033	0.036	0.032	0.83	0.93	6.8
ar7part	43_1a	2	0.036	0.043	0.038	0.044	0.039	0.81	0.92	1.2
Sum		1,177	529.258	142.856	107.543	146.275	112.225			
Mean		13	5.881	1.587	1.195	1.625	1.247	3.618	4.716	3.17
Sum (All)		2,660	3,048.373	434.853	334.603	448.424	349.69			
Mean (All)		15	16.749	2.389	1.838	2.464	1.921	6.798	8.717	4.3

between the Eager and Lazy algorithms on these benchmarks was quite negligible; both obtain a nontrivial speedup of around ×4.7 in analysis time, and ×3.6 in overall time, on average. When comparing mean analysis speedups of our approach and that of [4], we get a speedup that is ×1.5 larger. But, what is additionally interesting to note, is that we do not succeed on the same benchmarks as [4] does; the best 15 series in our work and theirs are completely disjoint. This suggests that the two methods are orthogonal.

Slowdowns are demonstrated for our worst 7 results. On the other hand, our top 7 results all demonstrate speedups of more than an order of magnitude, with an impressive max value of ×79.80. For each pair of successive revisions, we have computed their edit-distance by summing up the number of added, modified and deleted lines, and dividing by the total number of lines in the file. To compute the edit-distance of a series, we have computed the mean edit-distance of all revisions in it. We expected to see a correlation between the edit-distance of a series and the speedup obtained for it. In general, such a correlation does seems to exist; a speedup of greater than 4 is achieved mostly for revisions where the edit distance is small. But, this correlation is not definitive. For example, we had one series where the mean edit-distance was over 90slowdowns distribute evenly over the mean edit-distance size.

6 Related Work

The validation of evolving software has been the subject of extensive research over the years (see the book by Chockler et al. [10]). Several different problems have been studied in this context, e.g., analyzing the semantic difference between successive revisions [26] or determining which revision is responsible for a bug [1,21]. In this section, we will focus on the problem of formally verifying all program revisions.

A dominant approach to solve this problem is to only verify the first revision, and then prove that every pair of successive revisions is equivalent. It was suggested by Godlin and Strichman in [24], where they gave it the name *regression verification* and introduced an algorithm that is based on the theory of uninterpreted functions. Papers about regression verification are concerned with improving equivalence checking and increasing its applicability. In [2], a summary of program behaviors impacted by the change is computed for both programs, and then equivalence is checked on summaries alone. Similarly, in [5], checking equivalence is done gradually by partitioning the common input space of programs and checking equivalence separately for each set in the partition. In [13], a reduction is made from equivalence checking to Horn constraint solving. In [25] applicability is extended to pairs of recursive functions that are not in lock-step, and in [7] to multi-threaded concurrent programs. The work of [3] is focused on Programmable Logic Controllers, which are computing devices that control production in many safety-critical systems. Finally, [27] proposes a different notion of equivalence, which on top of the usual functional equivalence also considers runtime equivalence.

Another approach towards efficiently verifying all program revisions, which is the one we follow in this paper, is to use during each revision verification partial results obtained from previous revisions, in order to limit necessary analysis. Work in this field vary based on the underlying non-incremental verification technique used, which determines what information can be reused and how efficiently so. The work we find most closely related to ours is that of Beyer et al. [4], which suggests to reuse the abstraction precision in predicate abstraction.

Other techniques for reuse of verification results include reuse of function summaries for bounded model checking [7], contextual assumptions for assume-guarantee reasoning [15], parts of a proof or counter-example obtained through ic3 [9] and inductive invariants [12]. Also, incremental techniques for runtime verification of probabilistic systems modeled as Markov decision processes are developed in [14]. For the special case of component-based systems, [19] uses algebraic representations to minimize the number of individual components that need to be reverified. Last, the tool Green [28] facilitates reuse of SMT solver results for general purposes, and authors demonstrate how this could be beneficial for incremental program analysis.

7   Conclusion

We have presented a novel automata-based approach for incremental verification. Our approach relies on the method of [16,17] which uses a trace abstraction as a proof of correctness. Our idea is to reuse a trace abstraction by first translating it to the alphabet of the program under inspection, and then subtracting its automata from the control-flow automaton. We have defined a procedure, TRANSLATEAUTOMATON, for automata translation, and two algorithms for reuse of trace abstraction that differ in their strategy for automata subtraction. We have evaluated our approach on a set of previously established benchmarks on which we get significant speedups, thus demonstrating the usefulness of trace abstraction reuse.

References

1. Adler, J., Berryhill, R., Veneris, A.: Revision debug with non-linear version history in regression verification. In: IEEE International Verification and Security Workshop (IVSW), pp. 1–6. IEEE (2016)
2. Backes, J., Person, S., Rungta, N., Tkachuk, O.: Regression verification using impact summaries. In: Bartocci, E., Ramakrishnan, C.R. (eds.) SPIN 2013. LNCS, vol. 7976, pp. 99–116. Springer, Heidelberg (2013). https://doi.org/10.1007/978-3-642-39176-7_7
3. Beckert, B., Ulbrich, M., Vogel-Heuser, B., Weigl, A.: Regression verification for programmable logic controller software. In: Butler, M., Conchon, S., Zaïdi, F. (eds.) ICFEM 2015. LNCS, vol. 9407, pp. 234–251. Springer, Cham (2015). https://doi.org/10.1007/978-3-319-25423-4_15
4. Beyer, D., Löwe, S., Novikov, E., Stahlbauer, A., Wendler, P.: Precision reuse for efficient regression verification. In: Proceedings of the 2013 9th Joint Meeting on Foundations of Software Engineering, pp. 389–399 (2013)

5. Bohme, M., Oliveira, B.C.D.S., Roychoudhury, A., Böhme, M.: Partition-based regression verification. In: Proceedings of the 2013 International Conference on Software Engineering, pp. 302–311. IEEE Press (2013)
6. Brandin, B., Malik, R., Dietrich, P.: Incremental system verification and synthesis of minimally restrictive behaviours. In: Proceedings of the 2000 American Control Conference, vol. 6, pp. 4056–4061. IEEE (2000)
7. Chaki, S., Gurfinkel, A., Strichman, O.: Regression verification for multi-threaded programs. In: Kuncak, V., Rybalchenko, A. (eds.) VMCAI 2012. LNCS, vol. 7148, pp. 119–135. Springer, Heidelberg (2012). https://doi.org/10.1007/978-3-642-27940-9_9
8. Chang, K.-H., Papa, D.A., Markov, I.L., Bertacco, V.: InVerS: an incremental verification system with circuit similarity metrics and error visualization. In: 2007 8th International Symposium on Quality Electronic Design, ISQED 2007, pp. 487–494. IEEE (2007)
9. Chockler, H., Ivrii, A., Matsliah, A., Moran, S., Nevo, Z.: Incremental formal verification of hardware. In: Proceedings of the International Conference on Formal Methods in Computer-Aided Design, pp. 135–143. FMCAD Inc. (2011)
10. Chockler, H., Kroening, D., Mariani, L., Sharygina, N.: Validation of Evolving Software. Springer, Heidelberg (2015)
11. Dietsch, D., Heizmann, M., Musa, B., Nutz, A., Podelski, A.: Craig vs. Newton in software model checking. In: ESEC/FSE 2017, pp. 487–497 (2017)
12. Fedyukovich, G., Gurfinkel, A., Sharygina, N.: Incremental verification of compiler optimizations. In: NASA Formal Methods, pp. 300–306 (2014)
13. Felsing, D., Grebing, S., Klebanov, V., Rümmer, P., Ulbrich, M.: Automating regression verification. In: 29th IEEE/ACM International Conference on Automated Software Engineering, ASE 2014, pp. 349–360 (2014)
14. Forejt, V., Kwiatkowska, M., Parker, D., Qu, H., Ujma, M.: Incremental runtime verification of probabilistic systems. In: Qadeer, S., Tasiran, S. (eds.) RV 2012. LNCS, vol. 7687, pp. 314–319. Springer, Heidelberg (2013). https://doi.org/10.1007/978-3-642-35632-2_30
15. He, F., Mao, S., Wang, B.-Y.: Learning-based assume-guarantee regression verification. In: Chaudhuri, S., Farzan, A. (eds.) CAV 2016. LNCS, vol. 9779, pp. 310–328. Springer, Cham (2016). https://doi.org/10.1007/978-3-319-41528-4_17
16. Heizmann, M., Hoenicke, J., Podelski, A.: Refinement of trace abstraction. In: Palsberg, J., Su, Z. (eds.) SAS 2009. LNCS, vol. 5673, pp. 69–85. Springer, Heidelberg (2009). https://doi.org/10.1007/978-3-642-03237-0_7
17. Heizmann, M., Hoenicke, J., Podelski, A.: Software model checking for people who love automata. In: Sharygina, N., Veith, H. (eds.) CAV 2013. LNCS, vol. 8044, pp. 36–52. Springer, Heidelberg (2013). https://doi.org/10.1007/978-3-642-39799-8_2
18. Heizmann, M. et al.: Automizer and the search for perfect interpolants. In: TACAS 2018 (2018, to appear)
19. Johnson, K., Calinescu, R., Kikuchi, S.: An incremental verification framework for component-based software systems. In: Proceedings of the 16th International ACM SIGSOFT Symposium on Component-Based Software Engineering, pp. 33–42. ACM (2013)
20. Lakhnech, Y., Bensalem, S., Berezin, S., Owre, S.: Incremental verification by abstraction. In: Margaria, T., Yi, W. (eds.) TACAS 2001. LNCS, vol. 2031, pp. 98–112. Springer, Heidelberg (2001). https://doi.org/10.1007/3-540-45319-9_8
21. Maksimovic, D., Veneris, A., Poulos, Z.: Clustering-based revision debug in regression verification. In: Proceedings of the 33rd IEEE International Conference on Computer Design, ICCD 2015, pp. 32–37 (2015)

22. Meseguer, P.: Incremental verification of rule-based expert systems. In: Proceedings of the 10th European Conference on Artificial Intelligence, pp. 840–844. Wiley (1992)
23. Sery, O., Fedyukovich, G., Sharygina, N.: Incremental upgrade checking by means of interpolation-based function summaries. In: Formal Methods in Computer-Aided Design, FMCAD 2012, Cambridge, UK, 22–25 October 2012, pp. 114–121 (2012)
24. Strichman, O., Godlin, B.: Regression verification - a practical way to verify programs. In: Meyer, B., Woodcock, J. (eds.) VSTTE 2005. LNCS, vol. 4171, pp. 496–501. Springer, Heidelberg (2008). https://doi.org/10.1007/978-3-540-69149-5_54
25. Strichman, O., Veitsman, M.: Regression verification for unbalanced recursive functions. In: Fitzgerald, J., Heitmeyer, C., Gnesi, S., Philippou, A. (eds.) FM 2016. LNCS, vol. 9995, pp. 645–658. Springer, Cham (2016). https://doi.org/10.1007/978-3-319-48989-6_39
26. Trostanetski, A., Grumberg, O., Kroening, D.: Modular demand-driven analysis of semantic difference for program versions. In: Ranzato, F. (ed.) SAS 2017. LNCS, vol. 10422, pp. 405–427. Springer, Cham (2017). https://doi.org/10.1007/978-3-319-66706-5_20
27. Venkatesh, M.B.: A case study in non-functional regression verification (2016)
28. Visser, W., Geldenhuys, J., Dwyer, M.B.: Green: reducing, reusing and recycling constraints in program analysis. In: Proceedings of the ACM SIGSOFT 20th International Symposium on the Foundations of Software Engineering, pp. 58:1–58:11 (2012)

Volume-Based Merge Heuristics
for Disjunctive Numeric Domains

Andrew Ruef[1]([✉]), Kesha Hietala[1], and Arlen Cox[2]

[1] University of Maryland, College Park, USA
{awruef,kesha}@cs.umd.edu
[2] Center for Computing Sciences, Institute for Defense Analyses, Bowie, USA
ajcox3@super.org

Abstract. Static analysis of numeric programs allows proving important properties of programs such as a lack of buffer overflows, division by zero, or integer overflow. By using convex numeric abstractions, such as polyhedra, octagons, or intervals, representations of program states are concise and the analysis operations are efficient. Unfortunately, many sets of program states can only be very imprecisely represented with a single convex numeric abstraction. This means that many important properties cannot be proven using only these abstractions. One solution to this problem is to use powerset abstractions where a set of convex numeric abstractions represents the union rather than the hull of those state sets. This leads to a new challenge: when to merge elements of the powerset and when to keep them separate. We present a new methodology for determining when to merge based on counting and volume arguments. Unlike previous techniques, this heuristic directly represents losses in precision through hull computations. In this paper we develop these techniques and show their utility on a number of programs from the SV-COMP and WCET benchmark suites.

1 Introduction

A significant problem with common numeric abstraction domains such as intervals [11], octagons [31], and polyhedra [14] is that they are convex. A convex abstraction is unable to represent the absence of one or more concrete states within its volume. This causes problems, for instance, when attempting to prove that a division by zero is not possible because the set of all integers except zero is not representable with a single convex abstraction. To work around this problem, a common approach [34,36] is to use a powerset abstraction [13]. A *powerset abstraction* represents a non-convex set of states as a finite set of convex abstractions. Since (linear) convex abstractions are representable as a conjunction of hyperplanes, we refer to these powerset abstractions as *disjunction abstractions*. For instance, we can represent that x is equal to any integer except zero using a disjunction of two interval constraints: $x \leq -1 \vee x \geq 1$.

While disjunction abstractions solve the problem of representing holes within a convex numeric abstraction, they also introduce a new problem: performance.

© Springer Nature Switzerland AG 2018
A. Podelski (Ed.): SAS 2018, LNCS 11002, pp. 383–401, 2018.
https://doi.org/10.1007/978-3-319-99725-4_23

Instead of performing an operation on a single convex abstraction, the analysis must perform operations on each convex abstraction. Furthermore, if a disjunction is introduced at each branch in the program [35], the number of disjuncts is exponential in the number of branches. Loops cause further problems because they can effectively introduce an unbounded number of branches, leading to an analysis that does not terminate.

To resolve this problem we turn to merging. A *merge heuristic* is responsible for determining whether two convex numeric abstractions should be combined using a hulling operation or maintained as separate disjuncts. In [36], the authors propose a heuristic based on Hausdorff distance. In [34], the authors propose a heuristic based on the number of common hyperplanes. The problem with both of these approaches is that they do not relate directly to what the abstractions represent: concrete states.

This paper studies merge heuristics based on the number of concrete states that are affected by a potential merge. For instance, if two abstract states have no concrete states in common, then perhaps they should not be merged. Alternatively, if hulling two abstract states yields the same set of concrete states as taking their union, they should be merged as in [2].

In this paper we focus on *bounded polytope abstractions*, which are polytope abstractions with finite bounds. We study polytopes because, unlike intervals [20,39], appropriate merge heuristics for polytopes are non-obvious. Furthermore, operations on polytopes have higher complexity than operations on octagons or intervals and thus make differences between merge heuristics more obvious in empirical study. Regardless, we expect that the precision results would extend to other convex numeric abstractions. In order to study volume-based merge heuristics, we require computable volumes. Therefore we restrict polytopes to machine integer bounds with the assumption that integer overflow is checked. We make the following contributions.

- In Sect. 3 we develop heuristics based on the volume of the intersection of two polytopes relative to the volume of their union. We also develop heuristics based on the volume of the hull of two polytopes relative to the volume of their union.
- In Sect. 4 we describe how to use Markov Chain Monte Carlo algorithms to incrementally approximate relative volumes of polytopes, and we show how to use Barvinok's algorithm [5] to count integer points in polytopes. We also describe a segments-based affinity score that does not require a direct hull computation.
- In Sect. 5 we present a disjunctive abstract domain that utilizes various heuristics to determine which disjuncts to merge.
- In Sects. 6 and 7 we integrate the abstract domain into an analyzer and use that analyzer to produce invariants for a range of programs in the SV-COMP and WCET benchmark suites.

2   Overview and Example

Consider a typical forward abstract interpretation [12] of the program shown in Fig. 1a. The analysis should establish as strong an invariant as possible at the point where the branches A, B, and C have been joined together. We want to strike a balance between precision and performance: our invariant should be strong enough to allow us to prove interesting properties of the program, but we should not have to spend an unreasonable amount of computational power.

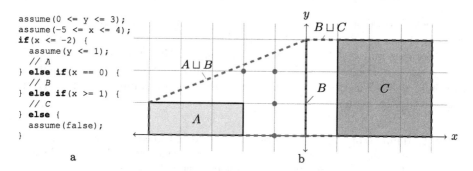

Fig. 1. Example of merging disjuncts. (a) Program that produces three disjuncts. (b) Three disjuncts shown as three convex polytopes. Red (resp. blue) dashed lines show the merge results of A and B (resp. B and C). Dots show integer points added in merging. (Color figure online)

Figure 1b shows the situation that arises. There are three disjoint polytopes. Each describes a range of values that can be assumed by x and y when the branches are joined together at the end of Fig. 1a. Now consider a case where we are allowed to describe the state using a disjunction of at most two polytopes. Then we must choose to merge two of A, B, or C. The question is, which two will result in the least loss of precision? The observation we make is that precision loss is related to volume. When the volume increases as a result of a merge, that represents a precision loss. The magnitude of the increase in volume is also related to the magnitude of the loss of precision. It is therefore desirable to merge the disjuncts that minimize the change in volume. In short: can we speculatively calculate or estimate the volume increase from a proposed disjunctive merge, and let that guide the management of our disjuncts? We will consider answering this question using two different volume calculation methods.

First, we consider an integer point counting method. We can see in Fig. 1b that merging A and B will cause four new points (shown in red) to be added to the approximation of the state space, while merging B and C will not result in any change in the number of integer points. Therefore we choose to merge disjuncts B and C while keeping A distinct.

Second, we consider a real approximation of the integer points methods. We can see that if we merge A and B, the volume increases by 7 (red dashed shape), whereas if we merge B and C the volume increases by 3 (blue dashed shape). Therefore we choose to merge disjuncts B and C while keeping A distinct.

In the remainder of the paper we precisely describe the comparison techniques used in this section. Both integer point methods and real approximation methods are considered.

3   Semantic Comparison of Polytopes

This section develops affinity scores between polytopes. An *affinity score* is a value in the range [0,1] assigned to a pair of polytopes where a 0 suggests that the polytopes may not be related and a 1 suggests that the polytopes are definitely related. Polytopes with an affinity score higher than a (user-specified) threshold will be merged. Table 1 summarizes the two affinity scoring mechanisms evaluated in this paper.

Table 1. Affinity scores measure the similarity between two convex polytopes and can be used to determine which polytopes to merge. We define $|A|_\mathbb{Z}$ to be the cardinality of $\{\, \mathbf{x} \in \mathbb{Z}^d \mid \mathbf{x} \in A \,\}$ and $|A|_\mathbb{R}$ to be the volume of the polytope A.

Affinity score	Integer	Real
Intersection volume	$i_\mathbb{Z}(A,B) = \dfrac{|A \cap B|_\mathbb{Z}}{|A \cup B|_\mathbb{Z}}$	$i_\mathbb{R}(A,B) = \dfrac{|A \cap B|_\mathbb{R}}{|A \cup B|_\mathbb{R}}$
Added hull volume	$h_\mathbb{Z}(A,B) = \dfrac{|A \cup B|_\mathbb{Z}}{|\mathrm{hull}(A,B)|_\mathbb{Z}}$	$h_\mathbb{R}(A,B) = \dfrac{|A \cup B|_\mathbb{R}}{|\mathrm{hull}(A,B)|_\mathbb{R}}$

Each affinity score is defined in two ways: over integers and over reals. For integers, the affinity score is given by the cardinality of point sets. For reals, the affinity score is given by the volume of the solids. The computation of both the cardinality of the point sets and the volume of the solids requires that the polytopes are bounded to avoid infinite results. Integer affinity scores are given a $\mathbb{Z}$ subscript and real affinity scores are given a $\mathbb{R}$ subscript.

To motivate the different affinity scoring systems, we use the examples shown in Fig. 2. Figure 2a shows two polytopes that are similar because they have a large

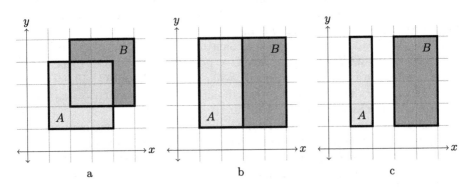

Fig. 2. Example polytopes that motivate different affinity scoring systems

overlap. Figure 2b shows two polytopes that are similar because they abut (and hence merging them will result in no loss of precision). During static analysis, we often encounter examples like the one in Fig. 2b because when we branch on an if statement, for the 'then' branch we assume one half-space and for the 'else' branch we assume the other half-space (in this case separated by $x = 3$). We also often encounter examples like Fig. 2c, which has a gap of size one. This is due to branching on integer variables: if we branch on $x \geq 3$, our else constraint is $x \leq 2$.

Definition 1 (Intersection volume affinity). *Intersection volume affinity is defined as the ratio between the volume of the intersection of the polytopes and the volume of the union of the polytopes. It is defined in the first row of Table 1.*

Intuitively, intersection volume is a good scoring mechanism because it merges polytopes that have large overlaps. The hull of two polytopes with a large intersection will not be significantly larger than the polytopes themselves. However, a small or non-existent intersection between two polytopes does not indicate anything about the size of their hull. What is particularly useful about this scoring mechanism is that the hulling operation can be skipped if unneeded. Since the hulling operation is potentially exponential time for arbitrary polytopes, this could lead to performance benefits.

Example 1 (Intersection volume affinity). For Fig. 2a, $i_{\mathbb{Z}}$ is $\frac{9}{23} \approx 0.39$ and $i_{\mathbb{R}}$ is $\frac{4}{14} \approx 0.29$. For Fig. 2b, $i_{\mathbb{Z}}$ is $\frac{1}{5} = 0.2$ and $i_{\mathbb{R}}$ is 0. For Fig. 2c, both $i_{\mathbb{Z}}$ and $i_{\mathbb{R}}$ are 0.

Definition 2 (Added hull volume affinity). *Added hull volume affinity is defined as the ratio between the volume of the union of the polytopes and the volume of the hull of the polytopes. It is defined in the second row of Table 1.*

Due to the situation that occurs in Figs. 2b and c, we also consider hull volume affinity, which corresponds directly to the volume/number of points that are gained through the hulling process. This scoring mechanism aims to minimize the total number of points represented by an abstraction.

Example 2 (Added hull volume affinity). For Fig. 2a, $h_{\mathbb{R}}$ is $\frac{14}{15} \approx 0.93$. For Fig. 2b, $h_{\mathbb{R}}$ is 1. For Fig. 2c, $h_{\mathbb{R}}$ is $\frac{12}{16} = 0.75$. For all three figures, $h_{\mathbb{Z}}$ is 1.

Other affinity scores are documented in the literature. The simplest affinity [23] is the null affinity, which always returns an affinity score of zero. Another affinity score [34] is the ratio between the number of half planes preserved by a hulling operation and the number of half planes in the two polytopes. This is biased to preserve complexity in the representation, but shares with the hull volume affinity the property that it tends to assign high scores to polytopes that do not add too many points in hulling. In [36] there is an affinity score that is based on the Hausdorff distance. This affinity tends to merge polytopes that are not too far apart, but does not consider points gained by the hulling operation.

4   Sampling and Counting Points

In this section we describe the techniques we use to implement affinity scores. Affinity scores are computed with one of two general techniques. They are either computed by counting integer points within polytopes or by calculating ratios of volumes of polytopes.

4.1   Integer-Point-Based Affinity

To implement $i_{\mathbb{Z}}$ and $h_{\mathbb{Z}}$ we need to be able to compute answers to problems of the form $|A|_{\mathbb{Z}} / |B|_{\mathbb{Z}}$. We accomplish this by computing individually $|A|_{\mathbb{Z}}$ and $|B|_{\mathbb{Z}}$ and then dividing. The key to doing this is the use of the Barvinok algorithm [5] and its corresponding tool [41]. The Barvinok algorithm has complexity $L^{O(d \, \log \, d)}$ for L input constraints and dimension d [33]. The Barvinok library (developed from PolyLib [30]) is an optimized implementation of this algorithm and can efficiently compute the precise cardinality of integer polytopes. The details of this algorithm are beyond the scope of this paper.

4.2   Volume-Ratio-Based Affinity

To implement $i_{\mathbb{R}}$ and $h_{\mathbb{R}}$ we need to be able to compute ratios of volumes of high-dimension polytopes. Directly computing the volume of high-dimension polytopes is a computationally complex problem and we need to do the operation twice for each merge candidate. Therefore, we develop the methodology used here more carefully.

For our purposes, it is not strictly necessary to compute volumes because the end result is not a volume, but rather a ratio of volumes. Exploiting this reduces the amount of computation that we have to do. If we can sample uniformly from the polytope in the denominator, we can count the number of samples that occur in the numerator to iteratively approximate the ratio of the volumes of the polytopes. To sample from a polytope, we borrow from techniques for approximating the volume of polytopes [17,27], which use Markov Chain Monte Carlo (MCMC) [28] sampling algorithms to produce a Markov chain whose limiting distribution is equal to a given distribution.

Definition 3 (Sampling intersection volume affinity). *Let $R(A)^n$ be an n-cardinality set of random points uniformly distributed in a polytope A. The sampling intersection volume ratio of polytopes A and B given n samples is*

$$i_{\mathbb{R}}^n(A, B) = \frac{|\{ x \in R(A \cup B)^n \mid x \in A \cap B \}|}{n}$$

Definition 4 (Sampling added hull volume affinity). *Given $R(A)^n$ as above, the sampling hull volume ratio of polytopes A and B given n samples is*

$$h_{\mathbb{R}}^n(A, B) = \frac{|\{ x \in R(\mathrm{hull}(A, B))^n \mid x \in A \cup B \}|}{n}$$

These definitions give iterative approximations of the affinity functions that become closer to the actual function as the number of samples increases. In the limit they compute the precise volume ratios given in Table 1.

The complexity of MCMC sampling is polynomial in the dimension of the polytope. Generating each sample is polynomial, and typically a polynomial number of samples is sufficient to get decent coverage of the polytope. However, the complexity of the hull operation is potentially exponential in the dimension of the polytope. Therefore the dominating factor in the complexity of the sampling hull volume affinity is the hull operation. The sampling intersection volume affinity is attractive because it does not incur this exponential cost. However, it does require uniform sampling from a union of two convex polytopes, which basic MCMC sampling does not support. We get around this with the following modification:

$$ i_{\mathbb{R}}^n(A, B) = \frac{\left| \left\{ x \in R(A)^{n/2} \cup R(B)^{n/2} \mid x \in A \cap B \right\} \right|}{n} $$

This only requires sampling from convex polytopes and is thus polynomial time, but results in increased sample density in the smaller polytope and in the intersecting region.

4.3   Segment-Sample Volume-Ratio-Based Affinity

To avoid the complexity of the hull operation used in the sampling hull volume affinity, we also define a segment-sample-based affinity. This affinity is inspired by the definition of convex hull, where every point on every line segment between points in the two polytopes is included in the hull.

Definition 5 (Segment-sample volume-ratio-based affinity). *Let* $S(A, B)^n = R(A)^n \times R(B)^n|_n$ *where* $R(A)^n$ *is as given above and* $\cdot|_n$ *randomly picks* n *elements of the set. Let* $\ell((x, y), A)$ *be the length of the line segment between* x *and* y *contained within the polytope* A. *Define* $|x - y|$ *to be the distance between* x *and* y. *The segment-sample volume-ratio-based affinity is*

$$ s_{\mathbb{R}}^n(A, B) = \frac{\sum_{\bar{s} \in \bar{S}} \ell(\bar{s}, A) + \ell(\bar{s}, B) - \ell(\bar{s}, A \cap B)}{\sum_{(x,y) \in \bar{s}} |x - y|} \quad \text{where } \bar{S} = S(A, B)^n. $$

This affinity's main interesting property is that it approximates the hull without actually computing the hull. As a result it has a polynomial time bound as opposed to an exponential time bound like other hull-based techniques. Unfortunately, this approximation is poor as the sampling is not uniform. Sampling end points uniformly from two polytopes individually does not yield a uniform sampling of segments between those polytopes. Because the segments on average end in the middle of each polytope, the portion of the polytopes that are farther away from each other may be underrepresented in the calculation. We include this heuristic here because we believe that it is an interesting approach despite its shortcomings.

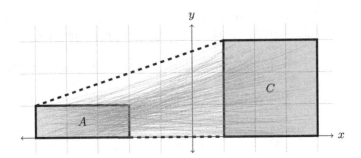

Fig. 3. The sampled segments approximate the hull of A and C non-uniformly. Note that the upper portion is underrepresented.

Example 3 (Segment-sample volume-ratio-based affinity). If we sample 300 segments, we get a picture like the one shown in Fig. 3. The segments in this figure do not cover the topmost part of hull of A and C (shown by dashed lines), but instead repeatedly cover the center of the hull. However, these segments can be computed without computing the hull itself, which means that hulling is not necessary to reason about the volume introduced by hulling.

4.4   Inflating Polytopes

With the volume-ratio-based affinities, there is the problem of abutment. When a conditional branch is interpreted, this splits the abstract state into two separate abstract states that may be re-merged with a disjunction. Identifying when these branches have come back together is important for reducing the number of disjuncts. Unfortunately, there are cases where an integer gap may be introduced, as shown in Fig. 2c. In this case, if the two abutting polytopes have a low total volume, the volume of the gap may outweigh the volume of the polytopes in the computation of the $h_{\mathbb{R}}$ affinity, and the two polytopes will be given a low score. Regardless of an integer gap, two abutting (but not intersecting) polytopes will be assigned a $i_{\mathbb{R}}$ affinity score of zero because their intersection volume is zero.

To avoid these issues, we use an inflation technique, which takes every face of the polytope and pushes it out by some amount. For example, in Fig. 2c, inflating by one will cause the two polytopes to have an intersection of width one. Now the $h_{\mathbb{R}}$ affinity score will be one, which is the same as $h_{\mathbb{Z}}$, and $i_{\mathbb{R}}$ will be nonzero. An inflation of 0.5 is sufficient to bridge the integer gap, but larger inflation values may be beneficial. For instance, in the case of intersection volume, a larger inflation can boost the affinity of nearby (but not intersecting) polytopes without boosting the affinity of far apart polytopes. This naturally biases closer polytopes to be merged.

5 Disjunctive Abstract Domain

A concrete state is a point in d-dimensional space $\mathbb{Z}^d$. Convex polytope abstract states $q, r \in D^\#$ are instances of an abstract domain. The concretization of an abstract state $\gamma(q)$ is a set of concrete states. An abstract domain is a lattice ordered by inclusion $\sqsubseteq$ that defines least upper bound $\sqcup$. An abstract domain defines monotone transfer functions f that map abstract states to other abstract states. Abstract domains also define a widening operator ∇ that predicts possible post-fixpoints and guarantees termination of the analysis.

We employ a typical disjunctive abstract domain. Disjunctive abstract states $Q = (q_1, \ldots, q_k), R = (r_1, \ldots, r_k) \in D^{\#^k}$ are k-element vectors of underlying convex numeric abstract states. The concretization is given as function of the underlying domain's concretization: $\gamma(Q) = \bigcup_{i \in [1,k]} \gamma(q_i)$ for $q_i \in Q$. Figure 4c shows the basic domain operations including join, a naive widening algorithm (for simplicity, not [1]), transfer function, and inclusion.

Following [19,36], we define disjunctive abstract domain operations using a selection function σ. The selection function shown in Fig. 4b determines which among a set of abstract states is most similar to another abstract state. To do this it makes three comparisons. The first two check if the parameter q is contained in any of the $r_i \in R$ or if any of the $r_i \in R$ are contained in q. If so, the least index is chosen. This takes care of initialization because $\bot$ is trivially contained in any q. The last comparison checks if some affinity score a indicates that the two abstract states have a similarity higher than some threshold Θ. The threshold Θ is a parameter to the analysis. If all three comparisons fail, the index containing the most similar abstract state will be selected. The threshold check is important to ensure that similar, but not contained, abstract states do not fill up all k positions first and then force dissimilar abstract states to choose the best of several poor choices.

Fn $K\,(Q : D^{\#^m}) : D^{\#^k}$
　$R \leftarrow \bot^k$
　for $i = 1$ **to** m **do**
　　$j \leftarrow \sigma(R, q_i)$
　　$r_j \leftarrow r_j \sqcup q_i$
　return R

a

Fn $\sigma\left(R : D^{\#^k},\ q : D^\#\right) : \{1 \ldots k\}$
　$(i_{max}, v_{max}) \leftarrow (0, 0)$
　for $i = 1$ **to** k **do**
　　$v \leftarrow a(q, r_i)$
　　if $q \sqsubseteq r_i \lor r_i \sqsubseteq q \lor v > \Theta$
　　then
　　　return i
　　if $v > v_{max}$ **then**
　　　$(i_{max}, v_{max}) \leftarrow (i, v)$
　return i_{max}

b

$Q \sqcup R = K(Q \cup R)$

$Q \nabla R = \bigcup_{i \in [1 \ldots k]} q_i \nabla r_i$

$f(Q) = K(\bigcup \{\, f(q) \mid q \in Q \,\})$

$Q \sqsubseteq R = \bigwedge_{q \in Q} \bigvee_{r \in R} q \sqsubseteq r$

c

Fig. 4. (a) Compaction function K and (b) corresponding selection function σ, where a is the affinity function. These are responsible for reducing the number of disjuncts in an abstract state down to k. (c) Domain operations join, widening, transfer function, and inclusion defined using K.

The σ function is then used by a compaction function K, which is shown in Fig. 4a, to reduce an overly large set of disjuncts down to a smaller set. This is necessary to ensure termination of abstract interpretation by preventing the number of disjunctions from growing indefinitely. The compaction function works by iteratively inserting elements from Q into a result disjunction R according to the selection function σ. All of the abstract domain operations are defined using this compaction function. They are implemented in the obvious way for a disjunctive abstract domain, and are compacted if too many disjuncts are produced by an operation. The soundness of this domain follows from definitions in prior work on disjunctive domains [36].

Example 4 (Compacting a disjunction). Consider the example shown in Fig. 1b. There are three disjuncts A, B, and C, but we wish to compact that to $k = 2$ disjuncts with a threshold $\Theta = 0.8$ and an affinity score $a = h_{\mathbb{Z}}$. To begin, A is placed into r_1 because $\bot \sqsubseteq A$. Next, B is placed into r_2 because $\bot \sqsubseteq B$ and the affinity score assigned to A and B is $0.75 < 0.8$. Finally, C is merged into r_2 because the affinity score of r_2 and C is $1.0 > 0.8$. This is significantly higher than the affinity score of r_1 and C, which is approximately 0.77.

6   Implementation

We implemented a disjunctive abstract domain in the CRAB C++ abstract interpretation framework [32], which builds upon Clang and LLVM version 3.8.0. C and C++ programs are compiled into LLVM IR and then optimized with a set of optimizations targeted at static analysis, such as pointer to array conversion [29]. The resulting LLVM IR files are then converted into a CRAB-specific intermediate representation for analysis with a selectable domain.

The disjunctive abstract domain is parameterized by the maximum number of disjuncts k, the similarity threshold Θ, and the choice of affinity scoring function a. The underlying numeric abstraction is the NewPolka abstraction from the APRON abstract domain library [26]. NewPolka is convenient because it provides fairly low-level access to the constraint matrix and separates equality constraints from inequality constraints. To circumvent problems with infinite volume polytopes, we impose reasonable machine integer bounds. All variables are restricted to be in the range -2^{63} to $2^{64} - 1$ to cover both signed and unsigned machine integers.

The null affinity scoring function 0 is trivially implemented: new polytopes are merged with either an existing polytope that wholly subsumes the new one, or if no such polytope is found the new polytope is added to the end. If there is no more room, the new polytope is merged with the last element in the disjunct. We also implemented an affinity measure that counts the number of common hyperplanes, c, as described in [34]. The $i_{\mathbb{Z}}$ and $h_{\mathbb{Z}}$ affinity functions are implemented as described in Sect. 4 using the Barvinok library [41] to implement integer counting within polytopes. The $i_{\mathbb{R}}$, $h_{\mathbb{R}}$ and $s_{\mathbb{R}}$ affinity scoring functions are implemented as described in Sect. 4 using our own implementation of polytope sampling (described in the next section). The $i_{\mathbb{R}}$, $h_{\mathbb{R}}$ and $s_{\mathbb{R}}$ scoring functions are additionally parameterized by the number of samples n. We scale the number of samples taken linearly with the number of dimensions in the polytope to ensure better coverage.

6.1 Random Sampling Within Polytopes

To implement the $R(A)^n$ operation we use a Markov Chain Monte Carlo (MCMC) technique called hit-and-run sampling [9,38], which performs a random walk to generate points within a polytope. We use hit-and-run sampling because of its relative ease of implementation. Note that hit-and-run sampling only guarantees uniformity in the limit, so our implementation, which uses a limited number of samples, does not provide completely uniform random sampling.

One challenge with hit-and-run sampling (or any technique that randomly explores the interior of a polytope) is how to handle zero-volume polytopes, which occur often in abstract interpretation. Zero-volume polytopes inhibit random walks because the probability of selecting a valid direction in which to step is zero. To get around this, we do a dimension reduction that converts a zero-volume polytope to a non-zero-volume polytope of lower dimension [10,16]. The lower-dimension polytope can then be sampled and each point mapped back to a point in the original polytope. These mapped points can then be used in one of the affinity scoring algorithms.

We also encounter difficulties with the representation of coefficients in the constraint matrices. For performance reasons it is desirable to use floating-point numbers in the constraint matrix. However, because the dynamic range of coefficients is very large, floating-point precision is insufficient and during sampling, rounding error may cause the invariant of the hit-and-run algorithm (that the current point is always inside the polytope) to be violated. To get around this, we represent coefficients using rational numbers. This gives us the precision we need, but adds significant overhead and makes it more difficult to do certain operations required by the hit-and-run algorithm, such as generating random points on a line segment.

We solve the problem of generating random points by introducing a new parameter m, which fixes the number of points that we can choose during any iteration of hit-and-run. To generate a random point on a line segment, we first split the segment into m sub-segments, and then choose an endpoint of a randomly selected sub-segment. Note that for a fixed number of samples, this limits the granularity of our samples. To get around some of the performance problems caused by using rational values we introduce another parameter, b, which is the batch size. The batch size determines how many points to sample from a segment once a hit-and-run direction has been chosen. This reduces the total number of directions sampled, and thus decreases the uniformity in exchange for increased performance.

7 Evaluation

In this section we evaluate the various affinity scores detailed in this paper. This evaluation attempts to answer the following research questions.

- **RQ1:** Does merging the most similar polytopes increase analysis precision?
- **RQ2:** Does sampling provide better performance characteristics than exact computation?
- **RQ3:** Is exact computation efficient enough for large-scale analysis?
- **RQ4:** Is sampling efficient enough for large-scale analysis?

7.1 Experimental Setup

To answer these research questions, we evaluate our implementation of the affinity scores listed in Table 2 on the SV-COMP [6] and WCET [21] benchmark suites. Specifically, we used the subset of programs from SV-COMP described in Table 3. We chose these benchmarks because they focus on numeric properties (e.g. `loops`) and represent interesting and significant programs (e.g. `busybox`). In total, we analyzed 170,090 lines of C code.

Table 2. Descriptions of the different affinity scores considered.

Affinity score	Description
0	Null affinity
c	Common hyperplanes [34]
$i_{\mathbb{Z}}$	Integer intersection volume
$h_{\mathbb{Z}}$	Integer added hull volume
$i_{\mathbb{R}}$	Sampling intersection volume
$h_{\mathbb{R}}$	Sampling added hull volume
$s_{\mathbb{R}}$	Segment-sample volume ratio

The benchmarks were executed on a 36-core, 72-thread Intel Xeon E5-2699 system with 512GB of RAM. We evaluated 72 benchmarks at a time and ran each benchmark five times to get an average for performance. Each benchmark was allowed up to 60 min of run time before being declared a time out.

We fixed the parameters in the following way based on a handful of small examples before evaluating on the full benchmark suite. The number of disjuncts k was limited to 3. The number of samples per dimension parameter n was set to 10. The number of segments parameter m was set to 1024. The batch size parameter b was set to 4. The threshold parameter Θ was set to 0.4. The inflation parameter was set to 0.5 for $h_{\mathbb{R}}$ and $s_{\mathbb{R}}$, 1.0 for $i_{\mathbb{R}}$, and 0 for $h_{\mathbb{Z}}$ and $i_{\mathbb{Z}}$. Recall that m and b are parameters used by our sampling implementation as described in Sect. 6. The evaluation proceeds with these settings.

Table 3. WCET and SV-COMP benchmark sets used for evaluation. Lines of code counted with `cloc`.

Dataset	LOC
wcet	907
loops	2866
ssh	60463
ntdrivers	39173
busybox-1.22.0	58997
loop-invgen	441
loop-acceleration	637
loop-industry-pattern	3114
array-industry-pattern	551
array-examples	2941
Total	170090

To evaluate precision, we compared the invariants inferred for each program point across all of the different analyses. For each pair of analyses M, N, we queried the number of program points where $M \sqsubseteq N$ and $M = N$. This comparison gives us a fine grained measurement of the relative precision of different analyzers. Instead of asking, for example, how many array bounds checks or other assertions were proven, we ask how about precision at every point in the program. An increase in precision would be valuable to any downstream client that sought to prove some numeric property of the program. We used the Yices SMT solver [15] to answer these queries. This query time is not counted as part of analysis time. Some M, N might be incomparable, and those are not represented in the table. One choice we have made in this experimental measurement is to not determine if either M or N are sufficient to prove a property about the program, but to instead compare the relative precision between the two invariants when they can be related. This choice was made due to the impact of improving precision early in an analysis and due to the relatively few properties to prove compared to the number of program points.

7.2   Results

The precision results are presented in Table 4. The performance results are presented in Table 5 and shown graphically in Fig. 5. We use this information to address the research questions.

RQ1. *Does merging the most similar polytopes increase analysis precision?* Table 4 shows that on average, yes. Both of the precise counting affinities produce more precise results 25% of the time, whereas the null affinity is more precise only 8% of the time. The sampling-based techniques fare slightly worse

Table 4. Ratio of program points where M is more precise than N. The upper diagonal is augmented with the percentage of when $M = N$.

| | | M | | | | | | | | | | | |
| | | 0 | c | | i_Z | | h_Z | | i_R | | h_R | | s_R | |
		⊏	⊏	=	⊏	=	⊏	=	⊏	=	⊏	=	⊏	=
N	0	-	.05	.64	.25	.42	.25	.42	.07	.79	.20	.43	.19	.45
	c	.18	-	-	.31	.36	.31	.36	.19	.58	.23	.42	.24	.43
	i_Z	.08	.03	-	-	-	0	1	.07	.45	.05	.33	.04	.42
	h_Z	.08	.03	-	0	-	-	-	.07	.45	.05	.33	.04	.42
	i_R	.02	.05	-	.23	-	.23	-	-	-	.18	.43	.18	.49
	h_R	.19	.14	-	.29	-	.29	-	.22	-	-	-	.12	.64
	s_R	.18	.13	-	.26	-	.26	-	.19	-	.08	-	-	-

Table 5. Aggregate performance of different analyzer configurations across all programs. Each program was analyzed 5 times. We took the mean of 5 runs and report on that mean when aggregating across all programs. Times reported are in seconds.

Analyzer	Mean	Min	Max	Median
0	5.375	0.242	79.291	0.866
c	7.883	0.254	240.350	0.786
i_Z	19.058	0.250	806.325	0.581
h_Z	33.202	0.250	1493.689	0.605
i_R	29.522	0.241	1204.348	4.013
h_R	56.186	0.243	932.781	7.236
s_R	86.074	0.254	1928.718	8.367

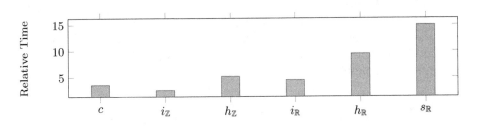

Fig. 5. Runtime performance of analyzer configurations relative to null affinity.

against the null affinity, scoring 7%, 20%, and 19% better, whereas the null affinity performs better 2%, 19%, and 18% of the time. However, the sampling-based techniques perform better against the c affinity measure in all cases. This suggests that when the volumetric comparison is precise (i.e. either i_Z or h_Z), there is a significant benefit over the basic strategy. This also suggests that either the number of samples or the specific samples that we chose were insufficient to identify the truly related polytopes.

RQ2. *Does sampling provide better performance characteristics than exact computation?* No. With the parameters that we have chosen, the performance is roughly comparable with the precise counting techniques generally being faster. Table 5 shows that the sampling techniques on average take twice as long as the precise counting techniques. However, for the added hull volume affinity scores ($h_\mathbb{Z}$ and $h_\mathbb{R}$), the maximum run time for the sampling technique is significantly better than the maximum run time for the precise counting technique. This suggests that the asymptotic complexity advantage of sampling pays off when the problem gets particularly difficult for precise counting. Even so, with the implementation we have developed and the parameters that we have chosen, the sampling techniques are generally not worth using.

RQ3. *Is exact computation efficient enough for large-scale analysis?* Yes. Table 5 shows that the exact computation techniques have non-trivial overhead over the null affinity case. However, depending on the situation, $i_\mathbb{Z}$ may provide a fair trade-off: a 4x increase in analysis time in exchange for invariants that are stronger 25% of the time. $h_\mathbb{Z}$ is less favorable: a 6x increase in analysis time for exactly the same 25% improvement in invariant strength.

RQ4. *Is sampling efficient enough for large-scale analysis?* Yes, though in its current state it is probably not worth using. Like $i_\mathbb{Z}$ and $h_\mathbb{Z}$, $i_\mathbb{R}$ and $h_\mathbb{R}$ are more expensive than the null affinity. In general a 6x overhead of $i_\mathbb{R}$ is not necessarily too expensive, although it depends on the situation. The 10x and 17x overheads of $h_\mathbb{R}$ and $s_\mathbb{R}$ are probably too expensive, especially as they seem to provide no precision benefit over the precise methods.

7.3 Limitations and Discussion

There are a number of limitations to our implementation, experimentation, and analysis. The most significant is the choice of parameters for the analysis. Ideally we would have chosen parameters for the sampling-based approaches on a large set of benchmarks. This limitation shows because, in the limit, the sampling should be similar to the exact counting methods. Due to the fact that the results are quite different, this suggests that we are not yet approaching that limit. We should probably increase the number of samples, increase the number of segments, or decrease the batch size to improve this result.

The choice of Θ is somewhat arbitrary. While the exact counting techniques do show a benefit with a Θ of 0.4, it is not clear that this is an optimum value. It is also not clear whether the sampling approaches should have different thresholds than the exact computation. It seems like that should be unnecessary, but we have not explored that space.

The results are somewhat unfairly biased against the sampling technique. The library for exact computation has been under development in some form for around 20 years. As a result it employs careful memory management for all of its computations to ensure that no extra memory is being allocated or freed. Furthermore it enjoys an optimized matrix library that has been custom built for this application and caching of intermediate results so that it can both avoid re-computation and re-allocation. In spot checks we have observed that the sampler is spending nearly 50% of its time doing memory allocation or freeing. If the sampler could manage memory more efficiently it may be possible to get it into the same realm of performance as the exact counting method.

We are currently using a fairly naive coordinate direction hit-and-run sampler. The reason for this was to increase the number of samples we could collect per second. It might be a fair trade to use a more advanced algorithm that is slower if it yielded more uniformly distributed samples. In particular, the coordinate direction hit-and-run sampler can get stuck in corners if a polytope is long and narrow and there is no coordinate direction that covers a large percentage of the space.

Finally, these results are dependent on the widening strategy. A poor choice when performing widening could easily cause one disjunct to go to top or close to top. Future disjuncts would be trivially merged with that particular disjunct resulting in an overall loss of precision. It is unclear how to account for this when analyzing results. While a loss of precision during widening is acceptable, it would be interesting to know how an ideal strategy would compare. Unfortunately, this is not possible.

8   Related Work

Disjunctions have been a widely studied topic. In abstract interpretation they were introduced with powerset domains in [13]. Jeannet [25] explored partitioning schemes for disjunctive invariants. More generally, the theory of disjunctive invariants is explored in [35]. This, along with [36], develops a relationship between disjunctive invariants and control flow path refinement. In effect, refining control flow such that multiple paths are presented for a single syntactic path is equivalent to a disjunctive analysis. This leads a significant quantity of work on control flow refinement [3,7,18,22,37], which can be viewed as applications of disjunctive techniques.

In [19] a theorem is given that a best disjunction merge policy can be statically computed. This theorem assumes that widening is not required and thus is not generally applicable to abstract interpretation. Furthermore, it is not obvious how to statically compute a merge policy in the context of a general abstract interpreter. [23] claims to do this but instead implements the null affinity score.

Model checking procedures [4,24] typically produce disjunctive invariants. The way they do this is different in its operation than what we present. They first analyze programs without any disjunctions and then introduce them by learning where a coarse abstraction has caused a property to not be proven.

While this approach is quite effective, it does not work for unguided analysis such as program understanding and it may not scale as well as non-refinement-based analyses such as Astrée [8].

We are most related to work that performs forward disjunctive analyses using numeric domains and no refinement. In [36], the authors use a similar formulation of the abstraction. The key difference is in the choice of merge heuristic. The choice in [36] is to merge according to a simplified Hausdorff distance, which is shown by [34] to be less desirable than other heuristics. In [34], the authors use a syntactic property of polytopes to decide merging. This technique counts the number of hyperplanes in common between an input polytope and the result of a join. Another possible merge heuristic is the similarity of Boolean variables. In [39], a binary decision diagram is used to determine which numeric domains should be merged and which should not.

Our merging heuristics are based on volume and counting computations for polytopes. Barvinok develops the core theory [5] for counting procedures. Approximate volume computations based on sampling are alternatively used [17,27]. The idea of using the Barvinok algorithm came from [40].

9 Conclusion

In this paper we have shown a number of new affinity scoring algorithms for determining which disjuncts should be merged in a disjunctive abstraction. The new affinity scoring algorithms are all based on points within the polytopes. Those points are either sampled or counted in order to compute proxies for polytope volume. We demonstrated that these techniques work by analyzing a large selection of benchmark programs. In the future we would like to further optimize sampling to make it more performant to determine if the difference in complexity yields tangible differences in performance. We would also like to explore adaptations of the segment sampling approach to find something that has some degree of uniformity.

References

1. Bagnara, R., Hill, P.M., Ricci, E., Zaffanella, E.: Precise widening operators for convex polyhedra. In: Cousot, R. (ed.) SAS 2003. LNCS, vol. 2694, pp. 337–354. Springer, Heidelberg (2003). https://doi.org/10.1007/3-540-44898-5_19
2. Bagnara, R., Hill, P.M., Zaffanella, E.: Exact join detection for convex polyhedra and other numerical abstractions. Comput. Geom. 43(5), 453–473 (2010)
3. Balakrishnan, G., Sankaranarayanan, S., Ivančić, F., Gupta, A.: Refining the control structure of loops using static analysis. In: EMSOFT (2009)
4. Ball, T., Majumdar, R., Millstein, T., Rajamani, S.K.: Automatic predicate abstraction of C programs. In: PLDI (2001)
5. Barvinok, A.I.: A polynomial time algorithm for counting integral points in polyhedra when the dimension is fixed. Math. Oper. Res. 19(4), 769–779 (1994)

6. Beyer, D.: Reliable and reproducible competition results with BenchExec and witnesses (report on SV-COMP 2016). In: Chechik, M., Raskin, J.-F. (eds.) TACAS 2016. LNCS, vol. 9636, pp. 887–904. Springer, Heidelberg (2016). https://doi.org/10.1007/978-3-662-49674-9_55

7. Beyer, D., Henzinger, T.A., Majumdar, R., Rybalchenko, A.: Path invariants. In: PLDI (2007)

8. Blanchet, B., et al.: Design and implementation of a special-purpose static program analyzer for safety-critical real-time embedded software. In: Mogensen, T.Æ., Schmidt, D.A., Sudborough, I.H. (eds.) The Essence of Computation. LNCS, vol. 2566, pp. 85–108. Springer, Heidelberg (2002). https://doi.org/10.1007/3-540-36377-7_5

9. Boneh, A., Golan, A.: Constraints' redundancy and feasible region boundedness by random feasible point generator (RFPG). In: Third European Congress on Operations Research, EURO III (1979)

10. Bromberger, M., Weidenbach, C.: Computing a complete basis for equalities implied by a system of LRA constraints. In: SMT, vol. 1617, pp. 15–30 (2016)

11. Cousot, P., Cousot, R.: Static determination of dynamic properties of programs. In: ISOP (1976)

12. Cousot, P., Cousot, R.: Abstract interpretation: a unified lattice model for static analysis of programs by construction or approximation of fixpoints. In: POPL (1977)

13. Cousot, P., Cousot, R.: Systematic design of program analysis frameworks. In: POPL (1979)

14. Cousot, P., Halbwachs, N.: Automatic discovery of linear restraints among variables of a program. In: POPL (1978)

15. Dutertre, B., De Moura, L.: The Yices SMT solver 2(2), pp. 1–2 (2006). Tool paper http://yices.csl.sri.com/tool-paper.pdf

16. Dutertre, B., de Moura, L.: A fast linear-arithmetic solver for DPLL(T). In: Ball, T., Jones, R.B. (eds.) CAV 2006. LNCS, vol. 4144, pp. 81–94. Springer, Heidelberg (2006). https://doi.org/10.1007/11817963_11

17. Dyer, M., Frieze, A., Kannan, R.: A random polynomial-time algorithm for approximating the volume of convex bodies. J. ACM **38**(1), 1–17 (1991)

18. Gulwani, S., Jain, S., Koskinen, E.: Control-flow refinement and progress invariants for bound analysis. In: PLDI (2009)

19. Gulwani, S., Zuleger, F.: The reachability-bound problem. In: PLDI (2010)

20. Gurfinkel, A., Chaki, S.: BOXES: a symbolic abstract domain of boxes. In: Cousot, R., Martel, M. (eds.) SAS 2010. LNCS, vol. 6337, pp. 287–303. Springer, Heidelberg (2010). https://doi.org/10.1007/978-3-642-15769-1_18

21. Gustafsson, J., Betts, A., Ermedahl, A., Lisper, B.: The mälardalen wcet benchmarks: Past, present and future. In: OASIcs-OpenAccess Series in Informatics. vol. 15. Schloss Dagstuhl-Leibniz-Zentrum fuer Informatik (2010)

22. Handjieva, M., Tzolovski, S.: Refining static analyses by trace-based partitioning using control flow. In: Levi, G. (ed.) SAS 1998. LNCS, vol. 1503, pp. 200–214. Springer, Heidelberg (1998). https://doi.org/10.1007/3-540-49727-7_12

23. Henry, J., Monniaux, D., Moy, M.: Succinct representations for abstract interpretation. In: Miné, A., Schmidt, D. (eds.) SAS 2012. LNCS, vol. 7460, pp. 283–299. Springer, Heidelberg (2012). https://doi.org/10.1007/978-3-642-33125-1_20

24. Henzinger, T.A., Jhala, R., Majumdar, R., Sutre, G.: Lazy abstraction. In: POPL (2002)

25. Jeannet, B.: Dynamic partitioning in linear relation analysis: application to the verification of reactive systems. Formal Methods Syst. Des. **23**(1), 5–37 (2003)

26. Jeannet, B., Miné, A.: APRON: a library of numerical abstract domains for static analysis. In: Bouajjani, A., Maler, O. (eds.) CAV 2009. LNCS, vol. 5643, pp. 661–667. Springer, Heidelberg (2009). https://doi.org/10.1007/978-3-642-02658-4_52

27. Kannan, R., Lovász, L., Simonovits, M.: Random walks and an o*(n5) volume algorithm for convex bodies. Random Struct. Algorithms **11**(1), 1–50 (1997)

28. Kroese, D.P., Taimre, T., Botev, Z.I.: Markov Chain Monte Carlo, Chap. 6, pp. 225–280. Wiley, New York (2011)

29. Lattner, C.: Macroscopic data structure analysis and optimization. Ph.D. thesis, UIUC (2005)

30. Loechner, V.: Polylib: A library for manipulating parameterized polyhedra. Technical report, Université Louis Pasteur de Strasbourg (1999)

31. Miné, A.: The octagon abstract domain. High. Order Symb. Comput. **19**(1), 31–100 (2006)

32. Navas, J.A.: CRAB: a language-agnostic library for static analysis (2018). https://github.com/seahorn/crab

33. Pak, I., Panova, G.: On the complexity of computing Kronecker coefficients. Comput. Complex. **26**(1), 1–36 (2017)

34. Popeea, C., Chin, W.-N.: Inferring disjunctive postconditions. In: Okada, M., Satoh, I. (eds.) ASIAN 2006. LNCS, vol. 4435, pp. 331–345. Springer, Heidelberg (2007). https://doi.org/10.1007/978-3-540-77505-8_26

35. Rival, X., Mauborgne, L.: The trace partitioning abstract domain. TOPLAS **29**(5), 26 (2007)

36. Sankaranarayanan, S., Ivančić, F., Shlyakhter, I., Gupta, A.: Static analysis in disjunctive numerical domains. In: Yi, K. (ed.) SAS 2006. LNCS, vol. 4134, pp. 3–17. Springer, Heidelberg (2006). https://doi.org/10.1007/11823230_2

37. Sharma, R., Dillig, I., Dillig, T., Aiken, A.: Simplifying loop invariant generation using splitter predicates. In: Gopalakrishnan, G., Qadeer, S. (eds.) CAV 2011. LNCS, vol. 6806, pp. 703–719. Springer, Heidelberg (2011). https://doi.org/10.1007/978-3-642-22110-1_57

38. Smith, R.L.: Monte Carlo procedures for generating random feasible solutions to mathematical programs. In: ORSA/TIMS Conference, May 1980

39. Sotin, P., Jeannet, B., Védrine, F., Goubault, E.: Policy iteration within logico-numerical abstract domains. In: Bultan, T., Hsiung, P.-A. (eds.) ATVA 2011. LNCS, vol. 6996, pp. 290–305. Springer, Heidelberg (2011). https://doi.org/10.1007/978-3-642-24372-1_21

40. Sweet, I., Trilla, J.M.C., Scherrer, C., Hicks, M., Magill, S.: What's the over/under? Probabilistic bounds on information leakage. In: Bauer, L., Küsters, R. (eds.) POST 2018. LNCS, vol. 10804, pp. 3–27. Springer, Cham (2018). https://doi.org/10.1007/978-3-319-89722-6_1

41. Verdoolaege, S., Seghir, R., Beyls, K., Loechner, V., Bruynooghe, M.: Counting integer points in parametric polytopes using Barvinok's rational functions. Algorithmica **48**(1), 37–66 (2007)

Abstract Interpretation
of CTL Properties

Caterina Urban$^{(\boxtimes)}$, Samuel Ueltschi, and Peter Müller

Department of Computer Science, ETH Zurich, Zurich, Switzerland
caterina.urban@inf.ethz.ch

Abstract. CTL is a temporal logic commonly used to express program properties. Most of the existing approaches for proving CTL properties only support certain classes of programs, limit their scope to a subset of CTL, or do not directly support certain existential CTL formulas. This paper presents an abstract interpretation framework for proving CTL properties that does not suffer from these limitations. Our approach automatically infers sufficient preconditions, and thus provides useful information even when a program satisfies a property only for some inputs. We systematically derive a program semantics that precisely captures CTL properties by abstraction of the operational trace semantics of a program. We then leverage existing abstract domains based on piecewise-defined functions to derive decidable abstractions that are suitable for static program analysis. To handle existential CTL properties, we augment these abstract domains with under-approximating operators. We implemented our approach in a prototype static analyzer. Our experimental evaluation demonstrates that the analysis is effective, even for CTL formulas with non-trivial nesting of universal and existential path quantifiers, and performs well on a wide variety of benchmarks.

1 Introduction

Computation tree logic (CTL) [6] is a temporal logic introduced by Clarke and Emerson to overcome certain limitations of linear temporal logic (LTL) [33] for program specification purposes. Most of the existing approaches for proving program properties expressed in CTL have limitations that restrict their applicability: they are limited to finite-state programs [7] or to certain classes of infinite-state programs (e.g., pushdown systems [36]), they limit their scope to a subset of CTL (e.g., the universal fragment of CTL [11]), or support existential path quantifiers only indirectly by considering their universal dual [8].

In this paper, we propose a new static analysis method for proving CTL properties that does not suffer from any of these limitations. We set our work in the framework of *abstract interpretation* [16], a general theory of semantic approximation that provides a basis for various successful industrial-scale tools

© Springer Nature Switzerland AG 2018
A. Podelski (Ed.): SAS 2018, LNCS 11002, pp. 402–422, 2018.
https://doi.org/10.1007/978-3-319-99725-4_24

```
while ¹( rand() ) {
    ²x := 1
    ³n := rand()
    while ⁴( n > 0 ) { ⁵n := n – 1 }
    ⁶x := 0
}
while ⁷( true ) {}⁸
```

Fig. 1. Standard lock acquire/release-style program [12], where rand() is a random number generation function. Assignments x := 1 and x := 0 are acting as acquire and release, respectively. We want to prove the CTL property $AG(x = 1 \Rightarrow A(true\ U\ x = 0))$ expressing that whenever a lock is acquired (x = 1) it is eventually released (x = 0). We assume that initially x = 0.

(e.g., Astrée [3]). We generalize an existing abstract interpretation framework for proving termination [18] and other liveness properties [41].

Following the theory of abstract interpretation [14], we abstract away from irrelevant details about the execution of a program and systematically derive a program semantics that is *sound and complete* for proving a CTL property. The semantics is a function defined over the programs states that satisfy the CTL formula. The value of the semantics for a CTL formula that expresses a liveness property (e.g., $A(true\ U\ \phi)$) gives an upper bound on the number of program execution steps needed to reach a desirable state (i.e., a state satisfying ϕ for $A(true\ U\ \phi)$). The semantics for any other CTL formula is the constant function equal to zero over its domain. We define the semantics inductively on the structure of a CTL formula, and we express it in a constructive fixpoint form starting from the functions defined for its sub-formulas.

Further sound abstractions suitable for static program analysis are derived by *fixpoint approximation* [14]. We leverage existing numerical abstract domains based on piecewise-defined functions [39], which we augment with novel under-approximating operators to directly handle existential CTL formulas. The piecewise-defined function for a CTL formula is automatically inferred through *backward analysis* by building upon the piecewise-defined functions for its sub-formulas. It over-approximates the value of the corresponding concrete semantics and, by under-approximating its domain of definition, yields a *sufficient precondition* for the CTL property. We prove the soundness of the analysis, meaning that all program executions respecting the inferred precondition indeed satisfy the CTL property. A program execution that does not respect the precondition might or might not satisfy the property.

To briefly illustrate our approach, let us consider the acquire/release-style program shown in Fig. 1, and the CTL formula $AG(x = 1 \Rightarrow A(true\ U\ x = 0))$. The analysis begins from the atomic propositions x = 1 and x = 0 and, for each program control point, it infers a piecewise-defined function that is only defined when x is one or zero, respectively. It then continues to the sub-formula

A(*true* U x = 0) for which, building upon the function obtained for x = 0, it infers the following interesting function at program point 4:

$$\lambda x.\lambda n. \begin{cases} 0 & x = 0 \\ 2 & x \neq 0 \wedge n \leq 0 \\ 2n + 2 & \text{otherwise} \end{cases} \tag{1.1}$$

The function indicates that the sub-formula x = 0 is either satisfied trivially (when x is already zero), or in at most 2 program execution steps when $n \leq 0$ (and thus the loop at program point 4 is not entered) and $2n + 2$ steps when $n > 0$ (and thus the loop is entered). The analysis then proceeds to x = 1 ⇒ A(*true* U x = 0), i.e., x ≠ 1 ∨ A(*true* U x = 0). The inferred function for the sub-formula x ≠ 1 is only defined over the complement of the domain of the one obtained for x = 1. The disjunction combines this function with the one obtained for A(*true* U x = 0) by taking the union over the function domains and the maximum over the function values. The result at program point 4 is the same function obtained for A(*true* U x = 0). Finally, the analysis can proceed to the initial formula AG(x = 1 ⇒ A(*true* U x = 0)). The function at program point 4 remains the same but its value now indicates the maximum number of steps needed until the *next state* that satisfies x = 0. The function inferred at the beginning of the program proves that the program satisfies the CTL formula AG(x = 1 ⇒ A(*true* U x = 0)) unless x has initial value one. Indeed, in such a case, the program does not satisfy the formula since the loop at program point 1 might never execute. Thus, the inferred precondition is the weakest precondition for the CTL property AG(x = 1 ⇒ A(*true* U x = 0)).

We implemented our approach in the prototype static analyzer FUNCTION [13]. Our experimental evaluation demonstrates that the analysis is effective, even for CTL formulas with non-trivial nesting of universal and existential path quantifiers, and performs well on a wide variety of benchmarks.

2   Trace Semantics

We model the operational semantics of a program as a *transition system* $\langle \Sigma, \tau \rangle$ where Σ is a (potentially infinite) set of program states, and the transition relation $\tau \subseteq \Sigma \times \Sigma$ describes the possible transitions between states. The set of *final states* of the program is $\Omega \stackrel{\text{def}}{=} \{s \in \Sigma \mid \forall s' \in \Sigma : \langle s, s' \rangle \notin \tau\}$.

Given a transition system $\langle \Sigma, \tau \rangle$, the function pre: $\mathcal{P}(\Sigma) \to \mathcal{P}(\Sigma)$ maps a given set of states X to the set of their predecessors with respect to τ:pre$(X) \stackrel{\text{def}}{=} \{s \in \Sigma \mid \exists s' \in X : \langle s, s' \rangle \in \tau\}$, and the function $\widetilde{\text{pre}}: \mathcal{P}(\Sigma) \to \mathcal{P}(\Sigma)$ maps a given set of states X to the set of states whose successors with respect to τ are all in X: $\widetilde{\text{pre}}(X) \stackrel{\text{def}}{=} \{s \in \Sigma \mid \forall s' \in \Sigma : \langle s, s' \rangle \in \tau \Rightarrow s' \in X\}$.

In the following, given a set S, let $S^n \stackrel{\text{def}}{=} \{s_0 \cdots s_{n-1} \mid \forall i < n : s_i \in S\}$ be the set of all sequences of exactly n elements from S. We write ε to denote the empty sequence, i.e., $S^0 \stackrel{\text{def}}{=} \{\varepsilon\}$. Let $S^* \stackrel{\text{def}}{=} \bigcup_{n \in \mathbb{N}} S^n$ be the set of all finite sequences, $S^+ \overset{\text{def}}{=} S^* \setminus S^0$ be the set of all non-empty finite sequences, S^ω be the set of all infinite sequences, $S^{+\infty} \overset{\text{def}}{=} S^+ \cup S^\omega$ be the set of all non-empty finite or infinite sequences and $S^{*\infty} \overset{\text{def}}{=} S^* \cup S^\omega$ be the set of all finite or infinite sequences of elements from S. We write $\sigma\sigma'$ for the concatenation of two sequences $\sigma, \sigma' \in S^{*\infty}$ (with $\sigma\varepsilon = \varepsilon\sigma = \sigma$, and $\sigma\sigma' = \sigma$ if $\sigma \in S^\omega$), $T^+ \overset{\text{def}}{=} T \cap S^+$ for the selection of the non-empty finite sequences of $T \subseteq S^{*\infty}$, $T^\omega \overset{\text{def}}{=} T \cap S^\omega$ for the selection of the infinite sequences of $T \subseteq S^{*\infty}$, and $T \, ; \, T' \overset{\text{def}}{=} \{\sigma s \sigma' \mid s \in S, \sigma s \in T, s\sigma' \in T'\}$ for the merging of sets of sequences $T \subseteq S^+$ and $T' \subseteq S^{+\infty}$, when a finite sequence in T terminates with the initial state of a sequence in T'.

Given a transition system $\langle \Sigma, \tau \rangle$, a *trace* is a non-empty sequence of program states described by the transition relation τ, that is, $\langle s, s' \rangle \in \tau$ for each pair of consecutive states $s, s' \in \Sigma$ in the sequence. The set of final states Ω and the transition relation τ can be understood as sets of traces of length one and two, respectively. The *maximal trace semantics* $\Lambda \in \mathcal{P}(\Sigma^{+\infty})$ generated by a transition system is the union of all non-empty finite traces that are terminating with a final state in Ω, and all infinite traces. It can be expressed as a least fixpoint in the complete lattice $\langle \mathcal{P}(\Sigma^{+\infty}), \sqsubseteq, \sqcup, \sqcap, \Sigma^\omega, \Sigma^+ \rangle$ [14]:

$$\Lambda = \text{lfp}^{\sqsubseteq} \, \lambda T . \Omega \cup (\tau \, ; \, T) \tag{2.1}$$

where the computational order is $T_1 \sqsubseteq T_2 \overset{\text{def}}{=} T_1^+ \subseteq T_2^+ \land T_1^\omega \supseteq T_2^\omega$.

The maximal trace semantics carries all information about a program and fully describes its behavior. However, reasoning about a particular property of a program is facilitated by the design of a semantics that abstracts away from irrelevant details about program executions. In the paper, we use *abstract interpretation* [16] to systematically derive, by abstraction of the maximal trace semantics, a sound and complete semantics that precisely captures exactly and only the needed information to reason about CTL properties.

3   Computation Tree Logic

CTL is also known as *branching* temporal logic; its semantics is based on a branching notion of time: at each moment there may be several possible successor program states and thus each moment of time might have several different possible futures. Accordingly, the interpretation of CTL formulas is defined in terms of program states, as opposed to the interpretation of LTL formulas in terms of traces. This section gives a brief introduction into the syntax and semantics of CTL. We refer to [1] for further details.

We assume a set of atomic propositions describing properties of program states. Formulas in CTL are formed according to the following grammar:

$$\phi ::= a \mid \neg\phi \mid \phi \land \phi \mid \phi \lor \phi \mid \text{AX}\phi \mid \text{AG}\phi \mid \text{A}(\phi \, \text{U} \, \phi) \mid \text{EX}\phi \mid \text{EG}\phi \mid \text{E}(\phi \, \text{U} \, \phi)$$

where a is an atomic proposition. The universal quantifier (denoted A) and the existential quantifier (denoted E) allow expressing properties of *all* or *some* traces that start in a state. In the following, we often use Q to mean either A or E. The *next* temporal operator (denoted X) allows expressing properties about the next program state in a trace. The *globally* operator (denoted G) allow expressing properties that should hold always (i.e., for all states) on a trace. The *until* temporal operator (denoted U) allows expressing properties that should hold eventually on a trace, and always until then. We omit the *finally* temporal operator (denoted F) since a formula of the form $QF\phi$ can be equivalently expressed as $Q(true\ U\ \phi)$.

The semantics of formulas in CTL is formally given by a satisfaction relation $\models$ between program states and CTL formulas. In the following, we write $s \models \phi$ if and only if the formula ϕ holds in the program state $s \in \Sigma$. We assume that the satisfaction relation for atomic propositions is given. The satisfaction relation for other CTL formulas is formally defined as follows:

$$
\begin{aligned}
s &\models \neg\phi & &\Leftrightarrow & \neg&(s \models \phi) \\
s &\models \phi_1 \wedge \phi_2 & &\Leftrightarrow & s &\models \phi_1 \wedge s \models \phi_2 \\
s &\models \phi_1 \vee \phi_2 & &\Leftrightarrow & s &\models \phi_1 \vee s \models \phi_2 \\
s &\models A\varphi & &\Leftrightarrow & \forall\sigma &\in T(s): \sigma \models \varphi \\
s &\models E\varphi & &\Leftrightarrow & \exists\sigma &\in T(s): \sigma \models \varphi
\end{aligned}
\tag{3.1}
$$

where $T(s) \in \mathcal{P}(\Sigma^{+\infty})$ denotes the set of all program traces starting in the state $s \in \Sigma$. The semantics of trace formulas φ is defined below:

$$
\begin{aligned}
\sigma &\models X\phi & &\Leftrightarrow & \sigma[1] &\models \phi \\
\sigma &\models G\phi & &\Leftrightarrow & \forall 0 \leq i&: \sigma[i] \models \phi \\
\sigma &\models \phi_1 U \phi_2 & &\Leftrightarrow & \exists 0 \leq i&: \sigma[i] \models \phi_2 \wedge \forall 0 \leq j < i: \sigma[j] \models \phi_1
\end{aligned}
\tag{3.2}
$$

where $\sigma[i]$ denotes the program state at position i on the trace $\sigma \in \Sigma^{+\infty}$. We refer to [1] for further details.

4   Program Semantics for CTL Properties

In the following, we derive a program semantics that is *sound and complete* for proving a CTL property. We define the semantics inductively on the structure of a CTL formula. More specifically, for each formula ϕ, we define the *CTL abstraction* $\alpha_\phi: \mathcal{P}(\Sigma^{+\infty}) \to (\Sigma \rightharpoonup \mathbb{O})$ which extracts a partial function $f: \Sigma \rightharpoonup \mathbb{O}$ from program states to ordinals from a given set of sequences $T \in \mathcal{P}(\Sigma^{+\infty})$ by building upon the CTL abstractions of the sub-formulas of ϕ. The domain of f coincides with the set of program states that satisfy ϕ. Ordinal values are needed to support programs with possibly unbounded non-determinism [18]. The definition of α_ϕ for each CTL formula is summarized in Fig. 2 and explained in more detail below. We use the CTL abstraction to define the program semantics $\Lambda_\phi: \Sigma \rightharpoonup \mathbb{O}$ for a formula ϕ by abstraction of the maximal trace semantics Λ.

Definition 1. *Given a CTL formula ϕ and the corresponding CTL abstraction $\alpha_\phi: \mathcal{P}(\Sigma^{+\infty}) \to (\Sigma \rightharpoonup \mathbb{O})$, the program semantics $\Lambda_\phi: \Sigma \rightharpoonup \mathbb{O}$ for ϕ is defined as $\Lambda_\phi \overset{def}{=} \alpha_\phi(\Lambda)$, where Λ is the maximal trace semantics (cf. Eq. 2.1).*

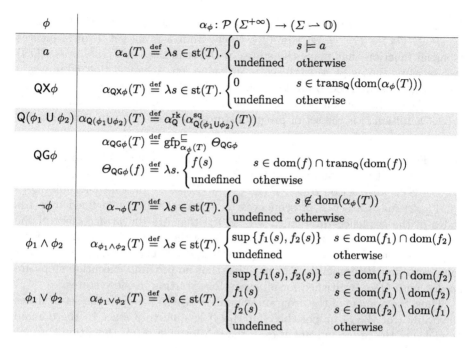

Fig. 2. CTL abstraction $\alpha_\phi \colon \mathcal{P}\left(\Sigma^{+\infty}\right) \to (\Sigma \rightharpoonup \mathbb{O})$ for each CTL formula ϕ. The function trans_Q stands for pre, if Q is E, or $\widetilde{\mathrm{pre}}$, if Q is A (cf. Sect. 2). The *state function* $\mathrm{st} \colon \mathcal{P}\left(\Sigma^{+\infty}\right) \to \mathcal{P}\left(\Sigma\right)$ collects all states of a given set of sequences T: $\mathrm{st}(T) \overset{\mathrm{def}}{=} \{s \in \Sigma \mid \exists \sigma' \in \Sigma^*, \sigma'' \in \Sigma^{*\infty} : \sigma's\sigma'' \in T\}$. The *ranking abstraction* $\alpha_Q^{\mathrm{rk}} \colon \mathcal{P}\left(\Sigma^+\right) \to (\Sigma \rightharpoonup \mathbb{O})$ is defined in Eq. 4.1, while the *subsequence abstraction* $\alpha_{\mathsf{QF}\phi}^{\mathrm{sq}} \colon \mathcal{P}\left(\Sigma^{+\infty}\right) \to \mathcal{P}\left(\Sigma^+\right)$ is defined in Eqs. 4.2 and 4.3. In the last two rows, $f_1 \overset{\mathrm{def}}{=} \alpha_{\phi_1}(T)$ and $f_2 \overset{\mathrm{def}}{=} \alpha_{\phi_2}(T)$.

Remarks. It may seem unintuitive to define Λ_ϕ starting from program traces rather than program states (as in Sect. 3). The reason behind this deliberate choice is that it allows placing Λ_ϕ in the hierarchy of semantics defined by Cousot [14], which is a uniform framework that makes program semantics easily comparable and facilitates explaining the similarities and correspondences between semantic models. Specifically, this enables the comparison with existing semantics for termination [18] and other liveness properties [41] (cf. Sect. 7).

It may also seem unnecessary to define Λ_ϕ to be a function. However, this choice yields a uniform treatment of CTL formulas independently of whether they express safety or liveness properties (or a combination of these). Additionally, it allows leveraging existing abstract domains [38, 39] (cf. Sect. 5) to obtain a sound static analysis for CTL properties. In particular, the proof of the soundness of the static analysis (cf. Theorem 2 and [38] for more details) requires reasoning both about the domain of Λ_ϕ as well as its value.

Atomic Propositions. For an atomic proposition a, the CTL abstraction $\alpha_a \colon \mathcal{P}(\Sigma^{+\infty}) \rightarrow (\Sigma \rightharpoonup \mathbb{O})$ simply extracts from a given set T of sequences a partial function that maps the states of the sequences in T (i.e., $s \in \mathrm{st}(T)$) that satisfy a (i.e., $s \models a$) to the constant value zero, meaning that no program execution steps are needed until a is satisfied for all executions starting in those states. Thus, the domain of the corresponding program semantics $\Lambda_a \colon \Sigma \rightharpoonup \mathbb{O}$ is (cf. Definition 1) is the set of program states that satisfy a (since $\mathrm{st}(\Lambda) = \Sigma$).

Next-Formulas. Next-formulas $\mathsf{Q}\mathsf{X}\phi$ express that the next state of all traces (if Q is A) or at least one trace (if Q is E) satisfies ϕ.

The CTL abstraction $\alpha_{\mathsf{Q}\mathsf{X}\phi} \colon \mathcal{P}(\Sigma^{+\infty}) \rightarrow (\Sigma \rightharpoonup \mathbb{O})$ for a next-formula $\mathsf{Q}\mathsf{X}\phi$ (cf. Fig. 2) maps a set T of sequences to a partial function defined over the states of the sequences in T (i.e., $s \in \mathrm{st}(T)$) that are the *predecessors* of the states that satisfy ϕ, that is, the predecessors of the states in the domain of the CTL abstraction for ϕ (i.e., $s \in \mathrm{trans}_{\mathsf{Q}}(\mathrm{dom}(\alpha_\phi(T)))$). The function has constant value zero over its domain, again meaning that no program execution steps are needed until $\mathsf{Q}\mathsf{X}\phi$ is satisfied for all executions starting in those states.

Thus, the domain of the program semantics $\Lambda_{\mathsf{Q}\mathsf{X}\phi} \colon \Sigma \rightharpoonup \mathbb{O}$ is the set of states inevitably (for $\Lambda_{\mathsf{A}\mathsf{X}\phi}$) or possibly (for $\Lambda_{\mathsf{E}\mathsf{X}\phi}$) leading to a state in the domain $\mathrm{dom}(\Lambda_\phi)$ of the program semantics of the sub-formula ϕ (cf. Definition 1).

Until-Formulas. Until-formulas $\mathsf{Q}(\phi_1 \ \mathsf{U} \ \phi_2)$ express that some desired state (i.e., a state satisfying the sub-formula ϕ_2) is eventually reached during program execution, either in all traces (if Q is A) or in at least one trace (if Q is E), and the sub-formula ϕ_1 is satisfied in all program states encountered until then. Thus, we can observe that an until-formula is satisfied by *finite* subsequences of possibly *infinite* program traces. To reason about subsequences, we define the *subsequence function* $\mathrm{sq} \colon \mathcal{P}(\Sigma^{+\infty}) \rightarrow \mathcal{P}(\Sigma^{+})$ which extracts all finite subsequences of a given set of sequences $T \colon \mathrm{sq}(T) \overset{\mathrm{def}}{=} \{\sigma \in \Sigma^{+} \mid \exists \sigma' \in \Sigma^{*}, \sigma'' \in \Sigma^{*\infty} : \sigma'\sigma\sigma'' \in T\}$. In the following, given a formula $\mathsf{Q}(\phi_1 \ \mathsf{U} \ \phi_2)$, we define the corresponding *subsequence abstraction* $\alpha^{\mathrm{sq}}_{\mathsf{Q}(\phi_1 \mathsf{U} \phi_2)} \colon \mathcal{P}(\Sigma^{+\infty}) \rightarrow \mathcal{P}(\Sigma^{+})$ which extracts the finite subsequences that satisfy $\mathsf{Q}(\phi_1 \ \mathsf{U} \ \phi_2)$ from of a set of sequences T. We can then use $\alpha^{\mathrm{sq}}_{\mathsf{Q}(\phi_1 \mathsf{U} \phi_2)}$ to define the CTL abstraction $\alpha_{\mathsf{Q}(\phi_1 \mathsf{U} \phi_2)} \colon \mathcal{P}(\Sigma^{+\infty}) \rightarrow (\Sigma \rightharpoonup \mathbb{O})$ as shown in Fig. 2. The *ranking abstraction* $\alpha^{\mathrm{rk}}_{\mathsf{Q}} \colon \mathcal{P}(\Sigma^{+}) \rightarrow (\Sigma \rightharpoonup \mathbb{O})$ is:

$$\alpha^{\mathrm{rk}}_{\mathsf{Q}}(T) \overset{\mathrm{def}}{=} \alpha^{\mathrm{v}}_{\mathsf{Q}}(\vec{\alpha}(T)) \tag{4.1}$$

where $\vec{\alpha} \colon \mathcal{P}(\Sigma^{+}) \rightarrow \mathcal{P}(\Sigma) \times \mathcal{P}(\Sigma \times \Sigma)$ extracts from a given set of non-empty finite sequences T the smallest transition system $\langle S, r \rangle$ that generates $T \colon \vec{\alpha}(T) \overset{\mathrm{def}}{=} \langle \mathrm{st}(T), \{\langle s, s' \rangle \in \Sigma \times \Sigma \mid \exists \sigma \in \Sigma^{*}, \sigma' \in \Sigma^{*\infty} : \sigma ss'\sigma' \in T\} \rangle$ and the function $\alpha^{\mathrm{v}}_{\mathsf{Q}} \colon \mathcal{P}(\Sigma) \times \mathcal{P}(\Sigma \times \Sigma) \rightarrow (\Sigma \rightharpoonup \mathbb{O})$ provides the rank of the elements in the domain of the transition relation of the transition system:

$$\alpha_Q^v \langle S, r \rangle s \overset{\text{def}}{=} \begin{cases} 0 & \forall s' \in S : \langle s, s' \rangle \notin r \\ \text{bnd}_Q \left\{ \alpha_Q^v \langle S, r \rangle s' + 1 \,\middle|\, \begin{matrix} s \neq s', \langle s, s' \rangle \in r, \\ s' \in \text{dom}(\alpha_Q^v \langle S, r \rangle) \end{matrix} \right\} & \text{otherwise} \end{cases}$$

where bnd_Q stands for sup, if Q is A, or inf, if Q is E. The CTL abstraction $\alpha_{A(\phi_1 U \phi_2)}$ (resp. $\alpha_{E(\phi_1 U \phi_2)}$) maps the states $\text{st}(T)$ of a given set of sequences T that satisfy $Q(\phi_1 \cup \phi_2)$ to an upper bound (resp. lower bound) on the number of program execution steps until the sub-formula ϕ_2 is satisfied, for all (resp. at least one of the) executions starting in those states.

Existential Until-Formulas. The subsequence abstraction $\alpha_{E(\phi_1 U \phi_2)}^{sq}$ for a formula $E(\phi_1 \cup \phi_2)$ extracts from a given a set of sequences T the finite subsequence of states that terminate in a state satisfying ϕ_2 and all predecessor states satisfy ϕ_1 (and not ϕ_2). It is defined as follows:

$$\alpha_{E(\phi_1 U \phi_2)}^{sq}(T) \overset{\text{def}}{=} \overline{\alpha}_{E(\phi_1 U \phi_2)}[\text{dom}(\alpha_{\phi_1}(T))][\text{dom}(\alpha_{\phi_2}(T))]T$$
$$\overline{\alpha}_{E(\phi_1 U \phi_2)}[S_1][S_2]T \overset{\text{def}}{=} \{\sigma s \in \text{sq}(T) \mid \sigma \in (S_1 \setminus S_2)^*, s \in S_2\} \tag{4.2}$$

where S_1 is the set of states that satisfy the sub-formula ϕ_1 (i.e., $\text{dom}(\alpha_{\phi_1}(T))$), and S_2 is the set of desired states (i.e., $\text{dom}(\alpha_{\phi_2}(T))$).

Universal Until-Formulas. A finite subsequence of states satisfies a universal until-formula $A(\phi_1 \cup \phi_2)$ if and only if it terminates in a state satisfying ϕ_2, all predecessor states satisfy ϕ_1, *and all other sequences with a common prefix also terminate in a state satisfying ϕ_2 (and all its predecessors satisfy ϕ_1)*, i.e., the program reaches a desired state (via states that satisfy ϕ_1) independently of the non-deterministic choices made during execution. We define the *neighborhood* of a sequence of states σ in a given set T as the set of sequences $\sigma' \in T$ with a common prefix with σ: $\text{nbhd}(\sigma, T) \overset{\text{def}}{=} \{\sigma' \in T \mid \text{pf}(\sigma) \cap \text{pf}(\sigma') \neq \emptyset\}$, where the *prefixes function* $\text{pf} \colon \Sigma^{+\infty} \to \mathcal{P}(\Sigma^{+\infty})$ yields the set of non-empty prefixes of a sequence $\sigma \in \Sigma^{+\infty}$: $\text{pf}(\sigma) \overset{\text{def}}{=} \{\sigma' \in \Sigma^{+\infty} \mid \exists \sigma'' \in \Sigma^{*\infty} : \sigma = \sigma'\sigma''\}$.

We can now defined the subsequence abstraction $\alpha_{A(\phi_1 U \phi_2)}^{sq}$:

$$\alpha_{A(\phi_1 U \phi_2)}^{sq}(T) \overset{\text{def}}{=} \overline{\alpha}_{A(\phi_1 U \phi_2)}[\text{dom}(\alpha_{\phi_1}(T))][\text{dom}(\alpha_{\phi_2}(T))]T$$
$$\overline{\alpha}_{A(\phi_1 U \phi_2)}[S_1][S_2]T \overset{\text{def}}{=} \left\{ \sigma s \in \text{sq}(T) \,\middle|\, \begin{matrix} \sigma \in (S_1 \setminus S_2)^*, s \in S_2, \\ \text{nbhd}(\sigma, \text{sf}(T) \cap \overline{S_2}^{+\infty}) = \emptyset, \\ \text{nbhd}(\sigma, \text{sf}(T) \cap Z) = \emptyset \end{matrix} \right\} \tag{4.3}$$

where the *suffixes function* $\text{sf} \colon \mathcal{P}(\Sigma^{+\infty}) \to \mathcal{P}(\Sigma^{+\infty})$ yields the set of non-empty suffixes of a set of sequences T: $\text{sf}(T) \overset{\text{def}}{=} \bigcup \{\sigma \in \Sigma^{+\infty} \mid \exists \sigma' \in \Sigma^* : \sigma'\sigma \in T\}$, and $Z \overset{\text{def}}{=} \{\sigma s \sigma' \in \Sigma^{+\infty} \mid \sigma \in \Sigma^* \wedge s \in \overline{S_1 \cup S_2} \wedge \sigma' \in \Sigma^{+\infty}\}$ is the set of sequences of states in which at least one state satisfies neither ϕ_1 nor ϕ_2. The last two conjuncts in the definition of the helper function $\overline{\alpha}_{A(\phi_1 \cup \phi_2)}[S_1][S_2]$ ensure that a finite subsequence satisfies $A(\phi_1 \cup \phi_2)$ only if it does not have a common prefix with any subsequence of T that never reaches a desired state in S_2 (i.e., $\text{nbhd}(\sigma, \text{sf}(T) \cap \overline{S_2}^{+\infty}) = \emptyset$) and with any subsequence that contains a state that does not belong to S_1 and S_2 (i.e., $\text{nbhd}(\sigma, \text{sf}(T) \cap Z) = \emptyset$).

Example 1. Let us consider again the acquire/release program of Fig. 1 and let T be the set of its traces. The suffixes starting at program point 2 of the traces in T can be visualized as follows:

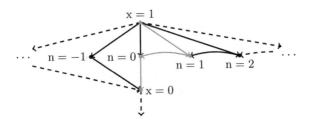

Observe that these sequences form a neighborhood in the set $\text{sf}(T)$ of suffixes of T (i.e., the set of all these sequences is the neighborhood $\text{nbhd}(\sigma, \text{sf}(T))$ of any sequence σ in the set). In the following, we write x_i and n_i for the states denoted above by $x = i$ and $n = i$, respectively.

Let us consider the universal until-formula $A(x = 1 \cup x = 0)$. The set of desired states is $S_2 = \{x_0\}$ and $S_1 = \{x_1\} \cup \{n_i \mid i \in \mathbb{Z}\}$ is the set of states that satisfy $x = 1$. All sequences in the neighborhood have prefixes of the form σs where $\sigma = x_1 \cdots \in (S_1 \cap \overline{S_2})^*$ and $s = x_0 \in S_2$. Thus, the neighborhood of any subsequence σs does not contain sequences in $\overline{S_2}^{+\infty}$ that never reach the desired state x_0 (i.e., $\text{nbhd}(\sigma s, \text{sf}(T) \cap \overline{S_2}^{+\infty}) = \emptyset$). Furthermore, the neighborhood does not contain sequences in Z in which at least one state neither satisfies $x = 1$ nor $x = 0$ (i.e., $\text{nbhd}(\sigma, \text{sf}(T) \cap Z) = \emptyset$). Therefore, the until-formula $A(x = 1 \cup x = 0)$ is satisfied at program point 2.

Let us consider now the formula $A(x = 1 \wedge 0 \leq n \cup x = 0)$. Again, all sequences in the neighborhood eventually reach the desired state x_0. However, in this case, the set S_1 is limited to states with non-negative values for n, i.e., $S_1 = \{x_1\} \cup \{n_i \mid 0 \leq i\}$. Thus, the neighborhood also contains sequences in which at least one state satisfies neither $x = 1 \wedge 0 \leq n$ nor $x = 0$ (e.g., the sequence $x_1 n_{-1} \ldots$). Hence $A(x = 1 \wedge 0 \leq n \cup x = 0)$ is not satisfied at program point 2 since $\text{nbhd}(\sigma, \text{sf}(T) \cap Z) \neq \emptyset$. Instead, the existential until-formula $E(x = 1 \wedge 0 \leq n \cup x = 0)$ is satisfied since, for instance, the subsequence σs where $\sigma = x_1 n_1$ and $s = x_0$ satisfies $(x = 1 \wedge 0 \leq n \cup x = 0)$.

Until Program Semantics. We now have all the ingredients that define the program semantics $\Lambda_{Q(\phi_1 \cup \phi_2)} \colon \Sigma \rightharpoonup \mathbb{O}$ for an until-formula $Q(\phi_1 \cup \phi_2)$ (cf. Definition 1). Let $\langle \Sigma \rightharpoonup \mathbb{O}, \sqsubseteq \rangle$ be the partially ordered set for the computational order $f_1 \sqsubseteq f_2 \Leftrightarrow \text{dom}(f_1) \subseteq \text{dom}(f_2) \wedge \forall x \in \text{dom}(f_1) \colon f_1(x) \leq f_2(x)$. The program semantics $\Lambda_{\mathsf{Q}(\phi_1 \mathsf{U} \phi_2)}$ can be expressed as a least fixpoint in $\langle \Sigma \rightharpoonup \mathbb{O}, \sqsubseteq \rangle$ as:

$$\Lambda_{\mathsf{Q}(\phi_1 \mathsf{U} \phi_2)} = \mathrm{lfp}_{\dot{\emptyset}}^{\sqsubseteq} \Theta_{\mathsf{Q}(\phi_1 \mathsf{U} \phi_2)} [\mathrm{dom}(\Lambda_{\phi_1})][\mathrm{dom}(\Lambda_{\phi_2})]$$

$$\Theta_{\mathsf{Q}(\phi_1 \mathsf{U} \phi_2)}[S_1][S_2] f \overset{\text{def}}{=} \lambda s. \begin{cases} 0 & s \in S_2 \\ \mathrm{bnd}_{\mathsf{Q}} \{ f(s') + 1 \mid \langle s, s' \rangle \in \tau \} & s \in S_1 \wedge s \notin S_2 \wedge \\ & s \in \mathrm{trans}_{\mathsf{Q}}(\mathrm{dom}(f)) \\ \text{undefined} & \text{otherwise} \end{cases}$$

$$(4.4)$$

where $\dot{\emptyset}$ is the totally undefined function. The program semantics $\Lambda_{\mathsf{A}(\phi_1 \mathsf{U} \phi_2)}$ (resp. $\Lambda_{\mathsf{E}(\phi_1 \mathsf{U} \phi_2)}$) is a well-founded function mapping each program state in $\mathrm{dom}(\Lambda_{\phi_1})$ inevitably (resp. possibly) leading to a desirable state in $\mathrm{dom}(\Lambda_{\phi_2})$ to an ordinal, which represents an upper bound (resp. lower bound) on the number of program execution steps needed until a desirable state is reached.

Globally-Formulas. Globally-formulas $\mathsf{QG}\phi$ express that ϕ holds indefinitely in all traces (if Q is A) or at least one trace (if Q is E) starting in a state.

The definition of the CTL abstraction $\alpha_{\mathsf{QG}\phi} \colon \mathcal{P}(\Sigma^{+\infty}) \rightarrow (\Sigma \rightharpoonup \mathbb{O})$ for $\mathsf{QG}\phi$ given in Fig. 2 retains the value of the CTL abstraction corresponding to the sub-formula ϕ. Intuitively, each iteration discards the states that satisfy ϕ (i.e., the states in $\mathrm{dom}(\alpha_\phi(T))$) but branch to (sub)sequences of T that do not satisfy $\mathsf{QG}\phi$. Preserving the value of α_ϕ provides more information than just mapping each state to the constant value zero. For instance, the CTL abstraction $\alpha_{\mathsf{AGAF}\phi}$ for a globally-formula $\mathsf{AGAF}\phi$ provides an upper bound on the number of program execution steps needed until the *next occurrence* of ϕ is satisfied, for all executions starting in the corresponding state.

The corresponding program semantics $\Lambda_{\mathsf{QG}\phi} \colon \Sigma \rightharpoonup \mathbb{O}$ (cf. Definition 1) preserves the value of Λ_ϕ for each state satisfying the sub-formula ϕ and inevitably (if Q is A) or possibly (if Q is E) leading only to other states that also satisfy ϕ.

Other Formulas. We are left with describing the CTL abstraction of $\neg \phi$, $\phi \wedge \phi$, and $\phi \vee \phi$ defined in Fig. 2. For a negation $\neg \phi$, the CTL abstraction $\alpha_{\neg \phi}$ maps each program state that does not satisfy ϕ to the value zero. The CTL abstraction for a binary formula $\phi_1 \wedge \phi_2$ or $\phi_1 \vee \phi_2$ retains the largest value of the functions Λ_{ϕ_1} and Λ_{ϕ_2} for each program state satisfying both ϕ_1 and ϕ_2; for a disjunction $\phi_1 \vee \phi_2$, it also retains the value of the function for each program state satisfying either sub-formula.

Theorem 1. *A program satisfies a CTL formula ϕ for all traces starting from a given set of states $\mathcal{I}$ if and only if $\mathcal{I} \subseteq \mathrm{dom}(\Lambda_\phi)$.*

Proof. The proof proceeds by induction over the structure of the CTL formula ϕ. The base case are atomic propositions a for which the proof is immediate.

For a next-formulas $\mathsf{QX}\phi$, by induction hypothesis, $\mathrm{dom}(\Lambda_\phi)$ coincides with the set of states that satisfy ϕ. By Definition 1 and the definition of $\alpha_{\mathsf{QX}\phi}$ in Fig. 2, the domain of $\Lambda_{\mathsf{QX}\phi}$ coincides with $\mathrm{trans}_{\mathsf{Q}}(\mathrm{dom}(\alpha_\phi(T)))$. Thus, by definition of $\mathrm{trans}_{\mathsf{Q}}$, we have that $\mathrm{dom}(\Lambda_{\mathsf{QX}\phi})$ coincides with the set of states that satisfy $\mathsf{QX}\phi$ (cf. Eqs. 3.1 and 3.2).

For an until-formula $\mathsf{Q}(\phi_1 \mathbin{\mathsf{U}} \phi_2)$, by induction hypothesis, $\mathrm{dom}(\Lambda_{\phi_1})$ and $\mathrm{dom}(\Lambda_{\phi_2})$ coincide with the set of states that satisfy ϕ_1 and ϕ_2, respectively. We have $\Lambda_{\mathsf{Q}(\phi_1 \mathbin{\mathsf{U}} \phi_2)} = \Theta_{\mathsf{Q}(\phi_1\mathsf{U}\phi_2)}[\mathrm{dom}(\Lambda_{\phi_1})][\mathrm{dom}(\Lambda_{\phi_2})](\Lambda_{\mathsf{Q}}(\phi_1 \mathbin{\mathsf{U}} \phi_2))$ from Eq. 4.4. Therefore, by definition of $\Theta_{\mathsf{Q}(\phi_1\mathsf{U}\phi_2)}$, $\mathrm{dom}(\Lambda_{\mathsf{Q}}(\phi_1 \mathbin{\mathsf{U}} \phi_2))$ coincides with the states that satisfy ϕ_2 and all states that satisfy ϕ_1 and inevitably (if Q is A) or possibly (if Q is E) lead to states that satisfy ϕ_2. So $\mathrm{dom}(\Lambda_{\mathsf{Q}}(\phi_1 \mathbin{\mathsf{U}} \phi_2))$ coincides with the states that satisfy $\mathsf{Q}(\phi_1 \mathbin{\mathsf{U}} \phi_2)$ (cf. Eqs. 3.1 and 3.2).

For a globally-formula $\mathsf{QG}\phi$, by induction hypothesis, $\mathrm{dom}(\Lambda_\phi)$ coincides with the set of states that satisfy ϕ. By Definition 1 and the definition of $\alpha_{\mathsf{QG}\phi}$ in Fig. 2, we have that $\Lambda_{\mathsf{QG}\phi} = \Theta_{\mathsf{QG}\phi}(\Lambda_{\mathsf{QG}\phi})$. Therefore, by definition of $\Theta_{\mathsf{QG}\phi}$, we have that $\mathrm{dom}(\Lambda_{\mathsf{QG}\phi})$ coincides with the states that satisfy ϕ inevitably (if Q is A) or possibly (if Q is E) lead to other states that satisfy ϕ. So $\mathrm{dom}(\Lambda_{\mathsf{QG}\phi})$ coincides with the states that satisfy $\mathsf{QG}\phi$ (cf. Eqs. 3.1 and 3.2).

Finally, all other cases ($\neg\phi$, $\phi_1 \wedge \phi_2$, and $\phi_1 \vee \phi_2$) follow immediately from the induction hypothesis, the semantics of the CTL formulas (cf. Eq. 3.1) and the definition of the corresponding program semantics (cf. Definition 1 and the CTL abstractions in Fig. 2). □

The program semantics for a CTL formula is not computable when the program state space is infinite. In the next section, we present decidable abstractions by means of piecewise-defined functions [38,39].

5   Static Analysis for CTL Properties

We recall here the features of the abstract domain of piecewise-defined functions [39] that are relevant for our purposes, and describe the new elements that we need to introduce to obtain a static analysis for proving CTL properties. We refer to [38] for an exhaustive presentation of the original abstract domain.

For illustration, we model a program using a control flow graph $\langle \mathcal{L}, E \rangle$, where $\mathcal{L}$ is the set of program points and $E \subseteq \mathcal{L} \times A \times \mathcal{L}$ is the set of edges in the control flow graph. Each edge is labeled by an action $s \in A$; possible actions are skip, a boolean condition b, or an assignment $x := e$. In the following, we write $out(l)$ to denote the set of outgoing edges from a program point l.

Piecewise-Defined Functions Abstract Domain. An element $t \in \mathcal{T}$ of the abstract domain is a piecewise-defined partial function represented by a *decision tree*, where the decision nodes are labeled by linear constraints over the program variables, and the leaf nodes are labeled by functions of the program variables. The decision nodes recursively partition the space of possible values of the program variables, and the leaf nodes represent the value of the function corresponding to each partition. An example of (simplified) decision tree representation of a piecewise-defined function is shown in Fig. 3.

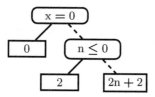

Fig. 3. Simplified decision tree representation of the piecewise-defined function inferred at program point 4 of the program of Fig. 1 (cf. Eq. 1.1). Each constraint is satisfied by the left subtree of the decision node, while the right subtree satisfies its negation. The leaves represent partial functions whose domain is determined by the constraints satisfied along the path to the leaf.

Specifically, the decision nodes are labeled by linear constraints supported by an existing underlying numerical domain, i.e., interval [15] constraints (of the form $\pm x \leq c$), octagonal [30] constraints (of the form $\pm x_i \pm x_j \leq c$), or polyhedral [19] constraints (of the form $c_1 \cdot x_1 + \cdots + c_k \cdot x_k \leq c_{k+1}$). The leaf nodes are labeled by *affine functions* of the program variables (of the form $m_1 \cdot x_1 + \cdots + m_k \cdot x_k + q$), or the special elements $\bot$ and $\top$, which explicitly represent undefined functions. The element $\top$ is introduced to manifest an irrecoverable precision loss of the analysis. We also support *lexicographic* affine *functions* $(f_k, \ldots, f_1, f_0)$ in the isomorphic form of ordinals $\omega^k \cdot f_k + \cdots + \omega \cdot f_1 + f_0$ [29,40].

The partitioning is dynamic: during the analysis of a control flow graph, partitions (i.e. decision nodes and constraints) are modified by assignments and split (i.e., added) by boolean conditions and when merging control flows. More specifically, for each action $s \in A$, we define sound over-approximating abstract transformers $[\![s]\!]_o : \mathcal{T} \to \mathcal{T}$ as well as *new under-approximating abstract transformers* $[\![s]\!]_u : \mathcal{T} \to \mathcal{T}$. These transformers always increase by one the value of the functions labeling the leaves of a given decision tree to count the number of executed program steps (i.e., actions in the control flow graph). The transformers for boolean conditions and assignments additionally modify the decision nodes by building upon the underlying numerical abstract domain. For instance, the abstract transformer $[\![b]\!]_o$ (resp. $[\![b]\!]_u$) for a boolean condition b uses the underlying numerical domain to obtain an over-approximation (resp. an under-approximation) of b as a set of linear constraints; then it adds these constraints to the given decision tree and discards the paths that become unfeasible (because they do not satisfy the added constraints). Let $\{n \leq 0\}$ (resp. $\{n = 0\}$) be the set of constraints obtained by $[\![b]\!]_o$ (resp. $[\![b]\!]_u$) for the boolean condition $b \equiv n \leq 0 \wedge n\%2 = 0$; then, given the right subtree in Fig. 3, $[\![b]\!]_o$ (resp. $[\![b]\!]_u$) would discard the path leading to the leaf with value $2n+2$ by replacing it with a leaf with undefined value $\bot$ (resp. replace $n \leq 0$ with $n = 0$ and replace $2n+2$ with $\bot$). Decision trees are merged using either the approximation join $\curlyvee$ or the computational join $\sqcup$. Both join operators add missing decision nodes from either of the given trees; $\curlyvee$ retains the leaves that are labeled with an undefined function in at least one of the given trees, while $\sqcup$ preserves the leaves that are labeled with a defined function over the leaves labeled with $\bot$ (but preserves the leaves labeled with $\top$ over all other leaves). To minimize the cost of the analysis and to enforce termination, a (dual) widening operator limits the height of the decision trees and the number of maintained partitions.

$$\Lambda_a^\natural \stackrel{\text{def}}{=} \lambda l.\ \text{RESET}\ [\![a]\!]\ (\bot) \tag{5.1}$$

$$\Lambda_{\mathsf{Q}\mathsf{X}\phi}^\natural \stackrel{\text{def}}{=} \lambda l.\ \text{ZERO}\left(\bigsqcup_{(l,s,l')\in out(l)}^{\mathsf{Q}} [\![s]\!]_{\mathsf{Q}}\ (\Lambda_\phi^\natural(l'))\right) \tag{5.2}$$

$$\Lambda_{\mathsf{Q}(\phi_1\mathsf{U}\phi_2)}^\natural \stackrel{\text{def}}{=} \text{lfp}_{\lambda l.\bot}^\natural\ \lambda m.\ \lambda l.\ \text{UNTIL}\left[\!\left[\Lambda_{\phi_1}^\natural(l),\Lambda_{\phi_2}^\natural(l)\right]\!\right]\left(\bigsqcup_{(l,s,l')\in out(l)}^{\mathsf{Q}} [\![s]\!]_{\mathsf{Q}}\ (m(l'))\right) \tag{5.3}$$

$$\Lambda_{\mathsf{Q}\mathsf{G}\phi}^\natural \stackrel{\text{def}}{=} \text{gfp}_{\Lambda_\phi^\natural}^\natural\ \lambda m.\ \lambda l.\ \text{MASK}\left[\!\left[\bigsqcup_{(l,s,l')\in out(l)}^{\mathsf{Q}} [\![s]\!]_{\mathsf{Q}}\ (m(l'))\right]\!\right](m(l)) \tag{5.4}$$

$$\Lambda_{\neg\phi}^\natural \stackrel{\text{def}}{=} \lambda l.\ \text{COMPLEMENT}(\Lambda_\phi^\natural(l)) \tag{5.5}$$

$$\Lambda_{\phi_1\wedge\phi_2}^\natural \stackrel{\text{def}}{=} \lambda l.\ \Lambda_{\phi_1}^\natural(l)\ \curlyvee\ \Lambda_{\phi_2}^\natural(l) \tag{5.6}$$

$$\Lambda_{\phi_1\vee\phi_2}^\natural \stackrel{\text{def}}{=} \lambda l.\ \Lambda_{\phi_1}^\natural(l)\ \sqcup\ \Lambda_{\phi_2}^\natural(l) \tag{5.7}$$

Fig. 4. Abstract program semantics $\Lambda_\phi^\natural$ for each CTL formula ϕ. The join operator $\bigsqcup^{\mathsf{Q}}$ and the abstract transformer $[\![s]\!]_{\mathsf{Q}}$ respectively stand for $\sqcup$ and $[\![s]\!]_u$, if Q is E, or $\curlyvee$ and $[\![s]\!]_o$, if Q is A. With abuse of notation, we use $\bot$ to denote a decision tree with a single undefined leaf node.

Abstract Program Semantics for CTL Properties. The abstract program semantics $\Lambda_\phi^\natural \colon \mathcal{L} \to \mathcal{T}$ for a CTL formula ϕ maps each program point $l \in \mathcal{L}$ to an element $t \in \mathcal{T}$ of the piecewise-defined functions abstract domain. The definition of $\Lambda_\phi^\natural$ for each CTL formula ϕ is summarized in Fig. 4 and explained in some detail below. More details and formal definitions can be found in [37,38].

The analysis starts with the totally undefined function (i.e., a decision tree that consists of a single leaf with undefined value $\bot$) at the final program points (i.e., nodes without outgoing edges in the control flow graph). Then it proceeds backwards through the control flow graph, taking the encountered actions into account, and joining decision trees when merging control flows. For existential CTL properties, the analysis uses the under-approximating abstract transformers $[\![s]\!]_u$ for each action s, to ensure that program states that do not satisfy the CTL property are discarded (i.e., removed from the domain of the current piecewise-defined function), and joins decision trees using the computational join $\sqcup$, to ensure that the current piecewise-defined function remains defined over states that satisfy the CTL property in at least one of the merged control flows. Dually, for universal CTL properties, the analysis uses the over-approximating abstract transformers $[\![s]\!]_o$ and joins decision trees using the approximation join $\curlyvee$, to ensure that the current piecewise-defined function remains defined only over states that satisfy the CTL property in all of the merged control flows.

At each program point, the analysis additionally performs operations that are specific to the considered CTL formula ϕ. For an atomic proposition a (cf. Eq. 5.1), the analysis performs a RESET $[\![a]\!]$ operation, which is analogous to the under-approximating transformer for boolean conditions but additionally replaces all the leaves that satisfy a with leaves labeled with the function with value zero. For example, given the atomic proposition $n = 0$ and the right sub-tree in Fig. 3, RESET $[\![n = 0]\!]$ would replace the constraint $n \leq 0$ with $n = 0$, the leaf $2n + 2$ with $\perp$ and the leaf 2 with 0. For a next-formula $\mathsf{QX}\phi$ (cf. Eq. 5.2), the analysis approximates the effect of the transition from each program point l to each successor program point l' and performs a ZERO operation to replace all defined functions labeling the leaves of the so obtained decision tree with the function with value zero. For an until-formula $\mathsf{Q}(\phi_1 \; \mathsf{U} \; \phi_2)$ (cf. Eq. 5.4), the analysis performs an ascending iteration with widening [13]. At each iteration, the analysis approximates the effect of the transition from each program point l to each successor program point l' and performs an UNTIL operation to model the until temporal operator: UNTIL replaces with the function with value zero all leaves that correspond to defined leaves in the decision tree $\Lambda^\natural_{\phi_2}(l)$ obtained for ϕ_2, and retains all leaves that are labeled with an undefined function in both $\Lambda^\natural_{\phi_1}(l)$ and $\Lambda^\natural_{\phi_1}(l)$. For a globally-formula $\mathsf{QG}\phi$ (cf. Eq. 5.5), the analysis performs a descending iteration with dual widening [41], starting from the abstract semantics $\Lambda^\natural_\phi$ obtained for ϕ. At each iteration, the MASK operation models the globally temporal operator: it discards all defined partitions in $\Lambda^\natural_\phi(l)$ that become undefined as a result of the transition from each program point l to each successor program point l'; at the limit, the only defined partitions are those that remain defined across transitions and thus satisfy the globally-formula. For a negation formula $\neg\phi$ (cf. Eq. 5.5), the analysis performs a COMPLEMENT operation on the decision tree $\Lambda^\natural_\phi(l)$ obtained for ϕ at each program point l; COMPLEMENT replaces all defined functions labeling the leaves of a decision tree with $\perp$, and all $\perp$ with the function with value zero. Note that $\Lambda^\natural_\phi$ is an abstraction of Λ_ϕ and thus not all undefined partitions in $\Lambda^\natural_\phi$ necessarily correspond to undefined partitions in Λ_ϕ. Leaves that are undefined in $\Lambda^\natural_\phi$ due to this uncertainty are labeled with $\top$, and are left unchanged by COMPLEMENT to guarantee the soundness of the analysis. Finally, for binary formulas $\phi_1 \wedge \phi_2$ and $\phi_1 \vee \phi_2$, the abstract semantics $\Lambda^\natural_{\phi_1 \wedge \phi_2}$ and $\Lambda^\natural_{\phi_1 \vee \phi_2}$ (cf. Eqs. 5.6 and 5.7) merge the decision trees obtained for ϕ_1 and ϕ_2 using the approximation join $\curlyvee$ and the computational join $\sqcup$, respectively.

The abstract program semantics $\Lambda^\natural_\phi$ for each CTL formula ϕ is *sound* with respect to the approximation order $f_1 \preccurlyeq f_2 \Leftrightarrow \mathrm{dom}(f_1) \supseteq \mathrm{dom}(f_2) \wedge \forall x \in \mathrm{dom}(f_1) : f_1(x) \leq f_2(x)$, which means that the abstract semantics $\Lambda^\natural_\phi$ *over-approximates* the value of the concrete semantics Λ_ϕ and *under-approximates* its domain of definition $\mathrm{dom}(\Lambda_\phi)$. In this way, the abstraction provides sufficient preconditions for the CTL property ϕ: if the abstraction is defined for a state then that state satisfies ϕ.

Theorem 2. *A program satisfies a CTL formula ϕ for all traces starting from a given set of states $\mathcal{I}$ if $\mathcal{I} \subseteq \mathrm{dom}(\gamma(\Lambda_\phi^\natural))$.*

Proof. (Sketch). The proof proceeds by induction over the structure of the formula ϕ. The base case are atomic propositions for which the proof is immediate.

For a next-formula $\mathsf{QX}\phi$, by induction hypothesis, $\mathrm{dom}(\Lambda_\phi^\natural)$ is a subset of the set of states that satisfy ϕ. Using the over-approximating transformers $[\![s]\!]_o$ together with the approximation join $\curlyvee$ (resp. the under-approximating transformers $[\![s]\!]_u$ together with the computational join $\sqcup$) ensures that $\Lambda_{\mathsf{QX}\phi}^\natural$ soundly under-approximates the set of states that satisfy $\mathsf{QX}\phi$.

For an until-formula $\mathsf{Q}(\phi_1 \mathrel{\mathsf{U}} \phi_2)$, by induction hypothesis, $\mathrm{dom}(\Lambda_{\phi_1}^\natural)$ and $\mathrm{dom}(\Lambda_{\phi_2}^\natural)$ are a subset of the set of states that satisfy ϕ_1 and ϕ_2, respectively. By definition, $\Lambda_{\mathsf{Q}(\phi_1 \mathsf{U}\phi_2)}$ is the limit of an ascending iteration sequence using widening. Again, using the over-approximating transformers $[\![s]\!]_o$ together with the approximation join $\curlyvee$ (resp. the under-approximating transformers $[\![s]\!]_u$ together with the computational join $\sqcup$) guarantees the soundness of the analysis with respect to each transition. The soundness of each iteration without widening is then guaranteed by the definition of the UNTIL operation. The iterations with widening are allowed to be unsound but the limit of the iterations (i.e., $\Lambda_{\mathsf{Q}(\phi_1 \mathsf{U}\phi_2)}$) is guaranteed to soundly under-approximate the set of states that satisfy $(\phi_1 \mathrel{\mathsf{U}} \phi_2)$. We refer to [38] for a detailed proof for formulas of the form $(\mathit{true} \mathrel{\mathsf{U}} \phi_2)$. The generalization to $(\phi_1 \mathrel{\mathsf{U}} \phi_2)$ is trivial.

For a globally-formula $\mathsf{QG}\phi$, $\Lambda_{\mathsf{QG}\phi}$ is the limit of a descending iteration sequence with dual widening, starting from $\Lambda_\phi^\natural$, which soundly under-approximates the set of states that satisfy ϕ. The soundness of each iteration is guaranteed by the definition of the MASK operation and the dual widening operator (see [38]).

The case of a negation $\neg\phi$ is non-trivial since, by induction hypothesis, $\mathrm{dom}(\Lambda_\phi^\natural)$ is a subset of the set of states that satisfy ϕ. Specifically, $\Lambda_\phi^\natural$ maps each program point $l \in \mathcal{L}$ to a decision tree whose leaves determine this under-approximation: leaves labeled with $\bot$ represent states that do not satisfy ϕ while leaves labeled with $\top$ represent states that may or may not satisfy ϕ. The COMPLEMENT operation performed by $\Lambda_{\neg\phi}^\natural$ only considers leaves labeled by $\bot$ and ignores (i.e., leaves unchanged) leaves labeled by $\top$. Thus, $\Lambda_{\neg\phi}^\natural$ soundly under-approximates the set of states that satisfy $\neg\phi$.

Finally, for binary formulas $\phi_1 \wedge \phi_2$ and $\phi_1 \vee \phi_2$, the proof follows immediately from the definition of the approximation join $\curlyvee$ and the computational join $\sqcup$ used in the definition of $\Lambda_{\phi_1 \wedge \phi_2}^\natural$ and $\Lambda_{\phi_1 \vee \phi_2}^\natural$, respectively. $\square$

6   Implementation

The proposed static analysis method for proving CTL properties is implemented in the prototype static analyzer FUNCTION [13].

The implementation is in OCAML and consists of around 9K lines of code. The current front-end of FUNCTION accepts non-deterministic programs written in a C-like syntax (without support for pointers, struct and union types). The only basic data type is mathematical integers. FUNCTION accepts CTL properties written using a syntax similar to the one used in the rest of this paper, with atomic propositions written as C-like pure expressions. The abstract domain of piecewise-defined functions builds on the numerical abstract domains provided by the APRON library [24], and the under-approximating numerical operators provided by the BANAL static analyzer [31].

The analysis is performed backwards on the control flow graph of a program with a standard worklist algorithm [32], using widening and dual widening at loop heads. Non-recursive function calls are inlined, while recursion is supported by augmenting the control flow graphs with call and return edges. The precision of the analysis can be tuned by choosing the underlying numerical abstract domain, by activating the extension to ordinal-value functions [40], and by adjusting the precision of the widening [13] and the widening delay. It is also possible to refine the analysis by considering only reachable states.

Experimental Evaluation. We evaluated our technique on a number of test cases obtained from various sources, and compared FUNCTION against T2 [8] and ULTIMATE LTL AUTOMIZER [20] as well as E-HSF [4], and the prototype implementation from [10]. Figs. 5 and 6 show an excerpt of the results, which demonstrates the differences between FUNCTION, T2 [8] and ULTIMATE LTL AUTOMIZER. The first set of test cases are programs that we used to test our implementation. The second and third set were collected from [25] and the web

No	Program	CTL Property	Result	Time
1.1	and_test.c	$AGAF(n = 1) \wedge AF(n = 0)$	✓	0.05s
1.2	and_test.c	$EGAF(n = 1)$	✓	0.05s
1.4	global_test.c	$AGEF(x \leq -10)$	✓	0.15s
1.7	or_test.c	$AFEG(x < -100) \vee AF(x = 20)$	✓	0.05s
1.8	may_term...	$EF(exit : true)$	✗	-
1.9	until_test.c	$A(x \geq y \, U \, x = y)$	✓	0.03s
1.11	fin_ex.c	$EGEF(n = 1)$	✓	0.04s
1.12	until_ex.c	$E(x \geq y \, U \, x = y)$	✓	0.03s
2.3	win4.c	$AFAG(WItemsNum \geq 1)$	✓	0.15s
2.4	toylin.c	$(c \leq 5 \wedge c > 0) \vee AF(resp > 5)$	✗	-
3.9	cb5_safe.c	$A(i = 0 \, U \, (A(i = 1 \, U \, AG(i = 3)) \vee AG(i = 1)))$	✗	-
3.14	timer...	$\neg AG(timer = 0 \Rightarrow AF(output = 1))$	✗	-
3.15	togglec...	$AG(AF(t = 1) \wedge AF(t = 0))$	✗	-
4.1	Bangalore...	$EF(x < 0)$	✗	-
4.2	Ex02...	$i < 5 \Rightarrow AF(exit : true)$	✓	0.04s
4.3	Ex07...	$AFEG(i = 0)$	✓	0.1s
4.4	java_Seq...	$EF(AF(j \geq 21) \wedge i = 100)$	✓	0.3s
4.5	Madrid...	$AF(x = 7 \wedge EFAG(x = 2))$	✓	0.02s

Fig. 5. Evaluation of FUNCTION on selected test cases collected from various sources. All test cases were analyzed using polyhedral constraints for the decision nodes, and affine functions for the leaf nodes of the decision tree.

No	FuncTion	T2 [8]	Ultimate LTL Automizer [20]
1.1	✓	✗	✓
1.2	✓	✗	-
1.4	✓	✗	-
1.7	✓	✗ (error)	-
1.8	✗	✓	-
1.9	✓	✗	✓
1.11	✓	✗	-
1.12	✓	✗ (no implementation)	-
2.3	✓	✗	✓
2.4	✗	✗	✓
3.9	✗	-	✓
3.14	✗	-	✓
3.15	✗	-	✓
4.1	✗	✓	-
4.2	✓	✗ (out of memory)	✓
4.3	✓	✗	-
4.4	✓	✗ (error)	-
4.5	✓	✗	-

Fig. 6. Differences between FuncTion, T2, and Ultimate LTL Automizer.

interface of Ultimate LTL Automizer [20]. The fourth set are examples from the termination category of the 6th International Competition on Software Verification (SV-COMP 2017). The experiments were conducted on an Intel i7-6600U processor with 20 GB of RAM on Arch Linux with Linux 4.11 and OCaml 4.04.1.

FuncTion passes all test cases with the exception of 2.4, 3.9, 3.14, and 3.15, which fail due to imprecisions introduced by the widening, and 1.8 and 4.1, which fail due to an unfortunate interaction of the under-approximations needed for existential properties and non-deterministic assignments in the programs. However, note that for these test cases we still get some useful information. For instance, for 3.15, FuncTion infers that the CTL property is satisfied if $x < 0$.

In Fig. 6, the missing results for T2 are due to a missing conversion of the test cases to the T2 input format. The comparison with Ultimate LTL Automizer is limited to the test cases where the CTL property can be equivalently expressed in LTL (i.e., universal CTL properties). The results show that only FuncTion succeeds on numerous test cases (1.2, 1.4, 1.7, 1.11, 1.12, 4.3, 4.4, and 4.5). Ultimate LTL Automizer performs well on the supported test cases, but FuncTion still succeeds on most of the test cases provided by Ultimate LTL Automizer (not shown in Fig. 6, since there are no differences between the results of FuncTion and Ultimate LTL Automizer). Overall, none of the tools subsumes the others. In fact, we observe that their combination is more powerful than any of the tools alone, as it would succeed on all test cases.

Finally, FuncTion only succeeds on two of the industrial benchmarks from [10], while T2, E-HSF and [10] fare much better (see [8, Fig. 11]). The reason for the poor performance is that in these benchmarks the effect of function calls is modeled as a non-deterministic assignment and this heavily impacts the precision of FUNCTION. We are confident that we would obtain better results on the original benchmarks, where function calls are not abstracted away.

7 Related Work

In the recent past, a large body of work has been devoted to proving CTL properties of programs. The problem has been extensively studied for finite-state programs [7,26, etc.], while most of the existing approaches for infinite-state systems have limitations that restrict their applicability. For instance, they only support certain classes of programs [36], or they limit their scope to a subset of CTL [11], or to a single CTL property such as termination [27,34, etc.] or non-termination [2,5, etc.]. Our approach does not suffer from these limitations.

Some other approaches for proving CTL properties do not reliably support CTL formulas with arbitrary nesting of universal and existential path quantifiers [23], or support existential path quantifiers only indirectly by building upon recent work for proving non-termination [22], or by considering their universal dual [8]. In particular, the latter approach is problematic: since the universal dual of an existential until formula is non-trivial to define, the current implementation of T2 does not support such formulas (see Fig. 6). Other indirect approaches [4,10] perform unnecessary computations that result in slower runtimes (see [8, Fig. 12]). In comparison to all these approaches, our approach provides strictly more information in the form of a ranking function whose domain gives a precondition for a given CTL property and whose value estimates the number of program execution steps until the property is satisfied.

In [17], Cousot and Cousot define a trace-based semantics for a very general temporal language which subsumes LTL and CTL; this is subsequently abstracted to a state-based semantics. The abstraction has been later shown to be incomplete by Giacobazzi and Ranzato [21]. In contrast to the work of Cousot and Cousot, we do not define a trace-based semantics for CTL. The semantics that we propose is close to their state-based semantics in that their state-based semantics coincides with the domain of the functions that we define. Note that Theorem 1 is not in contrast with the result of Giacobazzi and Ranzato because completeness is proven with respect to the state-based semantics of CTL.

Finally, our abstract interpretation framework generalizes an existing framework [41] for proving guarantee and recurrence properties of programs [28]. Guarantee and recurrence properties are equivalently expressed in CTL as $\mathsf{A}(true \ \mathsf{U} \ \phi)$ and $\mathsf{AGA}(true \ \mathsf{U} \ \phi)$, respectively. In fact, we rediscover the guarantee and recurrence program semantics defined in [41] as instances of our framework: the guarantee semantics coincides with $\Lambda_{\mathsf{A}(true\mathsf{U}\phi)}$ (cf. Sect. 4) and the recurrence semantics coincides with $\Lambda_{\mathsf{AGA}(true\mathsf{U}\phi)}$ (cf. Sect. 4). The common insight with our work is the observation that CTL (sub)formulas are satisfied by finite subsequences (which can also be single states) of possibly infinite sequences. The program semantics for these (sub)formulas then counts the number of steps in these subsequences. Our work generalizes this idea to all CTL formulas and integrates the corresponding semantics in a uniform framework.

8   Conclusion and Future Work

In this paper, we have presented a new static analysis method for inferring preconditions for CTL properties of programs that overcomes the limitations of existing approaches. We have derived our static analysis within the framework of abstract interpretation by abstraction of the operational trace semantics of a program. Using experimental evidence, we have shown that our analysis is effective and performs well on a wide variety of benchmarks, and is able to prove CTL properties that are out of reach for state-of-the-art tools.

It remains for future work to investigate and improve the precision of the analysis in the presence of non-deterministic program assignments. We also plan to support LTL properties [20] or, more generally, CTL* properties [9]. This requires some form of trace partitioning [35] as the interpretation of LTL formulas is defined in terms of program executions instead of program states as CTL.

References

1. Baier, C., Katoen, J.P.: Principles of Model Checking. MIT Press, Cambridge (2008)
2. Bakhirkin, A., Piterman, N.: Finding recurrent sets with backward analysis and trace partitioning. In: Chechik, M., Raskin, J.-F. (eds.) TACAS 2016. LNCS, vol. 9636, pp. 17–35. Springer, Heidelberg (2016). https://doi.org/10.1007/978-3-662-49674-9_2
3. Bertrane, J., Cousot, P., Cousot, R., Feret, J., Mauborgne, L., Miné, A., Rival, X.: Static analysis and verification of aerospace software by abstract interpretation. In: AIAA, pp. 1–38 (2010)
4. Beyene, T.A., Popeea, C., Rybalchenko, A.: Solving existentially quantified horn clauses. In: Sharygina, N., Veith, H. (eds.) CAV 2013. LNCS, vol. 8044, pp. 869–882. Springer, Heidelberg (2013). https://doi.org/10.1007/978-3-642-39799-8_61
5. Chen, H.-Y., Cook, B., Fuhs, C., Nimkar, K., O'Hearn, P.: Proving nontermination via safety. In: Ábrahám, E., Havelund, K. (eds.) TACAS 2014. LNCS, vol. 8413, pp. 156–171. Springer, Heidelberg (2014). https://doi.org/10.1007/978-3-642-54862-8_11
6. Clarke, E.M., Emerson, E.A.: Design and synthesis of synchronization skeletons using branching time temporal logic. In: Kozen, D. (ed.) Logic of Programs 1981. LNCS, vol. 131, pp. 52–71. Springer, Heidelberg (1982). https://doi.org/10.1007/BFb0025774
7. Clarke, E.M., Emerson, E.A., Sistla, A.P.: Automatic verification of finite-state concurrent systems using temporal logic specifications. ACM Trans. Program. Lang. Syst. 8(2), 244–263 (1986)
8. Cook, B., Khlaaf, H., Piterman, N.: Faster temporal reasoning for infinite-state programs. In: FMCAD, pp. 75–82 (2014)
9. Cook, B., Khlaaf, H., Piterman, N.: On automation of CTL* verification for infinite-state systems. In: Kroening, D., Păsăreanu, C.S. (eds.) CAV 2015. LNCS, vol. 9206, pp. 13–29. Springer, Cham (2015). https://doi.org/10.1007/978-3-319-21690-4_2
10. Cook, B., Koskinen, E.: Reasoning about nondeterminism in programs. In: PLDI, pp. 219–230 (2013)

11. Cook, B., Koskinen, E., Vardi, M.: Temporal property verification as a program analysis task. In: Gopalakrishnan, G., Qadeer, S. (eds.) CAV 2011. LNCS, vol. 6806, pp. 333–348. Springer, Heidelberg (2011). https://doi.org/10.1007/978-3-642-22110-1_26
12. Cook, B., Koskinen, E., Vardi, M.Y.: Temporal property verification as a program analysis task - extended version. Formal Methods Syst. Des. **41**(1), 66–82 (2012)
13. Courant, N., Urban, C.: Precise widening operators for proving termination by abstract interpretation. In: Legay, A., Margaria, T. (eds.) TACAS 2017. LNCS, vol. 10205, pp. 136–152. Springer, Heidelberg (2017). https://doi.org/10.1007/978-3-662-54577-5_8
14. Cousot, P.: Constructive design of a hierarchy of semantics of a transition system by abstract interpretation. Theoret. Comput. Sci. **277**(1–2), 47–103 (2002)
15. Cousot, P., Cousot, R.: Static determination of dynamic properties of programs. In: Symposium on Programming, pp. 106–130 (1976)
16. Cousot, P., Cousot, R.: Abstract interpretation: a unified lattice model for static analysis of programs by construction or approximation of fixpoints. In: POPL, pp. 238–252 (1977)
17. Cousot, P., Cousot, R.: Temporal abstract interpretation. In: POPL, pp. 12–25 (2000)
18. Cousot, P., Cousot, R.: An abstract interpretation framework for termination. In: POPL, pp. 245–258(2012)
19. Cousot, P., Halbwachs, N.: Automatic discovery of linear restraints among variables of a program. In: POPL, pp. 84–96 (1978)
20. Dietsch, D., Heizmann, M., Langenfeld, V., Podelski, A.: Fairness modulo theory: a new approach to LTL software model checking. In: Kroening, D., Păsăreanu, C.S. (eds.) CAV 2015. LNCS, vol. 9206, pp. 49–66. Springer, Cham (2015). https://doi.org/10.1007/978-3-319-21690-4_4
21. Giacobazzi, R., Ranzato, F.: Incompleteness of states w.r.t. traces in model checking. Inf. Comput. **204**(3), 376–407 (2006)
22. Gupta, A., Henzinger, T.A., Majumdar, R., Rybalchenko, A., Xu, R.: Proving non-termination. In: POPL, pp. 147–158 (2008)
23. Gurfinkel, A., Wei, O., Chechik, M.: Yasm: a software model-checker for verification and refutation. In: CAV, pp. 170–174 (2006)
24. Jeannet, B., Miné, A.: Apron: a library of numerical abstract domains for static analysis. In: Bouajjani, A., Maler, O. (eds.) CAV 2009. LNCS, vol. 5643, pp. 661–667. Springer, Heidelberg (2009). https://doi.org/10.1007/978-3-642-02658-4_52
25. Koskinen, E.: Temporal verification of programs. Ph.D. thesis, University of Cambridge, November 2012
26. Kupferman, O., Vardi, M.Y., Wolper, P.: An automata-theoretic approach to branching-time model checking. J. ACM **47**(2), 312–360 (2000)
27. Lee, C.S., Jones, N.D., Ben-Amram, A.M.: The size-change principle for program termination. In: POPL, pp. 81–92 (2001)
28. Manna, Z., Pnueli, A.: A hierarchy of temporal properties. In: PODC, pp. 377–410 (1990)
29. Manna, Z., Pnueli, A.: The Temporal Verification of Reactive Systems: Progress (1996)
30. Miné, A.: The octagon abstract domain. High. Order Symbolic Comput. **19**(1), 31–100 (2006)
31. Miné, A.: Inferring sufficient conditions with backward polyhedral under-approximations. Electron. Notes Theor. Comput. Sci. **287**, 89–100 (2012)

32. Nielson, F., Nielson, H.R., Hankin, C.: Principles of Program Analysis. Springer, (1999)
33. Pnueli, A.: The temporal logic of programs. In: FOCS, pp. 46–57 (1977)
34. Podelski, A., Rybalchenko, A.: Transition invariants. In: LICS, pp. 32–41 (2004)
35. Rival, X., Mauborgne, L.: The trace partitioning abstract domain. ACM TOPLAS **29**(5), 26 (2007)
36. Song, F., Touili, T.: Efficient CTL model-checking for pushdown systems. Theoret. Comput. Sci. **549**, 127–145 (2014)
37. Ueltschi, S.: Proving temporal properties by abstract interpretation. Master's thesis, ETH Zurich, Zurich, Switzerland (2017)
38. Urban, C.: Static Analysis by abstract interpretation of functional temporal properties of programs. Ph.D. thesis, École Normale Supérieure, Paris, France, July 2015
39. Urban, C., Miné, A.: A decision tree abstract domain for proving conditional termination. In: SAS, pp. 302–318 (2014)
40. Urban, C., Miné, A.: An abstract domain to infer ordinal-valued ranking functions. In: ESOP, pp. 412–431 (2014)
41. Urban, C., Miné, A.: Inference of ranking functions for proving temporal properties by abstract interpretation. Comput. Lang. Syst. Struct. **47**, 77–103 (2017)

Inductive Termination Proofs with Transition Invariants and Their Relationship to the Size-Change Abstraction

Florian Zuleger[(⊠)]

TU Wien, Vienna, Austria
zuleger@forsyte.at

Abstract. Transition invariants are a popular technique for automated termination analysis. A transition invariant is a covering of the transitive closure of the transition relation of a program by a finite number of well-founded relations. The covering is usually established by an inductive proof using transition predicate abstraction. Such inductive termination proofs have the structure of a finite automaton. These automata, which we call transition automata, offer a rich structure that has not been exploited in previous publications. We establish a new connection between transition automata and the size-change abstraction, which is another widespread technique for automated termination analysis. In particular, we are able to transfer recent results on automated complexity analysis with the size-change abstraction to transition invariants.

1 Introduction

The last decade has seen considerable interest in automated techniques for proving the termination of programs. Notably, the TERMINATOR termination analyzer [14] has been able to analyze device drivers with several thousand lines of code. The analysis in [14] uses the termination criterion suggested by Rybalchenko and Podelski in [25] (for a discussion of earlier work that implicitly used the same principle we refer the reader to [6]): In order to show the well-foundedness of a relation R, it is sufficient to find a finite number of well-founded relations $R_1, \ldots, R_k$ with

$$R^+ \subseteq R_1 \cup \cdots \cup R_k \qquad (*)$$

where R^+ denotes the transitive closure of R.

An essential difficulty in using the above criterion lies in establishing the condition $(*)$, as reasoning about the transitive closure R^+ usually requires induction. For this reason, not only the above criterion but also an inductive argument for establishing $(*)$ was suggested in [25]. The inductive argument was further developed in [26], where the use of *transition predicate abstraction* (TPA) has been suggested for establishing condition $(*)$. TPA is the basis for

© Springer Nature Switzerland AG 2018
A. Podelski (Ed.): SAS 2018, LNCS 11002, pp. 423–444, 2018.
https://doi.org/10.1007/978-3-319-99725-4_25

the termination analysis in TERMINATOR. The starting point of our research are the inductive termination proofs with TPA, which have the structure of finite automata (as already observed in [26]). These automata, which we call *transition automata*, offer a rich structure that has not been exploited in previous publications. It is precisely this automaton structure, which allows us to connect inductive termination proofs with TPA to the size-change abstraction, and transfer recent results on automated complexity analysis.

We contrast our approach with the fascinating line of work [6,30,32], which aims at bounding the height of the relation R in terms of the height of the relations $R_1, \ldots, R_k$. In order to derive such bounds, [6,30] replace Ramsey's theorem, which has been used to prove (*) in [25], by more fine-grained Ramsey-like arguments. In this paper, we show that *inductive* termination proofs with TPA do not need to rely on Ramsey's theorem and can be analyzed solely by *automata-theoretic techniques*.

Size-change abstraction (SCA), introduced by Ben-Amram, Lee and Jones in [22], is another wide-spread technique for automated termination analysis. SCA has been employed for the analysis of functional [22,23], logical [31] and imperative [3,10] programs and term rewriting systems [9], and is implemented in the industrial-strength systems ACL2 [23] and Isabelle [20]. Recently, SCA has also been used for resource bound and complexity analysis of imperative programs [34]. SCA is attractive because of several strong theoretical results on termination analysis [22], complexity analysis [12,33] and the existence of ranking functions [5,33]. The success of SCA has also inspired generalizations to richer classes of constraints [4,5,7]. The connection between TPA and SCA has been the subject of previous research [19], which contains first results but does not exploit the automaton structure of inductive termination proofs. In this paper, we make the following contributions:

Result 1: Our main result (Theorem 7) makes it possible to transfer recent results on automated complexity analysis with the size-change abstraction [12] to transition automata. In particular, we obtain a complete and effective characterization of asymptotic complexity analysis with transition automata. This result holds the potential for the design of new automated complexity analyzers, for example, by extracting complexity bounds from the inductive termination proofs computed by TERMINATOR. We illustrate our result in the following. We consider the programs P_1 and P_2 given by Examples 1 and 2 in Fig. 1. One can model the transition relation of P_1 by the predicate $x' = x - 1 \wedge y' = N \vee x' = x \wedge y' = y - 1$ and the transition relation of P_2 by the predicate $x' = x - 1 \wedge y' = y \vee x' = x \wedge y' = y - 1$. The two relations R_1 and R_2 given by the predicates $x' < x$ resp. $y' < y$ are a transition invariant for both programs; we give an inductive proof which establishes condition (*) for both programs in Sect. 3. For motivation of our results we state here the relation to [6]: With the program invariant $x \leq N \wedge y \leq N$ (which can be computed by standard techniques such as Octagon analysis [24]), the result of [6] allows us to obtain the quadratic bound $O(N^2)$ on the complexity of both programs from the transition invariant given by the relations R_1 and R_2. However, this bound is imprecise for

```
Example 1.
    main(nat N) {
        nat x = N; nat y = N;
        while (x>0 ∧ y>0) {
            if(?){ //transition a₁
                x--; y = N;
            }
            else { //transition a₂
                y--;
    } } }
```

```
Example 2.
    main(nat N) {
        nat x = N; nat y = N;
        while (x>0 ∧ y>0) {
            if(?){ //transition a₁
                x--;
            }
            else { //transition a₂
                y--;
    } } }
```

Fig. 1. The ? in the condition represents non-deterministic choice.

P_2, which has linear complexity. There is no hope in improving the bound for P_2, because the result of [6] just relies on R_1 and R_2. In this paper, we demonstrate that the inductive termination proof offers more structure. We show that just by analyzing the automaton structure of the proof we can deduce the linear bound $O(N)$ for P_2.

Result 2: Following [26] we examine a first termination criterion based on the universality of transition automata and show that the universality of the transition automaton implies the termination of the program under analysis (Theorem 2). We then show that transition automata admit a *more general* termination criterion based on the definition of an associated Büchi-automaton (Theorems 1 and 3). This more general termination criterion has the advantage that fewer predicates are needed for the termination proof (Example 7). We finally show that this new criterion is in fact the *most general* termination criterion admitted by transition automata (Theorem 4).

Result 3: We connect transition automata to the size-change abstraction in Sect. 6. In particular, we show how to transfer several results from the size-change abstraction to transition automata, demonstrating that techniques from SCA are applicable for the analysis of inductive termination proofs with transition predicate abstraction. This is of fundamental interest for understanding the relationship of both termination principles, because transition invariants have been suggested in [25] as a generalization of size-change termination proofs (and indeed later work has formally established that every size-change termination proof can be mimicked by a transition invariant termination proof [19]).

Organization of the Paper. Section 2 gives the basic definitions. Section 3 reviews transition predicate abstraction as introduced in [26]. Section 4 introduces transition automata and gives termination criteria. Section 5 reviews the size-change abstraction. Section 6 defines 'canonical' programs for transition automata and transfers results from the size-change abstraction to transition automata. Section 7 concludes.

2 Basic Definitions

We use $\circ$ to denote the usual *product* of relations, i.e., given two relations $B_1, B_2 \subseteq A \times A$ we define $B_1 \circ B_2 = \{(a_1, a_3) \mid$ there is an $a_2 \in A$ with $(a_1, a_2) \in B_1$ and $(a_2, a_3) \in B_2\}$. Let $B \subseteq A \times A$ be a relation. B is *well-founded* if there is no infinite sequence of states $a_1 a_2 \cdots$ with $(a_i, a_{i+1}) \in B$ for all i. The *transitive closure* of B is defined by $B^+ = \bigcup_{i \geq 1} B^i$, where $B^0 = \{(a, a) \mid a \in A\}$, $B^{i+1} = B^i \circ B$. Let $B \subseteq A \times A$ be a well-founded relation. For every element $a \in A$ we inductively define its *ordinal height* $\|a\|_B$ by setting $\|a\|_B = \sup_{(a,b) \in B} \|b\|_B + 1$, where sup over the empty set evaluates to 0. We note that $\|\cdot\|_B$ is well-defined because B is well-founded. We define the *ordinal height* of relation B as $\|B\| = \sup_{a \in A} \|a\|_B + 1$.

2.1 Automata

A *finite automaton* $A = \langle Q, \Sigma, \delta, \iota, F \rangle$ consists of a finite set of *states*, a finite alphabet Σ, a *transition relation* $\delta : \Sigma \to 2^{Q \times Q}$, an *initial state* $\iota \in Q$, and a set of final states $F \subseteq Q$. Automaton A is *deterministic* if for every $\tau \in Q$ and $a \in \Sigma$ there is at most one $\tau' \in Q$ such that $(\tau, \tau') \in \delta(a)$. We also write $\tau \xrightarrow{a} \tau'$ for $(\tau, \tau') \in \delta(a)$. We extend the transition relation to words and define $\delta(w) = \delta(a_1) \circ \cdots \circ \delta(a_l)$ for every $w = a_1 \cdots a_l \in \Sigma^*$. A *run* of A is a finite sequence $r = \iota \xrightarrow{a_1} \tau_1 \xrightarrow{a_2} \tau_2 \cdots \xrightarrow{a_l} \tau_l$. r is *accepting* if $\tau_l \in F$. Automaton A *accepts* a finite word $w \in \Sigma^*$ if there is an accepting run $r = \iota \xrightarrow{a_1} \tau_1 \xrightarrow{a_2} \tau_2 \cdots \xrightarrow{a_l} \tau_l$ such that $w = a_1 \cdots a_l$. We denote by $\mathcal{L}(A) = \{w \in \Sigma^* \mid A \text{ accepts } w\}$ the *language* of words accepted by A. Automaton A is *universal* if $\mathcal{L}(A) = \Sigma^*$.

A *Büchi automaton* $A = \langle Q, \Sigma, \delta, \iota \rangle$ consists of a finite set of *states*, a finite alphabet Σ, a *transition relation* $\delta : \Sigma \to 2^{Q \times \{\geq, >\} \times Q}$, and an *initial state* $\iota \in Q$. We also write $\tau \xrightarrow[d]{a} \tau'$ for $(\tau, d, \tau') \in \delta(a)$. A *run* of A is an infinite sequence $r = \iota \xrightarrow[d_1]{a_1} \tau_1 \xrightarrow[d_2]{a_2} \tau_2 \cdots$. r is *accepting* if $d_i = >$ for infinitely many i. Automaton A *accepts* an infinite word $w \in \Sigma^\omega$ if there is an accepting run $r = \iota \xrightarrow[d_1]{a_1} \tau_1 \xrightarrow[d_2]{a_2} \tau_2 \cdots$ such that $w = a_1 a_2 \cdots$. We denote by $\mathcal{L}(A) = \{w \in \Sigma^\omega \mid A \text{ accepts } w\}$ the *language* accepted by A. Automaton A is *universal* if $\mathcal{L}(A) = \Sigma^\omega$.

Remark. We use this slightly unusual presentation of automata in order to conveniently represent the connection between automata and the size-change abstraction later on. In particular, this connection is the reason for using the symbols $\{\geq, >\}$ instead of $\{0, 1\}$ for (non-)accepting transitions.

2.2 Programs

A *program* $P = \langle St, I, \Sigma, \rho \rangle$ consists of a set of *states* St, a set of initial states $I \subseteq St$, a finite set of *transitions* Σ, and a *labeling function* $\rho : \Sigma \to 2^{St \times St}$, which maps every transition $a \in \Sigma$ to a *transition relation* $\rho(a) \subseteq St \times St$.

We extend the labeling function ρ to finite words over Σ and set $\rho(\pi) = \rho(a_1) \circ \rho(a_2) \circ \cdots \circ \rho(a_l)$ for a finite word $\pi = a_1 a_2 \cdots a_l$. A *computation* of P is a (finite or infinite) sequence $s_1 \xrightarrow{a_1} s_2 \xrightarrow{a_2} \cdots$ such that $s_1 \in I$ and $(s_i, s_{i+1}) \in \rho(a_i)$ for all i. Program P *terminates* if there is no infinite computation of P. A relation $T \subseteq St \times St$ is a *transition invariant* for P if $(\bigcup_{a \in \Sigma} \rho(a))^+ \subseteq T$. For a finite computation $s_1 \xrightarrow{a_1} s_2 \xrightarrow{a_2} \cdots s_{l+1}$ we call l the *length* of the computation.

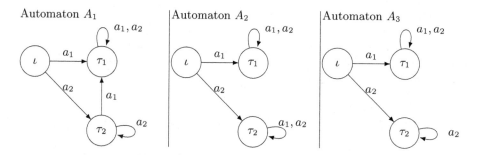

Fig. 2. Pictures of proof structures/transition automata.

Variables and Predicates. A common program model is to consider some finite set of *variables* Var and define the set of states $St = Var \to \alpha$ as the mappings from Var to some *domain* α. Sets of states can then be described by predicates over Var and transition relations by predicates over $Var \cup Var'$, where Var' denotes the set of *primed* versions of the variables in Var. Given a predicate p over Var, we write $\sigma \models p$ for $\sigma \in St$ if p is true when each variable $x \in Var$ is replaced by $\sigma(x)$; given a predicate p over $Var \cup Var'$, we write $\sigma, \varsigma \models p$ for $\sigma, \varsigma \in St$ if p is true when each variable $x \in Var$ is replaced by $\sigma(x)$ and each variable $x' \in Var'$ is replaced by $\varsigma(x)$. Given a set of predicates $Pred$ over Var, we write $Rel(Pred) = \{\sigma \in St \mid \sigma \models p \text{ for all } p \in Pred\}$ for the states which satisfy all predicates in $Pred$. Given a set of predicates $Pred$ over $Var \cup Var'$, we write $Rel(Pred) = \{(\sigma, \varsigma) \in St \times St \mid \sigma, \varsigma \models p \text{ for all } p \in Pred\}$ for the pairs of states which satisfy all predicates in $Pred$. We will also write $Rel_\alpha(Pred)$ in case we want to highlight the domain α.

Example 3. We now express the two programs from Fig. 1 in the above notation. For both programs, we consider the set of variables $Var = \{x, y\}$ and treat N as a symbolic constant. We choose the domain $\alpha = \omega$ according to the type **nat** of x and y. For both programs we model each branch of the if-statement as one transition. We set $P_i = \langle \{x, y\} \to \alpha, Rel_\alpha(\{x = N, y = N\}), \{a_1, a_2\}, \rho_i \rangle$, for $i = 1, 2$, where we define the labeling functions ρ_i using $C = \{x > 0, y > 0\}$:

$$\rho_1(a_1) = Rel_\alpha(C \cup \{x' = x - 1, y' = \mathbf{N}\}), \rho_1(a_2) = Rel_\alpha(C \cup \{x' = x, y' = y - 1\}),$$
$$\rho_2(a_1) = Rel_\alpha(C \cup \{x' = x - 1, y' = \mathbf{y}\}), \rho_2(a_2) = Rel_\alpha(C \cup \{x' = x, y' = y - 1\}),$$

3   Transition Predicate Abstraction

In this section, we review the definitions and results from [26] in order to motivate our generalizations in Sect. 4. The development in [26] also considers fairness requirements, which are not relevant for this paper and therefore left out.

Abstract-Transition Programs. We fix some program $P = \langle St, I, \Sigma, \rho \rangle$. We split up the definition of abstract-transition programs (see Definition 3 of [26]) into two parts: proof structures and proof labelings. A *proof structure* is a finite automaton $A = \langle Q, \Sigma, \delta, \iota, \_ \rangle$, where $\delta(a) \subseteq Q \times (Q \setminus \{\iota\})$ for all $a \in \Sigma$. For the moment, we ignore the acceptance condition; we will use it later on. A *proof labeling* $rel : Q \to 2^{St \times St}$ maps every state $\tau \in Q$ of a proof structure to a *transition relation* $rel(\tau) \subseteq St \times St$. A proof labeling is *inductive* if

$$rel(\iota) = Id_{St}, \qquad \text{and}$$
$$rel(\tau) \circ \rho(a) \subseteq rel(\tau'), \qquad \text{for all } (\tau, \tau') \in \delta(a) \text{ and for all } a \in \Sigma,$$

where Id_{St} is the identity relation over St. An *abstract-transition program* $P^{\#} = (A, rel)$ is a pair of a proof structure A and an inductive proof labeling.

Abstract-transition program are constructed from a fixed finite set of transition predicates that describe transition relations (see Sect. 4 of [26]). The resulting abstract-transition programs have the following properties:

- (P1) The proof structure is a *deterministic* automaton (see Sect. 5.1 of [26]).
- (P2) For every word $a_1 a_2 \cdots a_n$ with $\rho(a_1 a_2 \cdots a_n) \neq \emptyset$ there is a run $\iota \xrightarrow{a_1} \tau_1 \xrightarrow{a_2} \tau_2 \cdots \xrightarrow{a_n} \tau_n$ of A (see Lemma 1 from [26]).
- (P3) Every state $\tau \in Q \setminus \{\iota\}$ is reachable from ι (the reader can check that the abstraction algorithm of [26] starts from the initial state ι and adds only states which are reachable from ι).

We now state the core theorem of [26]; for illustration purposes, we also state its proof, which is based on condition (*), in the notation of this paper:

Theorem 1 (Theorem 1 of [26]). *Let* $P^{\#} = (A, rel)$ *be an abstract program with property (P2). Then,* $\bigcup_{\tau \in Q \setminus \{\iota\}} rel(\tau)$ *is a transition invariant for* P. *If* $rel(\tau)$ *is well-founded for every state* $\tau \in Q \setminus \{\iota\}$, *then* P *terminates.*

Proof. For the first claim, we consider some $(s, s') \in \rho(a_1 a_2 \cdots a_n)$ for some word $a_1 a_2 \cdots a_n$ with $n \geq 1$. By property (P2) we have that there is a run $\iota \xrightarrow{a_1} \tau_1 \xrightarrow{a_2} \tau_2 \cdots \xrightarrow{a_n} \tau_n$ of A. By the definition of an inductive proof labeling we have $\rho(a_1 a_2 \cdots a_n) \subseteq rel(\tau_n)$. Thus, we get that $(s, s') \in rel(\tau_n)$. Hence, we get $(\bigcup_{a \in \Sigma} \rho(a))^+ \subseteq \bigcup_{\tau \in Q \setminus \{\iota\}} rel(\tau)$. The second claim then directly follows from the first claim based on condition (*). □

Example 4. We will define an abstract-transition program for P_1. Let A_1 be the proof structure from Fig. 2. Let rel_1 be the proof labeling defined by $rel_1(\tau_1) = Rel_\alpha(\{x' < x\})$ and $rel_1(\tau_2) = Rel_\alpha(\{x' = x, y' < y\})$, where $\alpha = \omega$. It is easy to verify that rel_1 is inductive. Hence, $P_1^\# = (A_1, rel_1)$ is an abstract-transition program. Moreover, $rel_1(\tau_1)$ and $rel_1(\tau_2)$ are well-founded due to the predicates $x' < x$ and $y' < y$. The abstraction algorithm of [26] precisely computes $P_1^\#$ when called with the set of predicates $Pred = \{x' < x, x' = x, y' < y\}$.

Example 5. We will define an abstract-transition program for P_2. Let A_2 be the proof structure from Fig. 2. Let rel_2 be the proof labeling defined by $rel_2(\tau_1) = Rel_\alpha(\{x' < x\})$ and $rel_2(\tau_2) = Rel_\alpha(\{y' < y\})$, where $\alpha = \omega$. It is easy to verify that rel_2 is inductive. Hence, $P_2^\# = (A_2, rel_2)$ is an abstract-transition program. Moreover, $rel_2(\tau_1)$ and $rel_2(\tau_2)$ are well-founded due to the predicates $x' < x$ and $y' < y$. The abstraction algorithm of [26] precisely computes $P_2^\#$ when called with the set of predicates $Pred = \{x' < x, y' < y\}$.

Remark. The above proof of Theorem 1 only relies on property (P2). However, properties (P1) and (P3) explain the requirement that every non-initial state needs to be labelled by a well-founded relation: by (P3) every state $\tau \in Q \setminus \{\iota\}$ is reachable by some word $a_1 a_2 \cdots a_n$; by (P1) the word $a_1 a_2 \cdots a_n$ necessarily reaches τ; hence, τ needs to be labelled by some well-founded relation. In this paper, we will generalize Theorem 1 of [26] to non-deterministic proof structures; for such proof structures it will make sense to also consider proof labelings where not every state is labelled by some well-founded relation.

Remark. We further note that we can w.l.o.g. strengthen property (P2) to property (P2'): For every word $a_1 a_2 \cdots a_n$ there is a run $\iota \xrightarrow{a_1} \tau_1 \xrightarrow{a_2} \tau_2 \cdots \xrightarrow{a_n} \tau_n$ of A. We show the following: Let $P^\# = (A, rel)$ be an abstract-transition program with property (P2). Then we can extend $P^\#$ to some abstract-transition program (A', rel') with property (P2'). Further, if $rel(\tau)$ is well-founded for every non-initial state τ, then $rel'(\tau)$ is well-founded for every non-initial state τ.

We extend A to A' by adding a sink state $\tau_\emptyset$, which has self-loops for every $a \in \Sigma$; for every state τ and $a \in \Sigma$ we add an a-transition from τ to $\tau_\emptyset$ if τ does not have a a-successor. We extend rel to rel' by setting $rel'(\tau_\emptyset) = \emptyset$. It is easy to see that (P1)–(P3) ensure that rel' is inductive and that (A', rel') has property (P2'). Further $rel'(\tau_\emptyset) = \emptyset$ is well-founded; hence, the second claims holds.

Invariants. An *invariant* for a program $P = \langle St, I, \Sigma, \rho \rangle$ is a set $Inv \subseteq St$ such that (1) $I \subseteq Inv$ and (2) $\{\sigma \in St \mid$ there is a $\sigma' \in Inv$ with $(\sigma', \sigma) \in \rho(a)\} \subseteq Inv$ for all $a \in \Sigma$. For example, $Inv = Rel_\alpha(\{x \le N, y \le N\})$ is an invariant for P_1 and P_2. Invariants can be used to strengthen the transition relations of a program by restricting the transition relations to states from the invariant: Given an invariant Inv for P we define $P_{strengthen} = \langle St, I, \Sigma, \rho_{strengthen} \rangle$, where $\rho_{strengthen}(a) = \rho(a) \cap (Inv \times Inv)$ for all $a \in \Sigma$. Clearly, P and $P_{strengthen}$ have the same computations. However, working with $P_{strengthen}$ for termination resp. complexity analysis is often beneficial because of the restricted transition relations. Indeed, strengthening the transition relation is often necessary to find a termination proof. For example, the TERMINATOR termination analyzer [14] alternates between strengthening the transition relation and constructing a transition invariant. Similarly, complexity analyzers from the literature commonly employ invariant analysis as a subroutine either before or during the analysis [1,2,16–18,29,34]. The problem of computing invariants is orthogonal to the development in this paper. In our examples on complexity analysis we assume that appropriate invariants – such as $Inv = Rel_\alpha(\{x \leq N, y \leq N\})$ for P_1 and P_2 – can be computed by standard techniques such as Octagon analysis [24].

4   Transition Abstraction

In this section, we take another view on the result of [26] that we presented in the last section. On the one hand we aim at generalizing the termination analysis of [26] to non-deterministic proof structures. On the other hand we do not only want to reason about a single proof labeling but all possible proof labelings; to this end we will define a minimal inductive proof labeling. We fix a program $P = \langle St, I, \Sigma, \rho \rangle$ for the rest of this section.

A *transition automaton* $A = \langle Q, \Sigma, \delta, \iota, F \rangle$ is a finite automaton, where $\delta(a) \subseteq Q \times (Q \setminus \{\iota\})$ for all $a \in \Sigma$ and $F \subseteq Q \setminus \{\iota\}$. We point out that a transition automaton is a proof structure with final states.

Let $A = \langle Q, \Sigma, \delta, \iota, F \rangle$ be a transition automaton. We define a proof labeling $rel_{min} : Q \to 2^{St \times St}$ which precisely follows the structure of A: We set $rel_{min}(\iota) = Id_{St}$, and for each $\tau \in Q \setminus \{\iota\}$ we set

$$rel_{min}(\tau) = \bigcup_{\text{word } \pi \text{ with } (\iota, \tau) \in \delta(\pi)} \rho(\pi),$$

i.e., $rel_{min}(\tau)$ is the union of the transition relations along all words with a run from the initial state to τ.

We now state the central definition of this section:

Definition 1 (Transition Abstraction). A transition automaton A is a *transition abstraction* of program P if $rel_{min}(\tau)$ is well-founded for each $\tau \in F$.

The notion of transition automata is motivated by Theorem 2, which extends the termination criterion of [26] to non-deterministic proof structures. Proposition 3 below states that Theorem 2 indeed is an extension of Theorem 1 of [26].

Theorem 2. *Let A be a transition automaton that is a transition abstraction of program P. If A is universal, then P terminates.*

Proof (Sketch). The theorem can be proved in the same way as Theorem 1 of [26] whose proof we presented in Sect. 3 based on an application of condition (*); we will later give a proof purely based on automata-theoretic techniques.   □

We first show that rel_{min} is the minimal inductive proof labeling:

Proposition 1. rel_{min} *is inductive.*

Proof. We consider some $(\tau, \tau') \in \delta(a)$. We consider some word π with $(\iota, \tau) \in \delta(\pi)$. Then, πa is a word with $(\iota, \tau') \in \delta(\pi a)$. Hence, $\rho(\pi a) \subseteq rel_{min}(\tau')$. Because this holds for all such words π, we get $rel_{min}(\tau) \circ \rho(a) \subseteq rel_{min}(\tau')$.   □

Proposition 2. *Let $rel : Q \to 2^{St \times St}$ be some inductive proof labeling. Then, $rel_{min}(\tau) \subseteq rel(\tau)$ for all $\tau \in Q$.*

Proof. We note that $rel_{min}(\iota) = rel(\iota) = Id_{St}$. We will show that for all non-empty words π that $(\iota, \tau) \in \delta(\pi)$ implies $\rho(\pi) \subseteq rel(\tau)$. The proof proceeds by induction on the length of the word. For the induction start, we consider a word $\pi = a$ consisting of a single letter: Because rel is inductive, we have $\rho(a) = Id_{St} \circ \rho(a) = rel(\iota) \circ \rho(a) \subseteq rel(\tau)$ for all $(\iota, \tau) \in \delta(a)$. For the induction step, we consider a word $\pi = \pi' a$ with non-empty π': We fix some $(\iota, \tau) \in \delta(\pi' a)$. There is some $(\tau, \tau') \in \delta(a)$ with $(\tau', \tau) \in \delta(a)$ and $(\iota, \tau') \in \delta(\pi')$. By induction assumption we have $\rho(\pi') \subseteq rel(\tau')$. Because rel is inductive, we have $rel(\tau') \circ \rho(a) \subseteq rel(\tau)$. Thus, $\rho(\pi' a) = \rho(\pi') \circ \rho(a) \subseteq rel(\tau)$.   □

With Proposition 2 we are now able to relate transition automata to the abstract-transition programs presented in the last section:

Proposition 3. *Let $A = \langle Q, \Sigma, \delta, \iota, \_ \rangle$ be a proof structure with property (P2'). Let rel be an inductive proof labeling such that $rel(\tau)$ is well-founded for every state $\tau \in Q \setminus \{\iota\}$. With the set of final states $F = Q \setminus \{\iota\}$, the proof structure A is a transition abstraction of program P; further, A is universal.*

Proof. By Proposition 2 we have $rel_{min}(\tau) \subseteq rel(\tau)$ for all $\tau \in Q$. Hence, A is a transition automaton. By property (P2'), the automaton A has a run for every word; with $F = Q \setminus \{\iota\}$ each such run is accepting. Hence, A is universal.   □

Example 6. In Examples 4 and 5 we have argued that $P_1^{\#} = (A_1, rel_1)$ and $P_2^{\#} = (A_2, rel_2)$ are abstract-transition programs for P_1 resp. P_2. We now consider A_1 and A_2 as transition automata, defining the final states by $F = \{\tau_1, \tau_2\}$. By Proposition 3, A_1 and A_2 are transition abstractions for P_1 resp. P_2 and Theorem 2 can be applied.

We now define a transition automaton for program P_1 that is different from the transition automaton A_1 considered in Example 6:

Example 7. Let A_3 be the automaton from Fig. 2 with the set of final states $F = \{\tau_1, \tau_2\}$. We now argue that the transition automaton A_3 is a transition abstraction of P_1. In order to reason about the well-foundedness of $rel_{min}(\tau_1)$ and $rel_{min}(\tau_2)$, which are required by the definition of transition abstraction, we make use of Proposition 2 as a proof principle: it is sufficient to define an inductive proof labeling rel_3 and argue that $rel_3(\tau_1)$ and $rel_3(\tau_2)$ are well-founded.

We define rel_3 by setting $rel_3(\tau_1) = Rel_\alpha(\{x' < x\})$ and $rel_3(\tau_2) = Rel_\alpha(\{y' < y\})$ with $\alpha = \omega$. It is easy to verify that rel_3 is inductive. Moreover, $rel_3(\tau_1)$ and $rel_3(\tau_2)$ are well-founded due to the predicates $x' < x$ and $y' < y$. We conclude that A_3 is a transition abstraction of P_1. We observe that automaton A_3 (resp. A_3') is not universal, and Theorem 2 cannot be applied.

Remark. We relate A_3 to the abstraction algorithm of [26]. We extend A_3 to the automaton A_3' by adding a non-final state τ_{true}; we add an a_1-transition from τ_2

to τ_{true} and self-loops to τ_{true} for a_1 and a_2. We set $rel_3(\tau_{true}) = Rel_\alpha(\{true\}) = St \times St$ (note that $St \times St$ is not well-founded). The abstraction algorithm of [26] will exactly compute the abstract-transition program $P_3^\# = (A_3', rel_3)$ when called with the set of predicates $Pred = \{x' < x, y' < y\}$; we work with automaton A_3 instead of A_3' because it has one state less and is easier to represent.

Remark. In the next subsection, we will establish the more general criterion of factor-termination, which is satisfied by automaton A_3 (resp. A_3'). Hence, we obtain a new termination proof for the program P_1, which has the advantage to use fewer predicates than the termination proof in Example 4: we contrast the set of predicates $Pred = \{x' < x, y' < y\}$ used in Example 7 with the set $Pred = \{x' < x, x' = x, y' < y\}$ used in Example 4.

4.1   Factor Termination

In this section, we introduce the criterion of factor-termination. We first introduce the criterion and then argue that factor-termination is a more general termination criterion than universality. Finally, we state that factor-termination is in fact the most general termination criterion based on transition abstraction.

The intuition behind the criterion of factor-termination is as follows: Given a transition automaton $A = \langle Q, \Sigma, \delta, \iota, F \rangle$, we directly use the well-foundedness of the relations $rel_{min}(\tau)$, for final state $\tau \in F$. We check for every infinite word $\pi \in \Sigma^\omega$ if there is a $\tau \in F$ and a factorization $\pi = \pi_0 \pi_1 \pi_2 \cdots$ into finite words π_i such that A has a run from ι to τ on π_i for all $i \geq 1$. Such a factorization implies that there cannot be an infinite sequence of states $s_1 s_2 \ldots$ with $(s_i, s_{i+1}) \in \delta(\pi_i) \subseteq rel_{min}(\tau)$ because this would contradict the well-foundedness of $rel_{min}(\tau)$.

We implement the above idea with Büchi-automata. We fix some transition automaton $A = \langle Q, \Sigma, \delta, \iota, F \rangle$ for which we will define a Büchi-automaton $\mathcal{F}(A)$, which is composed of Büchi-automata A_τ, for every $\tau \in F$, and an additional initial state κ. $\mathcal{F}(A)$ can non-deterministically wait in κ a finite amount of time before moving to one of the automata A_τ. Each A_τ checks for a factorization with regard to $\tau \in F$. We first formally define the automata A_τ and then $\mathcal{F}(A)$.

We start with an intuition for the construction of A_τ. We take a copy of A where all copied transitions are non-accepting. We obtain A_τ by adding additional accepting transitions that allow the automaton A_τ to move back to the initial state whenever it could move to τ. The additional transitions allow A_τ to guess the beginning of a new factor; the Büchi-condition guarantees that an accepting run factorizes an infinite word into infinitely many finite words.

Formally, we define $A_\tau = \langle Q \times \{\tau\}, \Sigma, \delta_\tau, (\iota, \tau) \rangle$, where for all $a \in \Sigma$ we set

$$\delta_\tau(a) = \{((\tau', \tau), \geq, (\tau'', \tau)) \mid (\tau', \tau'') \in \delta(a)\} \cup \{((\tau', \tau), >, (\iota, \tau)) \mid (\tau', \tau) \in \delta(a)\}.$$

We state the main property of the automata A_τ:

Proposition 4. A_τ *accepts* $\pi \in \Sigma^\omega$ *iff there is a factorization* $\pi = \pi_1 \pi_2 \cdots$ *into finite words* π_i *such that A has a run from ι to τ on π_i for all i.*

Proof. Let r be an accepting run of A_τ on π. Hence, we can factor $\pi = \pi_1\pi_2\cdots$ into finite words π_i such that the accepting transitions of r exactly correspond to the last letters of the words π_i. We observe that the only accepting transitions are of shape $((\tau',\tau),>,(\iota,\tau))$ for $(\tau',\tau) \in \delta(a)$ (we denote this condition by $(\#)$). Further, automaton A_τ mimics A on the non-accepting transitions. Hence, on each word π_i the run r mimics a run of A except for the last transition; however, the condition $(\#)$ guarantees that A can move to τ with the last letter of π_i. $\square$

The *factorization automaton* is the Büchi-automaton $\mathcal{F}(A) = \langle G, \Sigma, \Gamma, \kappa \rangle$, where the set of states $G = (Q \times F) \cup \{\kappa\}$ consists of pairs of an automaton state and a final state plus a fresh initial state κ. We define the transition relation Γ by $\Gamma(a) = \Gamma_1(a) \cup \Gamma_2(a) \cup \Gamma_3(a)$ for all $a \in \Sigma$, where

$$\Gamma_1(a) = \bigcup_{\tau \in F} \delta_\tau(a), \Gamma_2(a) = \{(\kappa,\geq,\kappa)\}, \text{ and } \Gamma_3(a) = \{(\kappa,\geq,(\iota,\tau)) \mid \tau \in F\}.$$

The factorization automaton $\mathcal{F}(A)$ can be understood as the disjoint union of the initial state κ and the Büchi-automata A_τ; the state κ allows $\mathcal{F}(A)$ to wait in κ a finite amount of time before moving to the initial state of some A_τ.

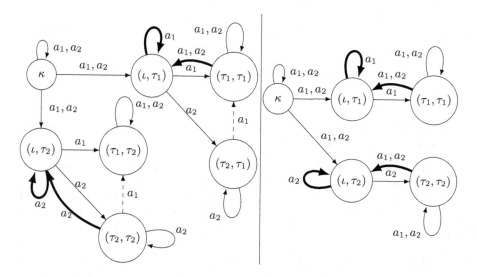

Fig. 3. On the left: Automata $\mathcal{F}(A_1)$ and $\mathcal{F}(A_3)$, which have the same states and transitions except for the dashed transitions which only belong to $\mathcal{F}(A_1)$. On the right: Automaton $\mathcal{F}(A_2)$. Bold arrows denote accepting transitions.

Example 8. We draw the factor-automata of A_1, A_2 and A_3 in Fig. 3.

We are now able to formally state our new termination criterion: Transition automaton A satisfies the *factor-termination* criterion if $\mathcal{F}(A)$ is universal. This notion is justified by Theorem 3 below:

Theorem 3. *Let $A = \langle Q, \Sigma, \delta, \iota, F \rangle$ be a transition automaton and let $P = \langle St, I, \Sigma, \rho \rangle$ be a program such that A is a transition abstraction of P. If A satisfies the factor-termination criterion, then P terminates.*

Proof. We assume that $\mathcal{F}(A)$ is universal and that P does not terminate. Then there is an infinite computation $t = s_1 \xrightarrow{a_1} s_2 \xrightarrow{a_2} \cdots$ of P. We consider the associated word $\pi = a_1 a_2 \cdots$. Because $\mathcal{F}(A)$ is universal, the word π is accepted by some run r. Word $\pi = \pi_a \pi_b$ can be split in a finite prefix π_a and an infinite suffix π_b such that $\mathcal{F}(A)$ stays in κ while reading π_a before leaving κ and then reading π_b. We further see that while reading π_b, $\mathcal{F}(A)$ stays within A_τ for some $\tau \in F$. By Proposition 4, there is a factorization $\pi_b = \pi_1 \pi_2 \cdots$ such that A has a run on each π_j from ι to τ. We split t into corresponding subcomputations

$$t_j = s_{i_j} \xrightarrow{a_{i_j}} \cdots s_{i_{j+1}-1} \xrightarrow{a_{i_{j+1}-1}} s_{i_{j+1}}$$

with $\pi_j = a_{i_j} \cdots a_{i_{j+1}-1}$. Hence, we have $(s_{i_j}, s_{i_{j+1}}) \in \rho(\pi_j) \subseteq rel_{min}(\tau)$ for all j. This gives us an infinite sequence $s_{i_1} s_{i_2} \cdots$ with $(s_{i_j}, s_{i_j+1}) \in rel_{min}(\tau)$. However, this results in a contradiction, because $rel_{min}(\tau)$ is well-founded by the assumption that A is a transition abstraction of P. $\square$

Next, we show that the universality of a transition automaton A implies the factor-termination of A; the proof uses the fundamental fact that a Büchi-automaton is universal iff it accepts all ultimately-periodic words:

Lemma 1. *Let A be a transition automaton. If A is universal, then A satisfies the factor-termination criterion.*

Proof. We assume that A is universal. We will show that $\mathcal{F}(A)$ accepts all ultimately-periodic words. Let u, v be two finite words over Σ and consider the ultimately-periodic word uv^ω. Since A is universal there is an accepting run of A ending in some final state $\tau \in F$. We will use this run to construct an accepting run of $\mathcal{F}(A)$. In order to accept uv^ω, the automaton $\mathcal{F}(A)$ reads the word u staying in the initial state κ and moving to (ι, τ) with the last letter of u (we tacitly assume here that the length of u is at least one; however this is without loss of generality as we can consider the word uv instead of u); $\mathcal{F}(A)$ then reads the word v, mimicking the accepting run of A in A_τ, and moving to state (ι, τ) with the last letter of v; A_τ then reads the next occurrence of v in the same way; we note that the last transition, with which the automaton returns to the initial state (ι, τ), is accepting; thus the constructed run on uv^ω is accepting. $\square$

Remark. The combination of Theorem 3 and Lemma 1 provides an alternative proof of Theorem 2. We highlight that the proof of Lemma 1 proceeds purely by automata-theoretic techniques and does not make use of condition (*); in particular, Ramsey's theorem is not needed to prove Theorem 1 of [26].

We now establish that factor-termination is a *strictly* more general termination criterion than universality:

Example 9. Let A_3 be the automaton from Example 7, where we have established that A_3 is a transition abstraction of P_1 and that A_3 is not universal. We have drawn $\mathcal{F}(A_3)$ in Fig. 3. It remains to argue that $\mathcal{F}(A_3)$ is universal.

We show that $\mathcal{F}(A_3)$ is universal by a case distinction: Assume a word contains infinitely many a_1. $\mathcal{F}(A_3)$ waits for the first a_1 and moves to (ι, τ_1) just before the first a_1; with the first a_1, $\mathcal{F}(A_3)$ moves to (τ_1, τ_1); then $\mathcal{F}(A_3)$ again waits for the next a_1, moving to (ι, τ_1) just before the next a_1, and so on. An infinite word that does not contain infinitely many a_1, only contains a_2 from some point on; $\mathcal{F}(A_3)$ accepts such a word by waiting in the initial state κ until there are only a_2 left and then moves to (ι, τ_2); $\mathcal{F}(A_3)$ then can stay in (ι, τ_2) while continuing to read the letters a_2.

We finally state that factor-termination is the most general termination criterion based on transition abstraction:

Theorem 4. *Let A be a transition automaton that does not satisfy the factor-termination criterion. Then there is a program P such that A is a transition abstraction of P, but P does not terminate.*

We prove Theorem 4 (see Corollary 2) and further results in Sect. 6 based on the close relationship of factorization automata and the size-change abstraction. We first introduce the size-change abstraction in the next subsection.

5   Size-Change Abstraction

Size-change abstraction (SCA) can be seen as an instantiation of (transition-) predicate abstraction with a restricted class of predicates: a *size-change predicate* over some set of variables Var is an inequality $x \rhd y'$ with $x, y \in Var$, where $\rhd$ is either $>$ or $\geq$ (recall that $y' \in Var'$ denotes the primed version of y). A *size-change relation* (SCR) is a set of size-change predicates over Var. A *size-change system* (SCS) $S = \langle Var, \Sigma, \lambda \rangle$ consists of a set of *variables* Var, a finite set of *transitions* Σ and a *labeling function* λ, which maps every transition $a \in \Sigma$ to a SCR $\lambda(a)$ over Var.

The SCA methodology requires an abstraction mechanism that abstracts programs to SCSs. Various static analyzes have been proposed in the literature which perform such an abstraction [3,9,10,20,22,23,31,34]. In this paper, we are not concerned with how to abstract programs to SCSs (and thus we do not describe an abstraction mechanism for programs). Rather, we will use results on the strength of SCA [12,21] for the analysis of transition automata.

Results on the strength of SCA directly interpret SCSs as (abstract) programs, which can be seen as 'most general programs' that satisfies all the size-change predicates. We now state the interpretation of SCSs as programs for which we make use of the variable mappings and predicate interpretations defined in

Sect. 3. An SCS $S = \langle Var, \Sigma, \lambda \rangle$ defines a program $\mathcal{P}_\alpha(S) = \langle St, St, \Sigma, \rho \rangle$, where $St = Var \to \alpha$ and $\rho(a) = Rel_\alpha(\lambda(a))$ for all $a \in \Sigma$; the program $\mathcal{P}_\alpha(S)$ is parameterized by some domain α that we require to be well-founded.

We will build on theoretical results for SCA which have been obtained by automata-theoretic techniques (we refer the interested reader to [13] for an overview). We begin by stating the syntactic termination criterion of [22]. Let $S = \langle Var, \Sigma, \lambda \rangle$ be an SCS. We define the Büchi-automaton $DESC(S) = \langle D, \Sigma, \mu, \kappa \rangle$, where the set of states $D = Var \cup \{\kappa\}$ consists of the variables and a fresh initial state κ, the alphabet Σ is the same as the alphabet of S, the transition relation μ is defined by $\mu(a) = \mu_1(a) \cup \mu_2(a) \cup \mu_3(a)$ for all $a \in \Sigma$, where $\mu_1(a) = \lambda(a)$, $\mu_2(a) = \{(\kappa, \geq, \kappa)\}$ and $\mu_3(a) = \{(\kappa, \geq, x) \mid x \in Var\}$. Intuitively the automaton $DESC(S)$ waits a finite amount of time in the initial state κ and then starts to trace a chain of inequalities $x_1 \vartriangleright_1 x_2 \vartriangleright_2 x_3 \cdots$ between the variables of S. The Büchi-acceptance condition ensures that $\vartriangleright_i = {>}$ infinitely often. Now we are ready to define the syntactic termination criterion of [22]: SCS S has *infinite descent* if $DESC(S)$ is universal. This criterion is sound and complete:

Theorem 5 ([21,22]). *S has infinite descent iff $\mathcal{P}_\alpha(S)$ terminates over all domains α. Moreover, if S does not have infinite descent, then $\mathcal{P}_\alpha(S)$ does not terminate for some domain $\alpha < \omega$ (i.e., $\mathcal{P}_\alpha(S)$ does not terminate when variables take values in some initial segment $\alpha = [0, N]$ of the natural numbers).*

While the original motivation for studying SCA has been termination analysis, we recently extended the theoretical results on SCA to complexity analysis:

Theorem 6 ([12]). *Let S be an SCS that is size-change terminating. Then there effectively is a rational number $z \geq 1$ such that the length of the longest run of $\mathcal{P}_{[0,N]}(S)$ is of asymptotic order $\Theta(N^z)$ for natural numbers N.*

Our result provides a complete characterization of the complexity bounds arising from SCA and gives an effective algorithm for computing the exact asymptotic bound of a given abstract program. The proof of Theorem 6 proceeds by rephrasing the question of complexity analysis for SCSs as a question about the asymptotic behaviour of max-plus automata. The main induction of the proof relies on the Factorization Forest Theorem [28], which is a powerful strengthening of Ramsey's Theorem for finite semigroups that offers a deep insight into their structure (see [11] for an overview).

6   Canonical Programs for Transition Automata

In this section, we will relate transition abstraction and SCA. We will describe the extraction of a size-change system $S = \mathcal{S}(A)$ from a transition automaton A. We will argue that the associated program $\mathcal{P}_\alpha(S)$ is *canonical* for A. We will prove three results that justify the use of the word 'canonical':

1. We show that the criterion of factor-termination for A agrees with the criterion of infinite descent for S (Corollary 1).

2. We show that A is a transition abstraction of $\mathcal{P}_\alpha(S)$ for all domains α (Proposition 5). This result allows us to establish that factor-termination is the most general termination criterion (Corollary 2).

3. If A is a transition abstraction for some program P, then every run of P can be mimicked by a run of $\mathcal{P}_\alpha(S)$, where the domain α depends on P and needs to be chosen appropriately (Lemma 3). This result allows us to transfer the result on complexity analysis for SCSs (see Theorem 6) to transition automata (Theorem 7).

6.1   Extracting Size-Change Systems from Transition Automata

We fix some transition automaton $A = \langle Q, \Sigma, \delta, \iota, F \rangle$. Let $\mathcal{F}(A) = \langle G, \Sigma, \Gamma, \kappa \rangle$ be the associated factorization automaton, where $G = Q \times F \cup \{\kappa\}$ and $\Gamma(a) = \Gamma_1(a) \cup \Gamma_2(a) \cup \Gamma_3(a)$ for all $a \in \Sigma$. We extract the associated size-change system from $\mathcal{F}(A)$ and define $\mathcal{S}(A) = \langle Var, \Sigma, \lambda \rangle$ by setting $Var = Q \times F$ and $\lambda(a) = \Gamma_1(a)$ for all $a \in \Sigma$ (i.e., $\mathcal{S}(A)$ is obtained from automaton $\mathcal{F}(A)$ by restriction to the non-initial states).

Example 10. We consider the transition automaton A_2. We have drawn $\mathcal{F}(A_2)$ in Fig. 3. We now state the size-change system extracted from $\mathcal{F}(A_2)$: We have $\mathcal{S}(A_2) = \langle \{\iota, \tau_1, \tau_2\} \times \{\tau_1, \tau_2\}, \{a_1, a_2\}, \lambda \rangle$, where λ is given by

- $\lambda(a_1) = \{(\iota, \tau_1) \geq (\tau_1, \tau_1)', (\tau_1, \tau_1) \geq (\tau_1, \tau_1)', (\tau_2, \tau_2) \geq (\tau_2, \tau_2)',$
  $\qquad (\iota, \tau_1) > (\iota, \tau_1)', (\tau_1, \tau_1) > (\iota, \tau_1)', (\tau_2, \tau_2) > (\iota, \tau_2)'\}$,
- $\lambda(a_2) = \{(\tau_1, \tau_1) \geq (\tau_1, \tau_1)', (\iota, \tau_2) \geq (\tau_2, \tau_2)', (\tau_2, \tau_2) \geq (\tau_2, \tau_2)',$
  $\qquad (\tau_1, \tau_1) > (\iota, \tau_1)', (\iota, \tau_2) > (\iota, \tau_2)', (\tau_2, \tau_2) > (\iota, \tau_2)'\}$.

Example 11. We consider the transition automaton A_3. We have drawn $\mathcal{F}(A_3)$ in Fig. 3. We now state the size-change system extracted from $\mathcal{F}(A_3)$. We have $\mathcal{S}(A_3) = \langle \{\iota, \tau_1, \tau_2\} \times \{\tau_1, \tau_2\}, \{a_1, a_2\}, \lambda \rangle$, where λ is given by

- $\lambda(a_1) = \{(\iota, \tau_1) \geq (\tau_1, \tau_1)', (\tau_1, \tau_1) \geq (\tau_1, \tau_1)', (\iota, \tau_2) \geq (\tau_1, \tau_2)',$
  $\qquad (\tau_1, \tau_2) \geq (\tau_1, \tau_2)', (\iota, \tau_1) > (\iota, \tau_1)', (\tau_1, \tau_1) > (\iota, \tau_1)'\}$,
- $\lambda(a_2) = \{(\tau_1, \tau_1) \geq (\tau_1, \tau_1)', (\iota, \tau_1) \geq (\tau_2, \tau_1)', (\tau_2, \tau_1) \geq (\tau_2, \tau_1)',$
  $\qquad (\tau_1, \tau_2) \geq (\tau_1, \tau_2)', (\iota, \tau_2) \geq (\tau_2, \tau_2)', (\tau_2, \tau_2) \geq (\tau_2, \tau_2)',$
  $\qquad (\tau_1, \tau_1) > (\iota, \tau_1)', (\iota, \tau_2) > (\iota, \tau_2)', (\tau_2, \tau_2) > (\iota, \tau_2)'\}$.

We comment on the intuition behind the definition of the SCS $S = \mathcal{S}(A)$. The underlying idea has been to obtain a close correspondence between $DESC(S)$ and $\mathcal{F}(A)$. Indeed, $DESC(S)$ and $\mathcal{F}(A)$ are almost identical, the only difference is that the initial state of $DESC(S)$ allows moving to every state, whereas the initial state of $\mathcal{F}(A)$ only allows moving to the initial states of the components A_τ. However, this difference does not change the set of accepted words, as we prove in the next lemma:

Lemma 2. *Let* $S = \mathcal{S}(A)$ *be the SCS extracted from* A. *Then* $\mathcal{L}(\mathcal{F}(A)) = \mathcal{L}(DESC(S))$.

Proof. We recall $DESC(S) = \langle D, \Sigma, \mu, \kappa \rangle$, where $D = Var \cup \{\kappa\}$ and $\mu(a) = \mu_1(a) \cup \mu_2(a) \cup \mu_3(a)$ for all $a \in \Sigma$. We see that both automata have the same set of states $G = D = Q \times F \cup \{\kappa\}$. From the definition of $\mathcal{F}(A)$ and $DESC(S)$ we further have that $\Gamma_1(a) = \mu_1(a)$, $\Gamma_2(a) = \mu_2(a)$ and $\Gamma_3(a) \subseteq \mu_3(a)$ for all $a \in \Sigma$.

Thus, we get $\mathcal{L}(\mathcal{F}(A)) \subseteq \mathcal{L}(DESC(S))$ because every run of A is also a run of $DESC(S)$. We now show $\mathcal{L}(\mathcal{F}(A)) \supseteq \mathcal{L}(DESC(S))$: Let π be some word accepted by $DESC(S)$ and let r be an accepting run of $DESC(S)$ on π. We can choose some factorization $\pi = \pi_1 \pi_2$ such that the last transition in r when reading π_1 is accepting. We note that after reading π_1, $DESC(S)$ must be in some state $(\iota, \_)$ because accepting transition always move to some state where the first component is ι. We further note that while reading π_2, $DESC(S)$ only uses transitions from μ_1, because there is no transition returning to κ. Hence, the accepting run r of $DESC(S)$ can be mimicked by $\mathcal{F}(A)$ as follows: $\mathcal{F}(A)$ waits in the initial state κ while reading π_1 and then moves to the state $(\iota, \_)$ with the last letter of π_1. After that $\mathcal{F}(A)$ follows the accepting run of $DESC(S)$ on π_2, which can be done because of $\Gamma_1 = \mu_1$. $\square$

As immediate corollary we get the equivalence of the termination conditions:

Corollary 1. *A has factor termination iff S has infinite descent.*

6.2   Factor-Termination Is the Most General Termination Criterion

We consider the size-change system $S = \mathcal{S}(A)$ extracted from transition automaton A. Our next result is that A is a transition abstraction for the program $\mathcal{P}_\alpha(S)$ associated to S. The crucial insight is that S exactly implements the minimal requirements to satisfy the condition of transition abstraction: the inequalities of S exactly follow the transition relation of A, where strict inequalities ensure that the value of variable (ι, τ) decreases iff A visits an accepting state τ.

Proposition 5. *A is a transition abstraction of $\mathcal{P}_\alpha(S)$ for all domains α.*

Proof. Let α be some well-founded domain. We will show that A is a transition abstraction of $\mathcal{P}_\alpha(S)$ using Proposition 2 as proof principle. For this we define a size-change relation T_τ for each $\tau \in Q \setminus \{\iota\}$. We set $T_\tau = \{(\iota, \tau') \geq (\tau, \tau') \mid \tau' \in F\} \cup T_\tau^{dec}$, where $T_\tau^{dec} = \{(\iota, \tau) > (\iota, \tau)\}$, if $\tau \in F$, and $T_\tau^{dec} = \emptyset$, otherwise. It is easy to check that we have $Rel_\alpha(T_\tau) \circ Rel_\alpha(\lambda(a)) \subseteq Rel_\alpha(T_{\tau'})$ for all $(\tau, \tau') \in \delta(a)$. We now apply Proposition 2 and get $rel_{min}(\tau) \subseteq Rel_\alpha(T_\tau)$ for all $\tau \in Q$.

It remains to argue that the relations $rel_{min}(\tau)$ are well-founded for all $\tau \in F$. This follows from $rel_{min}(\tau) \subseteq Rel_\alpha(T_\tau)$ and the fact that $Rel_\alpha(T_\tau)$ is well-founded due to the predicate T_τ^{dec}, which ensures the decrease of variable (ι, τ). $\square$

We are now in a position to prove Theorem 4, i.e., that factor termination is the most general termination criterion for transition abstraction:

Corollary 2. *Let A be a transition automaton that does not satisfy the factor-termination criterion. Then A is a transition abstraction of $\mathcal{P}_\alpha(S)$ for all domains α, but $\mathcal{P}_\alpha(S)$ does not terminate for some $\alpha < \omega$.*

Proof. From Corollary 1 we get that S does not satisfy the infinite descent criterion because A does not satisfy the factor-termination criterion. By Theorem 5 we know that the program $\mathcal{P}_\alpha(S)$ does not terminate for some $\alpha < \omega$ because S does not size-change terminate. We have that A is a transition abstraction of $\mathcal{P}_\alpha(S)$ by Proposition 5.   □

6.3   Complexity Analysis with Transition Automata

Let $A = \langle Q, \Sigma, \delta, \iota, F \rangle$ be a transition automaton and $P = \langle St, I, \Sigma, \rho \rangle$ be a program such that A is a transition abstraction of P. Let $S = \mathcal{S}(A) = \langle Var, \Sigma, \lambda \rangle$ be the SCS extracted from A. We will show that every run of P can be mimicked by a run of $\mathcal{P}_\alpha(S)$, where the domain α depends on P and needs to be chosen appropriately. We first introduce the machinery necessary to define α.

We define the *height* of a transition abstraction as the maximum of the heights of the well-founded relations $rel_{min}(\tau)$, i.e., we set

$$height(A, P) = \max_{\tau \in F} \| rel_{min}(\tau) \| .$$

We set $height^\bullet(A, P) = height(A, P) + 1$; we work with $height^\bullet(A, P)$, which differs from $height(A, P)$ by plus one for technical convenience; however, the difference of plus one is not important for our results on asymptotic complexity analysis.

We introduce another auxiliary definition. For every pair $(\tau', \tau) \in Q \times F$ we define a relation $Succ_P(\tau', \tau) \subseteq St \times St$ by setting

$$Succ_P(\tau', \tau) = \bigcup_{\text{word } \pi \text{ with } (\tau', \tau) \in \delta(\pi)} \rho(\pi).$$

We note that $Succ_P(\iota, \tau) = rel_{min}(\tau)$ for all $\tau \in F$.

For every pair $(\tau', \tau) \in Q \times F$ we define a function $rank_{\tau', \tau} : St \to height^\bullet(A, P)$ that maps a state $s \in St$ to an ordinal below $height^\bullet(A, P)$, by setting

$$rank_{\tau', \tau}(s) = \sup_{(s, s') \in Succ_P(\tau', \tau)} \| s' \|_{rel_{min}(\tau)} + 1,$$

where the sup over the empty set evaluates to 0. The following proposition is immediate from the definitions:

Proposition 6. *We have $rank_{\iota, \tau}(s) = \| s \|_{rel_{min}(\tau)}$ for all $s \in St$.*

Proof. Let $s \in St$ be some state. From the definition of $Succ_P$ we get $Succ_P(\iota, \tau) = rel_{min}(\tau)$. Thus, we get $rank_{\iota,\tau}(s) = \sup_{(s,s') \in Succ_P(\iota,\tau)} \|s'\|_{rel_{min}(\tau)} + 1 = \sup_{(s,s') \in rel_{min}(\tau)} \|s'\|_{rel_{min}(\tau)} + 1 = \|s\|_{rel_{min}(\tau)}$. □

For every $s \in St$ we define a valuation $\sigma_s : Q \times F \to height^\bullet(A, P)$ by setting $\sigma_s(\tau', \tau) = rank_{\tau',\tau}(s)$.

Lemma 3. *Let $\alpha = height^\bullet(A, P)$. For all pairs of states $(s, s') \in \rho(a)$, where $a \in \Sigma$, we have $(\sigma_s, \sigma_{s'}) \in Rel_\alpha(\lambda(a))$.*

Proof. Let $a \in \Sigma$ be some transition and let $(s, s') \in \rho(a)$ be a pair of states in the associated transition relation.

We consider an inequality $(\tau, \tau'') \geq (\tau', \tau'')' \in \lambda(a)$. By definition of $\lambda(a)$ we have $(\tau, \tau') \in \delta(a)$. From this we get $\{(s, s')\} \circ Succ_P(\tau', \tau'') \subseteq Succ_P(\tau, \tau'')$ because for every word π such that $(\tau', \tau'') \in \delta(\pi)$ we have that $(\tau, \tau'') \in \delta(a \cdot \pi)$ and thus $(s', s'') \in \rho(\pi)$ implies $(s, s'') \in \rho(a \cdot \pi)$. Hence, we get $\sigma_s(\tau, \tau'') = rank_{\tau,\tau''}(s) = \sup_{(s,s'') \in Succ_P(\tau,\tau'')} \|s''\|_{rel_{min}(\tau'')} + 1 \geq \sup_{(s',s'') \in Succ_P(\tau',\tau'')} \|s''\|_{rel_{min}(\tau'')} + 1 = rank_{\tau',\tau''}(s') = \sigma_{s'}(\tau', \tau'')$.

We consider an inequality $(\tau', \tau) > (\iota, \tau)' \in \lambda(a)$. By definition of $\lambda(a)$ we have $(\tau', \tau) \in \delta(a)$. From this we get $(s, s') \in \rho(a) \subseteq Succ_P(\tau', \tau)$. From Proposition 6 we have $rank_{\iota,\tau}(s') = \|s'\|_{rel_{min}(\tau)}$. Hence, we get $\sigma_s(\tau', \tau) = rank_{\tau',\tau}(s) = \sup_{(s,s'') \in Succ_P(\tau',\tau)} \|s''\|_{rel_{min}(\tau)} + 1 > \|s'\|_{rel_{min}(\tau)} = rank_{\iota,\tau}(s') = \sigma_{s'}(\iota, \tau)$. □

We immediately obtain the following corollary:

Corollary 3. *Let $\alpha = height^\bullet(A, P)$. Let $s_1 \xrightarrow{a_1} s_2 \xrightarrow{a_2} \cdots$ be a computation of P. Then, $\sigma_{s_1} \xrightarrow{a_1} \sigma_{s_2} \xrightarrow{a_2} \cdots$ is a computation of $\mathcal{P}_\alpha(S)$.*

Finally, we are in a position to transfer Theorem 6:

Theorem 7. *Let A be a transition automaton that satisfies the factor-termination termination criterion. Let $S = \mathcal{S}(A)$. Let z be the rational number obtained from Theorem 6 for S.*

Let $P = \langle St, I_N, \Sigma, \rho \rangle$ be a program whose set of initial states I_N is parameterized by natural number $N \in \mathbb{N}$, such that A is a transition abstraction of P and $height(A, P) = O(N)$. Then, the length of the longest computation of P is of asymptotic order $O(N^z)$.

Moreover, A is a transition abstraction for $\mathcal{P}_{[0,N]}(S)$ and the length of the longest computation of $\mathcal{P}_{[0,N]}(S)$ is of asymptotic order $\Theta(N^z)$.

Proof. By Proposition 5, A is a transition abstraction of $\mathcal{P}_{[0,N]}(S)$ for all $N \in \mathbb{N}$. From Theorem 6 we have that the longest computation of $\mathcal{P}_{[0,N]}(S)$ is of asymptotic order $\Theta(N^z)$.

Because of $height(A, P) = O(N)$, we can find some $a, b \in \mathbb{N}$ such that $height(A, P) \leq a \cdot N + b$ for all $N \in \mathbb{N}$. By Corollary 3, for every computation of P_N there is a computation of $\mathcal{P}_{[0,a \cdot N+b]}(S)$ of equal length. Hence, the longest computation of P_N is of asymptotic order $O((a \cdot N + b)^z) = O(N^z)$. □

We highlight that Theorem 7 gives a complete characterization of the complexity bounds obtainable with transition abstraction and provides an effective algorithm for computing these complexity bounds.

Theorem 7 allows us to derive the precise complexity for P_1 and P_2:

Example 12. We consider the size-change system $S = \mathcal{S}(A_2)$, which we have extracted in Example 10 from transition automaton A_2. Theorem 6 allows us to derive that $\mathcal{P}_{[0,N]}(S)$ has complexity $\Theta(N)$. In Example 5 we defined an abstract-transition program (A_2, rel_2) for P_2; the inductive proof labeling rel_2 in conjunction with the invariant $Inv = Rel_\alpha(\{x \leq N, y \leq N\})$ implies that $height(A_2, P_2) = N$. Hence, we can apply Theorem 7 and infer that P_2 has complexity $O(N)$, which is the precise asymptotic complexity of P_2.

We consider the size-change system $S = \mathcal{S}(A_3)$, which we have extracted in Example 11 from transition automaton A_3. Theorem 6 allows us to derive that $\mathcal{P}_{[0,N]}(S)$ has complexity $\Theta(N^2)$. In Example 4 we defined an abstract-transition program (A_1, rel_1) for P_1; the inductive proof labeling rel_1 in conjunction with the invariant $Inv = Rel_\alpha(\{x \leq N, y \leq N\})$ implies that $height(A_1, P_1) = N$. Hence, we can apply Theorem 7 and infer that P_2 has complexity $O(N^2)$, which is the precise asymptotic complexity of P_2.

7   Future Directions and Conclusion

In this paper, we have established a new connection between transition automata and the size-change abstraction. Our results suggest that all tools which implement termination analysis with transition invariants based on an inductive argument (such as TERMINATOR) can be retro-fitted to be complexity analyzers, which is an interesting direction for further research: While this paper has investigated what information can be extracted from a fixed proof (i.e., from a fixed set of transition predicates), there is also the question of what strategy for predicate selection gives the best results. We have seen that the predicates $x' < x$ and $y' < y$ allow inferring the linear complexity of P_2; these predicates are simple and can be extracted from the if- resp. else branch of P_2 by simple heuristics. On the other hand, the predicate $x' + y' < x + y$ allows establishing the linear complexity of P_2 using a single predicate; this predicate, however, is more complex and requires more complicated heuristics for extraction. Finding the right balance in predicate selection is an interesting topic for future research.

Ranking function construction is an alternative technique for termination proofs: [33] states a complete construction for deterministic size-change systems. [8,15] describes practical but incomplete constructions for general programs based on transition predicate abstraction. [15] states an example which has a transition invariant but no lexicographic ranking function over linear expressions; it is interesting to better understand the connection between the different termination proof techniques and investigate under which conditions ranking functions can be constructed.

Our results on transition abstraction and the previous results on size-change abstraction heavily rely on automata-theoretic techniques. We speculate that the study of the automaton structure of other inductive proofs, such as *cyclic proofs* [27], might also yield interesting results.

Acknowledgements. This article is dedicated to the memory of Helmut Veith who proposed to me the PhD topic of automatic derivation of loop bounds. Our initial idea was to extend the termination analysis of TERMINATOR. With this article I managed to return to this original idea.

References

1. Albert, E., Arenas, P., Genaim, S., Puebla, G., Zanardini, D.: Cost analysis of object-oriented bytecode programs. Theor. Comput. Sci. **413**(1), 142–159 (2012)
2. Alias, C., Darte, A., Feautrier, P., Gonnord, L.: Multi-dimensional rankings, program termination, and complexity bounds of flowchart programs. In: Cousot, R., Martel, M. (eds.) SAS 2010. LNCS, vol. 6337, pp. 117–133. Springer, Heidelberg (2010). https://doi.org/10.1007/978-3-642-15769-1_8
3. Anderson, H., Khoo, S.-C.: Affine-based size-change termination. In: Ohori, A. (ed.) APLAS 2003. LNCS, vol. 2895, pp. 122–140. Springer, Heidelberg (2003). https://doi.org/10.1007/978-3-540-40018-9_9
4. Ben-Amram, A.M.: Size-change termination with difference constraints. ACM Trans. Program. Lang. Syst. **30**(3), 1–30 (2008)
5. Ben-Amram, A.M.: Monotonicity constraints for termination in the integer domain. Log. Methods Comput. Sci. **7**(3), 1–43 (2011)
6. Blass, A., Gurevich, Y.: Program termination and well partial orderings. ACM Trans. Comput. Log. **9**(3), 18:1–18:26 (2008)
7. Bozzelli, L., Pinchinat, S.: Verification of gap-order constraint abstractions of counter systems. In: VMCAI, pp. 88–103 (2012)
8. Brockschmidt, M., Cook, B., Fuhs, C.: Better termination proving through cooperation. In: Sharygina, N., Veith, H. (eds.) CAV 2013. LNCS, vol. 8044, pp. 413–429. Springer, Heidelberg (2013). https://doi.org/10.1007/978-3-642-39799-8_28
9. Codish, M., Fuhs, C., Giesl, J., Schneider-Kamp, P.: Lazy abstraction for size-change termination. In: Fermüller, C.G., Voronkov, A. (eds.) LPAR 2010. LNCS, vol. 6397, pp. 217–232. Springer, Heidelberg (2010). https://doi.org/10.1007/978-3-642-16242-8_16
10. Codish, M., Gonopolskiy, I., Ben-Amram, A.M., Fuhs, C., Giesl, J.: Sat-based termination analysis using monotonicity constraints over the integers. TPLP **11**(4–5), 503–520 (2011)
11. Colcombet, T.: Factorisation forests for infinite words. In: Csuhaj-Varjú, E., Ésik, Z. (eds.) FCT 2007. LNCS, vol. 4639, pp. 226–237. Springer, Heidelberg (2007). https://doi.org/10.1007/978-3-540-74240-1_20
12. Colcombet, T., Daviaud, L., Zuleger, F.: Size-change abstraction and max-plus automata. In: Csuhaj-Varjú, E., Dietzfelbinger, M., Ésik, Z. (eds.) MFCS 2014. LNCS, vol. 8634, pp. 208–219. Springer, Heidelberg (2014). https://doi.org/10.1007/978-3-662-44522-8_18
13. Colcombet, T., Daviaud, L., Zuleger, F.: Automata and program analysis. In: Klasing, R., Zeitoun, M. (eds.) FCT 2017. LNCS, vol. 10472, pp. 3–10. Springer, Heidelberg (2017). https://doi.org/10.1007/978-3-662-55751-8_1
14. Cook, B., Podelski, A., Rybalchenko, A.: Termination proofs for systems code. In: PLDI, pp. 415–426 (2006)

15. Cook, B., See, A., Zuleger, F.: Ramsey vs. lexicographic termination proving. In: Piterman, N., Smolka, S.A. (eds.) TACAS 2013. LNCS, vol. 7795, pp. 47–61. Springer, Heidelberg (2013). https://doi.org/10.1007/978-3-642-36742-7_4
16. Flores-Montoya, A., Hähnle, R.: Resource analysis of complex programs with cost equations. In: Garrigue, J. (ed.) APLAS 2014. LNCS, vol. 8858, pp. 275–295. Springer, Cham (2014). https://doi.org/10.1007/978-3-319-12736-1_15
17. Giesl, J., Aschermann, C., Brockschmidt, M., Emmes, F., Frohn, F., Fuhs, C., Hensel, J., Otto, C., Plücker, M., Schneider-Kamp, P., Ströder, T., Swiderski, S., Thiemann, R.: Analyzing program termination and complexity automatically with aprove. J. Autom. Reason. **58**(1), 3–31 (2017)
18. Gulwani, S., Zuleger, F.: The reachability-bound problem. In: PLDI, pp. 292–304 (2010)
19. Heizmann, M., Jones, N.D., Podelski, A.: Size-change termination and transition invariants. In: Cousot, R., Martel, M. (eds.) SAS 2010. LNCS, vol. 6337, pp. 22–50. Springer, Heidelberg (2010). https://doi.org/10.1007/978-3-642-15769-1_4
20. Krauss, A.: Certified size-change termination. In: Pfenning, F. (ed.) CADE 2007. LNCS (LNAI), vol. 4603, pp. 460–475. Springer, Heidelberg (2007). https://doi.org/10.1007/978-3-540-73595-3_34
21. Lee, C.S.: Ranking functions for size-change termination. ACM Trans. Program. Lang. Syst. **31**(3), 10:1–10:42 (2009)
22. Lee, C.S., Jones, N.D., Ben-Amram, A.M.: The size-change principle for program termination. In: POPL, pp. 81–92 (2001)
23. Manolios, P., Vroon, D.: Termination analysis with calling context graphs. In: Ball, T., Jones, R.B. (eds.) CAV 2006. LNCS, vol. 4144, pp. 401–414. Springer, Heidelberg (2006). https://doi.org/10.1007/11817963_36
24. Miné, A.: The octagon abstract domain. High. Order Symb. Comput. **19**(1), 31–100 (2006)
25. Podelski, A., Rybalchenko, A.: Transition invariants. In: LICS, pp. 32–41 (2004)
26. Podelski, A., Rybalchenko, A.: Transition predicate abstraction and fair termination. ACM Trans. Program. Lang. Syst. **29**(3), 15 (2007)
27. Rowe, R.N.S., Brotherston, J.: Automatic cyclic termination proofs for recursive procedures in separation logic. In: CPP, pp. 53–65 (2017)
28. Simon, I.: Factorization forests of finite height. Theor. Comput. Sci. **72**(1), 65–94 (1990)
29. Sinn, M., Zuleger, F., Veith, H.: Complexity and resource bound analysis of imperative programs using difference constraints. J. Autom. Reason. **59**(1), 3–45 (2017)
30. Steila, S., Yokoyama, K.: Reverse mathematical bounds for the termination theorem. Ann. Pure Appl. Logic **167**(12), 1213–1241 (2016)
31. Vidal, G.: Quasi-terminating logic programs for ensuring the termination of partial evaluation. In: PEPM, pp. 51–60 (2007)
32. Vytiniotis, D., Coquand, T., Wahlstedt, D.: Stop when you are almost-full: adventures in constructive termination. In: Beringer, L., Felty, A. (eds.) ITP 2012. LNCS, vol. 7406, pp. 250–265. Springer, Heidelberg (2012). https://doi.org/10.1007/978-3-642-32347-8_17

33. Zuleger, F.: Asymptotically precise ranking functions for deterministic size-change systems. In: Beklemishev, L.D., Musatov, D.V. (eds.) CSR 2015. LNCS, vol. 9139, pp. 426–442. Springer, Cham (2015). https://doi.org/10.1007/978-3-319-20297-6_27

34. Zuleger, F., Gulwani, S., Sinn, M., Veith, H.: Bound analysis of imperative programs with the size-change abstraction. In: Yahav, E. (ed.) SAS 2011. LNCS, vol. 6887, pp. 280–297. Springer, Heidelberg (2011). https://doi.org/10.1007/978-3-642-23702-7_22

Author Index

Printed in the United States
By Bookmasters